ADAM BEDE

GEORGE ELIOT

Happy Hour Books

Published by:
HAPPY HOUR BOOKS
www.happyhoursbooks.com
email: happyhourbooks1@gmail.com

First published by Happy Hour Books 2024

Title : Adam Bede
Paperback ISBN : 9789358482287
Hardback ISBN : 9789358488432

BOOK FIRST

Chapter I
The Workshop

With a single drop of ink for a mirror, the Egyptian sorcerer undertakes to reveal to any chance comer far-reaching visions of the past. This is what I undertake to do for you, reader. With this drop of ink at the end of my pen, I will show you the roomy workshop of Mr. Jonathan Burge, carpenter and builder, in the village of Hayslope, as it appeared on the eighteenth of June, in the year of our Lord 1799.

The afternoon sun was warm on the five workmen there, busy upon doors and window-frames and wainscoting. A scent of pine-wood from a tentlike pile of planks outside the open door mingled itself with the scent of the elder-bushes which were spreading their summer snow close to the open window opposite; the slanting sunbeams shone through the transparent shavings that flew before the steady plane, and lit up the fine grain of the oak panelling which stood propped against the wall. On a heap of those soft shavings a rough, grey shepherd dog had made himself a pleasant bed, and was lying with his nose between his fore-paws, occasionally wrinkling his brows to cast a glance at the tallest of the five workmen, who was carving a shield in the centre of a wooden mantelpiece. It was to this workman that the strong barytone belonged which was heard above the sound of plane and hammer singing—

Awake, my soul, and with the sun
Thy daily stage of duty run;
Shake off dull sloth...

Here some measurement was to be taken which required more concentrated attention, and the sonorous voice subsided into a low whistle; but it presently broke out again with renewed vigour—

Let all thy converse be sincere,
Thy conscience as the noonday clear.

Such a voice could only come from a broad chest, and the broad chest belonged to a large-boned, muscular man nearly six feet high, with a back so flat and a head so well poised that when he drew himself up to take a more distant survey of his work, he had the air of a soldier standing at ease. The sleeve rolled up above the elbow showed an arm that was likely to win the prize for feats of strength; yet the long supple hand, with its broad finger-tips, looked ready for works of skill. In his tall stalwartness Adam Bede was a Saxon, and justified his name; but the jet-black hair, made the more noticeable by its contrast with the light paper cap, and the keen glance of the dark eyes that shone from under strongly marked, prominent and mobile eyebrows, indicated a mixture of Celtic blood. The face was large and roughly hewn, and when in repose had no other beauty than such as belongs to an expression of good-humoured honest intelligence.

It is clear at a glance that the next workman is Adam's brother. He is nearly as tall; he has the same type of features, the same hue of hair and complexion; but the strength of the family likeness seems only to render more conspicuous the remarkable difference of expression both in form and face. Seth's broad shoulders have a slight stoop; his eyes are grey; his eyebrows have less prominence and more repose than his brother's; and his glance, instead of being keen, is confiding and benign. He has thrown off his paper cap, and you see that his hair is not thick and straight, like Adam's, but thin and wavy, allowing you to discern the exact contour of a coronal arch that predominates very decidedly over the brow.

The idle tramps always felt sure they could get a copper from Seth; they scarcely ever spoke to Adam.

The concert of the tools and Adam's voice was at last broken by Seth, who, lifting the door at which he had been working intently, placed it against the wall, and said, "There! I've finished my door to-day, anyhow."

The workmen all looked up; Jim Salt, a burly, red-haired man known as Sandy Jim, paused from his planing, and Adam said to Seth, with a sharp glance of surprise, "What! Dost think thee'st finished the door?"

"Aye, sure," said Seth, with answering surprise; "what's awanting to't?"

A loud roar of laughter from the other three workmen made Seth look round confusedly. Adam did not join in the laughter, but there was a slight smile on his face as he said, in a gentler tone than before, "Why, thee'st forgot the panels."

The laughter burst out afresh as Seth clapped his hands to his head, and coloured over brow and crown.

"Hoorray!" shouted a small lithe fellow called Wiry Ben, running forward and seizing the door. "We'll hang up th' door at fur end o' th' shop an' write on't 'Seth Bede, the Methody, his work.' Here, Jim, lend's hould o' th' red pot."

"Nonsense!" said Adam. "Let it alone, Ben Cranage. You'll mayhap be making such a slip yourself some day; you'll laugh o' th' other side o' your mouth then."

"Catch me at it, Adam. It'll be a good while afore my head's full o' th' Methodies," said Ben.

"Nay, but it's often full o' drink, and that's worse."

Ben, however, had now got the "red pot" in his hand, and was about to begin writing his inscription, making, by way of preliminary, an imaginary S in the air.

"Let it alone, will you?" Adam called out, laying down his tools, striding up to Ben, and seizing his right shoulder. "Let it alone, or I'll shake the soul out o' your body."

Ben shook in Adam's iron grasp, but, like a plucky small man as he was, he didn't mean to give in. With his left hand he snatched the brush from his powerless right, and made a movement as if he would perform the feat of writing with his left. In a moment Adam turned him round, seized his other shoulder, and, pushing him along, pinned him against the wall. But now Seth spoke.

"Let be, Addy, let be. Ben will be joking. Why, he's i' the right to laugh at me—I canna help laughing at myself."

"I shan't loose him till he promises to let the door alone," said Adam.

"Come, Ben, lad," said Seth, in a persuasive tone, "don't let's have a quarrel about it. You know Adam will have his way. You may's well try to turn a waggon in a narrow lane. Say you'll leave the door alone, and make an end on't."

"I binna frighted at Adam," said Ben, "but I donna mind sayin' as I'll let 't alone at your askin', Seth."

"Come, that's wise of you, Ben," said Adam, laughing and relaxing his grasp.

They all returned to their work now; but Wiry Ben, having had the worst in the bodily contest, was bent on retrieving that humiliation by a success in sarcasm.

"Which was ye thinkin' on, Seth," he began—"the pretty parson's face or her sarmunt, when ye forgot the panels?"

"Come and hear her, Ben," said Seth, good-humouredly; "she's going to preach on the Green to-night; happen ye'd get something to think on yourself then, instead o' those wicked songs you're so fond on. Ye might get religion, and that 'ud be the best day's earnings y' ever made."

"All i' good time for that, Seth; I'll think about that when I'm a-goin' to settle i' life; bachelors doesn't want such heavy earnin's. Happen I shall do the coortin' an' the religion both together, as *ye* do, Seth; but ye wouldna ha' me get converted an' chop in atween ye an' the pretty preacher, an' carry her aff?"

"No fear o' that, Ben; she's neither for you nor for me to win, I doubt. Only you come and hear her, and you won't speak lightly on her again."

"Well, I'm half a mind t' ha' a look at her to-night, if there isn't good company at th' Holly Bush. What'll she take for her text? Happen ye can tell me, Seth, if so be as I shouldna come up i' time for't. Will't be—what come ye out for to see? A prophetess? Yea, I say unto you, and more than a prophetess—a uncommon pretty young woman."

"Come, Ben," said Adam, rather sternly, "you let the words o' the Bible alone; you're going too far now."

"What! Are *ye* a-turnin' roun', Adam? I thought ye war dead again th' women preachin', a while agoo?"

"Nay, I'm not turnin' noway. I said nought about the women preachin'. I said, You let the Bible alone: you've got a jest-book, han't you, as you're rare and proud on? Keep your dirty fingers to that."

"Why, y' are gettin' as big a saint as Seth. Y' are goin' to th' preachin' to-night, I should think. Ye'll do finely t' lead the singin'. But I don' know what Parson Irwine 'ull say at his gran' favright Adam Bede a-turnin' Methody."

"Never do you bother yourself about me, Ben. I'm not a-going to turn Methodist any more nor you are—though it's like enough you'll turn to something worse. Mester Irwine's got more sense nor to meddle wi' people's doing as they like in religion. That's between themselves and God, as he's said to me many a time."

"Aye, aye; but he's none so fond o' your dissenters, for all that."

"Maybe; I'm none so fond o' Josh Tod's thick ale, but I don't hinder you from making a fool o' yourself wi't."

There was a laugh at this thrust of Adam's, but Seth said, very seriously. "Nay, nay, Addy, thee mustna say as anybody's religion's like thick ale. Thee dostna believe but what the dissenters and the Methodists have got the root o' the matter as well as the church folks."

"Nay, Seth, lad; I'm not for laughing at no man's religion. Let 'em follow their consciences, that's all. Only I think it 'ud be better if their consciences 'ud let 'em stay quiet i' the church—there's a deal to be learnt there. And there's such a thing as being oversperitial; we must have something beside Gospel i' this world. Look at the canals, an' th' aqueduc's, an' th' coal-pit engines, and Arkwright's mills there at Cromford; a man must learn summat beside Gospel to make them things, I reckon. But t' hear some o' them preachers, you'd think as a man must be doing nothing all's life but shutting's eyes and looking what's agoing on inside him. I know a man must have the love o' God in his soul, and the Bible's God's word. But what does the Bible say? Why, it says as God put his sperrit into the workman as built the tabernacle, to make him do all the carved work and things as wanted a nice hand. And this is my way o' looking at it: there's the sperrit o' God in all things and all times—weekday as well as Sunday—and i' the great works and inventions, and i' the figuring and the mechanics. And God helps us with our headpieces and our hands as well as with our souls; and if a man does bits o' jobs out o' working hours—builds a oven for 's wife to save her from going to the bakehouse, or scrats at his bit o' garden and makes two potatoes grow istead o' one, he's doin' more good, and he's just as near to God, as if he was running after some preacher and a-praying and a-groaning."

"Well done, Adam!" said Sandy Jim, who had paused from his planing to shift his planks while Adam was speaking; "that's the best sarmunt I've heared this long while. By th' same token, my wife's been a-plaguin' on me to build her a oven this twelvemont."

"There's reason in what thee say'st, Adam," observed Seth, gravely. "But thee know'st thyself as it's hearing the preachers thee find'st so much fault with has turned many an idle fellow into an industrious un. It's the preacher as empties th' alehouse; and if a man gets religion, he'll do his work none the worse for that."

"On'y he'll lave the panels out o' th' doors sometimes, eh, Seth?" said Wiry Ben.

"Ah, Ben, you've got a joke again' me as 'll last you your life. But it isna religion as was i' fault there; it was Seth Bede, as was allays a wool-gathering chap, and religion hasna cured him, the more's the pity."

"Ne'er heed me, Seth," said Wiry Ben, "y' are a down-right good-hearted chap, panels or no panels; an' ye donna set up your bristles at every bit o' fun, like some o' your kin, as is mayhap cliverer."

"Seth, lad," said Adam, taking no notice of the sarcasm against himself, "thee mustna take me unkind. I wasna driving at thee in what I said just now. Some 's got one way o' looking at things and some 's got another."

"Nay, nay, Addy, thee mean'st me no unkindness," said Seth, "I know that well enough. Thee't like thy dog Gyp—thee bark'st at me sometimes, but thee allays lick'st my hand after."

All hands worked on in silence for some minutes, until the church clock began to strike six. Before the first stroke had died away, Sandy Jim had loosed his plane and was reaching his jacket; Wiry Ben had left a screw half driven in, and thrown his screwdriver into his tool-basket; Mum Taft, who, true to his name, had kept silence throughout the previous conversation, had flung down his hammer as he was in the act of lifting it; and Seth, too, had straightened his back, and was putting out his hand towards his paper cap. Adam alone had gone on with his work as if nothing had happened. But observing the cessation of the tools, he looked up, and said, in a tone of indignation, "Look there, now! I can't abide to see men throw away their tools i' that way, the minute the clock begins to strike, as if they took no pleasure i' their work and was afraid o' doing a stroke too much."

Seth looked a little conscious, and began to be slower in his preparations for going, but Mum Taft broke silence, and said, "Aye, aye, Adam lad, ye talk like a young un. When y' are six-an'-forty like me, istid o' six-an'-twenty, ye wonna be so flush o' workin' for nought."

"Nonsense," said Adam, still wrathful; "what's age got to do with it, I wonder? Ye arena getting stiff yet, I reckon. I hate to see a man's arms drop down as if he was shot, before the clock's fairly struck, just as if he'd never a bit o' pride and delight in 's work. The very grindstone 'ull go on turning a bit after you loose it."

"Bodderation, Adam!" exclaimed Wiry Ben; "lave a chap aloon, will 'ee? Ye war afinding faut wi' preachers a while agoo—y' are fond enough o' preachin' yoursen. Ye may like work better nor play, but I like play better nor work; that'll 'commodate ye—it laves ye th' more to do."

With this exit speech, which he considered effective, Wiry Ben shouldered his basket and left the workshop, quickly followed by Mum Taft and Sandy Jim. Seth lingered, and looked wistfully at Adam, as if he expected him to say something.

"Shalt go home before thee go'st to the preaching?" Adam asked, looking up.

"Nay; I've got my hat and things at Will Maskery's. I shan't be home before going for ten. I'll happen see Dinah Morris safe home, if she's willing. There's nobody comes with her from Poyser's, thee know'st."

"Then I'll tell mother not to look for thee," said Adam.

"Thee artna going to Poyser's thyself to-night?" said Seth rather timidly, as he turned to leave the workshop.

"Nay, I'm going to th' school."

Hitherto Gyp had kept his comfortable bed, only lifting up his head and watching Adam more closely as he noticed the other workmen departing. But no sooner did Adam put his ruler in his pocket, and begin to twist his apron round his waist, than Gyp ran forward and looked up in his master's face with patient expectation. If Gyp had had a tail he would doubtless have wagged it, but being destitute of that vehicle for his emotions, he was like many other worthy personages, destined to appear more phlegmatic than nature had made him.

“What! Art ready for the basket, eh, Gyp?” said Adam, with the same gentle modulation of voice as when he spoke to Seth.

Gyp jumped and gave a short bark, as much as to say, “Of course.” Poor fellow, he had not a great range of expression.

The basket was the one which on workdays held Adam’s and Seth’s dinner; and no official, walking in procession, could look more resolutely unconscious of all acquaintances than Gyp with his basket, trotting at his master’s heels.

On leaving the workshop Adam locked the door, took the key out, and carried it to the house on the other side of the woodyard. It was a low house, with smooth grey thatch and buff walls, looking pleasant and mellow in the evening light. The leaded windows were bright and speckless, and the door-stone was as clean as a white boulder at ebb tide. On the door-stone stood a clean old woman, in a dark-striped linen gown, a red kerchief, and a linen cap, talking to some speckled fowls which appeared to have been drawn towards her by an illusory expectation of cold potatoes or barley. The old woman’s sight seemed to be dim, for she did not recognize Adam till he said, “Here’s the key, Dolly; lay it down for me in the house, will you?”

“Aye, sure; but wunna ye come in, Adam? Miss Mary’s i’ th’ house, and Mester Burge ’ull be back anon; he’d be glad t’ ha’ ye to supper wi’m, I’ll be’s warrand.”

“No, Dolly, thank you; I’m off home. Good evening.”

Adam hastened with long strides, Gyp close to his heels, out of the workyard, and along the highroad leading away from the village and down to the valley. As he reached the foot of the slope, an elderly horseman, with his portmanteau strapped behind him, stopped his horse when Adam had passed him, and turned round to have another long look at the stalwart workman in paper cap, leather breeches, and dark-blue worsted stockings.

Adam, unconscious of the admiration he was exciting, presently struck across the fields, and now broke out into the tune which had all day long been running in his head:

Let all thy converse be sincere,
Thy conscience as the noonday clear;
For God’s all-seeing eye surveys
Thy secret thoughts, thy works and ways.

Chapter II
The Preaching

About a quarter to seven there was an unusual appearance of excitement in the village of Hayslope, and through the whole length of its little street, from the Donnithorne Arms to the churchyard gate, the inhabitants had evidently been drawn out of their houses by something more than the pleasure of lounging in the evening sunshine. The Donnithorne Arms stood at the entrance of the village, and a small farmyard and stackyard which flanked it, indicating that there was a pretty take of land attached to the inn, gave the traveller a promise of good feed for himself and his horse, which might well console him for the ignorance in which the weather-beaten sign left him as to the heraldic bearings of that ancient family, the Donnithornes. Mr. Casson, the landlord, had been for some time standing at the door with his hands in his pockets, balancing himself on his heels and toes and looking towards a piece of unenclosed ground, with a maple in the middle of it, which he knew to be the destination of certain grave-looking men and women whom he had observed passing at intervals.

Mr. Casson's person was by no means of that common type which can be allowed to pass without description. On a front view it appeared to consist principally of two spheres, bearing about the same relation to each other as the earth and the moon: that is to say, the lower sphere might be said, at a rough guess, to be thirteen times larger than the upper which naturally performed the function of a mere satellite and tributary. But here the resemblance ceased, for Mr. Casson's head was not at all a melancholy-looking satellite nor was it a "spotty globe," as Milton has irreverently called the moon; on the contrary, no head and face could look more sleek and healthy, and its expression—which was chiefly confined to a pair of round and ruddy cheeks, the slight knot and interruptions forming the nose and eyes being scarcely worth mention—was one of jolly contentment, only tempered by that sense of personal dignity which usually made itself felt in his attitude and bearing. This sense of dignity could hardly be considered excessive in a man who had been butler to "the family" for fifteen years, and who, in his present high position, was necessarily very much in contact with his inferiors. How to reconcile his dignity with the satisfaction of his curiosity by walking towards the Green was the problem that Mr. Casson had been revolving in his mind for the last five minutes; but when he had partly solved it by taking his hands out of his pockets, and thrusting them into the armholes of his waistcoat, by throwing his head on one side, and providing himself with an air of contemptuous indifference to whatever might fall under his notice, his thoughts were diverted by the approach of the horseman whom we lately saw pausing to have another look at our friend Adam, and who now pulled up at the door of the Donnithorne Arms.

"Take off the bridle and give him a drink, ostler," said the traveller to the lad in a smock-frock, who had come out of the yard at the sound of the horse's hoofs.

"Why, what's up in your pretty village, landlord?" he continued, getting down. "There seems to be quite a stir."

"It's a Methodis' preaching, sir; it's been gev hout as a young woman's a-going to preach on the Green," answered Mr. Casson, in a treble and wheezy voice, with a slightly mincing accent. "Will you please to step in, sir, an' tek somethink?"

"No, I must be getting on to Rosseter. I only want a drink for my horse. And what does your parson say, I wonder, to a young woman preaching just under his nose?"

"Parson Irwine, sir, doesn't live here; he lives at Brox'on, over the hill there. The parsonage here's a tumble-down place, sir, not fit for gentry to live in. He comes here to preach of a Sunday afternoon, sir, an' puts up his hoss here. It's a grey cob, sir, an' he sets great store by't. He's allays put up his hoss here, sir, iver since before I hed the Donnithorne Arms. I'm not this countryman, you may tell by my tongue, sir. They're cur'ous talkers i' this country, sir; the gentry's hard work to hunderstand 'em. I was brought hup among the gentry, sir, an' got the turn o' their tongue when I was a bye. Why, what do you think the folks here says for 'hevn't you?'—the gentry, you know, says, 'hevn't you'—well, the people about here says 'hanna yey.' It's what they call the dileck as is spoke hereabout, sir. That's what I've heared Squire Donnithorne say many a time; it's the dileck, says he."

"Aye, aye," said the stranger, smiling. "I know it very well. But you've not got many Methodists about here, surely—in this agricultural spot? I should have thought there would hardly be such a thing as a Methodist to be found about here. You're all farmers, aren't you? The Methodists can seldom lay much hold on *them*."

"Why, sir, there's a pretty lot o' workmen round about, sir. There's Mester Burge as owns the timber-yard over there, he underteks a good bit o' building an' repairs. An' there's the stone-pits not far off. There's plenty of emply i' this countryside, sir. An' there's a fine batch o' Methodisses at Treddles'on—that's the market town about three mile off—you'll maybe ha' come through it, sir. There's pretty nigh a score of 'em on the Green now, as come from there. That's where our people gets it from, though there's only two men of 'em in all Hayslope: that's Will Maskery, the wheelwright, and Seth Bede, a young man as works at the carpenterin'."

"The preacher comes from Treddleston, then, does she?"

"Nay, sir, she comes out o' Stonyshire, pretty nigh thirty mile off. But she's a-visitin' hereabout at Mester Poyser's at the Hall Farm—it's them barns an' big walnut-trees, right away to the left, sir. She's own niece to Poyser's wife, an' they'll be fine an' vexed at her for making a fool of herself i' that way. But I've heared as there's no holding these Methodisses when the maggit's once got i' their head: many of 'em goes stark starin' mad wi' their religion. Though this young woman's quiet enough to look at, by what I can make out; I've not seen her myself."

"Well, I wish I had time to wait and see her, but I must get on. I've been out of my way for the last twenty minutes to have a look at that place in the valley. It's Squire Donnithorne's, I suppose?"

"Yes, sir, that's Donnithorne Chase, that is. Fine hoaks there, isn't there, sir? I should know what it is, sir, for I've lived butler there a-going i' fifteen year. It's Captain Donnithorne as is th' heir, sir—Squire Donnithorne's grandson. He'll be comin' of hage this 'ay-'arvest, sir, an' we shall hev fine doin's. He owns all the land about here, sir, Squire Donnithorne does."

"Well, it's a pretty spot, whoever may own it," said the traveller, mounting his horse; "and one meets some fine strapping fellows about too. I met as fine a young fellow as ever I saw in my life, about half an hour ago, before I came up the hill—a carpenter, a tall, broad-shouldered fellow with black hair and black eyes, marching along like a soldier. We want such fellows as he to lick the French."

"Aye, sir, that's Adam Bede, that is, I'll be bound—Thias Bede's son everybody knows him hereabout. He's an uncommon clever stiddy fellow, an' wonderful strong. Lord bless you, sir—if you'll hexcuse me for saying so—he can walk forty mile a-day, an' lift a matter o' sixty ston'. He's an uncommon favourite wi' the gentry, sir: Captain Donnithorne and Parson Irwine meks a fine fuss wi' him. But he's a little lifted up an' peppery-like."

"Well, good evening to you, landlord; I must get on."

"Your servant, sir; good evenin'."

The traveller put his horse into a quick walk up the village, but when he approached the Green, the beauty of the view that lay on his right hand, the singular contrast presented by the groups of villagers with the knot of Methodists near the maple, and perhaps yet more, curiosity to see the young female preacher, proved too much for his anxiety to get to the end of his journey, and he paused.

The Green lay at the extremity of the village, and from it the road branched off in two directions, one leading farther up the hill by the church, and the other winding gently down towards the valley. On the side of the Green that led towards the church, the broken line of thatched cottages was continued nearly to the churchyard gate; but on the opposite northwestern side, there was nothing to obstruct the view of gently swelling meadow, and wooded valley, and dark masses of distant hill. That rich undulating district of Loamshire to which Hayslope belonged lies close to a grim outskirt of Stonyshire, overlooked by its barren hills as a pretty blooming sister may sometimes be seen linked in the arm of a rugged, tall, swarthy brother; and in two or three hours' ride the traveller might exchange a bleak treeless region, intersected by lines of cold grey stone, for one where his road wound under the shelter of woods, or up swelling hills, muffled with hedgerows and long meadow-grass and thick corn; and where at every turn he came upon some fine old country-seat nestled in the valley or crowning the slope, some homestead with its long length of barn and its cluster of golden ricks, some grey steeple looking out from a pretty confusion of trees and thatch and dark-red tiles. It was just such a picture as this last that Hayslope Church had made to the traveller as he began to mount the gentle slope leading to its pleasant uplands, and now from his station near the Green he had before him in one view nearly all the other typical features of this pleasant land. High up against the horizon were the huge conical masses of hill, like giant mounds intended to fortify this region of corn and grass against the keen and hungry winds of the north; not distant enough to be clothed in purple mystery, but with sombre greenish sides visibly specked with sheep, whose motion was only revealed by memory, not detected by sight; wooed from day to day by the changing hours, but responding with no change in themselves—left for ever grim and sullen after the flush of morning, the winged gleams of the April noonday, the parting crimson glory of the ripening summer sun. And directly below them the eye rested on a more advanced line of hanging woods, divided by bright patches of pasture or furrowed crops, and not yet deepened into the uniform leafy curtains of high summer, but still showing the warm tints of the young oak and the tender green of the ash and lime. Then came the valley, where the woods grew thicker, as if they had rolled down and hurried together from the patches left smooth on the slope, that they might take the better care of the tall mansion which lifted its parapets and sent its faint blue summer smoke among them. Doubtless there was a large sweep of park and a broad glassy pool in front of that mansion, but the swelling slope of meadow would not let our traveller see them from the village green. He saw instead a foreground which was just as lovely—the level sunlight lying like transparent gold among the gently curving stems of the feathered grass and the tall red sorrel, and the white ambels of the hemlocks lining the bushy hedgerows. It was that moment in summer when the sound of the scythe being whetted makes us cast more lingering looks at the flower-sprinkled tresses of the meadows.

He might have seen other beauties in the landscape if he had turned a little in his saddle and looked eastward, beyond Jonathan Burge's pasture and woodyard towards the green corn-fields and walnut-trees of the Hall Farm; but apparently there was more interest for him in the living groups close at hand. Every generation in the village was there, from old "Feyther Taft" in his brown worsted night-cap, who was bent nearly double, but seemed tough enough to keep on his legs a long while, leaning on his short stick, down to the babies with their little round heads lolling forward in quilted linen caps. Now and then there was a new arrival; perhaps a slouching labourer, who, having eaten his supper, came out to look at the unusual scene with a slow bovine gaze, willing to hear what any one had to say in explanation of it, but by no means excited enough to ask a question. But all took care not to join the Methodists on the Green, and identify themselves in that way with the expectant audience, for there was not one of them that would not have disclaimed the imputation of having come out to hear the "preacher woman"—they had only come out to see "what war a-goin' on, like." The men were chiefly gathered in the neighbourhood of the blacksmith's shop. But do not imagine them gathered in a knot. Villagers never swarm: a whisper is unknown among them, and they seem almost as incapable of an undertone as a cow or a stag. Your true rustic turns his back on his interlocutor, throwing a question over his shoulder as if he meant to run away from the answer, and walking a step or two farther off when the interest of the dialogue culminates. So the group in the vicinity of the blacksmith's door was by no means a close one, and formed no screen in front of Chad Cranage, the blacksmith himself, who stood with his black brawny arms folded, leaning against the door-post, and occasionally sending forth a bellowing laugh at his own jokes, giving them a marked preference over the sarcasms of Wiry Ben, who had renounced the pleasures of the Holly Bush for the sake of seeing life under a new form. But both styles of wit were treated with equal contempt by Mr. Joshua Rann. Mr. Rann's leathern apron and subdued griminess can leave no one in any doubt that he is the village shoemaker; the thrusting out of his chin and stomach and the twirling of his thumbs are more subtle indications, intended to prepare unwary strangers for the discovery that they are in the presence of the parish clerk. "Old Joshway," as he is irreverently called by his neighbours, is in a state of simmering indignation; but he has not yet opened his lips except to say, in a resounding bass undertone, like the tuning of a violoncello, "Sehon, King of the Amorites; for His mercy endureth for ever; and Og the King of Basan: for His mercy endureth for ever"—a quotation which may seem to have slight bearing on the present occasion, but, as with every other anomaly, adequate knowledge will show it to be a natural sequence. Mr. Rann was inwardly maintaining the dignity of the Church in the face of this scandalous irruption of Methodism, and as that dignity was bound up with his own sonorous utterance of the responses, his argument naturally suggested a quotation from the psalm he had read the last Sunday afternoon.

The stronger curiosity of the women had drawn them quite to the edge of the Green, where they could examine more closely the Quakerlike costume and odd deportment of the female Methodists. Underneath the maple there was a small cart, which had been brought from the wheelwright's to serve as a pulpit, and round this a couple of benches and a few chairs had been placed. Some of the Methodists were resting on these, with their eyes closed, as if wrapt in prayer or meditation. Others chose to continue standing, and had turned their faces towards the villagers with a look of melancholy compassion, which was highly amusing to Bessy Cranage, the blacksmith's buxom daughter, known to her neighbours as Chad's Bess, who wondered "why the folks war amakin' faces a that'ns." Chad's Bess was the object of peculiar compassion, because her hair, being turned back under a cap which was set at the top of her head, exposed to view an ornament of which she was much prouder than of her red cheeks—namely, a pair of large round ear-rings with false garnets in them, ornaments condemned not only by the Methodists, but by her own cousin and namesake Timothy's Bess, who, with much cousinly feeling, often wished "them ear-rings" might come to good.

Timothy's Bess, though retaining her maiden appellation among her familiars, had long been the wife of Sandy Jim, and possessed a handsome set of matronly jewels, of which it is enough to mention the heavy baby she was rocking in her arms, and the sturdy fellow of five in knee-breeches, and red legs, who had a rusty milk-can round his neck by way of drum, and was very carefully avoided by Chad's small terrier. This young olive-branch, notorious under the name of Timothy's Bess's Ben, being of an inquiring disposition, unchecked by any false modesty, had advanced beyond the group of women and children, and was walking round the Methodists, looking up in their faces with his mouth wide open, and beating his stick against the milk-can by way of musical accompaniment. But one of the elderly women bending down to take him by the shoulder, with an air of grave remonstrance, Timothy's Bess's Ben first kicked out vigorously, then took to his heels and sought refuge behind his father's legs.

"Ye gallows young dog," said Sandy Jim, with some paternal pride, "if ye donna keep that stick quiet, I'll tek it from ye. What dy'e mane by kickin' foulks?"

"Here! Gie him here to me, Jim," said Chad Cranage; "I'll tie hirs up an' shoe him as I do th' hosses. Well, Mester Casson," he continued, as that personage sauntered up towards the group of men, "how are ye t' naight? Are ye coom t' help groon? They say folks allays groon when they're hearkenin' to th' Methodys, as if they war bad i' th' inside. I mane to groon as loud as your cow did th' other naight, an' then the praicher 'ull think I'm i' th' raight way."

“I’d advise you not to be up to no nonsense, Chad,” said Mr. Casson, with some dignity; “Poyser wouldn’t like to hear as his wife’s niece was treated any ways disrespectful, for all he mayn’t be fond of her taking on herself to preach.”

“Aye, an’ she’s a pleasant-looked un too,” said Wiry Ben. “I’ll stick up for the pretty women preachin’; I know they’d persuade me over a deal sooner nor th’ ugly men. I shouldna wonder if I turn Methody afore the night’s out, an’ begin to coort the preacher, like Seth Bede.”

“Why, Seth’s looking rether too high, I should think,” said Mr. Casson. “This woman’s kin wouldn’t like her to demean herself to a common carpenter.”

“Tchu!” said Ben, with a long treble intonation, “what’s folks’s kin got to do wi’t? Not a chip. Poyser’s wife may turn her nose up an’ forget bygones, but this Dinah Morris, they tell me, ’s as poor as iver she was—works at a mill, an’s much ado to keep hersen. A strappin’ young carpenter as is a ready-made Methody, like Seth, wouldna be a bad match for her. Why, Poysers make as big a fuss wi’ Adam Bede as if he war a nevvy o’ their own.”

“Idle talk! idle talk!” said Mr. Joshua Rann. “Adam an’ Seth’s two men; you wunna fit them two wi’ the same last.”

“Maybe,” said Wiry Ben, contemptuously, “but Seth’s the lad for me, though he war a Methody twice o’er. I’m fair beat wi’ Seth, for I’ve been teasin’ him iver sin’ we’ve been workin’ together, an’ he bears me no more malice nor a lamb. An’ he’s a stout-hearted feller too, for when we saw the old tree all afire a-comin’ across the fields one night, an’ we thought as it war a boguy, Seth made no more ado, but he up to’t as bold as a constable. Why, there he comes out o’ Will Maskery’s; an’ there’s Will hisself, lookin’ as meek as if he couldna knock a nail o’ the head for fear o’ hurtin’t. An’ there’s the pretty preacher woman! My eye, she’s got her bonnet off. I mun go a bit nearer.”

Several of the men followed Ben’s lead, and the traveller pushed his horse on to the Green, as Dinah walked rather quickly and in advance of her companions towards the cart under the maple-tree. While she was near Seth’s tall figure, she looked short, but when she had mounted the cart, and was away from all comparison, she seemed above the middle height of woman, though in reality she did not exceed it—an effect which was due to the slimness of her figure and the simple line of her black stuff dress. The stranger was struck with surprise as he saw her approach and mount the cart—surprise, not so much at the feminine delicacy of her appearance, as at the total absence of self-consciousness in her demeanour. He had made up his mind to see her advance with a measured step and a demure solemnity of countenance; he had felt sure that her face would be mantled with the smile of conscious saintship, or else charged with denunciatory bitterness. He knew but two types of Methodist—the ecstatic and the bilious. But

Dinah walked as simply as if she were going to market, and seemed as unconscious of her outward appearance as a little boy: there was no blush, no tremulousness, which said, "I know you think me a pretty woman, too young to preach"; no casting up or down of the eyelids, no compression of the lips, no attitude of the arms that said, "But you must think of me as a saint." She held no book in her ungloved hands, but let them hang down lightly crossed before her, as she stood and turned her grey eyes on the people. There was no keenness in the eyes; they seemed rather to be shedding love than making observations; they had the liquid look which tells that the mind is full of what it has to give out, rather than impressed by external objects. She stood with her left hand towards the descending sun, and leafy boughs screened her from its rays; but in this sober light the delicate colouring of her face seemed to gather a calm vividness, like flowers at evening. It was a small oval face, of a uniform transparent whiteness, with an egg-like line of cheek and chin, a full but firm mouth, a delicate nostril, and a low perpendicular brow, surmounted by a rising arch of parting between smooth locks of pale reddish hair. The hair was drawn straight back behind the ears, and covered, except for an inch or two above the brow, by a net Quaker cap. The eyebrows, of the same colour as the hair, were perfectly horizontal and firmly pencilled; the eyelashes, though no darker, were long and abundant—nothing was left blurred or unfinished. It was one of those faces that make one think of white flowers with light touches of colour on their pure petals. The eyes had no peculiar beauty, beyond that of expression; they looked so simple, so candid, so gravely loving, that no accusing scowl, no light sneer could help melting away before their glance. Joshua Rann gave a long cough, as if he were clearing his throat in order to come to a new understanding with himself; Chad Cranage lifted up his leather skull-cap and scratched his head; and Wiry Ben wondered how Seth had the pluck to think of courting her.

"A sweet woman," the stranger said to himself, "but surely nature never meant her for a preacher."

Perhaps he was one of those who think that nature has theatrical properties and, with the considerate view of facilitating art and psychology, "makes up," her characters, so that there may be no mistake about them. But Dinah began to speak.

"Dear friends," she said in a clear but not loud voice "let us pray for a blessing."

She closed her eyes, and hanging her head down a little continued in the same moderate tone, as if speaking to some one quite near her: "Saviour of sinners! When a poor woman laden with sins, went out to the well to draw water, she found Thee sitting at the well. She knew Thee not; she had not sought Thee; her mind was dark; her life was unholy. But Thou didst speak to her, Thou didst teach her, Thou didst show her that her life lay open before Thee, and yet Thou wast ready to give her that blessing which she had never sought. Jesus, Thou art in the midst of us, and Thou knowest all men: if there is any here like that poor woman—if their minds are dark, their lives unholy—if they have come out not seeking Thee, not desiring to be taught; deal with them according to the free mercy which Thou didst show to her. Speak to them, Lord, open their ears to my message, bring their sins to their minds, and make them thirst for that salvation which Thou art ready to give.

"Lord, Thou art with Thy people still: they see Thee in the night-watches, and their hearts burn within them as Thou talkest with them by the way. And Thou art near to those who have not known Thee: open their eyes that they may see Thee—see Thee weeping over them, and saying 'Ye will not come unto me that ye might have life'—see Thee hanging on the cross and saying, 'Father, forgive them, for they know not what they do'—see Thee as Thou wilt come again in Thy glory to judge them at the last. Amen."

Dinah opened her eyes again and paused, looking at the group of villagers, who were now gathered rather more closely on her right hand.

"Dear friends," she began, raising her voice a little, "you have all of you been to church, and I think you must have heard the clergyman read these words: 'The Spirit of the Lord is upon me, because he hath anointed me to preach the gospel to the poor.' Jesus Christ spoke those words—he said he came *to preach the Gospel to the poor:* I don't know whether you ever thought about those words much, but I will tell you when I remember first hearing them. It was on just such a sort of evening as this, when I was a little girl, and my aunt as brought me up took me to hear a good man preach out of doors, just as we are here. I remember his face well: he was a very old man, and had very long white hair; his voice was very soft and beautiful, not like any voice I had ever heard before. I was a little girl and scarcely knew anything, and this old man seemed to me such a different sort of a man from anybody I had ever seen before that I thought he had perhaps come down from the sky to preach to us, and I said, 'Aunt, will he go back to the sky to-night, like the picture in the Bible?'

"That man of God was Mr. Wesley, who spent his life in doing what our blessed Lord did—preaching the Gospel to the poor—and he entered into his rest eight years ago. I came to know more about him years after, but I was a foolish thoughtless child then, and I remembered only one thing he told us in his sermon. He told us as 'Gospel' meant 'good news.' The Gospel, you know, is what the Bible tells us about God.

"Think of that now! Jesus Christ did really come down from heaven, as I, like a silly child, thought Mr. Wesley did; and what he came down for was to tell good news about God to the poor. Why, you and me, dear friends, are poor. We have been brought up in poor cottages and have been reared on oat-cake, and lived coarse; and we haven't been to school much, nor read books, and we don't know much about anything but what happens just round us. We are just the sort of people that want to hear good news. For when anybody's well off, they don't much mind about hearing news from distant parts; but if a poor man or woman's in trouble and has hard work to make out a living, they like to have a letter to tell 'em they've got a friend as will help 'em. To be sure, we can't help knowing something about God, even if we've never heard the Gospel, the good news that our Saviour brought us. For we know everything comes from God: don't you say almost every day, 'This and that will happen, please God,' and 'We shall begin to cut the grass soon, please God to send us a little more sunshine'? We know very well we are altogether in the hands of God. We didn't bring ourselves into the world, we can't keep ourselves alive while we're sleeping; the daylight, and the wind, and the corn, and the cows to give us milk—everything we have comes from God. And he gave us our souls and put love between parents and children, and husband and wife. But is that as much as we want to know about God? We see he is great and mighty, and can do what he will: we are lost, as if we was struggling in great waters, when we try to think of him.

"But perhaps doubts come into your mind like this: Can God take much notice of us poor people? Perhaps he only made the world for the great and the wise and the rich. It doesn't cost him much to give us our little handful of victual and bit of clothing; but how do we know he cares for us any more than we care for the worms and things in the garden, so as we rear our carrots and onions? Will God take care of us when we die? And has he any comfort for us when we are lame and sick and helpless? Perhaps, too, he is angry with us; else why does the blight come, and the bad harvests, and the fever, and all sorts of pain and trouble? For our life is full of trouble, and if God sends us good, he seems to send bad too. How is it? How is it?

"Ah, dear friends, we are in sad want of good news about God; and what does other good news signify if we haven't that? For everything else comes to an end, and when we die we leave it all. But God lasts when everything else is gone. What shall we do if he is not our friend?"

Then Dinah told how the good news had been brought, and how the mind of God towards the poor had been made manifest in the life of Jesus, dwelling on its lowliness and its acts of mercy.

"So you see, dear friends," she went on, "Jesus spent his time almost all in doing good to poor people; he preached out of doors to them, and he made friends of poor workmen, and taught them and took pains with them. Not but what he did good to the rich too, for he was full of love to all men, only he saw as the poor were more in want of his help. So he cured the lame and the sick and the blind, and he worked miracles to feed the hungry because, he said, he was sorry for them; and he was very kind to the little children and comforted those who had lost their friends; and he spoke very tenderly to poor sinners that were sorry for their sins.

"Ah, wouldn't you love such a man if you saw him—if he were here in this village? What a kind heart he must have! What a friend he would be to go to in trouble! How pleasant it must be to be taught by him.

"Well, dear friends, who *was* this man? Was he only a good man—a very good man, and no more—like our dear Mr. Wesley, who has been taken from us?... He was the Son of God—'in the image of the Father,' the Bible says; that means, just like God, who is the beginning and end of all things—the God we want to know about. So then, all the love that Jesus showed to the poor is the same love that God has for us. We can understand what Jesus felt, because he came in a body like ours and spoke words such as we speak to each other. We were afraid to think what God was before—the God who made the world and the sky and the thunder and lightning. We could never see him; we could only see the things he had made; and some of these things was very terrible, so as we might well tremble when we thought of him. But our blessed Saviour has showed us what God is in a way us poor ignorant people can understand; he has showed us what God's heart is, what are his feelings towards us.

"But let us see a little more about what Jesus came on earth for. Another time he said, 'I came to seek and to save that which was lost'; and another time, 'I came not to call the righteous but sinners to repentance.'

"The *lost!... Sinners!...* Ah, dear friends, does that mean you and me?"

Hitherto the traveller had been chained to the spot against his will by the charm of Dinah's mellow treble tones, which had a variety of modulation like that of a fine instrument touched with the unconscious skill of musical instinct. The simple things she said seemed like novelties, as a melody strikes us with a new feeling when we hear it sung by the pure voice of a boyish chorister; the quiet depth of conviction with which she spoke seemed in itself an evidence for the truth of her message. He saw that she had thoroughly arrested her hearers. The villagers had pressed nearer to her, and there was no longer anything but grave attention on all faces. She spoke slowly, though quite fluently, often pausing after a question, or before any transition of ideas. There was no change of attitude, no gesture; the effect of her speech was produced entirely by the inflections of her voice, and when she came to the question, "Will God take care of us when we die?" she uttered it in such a tone of plaintive appeal that the tears came into some of the hardest eyes. The stranger had ceased to doubt, as he had done at the first glance, that she could fix the attention of her rougher hearers, but still he wondered whether she could have that power of rousing their more violent emotions, which must surely be a necessary seal of her vocation as a Methodist preacher, until she came to the words, "Lost!—Sinners!" when there was a great change in her voice and manner. She had made a long pause before the exclamation, and the pause seemed to be filled by agitating thoughts that showed themselves in her features. Her pale face became paler; the circles under her eyes deepened, as they did when tears half-gather without falling; and the mild loving eyes took an expression of appalled pity, as if she had suddenly discerned a destroying angel hovering over the heads of the people. Her voice became deep and muffled, but there was still no gesture. Nothing could be less like the ordinary type of the Ranter than Dinah. She was not preaching as she heard others preach, but speaking directly from her own emotions and under the inspiration of her own simple faith.

But now she had entered into a new current of feeling. Her manner became less calm, her utterance more rapid and agitated, as she tried to bring home to the people their guilt, their wilful darkness, their state of disobedience to God—as she dwelt on the hatefulness of sin, the Divine holiness, and the sufferings of the Saviour, by which a way had been opened for their salvation. At last it seemed as if, in her yearning desire to reclaim the lost sheep, she could not be satisfied by addressing her hearers as a body. She appealed first to one and then to another, beseeching them with tears to turn to God while there was yet time; painting to them the desolation of their souls, lost in sin, feeding on the husks of this miserable world, far away from God their Father; and then the love of the Saviour, who was waiting and watching for their return.

There was many a responsive sigh and groan from her fellow-Methodists, but the village mind does not easily take fire, and a little smouldering vague anxiety that might easily die out again was the utmost effect Dinah's preaching had wrought in them at present. Yet no one had retired, except the children and "old Feyther Taft," who being too deaf to catch many words, had some time ago gone back to his inglenook. Wiry Ben was feeling very uncomfortable, and almost wishing he had not come to hear Dinah; he thought what she said would haunt him somehow. Yet he couldn't help liking to look at her and listen to her, though he dreaded every moment that she would fix her eyes on him and address him in particular. She had already addressed Sandy Jim, who was now holding the baby to relieve his wife, and the big soft-hearted man had rubbed away some tears with his fist, with a confused intention of being a better fellow, going less to the Holly Bush down by the Stone-pits, and cleaning himself more regularly of a Sunday.

In front of Sandy Jim stood Chad's Bess, who had shown an unwonted quietude and fixity of attention ever since Dinah had begun to speak. Not that the matter of the discourse had arrested her at once, for she was lost in a puzzling speculation as to what pleasure and satisfaction there could be in life to a young woman who wore a cap like Dinah's. Giving up this inquiry in despair, she took to studying Dinah's nose, eyes, mouth, and hair, and wondering whether it was better to have such a sort of pale face as that, or fat red cheeks and round black eyes like her own. But gradually the influence of the general gravity told upon her, and she became conscious of what Dinah was saying. The gentle tones, the loving persuasion, did not touch her, but when the more severe appeals came she began to be frightened. Poor Bessy had always been considered a naughty girl; she was conscious of it; if it was necessary to be very good, it was clear she must be in a bad way. She couldn't find her places at church as Sally Rann could, she had often been tittering when she "curcheyed" to Mr. Irwine; and these religious deficiencies were accompanied by a corresponding slackness in the minor morals, for Bessy belonged unquestionably to that unsoaped lazy class of feminine characters with whom you may venture to "eat an egg, an apple, or a nut." All this she was generally conscious of, and hitherto had not been greatly ashamed of it. But now she began to feel very much as if the constable had come to take her up and carry her before the justice for some undefined offence. She had a terrified sense that God, whom she had always thought of as very far off, was very near to her, and that Jesus was close by looking at her, though she could not see him. For Dinah had that belief in visible manifestations of Jesus, which is common among the Methodists, and she communicated it irresistibly to her hearers: she made them feel that he was among them bodily, and might at any moment show himself to them in some way that would strike anguish and penitence into their hearts.

"See!" she exclaimed, turning to the left, with her eyes fixed on a point above the heads of the people. "See where our blessed Lord stands and weeps and stretches out his arms towards you. Hear what he says: 'How often would I have gathered you as a hen gathereth her chickens under her wings, and ye would not!'... and ye would not," she repeated, in a tone of pleading reproach, turning her eyes on the people again. "See the print of the nails on his dear hands and feet. It is your sins that made them! Ah! How pale and worn he looks! He has gone through all that great agony in the garden, when his soul was exceeding sorrowful even unto death, and the great drops of sweat fell like blood to the ground. They spat upon him and buffeted him, they scourged him, they mocked him, they laid the heavy cross on his bruised shoulders. Then they nailed him up. Ah, what pain! His lips are parched with thirst, and they mock him still in this great agony; yet with those parched lips he prays for them, 'Father, forgive them, for they know not what they do.' Then a horror of great darkness fell upon him, and he felt what sinners feel when they are for ever shut out from God. That was the last drop in the cup of bitterness. 'My God, my God!' he cries, 'why hast Thou forsaken me?'

"All this he bore for you! For you—and you never think of him; for you—and you turn your backs on him; you don't care what he has gone through for you. Yet he is not weary of toiling for you: he has risen from the dead, he is praying for you at the right hand of God—'Father, forgive them, for they know not what they do.' And he is upon this earth too; he is among us; he is there close to you now; I see his wounded body and his look of love."

Here Dinah turned to Bessy Cranage, whose bonny youth and evident vanity had touched her with pity.

"Poor child! Poor child! He is beseeching you, and you don't listen to him. You think of ear-rings and fine gowns and caps, and you never think of the Saviour who died to save your precious soul. Your cheeks will be shrivelled one day, your hair will be grey, your poor body will be thin and tottering! Then you will begin to feel that your soul is not saved; then you will have to stand before God dressed in your sins, in your evil tempers and vain thoughts. And Jesus, who stands ready to help you now, won't help you then; because you won't have him to be your Saviour, he will be your judge. Now he looks at you with love and mercy and says, 'Come to me that you may have life'; then he will turn away from you, and say, 'Depart from me into ever-lasting fire!'"

Poor Bessy's wide-open black eyes began to fill with tears, her great red cheeks and lips became quite pale, and her face was distorted like a little child's before a burst of crying.

"Ah, poor blind child!" Dinah went on, "think if it should happen to you as it once happened to a servant of God in the days of her vanity. *She* thought of her lace caps and saved all her money to buy 'em; she thought nothing about how she might get a clean heart and a right spirit—she only wanted to have better lace than other girls. And one day when she put her new cap on and looked in the glass, she saw a bleeding Face crowned with thorns. That face is looking at you now"—here Dinah pointed to a spot close in front of Bessy—"Ah, tear off those follies! Cast them away from you, as if they were stinging adders. They *are* stinging you—they are poisoning your soul—they are dragging you down into a dark bottomless pit, where you will sink for ever, and for ever, and for ever, further away from light and God."

Bessy could bear it no longer: a great terror was upon her, and wrenching her ear-rings from her ears, she threw them down before her, sobbing aloud. Her father, Chad, frightened lest he should be "laid hold on" too, this impression on the rebellious Bess striking him as nothing less than a miracle, walked hastily away and began to work at his anvil by way of reassuring himself. "Folks mun ha' hoss-shoes, praichin' or no praichin': the divil canna lay hould o' me for that," he muttered to himself.

But now Dinah began to tell of the joys that were in store for the penitent, and to describe in her simple way the divine peace and love with which the soul of the believer is filled—how the sense of God's love turns poverty into riches and satisfies the soul so that no uneasy desire vexes it, no fear alarms it: how, at last, the very temptation to sin is extinguished, and heaven is begun upon earth, because no cloud passes between the soul and God, who is its eternal sun.

"Dear friends," she said at last, "brothers and sisters, whom I love as those for whom my Lord has died, believe me, I know what this great blessedness is; and because I know it, I want you to have it too. I am poor, like you: I have to get my living with my hands; but no lord nor lady can be so happy as me, if they haven't got the love of God in their souls. Think what it is—not to hate anything but sin; to be full of love to every creature; to be frightened at nothing; to be sure that all things will turn to good; not to mind pain, because it is our Father's will; to know that nothing—no, not if the earth was to be burnt up, or the waters come and drown us—nothing could part us from God who loves us, and who fills our souls with peace and joy, because we are sure that whatever he wills is holy, just, and good.

"Dear friends, come and take this blessedness; it is offered to you; it is the good news that Jesus came to preach to the poor. It is not like the riches of this world, so that the more one gets the less the rest can have. God is without end; his love is without end—"

Its streams the whole creation reach,
So plenteous is the store;
Enough for all, enough for each,
Enough for evermore.

Dinah had been speaking at least an hour, and the reddening light of the parting day seemed to give a solemn emphasis to her closing words. The stranger, who had been interested in the course of her sermon as if it had been the development of a drama—for there is this sort of fascination in all sincere unpremeditated eloquence, which opens to one the inward drama of the speaker's emotions—now turned his horse aside and pursued his way, while Dinah said, "Let us sing a little, dear friends"; and as he was still winding down the slope, the voices of the Methodists reached him, rising and falling in that strange blending of exultation and sadness which belongs to the cadence of a hymn.

Chapter III
After the Preaching

In less than an hour from that time, Seth Bede was walking by Dinah's side along the hedgerow-path that skirted the pastures and green corn-fields which lay between the village and the Hall Farm. Dinah had taken off her little Quaker bonnet again, and was holding it in her hands that she might have a freer enjoyment of the cool evening twilight, and Seth could see the expression of her face quite clearly as he walked by her side, timidly revolving something he wanted to say to her. It was an expression of unconscious placid gravity—of absorption in thoughts that had no connection with the present moment or with her own personality—an expression that is most of all discouraging to a lover. Her very walk was discouraging: it had that quiet elasticity that asks for no support. Seth felt this dimly; he said to himself, "She's too good and holy for any man, let alone me," and the words he had been summoning rushed back again before they had reached his lips. But another thought gave him courage: "There's no man could love her better and leave her freer to follow the Lord's work." They had been silent for many minutes now, since they had done talking about Bessy Cranage; Dinah seemed almost to have forgotten Seth's presence, and her pace was becoming so much quicker that the sense of their being only a few minutes' walk from the yard-gates of the Hall Farm at last gave Seth courage to speak.

"You've quite made up your mind to go back to Snowfield o' Saturday, Dinah?"

"Yes," said Dinah, quietly. "I'm called there. It was borne in upon my mind while I was meditating on Sunday night, as Sister Allen, who's in a decline, is in need of me. I saw her as plain as we see that bit of thin white cloud, lifting up her poor thin hand and beckoning to me. And this morning when I opened the Bible for direction, the first words my eyes fell on were, 'And after we had seen the vision, immediately we endeavoured to go into Macedonia.' If it wasn't for that clear showing of the Lord's will, I should be loath to go, for my heart yearns over my aunt and her little ones, and that poor wandering lamb Hetty Sorrel. I've been much drawn out in prayer for her of late, and I look on it as a token that there may be mercy in store for her."

"God grant it," said Seth. "For I doubt Adam's heart is so set on her, he'll never turn to anybody else; and yet it 'ud go to my heart if he was to marry her, for I canna think as she'd make him happy. It's a deep mystery—the way the heart of man turns to one woman out of all the rest he's seen i' the world, and makes it easier for him to work seven year for *her*, like Jacob did for Rachel, sooner than have any other woman for th' asking. I often think of them words, 'And Jacob served seven years for Rachel; and they seemed to him but a few days for the love he had to her.' I know those words 'ud come true with me, Dinah, if so be you'd give me hope as I might win you after seven years was over. I know you think a husband 'ud be taking up too much o' your thoughts, because St. Paul says, 'She that's married careth for the things of the world how she may please her husband'; and may happen you'll think me overbold to speak to you about it again, after what you told me o' your mind last Saturday. But I've been thinking it over again by night and by day, and I've prayed not to be blinded by my own desires, to think what's only good for me must be good for you too. And it seems to me there's more texts for your marrying than ever you can find against it. For St. Paul says as plain as can be in another place, 'I will that the younger women marry, bear children, guide the house, give none occasion to the adversary to speak reproachfully'; and then 'two are better than one'; and that holds good with marriage as well as with other things. For we should be o' one heart and o' one mind, Dinah. We both serve the same Master, and are striving after the same gifts; and I'd never be the husband to make a claim on you as could interfere with your doing the work God has fitted you for. I'd make a shift, and fend indoor and out, to give you more liberty—more than you can have now, for you've got to get your own living now, and I'm strong enough to work for us both."

When Seth had once begun to urge his suit, he went on earnestly and almost hurriedly, lest Dinah should speak some decisive word before he had poured forth all the arguments he had prepared. His cheeks became flushed as he went on, his mild grey eyes filled with tears, and his voice trembled as he spoke the last sentence. They had reached one of those very narrow passes between two tall stones, which performed the office of a stile in Loamshire, and Dinah paused as she turned towards Seth and said, in her tender but calm treble notes, "Seth Bede, I thank you for your love towards me, and if I could think of any man as more than a Christian brother, I think it would be you. But my heart is not free to marry. That is good for other women, and it is a great and a blessed thing to be a wife and mother; but 'as God has distributed to every man, as the Lord hath called every man, so let him walk.' God has called me to minister to others, not to have any joys or sorrows of my own, but to rejoice with them that do rejoice, and to weep with those that weep. He has called me to speak his word, and he has greatly owned my work. It could only be on a very clear showing that I could leave the brethren and sisters at Snowfield, who are favoured with very little of this world's good; where the trees are few, so that a child might count them, and there's very hard living for the poor in the winter. It has been given me to help, to comfort, and strengthen the little flock there and to call in many wanderers; and my soul is filled with these things from my rising up till my lying down. My life is too short, and God's work is too great for me to think of making a home for myself in this world. I've not turned a deaf ear to your words, Seth, for when I saw as your love was given to me, I thought it might be a leading of Providence for me to change my way of life, and that we should be fellow-helpers; and I spread the matter before the Lord. But whenever I tried to fix my mind on marriage, and our living together, other thoughts always came in—the times when I've prayed by the sick and dying, and the happy hours I've had preaching, when my heart was filled with love, and the Word was given to me abundantly. And when I've opened the Bible for direction, I've always lighted on some clear word to tell me where my work lay. I believe what you say, Seth, that you would try to be a help and not a hindrance to my work; but I see that our marriage is not God's will—He draws my heart another way. I desire to live and die without husband or children. I seem to have no room in my soul for wants and fears of my own, it has pleased God to fill my heart so full with the wants and sufferings of his poor people."

Seth was unable to reply, and they walked on in silence. At last, as they were nearly at the yard-gate, he said, "Well, Dinah, I must seek for strength to bear it, and to endure as seeing Him who is invisible. But I feel now how weak my faith is. It seems as if, when you are gone, I could never joy in anything any more. I think it's something passing the love of women as I feel for you, for I could be content without your marrying me if I could go and live at Snowfield and be near you. I trusted as the strong love God has given me towards you was a leading for us both; but it seems it was only meant for my trial. Perhaps I feel more for you than I ought to feel for any creature, for I often can't help saying of you what the hymn says—

In darkest shades if she appear,
My dawning is begun;
She is my soul's bright morning-star,
And she my rising sun.

That may be wrong, and I am to be taught better. But you wouldn't be displeased with me if things turned out so as I could leave this country and go to live at Snowfield?"

"No, Seth; but I counsel you to wait patiently, and not lightly to leave your own country and kindred. Do nothing without the Lord's clear bidding. It's a bleak and barren country there, not like this land of Goshen you've been used to. We mustn't be in a hurry to fix and choose our own lot; we must wait to be guided."

"But you'd let me write you a letter, Dinah, if there was anything I wanted to tell you?"

"Yes, sure; let me know if you're in any trouble. You'll be continually in my prayers."

They had now reached the yard-gate, and Seth said, "I won't go in, Dinah, so farewell." He paused and hesitated after she had given him her hand, and then said, "There's no knowing but what you may see things different after a while. There may be a new leading."

"Let us leave that, Seth. It's good to live only a moment at a time, as I've read in one of Mr. Wesley's books. It isn't for you and me to lay plans; we've nothing to do but to obey and to trust. Farewell."

Dinah pressed his hand with rather a sad look in her loving eyes, and then passed through the gate, while Seth turned away to walk lingeringly home. But instead of taking the direct road, he chose to turn back along the fields through which he and Dinah had already passed; and I think his blue linen handkerchief was very wet with tears long before he had made up his mind that it was time for him to set his face steadily homewards. He was but three-and-twenty, and had only just learned what it is to love—to love with that adoration which a young man gives to a woman whom he feels to be greater and better than himself. Love of this sort is hardly distinguishable from religious feeling. What deep and worthy love is so, whether of woman or child, or art or music. Our caresses, our tender words, our still rapture under the influence of autumn sunsets, or pillared vistas, or calm majestic statues, or Beethoven symphonies all bring with them the consciousness that they are mere waves and ripples in an unfathomable ocean of love and beauty; our emotion in its keenest moment passes from expression into silence, our love at its highest flood rushes beyond its object and loses itself in the sense of divine mystery. And this blessed gift of venerating love has been given to too many humble craftsmen since the world began for us to feel any surprise that it should have existed in the soul of a Methodist carpenter half a century ago, while there was yet a lingering after-glow from the time when Wesley and his fellow-labourer fed on the hips and haws of the Cornwall hedges, after exhausting limbs and lungs in carrying a divine message to the poor.

That afterglow has long faded away; and the picture we are apt to make of Methodism in our imagination is not an amphitheatre of green hills, or the deep shade of broad-leaved sycamores, where a crowd of rough men and weary-hearted women drank in a faith which was a rudimentary culture, which linked their thoughts with the past, lifted their imagination above the sordid details of their own narrow lives, and suffused their souls with the sense of a pitying, loving, infinite Presence, sweet as summer to the houseless needy. It is too possible that to some of my readers Methodism may mean nothing more than low-pitched gables up dingy streets, sleek grocers, sponging preachers, and hypocritical jargon—elements which are regarded as an exhaustive analysis of Methodism in many fashionable quarters.

That would be a pity; for I cannot pretend that Seth and Dinah were anything else than Methodists—not indeed of that modern type which reads quarterly reviews and attends in chapels with pillared porticoes, but of a very old-fashioned kind. They believed in present miracles, in instantaneous conversions, in revelations by dreams and visions; they drew lots, and sought for Divine guidance by opening the Bible at hazard; having a literal way of interpreting the Scriptures, which is not at all sanctioned by approved commentators; and it is impossible for me to represent their diction as correct, or their instruction as liberal. Still—if I have read religious history aright—faith, hope, and charity have not always been found in a direct ratio with a sensibility to the three concords, and it is possible—thank Heaven!—to have very erroneous theories and very sublime feelings. The raw bacon which clumsy Molly spares from her own scanty store that she may carry it to her neighbour's child to "stop the fits," may be a piteously inefficacious remedy; but the generous stirring of neighbourly kindness that prompted the deed has a beneficent radiation that is not lost.

Considering these things, we can hardly think Dinah and Seth beneath our sympathy, accustomed as we may be to weep over the loftier sorrows of heroines in satin boots and crinoline, and of heroes riding fiery horses, themselves ridden by still more fiery passions.

Poor Seth! He was never on horseback in his life except once, when he was a little lad, and Mr. Jonathan Burge took him up behind, telling him to "hold on tight"; and instead of bursting out into wild accusing apostrophes to God and destiny, he is resolving, as he now walks homewards under the solemn starlight, to repress his sadness, to be less bent on having his own will, and to live more for others, as Dinah does.

Chapter IV
Home and Its Sorrows

A green valley with a brook running through it, full almost to overflowing with the late rains, overhung by low stooping willows. Across this brook a plank is thrown, and over this plank Adam Bede is passing with his undoubting step, followed close by Gyp with the basket; evidently making his way to the thatched house, with a stack of timber by the side of it, about twenty yards up the opposite slope.

The door of the house is open, and an elderly woman is looking out; but she is not placidly contemplating the evening sunshine; she has been watching with dim eyes the gradually enlarging speck which for the last few minutes she has been quite sure is her darling son Adam. Lisbeth Bede loves her son with the love of a woman to whom her first-born has come late in life. She is an anxious, spare, yet vigorous old woman, clean as a snowdrop. Her grey hair is turned neatly back under a pure linen cap with a black band round it; her broad chest is covered with a buff neckerchief, and below this you see a sort of short bedgown made of blue-checkered linen, tied round the waist and descending to the hips, from whence there is a considerable length of linsey-woolsey petticoat. For Lisbeth is tall, and in other points too there is a strong likeness between her and her son Adam. Her dark eyes are somewhat dim now—perhaps from too much crying—but her broadly marked eyebrows are still black, her teeth are sound, and as she stands knitting rapidly and unconsciously with her work-hardened hands, she has as firmly upright an attitude as when she is carrying a pail of water on her head from the spring. There is the same type of frame and the same keen activity of temperament in mother and son, but it was not from her that Adam got his well-filled brow and his expression of large-hearted intelligence.

Family likeness has often a deep sadness in it. Nature, that great tragic dramatist, knits us together by bone and muscle, and divides us by the subtler web of our brains; blends yearning and repulsion; and ties us by our heart-strings to the beings that jar us at every movement. We hear a voice with the very cadence of our own uttering the thoughts we despise; we see eyes—ah, so like our mother's!—averted from us in cold alienation; and our last darling child startles us with the air and gestures of the sister we parted from in bitterness long years ago. The father to whom we owe our best heritage—the mechanical instinct, the keen sensibility to harmony, the unconscious skill of the modelling hand—galls us and puts us to shame by his daily errors; the long-lost mother, whose face we begin to see in the glass as our own wrinkles come, once fretted our young souls with her anxious humours and irrational persistence.

It is such a fond anxious mother's voice that you hear, as Lisbeth says, "Well, my lad, it's gone seven by th' clock. Thee't allays stay till the last child's born. Thee wants thy supper, I'll warrand. Where's Seth? Gone arter some o's chapellin', I reckon?"

"Aye, aye, Seth's at no harm, mother, thee mayst be sure. But where's father?" said Adam quickly, as he entered the house and glanced into the room on the left hand, which was used as a workshop. "Hasn't he done the coffin for Tholer? There's the stuff standing just as I left it this morning."

"Done the coffin?" said Lisbeth, following him, and knitting uninterruptedly, though she looked at her son very anxiously. "Eh, my lad, he went aff to Treddles'on this forenoon, an's niver come back. I doubt he's got to th' 'Waggin Overthrow' again."

A deep flush of anger passed rapidly over Adam's face. He said nothing, but threw off his jacket and began to roll up his shirt-sleeves again.

"What art goin' to do, Adam?" said the mother, with a tone and look of alarm. "Thee wouldstna go to work again, wi'out ha'in thy bit o' supper?"

Adam, too angry to speak, walked into the workshop. But his mother threw down her knitting, and, hurrying after him, took hold of his arm, and said, in a tone of plaintive remonstrance, "Nay, my lad, my lad, thee munna go wi'out thy supper; there's the taters wi' the gravy in 'em, just as thee lik'st 'em. I saved 'em o' purpose for thee. Come an' ha' thy supper, come."

"Let be!" said Adam impetuously, shaking her off and seizing one of the planks that stood against the wall. "It's fine talking about having supper when here's a coffin promised to be ready at Brox'on by seven o'clock to-morrow morning, and ought to ha' been there now, and not a nail struck yet. My throat's too full to swallow victuals."

"Why, thee canstna get the coffin ready," said Lisbeth. "Thee't work thyself to death. It 'ud take thee all night to do't."

"What signifies how long it takes me? Isn't the coffin promised? Can they bury the man without a coffin? I'd work my right hand off sooner than deceive people with lies i' that way. It makes me mad to think on't. I shall overrun these doings before long. I've stood enough of 'em."

Poor Lisbeth did not hear this threat for the first time, and if she had been wise she would have gone away quietly and said nothing for the next hour. But one of the lessons a woman most rarely learns is never to talk to an angry or a drunken man. Lisbeth sat down on the chopping bench and began to cry, and by the time she had cried enough to make her voice very piteous, she burst out into words.

"Nay, my lad, my lad, thee wouldstna go away an' break thy mother's heart, an' leave thy feyther to ruin. Thee wouldstna ha' 'em carry me to th' churchyard, an' thee not to follow me. I shanna rest i' my grave if I donna see thee at th' last; an' how's they to let thee know as I'm a-dyin', if thee't gone a-workin' i' distant parts, an' Seth belike gone arter thee, and thy feyther not able to hold a pen for's hand shakin', besides not knowin' where thee art? Thee mun forgie thy feyther—thee munna be so bitter again' him. He war a good feyther to thee afore he took to th' drink. He's a clever workman, an' taught thee thy trade, remember, an's niver gen me a blow nor so much as an ill word—no, not even in 's drink. Thee wouldstna ha' 'm go to the workhus—thy own feyther—an' him as was a fine-growed man an' handy at everythin' amost as thee art thysen, five-an'-twenty 'ear ago, when thee wast a baby at the breast."

Lisbeth's voice became louder, and choked with sobs—a sort of wail, the most irritating of all sounds where real sorrows are to be borne and real work to be done. Adam broke in impatiently.

"Now, Mother, don't cry and talk so. Haven't I got enough to vex me without that? What's th' use o' telling me things as I only think too much on every day? If I didna think on 'em, why should I do as I do, for the sake o' keeping things together here? But I hate to be talking where it's no use: I like to keep my breath for doing i'stead o' talking."

"I know thee dost things as nobody else 'ud do, my lad. But thee't allays so hard upo' thy feyther, Adam. Thee think'st nothing too much to do for Seth: thee snapp'st me up if iver I find faut wi' th' lad. But thee't so angered wi' thy feyther, more nor wi' anybody else."

"That's better than speaking soft and letting things go the wrong way, I reckon, isn't it? If I wasn't sharp with him he'd sell every bit o' stuff i' th' yard and spend it on drink. I know there's a duty to be done by my father, but it isn't my duty to encourage him in running headlong to ruin. And what has Seth got to do with it? The lad does no harm as I know of. But leave me alone, Mother, and let me get on with the work."

Lisbeth dared not say any more; but she got up and called Gyp, thinking to console herself somewhat for Adam's refusal of the supper she had spread out in the loving expectation of looking at him while he ate it, by feeding Adam's dog with extra liberality. But Gyp was watching his master with wrinkled brow and ears erect, puzzled at this unusual course of things; and though he glanced at Lisbeth when she called him, and moved his fore-paws uneasily, well knowing that she was inviting him to supper, he was in a divided state of mind, and remained seated on his haunches, again fixing his eyes anxiously on his master. Adam noticed Gyp's mental conflict, and though his anger had made him less tender than usual to his mother, it did not prevent him from caring as much as usual for his dog. We are apt to be kinder to the brutes that love us than to the women that love us. Is it because the brutes are dumb?

"Go, Gyp; go, lad!" Adam said, in a tone of encouraging command; and Gyp, apparently satisfied that duty and pleasure were one, followed Lisbeth into the house-place.

But no sooner had he licked up his supper than he went back to his master, while Lisbeth sat down alone to cry over her knitting. Women who are never bitter and resentful are often the most querulous; and if Solomon was as wise as he is reputed to be, I feel sure that when he compared a contentious woman to a continual dropping on a very rainy day, he had not a vixen in his eye—a fury with long nails, acrid and selfish. Depend upon it, he meant a good creature, who had no joy but in the happiness of the loved ones whom she contributed to make uncomfortable, putting by all the tid-bits for them and spending nothing on herself. Such a woman as Lisbeth, for example—at once patient and complaining, self-renouncing and exacting, brooding the livelong day over what happened yesterday and what is likely to happen to-morrow, and crying very readily both at the good and the evil. But a certain awe mingled itself with her idolatrous love of Adam, and when he said, "Leave me alone," she was always silenced.

So the hours passed, to the loud ticking of the old day-clock and the sound of Adam's tools. At last he called for a light and a draught of water (beer was a thing only to be drunk on holidays), and Lisbeth ventured to say as she took it in, "Thy supper stan's ready for thee, when thee lik'st."

"Donna thee sit up, mother," said Adam, in a gentle tone. He had worked off his anger now, and whenever he wished to be especially kind to his mother, he fell into his strongest native accent and dialect, with which at other times his speech was less deeply tinged. "I'll see to Father when he comes home; maybe he wonna come at all to-night. I shall be easier if thee't i' bed."

"Nay, I'll bide till Seth comes. He wonna be long now, I reckon."

It was then past nine by the clock, which was always in advance of the days, and before it had struck ten the latch was lifted and Seth entered. He had heard the sound of the tools as he was approaching.

"Why, Mother," he said, "how is it as Father's working so late?"

"It's none o' thy feyther as is a-workin'—thee might know that well anoof if thy head warna full o' chapellin'—it's thy brother as does iverything, for there's niver nobody else i' th' way to do nothin'."

Lisbeth was going on, for she was not at all afraid of Seth, and usually poured into his ears all the querulousness which was repressed by her awe of Adam. Seth had never in his life spoken a harsh word to his mother, and timid people always wreak their peevishness on the gentle. But Seth, with an anxious look, had passed into the workshop and said, "Addy, how's this? What! Father's forgot the coffin?"

"Aye, lad, th' old tale; but I shall get it done," said Adam, looking up and casting one of his bright keen glances at his brother. "Why, what's the matter with thee? Thee't in trouble."

Seth's eyes were red, and there was a look of deep depression on his mild face.

"Yes, Addy, but it's what must be borne, and can't be helped. Why, thee'st never been to the school, then?"

"School? No, that screw can wait," said Adam, hammering away again.

"Let me take my turn now, and do thee go to bed," said Seth.

"No, lad, I'd rather go on, now I'm in harness. Thee't help me to carry it to Brox'on when it's done. I'll call thee up at sunrise. Go and eat thy supper, and shut the door so as I mayn't hear Mother's talk."

Seth knew that Adam always meant what he said, and was not to be persuaded into meaning anything else. So he turned, with rather a heavy heart, into the house-place.

"Adam's niver touched a bit o' victual sin' home he's come," said Lisbeth. "I reckon thee'st hed thy supper at some o' thy Methody folks."

"Nay, Mother," said Seth, "I've had no supper yet."

"Come, then," said Lisbeth, "but donna thee ate the taters, for Adam 'ull happen ate 'em if I leave 'em stannin'. He loves a bit o' taters an' gravy. But he's been so sore an' angered, he wouldn't ate 'em, for all I'd putten 'em by o' purpose for him. An' he's been a-threatenin' to go away again," she went on, whimpering, "an' I'm fast sure he'll go some dawnin' afore I'm up, an' niver let me know aforehand, an' he'll niver come back again when once he's gone. An' I'd better niver ha' had a son, as is like no other body's son for the deftness an' th' handiness, an' so looked on by th' grit folks, an' tall an' upright like a poplar-tree, an' me to be parted from him an' niver see 'm no more."

"Come, Mother, donna grieve thyself in vain," said Seth, in a soothing voice. "Thee'st not half so good reason to think as Adam 'ull go away as to think he'll stay with thee. He may say such a thing when he's in wrath—and he's got excuse for being wrathful sometimes—but his heart 'ud never let him go. Think how he's stood by us all when it's been none so easy—paying his savings to free me from going for a soldier, an' turnin' his earnin's into wood for father, when he's got plenty o' uses for his money, and many a young man like him 'ud ha' been married and settled before now. He'll never turn round and knock down his own work, and forsake them as it's been the labour of his life to stand by."

"Donna talk to me about's marr'in'," said Lisbeth, crying afresh. "He's set's heart on that Hetty Sorrel, as 'ull niver save a penny, an' 'ull toss up her head at's old mother. An' to think as he might ha' Mary Burge, an' be took partners, an' be a big man wi' workmen under him, like Mester Burge—Dolly's told me so o'er and o'er again—if it warna as he's set's heart on that bit of a wench, as is o' no more use nor the gillyflower on the wall. An' he so wise at bookin' an' figurin', an' not to know no better nor that!"

"But, Mother, thee know'st we canna love just where other folks 'ud have us. There's nobody but God can control the heart of man. I could ha' wished myself as Adam could ha' made another choice, but I wouldn't reproach him for what he can't help. And I'm not sure but what he tries to o'ercome it. But it's a matter as he doesn't like to be spoke to about, and I can only pray to the Lord to bless and direct him."

"Aye, thee't allays ready enough at prayin', but I donna see as thee gets much wi' thy prayin'. Thee wotna get double earnin's o' this side Yule. Th' Methodies 'll niver make thee half the man thy brother is, for all they're a-makin' a preacher on thee."

"It's partly truth thee speak'st there, Mother," said Seth, mildly; "Adam's far before me, an's done more for me than I can ever do for him. God distributes talents to every man according as He sees good. But thee mustna undervally prayer. Prayer mayna bring money, but it brings us what no money can buy—a power to keep from sin and be content with God's will, whatever He may please to send. If thee wouldst pray to God to help thee, and trust in His goodness, thee wouldstna be so uneasy about things."

"Unaisy? I'm i' th' right on't to be unaisy. It's well seen on *thee* what it is niver to be unaisy. Thee't gi' away all thy earnin's, an' niver be unaisy as thee'st nothin' laid up again' a rainy day. If Adam had been as aisy as thee, he'd niver ha' had no money to pay for thee. Take no thought for the morrow—take no thought—that's what thee't allays sayin'; an' what comes on't? Why, as Adam has to take thought for thee."

"Those are the words o' the Bible, Mother," said Seth. "They don't mean as we should be idle. They mean we shouldn't be overanxious and worreting ourselves about what'll happen to-morrow, but do our duty and leave the rest to God's will."

"Aye, aye, that's the way wi' thee: thee allays makes a peck o' thy own words out o' a pint o' the Bible's. I donna see how thee't to know as 'take no thought for the morrow' means all that. An' when the Bible's such a big book, an' thee canst read all thro't, an' ha' the pick o' the texes, I canna think why thee dostna pick better words as donna mean so much more nor they say. Adam doesna pick a that'n; I can understan' the tex as he's allays a-sayin', 'God helps them as helps theirsens.'"

"Nay, Mother," said Seth, "that's no text o' the Bible. It comes out of a book as Adam picked up at the stall at Treddles'on. It was wrote by a knowing man, but overworldly, I doubt. However, that saying's partly true; for the Bible tells us we must be workers together with God."

"Well, how'm I to know? It sounds like a tex. But what's th' matter wi' th' lad? Thee't hardly atin' a bit o' supper. Dostna mean to ha' no more nor that bit o' oat-cake? An' thee lookst as white as a flick o' new bacon. What's th' matter wi' thee?"

"Nothing to mind about, Mother; I'm not hungry. I'll just look in at Adam again, and see if he'll let me go on with the coffin."

"Ha' a drop o' warm broth?" said Lisbeth, whose motherly feeling now got the better of her "nattering" habit. "I'll set two-three sticks a-light in a minute."

"Nay, Mother, thank thee; thee't very good," said Seth, gratefully; and encouraged by this touch of tenderness, he went on: "Let me pray a bit with thee for Father, and Adam, and all of us—it'll comfort thee, happen, more than thee thinkst."

"Well, I've nothin' to say again' it."

Lisbeth, though disposed always to take the negative side in her conversations with Seth, had a vague sense that there was some comfort and safety in the fact of his piety, and that it somehow relieved her from the trouble of any spiritual transactions on her own behalf.

So the mother and son knelt down together, and Seth prayed for the poor wandering father and for those who were sorrowing for him at home. And when he came to the petition that Adam might never be called to set up his tent in a far country, but that his mother might be cheered and comforted by his presence all the days of her pilgrimage, Lisbeth's ready tears flowed again, and she wept aloud.

When they rose from their knees, Seth went to Adam again and said, "Wilt only lie down for an hour or two, and let me go on the while?"

"No, Seth, no. Make Mother go to bed, and go thyself."

Meantime Lisbeth had dried her eyes, and now followed Seth, holding something in her hands. It was the brown-and-yellow platter containing the baked potatoes with the gravy in them and bits of meat which she had cut and mixed among them. Those were dear times, when wheaten bread and fresh meat were delicacies to working people. She set the dish down rather timidly on the bench by Adam's side and said, "Thee canst pick a bit while thee't workin'. I'll bring thee another drop o' water."

"Aye, Mother, do," said Adam, kindly; "I'm getting very thirsty."

In half an hour all was quiet; no sound was to be heard in the house but the loud ticking of the old day-clock and the ringing of Adam's tools. The night was very still: when Adam opened the door to look out at twelve o'clock, the only motion seemed to be in the glowing, twinkling stars; every blade of grass was asleep.

Bodily haste and exertion usually leave our thoughts very much at the mercy of our feelings and imagination; and it was so to-night with Adam. While his muscles were working lustily, his mind seemed as passive as a spectator at a diorama: scenes of the sad past, and probably sad future, floating before him and giving place one to the other in swift succession.

He saw how it would be to-morrow morning, when he had carried the coffin to Broxton and was at home again, having his breakfast: his father perhaps would come in ashamed to meet his son's glance—would sit down, looking older and more tottering than he had done the morning before, and hang down his head, examining the floor-quarries; while Lisbeth would ask him how he supposed the coffin had been got ready, that he had slinked off and left undone—for Lisbeth was always the first to utter the word of reproach, although she cried at Adam's severity towards his father.

"So it will go on, worsening and worsening," thought Adam; "there's no slipping uphill again, and no standing still when once you 've begun to slip down." And then the day came back to him when he was a little fellow and used to run by his father's side, proud to be taken out to work, and prouder still to hear his father boasting to his fellow-workmen how "the little chap had an uncommon notion o' carpentering." What a fine active fellow his father was then! When people asked Adam whose little lad he was, he had a sense of distinction as he answered, "I'm Thias Bede's lad." He was quite sure everybody knew Thias Bede—didn't he make the wonderful pigeon-house at Broxton parsonage? Those were happy days, especially when Seth, who was three years the younger, began to go out working too, and Adam began to be a teacher as well as a learner. But then came the days of sadness, when Adam was someway on in his teens, and Thias began to loiter at the public-houses, and Lisbeth began to cry at home, and to pour forth her plaints in the hearing of her sons. Adam remembered well the night of shame and anguish when he first saw his father quite wild and foolish, shouting a song out fitfully among his drunken companions at the "Waggon Overthrown." He had run away once when he was only eighteen, making his escape in the morning twilight with a little blue bundle over his shoulder, and his "mensuration book" in his pocket, and saying to himself very decidedly that he could bear the vexations of home no longer—he would go and seek his fortune, setting up his stick at the crossways and bending his steps the way it fell. But by the time he got to Stoniton, the thought of his mother and Seth, left behind to endure everything without him, became too importunate, and his resolution failed him. He came back the next day, but the misery and terror his mother had gone through in those two days had haunted her ever since.

"No!" Adam said to himself to-night, "that must never happen again. It 'ud make a poor balance when my doings are cast up at the last, if my poor old mother stood o' the wrong side. My back's broad enough and strong enough; I should be no better than a coward to go away and leave the troubles to be borne by them as aren't half so able. 'They that are strong ought to bear the infirmities of those that are weak, and not to please themselves.' There's a text wants no candle to show't; it shines by its own light. It's plain enough you get into the wrong road i' this life if you run after this and that only for the sake o' making things easy and pleasant to yourself. A pig may poke his nose into the trough and think o' nothing outside it; but if you've got a man's heart and soul in you, you can't be easy a-making your own bed an' leaving the rest to lie on the stones. Nay, nay, I'll never slip my neck out o' the yoke, and leave the load to be drawn by the weak uns. Father's a sore cross to me, an's likely to be for many a long year to come. What then? I've got th' health, and the limbs, and the sperrit to bear it."

At this moment a smart rap, as if with a willow wand, was given at the house door, and Gyp, instead of barking, as might have been expected, gave a loud howl. Adam, very much startled, went at once to the door and opened it. Nothing was there; all was still, as when he opened it an hour before; the leaves were motionless, and the light of the stars showed the placid fields on both sides of the brook quite empty of visible life. Adam walked round the house, and still saw nothing except a rat which darted into the woodshed as he passed. He went in again, wondering; the sound was so peculiar that the moment he heard it it called up the image of the willow wand striking the door. He could not help a little shudder, as he remembered how often his mother had told him of just such a sound coming as a sign when some one was dying. Adam was not a man to be gratuitously superstitious, but he had the blood of the peasant in him as well as of the artisan, and a peasant can no more help believing in a traditional superstition than a horse can help trembling when he sees a camel. Besides, he had that mental combination which is at once humble in the region of mystery and keen in the region of knowledge: it was the depth of his reverence quite as much as his hard common sense which gave him his disinclination to doctrinal religion, and he often checked Seth's argumentative spiritualism by saying, "Eh, it's a big mystery; thee know'st but little about it." And so it happened that Adam was at once penetrating and credulous. If a new building had fallen down and he had been told that this was a divine judgment, he would have said, "May be; but the bearing o' the roof and walls wasn't right, else it wouldn't ha' come down"; yet he believed in dreams and prognostics, and to his dying day he bated his breath a little when he told the story of the stroke with the willow wand. I tell it as he told it, not attempting to reduce it to its natural elements—in our eagerness to explain impressions, we often lose our hold of the sympathy that comprehends them.

But he had the best antidote against imaginative dread in the necessity for getting on with the coffin, and for the next ten minutes his hammer was ringing so uninterruptedly, that other sounds, if there were any, might well be overpowered. A pause came, however, when he had to take up his ruler, and now again came the strange rap, and again Gyp howled. Adam was at the door without the loss of a moment; but again all was still, and the starlight showed there was nothing but the dew-laden grass in front of the cottage.

Adam for a moment thought uncomfortably about his father; but of late years he had never come home at dark hours from Treddleston, and there was every reason for believing that he was then sleeping off his drunkenness at the "Waggon Overthrown." Besides, to Adam, the conception of the future was so inseparable from the painful image of his father that the fear of any fatal accident to him was excluded by the deeply infixed fear of his continual degradation. The next thought that occurred to him was one that made him slip off his shoes and tread lightly upstairs, to listen at the bedroom doors. But both Seth and his mother were breathing regularly.

Adam came down and set to work again, saying to himself, "I won't open the door again. It's no use staring about to catch sight of a sound. Maybe there's a world about us as we can't see, but th' ear's quicker than the eye and catches a sound from't now and then. Some people think they get a sight on't too, but they're mostly folks whose eyes are not much use to 'em at anything else. For my part, I think it's better to see when your perpendicular's true than to see a ghost."

Such thoughts as these are apt to grow stronger and stronger as daylight quenches the candles and the birds begin to sing. By the time the red sunlight shone on the brass nails that formed the initials on the lid of the coffin, any lingering foreboding from the sound of the willow wand was merged in satisfaction that the work was done and the promise redeemed. There was no need to call Seth, for he was already moving overhead, and presently came downstairs.

"Now, lad," said Adam, as Seth made his appearance, "the coffin's done, and we can take it over to Brox'on, and be back again before half after six. I'll take a mouthful o' oat-cake, and then we'll be off."

The coffin was soon propped on the tall shoulders of the two brothers, and they were making their way, followed close by Gyp, out of the little woodyard into the lane at the back of the house. It was but about a mile and a half to Broxton over the opposite slope, and their road wound very pleasantly along lanes and across fields, where the pale woodbines and the dog-roses were scenting the hedgerows, and the birds were twittering and trilling in the tall leafy boughs of oak and elm. It was a strangely mingled picture—the fresh youth of the summer morning, with its Edenlike peace and loveliness, the stalwart strength of the two brothers in their rusty working clothes, and the long coffin on their shoulders. They paused for the last time before a small farmhouse outside the village of Broxton. By six o'clock the task was done, the coffin nailed down, and Adam and Seth were on their way home. They chose a shorter way homewards, which would take them across the fields and the brook in front of the house. Adam had not mentioned to Seth what had happened in the night, but he still retained sufficient impression from it himself to say, "Seth, lad, if Father isn't come home by the time we've had our breakfast, I think it'll be as well for thee to go over to Treddles'on and look after him, and thee canst get me the brass wire I want. Never mind about losing an hour at thy work; we can make that up. What dost say?"

"I'm willing," said Seth. "But see what clouds have gathered since we set out. I'm thinking we shall have more rain. It'll be a sore time for th' haymaking if the meadows are flooded again. The brook's fine and full now: another day's rain 'ud cover the plank, and we should have to go round by the road."

They were coming across the valley now, and had entered the pasture through which the brook ran.

"Why, what's that sticking against the willow?" continued Seth, beginning to walk faster. Adam's heart rose to his mouth: the vague anxiety about his father was changed into a great dread. He made no answer to Seth, but ran forward preceded by Gyp, who began to bark uneasily; and in two moments he was at the bridge.

This was what the omen meant, then! And the grey-haired father, of whom he had thought with a sort of hardness a few hours ago, as certain to live to be a thorn in his side was perhaps even then struggling with that watery death! This was the first thought that flashed through Adam's conscience, before he had time to seize the coat and drag out the tall heavy body. Seth was already by his side, helping him, and when they had it on the bank, the two sons in the first moment knelt and looked with mute awe at the glazed eyes, forgetting that there was need for action—forgetting everything but that their father lay dead before them. Adam was the first to speak.

"I'll run to Mother," he said, in a loud whisper. "I'll be back to thee in a minute."

Poor Lisbeth was busy preparing her sons' breakfast, and their porridge was already steaming on the fire. Her kitchen always looked the pink of cleanliness, but this morning she was more than usually bent on making her hearth and breakfast-table look comfortable and inviting.

"The lads 'ull be fine an' hungry," she said, half-aloud, as she stirred the porridge. "It's a good step to Brox'on, an' it's hungry air o'er the hill—wi' that heavy coffin too. Eh! It's heavier now, wi' poor Bob Tholer in't. Howiver, I've made a drap more porridge nor common this mornin'. The feyther 'ull happen come in arter a bit. Not as he'll ate much porridge. He swallers sixpenn'orth o' ale, an' saves a hap'orth o' por-ridge—that's his way o' layin' by money, as I've told him many a time, an' am likely to tell him again afore the day's out. Eh, poor mon, he takes it quiet enough; there's no denyin' that."

But now Lisbeth heard the heavy "thud" of a running footstep on the turf, and, turning quickly towards the door, she saw Adam enter, looking so pale and overwhelmed that she screamed aloud and rushed towards him before he had time to speak.

"Hush, Mother," Adam said, rather hoarsely, "don't be frightened. Father's tumbled into the water. Belike we may bring him round again. Seth and me are going to carry him in. Get a blanket and make it hot as the fire."

In reality Adam was convinced that his father was dead but he knew there was no other way of repressing his mother's impetuous wailing grief than by occupying her with some active task which had hope in it.

He ran back to Seth, and the two sons lifted the sad burden in heart-stricken silence. The wide-open glazed eyes were grey, like Seth's, and had once looked with mild pride on the boys before whom Thias had lived to hang his head in shame. Seth's chief feeling was awe and distress at this sudden snatching away of his father's soul; but Adam's mind rushed back over the past in a flood of relenting and pity. When death, the great Reconciler, has come, it is never our tenderness that we repent of, but our severity.

Chapter V
The Rector

Before twelve o'clock there had been some heavy storms of rain, and the water lay in deep gutters on the sides of the gravel walks in the garden of Broxton Parsonage; the great Provence roses had been cruelly tossed by the wind and beaten by the rain, and all the delicate-stemmed border flowers had been dashed down and stained with the wet soil. A melancholy morning—because it was nearly time hay-harvest should begin, and instead of that the meadows were likely to be flooded.

But people who have pleasant homes get indoor enjoyments that they would never think of but for the rain. If it had not been a wet morning, Mr. Irwine would not have been in the dining-room playing at chess with his mother, and he loves both his mother and chess quite well enough to pass some cloudy hours very easily by their help. Let me take you into that dining-room and show you the Rev. Adolphus Irwine, Rector of Broxton, Vicar of Hayslope, and Vicar of Blythe, a pluralist at whom the severest Church reformer would have found it difficult to look sour. We will enter very softly and stand still in the open doorway, without awaking the glossy-brown setter who is stretched across the hearth, with her two puppies beside her; or the pug, who is dozing, with his black muzzle aloft, like a sleepy president.

The room is a large and lofty one, with an ample mullioned oriel window at one end; the walls, you see, are new, and not yet painted; but the furniture, though originally of an expensive sort, is old and scanty, and there is no drapery about the window. The crimson cloth over the large dining-table is very threadbare, though it contrasts pleasantly enough with the dead hue of the plaster on the walls; but on this cloth there is a massive silver waiter with a decanter of water on it, of the same pattern as two larger ones that are propped up on the sideboard with a coat of arms conspicuous in their centre. You suspect at once that the inhabitants of this room have inherited more blood than wealth, and would not be surprised to find that Mr. Irwine had a finely cut nostril and upper lip; but at present we can only see that he has a broad flat back and an abundance of powdered hair, all thrown backward and tied behind with a black ribbon—a bit of conservatism in costume which tells you that he is not a young man. He will perhaps turn round by and by, and in the meantime we can look at that stately old lady, his mother, a beautiful aged brunette, whose rich-toned complexion is well set off by the complex wrappings of pure white cambric and lace about her head and neck. She is as erect in her comely embonpoint as a statue of Ceres; and her dark face, with its delicate aquiline nose, firm proud mouth, and small, intense, black eye, is so keen and sarcastic in its expression that you instinctively substitute a pack of cards for the chess-men and imagine her telling your fortune. The small brown hand with which she is lifting her queen is laden with pearls, diamonds, and turquoises; and a large black veil is very carefully adjusted over the crown of her cap, and falls in sharp contrast on the white folds about her neck. It must take a long time to dress that old lady in the morning! But it seems a law of nature that she should be dressed so: she is clearly one of those children of royalty who have never doubted their right divine and never met with any one so absurd as to question it.

"There, Dauphin, tell me what that is!" says this magnificent old lady, as she deposits her queen very quietly and folds her arms. "I should be sorry to utter a word disagreeable to your feelings."

"Ah, you witch-mother, you sorceress! How is a Christian man to win a game off you? I should have sprinkled the board with holy water before we began. You've not won that game by fair means, now, so don't pretend it."

"Yes, yes, that's what the beaten have always said of great conquerors. But see, there's the sunshine falling on the board, to show you more clearly what a foolish move you made with that pawn. Come, shall I give you another chance?"

"No, Mother, I shall leave you to your own conscience, now it's clearing up. We must go and plash up the mud a little, mus'n't we, Juno?" This was addressed to the brown setter, who had jumped up at the sound of the voices and laid her nose in an insinuating way on her master's leg. "But I must go upstairs first and see Anne. I was called away to Tholer's funeral just when I was going before."

"It's of no use, child; she can't speak to you. Kate says she has one of her worst headaches this morning."

"Oh, she likes me to go and see her just the same; she's never too ill to care about that."

If you know how much of human speech is mere purposeless impulse or habit, you will not wonder when I tell you that this identical objection had been made, and had received the same kind of answer, many hundred times in the course of the fifteen years that Mr. Irwine's sister Anne had been an invalid. Splendid old ladies, who take a long time to dress in the morning, have often slight sympathy with sickly daughters.

But while Mr. Irwine was still seated, leaning back in his chair and stroking Juno's head, the servant came to the door and said, "If you please, sir, Joshua Rann wishes to speak with you, if you are at liberty."

“Let him be shown in here,” said Mrs. Irwine, taking up her knitting. “I always like to hear what Mr. Rann has got to say. His shoes will be dirty, but see that he wipes them Carroll.”

In two minutes Mr. Rann appeared at the door with very deferential bows, which, however, were far from conciliating Pug, who gave a sharp bark and ran across the room to reconnoitre the stranger’s legs; while the two puppies, regarding Mr. Rann’s prominent calf and ribbed worsted stockings from a more sensuous point of view, plunged and growled over them in great enjoyment. Meantime, Mr. Irwine turned round his chair and said, “Well, Joshua, anything the matter at Hayslope, that you’ve come over this damp morning? Sit down, sit down. Never mind the dogs; give them a friendly kick. Here, Pug, you rascal!”

It is very pleasant to see some men turn round; pleasant as a sudden rush of warm air in winter, or the flash of firelight in the chill dusk. Mr. Irwine was one of those men. He bore the same sort of resemblance to his mother that our loving memory of a friend’s face often bears to the face itself: the lines were all more generous, the smile brighter, the expression heartier. If the outline had been less finely cut, his face might have been called jolly; but that was not the right word for its mixture of bonhomie and distinction.

“Thank Your Reverence,” answered Mr. Rann, endeavouring to look unconcerned about his legs, but shaking them alternately to keep off the puppies; “I’ll stand, if you please, as more becoming. I hope I see you an’ Mrs. Irwine well, an’ Miss Irwine—an’ Miss Anne, I hope’s as well as usual.”

“Yes, Joshua, thank you. You see how blooming my mother looks. She beats us younger people hollow. But what’s the matter?”

“Why, sir, I had to come to Brox’on to deliver some work, and I thought it but right to call and let you know the goins-on as there’s been i’ the village, such as I hanna seen i’ my time, and I’ve lived in it man and boy sixty year come St. Thomas, and collected th’ Easter dues for Mr. Blick before Your Reverence come into the parish, and been at the ringin’ o’ every bell, and the diggin’ o’ every grave, and sung i’ the choir long afore Bartle Massey come from nobody knows where, wi’ his counter-singin’ and fine anthems, as puts everybody out but himself—one takin’ it up after another like sheep a-bleatin’ i’ th’ fold. I know what belongs to bein’ a parish clerk, and I know as I should be wantin’ i’ respect to Your Reverence, an’ church, an’ king, if I was t’ allow such goins-on wi’out speakin’. I was took by surprise, an’ knowed nothin’ on it beforehand, an’ I was so flustered, I was clean as if I’d lost my tools. I hanna slep’ more nor four hour this night as is past an’ gone; an’ then it was nothin’ but nightmare, as tired me worse nor wakin’.”

"Why, what in the world is the matter, Joshua? Have the thieves been at the church lead again?"

"Thieves! No, sir—an' yet, as I may say, it *is* thieves, an' a-thievin' the church, too. It's the Methodisses as is like to get th' upper hand i' th' parish, if Your Reverence an' His Honour, Squire Donnithorne, doesna think well to say the word an' forbid it. Not as I'm a-dictatin' to you, sir; I'm not forgettin' myself so far as to be wise above my betters. Howiver, whether I'm wise or no, that's neither here nor there, but what I've got to say I say—as the young Methodis woman as is at Mester Poyser's was a-preachin' an' a-prayin' on the Green last night, as sure as I'm a-stannin' afore Your Reverence now."

"Preaching on the Green!" said Mr. Irwine, looking surprised but quite serene. "What, that pale pretty young woman I've seen at Poyser's? I saw she was a Methodist, or Quaker, or something of that sort, by her dress, but I didn't know she was a preacher."

"It's a true word as I say, sir," rejoined Mr. Rann, compressing his mouth into a semicircular form and pausing long enough to indicate three notes of exclamation. "She preached on the Green last night; an' she's laid hold of Chad's Bess, as the girl's been i' fits welly iver sin'."

"Well, Bessy Cranage is a hearty-looking lass; I daresay she'll come round again, Joshua. Did anybody else go into fits?"

"No, sir, I canna say as they did. But there's no knowin' what'll come, if we're t' have such preachin's as that a-goin' on ivery week—there'll be no livin' i' th' village. For them Methodisses make folks believe as if they take a mug o' drink extry, an' make theirselves a bit comfortable, they'll have to go to hell for't as sure as they're born. I'm not a tipplin' man nor a drunkard—nobody can say it on me—but I like a extry quart at Easter or Christmas time, as is nat'ral when we're goin' the rounds a-singin', an' folks offer't you for nothin'; or when I'm a-collectin' the dues; an' I like a pint wi' my pipe, an' a neighbourly chat at Mester Casson's now an' then, for I was brought up i' the Church, thank God, an' ha' been a parish clerk this two-an'-thirty year: I should know what the church religion is."

"Well, what's your advice, Joshua? What do you think should be done?"

"Well, Your Reverence, I'm not for takin' any measures again' the young woman. She's well enough if she'd let alone preachin'; an' I hear as she's a-goin' away back to her own country soon. She's Mr. Poyser's own niece, an' I donna wish to say what's anyways disrespectful o' th' family at th' Hall Farm, as I've measured for shoes, little an' big, welly iver sin' I've been a shoemaker. But there's that Will Maskery, sir as is the rampageousest Methodis as can be, an' I make no doubt it was him as stirred up th' young woman to preach last night, an' he'll be a-bringin' other folks to preach from Treddles'on, if his comb isn't cut a bit; an' I think as he should be let know as he isna t' have the makin' an' mendin' o' church carts an' implemen's, let alone stayin' i' that house an' yard as is Squire Donnithorne's."

"Well, but you say yourself, Joshua, that you never knew any one come to preach on the Green before; why should you think they'll come again? The Methodists don't come to preach in little villages like Hayslope, where there's only a handful of labourers, too tired to listen to them. They might almost as well go and preach on the Binton Hills. Will Maskery is no preacher himself, I think."

"Nay, sir, he's no gift at stringin' the words together wi'out book; he'd be stuck fast like a cow i' wet clay. But he's got tongue enough to speak disrespectful about's neebors, for he said as I was a blind Pharisee—a-usin' the Bible i' that way to find nick-names for folks as are his elders an' betters!—and what's worse, he's been heard to say very unbecomin' words about Your Reverence; for I could bring them as 'ud swear as he called you a 'dumb dog,' an' a 'idle shepherd.' You'll forgi'e me for sayin' such things over again."

"Better not, better not, Joshua. Let evil words die as soon as they're spoken. Will Maskery might be a great deal worse fellow than he is. He used to be a wild drunken rascal, neglecting his work and beating his wife, they told me; now he's thrifty and decent, and he and his wife look comfortable together. If you can bring me any proof that he interferes with his neighbours and creates any disturbance, I shall think it my duty as a clergyman and a magistrate to interfere. But it wouldn't become wise people like you and me to be making a fuss about trifles, as if we thought the Church was in danger because Will Maskery lets his tongue wag rather foolishly, or a young woman talks in a serious way to a handful of people on the Green. We must 'live and let live,' Joshua, in religion as well as in other things. You go on doing your duty, as parish clerk and sexton, as well as you've always done it, and making those capital thick boots for your neighbours, and things won't go far wrong in Hayslope, depend upon it."

"Your Reverence is very good to say so; an' I'm sensable as, you not livin' i' the parish, there's more upo' my shoulders."

"To be sure; and you must mind and not lower the Church in people's eyes by seeming to be frightened about it for a little thing, Joshua. I shall trust to your good sense, now to take no notice at all of what Will Maskery says, either about you or me. You and your neighbours can go on taking your pot of beer soberly, when you've done your day's work, like good churchmen; and if Will Maskery doesn't like to join you, but to go to a prayer-meeting at Treddleston instead, let him; that's no business of yours, so long as he doesn't hinder you from doing what you like. And as to people saying a few idle words about us, we must not mind that, any more than the old church-steeple minds the rooks cawing about it. Will Maskery comes to church every Sunday afternoon, and does his wheelwright's business steadily in the weekdays, and as long as he does that he must be let alone."

"Ah, sir, but when he comes to church, he sits an' shakes his head, an' looks as sour an' as coxy when we're a-singin' as I should like to fetch him a rap across the jowl—God forgi'e me—an' Mrs. Irwine, an' Your Reverence too, for speakin' so afore you. An' he said as our Christmas singin' was no better nor the cracklin' o' thorns under a pot."

"Well, he's got a bad ear for music, Joshua. When people have wooden heads, you know, it can't be helped. He won't bring the other people in Hayslope round to his opinion, while you go on singing as well as you do."

"Yes, sir, but it turns a man's stomach t' hear the Scripture misused i' that way. I know as much o' the words o' the Bible as he does, an' could say the Psalms right through i' my sleep if you was to pinch me; but I know better nor to take 'em to say my own say wi'. I might as well take the Sacriment-cup home and use it at meals."

"That's a very sensible remark of yours, Joshua; but, as I said before——"

While Mr. Irwine was speaking, the sound of a booted step and the clink of a spur were heard on the stone floor of the entrance-hall, and Joshua Rann moved hastily aside from the doorway to make room for some one who paused there, and said, in a ringing tenor voice,

"Godson Arthur—may he come in?"

"Come in, come in, godson!" Mrs. Irwine answered, in the deep half-masculine tone which belongs to the vigorous old woman, and there entered a young gentleman in a riding-dress, with his right arm in a sling; whereupon followed that pleasant confusion of laughing interjections, and hand-shakings, and "How are you's?" mingled with joyous short barks and wagging of tails on the part of the canine members of the family, which tells that the visitor is on the best terms with the visited. The young gentleman was Arthur Donnithorne, known in Hayslope, variously, as "the young squire," "the heir," and "the captain." He was only a captain in the Loamshire Militia, but to the Hayslope tenants he was more intensely a captain than all the young gentlemen of the same rank in his Majesty's regulars—he outshone them as the planet Jupiter outshines the Milky Way. If you want to know more particularly how he looked, call to your remembrance some tawny-whiskered, brown-locked, clear-complexioned young Englishman whom you have met with in a foreign town, and been proud of as a fellow-countryman—well-washed, high-bred, white-handed, yet looking as if he could deliver well from ‘the left shoulder and floor his man: I will not be so much of a tailor as to trouble your imagination with the difference of costume, and insist on the striped waistcoat, long-tailed coat, and low top-boots.

Turning round to take a chair, Captain Donnithorne said, “But don’t let me interrupt Joshua’s business—he has something to say.”

“Humbly begging Your Honour’s pardon,” said Joshua, bowing low, “there was one thing I had to say to His Reverence as other things had drove out o’ my head.”

“Out with it, Joshua, quickly!” said Mr. Irwine.

“Belike, sir, you havena heared as Thias Bede’s dead—drownded this morning, or more like overnight, i’ the Willow Brook, again’ the bridge right i’ front o’ the house.”

“Ah!” exclaimed both the gentlemen at once, as if they were a good deal interested in the information.

“An’ Seth Bede’s been to me this morning to say he wished me to tell Your Reverence as his brother Adam begged of you particular t’ allow his father’s grave to be dug by the White Thorn, because his mother’s set her heart on it, on account of a dream as she had; an’ they’d ha’ come theirselves to ask you, but they’ve so much to see after with the crowner, an’ that; an’ their mother’s took on so, an’ wants ’em to make sure o’ the spot for fear somebody else should take it. An’ if Your Reverence sees well and good, I’ll send my boy to tell ’em as soon as I get home; an’ that’s why I make bold to trouble you wi’ it, His Honour being present.”

“To be sure, Joshua, to be sure, they shall have it. I’ll ride round to Adam myself, and see him. Send your boy, however, to say they shall have the grave, lest anything should happen to detain me. And now, good morning, Joshua; go into the kitchen and have some ale.”

“Poor old Thias!” said Mr. Irwine, when Joshua was gone. “I’m afraid the drink helped the brook to drown him. I should have been glad for the load to have been taken off my friend Adam’s shoulders in a less painful way. That fine fellow has been propping up his father from ruin for the last five or six years.”

“He’s a regular trump, is Adam,” said Captain Donnithorne. “When I was a little fellow, and Adam was a strapping lad of fifteen, and taught me carpentering, I used to think if ever I was a rich sultan, I would make Adam my grand-vizier. And I believe now he would bear the exaltation as well as any poor wise man in an Eastern story. If ever I live to be a large-acred man instead of a poor devil with a mortgaged allowance of pocket-money, I’ll have Adam for my right hand. He shall manage my woods for me, for he seems to have a better notion of those things than any man I ever met with; and I know he would make twice the money of them that my grandfather does, with that miserable old Satchell to manage, who understands no more about timber than an old carp. I've mentioned the subject to my grandfather once or twice, but for some reason or other he has a dislike to Adam, and *I* can do nothing. But come, Your Reverence, are you for a ride with me? It's splendid out of doors now. We can go to Adam's together, if you like; but I want to call at the Hall Farm on my way, to look at the whelps Poyser is keeping for me."

"You must stay and have lunch first, Arthur," said Mrs. Irwine. "It's nearly two. Carroll will bring it in directly."

"I want to go to the Hall Farm too," said Mr. Irwine, "to have another look at the little Methodist who is staying there. Joshua tells me she was preaching on the Green last night."

"Oh, by Jove!" said Captain Donnithorne, laughing. "Why, she looks as quiet as a mouse. There's something rather striking about her, though. I positively felt quite bashful the first time I saw her—she was sitting stooping over her sewing in the sunshine outside the house, when I rode up and called out, without noticing that she was a stranger, 'Is Martin Poyser at home?' I declare, when she got up and looked at me and just said, 'He's in the house, I believe: I'll go and call him,' I felt quite ashamed of having spoken so abruptly to her. She looked like St. Catherine in a Quaker dress. It's a type of face one rarely sees among our common people."

"I should like to see the young woman, Dauphin," said Mrs. Irwine. "Make her come here on some pretext or other."

"I don't know how I can manage that, Mother; it will hardly do for me to patronize a Methodist preacher, even if she would consent to be patronized by an idle shepherd, as Will Maskery calls me. You should have come in a little sooner, Arthur, to hear Joshua's denunciation of his neighbour Will Maskery. The old fellow wants me to excommunicate the wheelwright, and then deliver him over to the civil arm—that is to say, to your grandfather—to be turned out of house and yard. If I chose to interfere in this business, now, I might get up as pretty a story of hatred and persecution as the Methodists need desire to publish in the next number of their magazine. It wouldn't take me much trouble to persuade Chad Cranage and half a dozen other bull-headed fellows that they would be doing an acceptable service to the Church by hunting Will Maskery out of the village with rope-ends and pitchforks; and then, when I had furnished them with half a sovereign to get gloriously drunk after their exertions, I should have put the climax to as pretty a farce as any of my brother clergy have set going in their parishes for the last thirty years."

"It is really insolent of the man, though, to call you an 'idle shepherd' and a 'dumb dog,'" said Mrs. Irwine. "I should be inclined to check him a little there. You are too easy-tempered, Dauphin."

"Why, Mother, you don't think it would be a good way of sustaining my dignity to set about vindicating myself from the aspersions of Will Maskery? Besides, I'm not so sure that they *are* aspersions. I *am* a lazy fellow, and get terribly heavy in my saddle; not to mention that I'm always spending more than I can afford in bricks and mortar, so that I get savage at a lame beggar when he asks me for sixpence. Those poor lean cobblers, who think they can help to regenerate mankind by setting out to preach in the morning twilight before they begin their day's work, may well have a poor opinion of me. But come, let us have our luncheon. Isn't Kate coming to lunch?"

"Miss Irwine told Bridget to take her lunch upstairs," said Carroll; "she can't leave Miss Anne."

"Oh, very well. Tell Bridget to say I'll go up and see Miss Anne presently. You can use your right arm quite well now, Arthur," Mr. Irwine continued, observing that Captain Donnithorne had taken his arm out of the sling.

"Yes, pretty well; but Godwin insists on my keeping it up constantly for some time to come. I hope I shall be able to get away to the regiment, though, in the beginning of August. It's a desperately dull business being shut up at the Chase in the summer months, when one can neither hunt nor shoot, so as to make one's self pleasantly sleepy in the evening. However, we are to astonish the echoes on the 30th of July. My grandfather has given me *carte blanche* for once, and I promise you the entertainment shall be worthy of the occasion. The world will not see the grand epoch of my majority twice. I think I shall have a lofty throne for you, Godmamma, or rather two, one on the lawn and another in the ballroom, that you may sit and look down upon us like an Olympian goddess."

"I mean to bring out my best brocade, that I wore at your christening twenty years ago," said Mrs. Irwine. "Ah, I think I shall see your poor mother flitting about in her white dress, which looked to me almost like a shroud that very day; and it *was* her shroud only three months after; and your little cap and christening dress were buried with her too. She had set her heart on that, sweet soul! Thank God you take after your mother's family, Arthur. If you had been a puny, wiry, yellow baby, I wouldn't have stood godmother to you. I should have been sure you would turn out a Donnithorne. But you were such a broad-faced, broad-chested, loud-screaming rascal, I knew you were every inch of you a Tradgett."

“But you might have been a little too hasty there, Mother,” said Mr. Irwine, smiling. “Don’t you remember how it was with Juno’s last pups? One of them was the very image of its mother, but it had two or three of its father’s tricks notwithstanding. Nature is clever enough to cheat even you, Mother.”

“Nonsense, child! Nature never makes a ferret in the shape of a mastiff. You’ll never persuade me that I can’t tell what men are by their outsides. If I don’t like a man’s looks, depend upon it I shall never like *him*. I don’t want to know people that look ugly and disagreeable, any more than I want to taste dishes that look disagreeable. If they make me shudder at the first glance, I say, take them away. An ugly, piggish, or fishy eye, now, makes me feel quite ill; it’s like a bad smell.”

“Talking of eyes,” said Captain Donnithorne, “that reminds me that I’ve got a book I meant to bring you, Godmamma. It came down in a parcel from London the other day. I know you are fond of queer, wizardlike stories. It’s a volume of poems, ‘Lyrical Ballads.’ Most of them seem to be twaddling stuff, but the first is in a different style—‘The Ancient Mariner’ is the title. I can hardly make head or tail of it as a story, but it’s a strange, striking thing. I’ll send it over to you; and there are some other books that *you* may like to see, Irwine—pamphlets about Antinomianism and Evangelicalism, whatever they may be. I can’t think what the fellow means by sending such things to me. I’ve written to him to desire that from henceforth he will send me no book or pamphlet on anything that ends in *ism*.”

“Well, I don’t know that I’m very fond of *isms* myself; but I may as well look at the pamphlets; they let one see what is going on. I’ve a little matter to attend to, Arthur,” continued Mr. Irwine, rising to leave the room, “and then I shall be ready to set out with you.”

The little matter that Mr. Irwine had to attend to took him up the old stone staircase (part of the house was very old) and made him pause before a door at which he knocked gently. “Come in,” said a woman’s voice, and he entered a room so darkened by blinds and curtains that Miss Kate, the thin middle-aged lady standing by the bedside, would not have had light enough for any other sort of work than the knitting which lay on the little table near her. But at present she was doing what required only the dimmest light—sponging the aching head that lay on the pillow with fresh vinegar. It was a small face, that of the poor sufferer; perhaps it had once been pretty, but now it was worn and sallow. Miss Kate came towards her brother and whispered, “Don’t speak to her; she can’t bear to be spoken to to-day.” Anne’s eyes were closed, and her brow contracted as if from intense pain. Mr. Irwine went to the bedside and took up one of the delicate hands and kissed it, a slight pressure from the small fingers told him that it was worth-while to have come upstairs for the sake of doing that. He lingered a moment, looking at her, and then turned away and left the room, treading very gently—he had taken off his boots and put on slippers before he came upstairs. Whoever remembers how many things he has declined to do even for himself, rather than have the trouble of putting on or taking off his boots, will not think this last detail insignificant.

And Mr. Irwine's sisters, as any person of family within ten miles of Broxton could have testified, were such stupid, uninteresting women! It was quite a pity handsome, clever Mrs. Irwine should have had such commonplace daughters. That fine old lady herself was worth driving ten miles to see, any day; her beauty, her well-preserved faculties, and her old-fashioned dignity made her a graceful subject for conversation in turn with the King's health, the sweet new patterns in cotton dresses, the news from Egypt, and Lord Dacey's lawsuit, which was fretting poor Lady Dacey to death. But no one ever thought of mentioning the Miss Irwines, except the poor people in Broxton village, who regarded them as deep in the science of medicine, and spoke of them vaguely as "the gentlefolks." If any one had asked old Job Dummilow who gave him his flannel jacket, he would have answered, "the gentlefolks, last winter"; and widow Steene dwelt much on the virtues of the "stuff" the gentlefolks gave her for her cough. Under this name too, they were used with great effect as a means of taming refractory children, so that at the sight of poor Miss Anne's sallow face, several small urchins had a terrified sense that she was cognizant of all their worst misdemeanours, and knew the precise number of stones with which they had intended to hit Farmer Britton's ducks. But for all who saw them through a less mythical medium, the Miss Irwines were quite superfluous existences—inartistic figures crowding the canvas of life without adequate effect. Miss Anne, indeed, if her chronic headaches could have been accounted for by a pathetic story of disappointed love, might have had some romantic interest attached to her: but no such story had either been known or invented concerning her, and the general impression was quite in accordance with the fact, that both the sisters were old maids for the prosaic reason that they had never received an eligible offer.

Nevertheless, to speak paradoxically, the existence of insignificant people has very important consequences in the world. It can be shown to affect the price of bread and the rate of wages, to call forth many evil tempers from the selfish and many heroisms from the sympathetic, and, in other ways, to play no small part in the tragedy of life. And if that handsome, generous-blooded clergyman, the Rev. Adolphus Irwine, had not had these two hopelessly maiden sisters, his lot would have been shaped quite differently: he would very likely have taken a comely wife in his youth, and now, when his hair was getting grey under the powder, would have had tall sons and blooming daughters—such possessions, in short, as men commonly think will repay them for all the labour they take under the sun. As it was—having with all his three livings no more than seven hundred a-year, and seeing no way of keeping his splendid mother and his sickly sister, not to reckon a second sister, who was usually spoken of without any adjective, in such ladylike ease as became their birth and habits, and at the same time providing for a family of his own—he remained, you see, at the age of eight-and-forty, a bachelor, not making any merit of that renunciation, but saying laughingly, if any one alluded to it, that he made it an excuse for many indulgences which a wife would never have allowed him. And perhaps he was the only person in the world who did not think his sisters uninteresting and superfluous; for his was one of those large-hearted, sweet-blooded natures that never know a narrow or a grudging thought; Epicurean, if you will, with no enthusiasm, no self-scourging sense of duty; but yet, as you have seen, of a sufficiently subtle moral fibre to have an unwearying tenderness for obscure and monotonous suffering. It was his large-hearted indulgence that made him ignore his mother's hardness towards her daughters, which was the more striking from its contrast with her doting fondness towards himself; he held it no virtue to frown at irremediable faults.

See the difference between the impression a man makes on you when you walk by his side in familiar talk, or look at him in his home, and the figure he makes when seen from a lofty historical level, or even in the eyes of a critical neighbour who thinks of him as an embodied system or opinion rather than as a man. Mr. Roe, the "travelling preacher" stationed at Treddleston, had included Mr. Irwine in a general statement concerning the Church clergy in the surrounding district, whom he described as men given up to the lusts of the flesh and the pride of life; hunting and shooting, and adorning their own houses; asking what shall we eat, and what shall we drink, and wherewithal shall we be clothed?—careless of dispensing the bread of life to their flocks, preaching at best but a carnal and soul-benumbing morality, and trafficking in the souls of men by receiving money for discharging the pastoral office in parishes where they did not so much as look on the faces of the people more than once a-year. The ecclesiastical historian, too, looking into parliamentary reports of that period, finds honourable members zealous for the Church, and untainted with any sympathy for the "tribe of canting Methodists," making statements scarcely less melancholy than that of Mr. Roe. And it is impossible for me to say that Mr. Irwine was altogether belied by the generic classification assigned him. He really had no very lofty aims, no theological enthusiasm: if I were closely questioned, I should be obliged to confess that he felt no serious alarms about the souls of his parishioners, and would have thought it a mere loss of time to talk in a doctrinal and awakening manner to old "Feyther Taft," or even to Chad Cranage the blacksmith. If he had been in the habit of speaking theoretically, he would perhaps have said that the only healthy form religion could take in such minds was that of certain dim but strong emotions, suffusing themselves as a hallowing influence over the family affections and neighbourly duties. He thought the custom of baptism more important than its doctrine, and that the religious benefits the peasant drew from the church where his fathers worshipped and the sacred piece of turf where they lay buried were but slightly dependent on a clear understanding of the Liturgy or the sermon. Clearly the rector was not what is called in these days an "earnest" man: he was fonder of church history than of divinity, and had much more insight into men's characters than interest in their opinions; he was neither laborious, nor obviously self-denying, nor very copious in alms-giving, and his theology, you perceive, was lax. His mental palate, indeed, was rather pagan, and found a savouriness in a quotation from Sophocles or Theocritus that was quite absent from any text in Isaiah or Amos. But if you feed your young setter on raw flesh, how can you wonder at its retaining a relish for uncooked partridge in after-life? And Mr. Irwine's recollections of young enthusiasm and ambition were all associated with poetry and ethics that lay aloof from the Bible.

On the other hand, I must plead, for I have an affectionate partiality towards the rector's memory, that he was not vindictive—and some philanthropists have been so; that he was not intolerant—and there is a rumour that some zealous theologians have not been altogether free from that blemish; that although he would probably have declined to give his body to be burned in any public cause, and was far from bestowing all his goods to feed the poor, he had that charity which has sometimes been lacking to very illustrious virtue—he was tender to other men's failings, and unwilling to impute evil. He was one of those men, and they are not the commonest, of whom we can know the best only by following them away from the marketplace, the platform, and the pulpit, entering with them into their own homes, hearing the voice with which they speak to the young and aged about their own hearthstone, and witnessing their thoughtful care for the everyday wants of everyday companions, who take all their kindness as a matter of course, and not as a subject for panegyric.

Such men, happily, have lived in times when great abuses flourished, and have sometimes even been the living representatives of the abuses. That is a thought which might comfort us a little under the opposite fact—that it is better sometimes *not* to follow great reformers of abuses beyond the threshold of their homes.

But whatever you may think of Mr. Irwine now, if you had met him that June afternoon riding on his grey cob, with his dogs running beside him—portly, upright, manly, with a good-natured smile on his finely turned lips as he talked to his dashing young companion on the bay mare, you must have felt that, however ill he harmonized with sound theories of the clerical office, he somehow harmonized extremely well with that peaceful landscape.

See them in the bright sunlight, interrupted every now and then by rolling masses of cloud, ascending the slope from the Broxton side, where the tall gables and elms of the rectory predominate over the tiny whitewashed church. They will soon be in the parish of Hayslope; the grey church-tower and village roofs lie before them to the left, and farther on, to the right, they can just see the chimneys of the Hall Farm.

Chapter VI
The Hall Farm

Evidently that gate is never opened, for the long grass and the great hemlocks grow close against it, and if it were opened, it is so rusty that the force necessary to turn it on its hinges would be likely to pull down the square stone-built pillars, to the detriment of the two stone lionesses which grin with a doubtful carnivorous affability above a coat of arms surmounting each of the pillars. It would be easy enough, by the aid of the nicks in the stone pillars, to climb over the brick wall with its smooth stone coping; but by putting our eyes close to the rusty bars of the gate, we can see the house well enough, and all but the very corners of the grassy enclosure.

It is a very fine old place, of red brick, softened by a pale powdery lichen, which has dispersed itself with happy irregularity, so as to bring the red brick into terms of friendly companionship with the limestone ornaments surrounding the three gables, the windows, and the door-place. But the windows are patched with wooden panes, and the door, I think, is like the gate—it is never opened. How it would groan and grate against the stone floor if it were! For it is a solid, heavy, handsome door, and must once have been in the habit of shutting with a sonorous bang behind a liveried lackey, who had just seen his master and mistress off the grounds in a carriage and pair.

But at present one might fancy the house in the early stage of a chancery suit, and that the fruit from that grand double row of walnut-trees on the right hand of the enclosure would fall and rot among the grass, if it were not that we heard the booming bark of dogs echoing from great buildings at the back. And now the half-weaned calves that have been sheltering themselves in a gorse-built hovel against the left-hand wall come out and set up a silly answer to that terrible bark, doubtless supposing that it has reference to buckets of milk.

Yes, the house must be inhabited, and we will see by whom; for imagination is a licensed trespasser: it has no fear of dogs, but may climb over walls and peep in at windows with impunity. Put your face to one of the glass panes in the right-hand window: what do you see? A large open fireplace, with rusty dogs in it, and a bare boarded floor; at the far end, fleeces of wool stacked up; in the middle of the floor, some empty corn-bags. That is the furniture of the dining-room. And what through the left-hand window? Several clothes-horses, a pillion, a spinning-wheel, and an old box wide open and stuffed full of coloured rags. At the edge of this box there lies a great wooden doll, which, so far as mutilation is concerned, bears a strong resemblance to the finest Greek sculpture, and especially in the total loss of its nose. Near it there is a little chair, and the butt end of a boy's leather long-lashed whip.

The history of the house is plain now. It was once the residence of a country squire, whose family, probably dwindling down to mere spinsterhood, got merged in the more territorial name of Donnithorne. It was once the Hall; it is now the Hall Farm. Like the life in some coast town that was once a watering-place, and is now a port, where the genteel streets are silent and grass-grown, and the docks and warehouses busy and resonant, the life at the Hall has changed its focus, and no longer radiates from the parlour, but from the kitchen and the farmyard.

Plenty of life there, though this is the drowsiest time of the year, just before hay-harvest; and it is the drowsiest time of the day too, for it is close upon three by the sun, and it is half-past three by Mrs. Poyser's handsome eight-day clock. But there is always a stronger sense of life when the sun is brilliant after rain; and now he is pouring down his beams, and making sparkles among the wet straw, and lighting up every patch of vivid green moss on the red tiles of the cow-shed, and turning even the muddy water that is hurrying along the channel to the drain into a mirror for the yellow-billed ducks, who are seizing the opportunity of getting a drink with as much body in it as possible. There is quite a concert of noises; the great bull-dog, chained against the stables, is thrown into furious exasperation by the unwary approach of a cock too near the mouth of his kennel, and sends forth a thundering bark, which is answered by two fox-hounds shut up in the opposite cow-house; the old top-knotted hens, scratching with their chicks among the straw, set up a sympathetic croaking as the discomfited cock joins them; a sow with her brood, all very muddy as to the legs, and curled as to the tail, throws in some deep staccato notes; our friends the calves are bleating from the home croft; and, under all, a fine ear discerns the continuous hum of human voices.

For the great barn-doors are thrown wide open, and men are busy there mending the harness, under the superintendence of Mr. Goby, the "whittaw," otherwise saddler, who entertains them with the latest Treddleston gossip. It is certainly rather an unfortunate day that Alick, the shepherd, has chosen for having the whittaws, since the morning turned out so wet; and Mrs. Poyser has spoken her mind pretty strongly as to the dirt which the extra number of men's shoes brought into the house at dinnertime. Indeed, she has not yet recovered her equanimity on the subject, though it is now nearly three hours since dinner, and the house-floor is perfectly clean again; as clean as everything else in that wonderful house-place, where the only chance of collecting a few grains of dust would be to climb on the salt-coffer, and put your finger on the high mantel-shelf on which the glittering brass candlesticks are enjoying their summer sinecure; for at this time of year, of course, every one goes to bed while it is yet light, or at least light enough to discern the outline of objects after you have bruised your shins against them. Surely nowhere else could an oak clock-case and an oak table have got to such a polish by the hand: genuine "elbow polish," as Mrs. Poyser called it, for she thanked God she never had any of your varnished rubbish in her house. Hetty Sorrel often took the opportunity, when her aunt's back was turned, of looking at the pleasing reflection of herself in those polished surfaces, for the oak table was usually turned up like a screen, and was more for ornament than for use; and she could see herself sometimes in the great round pewter dishes that were ranged on the shelves above the long deal dinner-table, or in the hobs of the grate, which always shone like jasper.

Everything was looking at its brightest at this moment, for the sun shone right on the pewter dishes, and from their reflecting surfaces pleasant jets of light were thrown on mellow oak and bright brass—and on a still pleasanter object than these, for some of the rays fell on Dinah's finely moulded cheek, and lit up her pale red hair to auburn, as she bent over the heavy household linen which she was mending for her aunt. No scene could have been more peaceful, if Mrs. Poyser, who was ironing a few things that still remained from the Monday's wash, had not been making a frequent clinking with her iron and moving to and fro whenever she wanted it to cool; carrying the keen glance of her blue-grey eye from the kitchen to the dairy, where Hetty was making up the butter, and from the dairy to the back kitchen, where Nancy was taking the pies out of the oven. Do not suppose, however, that Mrs. Poyser was elderly or shrewish in her appearance; she was a good-looking woman, not more than eight-and-thirty, of fair complexion and sandy hair, well-shapen, light-footed. The most conspicuous article in her attire was an ample checkered linen apron, which almost covered her skirt; and nothing could be plainer or less noticeable than her cap and gown, for there was no weakness of which she was less tolerant than feminine vanity, and the preference of ornament to utility. The family likeness between her and her niece Dinah Morris, with the contrast between her keenness and Dinah's seraphic gentleness of expression, might have served a painter as an excellent suggestion for a Martha and Mary. Their eyes were just of the same colour, but a striking test of the difference in their operation was seen in the demeanour of Trip, the black-and-tan terrier, whenever that much-suspected dog unwarily exposed himself to the freezing arctic ray of Mrs. Poyser's glance. Her tongue was not less keen than her eye, and, whenever a damsel came within earshot, seemed to take up an unfinished lecture, as a barrel-organ takes up a tune, precisely at the point where it had left off.

The fact that it was churning day was another reason why it was inconvenient to have the whittaws, and why, consequently, Mrs. Poyser should scold Molly the housemaid with unusual severity. To all appearance Molly had got through her after-dinner work in an exemplary manner, had "cleaned herself" with great dispatch, and now came to ask, submissively, if she should sit down to her spinning till milking time. But this blameless conduct, according to Mrs. Poyser, shrouded a secret indulgence of unbecoming wishes, which she now dragged forth and held up to Molly's view with cutting eloquence.

"Spinning, indeed! It isn't spinning as you'd be at, I'll be bound, and let you have your own way. I never knew your equals for gallowsness. To think of a gell o' your age wanting to go and sit with half-a-dozen men! I'd ha' been ashamed to let the words pass over my lips if I'd been you. And you, as have been here ever since last Michaelmas, and I hired you at Treddles'on stattits, without a bit o' character—as I say, you might be grateful to be hired in that way to a respectable place; and you knew no more o' what belongs to work when you come here than the mawkin i' the field. As poor a two-fisted thing as ever I saw, you know you was. Who taught you to scrub a floor, I should like to know? Why, you'd leave the dirt in heaps i' the corners—anybody 'ud think you'd never been brought up among Christians. And as for spinning, why, you've wasted as much as your wage i' the flax you've spoiled learning to spin. And you've a right to feel that, and not to go about as gaping and as thoughtless as if you was beholding to nobody. Comb the wool for the whittaws, indeed! That's what you'd like to be doing, is it? That's the way with you—that's the road you'd all like to go, headlongs to ruin. You're never easy till you've got some sweetheart as is as big a fool as yourself: you think you'll be finely off when you're married, I daresay, and have got a three-legged stool to sit on, and never a blanket to cover you, and a bit o' oat-cake for your dinner, as three children are a-snatching at."

"I'm sure I donna want t' go wi' the whittaws," said Molly, whimpering, and quite overcome by this Dantean picture of her future, "on'y we allays used to comb the wool for 'n at Mester Ottley's; an' so I just axed ye. I donna want to set eyes on the whittaws again; I wish I may never stir if I do."

"Mr. Ottley's, indeed! It's fine talking o' what you did at Mr. Ottley's. Your missis there might like her floors dirted wi' whittaws for what I know. There's no knowing what people *wonna* like—such ways as I've heard of! I never had a gell come into my house as seemed to know what cleaning was; I think people live like pigs, for my part. And as to that Betty as was dairymaid at Trent's before she come to me, she'd ha' left the cheeses without turning from week's end to week's end, and the dairy thralls, I might ha' wrote my name on 'em, when I come downstairs after my illness, as the doctor said it was inflammation—it was a mercy I got well of it. And to think o' your knowing no better, Molly, and been here a-going i' nine months, and not for want o' talking to, neither—and what are you stanning there for, like a jack as is run down, instead o' getting your wheel out? You're a rare un for sitting down to your work a little while after it's time to put by."

"Munny, my iron's twite told; pease put it down to warm."

The small chirruping voice that uttered this request came from a little sunny-haired girl between three and four, who, seated on a high chair at the end of the ironing table, was arduously clutching the handle of a miniature iron with her tiny fat fist, and ironing rags with an assiduity that required her to put her little red tongue out as far as anatomy would allow.

"Cold, is it, my darling? Bless your sweet face!" said Mrs. Poyser, who was remarkable for the facility with which she could relapse from her official objurgatory to one of fondness or of friendly converse. "Never mind! Mother's done her ironing now. She's going to put the ironing things away."

"Munny, I tould 'ike to do into de barn to Tommy, to see de whittawd."

"No, no, no; Totty 'ud get her feet wet," said Mrs. Poyser, carrying away her iron. "Run into the dairy and see cousin Hetty make the butter."

"I tould 'ike a bit o' pum-take," rejoined Totty, who seemed to be provided with several relays of requests; at the same time, taking the opportunity of her momentary leisure to put her fingers into a bowl of starch, and drag it down so as to empty the contents with tolerable completeness on to the ironing sheet.

"Did ever anybody see the like?" screamed Mrs. Poyser, running towards the table when her eye had fallen on the blue stream. "The child's allays i' mischief if your back's turned a minute. What shall I do to you, you naughty, naughty gell?"

Totty, however, had descended from her chair with great swiftness, and was already in retreat towards the dairy with a sort of waddling run, and an amount of fat on the nape of her neck which made her look like the metamorphosis of a white suckling pig.

The starch having been wiped up by Molly's help, and the ironing apparatus put by, Mrs. Poyser took up her knitting which always lay ready at hand, and was the work she liked best, because she could carry it on automatically as she walked to and fro. But now she came and sat down opposite Dinah, whom she looked at in a meditative way, as she knitted her grey worsted stocking.

"You look th' image o' your Aunt Judith, Dinah, when you sit a-sewing. I could almost fancy it was thirty years back, and I was a little gell at home, looking at Judith as she sat at her work, after she'd done the house up; only it was a little cottage, Father's was, and not a big rambling house as gets dirty i' one corner as fast as you clean it in another—but for all that, I could fancy you was your Aunt

Judith, only her hair was a deal darker than yours, and she was stouter and broader i' the shoulders. Judith and me allays hung together, though she had such queer ways, but your mother and her never could agree. Ah, your mother little thought as she'd have a daughter just cut out after the very pattern o' Judith, and leave her an orphan, too, for Judith to take care on, and bring up with a spoon when *she* was in the graveyard at Stoniton. I allays said that o' Judith, as she'd bear a pound weight any day to save anybody else carrying a ounce. And she was just the same from the first o' my remembering her; it made no difference in her, as I could see, when she took to the Methodists, only she talked a bit different and wore a different sort o' cap; but she'd never in her life spent a penny on herself more than keeping herself decent."

"She was a blessed woman," said Dinah; "God had given her a loving, self-forgetting nature, and He perfected it by grace. And she was very fond of you too, Aunt Rachel. I often heard her talk of you in the same sort of way. When she had that bad illness, and I was only eleven years old, she used to say, 'You'll have a friend on earth in your Aunt Rachel, if I'm taken from you, for she has a kind heart,' and I'm sure I've found it so."

"I don't know how, child; anybody 'ud be cunning to do anything for you, I think; you're like the birds o' th' air, and live nobody knows how. I'd ha' been glad to behave to you like a mother's sister, if you'd come and live i' this country where there's some shelter and victual for man and beast, and folks don't live on the naked hills, like poultry a-scratching on a gravel bank. And then you might get married to some decent man, and there'd be plenty ready to have you, if you'd only leave off that preaching, as is ten times worse than anything your Aunt Judith ever did. And even if you'd marry Seth Bede, as is a poor wool-gathering Methodist and's never like to have a penny beforehand, I know your uncle 'ud help you with a pig, and very like a cow, for he's allays been good-natur'd to my kin, for all they're poor, and made 'em welcome to the house; and 'ud do for you, I'll be bound, as much as ever he'd do for Hetty, though she's his own niece. And there's linen in the house as I could well spare you, for I've got lots o' sheeting and table-clothing, and towelling, as isn't made up. There's a piece o' sheeting I could give you as that squinting Kitty spun—she was a rare girl to spin, for all she squinted, and the children couldn't abide her; and, you know, the spinning's going on constant, and there's new linen wove twice as fast as the old wears out. But where's the use o' talking, if ye wonna be persuaded, and settle down like any other woman in her senses, i'stead o' wearing yourself out with walking and preaching, and giving away every penny you get, so as you've nothing saved against sickness; and all the things you've got i' the world, I verily believe, 'ud go into a bundle no bigger nor a double cheese. And all because you've got notions i' your head about religion more nor what's i' the Catechism and the Prayer-book."

"But not more than what's in the Bible, Aunt," said Dinah.

"Yes, and the Bible too, for that matter," Mrs. Poyser rejoined, rather sharply; "else why shouldn't them as know best what's in the Bible—the parsons and people as have got nothing to do but learn it—do the same as you do? But, for the matter o' that, if everybody was to do like you, the world must come to a standstill; for if everybody tried to do without house and home, and with poor eating and drinking, and was allays talking as we must despise the things o' the world as you say, I should like to know where the pick o' the stock, and the corn, and the best new-milk cheeses 'ud have to go. Everybody 'ud be wanting bread made o' tail ends and everybody 'ud be running after everybody else to preach to 'em, istead o' bringing up their families, and laying by against a bad harvest. It stands to sense as that can't be the right religion."

"Nay, dear aunt, you never heard me say that all people are called to forsake their work and their families. It's quite right the land should be ploughed and sowed, and the precious corn stored, and the things of this life cared for, and right that people should rejoice in their families, and provide for them, so that this is done in the fear of the Lord, and that they are not unmindful of the soul's wants while they are caring for the body. We can all be servants of God wherever our lot is cast, but He gives us different sorts of work, according as He fits us for it and calls us to it. I can no more help spending my life in trying to do what I can for the souls of others, than you could help running if you heard little Totty crying at the other end of the house; the voice would go to your heart, you would think the dear child was in trouble or in danger, and you couldn't rest without running to help her and comfort her."

"Ah," said Mrs. Poyser, rising and walking towards the door, "I know it 'ud be just the same if I was to talk to you for hours. You'd make me the same answer, at th' end. I might as well talk to the running brook and tell it to stan' still."

The causeway outside the kitchen door was dry enough now for Mrs. Poyser to stand there quite pleasantly and see what was going on in the yard, the grey worsted stocking making a steady progress in her hands all the while. But she had not been standing there more than five minutes before she came in again, and said to Dinah, in rather a flurried, awe-stricken tone, "If there isn't Captain Donnithorne and Mr. Irwine a-coming into the yard! I'll lay my life they're come to speak about your preaching on the Green, Dinah; it's you must answer 'em, for I'm dumb. I've said enough a'ready about your bringing such disgrace upo' your uncle's family. I wouldn't ha' minded if you'd been Mr. Poyser's own niece—folks must put up wi' their own kin, as they put up wi' their own noses—it's their own flesh and blood. But to think of a niece o' mine being cause o' my husband's being turned out of his farm, and me brought him no fortin but my savin's——"

"Nay, dear Aunt Rachel," said Dinah gently, "you've no cause for such fears. I've strong assurance that no evil will happen to you and my uncle and the children from anything I've done. I didn't preach without direction."

"Direction! I know very well what you mean by direction," said Mrs. Poyser, knitting in a rapid and agitated manner. "When there's a bigger maggot than usual in your head you call it 'direction'; and then nothing can stir you—you look like the statty o' the outside o' Treddles'on church, a-starin' and a-smilin' whether it's fair weather or foul. I hanna common patience with you."

By this time the two gentlemen had reached the palings and had got down from their horses: it was plain they meant to come in. Mrs. Poyser advanced to the door to meet them, curtsying low and trembling between anger with Dinah and anxiety to conduct herself with perfect propriety on the occasion. For in those days the keenest of bucolic minds felt a whispering awe at the sight of the gentry, such as of old men felt when they stood on tiptoe to watch the gods passing by in tall human shape.

"Well, Mrs. Poyser, how are you after this stormy morning?" said Mr. Irwine, with his stately cordiality. "Our feet are quite dry; we shall not soil your beautiful floor."

"Oh, sir, don't mention it," said Mrs. Poyser. "Will you and the captain please to walk into the parlour?"

"No, indeed, thank you, Mrs. Poyser," said the captain, looking eagerly round the kitchen, as if his eye were seeking something it could not find. "I delight in your kitchen. I think it is the most charming room I know. I should like every farmer's wife to come and look at it for a pattern."

"Oh, you're pleased to say so, sir. Pray take a seat," said Mrs. Poyser, relieved a little by this compliment and the captain's evident good-humour, but still glancing anxiously at Mr. Irwine, who, she saw, was looking at Dinah and advancing towards her.

"Poyser is not at home, is he?" said Captain Donnithorne, seating himself where he could see along the short passage to the open dairy-door.

"No, sir, he isn't; he's gone to Rosseter to see Mr. West, the factor, about the wool. But there's Father i' the barn, sir, if he'd be of any use."

"No, thank you; I'll just look at the whelps and leave a message about them with your shepherd. I must come another day and see your husband; I want to have a consultation with him about horses. Do you know when he's likely to be at liberty?"

"Why, sir, you can hardly miss him, except it's o' Treddles'on market-day—that's of a Friday, you know. For if he's anywhere on the farm we can send for him in a minute. If we'd got rid o' the Scantlands, we should have no outlying fields; and I should be glad of it, for if ever anything happens, he's sure to be gone to the Scantlands. Things allays happen so contrairy, if they've a chance; and it's an unnat'ral thing to have one bit o' your farm in one county and all the rest in another."

"Ah, the Scantlands would go much better with Choyce's farm, especially as he wants dairyland and you've got plenty. I think yours is the prettiest farm on the estate, though; and do you know, Mrs. Poyser, if I were going to marry and settle, I should be tempted to turn you out, and do up this fine old house, and turn farmer myself."

"Oh, sir," said Mrs. Poyser, rather alarmed, "you wouldn't like it at all. As for farming, it's putting money into your pocket wi' your right hand and fetching it out wi' your left. As fur as I can see, it's raising victual for other folks and just getting a mouthful for yourself and your children as you go along. Not as you'd be like a poor man as wants to get his bread—you could afford to lose as much money as you liked i' farming—but it's poor fun losing money, I should think, though I understan' it's what the great folks i' London play at more than anything. For my husband heard at market as Lord Dacey's eldest son had lost thousands upo' thousands to the Prince o' Wales, and they said my lady was going to pawn her jewels to pay for him. But you know more about that than I do, sir. But, as for farming, sir, I canna think as you'd like it; and this house—the draughts in it are enough to cut you through, and it's my opinion the floors upstairs are very rotten, and the rats i' the cellar are beyond anything."

"Why, that's a terrible picture, Mrs. Poyser. I think I should be doing you a service to turn you out of such a place. But there's no chance of that. I'm not likely to settle for the next twenty years, till I'm a stout gentleman of forty; and my grandfather would never consent to part with such good tenants as you."

"Well, sir, if he thinks so well o' Mr. Poyser for a tenant I wish you could put in a word for him to allow us some new gates for the Five closes, for my husband's been asking and asking till he's tired, and to think o' what he's done for the farm, and's never had a penny allowed him, be the times bad or good. And as I've said to my husband often and often, I'm sure if the captain had anything to do with it, it wouldn't be so. Not as I wish to speak disrespectful o' them as have got the power i' their hands, but it's more than flesh and blood 'ull bear sometimes, to be toiling and striving, and up early and down late, and hardly sleeping a wink when you lie down for thinking as the cheese may swell, or the cows may slip their calf, or the wheat may grow green again i' the sheaf—and after all, at th' end o' the year, it's like as if you'd been cooking a feast and had got the smell of it for your pains."

Mrs. Poyser, once launched into conversation, always sailed along without any check from her preliminary awe of the gentry. The confidence she felt in her own powers of exposition was a motive force that overcame all resistance.

"I'm afraid I should only do harm instead of good, if I were to speak about the gates, Mrs. Poyser," said the captain, "though I assure you there's no man on the estate I would sooner say a word for than your husband. I know his farm is in better order than any other within ten miles of us; and as for the kitchen," he added, smiling, "I don't believe there's one in the kingdom to beat it. By the by, I've never seen your dairy: I must see your dairy, Mrs. Poyser."

"Indeed, sir, it's not fit for you to go in, for Hetty's in the middle o' making the butter, for the churning was thrown late, and I'm quite ashamed." This Mrs. Poyser said blushing, and believing that the captain was really interested in her milk-pans, and would adjust his opinion of her to the appearance of her dairy.

"Oh, I've no doubt it's in capital order. Take me in," said the captain, himself leading the way, while Mrs. Poyser followed.

Chapter VII
The Dairy

The dairy was certainly worth looking at: it was a scene to sicken for with a sort of calenture in hot and dusty streets—such coolness, such purity, such fresh fragrance of new-pressed cheese, of firm butter, of wooden vessels perpetually bathed in pure water; such soft colouring of red earthenware and creamy surfaces, brown wood and polished tin, grey limestone and rich orange-red rust on the iron weights and hooks and hinges. But one gets only a confused notion of these details when they surround a distractingly pretty girl of seventeen, standing on little pattens and rounding her dimpled arm to lift a pound of butter out of the scale.

Hetty blushed a deep rose-colour when Captain Donnithorne entered the dairy and spoke to her; but it was not at all a distressed blush, for it was inwreathed with smiles and dimples, and with sparkles from under long, curled, dark eyelashes; and while her aunt was discoursing to him about the limited amount of milk that was to be spared for butter and cheese so long as the calves were not all weaned, and a large quantity but inferior quality of milk yielded by the shorthorn, which had been bought on experiment, together with other matters which must be interesting to a young gentleman who would one day be a landlord, Hetty tossed and patted her pound of butter with quite a self-possessed, coquettish air, slyly conscious that no turn of her head was lost.

There are various orders of beauty, causing men to make fools of themselves in various styles, from the desperate to the sheepish; but there is one order of beauty which seems made to turn the heads not only of men, but of all intelligent mammals, even of women. It is a beauty like that of kittens, or very small downy ducks making gentle rippling noises with their soft bills, or babies just beginning to toddle and to engage in conscious mischief—a beauty with which you can never be angry, but that you feel ready to crush for inability to comprehend the state of mind into which it throws you. Hetty Sorrel's was that sort of beauty. Her aunt, Mrs. Poyser, who professed to despise all personal attractions and intended to be the severest of mentors, continually gazed at Hetty's charms by the sly, fascinated in spite of herself; and after administering such a scolding as naturally flowed from her anxiety to do well by her husband's niece—who had no mother of her own to scold her, poor thing!—she would often confess to her husband, when they were safe out of hearing, that she firmly believed, "the naughtier the little huzzy behaved, the prettier she looked."

It is of little use for me to tell you that Hetty's cheek was like a rose-petal, that dimples played about her pouting lips, that her large dark eyes hid a soft roguishness under their long lashes, and that her curly hair, though all pushed back under her round cap while she was at work, stole back in dark delicate rings on her forehead, and about her white shell-like ears; it is of little use for me to say how lovely was the contour of her pink-and-white neckerchief, tucked into her low plum-coloured stuff bodice, or how the linen butter-making apron, with its bib, seemed a thing to be imitated in silk by duchesses, since it fell in such charming lines, or how her brown stockings and thick-soled buckled shoes lost all that clumsiness which they must certainly have had when empty of her foot and ankle—of little use, unless you have seen a woman who affected you as Hetty affected her beholders, for otherwise, though you might conjure up the image of a lovely woman, she would not in the least resemble that distracting kittenlike maiden. I might mention all the divine charms of a bright spring day, but if you had never in your life utterly forgotten yourself in straining your eyes after the mounting lark, or in wandering through the still lanes when the fresh-opened blossoms fill them with a sacred silent beauty like that of fretted aisles, where would be the use of my descriptive catalogue? I could never make you know what I meant by a bright spring day. Hetty's was a spring-tide beauty; it was the beauty of young frisking things, round-limbed, gambolling, circumventing you by a false air of innocence—the innocence of a young star-browed calf, for example, that, being inclined for a promenade out of bounds, leads you a severe steeplechase over hedge and ditch, and only comes to a stand in the middle of a bog.

And they are the prettiest attitudes and movements into which a pretty girl is thrown in making up butter—tossing movements that give a charming curve to the arm, and a sideward inclination of the round white neck; little patting and rolling movements with the palm of the hand, and nice adaptations and finishings which cannot at all be effected without a great play of the pouting mouth and the dark eyes. And then the butter itself seems to communicate a fresh charm—it is so pure, so sweet-scented; it is turned off the mould with such a beautiful firm surface, like marble in a pale yellow light! Moreover, Hetty was particularly clever at making up the butter; it was the one performance of hers that her aunt allowed to pass without severe criticism; so she handled it with all the grace that belongs to mastery.

"I hope you will be ready for a great holiday on the thirtieth of July, Mrs. Poyser," said Captain Donnithorne, when he had sufficiently admired the dairy and given several improvised opinions on Swede turnips and shorthorns. "You know what is to happen then, and I shall expect you to be one of the guests who come earliest and leave latest. Will you promise me your hand for two dances, Miss Hetty? If I don't get your promise now, I know I shall hardly have a chance, for all the smart young farmers will take care to secure you."

Hetty smiled and blushed, but before she could answer, Mrs. Poyser interposed, scandalized at the mere suggestion that the young squire could be excluded by any meaner partners.

"Indeed, sir, you are very kind to take that notice of her. And I'm sure, whenever you're pleased to dance with her, she'll be proud and thankful, if she stood still all the rest o' th' evening."

"Oh no, no, that would be too cruel to all the other young fellows who can dance. But you will promise me two dances, won't you?" the captain continued, determined to make Hetty look at him and speak to him.

Hetty dropped the prettiest little curtsy, and stole a half-shy, half-coquettish glance at him as she said, "Yes, thank you, sir."

"And you must bring all your children, you know, Mrs. Poyser; your little Totty, as well as the boys. I want all the youngest children on the estate to be there—all those who will be fine young men and women when I'm a bald old fellow."

"Oh dear, sir, that 'ull be a long time first," said Mrs. Poyser, quite overcome at the young squire's speaking so lightly of himself, and thinking how her husband would be interested in hearing her recount this remarkable specimen of high-born humour. The captain was thought to be "very full of his jokes," and was a great favourite throughout the estate on account of his free manners. Every tenant was quite sure things would be different when the reins got into his hands—there was to be a millennial abundance of new gates, allowances of lime, and returns of ten per cent.

"But where *is* Totty to-day?" he said. "I want to see her."

"Where is the little un, Hetty?" said Mrs. Poyser. "She came in here not long ago."

"I don't know. She went into the brewhouse to Nancy, I think."

The proud mother, unable to resist the temptation to show her Totty, passed at once into the back kitchen, in search of her, not, however, without misgivings lest something should have happened to render her person and attire unfit for presentation.

"And do you carry the butter to market when you've made it?" said the Captain to Hetty, meanwhile.

"Oh no, sir; not when it's so heavy. I'm not strong enough to carry it. Alick takes it on horseback."

"No, I'm sure your pretty arms were never meant for such heavy weights. But you go out a walk sometimes these pleasant evenings, don't you? Why don't you have a walk in the Chase sometimes, now it's so green and pleasant? I hardly ever see you anywhere except at home and at church."

"Aunt doesn't like me to go a-walking only when I'm going somewhere," said Hetty. "But I go through the Chase sometimes."

"And don't you ever go to see Mrs. Best, the housekeeper? I think I saw you once in the housekeeper's room."

"It isn't Mrs. Best, it's Mrs. Pomfret, the lady's maid, as I go to see. She's teaching me tent-stitch and the lace-mending. I'm going to tea with her to-morrow afternoon."

The reason why there had been space for this *tête-à-tête* can only be known by looking into the back kitchen, where Totty had been discovered rubbing a stray blue-bag against her nose, and in the same moment allowing some liberal indigo drops to fall on her afternoon pinafore. But now she appeared holding her mother's hand—the end of her round nose rather shiny from a recent and hurried application of soap and water.

"Here she is!" said the captain, lifting her up and setting her on the low stone shelf. "Here's Totty! By the by, what's her other name? She wasn't christened Totty."

"Oh, sir, we call her sadly out of her name. Charlotte's her christened name. It's a name i' Mr. Poyser's family: his grandmother was named Charlotte. But we began with calling her Lotty, and now it's got to Totty. To be sure it's more like a name for a dog than a Christian child."

"Totty's a capital name. Why, she looks like a Totty. Has she got a pocket on?" said the captain, feeling in his own waistcoat pockets.

Totty immediately with great gravity lifted up her frock, and showed a tiny pink pocket at present in a state of collapse.

"It dot notin' in it," she said, as she looked down at it very earnestly.

"No! What a pity! Such a pretty pocket. Well, I think I've got some things in mine that will make a pretty jingle in it. Yes! I declare I've got five little round silver things, and hear what a pretty noise they make in Totty's pink pocket." Here he shook the pocket with the five sixpences in it, and Totty showed her teeth and wrinkled her nose in great glee; but, divining that there was nothing more to be got by staying, she jumped off the shelf and ran away to jingle her pocket in the hearing of Nancy, while her mother called after her, "Oh for shame, you naughty gell! Not to thank the captain for what he's given you I'm sure, sir, it's very kind of you; but she's spoiled shameful; her father won't have her said nay in anything, and there's no managing her. It's being the youngest, and th' only gell."

"Oh, she's a funny little fatty; I wouldn't have her different. But I must be going now, for I suppose the rector is waiting for me."

With a "good-bye," a bright glance, and a bow to Hetty Arthur left the dairy. But he was mistaken in imagining himself waited for. The rector had been so much interested in his conversation with Dinah that he would not have chosen to close it earlier; and you shall hear now what they had been saying to each other.

Chapter VIII
A Vocation

Dinah, who had risen when the gentlemen came in, but still kept hold of the sheet she was mending, curtsied respectfully when she saw Mr. Irwine looking at her and advancing towards her. He had never yet spoken to her, or stood face to face with her, and her first thought, as her eyes met his, was, "What a well-favoured countenance! Oh that the good seed might fall on that soil, for it would surely flourish." The agreeable impression must have been mutual, for Mr. Irwine bowed to her with a benignant deference, which would have been equally in place if she had been the most dignified lady of his acquaintance.

"You are only a visitor in this neighbourhood, I think?" were his first words, as he seated himself opposite to her.

"No, sir, I come from Snowfield, in Stonyshire. But my aunt was very kind, wanting me to have rest from my work there, because I'd been ill, and she invited me to come and stay with her for a while."

"Ah, I remember Snowfield very well; I once had occasion to go there. It's a dreary bleak place. They were building a cotton-mill there; but that's many years ago now. I suppose the place is a good deal changed by the employment that mill must have brought."

"It *is* changed so far as the mill has brought people there, who get a livelihood for themselves by working in it, and make it better for the tradesfolks. I work in it myself, and have reason to be grateful, for thereby I have enough and to spare. But it's still a bleak place, as you say, sir—very different from this country."

"You have relations living there, probably, so that you are attached to the place as your home?"

"I had an aunt there once; she brought me up, for I was an orphan. But she was taken away seven years ago, and I have no other kindred that I know of, besides my Aunt Poyser, who is very good to me, and would have me come and live in this country, which to be sure is a good land, wherein they eat bread without scarceness. But I'm not free to leave Snowfield, where I was first planted, and have grown deep into it, like the small grass on the hill-top."

"Ah, I daresay you have many religious friends and companions there; you are a Methodist—a Wesleyan, I think?"

"Yes, my aunt at Snowfield belonged to the Society, and I have cause to be thankful for the privileges I have had thereby from my earliest childhood."

"And have you been long in the habit of preaching? For I understand you preached at Hayslope last night."

"I first took to the work four years since, when I was twenty-one."

"Your Society sanctions women's preaching, then?"

"It doesn't forbid them, sir, when they've a clear call to the work, and when their ministry is owned by the conversion of sinners and the strengthening of God's people. Mrs. Fletcher, as you may have heard about, was the first woman to preach in the Society, I believe, before she was married, when she was Miss Bosanquet; and Mr. Wesley approved of her undertaking the work. She had a great gift, and there are many others now living who are precious fellow-helpers in the work of the ministry. I understand there's been voices raised against it in the Society of late, but I cannot but think their counsel will come to nought. It isn't for men to make channels for God's Spirit, as they make channels for the watercourses, and say, 'Flow here, but flow not there.'"

"But don't you find some danger among your people—I don't mean to say that it is so with you, far from it—but don't you find sometimes that both men and women fancy themselves channels for God's Spirit, and are quite mistaken, so that they set about a work for which they are unfit and bring holy things into contempt?"

"Doubtless it is so sometimes; for there have been evil-doers among us who have sought to deceive the brethren, and some there are who deceive their own selves. But we are not without discipline and correction to put a check upon these things. There's a very strict order kept among us, and the brethren and sisters watch for each other's souls as they that must give account. They don't go every one his own way and say, 'Am I my brother's keeper?'"

"But tell me—if I may ask, and I am really interested in knowing it—how you first came to think of preaching?"

"Indeed, sir, I didn't think of it at all—I'd been used from the time I was sixteen to talk to the little children, and teach them, and sometimes I had had my heart enlarged to speak in class, and was much drawn out in prayer with the sick. But I had felt no call to preach, for when I'm not greatly wrought upon, I'm too much given to sit still and keep by myself. It seems as if I could sit silent all day long with the thought of God overflowing my soul—as the pebbles lie bathed in the Willow Brook. For thoughts are so great—aren't they, sir? They seem to lie upon us like a deep flood; and it's my besetment to forget where I am and everything about me, and lose myself in thoughts that I could give no account of, for I could neither make a beginning nor ending of them in words. That was my way as long as I can remember; but sometimes it seemed as if speech came to me without any will of my own, and words were given to me that came out as the tears come, because our hearts are full and we can't help it. And those were always times of great blessing, though I had never thought it could be so with me before a congregation of people. But, sir, we are led on, like the little children, by a way that we know not. I was called to preach quite suddenly, and since then I have never been left in doubt about the work that was laid upon me."

"But tell me the circumstances—just how it was, the very day you began to preach."

"It was one Sunday I walked with brother Marlowe, who was an aged man, one of the local preachers, all the way to Hetton-Deeps—that's a village where the people get their living by working in the lead-mines, and where there's no church nor preacher, but they live like sheep without a shepherd. It's better than twelve miles from Snowfield, so we set out early in the morning, for it was summertime; and I had a wonderful sense of the Divine love as we walked over the hills, where there's no trees, you know, sir, as there is here, to make the sky look smaller, but you see the heavens stretched out like a tent, and you feel the everlasting arms around you. But before we got to Hetton, brother Marlowe was seized with a dizziness that made him afraid of falling, for he overworked himself sadly, at his years, in watching and praying, and walking so many miles to speak the Word, as well as carrying on his trade of linen-weaving. And when we got to the village, the people were expecting him, for he'd appointed the time and the place when he was there before, and such of them as cared to hear the Word of Life were assembled on a spot where the cottages was thickest, so as others might be drawn to come. But he felt as he couldn't stand up to preach, and he was forced to lie down in the first of the cottages we came to. So I went to tell the people, thinking we'd go into one of the houses, and I would read and pray with them. But as I passed along by the cottages and saw the aged and trembling women at the doors, and the hard looks of the men, who seemed to have their eyes no more filled with the sight of the Sabbath morning than if they had been dumb oxen that never looked up to the sky, I felt a great movement in my soul, and I trembled as if I was shaken by a strong spirit entering into my weak body. And I went to where the little flock of people was gathered together, and stepped on the low wall that was built against the green hillside, and I spoke the words that were given to me abundantly. And they all came round me out of all the cottages, and many wept over their sins, and have since been joined to the Lord. That was the beginning of my preaching, sir, and I've preached ever since."

Dinah had let her work fall during this narrative, which she uttered in her usual simple way, but with that sincere articulate, thrilling treble by which she always mastered her audience. She stooped now to gather up her sewing, and then went on with it as before. Mr. Irwine was deeply interested. He said to himself, "He must be a miserable prig who would act the pedagogue here: one might as well go and lecture the trees for growing in their own shape."

"And you never feel any embarrassment from the sense of your youth—that you are a lovely young woman on whom men's eyes are fixed?" he said aloud.

"No, I've no room for such feelings, and I don't believe the people ever take notice about that. I think, sir, when God makes His presence felt through us, we are like the burning bush: Moses never took any heed what sort of bush it was—he only saw the brightness of the Lord. I've preached to as rough ignorant people as can be in the villages about Snowfield—men that looked very hard and wild—but they never said an uncivil word to me, and often thanked me kindly as they made way for me to pass through the midst of them."

"*That* I can believe—that I can well believe," said Mr. Irwine, emphatically. "And what did you think of your hearers last night, now? Did you find them quiet and attentive?"

"Very quiet, sir, but I saw no signs of any great work upon them, except in a young girl named Bessy Cranage, towards whom my heart yearned greatly, when my eyes first fell on her blooming youth, given up to folly and vanity. I had some private talk and prayer with her afterwards, and I trust her heart is touched. But I've noticed that in these villages where the people lead a quiet life among the green pastures and the still waters, tilling the ground and tending the cattle, there's a strange deadness to the Word, as different as can be from the great towns, like Leeds, where I once went to visit a holy woman who preaches there. It's wonderful how rich is the harvest of souls up those high-walled streets, where you seemed to walk as in a prison-yard, and the ear is deafened with the sounds of worldly toil. I think maybe it is because the promise is sweeter when this life is so dark and weary, and the soul gets more hungry when the body is ill at ease."

"Why, yes, our farm-labourers are not easily roused. They take life almost as slowly as the sheep and cows. But we have some intelligent workmen about here. I daresay you know the Bedes; Seth Bede, by the by, is a Methodist."

"Yes, I know Seth well, and his brother Adam a little. Seth is a gracious young man—sincere and without offence; and Adam is like the patriarch Joseph, for his great skill and knowledge and the kindness he shows to his brother and his parents."

"Perhaps you don't know the trouble that has just happened to them? Their father, Matthias Bede, was drowned in the Willow Brook last night, not far from his own door. I'm going now to see Adam."

"Ah, their poor aged mother!" said Dinah, dropping her hands and looking before her with pitying eyes, as if she saw the object of her sympathy. "She will mourn heavily, for Seth has told me she's of an anxious, troubled heart. I must go and see if I can give her any help."

As she rose and was beginning to fold up her work, Captain Donnithorne, having exhausted all plausible pretexts for remaining among the milk-pans, came out of the dairy, followed by Mrs. Poyser. Mr. Irwine now rose also, and, advancing towards Dinah, held out his hand, and said, "Good-bye. I hear you are going away soon; but this will not be the last visit you will pay your aunt—so we shall meet again, I hope."

His cordiality towards Dinah set all Mrs. Poyser's anxieties at rest, and her face was brighter than usual, as she said, "I've never asked after Mrs. Irwine and the Miss Irwines, sir; I hope they're as well as usual."

"Yes, thank you, Mrs. Poyser, except that Miss Anne has one of her bad headaches to-day. By the by, we all liked that nice cream-cheese you sent us—my mother especially."

"I'm very glad, indeed, sir. It is but seldom I make one, but I remembered Mrs. Irwine was fond of 'em. Please to give my duty to her, and to Miss Kate and Miss Anne. They've never been to look at my poultry this long while, and I've got some beautiful speckled chickens, black and white, as Miss Kate might like to have some of amongst hers."

"Well, I'll tell her; she must come and see them. Good-bye," said the rector, mounting his horse.

"Just ride slowly on, Irwine," said Captain Donnithorne, mounting also. "I'll overtake you in three minutes. I'm only going to speak to the shepherd about the whelps. Good-bye, Mrs. Poyser; tell your husband I shall come and have a long talk with him soon."

Mrs. Poyser curtsied duly, and watched the two horses until they had disappeared from the yard, amidst great excitement on the part of the pigs and the poultry, and under the furious indignation of the bull-dog, who performed a Pyrrhic dance, that every moment seemed to threaten the breaking of his chain. Mrs. Poyser delighted in this noisy exit; it was a fresh assurance to her that the farm-yard was well guarded, and that no loiterers could enter unobserved; and it was not until the gate had closed behind the captain that she turned into the kitchen again, where Dinah stood with her bonnet in her hand, waiting to speak to her aunt, before she set out for Lisbeth Bede's cottage.

Mrs. Poyser, however, though she noticed the bonnet, deferred remarking on it until she had disburdened herself of her surprise at Mr. Irwine's behaviour.

"Why, Mr. Irwine wasn't angry, then? What did he say to you, Dinah? Didn't he scold you for preaching?"

"No, he was not at all angry; he was very friendly to me. I was quite drawn out to speak to him; I hardly know how, for I had always thought of him as a worldly Sadducee. But his countenance is as pleasant as the morning sunshine."

"Pleasant! and what else did y' expect to find him but pleasant?" said Mrs. Poyser impatiently, resuming her knitting. "I should think his countenance *is* pleasant indeed! And him a gentleman born, and's got a mother like a picter. You may go the country round and not find such another woman turned sixty-six. It's summat-like to see such a man as that i' the desk of a Sunday! As I say to Poyser, it's like looking at a full crop o' wheat, or a pasture with a fine dairy o' cows in it; it makes you think the world's comfortable-like. But as for such creaturs as you Methodisses run after, I'd as soon go to look at a lot o' bare-ribbed runts on a common. Fine folks they are to tell you what's right, as look as if they'd never tasted nothing better than bacon-sword and sour-cake i' their lives. But what did Mr. Irwine say to you about that fool's trick o' preaching on the Green?"

"He only said he'd heard of it; he didn't seem to feel any displeasure about it. But, dear aunt, don't think any more about that. He told me something that I'm sure will cause you sorrow, as it does me. Thias Bede was drowned last night in the Willow Brook, and I'm thinking that the aged mother will be greatly in need of comfort. Perhaps I can be of use to her, so I have fetched my bonnet and am going to set out."

"Dear heart, dear heart! But you must have a cup o' tea first, child," said Mrs. Poyser, falling at once from the key of B with five sharps to the frank and genial C. "The kettle's boiling—we'll have it ready in a minute; and the young uns 'ull be in and wanting theirs directly. I'm quite willing you should go and see th' old woman, for you're one as is allays welcome in trouble, Methodist or no Methodist; but, for the matter o' that, it's the flesh and blood folks are made on as makes the difference. Some cheeses are made o' skimmed milk and some o' new milk, and it's no matter what you call 'em, you may tell which is which by the look and the smell. But as to Thias Bede, he's better out o' the way nor in—God forgi' me for saying so—for he's done little this ten year but make trouble for them as belonged to him; and I think it 'ud be well for you to take a little bottle o' rum for th' old woman, for I daresay she's got never a drop o' nothing to comfort her inside. Sit down, child, and be easy, for you shan't stir out till you've had a cup o' tea, and so I tell you."

During the latter part of this speech, Mrs. Poyser had been reaching down the tea-things from the shelves, and was on her way towards the pantry for the loaf (followed close by Totty, who had made her appearance on the rattling of the tea-cups), when Hetty came out of the dairy relieving her tired arms by lifting them up, and clasping her hands at the back of her head.

“Molly,” she said, rather languidly, “just run out and get me a bunch of dock-leaves: the butter’s ready to pack up now.”

“D’ you hear what’s happened, Hetty?” said her aunt.

“No; how should I hear anything?” was the answer, in a pettish tone.

“Not as you’d care much, I daresay, if you did hear; for you’re too feather-headed to mind if everybody was dead, so as you could stay upstairs a-dressing yourself for two hours by the clock. But anybody besides yourself ’ud mind about such things happening to them as think a deal more of you than you deserve. But Adam Bede and all his kin might be drownded for what you’d care—you’d be perking at the glass the next minute.”

“Adam Bede—drowned?” said Hetty, letting her arms fall and looking rather bewildered, but suspecting that her aunt was as usual exaggerating with a didactic purpose.

“No, my dear, no,” said Dinah kindly, for Mrs. Poyser had passed on to the pantry without deigning more precise information. “Not Adam. Adam’s father, the old man, is drowned. He was drowned last night in the Willow Brook. Mr. Irwine has just told me about it.”

“Oh, how dreadful!” said Hetty, looking serious, but not deeply affected; and as Molly now entered with the dock-leaves, she took them silently and returned to the dairy without asking further questions.

Chapter IX
Hetty's World

While she adjusted the broad leaves that set off the pale fragrant butter as the primrose is set off by its nest of green I am afraid Hetty was thinking a great deal more of the looks Captain Donnithorne had cast at her than of Adam and his troubles. Bright, admiring glances from a handsome young gentleman with white hands, a gold chain, occasional regimentals, and wealth and grandeur immeasurable—those were the warm rays that set poor Hetty's heart vibrating and playing its little foolish tunes over and over again. We do not hear that Memnon's statue gave forth its melody at all under the rushing of the mightiest wind, or in response to any other influence divine or human than certain short-lived sunbeams of morning; and we must learn to accommodate ourselves to the discovery that some of those cunningly fashioned instruments called human souls have only a very limited range of music, and will not vibrate in the least under a touch that fills others with tremulous rapture or quivering agony.

Hetty was quite used to the thought that people liked to look at her. She was not blind to the fact that young Luke Britton of Broxton came to Hayslope Church on a Sunday afternoon on purpose that he might see her; and that he would have made much more decided advances if her uncle Poyser, thinking but lightly of a young man whose father's land was so foul as old Luke Britton's, had not forbidden her aunt to encourage him by any civilities. She was aware, too, that Mr. Craig, the gardener at the Chase, was over head and ears in love with her, and had lately made unmistakable avowals in luscious strawberries and hyperbolical peas. She knew still better, that Adam Bede—tall, upright, clever, brave Adam Bede—who carried such authority with all the people round about, and whom her uncle was always delighted to see of an evening, saying that "Adam knew a fine sight more o' the natur o' things than those as thought themselves his betters"—she knew that this Adam, who was often rather stern to other people and not much given to run after the lasses, could be made to turn pale or red any day by a word or a look from her. Hetty's sphere of comparison was not large, but she couldn't help perceiving that Adam was "something like" a man; always knew what to say about things, could tell her uncle how to prop the hovel, and had mended the churn in no time; knew, with only looking at it, the value of the chestnut-tree that was blown down, and why the damp came in the walls, and what they must do to stop the rats; and wrote a beautiful hand that you could read off, and could do figures in his head—a degree of accomplishment totally unknown among the richest farmers of that countryside. Not at all like that slouching Luke Britton, who, when she once walked with him all the way from Broxton to Hayslope, had only broken silence to remark that the grey goose had begun to lay. And as for Mr. Craig, the gardener, he was a sensible man enough, to be sure, but he was knock-kneed, and had a queer sort of sing-song in his talk; moreover, on the most charitable supposition, he must be far on the way to forty.

Hetty was quite certain her uncle wanted her to encourage Adam, and would be pleased for her to marry him. For those were times when there was no rigid demarcation of rank between the farmer and the respectable artisan, and on the home hearth, as well as in the public house, they might be seen taking their jug of ale together; the farmer having a latent sense of capital, and of weight in parish affairs, which sustained him under his conspicuous inferiority in conversation. Martin Poyser was not a frequenter of public houses, but he liked a friendly chat over his own home-brewed; and though it was pleasant to lay down the law to a stupid neighbour who had no notion how to make the best of his farm, it was also an agreeable variety to learn something from a clever fellow like Adam Bede. Accordingly, for the last three years—ever since he had superintended the building of the new barn—Adam had always been made welcome at the Hall Farm, especially of a winter evening, when the whole family, in patriarchal fashion, master and mistress, children and servants, were assembled in that glorious kitchen, at well-graduated distances from the blazing fire. And for the last two years, at least, Hetty had been in the habit of hearing her uncle say, "Adam Bede may be working for wage now, but he'll be a master-man some day, as sure as I sit in this chair. Mester Burge is in the right on't to want him to go partners and marry his daughter, if it's true what they say; the woman as marries him 'ull have a good take, be't Lady day or Michaelmas," a remark which Mrs. Poyser always followed up with her cordial assent. "Ah," she would say, "it's all very fine having a ready-made rich man, but mayhappen he'll be a ready-made fool; and it's no use filling your pocket full o' money if you've got a hole in the corner. It'll do you no good to sit in a spring-cart o' your own, if you've got a soft to drive you: he'll soon turn you over into the ditch. I allays said I'd never marry a man as had got no brains; for where's the use of a woman having brains of her own if she's tackled to a geck as everybody's a-laughing at? She might as well dress herself fine to sit back'ards on a donkey."

These expressions, though figurative, sufficiently indicated the bent of Mrs. Poyser's mind with regard to Adam; and though she and her husband might have viewed the subject differently if Hetty had been a daughter of their own, it was clear that they would have welcomed the match with Adam for a penniless niece. For what could Hetty have been but a servant elsewhere, if her uncle had not taken her in and brought her up as a domestic help to her aunt, whose health since the birth of Totty had not been equal to more positive labour than the superintendence of servants and children? But Hetty had never given Adam any steady encouragement. Even in the moments when she was most thoroughly conscious of his superiority to her other admirers, she had never brought herself to think of accepting him. She liked to feel that this strong, skilful, keen-eyed man was in her power, and would have been indignant if he had shown the least sign of slipping from under the yoke of her coquettish tyranny and attaching himself to the gentle Mary Burge, who would have been grateful enough for the most trifling notice from him. "Mary Burge, indeed! Such a sallow-faced girl: if she put on a bit of pink ribbon, she looked as yellow as a crow-flower and her hair was as straight as a hank of cotton." And always when Adam stayed away for several weeks from the Hall Farm, and otherwise made some show of resistance to his passion as a foolish one, Hetty took care to entice him back into the net by little airs of meekness and timidity, as if she were in trouble at his neglect. But as to marrying Adam, that was a very different affair! There was nothing in the world to tempt her to do that. Her cheeks never grew a shade deeper when his name was mentioned; she felt no thrill when she saw him passing along the causeway by the window, or advancing towards her unexpectedly in the footpath across the meadow; she felt nothing, when his eyes rested on her, but the cold triumph of knowing that he loved her and would not care to look at Mary Burge. He could no more stir in her the emotions that make the sweet intoxication of young love than the mere picture of a sun can stir the spring sap in the subtle fibres of the plant. She saw him as he was—a poor man with old parents to keep, who would not be able, for a long while to come, to give her even such luxuries as she shared in her uncle's house. And Hetty's dreams were all of luxuries: to sit in a carpeted parlour, and always wear white stockings; to have some large beautiful ear-rings, such as were all the fashion; to have Nottingham lace round the top of her gown, and something to make her handkerchief smell nice, like Miss Lydia Donnithorne's when she drew it out at church; and not to be obliged to get up early or be scolded by anybody. She thought, if Adam had been rich and could have given her these things, she loved him well enough to marry him.

But for the last few weeks a new influence had come over Hetty—vague, atmospheric, shaping itself into no self-confessed hopes or prospects, but producing a pleasant narcotic effect, making her tread the ground and go about her work in a sort of dream, unconscious of weight or effort, and showing her all things through a soft, liquid veil, as if she were living not in this solid world of brick and stone, but in a beatified world, such as the sun lights up for us in the waters. Hetty had become aware that Mr. Arthur Donnithorne would take a good deal of trouble for the chance of seeing her; that he always placed himself at church so as to have the fullest view of her both sitting and standing; that he was constantly finding reason for calling at the Hall Farm, and always would contrive to say something for the sake of making her speak to him and look at him. The poor child no more conceived at present the idea that the young squire could ever be her lover than a baker's pretty daughter in the crowd, whom a young emperor distinguishes by an imperial but admiring smile, conceives that she shall be made empress. But the baker's daughter goes home and dreams of the handsome young emperor, and perhaps weighs the flour amiss while she is thinking what a heavenly lot it must be to have him for a husband. And so, poor Hetty had got a face and a presence haunting her waking and sleeping dreams; bright, soft glances had penetrated her, and suffused her life with a strange, happy languor. The eyes that shed those glances were really not half so fine as Adam's, which sometimes looked at her with a sad, beseeching tenderness, but they had found a ready medium in Hetty's little silly imagination, whereas Adam's could get no entrance through that atmosphere. For three weeks, at least, her inward life had consisted of little else than living through in memory the looks and words Arthur had directed towards her—of little else than recalling the sensations with which she heard his voice outside the house, and saw him enter, and became conscious that his eyes were fixed on her, and then became conscious that a tall figure, looking down on her with eyes that seemed to touch her, was coming nearer in clothes of beautiful texture with an odour like that of a flower-garden borne on the evening breeze. Foolish thoughts! But all this happened, you must remember, nearly sixty years ago, and Hetty was quite uneducated—a simple farmer's girl, to whom a gentleman with a white hand was dazzling as an Olympian god. Until to-day, she had never looked farther into the future than to the next time Captain Donnithorne would come to the Farm, or the next Sunday when she should see him at church; but now she thought, perhaps he would try to meet her when she went to the Chase to-morrow—and if he should speak to her, and walk a little way, when nobody was by! That had never happened yet; and now her imagination, instead of retracing the past, was busy fashioning what would happen to-morrow—whereabout in the Chase she should see him coming towards her, how she should put her new rose-coloured ribbon on, which he had never seen, and what he would say to her to make her return his glance—a glance which she would be living through in her memory, over and over again, all the rest of the day.

In this state of mind, how could Hetty give any feeling to Adam's troubles, or think much about poor old Thias being drowned? Young souls, in such pleasant delirium as hers are as unsympathetic as butterflies sipping nectar; they are isolated from all appeals by a barrier of dreams—by invisible looks and impalpable arms.

While Hetty's hands were busy packing up the butter, and her head filled with these pictures of the morrow, Arthur Donnithorne, riding by Mr. Irwine's side towards the valley of the Willow Brook, had also certain indistinct anticipations, running as an undercurrent in his mind while he was listening to Mr. Irwine's account of Dinah—indistinct, yet strong enough to make him feel rather conscious when Mr. Irwine suddenly said, "What fascinated you so in Mrs.

Poyser's dairy, Arthur? Have you become an amateur of damp quarries and skimming dishes?"

Arthur knew the rector too well to suppose that a clever invention would be of any use, so he said, with his accustomed frankness, "No, I went to look at the pretty butter-maker Hetty Sorrel. She's a perfect Hebe; and if I were an artist, I would paint her. It's amazing what pretty girls one sees among the farmers' daughters, when the men are such clowns. That common, round, red face one sees sometimes in the men—all cheek and no features, like Martin Poyser's—comes out in the women of the family as the most charming phiz imaginable."

"Well, I have no objection to your contemplating Hetty in an artistic light, but I must not have you feeding her vanity and filling her little noddle with the notion that she's a great beauty, attractive to fine gentlemen, or you will spoil her for a poor man's wife—honest Craig's, for example, whom I have seen bestowing soft glances on her. The little puss seems already to have airs enough to make a husband as miserable as it's a law of nature for a quiet man to be when he marries a beauty. Apropos of marrying, I hope our friend Adam will get settled, now the poor old man's gone. He will only have his mother to keep in future, and I've a notion that there's a kindness between him and that nice modest girl, Mary Burge, from something that fell from old Jonathan one day when I was talking to him. But when I mentioned the subject to Adam he looked uneasy and turned the conversation. I suppose the love-making doesn't run smooth, or perhaps Adam hangs back till he's in a better position. He has independence of spirit enough for two men—rather an excess of pride, if anything."

"That would be a capital match for Adam. He would slip into old Burge's shoes and make a fine thing of that building business, I'll answer for him. I should like to see him well settled in this parish; he would be ready then to act as my grand-vizier when I wanted one. We could plan no end of repairs and improvements together. I've never seen the girl, though, I think—at least I've never looked at her."

"Look at her next Sunday at church—she sits with her father on the left of the reading-desk. You needn't look quite so much at Hetty Sorrel then. When I've made up my mind that I can't afford to buy a tempting dog, I take no notice of him, because if he took a strong fancy to me and looked lovingly at me, the struggle between arithmetic and inclination might become unpleasantly severe. I pique myself on my wisdom there, Arthur, and as an old fellow to whom wisdom had become cheap, I bestow it upon you."

"Thank you. It may stand me in good stead some day though I don't know that I have any present use for it. Bless me! How the brook has overflowed. Suppose we have a canter, now we're at the bottom of the hill."

That is the great advantage of dialogue on horseback; it can be merged any minute into a trot or a canter, and one might have escaped from Socrates himself in the saddle. The two friends were free from the necessity of further conversation till they pulled up in the lane behind Adam's cottage.

Chapter X
Dinah Visits Lisbeth

At five o'clock Lisbeth came downstairs with a large key in her hand: it was the key of the chamber where her husband lay dead. Throughout the day, except in her occasional outbursts of wailing grief, she had been in incessant movement, performing the initial duties to her dead with the awe and exactitude that belong to religious rites. She had brought out her little store of bleached linen, which she had for long years kept in reserve for this supreme use. It seemed but yesterday—that time so many midsummers ago, when she had told Thias where this linen lay, that he might be sure and reach it out for her when *she* died, for she was the elder of the two. Then there had been the work of cleansing to the strictest purity every object in the sacred chamber, and of removing from it every trace of common daily occupation. The small window, which had hitherto freely let in the frosty moonlight or the warm summer sunrise on the working man's slumber, must now be darkened with a fair white sheet, for this was the sleep which is as sacred under the bare rafters as in ceiled houses. Lisbeth had even mended a long-neglected and unnoticeable rent in the checkered bit of bed-curtain; for the moments were few and precious now in which she would be able to do the smallest office of respect or love for the still corpse, to which in all her thoughts she attributed some consciousness. Our dead are never dead to us until we have forgotten them: they can be injured by us, they can be wounded; they know all our penitence, all our aching sense that their place is empty, all the kisses we bestow on the smallest relic of their presence. And the aged peasant woman most of all believes that her dead are conscious. Decent burial was what Lisbeth had been thinking of for herself through years of thrift, with an indistinct expectation that she should know when she was being carried to the churchyard, followed by her husband and her sons; and now she felt as if the greatest work of her life were to be done in seeing that Thias was buried decently before her—under the white thorn, where once, in a dream, she had thought she lay in the coffin, yet all the while saw the sunshine above and smelt the white blossoms that were so thick upon the thorn the Sunday she went to be churched after Adam was born.

But now she had done everything that could be done to-day in the chamber of death—had done it all herself, with some aid from her sons in lifting, for she would let no one be fetched to help her from the village, not being fond of female neighbours generally; and her favourite Dolly, the old housekeeper at Mr. Burge's, who had come to condole with her in the morning as soon as she heard of Thias's death, was too dim-sighted to be of much use. She had locked the door, and now held the key in her hand, as she threw herself wearily into a chair that stood out of its place in the middle of the house floor, where in ordinary times she would never have consented to sit. The kitchen had had none of her attention that day; it was soiled with the tread of muddy shoes and untidy with clothes and other objects out of place. But what at another time would have been intolerable to Lisbeth's habits of order and cleanliness seemed to her now just what should be: it was right that things should look strange and disordered and wretched, now the old man had come to his end in that sad way; the kitchen ought not to look as if nothing had happened. Adam, overcome with the agitations and exertions of the day after his night of hard work, had fallen asleep on a bench in the workshop; and Seth was in the back kitchen making a fire of sticks that he might get the kettle to boil, and persuade his mother to have a cup of tea, an indulgence which she rarely allowed herself.

There was no one in the kitchen when Lisbeth entered and threw herself into the chair. She looked round with blank eyes at the dirt and confusion on which the bright afternoon's sun shone dismally; it was all of a piece with the sad confusion of her mind—that confusion which belongs to the first hours of a sudden sorrow, when the poor human soul is like one who has been deposited sleeping among the ruins of a vast city, and wakes up in dreary amazement, not knowing whether it is the growing or the dying day—not knowing why and whence came this illimitable scene of desolation, or why he too finds himself desolate in the midst of it.

At another time Lisbeth's first thought would have been, "Where is Adam?" but the sudden death of her husband had restored him in these hours to that first place in her affections which he had held six-and-twenty years ago. She had forgotten his faults as we forget the sorrows of our departed childhood, and thought of nothing but the young husband's kindness and the old man's patience. Her eyes continued to wander blankly until Seth came in and began to remove some of the scattered things, and clear the small round deal table that he might set out his mother's tea upon it.

"What art goin' to do?" she said, rather peevishly.

"I want thee to have a cup of tea, Mother," answered Seth, tenderly. "It'll do thee good; and I'll put two or three of these things away, and make the house look more comfortable."

"Comfortable! How canst talk o' ma'in' things comfortable? Let a-be, let a-be. There's no comfort for me no more," she went on, the tears coming when she began to speak, "now thy poor feyther's gone, as I'n washed for and mended, an' got's victual for him for thirty 'ear, an' him allays so pleased wi' iverything I done for him, an' used to be so handy an' do the jobs for me when I war ill an' cumbered wi' th' babby, an' made me the posset an' brought it upstairs as proud as could be, an' carried the lad as war as heavy as two children for five mile an' ne'er grumbled, all the way to Warson Wake, 'cause I wanted to go an' see my sister, as war dead an' gone the very next Christmas as e'er come. An' him to be drownded in the brook as we passed o'er the day we war married an' come home together, an' he'd made them lots o' shelves for me to put my plates an' things on, an' showed 'em me as proud as could be, 'cause he know'd I should be pleased. An' he war to die an' me not to know, but to be a-sleepin' i' my bed, as if I caredna nought about it. Eh! An' me to live to see that! An' us as war young folks once, an' thought we should do rarely when we war married. Let a-be, lad, let a-be! I wonna ha' no tay. I carena if I ne'er ate nor drink no more. When one end o' th' bridge tumbles down, where's th' use o' th' other stannin'? I may's well die, an' foller my old man. There's no knowin' but he'll want me."

Here Lisbeth broke from words into moans, swaying herself backwards and forwards on her chair. Seth, always timid in his behaviour towards his mother, from the sense that he had no influence over her, felt it was useless to attempt to persuade or soothe her till this passion was past; so he contented himself with tending the back kitchen fire and folding up his father's clothes, which had been hanging out to dry since morning—afraid to move about in the room where his mother was, lest he should irritate her further.

But after Lisbeth had been rocking herself and moaning for some minutes, she suddenly paused and said aloud to herself, "I'll go an' see arter Adam, for I canna think where he's gotten; an' I want him to go upstairs wi' me afore it's dark, for the minutes to look at the corpse is like the meltin' snow."

Seth overheard this, and coming into the kitchen again, as his mother rose from her chair, he said, "Adam's asleep in the workshop, mother. Thee'dst better not wake him. He was o'erwrought with work and trouble."

"Wake him? Who's a-goin' to wake him? I shanna wake him wi' lookin' at him. I hanna seen the lad this two hour—I'd welly forgot as he'd e'er growed up from a babby when's feyther carried him."

Adam was seated on a rough bench, his head supported by his arm, which rested from the shoulder to the elbow on the long planing-table in the middle of the workshop. It seemed as if he had sat down for a few minutes' rest and had fallen asleep without slipping from his first attitude of sad, fatigued thought. His face, unwashed since yesterday, looked pallid and clammy; his hair was tossed shaggily about his forehead, and his closed eyes had the sunken look which follows upon watching and sorrow. His brow was knit, and his whole face had an expression of weariness and pain. Gyp was evidently uneasy, for he sat on his haunches, resting his nose on his master's stretched-out leg, and dividing the time between licking the hand that hung listlessly down and glancing with a listening air towards the door. The poor dog was hungry and restless, but would not leave his master, and was waiting impatiently for some change in the scene. It was owing to this feeling on Gyp's part that, when Lisbeth came into the workshop and advanced towards Adam as noiselessly as she could, her intention not to awaken him was immediately defeated; for Gyp's excitement was too great to find vent in anything short of a sharp bark, and in a moment Adam opened his eyes and saw his mother standing before him. It was not very unlike his dream, for his sleep had been little more than living through again, in a fevered delirious way, all that had happened since daybreak, and his mother with her fretful grief was present to him through it all. The chief difference between the reality and the vision was that in his dream Hetty was continually coming before him in bodily presence—strangely mingling herself as an actor in scenes with which she had nothing to do. She was even by the Willow Brook; she made his mother angry by coming into the house; and he met her with her smart clothes quite wet through, as he walked in the rain to Treddleston, to tell the coroner. But wherever Hetty came, his mother was sure to follow soon; and when he opened his eyes, it was not at all startling to see her standing near him.

"Eh, my lad, my lad!" Lisbeth burst out immediately, her wailing impulse returning, for grief in its freshness feels the need of associating its loss and its lament with every change of scene and incident, "thee'st got nobody now but thy old mother to torment thee and be a burden to thee. Thy poor feyther 'ull ne'er anger thee no more; an' thy mother may's well go arter him—the sooner the better—for I'm no good to nobody now. One old coat 'ull do to patch another, but it's good for nought else. Thee'dst like to ha' a wife to mend thy clothes an' get thy victual, better nor thy old mother. An' I shall be nought but cumber, a-sittin' i' th' chimney-corner. (Adam winced and moved uneasily; he dreaded, of all things, to hear his mother speak of Hetty.) But if thy feyther had lived, he'd ne'er ha' wanted me to go to make room for another, for he could no more ha' done wi'out me nor one side o' the scissars can do wi'out th' other. Eh, we should ha' been both flung away together, an' then I shouldna ha' seen this day, an' one buryin' 'ud ha' done for us both."

Here Lisbeth paused, but Adam sat in pained silence—he could not speak otherwise than tenderly to his mother to-day, but he could not help being irritated by this plaint. It was not possible for poor Lisbeth to know how it affected Adam any more than it is possible for a wounded dog to know how his moans affect the nerves of his master. Like all complaining women, she complained in the expectation of being soothed, and when Adam said nothing, she was only prompted to complain more bitterly.

"I know thee couldst do better wi'out me, for thee couldst go where thee likedst an' marry them as thee likedst. But I donna want to say thee nay, let thee bring home who thee wut; I'd ne'er open my lips to find faut, for when folks is old an' o' no use, they may think theirsens well off to get the bit an' the sup, though they'n to swallow ill words wi't. An' if thee'st set thy heart on a lass as'll bring thee nought and waste all, when thee mightst ha' them as 'ud make a man on thee, I'll say nought, now thy feyther's dead an' drownded, for I'm no better nor an old haft when the blade's gone."

Adam, unable to bear this any longer, rose silently from the bench and walked out of the workshop into the kitchen. But Lisbeth followed him.

"Thee wutna go upstairs an' see thy feyther then? I'n done everythin' now, an' he'd like thee to go an' look at him, for he war allays so pleased when thee wast mild to him."

Adam turned round at once and said, "Yes, mother; let us go upstairs. Come, Seth, let us go together."

They went upstairs, and for five minutes all was silence. Then the key was turned again, and there was a sound of footsteps on the stairs. But Adam did not come down again; he was too weary and worn-out to encounter more of his mother's querulous grief, and he went to rest on his bed. Lisbeth no sooner entered the kitchen and sat down than she threw her apron over her head, and began to cry and moan and rock herself as before. Seth thought, "She will be quieter by and by, now we have been upstairs"; and he went into the back kitchen again, to tend his little fire, hoping that he should presently induce her to have some tea.

Lisbeth had been rocking herself in this way for more than five minutes, giving a low moan with every forward movement of her body, when she suddenly felt a hand placed gently on hers, and a sweet treble voice said to her, "Dear sister, the Lord has sent me to see if I can be a comfort to you."

Lisbeth paused, in a listening attitude, without removing her apron from her face. The voice was strange to her. Could it be her sister's spirit come back to her from the dead after all those years? She trembled and dared not look.

Dinah, believing that this pause of wonder was in itself a relief for the sorrowing woman, said no more just yet, but quietly took off her bonnet, and then, motioning silence to Seth, who, on hearing her voice, had come in with a beating heart, laid one hand on the back of Lisbeth's chair and leaned over her, that she might be aware of a friendly presence.

Slowly Lisbeth drew down her apron, and timidly she opened her dim dark eyes. She saw nothing at first but a face—a pure, pale face, with loving grey eyes, and it was quite unknown to her. Her wonder increased; perhaps it *was* an angel. But in the same instant Dinah had laid her hand on Lisbeth's again, and the old woman looked down at it. It was a much smaller hand than her own, but it was not white and delicate, for Dinah had never worn a glove in her life, and her hand bore the traces of labour from her childhood upwards. Lisbeth looked earnestly at the hand for a moment, and then, fixing her eyes again on Dinah's face, said, with something of restored courage, but in a tone of surprise, "Why, ye're a workin' woman!"

"Yes, I am Dinah Morris, and I work in the cotton-mill when I am at home."

"Ah!" said Lisbeth slowly, still wondering; "ye comed in so light, like the shadow on the wall, an' spoke i' my ear, as I thought ye might be a sperrit. Ye've got a'most the face o' one as is a-sittin' on the grave i' Adam's new Bible."

"I come from the Hall Farm now. You know Mrs. Poyser—she's my aunt, and she has heard of your great affliction, and is very sorry; and I'm come to see if I can be any help to you in your trouble; for I know your sons Adam and Seth, and I know you have no daughter; and when the clergyman told me how the hand of God was heavy upon you, my heart went out towards you, and I felt a command to come and be to you in the place of a daughter in this grief, if you will let me."

"Ah! I know who y' are now; y' are a Methody, like Seth; he's tould me on you," said Lisbeth fretfully, her overpowering sense of pain returning, now her wonder was gone. "Ye'll make it out as trouble's a good thing, like *he* allays does. But where's the use o' talkin' to me a-that'n? Ye canna make the smart less wi' talkin'. Ye'll ne'er make me believe as it's better for me not to ha' my old man die in's bed, if he must die, an' ha' the parson to pray by him, an' me to sit by him, an' tell him ne'er to mind th' ill words I've gi'en him sometimes when I war angered, an' to gi' him a bit an' a sup, as long as a bit an' a sup he'd swallow. But eh! To die i' the cold water, an' us close to him, an' ne'er to know; an' me a-sleepin', as if I ne'er belonged to him no more nor if he'd been a journeyman tramp from nobody knows where!"

Here Lisbeth began to cry and rock herself again; and Dinah said, "Yes, dear friend, your affliction is great. It would be hardness of heart to say that your trouble was not heavy to bear. God didn't send me to you to make light of your sorrow, but to mourn with you, if you will let me. If you had a table spread for a feast, and was making merry with your friends, you would think it was kind to let me come and sit down and rejoice with you, because you'd think I should like to share those good things; but I should like better to share in your trouble and your labour, and it would seem harder to me if you denied me that. You won't send me away? You're not angry with me for coming?"

"Nay, nay; angered! who said I war angered? It war good on you to come. An' Seth, why donna ye get her some tay? Ye war in a hurry to get some for me, as had no need, but ye donna think o' gettin' 't for them as wants it. Sit ye down; sit ye down. I thank you kindly for comin', for it's little wage ye get by walkin' through the wet fields to see an old woman like me.... Nay, I'n got no daughter o' my own—ne'er had one—an' I warna sorry, for they're poor queechy things, gells is; I allays wanted to ha' lads, as could fend for theirsens. An' the lads 'ull be marryin'—I shall ha' daughters eno', an' too many. But now, do ye make the tay as ye like it, for I'n got no taste i' my mouth this day—it's all one what I swaller—it's all got the taste o' sorrow wi't."

Dinah took care not to betray that she had had her tea, and accepted Lisbeth's invitation very readily, for the sake of persuading the old woman herself to take the food and drink she so much needed after a day of hard work and fasting.

Seth was so happy now Dinah was in the house that he could not help thinking her presence was worth purchasing with a life in which grief incessantly followed upon grief; but the next moment he reproached himself—it was almost as if he were rejoicing in his father's sad death. Nevertheless the joy of being with Dinah *would* triumph—it was like the influence of climate, which no resistance can overcome. And the feeling even suffused itself over his face so as to attract his mother's notice, while she was drinking her tea.

"Thee may'st well talk o' trouble bein' a good thing, Seth, for thee thriv'st on't. Thee look'st as if thee know'dst no more o' care an' cumber nor when thee wast a babby a-lyin' awake i' th' cradle. For thee'dst allays lie still wi' thy eyes open, an' Adam ne'er 'ud lie still a minute when he wakened. Thee wast allays like a bag o' meal as can ne'er be bruised—though, for the matter o' that, thy poor feyther war just such another. But *ye*'ve got the same look too" (here Lisbeth turned to Dinah). "I reckon it's wi' bein' a Methody. Not as I'm a-findin' faut wi' ye for't, for ye've no call to be frettin', an' somehow ye looken sorry too. Eh! Well, if the Methodies are fond o' trouble, they're like to thrive: it's a pity they canna ha't all, an' take it away from them as donna like it. I could ha' gi'en 'em plenty; for when I'd gotten my old man I war worreted from morn till night; and now he's gone, I'd be glad for the worst o'er again."

"Yes," said Dinah, careful not to oppose any feeling of Lisbeth's, for her reliance, in her smallest words and deeds, on a divine guidance, always issued in that finest woman's tact which proceeds from acute and ready sympathy; "yes, I remember too, when my dear aunt died, I longed for the sound of her bad cough in the nights, instead of the silence that came when she was gone. But now, dear friend, drink this other cup of tea and eat a little more."

"What!" said Lisbeth, taking the cup and speaking in a less querulous tone, "had ye got no feyther and mother, then, as ye war so sorry about your aunt?"

"No, I never knew a father or mother; my aunt brought me up from a baby. She had no children, for she was never married and she brought me up as tenderly as if I'd been her own child."

"Eh, she'd fine work wi' ye, I'll warrant, bringin' ye up from a babby, an' her a lone woman—it's ill bringin' up a cade lamb. But I daresay ye warna franzy, for ye look as if ye'd ne'er been angered i' your life. But what did ye do when your aunt died, an' why didna ye come to live in this country, bein' as Mrs. Poyser's your aunt too?"

Dinah, seeing that Lisbeth's attention was attracted, told her the story of her early life—how she had been brought up to work hard, and what sort of place Snowfield was, and how many people had a hard life there—all the details that she thought likely to interest Lisbeth. The old woman listened, and forgot to be fretful, unconsciously subject to the soothing influence of Dinah's face and voice. After a while she was persuaded to let the kitchen be made tidy; for Dinah was bent on this, believing that the sense of order and quietude around her would help in disposing Lisbeth to join in the prayer she longed to pour forth at her side. Seth, meanwhile, went out to chop wood, for he surmised that Dinah would like to be left alone with his mother.

Lisbeth sat watching her as she moved about in her still quick way, and said at last, "Ye've got a notion o' cleanin' up. I wouldna mind ha'in ye for a daughter, for ye wouldna spend the lad's wage i' fine clothes an' waste. Ye're not like the lasses o' this countryside. I reckon folks is different at Snowfield from what they are here."

"They have a different sort of life, many of 'em," said Dinah; "they work at different things—some in the mill, and many in the mines, in the villages round about. But the heart of man is the same everywhere, and there are the children of this world and the children of light there as well as elsewhere. But we've many more Methodists there than in this country."

"Well, I didna know as the Methody women war like ye, for there's Will Maskery's wife, as they say's a big Methody, isna pleasant to look at, at all. I'd as lief look at a tooad. An' I'm thinkin' I wouldna mind if ye'd stay an' sleep here, for I should like to see ye i' th' house i' th' mornin'. But mayhappen they'll be lookin for ye at Mester Poyser's."

"No," said Dinah, "they don't expect me, and I should like to stay, if you'll let me."

"Well, there's room; I'n got my bed laid i' th' little room o'er the back kitchen, an' ye can lie beside me. I'd be glad to ha' ye wi' me to speak to i' th' night, for ye've got a nice way o' talkin'. It puts me i' mind o' the swallows as was under the thack last 'ear when they fust begun to sing low an' soft-like i' th' mornin'. Eh, but my old man war fond o' them birds! An' so war Adam, but they'n ne'er comed again this 'ear. Happen they're dead too."

"There," said Dinah, "now the kitchen looks tidy, and now, dear Mother—for I'm your daughter to-night, you know—I should like you to wash your face and have a clean cap on. Do you remember what David did, when God took away his child from him? While the child was yet alive he fasted and prayed to God to spare it, and he would neither eat nor drink, but lay on the ground all night, beseeching God for the child. But when he knew it was dead, he rose up from the ground and washed and anointed himself, and changed his clothes, and ate and drank; and when they asked him how it was that he seemed to have left off grieving now the child was dead, he said, 'While the child was yet alive, I fasted and wept; for I said, Who can tell whether God will be gracious to me, that the child may live? But now he is dead, wherefore should I fast? Can I bring him back again? I shall go to him, but he shall not return to me.'"

"Eh, that's a true word," said Lisbeth. "Yea, my old man wonna come back to me, but I shall go to him—the sooner the better. Well, ye may do as ye like wi' me: there's a clean cap i' that drawer, an' I'll go i' the back kitchen an' wash my face. An' Seth, thee may'st reach down Adam's new Bible wi' th' picters in, an' she shall read us a chapter. Eh, I like them words—'I shall go to him, but he wonna come back to me.'"

Dinah and Seth were both inwardly offering thanks for the greater quietness of spirit that had come over Lisbeth. This was what Dinah had been trying to bring about, through all her still sympathy and absence from exhortation. From her girlhood upwards she had had experience among the sick and the mourning, among minds hardened and shrivelled through poverty and ignorance, and had gained the subtlest perception of the mode in which they could best be touched and softened into willingness to receive words of spiritual consolation or warning. As Dinah expressed it, "she was never left to herself; but it was always given her when to keep silence and when to speak." And do we not all agree to call rapid thought and noble impulse by the name of inspiration? After our subtlest analysis of the mental process, we must still say, as Dinah did, that our highest thoughts and our best deeds are all given to us.

And so there was earnest prayer—there was faith, love, and hope pouring forth that evening in the little kitchen. And poor, aged, fretful Lisbeth, without grasping any distinct idea, without going through any course of religious emotions, felt a vague sense of goodness and love, and of something right lying underneath and beyond all this sorrowing life. She couldn't understand the sorrow; but, for these moments, under the subduing influence of Dinah's spirit, she felt that she must be patient and still.

Chapter XI
In the Cottage

It was but half-past four the next morning when Dinah, tired of lying awake listening to the birds and watching the growing light through the little window in the garret roof, rose and began to dress herself very quietly, lest she should disturb Lisbeth. But already some one else was astir in the house, and had gone downstairs, preceded by Gyp. The dog's pattering step was a sure sign that it was Adam who went down; but Dinah was not aware of this, and she thought it was more likely to be Seth, for he had told her how Adam had stayed up working the night before. Seth, however, had only just awakened at the sound of the opening door. The exciting influence of the previous day, heightened at last by Dinah's unexpected presence, had not been counteracted by any bodily weariness, for he had not done his ordinary amount of hard work; and so when he went to bed; it was not till he had tired himself with hours of tossing wakefulness that drowsiness came, and led on a heavier morning sleep than was usual with him.

But Adam had been refreshed by his long rest, and with his habitual impatience of mere passivity, he was eager to begin the new day and subdue sadness by his strong will and strong arm. The white mist lay in the valley; it was going to be a bright warm day, and he would start to work again when he had had his breakfast.

"There's nothing but what's bearable as long as a man can work," he said to himself; "the natur o' things doesn't change, though it seems as if one's own life was nothing but change. The square o' four is sixteen, and you must lengthen your lever in proportion to your weight, is as true when a man's miserable as when he's happy; and the best o' working is, it gives you a grip hold o' things outside your own lot."

As he dashed the cold water over his head and face, he felt completely himself again, and with his black eyes as keen as ever and his thick black hair all glistening with the fresh moisture, he went into the workshop to look out the wood for his father's coffin, intending that he and Seth should carry it with them to Jonathan Burge's and have the coffin made by one of the workmen there, so that his mother might not see and hear the sad task going forward at home.

He had just gone into the workshop when his quick ear detected a light rapid foot on the stairs—certainly not his mother's. He had been in bed and asleep when Dinah had come in, in the evening, and now he wondered whose step this could be. A foolish thought came, and moved him strangely. As if it could be Hetty! She was the last person likely to be in the house. And yet he felt reluctant to go and look and have the clear proof that it was some one else. He stood leaning on a plank he had taken hold of, listening to sounds which his imagination interpreted for him so pleasantly that the keen strong face became suffused with a timid tenderness. The light footstep moved about the kitchen, followed by the sound of the sweeping brush, hardly making so much noise as the lightest breeze that chases the autumn leaves along the dusty path; and Adam's imagination saw a dimpled face, with dark bright eyes and roguish smiles looking backward at this brush, and a rounded figure just leaning a little to clasp the handle. A very foolish thought—it could not be Hetty; but the only way of dismissing such nonsense from his head was to go and see *who* it was, for his fancy only got nearer and nearer to belief while he stood there listening. He loosed the plank and went to the kitchen door.

"How do you do, Adam Bede?" said Dinah, in her calm treble, pausing from her sweeping and fixing her mild grave eyes upon him. "I trust you feel rested and strengthened again to bear the burden and heat of the day."

It was like dreaming of the sunshine and awaking in the moonlight. Adam had seen Dinah several times, but always at the Hall Farm, where he was not very vividly conscious of any woman's presence except Hetty's, and he had only in the last day or two begun to suspect that Seth was in love with her, so that his attention had not hitherto been drawn towards her for his brother's sake. But now her slim figure, her plain black gown, and her pale serene face impressed him with all the force that belongs to a reality contrasted with a preoccupying fancy. For the first moment or two he made no answer, but looked at her with the concentrated, examining glance which a man gives to an object in which he has suddenly begun to be interested. Dinah, for the first time in her life, felt a painful self-consciousness; there was something in the dark penetrating glance of this strong man so different from the mildness and timidity of his brother Seth. A faint blush came, which deepened as she wondered at it. This blush recalled Adam from his forgetfulness.

"I was quite taken by surprise; it was very good of you to come and see my mother in her trouble," he said, in a gentle grateful tone, for his quick mind told him at once how she came to be there. "I hope my mother was thankful to have you," he added, wondering rather anxiously what had been Dinah's reception.

"Yes," said Dinah, resuming her work, "she seemed greatly comforted after a while, and she's had a good deal of rest in the night, by times. She was fast asleep when I left her."

"Who was it took the news to the Hall Farm?" said Adam, his thoughts reverting to some one there; he wondered whether *she* had felt anything about it.

"It was Mr. Irwine, the clergyman, told me, and my aunt was grieved for your mother when she heard it, and wanted me to come; and so is my uncle, I'm sure, now he's heard it, but he was gone out to Rosseter all yesterday. They'll look for you there as soon as you've got time to go, for there's nobody round that hearth but what's glad to see you."

Dinah, with her sympathetic divination, knew quite well that Adam was longing to hear if Hetty had said anything about their trouble; she was too rigorously truthful for benevolent invention, but she had contrived to say something in which Hetty was tacitly included. Love has a way of cheating itself consciously, like a child who plays at solitary hide-and-seek; it is pleased with assurances that it all the while disbelieves. Adam liked what Dinah had said so much that his mind was directly full of the next visit he should pay to the Hall Farm, when Hetty would perhaps behave more kindly to him than she had ever done before.

"But you won't be there yourself any longer?" he said to Dinah.

"No, I go back to Snowfield on Saturday, and I shall have to set out to Treddleston early, to be in time for the Oakbourne carrier. So I must go back to the farm to-night, that I may have the last day with my aunt and her children. But I can stay here all to-day, if your mother would like me; and her heart seemed inclined towards me last night."

"Ah, then, she's sure to want you to-day. If mother takes to people at the beginning, she's sure to get fond of 'em; but she's a strange way of not liking young women. Though, to be sure," Adam went on, smiling, "her not liking other young women is no reason why she shouldn't like you."

Hitherto Gyp had been assisting at this conversation in motionless silence, seated on his haunches, and alternately looking up in his master's face to watch its expression and observing Dinah's movements about the kitchen. The kind smile with which Adam uttered the last words was apparently decisive with Gyp of the light in which the stranger was to be regarded, and as she turned round after putting aside her sweeping-brush, he trotted towards her and put up his muzzle against her hand in a friendly way.

"You see Gyp bids you welcome," said Adam, "and he's very slow to welcome strangers."

"Poor dog!" said Dinah, patting the rough grey coat, "I've a strange feeling about the dumb things as if they wanted to speak, and it was a trouble to 'em because they couldn't. I can't help being sorry for the dogs always, though perhaps there's no need. But they may well have more in them than they know how to make us understand, for we can't say half what we feel, with all our words."

Seth came down now, and was pleased to find Adam talking with Dinah; he wanted Adam to know how much better she was than all other women. But after a few words of greeting, Adam drew him into the workshop to consult about the coffin, and Dinah went on with her cleaning.

By six o'clock they were all at breakfast with Lisbeth in a kitchen as clean as she could have made it herself. The window and door were open, and the morning air brought with it a mingled scent of southernwood, thyme, and sweet-briar from the patch of garden by the side of the cottage. Dinah did not sit down at first, but moved about, serving the others with the warm porridge and the toasted oat-cake, which she had got ready in the usual way, for she had asked Seth to tell her just what his mother gave them for breakfast. Lisbeth had been unusually silent since she came downstairs, apparently requiring some time to adjust her ideas to a state of things in which she came down like a lady to find all the work done, and sat still to be waited on. Her new sensations seemed to exclude the remembrance of her grief. At last, after tasting the porridge, she broke silence:

"Ye might ha' made the parridge worse," she said to Dinah; "I can ate it wi'out its turnin' my stomach. It might ha' been a trifle thicker an' no harm, an' I allays putten a sprig o' mint in mysen; but how's ye t' know that? The lads arena like to get folks as 'll make their parridge as I'n made it for 'em; it's well if they get onybody as 'll make parridge at all. But ye might do, wi' a bit o' showin'; for ye're a stirrin' body in a mornin', an' ye've a light heel, an' ye've cleaned th' house well enough for a ma'shift."

"Makeshift, mother?" said Adam. "Why, I think the house looks beautiful. I don't know how it could look better."

"Thee dostna know? Nay; how's thee to know? Th' men ne'er know whether the floor's cleaned or cat-licked. But thee'lt know when thee gets thy parridge burnt, as it's like enough to be when I'n gi'en o'er makin' it. Thee'lt think thy mother war good for summat then."

"Dinah," said Seth, "do come and sit down now and have your breakfast. We're all served now."

"Aye, come an' sit ye down—do," said Lisbeth, "an' ate a morsel; ye'd need, arter bein' upo' your legs this hour an' half a'ready. Come, then," she added, in a tone of complaining affection, as Dinah sat down by her side, "I'll be loath for ye t' go, but ye canna stay much longer, I doubt. I could put up wi' ye i' th' house better nor wi' most folks."

"I'll stay till to-night if you're willing," said Dinah. "I'd stay longer, only I'm going back to Snowfield on Saturday, and I must be with my aunt to-morrow."

"Eh, I'd ne'er go back to that country. My old man come from that Stonyshire side, but he left it when he war a young un, an' i' the right on't too; for he said as there war no wood there, an' it 'ud ha' been a bad country for a carpenter."

"Ah," said Adam, "I remember father telling me when I was a little lad that he made up his mind if ever he moved it should be south'ard. But I'm not so sure about it. Bartle Massey says—and he knows the South—as the northern men are a finer breed than the southern, harder-headed and stronger-bodied, and a deal taller. And then he says in some o' those counties it's as flat as the back o' your hand, and you can see nothing of a distance without climbing up the highest trees. I couldn't abide that. I like to go to work by a road that'll take me up a bit of a hill, and see the fields for miles round me, and a bridge, or a town, or a bit of a steeple here and there. It makes you feel the world's a big place, and there's other men working in it with their heads and hands besides yourself."

"I like th' hills best," said Seth, "when the clouds are over your head and you see the sun shining ever so far off, over the Loamford way, as I've often done o' late, on the stormy days. It seems to me as if that was heaven where there's always joy and sunshine, though this life's dark and cloudy."

"Oh, I love the Stonyshire side," said Dinah; "I shouldn't like to set my face towards the countries where they're rich in corn and cattle, and the ground so level and easy to tread; and to turn my back on the hills where the poor people have to live such a hard life and the men spend their days in the mines away from the sunlight. It's very blessed on a bleak cold day, when the sky is hanging dark over the hill, to feel the love of God in one's soul, and carry it to the lonely, bare, stone houses, where there's nothing else to give comfort."

"Eh!" said Lisbeth, "that's very well for ye to talk, as looks welly like the snowdrop-flowers as ha' lived for days an' days when I'n gethered 'em, wi' nothin' but a drop o' water an' a peep o' daylight; but th' hungry foulks had better leave th' hungry country. It makes less mouths for the scant cake. But," she went on, looking at Adam, "donna thee talk o' goin' south'ard or north'ard, an' leavin' thy feyther and mother i' the churchyard, an' goin' to a country as they know nothin' on. I'll ne'er rest i' my grave if I donna see thee i' the churchyard of a Sunday."

"Donna fear, mother," said Adam. "If I hadna made up my mind not to go, I should ha' been gone before now."

He had finished his breakfast now, and rose as he was speaking.

"What art goin' to do?" asked Lisbeth. "Set about thy feyther's coffin?"

"No, mother," said Adam; "we're going to take the wood to the village and have it made there."

"Nay, my lad, nay," Lisbeth burst out in an eager, wailing tone; "thee wotna let nobody make thy feyther's coffin but thysen? Who'd make it so well? An' him as know'd what good work war, an's got a son as is the head o' the village an' all Treddles'on too, for cleverness."

"Very well, mother, if that's thy wish, I'll make the coffin at home; but I thought thee wouldstna like to hear the work going on."

"An' why shouldna I like 't? It's the right thing to be done. An' what's liking got to do wi't? It's choice o' mislikings is all I'n got i' this world. One morsel's as good as another when your mouth's out o' taste. Thee mun set about it now this mornin' fust thing. I wonna ha' nobody to touch the coffin but thee."

Adam's eyes met Seth's, which looked from Dinah to him rather wistfully.

"No, Mother," he said, "I'll not consent but Seth shall have a hand in it too, if it's to be done at home. I'll go to the village this forenoon, because Mr. Burge 'ull want to see me, and Seth shall stay at home and begin the coffin. I can come back at noon, and then he can go."

"Nay, nay," persisted Lisbeth, beginning to cry, "I'n set my heart on't as thee shalt ma' thy feyther's coffin. Thee't so stiff an' masterful, thee't ne'er do as thy mother wants thee. Thee wast often angered wi' thy feyther when he war alive; thee must be the better to him now he's gone. He'd ha' thought nothin' on't for Seth to ma's coffin."

"Say no more, Adam, say no more," said Seth, gently, though his voice told that he spoke with some effort; "Mother's in the right. I'll go to work, and do thee stay at home."

He passed into the workshop immediately, followed by Adam; while Lisbeth, automatically obeying her old habits, began to put away the breakfast things, as if she did not mean Dinah to take her place any longer. Dinah said nothing, but presently used the opportunity of quietly joining the brothers in the workshop.

They had already got on their aprons and paper caps, and Adam was standing with his left hand on Seth's shoulder, while he pointed with the hammer in his right to some boards which they were looking at. Their backs were turned towards the door by which Dinah entered, and she came in so gently that they were not aware of her presence till they heard her voice saying, "Seth Bede!" Seth started, and they both turned round. Dinah looked as if she did not see Adam, and fixed her eyes on Seth's face, saying with calm kindness, "I won't say farewell. I shall see you again when you come from work. So as I'm at the farm before dark, it will be quite soon enough."

"Thank you, Dinah; I should like to walk home with you once more. It'll perhaps be the last time."

There was a little tremor in Seth's voice. Dinah put out her hand and said, "You'll have sweet peace in your mind to-day, Seth, for your tenderness and long-suffering towards your aged mother."

She turned round and left the workshop as quickly and quietly as she had entered it. Adam had been observing her closely all the while, but she had not looked at him. As soon as she was gone, he said, "I don't wonder at thee for loving her, Seth. She's got a face like a lily."

Seth's soul rushed to his eyes and lips: he had never yet confessed his secret to Adam, but now he felt a delicious sense of disburdenment, as he answered, "Aye, Addy, I do love her—too much, I doubt. But she doesna love me, lad, only as one child o' God loves another. She'll never love any man as a husband—that's my belief."

"Nay, lad, there's no telling; thee mustna lose heart. She's made out o' stuff with a finer grain than most o' the women; I can see that clear enough. But if she's better than they are in other things, I canna think she'll fall short of 'em in loving."

No more was said. Seth set out to the village, and Adam began his work on the coffin.

"God help the lad, and me too," he thought, as he lifted the board. "We're like enough to find life a tough job—hard work inside and out. It's a strange thing to think of a man as can lift a chair with his teeth and walk fifty mile on end, trembling and turning hot and cold at only a look from one woman out of all the rest i' the world. It's a mystery we can give no account of; but no more we can of the sprouting o' the seed, for that matter."

Chapter XII
In the Wood

That same Thursday morning, as Arthur Donnithorne was moving about in his dressing-room seeing his well-looking British person reflected in the old-fashioned mirrors, and stared at, from a dingy olive-green piece of tapestry, by Pharaoh's daughter and her maidens, who ought to have been minding the infant Moses, he was holding a discussion with himself, which, by the time his valet was tying the black silk sling over his shoulder, had issued in a distinct practical resolution.

"I mean to go to Eagledale and fish for a week or so," he said aloud. "I shall take you with me, Pym, and set off this morning; so be ready by half-past eleven."

The low whistle, which had assisted him in arriving at this resolution, here broke out into his loudest ringing tenor, and the corridor, as he hurried along it, echoed to his favourite song from the Beggar's Opera, "When the heart of a man is oppressed with care." Not an heroic strain; nevertheless Arthur felt himself very heroic as he strode towards the stables to give his orders about the horses. His own approbation was necessary to him, and it was not an approbation to be enjoyed quite gratuitously; it must be won by a fair amount of merit. He had never yet forfeited that approbation, and he had considerable reliance on his own virtues. No young man could confess his faults more candidly; candour was one of his favourite virtues; and how can a man's candour be seen in all its lustre unless he has a few failings to talk of? But he had an agreeable confidence that his faults were all of a generous kind—impetuous, warm-blooded, leonine; never crawling, crafty, reptilian. It was not possible for Arthur Donnithorne to do anything mean, dastardly, or cruel. "No! I'm a devil of a fellow for getting myself into a hobble, but I always take care the load shall fall on my own shoulders." Unhappily, there is no inherent poetical justice in hobbles, and they will sometimes obstinately refuse to inflict their worst consequences on the prime offender, in spite of his loudly expressed wish. It was entirely owing to this deficiency in the scheme of things that Arthur had ever brought any one into trouble besides himself. He was nothing if not good-natured; and all his pictures of the future, when he should come into the estate, were made up of a prosperous, contented tenantry, adoring their landlord, who would be the model of an English gentleman—mansion in first-rate order, all elegance and high taste—jolly housekeeping, finest stud in Loamshire—purse open to all public objects—in short, everything as different as possible from what was now associated with the name of Donnithorne. And one of the first good actions he would perform in that future should be to increase Irwine's income for the vicarage of Hayslope, so that he might keep a carriage for his mother and sisters. His hearty affection for the rector dated from the age of frocks and trousers. It was an affection partly filial, partly fraternal—fraternal enough to make him like Irwine's company better than that of most younger men, and filial enough to make him shrink strongly from incurring Irwine's disapprobation.

You perceive that Arthur Donnithorne was "a good fellow"—all his college friends thought him such. He couldn't bear to see any one uncomfortable; he would have been sorry even in his angriest moods for any harm to happen to his grandfather; and his Aunt Lydia herself had the benefit of that soft-heartedness which he bore towards the whole sex. Whether he would have self-mastery enough to be always as harmless and purely beneficent as his good-nature led him to desire, was a question that no one had yet decided against him; he was but twenty-one, you remember, and we don't inquire too closely into character in the case of a handsome generous young fellow, who will have property enough to support numerous peccadilloes—who, if he should unfortunately break a man's legs in his rash driving, will be able to pension him handsomely; or if he should happen to spoil a woman's existence for her, will make it up to her with expensive *bon-bons*, packed up and directed by his own hand. It would be ridiculous to be prying and analytic in such cases, as if one were inquiring into the character of a confidential clerk. We use round, general, gentlemanly epithets about a young man of birth and fortune; and ladies, with that fine intuition which is the distinguishing attribute of their sex, see at once that he is "nice." The chances are that he will go through life without scandalizing any one; a seaworthy vessel that no one would refuse to insure. Ships, certainly, are liable to casualties, which sometimes make terribly evident some flaw in their construction that would never have been discoverable in smooth water; and many a "good fellow," through a disastrous combination of circumstances, has undergone a like betrayal.

But we have no fair ground for entertaining unfavourable auguries concerning Arthur Donnithorne, who this morning proves himself capable of a prudent resolution founded on conscience. One thing is clear: Nature has taken care that he shall never go far astray with perfect comfort and satisfaction to himself; he will never get beyond that border-land of sin, where he will be perpetually harassed by assaults from the other side of the boundary. He will never be a courtier of Vice, and wear her orders in his button-hole.

It was about ten o'clock, and the sun was shining brilliantly; everything was looking lovelier for the yesterday's rain. It is a pleasant thing on such a morning to walk along the well-rolled gravel on one's way to the stables, meditating an excursion. But the scent of the stables, which, in a natural state of things, ought to be among the soothing influences of a man's life, always brought with it some irritation to Arthur. There was no having his own way in the stables; everything was managed in the stingiest fashion. His grandfather persisted in retaining as head groom an old dolt whom no sort of lever could move out of his old habits, and who was allowed to hire a succession of raw Loamshire lads as his subordinates, one of whom had lately tested a new pair of shears by clipping an oblong patch on Arthur's bay mare. This state of things is naturally embittering; one can put up with annoyances in the house, but to have the stable made a scene of vexation and disgust is a point beyond what human flesh and blood can be expected to endure long together without danger of misanthropy.

Old John's wooden, deep-wrinkled face was the first object that met Arthur's eyes as he entered the stable-yard, and it quite poisoned for him the bark of the two bloodhounds that kept watch there. He could never speak quite patiently to the old blockhead.

"You must have Meg saddled for me and brought to the door at half-past eleven, and I shall want Rattler saddled for Pym at the same time. Do you hear?"

"Yes, I hear, I hear, Cap'n," said old John very deliberately, following the young master into the stable. John considered a young master as the natural enemy of an old servant, and young people in general as a poor contrivance for carrying on the world.

Arthur went in for the sake of patting Meg, declining as far as possible to see anything in the stables, lest he should lose his temper before breakfast. The pretty creature was in one of the inner stables, and turned her mild head as her master came beside her. Little Trot, a tiny spaniel, her inseparable companion in the stable, was comfortably curled up on her back.

"Well, Meg, my pretty girl," said Arthur, patting her neck, "we'll have a glorious canter this morning."

"Nay, your honour, I donna see as that can be," said John.

"Not be? Why not?"

"Why, she's got lamed."

"Lamed, confound you! What do you mean?"

"Why, th' lad took her too close to Dalton's hosses, an' one on 'em flung out at her, an' she's got her shank bruised o' the near foreleg."

The judicious historian abstains from narrating precisely what ensued. You understand that there was a great deal of strong language, mingled with soothing "who-ho's" while the leg was examined; that John stood by with quite as much emotion as if he had been a cunningly carved crab-tree walking-stick, and that

Arthur Donnithorne presently repassed the iron gates of the pleasure-ground without singing as he went.

He considered himself thoroughly disappointed and annoyed. There was not another mount in the stable for himself and his servant besides Meg and Rattler. It was vexatious; just when he wanted to get out of the way for a week or two. It seemed culpable in Providence to allow such a combination of circumstances. To be shut up at the Chase with a broken arm when every other fellow in his regiment was enjoying himself at Windsor—shut up with his grandfather, who had the same sort of affection for him as for his parchment deeds! And to be disgusted at every turn with the management of the house and the estate! In such circumstances a man necessarily gets in an ill humour, and works off the irritation by some excess or other. "Salkeld would have drunk a bottle of port every day," he muttered to himself, "but I'm not well seasoned enough for that. Well, since I can't go to Eagledale, I'll have a gallop on Rattler to Norburne this morning, and lunch with Gawaine."

Behind this explicit resolution there lay an implicit one. If he lunched with Gawaine and lingered chatting, he should not reach the Chase again till nearly five, when Hetty would be safe out of his sight in the housekeeper's room; and when she set out to go home, it would be his lazy time after dinner, so he should keep out of her way altogether. There really would have been no harm in being kind to the little thing, and it was worth dancing with a dozen ballroom belles only to look at Hetty for half an hour. But perhaps he had better not take any more notice of her; it might put notions into her head, as Irwine had hinted; though Arthur, for his part, thought girls were not by any means so soft and easily bruised; indeed, he had generally found them twice as cool and cunning as he was himself. As for any real harm in Hetty's case, it was out of the question: Arthur Donnithorne accepted his own bond for himself with perfect confidence.

So the twelve o'clock sun saw him galloping towards Norburne; and by good fortune Halsell Common lay in his road and gave him some fine leaps for Rattler. Nothing like "taking" a few bushes and ditches for exorcising a demon; and it is really astonishing that the Centaurs, with their immense advantages in this way, have left so bad a reputation in history.

After this, you will perhaps be surprised to hear that although Gawaine was at home, the hand of the dial in the courtyard had scarcely cleared the last stroke of three when Arthur returned through the entrance-gates, got down from the panting Rattler, and went into the house to take a hasty luncheon. But I believe there have been men since his day who have ridden a long way to avoid a rencontre, and then galloped hastily back lest they should miss it. It is the favourite stratagem of our passions to sham a retreat, and to turn sharp round upon us at the moment we have made up our minds that the day is our own.

"The cap'n's been ridin' the devil's own pace," said Dalton the coachman, whose person stood out in high relief as he smoked his pipe against the stable wall, when John brought up Rattler.

"An' I wish he'd get the devil to do's grooming for'n," growled John.

"Aye; he'd hev a deal haimabler groom nor what he has now," observed Dalton—and the joke appeared to him so good that, being left alone upon the scene, he continued at intervals to take his pipe from his mouth in order to wink at an imaginary audience and shake luxuriously with a silent, ventral laughter, mentally rehearsing the dialogue from the beginning, that he might recite it with effect in the servants' hall.

When Arthur went up to his dressing-room again after luncheon, it was inevitable that the debate he had had with himself there earlier in the day should flash across his mind; but it was impossible for him now to dwell on the remembrance—impossible to recall the feelings and reflections which had been decisive with him then, any more than to recall the peculiar scent of the air that had freshened him when he first opened his window. The desire to see Hetty had rushed back like an ill-stemmed current; he was amazed himself at the force with which this trivial fancy seemed to grasp him: he was even rather tremulous as he brushed his hair—pooh! it was riding in that break-neck way. It was because he had made a serious affair of an idle matter, by thinking of it as if it were of any consequence. He would amuse himself by seeing Hetty to-day, and get rid of the whole thing from his mind. It was all Irwine's fault. "If Irwine had said nothing, I shouldn't have thought half so much of Hetty as of Meg's lameness." However, it was just the sort of day for lolling in the Hermitage, and he would go and finish Dr. Moore's *Zeluco* there before dinner. The Hermitage stood in Fir-tree Grove—the way Hetty was sure to come in walking from the Hall Farm. So nothing could be simpler and more natural: meeting Hetty was a mere circumstance of his walk, not its object.

Arthur's shadow flitted rather faster among the sturdy oaks of the Chase than might have been expected from the shadow of a tired man on a warm afternoon, and it was still scarcely four o'clock when he stood before the tall narrow gate leading into the delicious labyrinthine wood which skirted one side of the Chase, and which was called Fir-tree Grove, not because the firs were many, but because they were few. It was a wood of beeches and limes, with here and there a light silver-stemmed birch—just the sort of wood most haunted by the nymphs: you see their white sunlit limbs gleaming athwart the boughs, or peeping from behind the smooth-sweeping outline of a tall lime; you hear their soft liquid laughter—but if you look with a too curious sacrilegious eye, they vanish behind the silvery beeches, they make you believe that their voice was only a running brooklet, perhaps they metamorphose themselves into a tawny squirrel that scampers away and mocks you from the topmost bough. It was not a grove with measured grass or rolled gravel for you to tread upon, but with narrow, hollow-shaped, earthy paths, edged with faint dashes of delicate moss—paths which look as if they were made by the free will of the trees and underwood, moving reverently aside to look at the tall queen of the white-footed nymphs.

It was along the broadest of these paths that Arthur Donnithorne passed, under an avenue of limes and beeches. It was a still afternoon—the golden light was lingering languidly among the upper boughs, only glancing down here and there on the purple pathway and its edge of faintly sprinkled moss: an afternoon in which destiny disguises her cold awful face behind a hazy radiant veil, encloses us in warm downy wings, and poisons us with violet-scented breath. Arthur strolled along carelessly, with a book under his arm, but not looking on the ground as meditative men are apt to do; his eyes *would* fix themselves on the distant bend in the road round which a little figure must surely appear before long. Ah! There she comes. First a bright patch of colour, like a tropic bird among the boughs; then a tripping figure, with a round hat on, and a small basket under her arm; then a deep-blushing, almost frightened, but bright-smiling girl, making her curtsy with a fluttered yet happy glance, as Arthur came up to her. If Arthur had had time to think at all, he would have thought it strange that he should feel fluttered too, be conscious of blushing too—in fact, look and feel as foolish as if he had been taken by surprise instead of meeting just what he expected. Poor things! It was a pity they were not in that golden age of childhood when they would have stood face to face, eyeing each other with timid liking, then given each other a little butterfly kiss, and toddled off to play together. Arthur would have gone home to his silk-curtained cot, and Hetty to her home-spun pillow, and both would have slept without dreams, and to-morrow would have been a life hardly conscious of a yesterday.

Arthur turned round and walked by Hetty's side without giving a reason. They were alone together for the first time. What an overpowering presence that first privacy is! He actually dared not look at this little butter-maker for the first minute or two. As for Hetty, her feet rested on a cloud, and she was borne along by warm zephyrs; she had forgotten her rose-coloured ribbons; she was no more conscious of her limbs than if her childish soul had passed into a water-lily, resting on a liquid bed and warmed by the midsummer sun-beams. It may seem a contradiction, but Arthur gathered a certain carelessness and confidence from his timidity: it was an entirely different state of mind from what he had expected in such a meeting with Hetty; and full as he was of vague feeling, there was room, in those moments of silence, for the thought that his previous debates and scruples were needless.

"You are quite right to choose this way of coming to the Chase," he said at last, looking down at Hetty; "it is so much prettier as well as shorter than coming by either of the lodges."

"Yes, sir," Hetty answered, with a tremulous, almost whispering voice. She didn't know one bit how to speak to a gentleman like Mr. Arthur, and her very vanity made her more coy of speech.

"Do you come every week to see Mrs. Pomfret?"

"Yes, sir, every Thursday, only when she's got to go out with Miss Donnithorne."

"And she's teaching you something, is she?"

"Yes, sir, the lace-mending as she learnt abroad, and the stocking-mending—it looks just like the stocking, you can't tell it's been mended; and she teaches me cutting-out too."

"What! are *you* going to be a lady's maid?"

"I should like to be one very much indeed." Hetty spoke more audibly now, but still rather tremulously; she thought, perhaps she seemed as stupid to Captain Donnithorne as Luke Britton did to her.

"I suppose Mrs. Pomfret always expects you at this time?"

"She expects me at four o'clock. I'm rather late to-day, because my aunt couldn't spare me; but the regular time is four, because that gives us time before Miss Donnithorne's bell rings."

"Ah, then, I must not keep you now, else I should like to show you the Hermitage. Did you ever see it?"

"No, sir."

"This is the walk where we turn up to it. But we must not go now. I'll show it you some other time, if you'd like to see it."

"Yes, please, sir."

"Do you always come back this way in the evening, or are you afraid to come so lonely a road?"

"Oh no, sir, it's never late; I always set out by eight o'clock, and it's so light now in the evening. My aunt would be angry with me if I didn't get home before nine."

"Perhaps Craig, the gardener, comes to take care of you?"

A deep blush overspread Hetty's face and neck. "I'm sure he doesn't; I'm sure he never did; I wouldn't let him; I don't like him," she said hastily, and the tears of vexation had come so fast that before she had done speaking a bright drop rolled down her hot cheek. Then she felt ashamed to death that she was crying, and for one long instant her happiness was all gone. But in the next she felt an arm steal round her, and a gentle voice said, "Why, Hetty, what makes you cry? I didn't mean to vex you. I wouldn't vex you for the world, you little blossom. Come, don't cry; look at me, else I shall think you won't forgive me."

Arthur had laid his hand on the soft arm that was nearest to him, and was stooping towards Hetty with a look of coaxing entreaty. Hetty lifted her long dewy lashes, and met the eyes that were bent towards her with a sweet, timid, beseeching look. What a space of time those three moments were while their eyes met and his arms touched her! Love is such a simple thing when we have only one-and-twenty summers and a sweet girl of seventeen trembles under our glance, as if she were a bud first opening her heart with wondering rapture to the morning. Such young unfurrowed souls roll to meet each other like two velvet peaches that touch softly and are at rest; they mingle as easily as two brooklets that ask for nothing but to entwine themselves and ripple with ever-interlacing curves in the leafiest hiding-places. While Arthur gazed into Hetty's dark beseeching eyes, it made no difference to him what sort of English she spoke; and even if hoops and powder had been in fashion, he would very likely not have been sensible just then that Hetty wanted those signs of high breeding.

But they started asunder with beating hearts: something had fallen on the ground with a rattling noise; it was Hetty's basket; all her little workwoman's matters were scattered on the path, some of them showing a capability of rolling to great lengths. There was much to be done in picking up, and not a word was spoken; but when Arthur hung the basket over her arm again, the poor child felt a strange difference in his look and manner. He just pressed her hand, and said, with a look and tone that were almost chilling to her, "I have been hindering you; I must not keep you any longer now. You will be expected at the house. Good-bye."

Without waiting for her to speak, he turned away from her and hurried back towards the road that led to the Hermitage, leaving Hetty to pursue her way in a strange dream that seemed to have begun in bewildering delight and was now passing into contrarieties and sadness. Would he meet her again as she came home? Why had he spoken almost as if he were displeased with her? And then run away so suddenly? She cried, hardly knowing why.

Arthur too was very uneasy, but his feelings were lit up for him by a more distinct consciousness. He hurried to the Hermitage, which stood in the heart of the wood, unlocked the door with a hasty wrench, slammed it after him, pitched *Zeluco* into the most distant corner, and thrusting his right hand into his pocket, first walked four or five times up and down the scanty length of the little room, and then seated himself on the ottoman in an uncomfortable stiff way, as we often do when we wish not to abandon ourselves to feeling.

He was getting in love with Hetty—that was quite plain. He was ready to pitch everything else—no matter where—for the sake of surrendering himself to this delicious feeling which had just disclosed itself. It was no use blinking the fact now—they would get too fond of each other, if he went on taking notice of her—and what would come of it? He should have to go away in a few weeks, and the poor little thing would be miserable. He *must not* see her alone again; he must keep out of her way. What a fool he was for coming back from Gawaine's!

He got up and threw open the windows, to let in the soft breath of the afternoon, and the healthy scent of the firs that made a belt round the Hermitage. The soft air did not help his resolution, as he leaned out and looked into the leafy distance. But he considered his resolution sufficiently fixed: there was no need to debate with himself any longer. He had made up his mind not to meet Hetty again; and now he might give himself up to thinking how immensely agreeable it would be if circumstances were different—how pleasant it would have been to meet her this evening as she came back, and put his arm round her again and look into her sweet face. He wondered if the dear little thing were thinking of him too—twenty to one she was. How beautiful her eyes were with the tear on their lashes! He would like to satisfy his soul for a day with looking at them, and he *must* see her again—he must see her, simply to remove any false impression from her mind about his manner to her just now. He would behave in a quiet, kind way to her—just to prevent her from going home with her head full of wrong fancies. Yes, that would be the best thing to do after all.

It was a long while—more than an hour before Arthur had brought his meditations to this point; but once arrived there, he could stay no longer at the Hermitage. The time must be filled up with movement until he should see Hetty again. And it was already late enough to go and dress for dinner, for his grandfather's dinner-hour was six.

Chapter XIII
Evening in the Wood

It happened that Mrs. Pomfret had had a slight quarrel with Mrs. Best, the housekeeper, on this Thursday morning—a fact which had two consequences highly convenient to Hetty. It caused Mrs. Pomfret to have tea sent up to her own room, and it inspired that exemplary lady's maid with so lively a recollection of former passages in Mrs. Best's conduct, and of dialogues in which Mrs. Best had decidedly the inferiority as an interlocutor with Mrs. Pomfret, that Hetty required no more presence of mind than was demanded for using her needle, and throwing in an occasional "yes" or "no." She would have wanted to put on her hat earlier than usual; only she had told Captain Donnithorne that she usually set out about eight o'clock, and if he *should* go to the Grove again expecting to see her, and she should be gone! Would he come? Her little butterfly soul fluttered incessantly between memory and dubious expectation. At last the minute-hand of the old-fashioned brazen-faced timepiece was on the last quarter to eight, and there was every reason for its being time to get ready for departure. Even Mrs. Pomfret's preoccupied mind did not prevent her from noticing what looked like a new flush of beauty in the little thing as she tied on her hat before the looking-glass.

"That child gets prettier and prettier every day, I do believe," was her inward comment. "The more's the pity. She'll get neither a place nor a husband any the sooner for it. Sober well-to-do men don't like such pretty wives. When I was a girl, I was more admired than if I had been so very pretty. However, she's reason to be grateful to me for teaching her something to get her bread with, better than farm-house work. They always told me I was good-natured—and that's the truth, and to my hurt too, else there's them in this house that wouldn't be here now to lord it over me in the housekeeper's room."

Hetty walked hastily across the short space of pleasure-ground which she had to traverse, dreading to meet Mr. Craig, to whom she could hardly have spoken civilly. How relieved she was when she had got safely under the oaks and among the fern of the Chase! Even then she was as ready to be startled as the deer that leaped away at her approach. She thought nothing of the evening light that lay gently in the grassy alleys between the fern, and made the beauty of their living green more visible than it had been in the overpowering flood of noon: she thought of nothing that was present. She only saw something that was possible: Mr. Arthur Donnithorne coming to meet her again along the Fir-tree Grove. That was the foreground of Hetty's picture; behind it lay a bright hazy something—days that were not to be as the other days of her life had been. It was as if she had been wooed by a river-god, who might any time take her to his wondrous halls below a watery heaven. There was no knowing what would come, since this strange entrancing delight had come. If a chest full of lace and satin and jewels had been sent her from some unknown source, how could she but have thought that her whole lot was going to change, and that to-morrow some still more bewildering joy would befall her? Hetty had never read a novel; if she had ever seen one, I think the words would have been too hard for her; how then could she find a shape for her expectations? They were as formless as the sweet languid odours of the garden at the Chase, which had floated past her as she walked by the gate.

She is at another gate now—that leading into Fir-tree Grove. She enters the wood, where it is already twilight, and at every step she takes, the fear at her heart becomes colder. If he should not come! Oh, how dreary it was—the thought of going out at the other end of the wood, into the unsheltered road, without having seen him. She reaches the first turning towards the Hermitage, walking slowly—he is not there. She hates the leveret that runs across the path; she hates everything that is not what she longs for. She walks on, happy whenever she is coming to a bend in the road, for perhaps he is behind it. No. She is beginning to cry: her heart has swelled so, the tears stand in her eyes; she gives one great sob, while the corners of her mouth quiver, and the tears roll down.

She doesn't know that there is another turning to the Hermitage, that she is close against it, and that Arthur Donnithorne is only a few yards from her, full of one thought, and a thought of which she only is the object. He is going to see Hetty again: that is the longing which has been growing through the last three hours to a feverish thirst. Not, of course, to speak in the caressing way into which he had unguardedly fallen before dinner, but to set things right with her by a kindness which would have the air of friendly civility, and prevent her from running away with wrong notions about their mutual relation.

If Hetty had known he was there, she would not have cried; and it would have been better, for then Arthur would perhaps have behaved as wisely as he had intended. As it was, she started when he appeared at the end of the side-alley, and looked up at him with two great drops rolling down her cheeks. What else could he do but speak to her in a soft, soothing tone, as if she were a bright-eyed spaniel with a thorn in her foot?

"Has something frightened you, Hetty? Have you seen anything in the wood? Don't be frightened—I'll take care of you now."

Hetty was blushing so, she didn't know whether she was happy or miserable. To be crying again—what did gentlemen think of girls who cried in that way? She felt unable even to say "no," but could only look away from him and wipe the tears from her cheek. Not before a great drop had fallen on her rose-coloured strings—she knew that quite well.

"Come, be cheerful again. Smile at me, and tell me what's the matter. Come, tell me."

Hetty turned her head towards him, whispered, "I thought you wouldn't come," and slowly got courage to lift her eyes to him. That look was too much: he must have had eyes of Egyptian granite not to look too lovingly in return.

"You little frightened bird! Little tearful rose! Silly pet! You won't cry again, now I'm with you, will you?"

Ah, he doesn't know in the least what he is saying. This is not what he meant to say. His arm is stealing round the waist again; it is tightening its clasp; he is bending his face nearer and nearer to the round cheek; his lips are meeting those pouting child-lips, and for a long moment time has vanished. He may be a shepherd in Arcadia for aught he knows, he may be the first youth kissing the first maiden, he may be Eros himself, sipping the lips of Psyche—it is all one.

There was no speaking for minutes after. They walked along with beating hearts till they came within sight of the gate at the end of the wood. Then they looked at each other, not quite as they had looked before, for in their eyes there was the memory of a kiss. But already something bitter had begun to mingle itself with the fountain of sweets: already Arthur was uncomfortable. He took his arm from Hetty's waist, and said, "Here we are, almost at the end of the Grove. I wonder how late it is," he added, pulling out his watch. "Twenty minutes past eight—but my watch is too fast. However, I'd better not go any further now. Trot along quickly with your little feet, and get home safely. Good-bye."

He took her hand, and looked at her half-sadly, half with a constrained smile. Hetty's eyes seemed to beseech him not to go away yet; but he patted her cheek and said "Good-bye" again. She was obliged to turn away from him and go on.

As for Arthur, he rushed back through the wood, as if he wanted to put a wide space between himself and Hetty. He would not go to the Hermitage again; he remembered how he had debated with himself there before dinner, and it had all come to nothing—worse than nothing. He walked right on into the Chase, glad to get out of the Grove, which surely was haunted by his evil genius. Those beeches and smooth limes—there was something enervating in the very sight of them; but the strong knotted old oaks had no bending languor in them—the sight of them would give a man some energy. Arthur lost himself among the narrow openings in the fern, winding about without seeking any issue, till the twilight deepened almost to night under the great boughs, and the hare looked black as it darted across his path.

He was feeling much more strongly than he had done in the morning: it was as if his horse had wheeled round from a leap and dared to dispute his mastery. He was dissatisfied with himself, irritated, mortified. He no sooner fixed his mind on the probable consequences of giving way to the emotions which had stolen over him to-day—of continuing to notice Hetty, of allowing himself any opportunity for such slight caresses as he had been betrayed into already—than he refused to believe such a future possible for himself. To flirt with Hetty was a very different affair from flirting with a pretty girl of his own station: that was understood to be an amusement on both sides, or, if it became serious, there was no obstacle to marriage. But this little thing would be spoken ill of directly, if she happened to be seen walking with him; and then those excellent people, the Poysers, to whom a good name was as precious as if they had the best blood in the land in their veins—he should hate himself if he made a scandal of that sort, on the estate that was to be his own some day, and among tenants by whom he liked, above all, to be respected. He could no more believe that he should so fall in his own esteem than that he should break both his legs and go on crutches all the rest of his life. He couldn't imagine himself in that position; it was too odious, too unlike him.

And even if no one knew anything about it, they might get too fond of each other, and then there could be nothing but the misery of parting, after all. No gentleman, out of a ballad, could marry a farmer's niece. There must be an end to the whole thing at once. It was too foolish.

And yet he had been so determined this morning, before he went to Gawaine's; and while he was there something had taken hold of him and made him gallop back. It seemed he couldn't quite depend on his own resolution, as he had thought he could; he almost wished his arm would get painful again, and then he should think of nothing but the comfort it would be to get rid of the pain. There was no knowing what impulse might seize him to-morrow, in this confounded place, where there was nothing to occupy him imperiously through the livelong day. What could he do to secure himself from any more of this folly?There was but one resource. He would go and tell Irwine—tell him everything. The mere act of telling it would make it seem trivial; the temptation would vanish, as the charm of fond words vanishes when one repeats them to the indifferent. In every way it would help him to tell Irwine. He would ride to Broxton Rectory the first thing after breakfast to-morrow.

Arthur had no sooner come to this determination than he began to think which of the paths would lead him home, and made as short a walk thither as he could. He felt sure he should sleep now: he had had enough to tire him, and there was no more need for him to think.

Chapter XIV
The Return Home

While that parting in the wood was happening, there was a parting in the cottage too, and Lisbeth had stood with Adam at the door, straining her aged eyes to get the last glimpse of Seth and Dinah, as they mounted the opposite slope.

"Eh, I'm loath to see the last on her," she said to Adam, as they turned into the house again. "I'd ha' been willin' t' ha' her about me till I died and went to lie by my old man. She'd make it easier dyin'—she spakes so gentle an' moves about so still. I could be fast sure that pictur' was drawed for her i' thy new Bible—th' angel a-sittin' on the big stone by the grave. Eh, I wouldna mind ha'in a daughter like that; but nobody ne'er marries them as is good for aught."

"Well, Mother, I hope thee wilt have her for a daughter; for Seth's got a liking for her, and I hope she'll get a liking for Seth in time."

"Where's th' use o' talkin' a-that'n? She caresna for Seth. She's goin' away twenty mile aff. How's she to get a likin' for him, I'd like to know? No more nor the cake 'ull come wi'out the leaven. Thy figurin' books might ha' tould thee better nor that, I should think, else thee mightst as well read the commin print, as Seth allays does."

"Nay, Mother," said Adam, laughing, "the figures tell us a fine deal, and we couldn't go far without 'em, but they don't tell us about folks's feelings. It's a nicer job to calculate *them*. But Seth's as good-hearted a lad as ever handled a tool, and plenty o' sense, and good-looking too; and he's got the same way o' thinking as Dinah. He deserves to win her, though there's no denying she's a rare bit o' workmanship. You don't see such women turned off the wheel every day."

"Eh, thee't allays stick up for thy brother. Thee'st been just the same, e'er sin' ye war little uns together. Thee wart allays for halving iverything wi' him. But what's Seth got to do with marryin', as is on'y three-an'-twenty? He'd more need to learn an' lay by sixpence. An' as for his desarving her—she's two 'ear older nor Seth: she's pretty near as old as thee. But that's the way; folks mun allays choose by contrairies, as if they must be sorted like the pork—a bit o' good meat wi' a bit o' offal."

To the feminine mind in some of its moods, all things that might be receive a temporary charm from comparison with what is; and since Adam did not want to marry Dinah himself, Lisbeth felt rather peevish on that score—as peevish as she would have been if he *had* wanted to marry her, and so shut himself out from Mary Burge and the partnership as effectually as by marrying Hetty.

It was more than half-past eight when Adam and his mother were talking in this way, so that when, about ten minutes later, Hetty reached the turning of the lane that led to the farmyard gate, she saw Dinah and Seth approaching it from the opposite direction, and waited for them to come up to her. They, too, like Hetty, had lingered a little in their walk, for Dinah was trying to speak words of comfort and strength to Seth in these parting moments. But when they saw Hetty, they paused and shook hands; Seth turned homewards, and Dinah came on alone.

"Seth Bede would have come and spoken to you, my dear," she said, as she reached Hetty, "but he's very full of trouble to-night."

Hetty answered with a dimpled smile, as if she did not quite know what had been said; and it made a strange contrast to see that sparkling self-engrossed loveliness looked at by Dinah's calm pitying face, with its open glance which told that her heart lived in no cherished secrets of its own, but in feelings which it longed to share with all the world. Hetty liked Dinah as well as she had ever liked any woman; how was it possible to feel otherwise towards one who always put in a kind word for her when her aunt was finding fault, and who was always ready to take Totty off her hands—little tiresome Totty, that was made such a pet of by every one, and that Hetty could see no interest in at all? Dinah had never said anything disapproving or reproachful to Hetty during her whole visit to the Hall Farm; she had talked to her a great deal in a serious way, but Hetty didn't mind that much, for she never listened: whatever Dinah might say, she almost always stroked Hetty's cheek after it, and wanted to do some mending for her. Dinah was a riddle to her; Hetty looked at her much in the same way as one might imagine a little perching bird that could only flutter from bough to bough, to look at the swoop of the swallow or the mounting of the lark; but she did not care to solve such riddles, any more than she cared to know what was meant by the pictures in the Pilgrim's Progress, or in the old folio Bible that Marty and Tommy always plagued her about on a Sunday.

Dinah took her hand now and drew it under her own arm.

"You look very happy to-night, dear child," she said. "I shall think of you often when I'm at Snowfield, and see your face before me as it is now. It's a strange thing—sometimes when I'm quite alone, sitting in my room with my eyes closed, or walking over the hills, the people I've seen and known, if it's only been for a few days, are brought before me, and I hear their voices and see them look and move almost plainer than I ever did when they were really with me so as I could touch them. And then my heart is drawn out towards them, and I feel their lot as if it was my own, and I take comfort in spreading it before the Lord and resting in His love, on their behalf as well as my own. And so I feel sure you will come before me."

She paused a moment, but Hetty said nothing.

"It has been a very precious time to me," Dinah went on, "last night and to-day—seeing two such good sons as Adam and Seth Bede. They are so tender and thoughtful for their aged mother. And she has been telling me what Adam has done, for these many years, to help his father and his brother; it's wonderful what a spirit of wisdom and knowledge he has, and how he's ready to use it all in behalf of them that are feeble. And I'm sure he has a loving spirit too. I've noticed it often among my own people round Snowfield, that the strong, skilful men are often the gentlest to the women and children; and it's pretty to see 'em carrying the little babies as if they were no heavier than little birds. And the babies always seem to like the strong arm best. I feel sure it would be so with Adam Bede. Don't you think so, Hetty?"

"Yes," said Hetty abstractedly, for her mind had been all the while in the wood, and she would have found it difficult to say what she was assenting to. Dinah saw she was not inclined to talk, but there would not have been time to say much more, for they were now at the yard-gate.

The still twilight, with its dying western red and its few faint struggling stars, rested on the farm-yard, where there was not a sound to be heard but the stamping of the cart-horses in the stable. It was about twenty minutes after sunset. The fowls were all gone to roost, and the bull-dog lay stretched on the straw outside his kennel, with the black-and-tan terrier by his side, when the falling-to of the gate disturbed them and set them barking, like good officials, before they had any distinct knowledge of the reason.

The barking had its effect in the house, for, as Dinah and Hetty approached, the doorway was filled by a portly figure, with a ruddy black-eyed face which bore in it the possibility of looking extremely acute, and occasionally contemptuous, on market-days, but had now a predominant after-supper expression of hearty good-nature. It is well known that great scholars who have shown the most pitiless acerbity in their criticism of other men's scholarship have yet been of a relenting and indulgent temper in private life; and I have heard of a learned man meekly rocking the twins in the cradle with his left hand, while with his right he inflicted the most lacerating sarcasms on an opponent who had betrayed a brutal ignorance of Hebrew. Weaknesses and errors must be forgiven—alas! they are not alien to us—but the man who takes the wrong side on the momentous subject of the Hebrew points must be treated as the enemy of his race. There was the same sort of antithetic mixture in Martin Poyser: he was of so excellent a disposition that he had been kinder and more respectful than ever to his old father since he had made a deed of gift of all his property, and no man judged his neighbours more charitably on all personal matters; but for a farmer, like Luke Britton, for example, whose fallows were not well cleaned, who didn't know the rudiments of hedging and ditching, and showed but a small share of judgment in the purchase of winter stock, Martin Poyser was as hard and implacable as the north-east wind. Luke Britton could not make a remark, even on the weather, but Martin Poyser detected in it a taint of that unsoundness and general ignorance which was palpable in all his farming operations. He hated to see the fellow lift the pewter pint to his mouth in the bar of the Royal George on market-day, and the mere sight of him on the other side of the road brought a severe and critical expression into his black eyes, as different as possible from the fatherly glance he bent on his two nieces as they approached the door. Mr. Poyser had smoked his evening pipe, and now held his hands in his pockets, as the only resource of a man who continues to sit up after the day's business is done.

"Why, lasses, ye're rather late to-night," he said, when they reached the little gate leading into the causeway. "The mother's begun to fidget about you, an' she's got the little un ill. An' how did you leave the old woman Bede, Dinah? Is she much down about the old man? He'd been but a poor bargain to her this five year."

"She's been greatly distressed for the loss of him," said Dinah, "but she's seemed more comforted to-day. Her son Adam's been at home all day, working at his father's coffin, and she loves to have him at home. She's been talking about him to me almost all the day. She has a loving heart, though she's sorely given to fret and be fearful. I wish she had a surer trust to comfort her in her old age."

"Adam's sure enough," said Mr. Poyser, misunderstanding Dinah's wish. "There's no fear but he'll yield well i' the threshing. He's not one o' them as is all straw and no grain. I'll be bond for him any day, as he'll be a good son to the last. Did he say he'd be coming to see us soon? But come in, come in," he added, making way for them; "I hadn't need keep y' out any longer."

The tall buildings round the yard shut out a good deal of the sky, but the large window let in abundant light to show every corner of the house-place.

Mrs. Poyser, seated in the rocking-chair, which had been brought out of the "right-hand parlour," was trying to soothe Totty to sleep. But Totty was not disposed to sleep; and when her cousins entered, she raised herself up and showed a pair of flushed cheeks, which looked fatter than ever now they were defined by the edge of her linen night-cap.

In the large wicker-bottomed arm-chair in the left-hand chimney-nook sat old Martin Poyser, a hale but shrunken and bleached image of his portly black-haired son—his head hanging forward a little, and his elbows pushed backwards so as to allow the whole of his forearm to rest on the arm of the chair. His blue handkerchief was spread over his knees, as was usual indoors, when it was not hanging over his head; and he sat watching what went forward with the quiet *outward* glance of healthy old age, which, disengaged from any interest in an inward drama, spies out pins upon the floor, follows one's minutest motions with an unexpectant purposeless tenacity, watches the flickering of the flame or the sun-gleams on the wall, counts the quarries on the floor, watches even the hand of the clock, and pleases itself with detecting a rhythm in the tick.

"What a time o' night this is to come home, Hetty!" said Mrs. Poyser. "Look at the clock, do; why, it's going on for half-past nine, and I've sent the gells to bed this half-hour, and late enough too; when they've got to get up at half after four, and the mowers' bottles to fill, and the baking; and here's this blessed child wi' the fever for what I know, and as wakeful as if it was dinner-time, and nobody to help me to give her the physic but your uncle, and fine work there's been, and half of it spilt on her night-gown—it's well if she's swallowed more nor 'ull make her worse i'stead o' better. But folks as have no mind to be o' use have allays the luck to be out o' the road when there's anything to be done."

"I did set out before eight, aunt," said Hetty, in a pettish tone, with a slight toss of her head. "But this clock's so much before the clock at the Chase, there's no telling what time it'll be when I get here."

"What! You'd be wanting the clock set by gentlefolks's time, would you? An' sit up burnin' candle, an' lie a-bed wi' the sun a-bakin' you like a cowcumber i' the frame? The clock hasn't been put forrard for the first time to-day, I reckon."

The fact was, Hetty had really forgotten the difference of the clocks when she told Captain Donnithorne that she set out at eight, and this, with her lingering pace, had made her nearly half an hour later than usual. But here her aunt's attention was diverted from this tender subject by Totty, who, perceiving at length that the arrival of her cousins was not likely to bring anything satisfactory to her in particular, began to cry, "Munny, munny," in an explosive manner.

"Well, then, my pet, Mother's got her, Mother won't leave her; Totty be a good dilling, and go to sleep now," said Mrs. Poyser, leaning back and rocking the chair, while she tried to make Totty nestle against her. But Totty only cried louder, and said, "Don't yock!" So the mother, with that wondrous patience which love gives to the quickest temperament, sat up again, and pressed her cheek against the linen night-cap and kissed it, and forgot to scold Hetty any longer.

"Come, Hetty," said Martin Poyser, in a conciliatory tone, "go and get your supper i' the pantry, as the things are all put away; an' then you can come and take the little un while your aunt undresses herself, for she won't lie down in bed without her mother. An' I reckon *you* could eat a bit, Dinah, for they don't keep much of a house down there."

"No, thank you, Uncle," said Dinah; "I ate a good meal before I came away, for Mrs. Bede would make a kettle-cake for me."

"I don't want any supper," said Hetty, taking off her hat. "I can hold Totty now, if Aunt wants me."

"Why, what nonsense that is to talk!" said Mrs. Poyser. "Do you think you can live wi'out eatin', an' nourish your inside wi' stickin' red ribbons on your head? Go an' get your supper this minute, child; there's a nice bit o' cold pudding i' the safe—just what you're fond of."

Hetty complied silently by going towards the pantry, and Mrs. Poyser went on speaking to Dinah.

"Sit down, my dear, an' look as if you knowed what it was to make yourself a bit comfortable i' the world. I warrant the old woman was glad to see you, since you stayed so long."

"She seemed to like having me there at last; but her sons say she doesn't like young women about her commonly; and I thought just at first she was almost angry with me for going."

"Eh, it's a poor look-out when th' ould folks doesna like the young uns," said old Martin, bending his head down lower, and seeming to trace the pattern of the quarries with his eye.

"Aye, it's ill livin' in a hen-roost for them as doesn't like fleas," said Mrs. Poyser. "We've all had our turn at bein' young, I reckon, be't good luck or ill."

"But she must learn to 'commodate herself to young women," said Mr. Poyser, "for it isn't to be counted on as Adam and Seth 'ull keep bachelors for the next ten year to please their mother. That 'ud be unreasonable. It isn't right for old nor young nayther to make a bargain all o' their own side. What's good for one's good all round i' the long run. I'm no friend to young fellows a-marrying afore they know the difference atween a crab an' a apple; but they may wait o'er long."

"To be sure," said Mrs. Poyser; "if you go past your dinner-time, there'll be little relish o' your meat. You turn it o'er an' o'er wi' your fork, an' don't eat it after all. You find faut wi' your meat, an' the faut's all i' your own stomach."

Hetty now came back from the pantry and said, "I can take Totty now, Aunt, if you like."

"Come, Rachel," said Mr. Poyser, as his wife seemed to hesitate, seeing that Totty was at last nestling quietly, "thee'dst better let Hetty carry her upstairs, while thee tak'st thy things off. Thee't tired. It's time thee wast in bed. Thee't bring on the pain in thy side again."

"Well, she may hold her if the child 'ull go to her," said Mrs. Poyser.

Hetty went close to the rocking-chair, and stood without her usual smile, and without any attempt to entice Totty, simply waiting for her aunt to give the child into her hands.

"Wilt go to Cousin Hetty, my dilling, while mother gets ready to go to bed? Then Totty shall go into Mother's bed, and sleep there all night."

Before her mother had done speaking, Totty had given her answer in an unmistakable manner, by knitting her brow, setting her tiny teeth against her underlip, and leaning forward to slap Hetty on the arm with her utmost force. Then, without speaking, she nestled to her mother again.

"Hey, hey," said Mr. Poyser, while Hetty stood without moving, "not go to Cousin Hetty? That's like a babby. Totty's a little woman, an' not a babby."

"It's no use trying to persuade her," said Mrs. Poyser. "She allays takes against Hetty when she isn't well. Happen she'll go to Dinah."

Dinah, having taken off her bonnet and shawl, had hitherto kept quietly seated in the background, not liking to thrust herself between Hetty and what was considered Hetty's proper work. But now she came forward, and, putting out her arms, said, "Come Totty, come and let Dinah carry her upstairs along with Mother: poor, poor Mother! she's so tired—she wants to go to bed."

Totty turned her face towards Dinah, and looked at her an instant, then lifted herself up, put out her little arms, and let Dinah lift her from her mother's lap. Hetty turned away without any sign of ill humour, and, taking her hat from the table, stood waiting with an air of indifference, to see if she should be told to do anything else.

"You may make the door fast now, Poyser; Alick's been come in this long while," said Mrs. Poyser, rising with an appearance of relief from her low chair. "Get me the matches down, Hetty, for I must have the rushlight burning i' my room. Come, Father."

The heavy wooden bolts began to roll in the house doors, and old Martin prepared to move, by gathering up his blue handkerchief, and reaching his bright knobbed walnut-tree stick from the corner. Mrs. Poyser then led the way out of the kitchen, followed by the grandfather, and Dinah with Totty in her arms—all going to bed by twilight, like the birds. Mrs. Poyser, on her way, peeped into the room where her two boys lay; just to see their ruddy round cheeks on the pillow, and to hear for a moment their light regular breathing.

"Come, Hetty, get to bed," said Mr. Poyser, in a soothing tone, as he himself turned to go upstairs. "You didna mean to be late, I'll be bound, but your aunt's been worrited to-day. Good-night, my wench, good-night."

Chapter XV
The Two Bed-Chambers

Hetty and Dinah both slept in the second story, in rooms adjoining each other, meagrely furnished rooms, with no blinds to shut out the light, which was now beginning to gather new strength from the rising of the moon—more than enough strength to enable Hetty to move about and undress with perfect comfort. She could see quite well the pegs in the old painted linen-press on which she hung her hat and gown; she could see the head of every pin on her red cloth pin-cushion; she could see a reflection of herself in the old-fashioned looking-glass, quite as distinct as was needful, considering that she had only to brush her hair and put on her night-cap. A queer old looking-glass! Hetty got into an ill temper with it almost every time she dressed. It had been considered a handsome glass in its day, and had probably been bought into the Poyser family a quarter of a century before, at a sale of genteel household furniture. Even now an auctioneer could say something for it: it had a great deal of tarnished gilding about it; it had a firm mahogany base, well supplied with drawers, which opened with a decided jerk and sent the contents leaping out from the farthest corners, without giving you the trouble of reaching them; above all, it had a brass candle-socket on each side, which would give it an aristocratic air to the very last. But Hetty objected to it because it had numerous dim blotches sprinkled over the mirror, which no rubbing would remove, and because, instead of swinging backwards and forwards, it was fixed in an upright position, so that she could only get one good view of her head and neck, and that was to be had only by sitting down on a low chair before her dressing-table. And the dressing-table was no dressing-table at all, but a small old chest of drawers, the most awkward thing in the world to sit down before, for the big brass handles quite hurt her knees, and she couldn't get near the glass at all comfortably. But devout worshippers never allow inconveniences to prevent them from performing their religious rites, and Hetty this evening was more bent on her peculiar form of worship than usual.

Having taken off her gown and white kerchief, she drew a key from the large pocket that hung outside her petticoat, and, unlocking one of the lower drawers in the chest, reached from it two short bits of wax candle—secretly bought at Treddleston—and stuck them in the two brass sockets. Then she drew forth a bundle of matches and lighted the candles; and last of all, a small red-framed shilling looking-glass, without blotches. It was into this small glass that she chose to look first after seating herself. She looked into it, smiling and turning her head on one side, for a minute, then laid it down and took out her brush and comb from an upper drawer. She was going to let down her hair, and make herself look like that picture of a lady in Miss Lydia Donnithorne's dressing-room. It was soon done, and the dark hyacinthine curves fell on her neck. It was not heavy, massive, merely rippling hair, but soft and silken, running at every opportunity into delicate rings. But she pushed it all backward to look like the picture, and form a dark curtain, throwing into relief her round white neck. Then she put down her brush and comb and looked at herself, folding her arms before her, still like the picture. Even the old mottled glass couldn't help sending back a lovely image, none the less lovely because Hetty's stays were not of white satin—such as I feel sure heroines must generally wear—but of a dark greenish cotton texture.

Oh yes! She was very pretty. Captain Donnithorne thought so. Prettier than anybody about Hayslope—prettier than any of the ladies she had ever seen visiting at the Chase—indeed it seemed fine ladies were rather old and ugly—and prettier than Miss Bacon, the miller's daughter, who was called the beauty of Treddleston. And Hetty looked at herself to-night with quite a different sensation from what she had ever felt before; there was an invisible spectator whose eye rested on her like morning on the flowers. His soft voice was saying over and over again those pretty things she had heard in the wood; his arm was round her, and the delicate rose-scent of his hair was with her still. The vainest woman is never thoroughly conscious of her own beauty till she is loved by the man who sets her own passion vibrating in return.

But Hetty seemed to have made up her mind that something was wanting, for she got up and reached an old black lace scarf out of the linen-press, and a pair of large ear-rings out of the sacred drawer from which she had taken her candles. It was an old old scarf, full of rents, but it would make a becoming border round her shoulders, and set off the whiteness of her upper arm. And she would take out the little ear-rings she had in her ears—oh, how her aunt had scolded her for having her ears bored!—and put in those large ones. They were but coloured glass and gilding, but if you didn't know what they were made of, they looked just as well as what the ladies wore. And so she sat down again, with the large ear-rings in her ears, and the black lace scarf adjusted round her shoulders. She looked down at her arms: no arms could be prettier down to a little way below the elbow—they were white and plump, and dimpled to match her cheeks; but towards the wrist, she thought with vexation that they were coarsened by butter-making and other work that ladies never did.

Captain Donnithorne couldn't like her to go on doing work: he would like to see her in nice clothes, and thin shoes, and white stockings, perhaps with silk clocks to them; for he must love her very much—no one else had ever put his arm round her and kissed her in that way. He would want to marry her and make a lady of her; she could hardly dare to shape the thought—yet how else could it be? Marry her quite secretly, as Mr. James, the doctor's assistant, married the doctor's niece, and nobody ever found it out for a long while after, and then it was of no use to be angry. The doctor had told her aunt all about it in Hetty's hearing. She didn't know how it would be, but it was quite plain the old Squire could never be told anything about it, for Hetty was ready to faint with awe and fright if she came across him at the Chase. He might have been earth-born, for what she knew. It had never entered her mind that he had been young like other men; he had always been the old Squire at whom everybody was frightened. Oh, it was impossible to think how it would be! But Captain Donnithorne would know; he was a great gentleman, and could have his way in everything, and could buy everything he liked. And nothing could be as it had been again: perhaps some day she should be a grand lady, and ride in her coach, and dress for dinner in a brocaded silk, with feathers in her hair, and her dress sweeping the ground, like Miss Lydia and Lady Dacey, when she saw them going into the dining-room one evening as she peeped through the little round window in the lobby; only she should not be old and ugly like Miss Lydia, or all the same thickness like Lady Dacey, but very pretty, with her hair done in a great many different ways, and sometimes in a pink dress, and sometimes in a white one—she didn't know which she liked best; and Mary Burge and everybody would perhaps see her going out in her carriage—or rather, they would *hear* of it: it was impossible to imagine these things happening at Hayslope in sight of her aunt. At the thought of all this splendour, Hetty got up from her chair, and in doing so caught the little red-framed glass with the edge of her scarf, so that it fell with a bang on the floor; but she was too eagerly occupied with her vision to care about picking it up; and after a momentary start, began to pace with a pigeon-like stateliness backwards and forwards along her room, in her coloured stays and coloured skirt, and the old black lace scarf round her shoulders, and the great glass ear-rings in her ears.

How pretty the little puss looks in that odd dress! It would be the easiest folly in the world to fall in love with her: there is such a sweet babylike roundness about her face and figure; the delicate dark rings of hair lie so charmingly about her ears and neck; her great dark eyes with their long eye-lashes touch one so strangely, as if an imprisoned frisky sprite looked out of them.

Ah, what a prize the man gets who wins a sweet bride like Hetty! How the men envy him who come to the wedding breakfast, and see her hanging on his arm in her white lace and orange blossoms. The dear, young, round, soft, flexible thing! Her heart must be just as soft, her temper just as free from angles, her character just as pliant. If anything ever goes wrong, it must be the husband's fault there: he can make her what he likes—that is plain. And the lover himself thinks so too: the little darling is so fond of him, her little vanities are so bewitching, he wouldn't consent to her being a bit wiser; those kittenlike glances and movements are just what one wants to make one's hearth a paradise. Every man under such circumstances is conscious of being a great physiognomist. Nature, he knows, has a language of her own, which she uses with strict veracity, and he considers himself an adept in the language. Nature has written out his bride's character for him in those exquisite lines of cheek and lip and chin, in those eyelids delicate as petals, in those long lashes curled like the stamen of a flower, in the dark liquid depths of those wonderful eyes. How she will dote on her children! She is almost a child herself, and the little pink round things will hang about her like florets round the central flower; and the husband will look on, smiling benignly, able, whenever he chooses, to withdraw into the sanctuary of his wisdom, towards which his sweet wife will look reverently, and never lift the curtain. It is a marriage such as they made in the golden age, when the men were all wise and majestic and the women all lovely and loving.

It was very much in this way that our friend Adam Bede thought about Hetty; only he put his thoughts into different words. If ever she behaved with cold vanity towards him, he said to himself it is only because she doesn't love me well enough; and he was sure that her love, whenever she gave it, would be the most precious thing a man could possess on earth. Before you despise Adam as deficient in penetration, pray ask yourself if you were ever predisposed to believe evil of any pretty woman—if you ever *could*, without hard head-breaking demonstration, believe evil of the *one* supremely pretty woman who has bewitched you. No: people who love downy peaches are apt not to think of the stone, and sometimes jar their teeth terribly against it.

Arthur Donnithorne, too, had the same sort of notion about Hetty, so far as he had thought of her nature of all. He felt sure she was a dear, affectionate, good little thing. The man who awakes the wondering tremulous passion of a young girl always thinks her affectionate; and if he chances to look forward to future years, probably imagines himself being virtuously tender to her, because the poor thing is so clingingly fond of him. God made these dear women so—and it is a convenient arrangement in case of sickness.

After all, I believe the wisest of us must be beguiled in this way sometimes, and must think both better and worse of people than they deserve. Nature has her language, and she is not unveracious; but we don't know all the intricacies of her syntax just yet, and in a hasty reading we may happen to extract the very opposite of her real meaning. Long dark eyelashes, now—what can be more exquisite? I find it impossible not to expect some depth of soul behind a deep grey eye with a long dark eyelash, in spite of an experience which has shown me that they may go along with deceit, peculation, and stupidity. But if, in the reaction of disgust, I have betaken myself to a fishy eye, there has been a surprising similarity of result. One begins to suspect at length that there is no direct correlation between eyelashes and morals; or else, that the eyelashes express the disposition of the fair one's grandmother, which is on the whole less important to us.

No eyelashes could be more beautiful than Hetty's; and now, while she walks with her pigeon-like stateliness along the room and looks down on her shoulders bordered by the old black lace, the dark fringe shows to perfection on her pink cheek. They are but dim ill-defined pictures that her narrow bit of an imagination can make of the future; but of every picture she is the central figure in fine clothes; Captain Donnithorne is very close to her, putting his arm round her, perhaps kissing her, and everybody else is admiring and envying her—especially Mary Burge, whose new print dress looks very contemptible by the side of Hetty's resplendent toilette. Does any sweet or sad memory mingle with this dream of the future—any loving thought of her second parents—of the children she had helped to tend—of any youthful companion, any pet animal, any relic of her own childhood even? Not one. There are some plants that have hardly any roots: you may tear them from their native nook of rock or wall, and just lay them over your ornamental flower-pot, and they blossom none the worse. Hetty could have cast all her past life behind her and never cared to be reminded of it again. I think she had no feeling at all towards the old house, and did not like the Jacobb's Ladder and the long row of hollyhocks in the garden better than other flowers—perhaps not so well. It was wonderful how little she seemed to care about waiting on her uncle, who had been a good father to her—she hardly ever remembered to reach him his pipe at the right time without being told, unless a visitor happened to be there, who would have a better opportunity of seeing her as she walked across the hearth. Hetty did not understand how anybody could be very fond of middle-aged people. And as for those tiresome children, Marty and Tommy and Totty, they had been the very nuisance of her life—as bad as buzzing insects that will come teasing you on a hot day when you want to be quiet. Marty, the eldest, was a baby when she first came to the farm, for the children born before him had died, and so Hetty had had them all three, one after the other, toddling by her side in the meadow, or playing about her on wet days in the half-empty rooms of the large old house. The boys were out of hand now, but Totty was still a day-long plague, worse than either of the others had been, because there was more fuss made about her. And there was no end to the making and mending of clothes. Hetty would have been glad to hear that she should never see a child again; they were worse than the nasty little lambs that the shepherd was always bringing in to be taken special care of in lambing time; for the lambs *were* got rid of sooner or later. As for the young chickens and turkeys, Hetty would have hated the very word "hatching," if her aunt had not bribed her to attend to the young poultry by promising her the proceeds of one out of every brood. The round downy chicks peeping out from under their mother's wing never touched Hetty with any pleasure; that was not the sort of prettiness she cared about, but she did care about the prettiness of the new things she would buy for herself at Treddleston Fair with the money they fetched. And yet she looked so dimpled, so charming, as she stooped down to put the soaked bread under the hen-coop, that you must have been a very acute personage indeed to suspect her of that hardness. Molly, the housemaid, with a turn-up nose and a protuberant jaw, was really a tender-hearted girl, and, as Mrs. Poyser said, a jewel to look after the poultry; but her stolid face showed nothing of this maternal delight, any more than a brown earthenware pitcher will show the light of the lamp within it.

It is generally a feminine eye that first detects the moral deficiencies hidden under the "dear deceit" of beauty, so it is not surprising that Mrs. Poyser, with her keenness and abundant opportunity for observation, should have formed a tolerably fair estimate of what might be expected from Hetty in the way of feeling, and in moments of indignation she had sometimes spoken with great openness on the subject to her husband.

"She's no better than a peacock, as 'ud strut about on the wall and spread its tail when the sun shone if all the folks i' the parish was dying: there's nothing seems to give her a turn i' th' inside, not even when we thought Totty had tumbled into the pit. To think o' that dear cherub! And we found her wi' her little shoes stuck i' the mud an' crying fit to break her heart by the far horse-pit. But Hetty never minded it, I could see, though she's been at the nussin' o' the child ever since it was a babby. It's my belief her heart's as hard as a pebble."

"Nay, nay," said Mr. Poyser, "thee mustn't judge Hetty too hard. Them young gells are like the unripe grain; they'll make good meal by and by, but they're squashy as yet. Thee't see Hetty 'll be all right when she's got a good husband and children of her own."

"*I* don't want to be hard upo' the gell. She's got cliver fingers of her own, and can be useful enough when she likes and I should miss her wi' the butter, for she's got a cool hand. An' let be what may, I'd strive to do my part by a niece o' yours—an' that I've done, for I've taught her everything as belongs to a house, an' I've told her her duty often enough, though, God knows, I've no breath to spare, an' that catchin' pain comes on dreadful by times. Wi' them three gells in the house I'd need have twice the strength to keep 'em up to their work. It's like having roast meat at three fires; as soon as you've basted one, another's burnin'."

Hetty stood sufficiently in awe of her aunt to be anxious to conceal from her so much of her vanity as could be hidden without too great a sacrifice. She could not resist spending her money in bits of finery which Mrs. Poyser disapproved; but she would have been ready to die with shame, vexation, and fright if her aunt had this moment opened the door, and seen her with her bits of candle lighted, and strutting about decked in her scarf and ear-rings. To prevent such a surprise, she always bolted her door, and she had not forgotten to do so to-night. It was well: for there now came a light tap, and Hetty, with a leaping heart, rushed to blow out the candles and throw them into the drawer. She dared not stay to take out her ear-rings, but she threw off her scarf, and let it fall on the floor, before the light tap came again. We shall know how it was that the light tap came, if we leave Hetty for a short time and return to Dinah, at the moment when she had delivered Totty to her mother's arms, and was come upstairs to her bedroom, adjoining Hetty's.

Dinah delighted in her bedroom window. Being on the second story of that tall house, it gave her a wide view over the fields. The thickness of the wall formed a broad step about a yard below the window, where she could place her chair. And now the first thing she did on entering her room was to seat herself in this chair and look out on the peaceful fields beyond which the large moon was rising, just above the hedgerow elms. She liked the pasture best where the milch cows were lying, and next to that the meadow where the grass was half-mown, and lay in silvered sweeping lines. Her heart was very full, for there was to be only one more night on which she would look out on those fields for a long time to come; but she thought little of leaving the mere scene, for, to her, bleak Snowfield had just as many charms. She thought of all the dear people whom she had learned to care for among these peaceful fields, and who would now have a place in her loving remembrance for ever. She thought of the struggles and the weariness that might lie before them in the rest of their life's journey, when she would be away from them, and know nothing of what was befalling them; and the pressure of this thought soon became too strong for her to enjoy the unresponding stillness of the moonlit fields. She closed her eyes, that she might feel more intensely the presence of a Love and Sympathy deeper and more tender than was breathed from the earth and sky. That was often Dinah's mode of praying in solitude. Simply to close her eyes and to feel herself enclosed by the Divine Presence; then gradually her fears, her yearning anxieties for others, melted away like ice-crystals in a warm ocean. She had sat in this way perfectly still, with her hands crossed on her lap and the pale light resting on her calm face, for at least ten minutes when she was startled by a loud sound, apparently of something falling in Hetty's room. But like all sounds that fall on our ears in a state of abstraction, it had no distinct character, but was simply loud and startling, so that she felt uncertain whether she had interpreted it rightly. She rose and listened, but all was quiet afterwards, and she reflected that Hetty might merely have knocked something down in getting into bed. She began slowly to undress; but now, owing to the suggestions of this sound, her thoughts became concentrated on Hetty—that sweet young thing, with life and all its trials before her—the solemn daily duties of the wife and mother—and her mind so unprepared for them all, bent merely on little foolish, selfish pleasures, like a child hugging its toys in the beginning of a long toilsome journey in which it will have to bear hunger and cold and unsheltered darkness. Dinah felt a double care for Hetty, because she shared Seth's anxious interest in his brother's lot, and she had not come to the conclusion that Hetty did not love Adam well enough to marry him. She saw too clearly the absence of any warm, self-devoting love in Hetty's nature to regard the coldness of her behaviour towards Adam as any indication that he was not the man she would like to have for a husband. And this blank in Hetty's nature, instead of exciting Dinah's dislike, only touched her with a deeper pity: the lovely face and form affected her as beauty always affects a pure and tender mind, free from selfish jealousies. It was an excellent divine gift, that gave a deeper pathos to the need, the sin, the sorrow with which it was mingled, as the canker in a lily-white bud is more grievous to behold than in a common pot-herb.

By the time Dinah had undressed and put on her night-gown, this feeling about Hetty had gathered a painful intensity; her imagination had created a thorny thicket of sin and sorrow, in which she saw the poor thing struggling torn and bleeding, looking with tears for rescue and finding none. It was in this way that Dinah's imagination and sympathy acted and reacted habitually, each heightening the other. She felt a deep longing to go now and pour into Hetty's ear all the words of tender warning and appeal that rushed into her mind. But perhaps Hetty was already asleep. Dinah put her ear to the partition and heard still some slight noises, which convinced her that Hetty was not yet in bed. Still she hesitated; she was not quite certain of a divine direction; the voice that told her to go to Hetty seemed no stronger than the other voice which said that Hetty was weary, and that going to her now in an unseasonable moment would only tend to close her heart more obstinately. Dinah was not satisfied without a more unmistakable guidance than those inward voices. There was light enough for her, if she opened her Bible, to discern the text sufficiently to know what it would say to her. She knew the physiognomy of every page, and could tell on what book she opened, sometimes on what chapter, without seeing title or number. It was a small thick Bible, worn quite round at the edges. Dinah laid it sideways on the window ledge, where the light was strongest, and then opened it with her forefinger. The first words she looked at were those at the top of the left-hand page: "And they all wept sore, and fell on Paul's neck and kissed him." That was enough for Dinah; she had opened on that memorable parting at Ephesus, when Paul had felt bound to open his heart in a last exhortation and warning. She hesitated no longer, but, opening her own door gently, went and tapped on Hetty's. We know she had to tap twice, because Hetty had to put out her candles and throw off her black lace scarf; but after the second tap the door was opened immediately. Dinah said, "Will you let me come in, Hetty?" and Hetty, without speaking, for she was confused and vexed, opened the door wider and let her in.

What a strange contrast the two figures made, visible enough in that mingled twilight and moonlight! Hetty, her cheeks flushed and her eyes glistening from her imaginary drama, her beautiful neck and arms bare, her hair hanging in a curly tangle down her back, and the baubles in her ears. Dinah, covered with her long white dress, her pale face full of subdued emotion, almost like a lovely corpse into which the soul has returned charged with sublimer secrets and a sublimer love. They were nearly of the same height; Dinah evidently a little the taller as she put her arm round Hetty's waist and kissed her forehead.

"I knew you were not in bed, my dear," she said, in her sweet clear voice, which was irritating to Hetty, mingling with her own peevish vexation like music with jangling chains, "for I heard you moving; and I longed to speak to you again to-night, for it is the last but one that I shall be here, and we don't know what may happen to-morrow to keep us apart. Shall I sit down with you while you do up your hair?"

"Oh yes," said Hetty, hastily turning round and reaching the second chair in the room, glad that Dinah looked as if she did not notice her ear-rings.

Dinah sat down, and Hetty began to brush together her hair before twisting it up, doing it with that air of excessive indifference which belongs to confused self-consciousness. But the expression of Dinah's eyes gradually relieved her; they seemed unobservant of all details.

"Dear Hetty," she said, "It has been borne in upon my mind to-night that you may some day be in trouble—trouble is appointed for us all here below, and there comes a time when we need more comfort and help than the things of this life can give. I want to tell you that if ever you are in trouble, and need a friend that will always feel for you and love you, you have got that friend in Dinah Morris at Snowfield, and if you come to her, or send for her, she'll never forget this night and the words she is speaking to you now. Will you remember it, Hetty?"

"Yes," said Hetty, rather frightened. "But why should you think I shall be in trouble? Do you know of anything?"

Hetty had seated herself as she tied on her cap, and now Dinah leaned forwards and took her hands as she answered, "Because, dear, trouble comes to us all in this life: we set our hearts on things which it isn't God's will for us to have, and then we go sorrowing; the people we love are taken from us, and we can joy in nothing because they are not with us; sickness comes, and we faint under the burden of our feeble bodies; we go astray and do wrong, and bring ourselves into trouble with our fellow-men. There is no man or woman born into this world to whom some of these trials do not fall, and so I feel that some of them must happen to you; and I desire for you, that while you are young you should seek for strength from your Heavenly Father, that you may have a support which will not fail you in the evil day."

Dinah paused and released Hetty's hands that she might not hinder her. Hetty sat quite still; she felt no response within herself to Dinah's anxious affection; but Dinah's words uttered with solemn pathetic distinctness, affected her with a chill fear. Her flush had died away almost to paleness; she had the timidity of a luxurious pleasure-seeking nature, which shrinks from the hint of pain. Dinah saw the effect, and her tender anxious pleading became the more earnest, till Hetty, full of a vague fear that something evil was some time to befall her, began to cry.

It is our habit to say that while the lower nature can never understand the higher, the higher nature commands a complete view of the lower. But I think the higher nature has to learn this comprehension, as we learn the art of vision, by a good deal of hard experience, often with bruises and gashes incurred in taking things up by the wrong end, and fancying our space wider than it is. Dinah had never seen Hetty affected in this way before, and, with her usual benignant hopefulness, she trusted it was the stirring of a divine impulse. She kissed the sobbing thing, and began to cry with her for grateful joy. But Hetty was simply in that excitable state of mind in which there is no calculating what turn the feelings may take from one moment to another, and for the first time she became irritated under Dinah's caress. She pushed her away impatiently, and said, with a childish sobbing voice, "Don't talk to me so, Dinah. Why do you come to frighten me? I've never done anything to you. Why can't you let me be?"

Poor Dinah felt a pang. She was too wise to persist, and only said mildly, "Yes, my dear, you're tired; I won't hinder you any longer. Make haste and get into bed. Good-night."

She went out of the room almost as quietly and quickly as if she had been a ghost; but once by the side of her own bed, she threw herself on her knees and poured out in deep silence all the passionate pity that filled her heart.

As for Hetty, she was soon in the wood again—her waking dreams being merged in a sleeping life scarcely more fragmentary and confused.

Chapter XVI
Links

Arthur Donnithorne, you remember, is under an engagement with himself to go and see Mr. Irwine this Friday morning, and he is awake and dressing so early that he determines to go before breakfast, instead of after. The rector, he knows, breakfasts alone at half-past nine, the ladies of the family having a different breakfast-hour; Arthur will have an early ride over the hill and breakfast with him. One can say everything best over a meal.

The progress of civilization has made a breakfast or a dinner an easy and cheerful substitute for more troublesome and disagreeable ceremonies. We take a less gloomy view of our errors now our father confessor listens to us over his egg and coffee. We are more distinctly conscious that rude penances are out of the question for gentlemen in an enlightened age, and that mortal sin is not incompatible with an appetite for muffins. An assault on our pockets, which in more barbarous times would have been made in the brusque form of a pistol-shot, is quite a well-bred and smiling procedure now it has become a request for a loan thrown in as an easy parenthesis between the second and third glasses of claret.

Still, there was this advantage in the old rigid forms, that they committed you to the fulfilment of a resolution by some outward deed: when you have put your mouth to one end of a hole in a stone wall and are aware that there is an expectant ear at the other end, you are more likely to say what you came out with the intention of saying than if you were seated with your legs in an easy attitude under the mahogany with a companion who will have no reason to be surprised if you have nothing particular to say.

However, Arthur Donnithorne, as he winds among the pleasant lanes on horseback in the morning sunshine, has a sincere determination to open his heart to the rector, and the swirling sound of the scythe as he passes by the meadow is all the pleasanter to him because of this honest purpose. He is glad to see the promise of settled weather now, for getting in the hay, about which the farmers have been fearful; and there is something so healthful in the sharing of a joy that is general and not merely personal, that this thought about the hay-harvest reacts on his state of mind and makes his resolution seem an easier matter. A man about town might perhaps consider that these influences were not to be felt out of a child's story-book; but when you are among the fields and hedgerows, it is impossible to maintain a consistent superiority to simple natural pleasures.

Arthur had passed the village of Hayslope and was approaching the Broxton side of the hill, when, at a turning in the road, he saw a figure about a hundred yards before him which it was impossible to mistake for any one else than Adam Bede, even if there had been no grey, tailless shepherd-dog at his heels. He was striding along at his usual rapid pace, and Arthur pushed on his horse to overtake him, for he retained too much of his boyish feeling for Adam to miss an opportunity of chatting with him. I will not say that his love for that good fellow did not owe some of its force to the love of patronage: our friend Arthur liked to do everything that was handsome, and to have his handsome deeds recognized.

Adam looked round as he heard the quickening clatter of the horse's heels, and waited for the horseman, lifting his paper cap from his head with a bright smile of recognition. Next to his own brother Seth, Adam would have done more for Arthur Donnithorne than for any other young man in the world. There was hardly anything he would not rather have lost than the two-feet ruler which he always carried in his pocket; it was Arthur's present, bought with his pocket-money when he was a fair-haired lad of eleven, and when he had profited so well by Adam's lessons in carpentering and turning as to embarrass every female in the house with gifts of superfluous thread-reels and round boxes. Adam had quite a pride in the little squire in those early days, and the feeling had only become slightly modified as the fair-haired lad had grown into the whiskered young man. Adam, I confess, was very susceptible to the influence of rank, and quite ready to give an extra amount of respect to every one who had more advantages than himself, not being a philosopher or a proletaire with democratic ideas, but simply a stout-limbed clever carpenter with a large fund of reverence in his nature, which inclined him to admit all established claims unless he saw very clear grounds for questioning them. He had no theories about setting the world to rights, but he saw there was a great deal of damage done by building with ill-seasoned timber—by ignorant men in fine clothes making plans for outhouses and workshops and the like without knowing the bearings of things—by slovenly joiners' work, and by hasty contracts that could never be fulfilled without ruining somebody; and he resolved, for his part, to set his face against such doings. On these points he would have maintained his opinion against the largest landed proprietor in Loamshire or Stonyshire either; but he felt that beyond these it would be better for him to defer to people who were more knowing than himself. He saw as plainly as possible how ill the woods on the estate were managed, and the shameful state of the farm-buildings; and if old Squire Donnithorne had asked him the effect of this mismanagement, he would have spoken his opinion without flinching, but the impulse to a respectful demeanour towards a "gentleman" would have been strong within him all the while. The word "gentleman" had a spell for Adam, and, as he often said, he "couldn't abide a fellow who thought he made himself fine by being coxy to's betters." I must remind you again that Adam had the blood of the peasant in his veins, and that since he was in his prime half a century ago, you must expect some of his characteristics to be obsolete.

Towards the young squire this instinctive reverence of Adam's was assisted by boyish memories and personal regard so you may imagine that he thought far more of Arthur's good qualities, and attached far more value to very slight actions of his, than if they had been the qualities and actions of a common workman like himself. He felt sure it would be a fine day for everybody about Hayslope when the young squire came into the estate—such a generous open-hearted disposition as he had, and an "uncommon" notion about improvements and repairs, considering he was only just coming of age. Thus there was both respect and affection in the smile with which he raised his paper cap as Arthur Donnithorne rode up.

"Well, Adam, how are you?" said Arthur, holding out his hand. He never shook hands with any of the farmers, and Adam felt the honour keenly. "I could swear to your back a long way off. It's just the same back, only broader, as when you used to carry me on it. Do you remember?"

"Aye, sir, I remember. It 'ud be a poor look-out if folks didn't remember what they did and said when they were lads. We should think no more about old friends than we do about new uns, then."

"You're going to Broxton, I suppose?" said Arthur, putting his horse on at a slow pace while Adam walked by his side. "Are you going to the rectory?"

"No, sir, I'm going to see about Bradwell's barn. They're afraid of the roof pushing the walls out, and I'm going to see what can be done with it before we send the stuff and the workmen."

"Why, Burge trusts almost everything to you now, Adam, doesn't he? I should think he will make you his partner soon. He will, if he's wise."

"Nay, sir, I don't see as he'd be much the better off for that. A foreman, if he's got a conscience and delights in his work, will do his business as well as if he was a partner. I wouldn't give a penny for a man as 'ud drive a nail in slack because he didn't get extra pay for it."

"I know that, Adam; I know you work for him as well as if you were working for yourself. But you would have more power than you have now, and could turn the business to better account perhaps. The old man must give up his business sometime, and he has no son; I suppose he'll want a son-in-law who can take to it. But he has rather grasping fingers of his own, I fancy. I daresay he wants a man who can put some money into the business. If I were not as poor as a rat, I would gladly invest some money in that way, for the sake of having you settled on the estate. I'm sure I should profit by it in the end. And perhaps I shall be better off in a year or two. I shall have a larger allowance now I'm of age; and when I've paid off a debt or two, I shall be able to look about me."

"You're very good to say so, sir, and I'm not unthankful. But"—Adam continued, in a decided tone—"I shouldn't like to make any offers to Mr. Burge, or t' have any made for me. I see no clear road to a partnership. If he should ever want to dispose of the business, that 'ud be a different matter. I should be glad of some money at a fair interest then, for I feel sure I could pay it off in time."

"Very well, Adam," said Arthur, remembering what Mr. Irwine had said about a probable hitch in the love-making between Adam and Mary Burge, "we'll say no more about it at present. When is your father to be buried?"

"On Sunday, sir; Mr. Irwine's coming earlier on purpose. I shall be glad when it's over, for I think my mother 'ull perhaps get easier then. It cuts one sadly to see the grief of old people; they've no way o' working it off, and the new spring brings no new shoots out on the withered tree."

"Ah, you've had a good deal of trouble and vexation in your life, Adam. I don't think you've ever been hare-brained and light-hearted, like other youngsters. You've always had some care on your mind."

"Why, yes, sir; but that's nothing to make a fuss about. If we're men and have men's feelings, I reckon we must have men's troubles. We can't be like the birds, as fly from their nest as soon as they've got their wings, and never know their kin when they see 'em, and get a fresh lot every year. I've had enough to be thankful for: I've allays had health and strength and brains to give me a delight in my work; and I count it a great thing as I've had Bartle Massey's night-school to go to. He's helped me to knowledge I could never ha' got by myself."

"What a rare fellow you are, Adam!" said Arthur, after a pause, in which he had looked musingly at the big fellow walking by his side. "I could hit out better than most men at Oxford, and yet I believe you would knock me into next week if I were to have a battle with you."

"God forbid I should ever do that, sir," said Adam, looking round at Arthur and smiling. "I used to fight for fun, but I've never done that since I was the cause o' poor Gil Tranter being laid up for a fortnight. I'll never fight any man again, only when he behaves like a scoundrel. If you get hold of a chap that's got no shame nor conscience to stop him, you must try what you can do by bunging his eyes up."

Arthur did not laugh, for he was preoccupied with some thought that made him say presently, "I should think now, Adam, you never have any struggles within yourself. I fancy you would master a wish that you had made up your mind it was not quite right to indulge, as easily as you would knock down a drunken fellow who was quarrelsome with you. I mean, you are never shilly-shally, first making up your mind that you won't do a thing, and then doing it after all?"

"Well," said Adam, slowly, after a moment's hesitation, "no. I don't remember ever being see-saw in that way, when I'd made my mind up, as you say, that a thing was wrong. It takes the taste out o' my mouth for things, when I know I should have a heavy conscience after 'em. I've seen pretty clear, ever since I could cast up a sum, as you can never do what's wrong without breeding sin and trouble more than you can ever see. It's like a bit o' bad workmanship—you never see th' end o' the mischief it'll do. And it's a poor look-out to come into the world to make your fellow-creatures worse off instead o' better. But there's a difference between the things folks call wrong. I'm not for making a sin of every little fool's trick, or bit o' nonsense anybody may be let into, like some o' them dissenters. And a man may have two minds whether it isn't worthwhile to get a bruise or two for the sake of a bit o' fun. But it isn't my way to be see-saw about anything: I think my fault lies th' other way. When I've said a thing, if it's only to myself, it's hard for me to go back."

"Yes, that's just what I expected of you," said Arthur. "You've got an iron will, as well as an iron arm. But however strong a man's resolution may be, it costs him something to carry it out, now and then. We may determine not to gather any cherries and keep our hands sturdily in our pockets, but we can't prevent our mouths from watering."

"That's true, sir, but there's nothing like settling with ourselves as there's a deal we must do without i' this life. It's no use looking on life as if it was Treddles'on Fair, where folks only go to see shows and get fairings. If we do, we shall find it different. But where's the use o' me talking to you, sir? You know better than I do."

"I'm not so sure of that, Adam. You've had four or five years of experience more than I've had, and I think your life has been a better school to you than college has been to me."

"Why, sir, you seem to think o' college something like what Bartle Massey does. He says college mostly makes people like bladders—just good for nothing but t' hold the stuff as is poured into 'em. But he's got a tongue like a sharp blade, Bartle has—it never touches anything but it cuts. Here's the turning, sir. I must bid you good-morning, as you're going to the rectory."

"Good-bye, Adam, good-bye."

Arthur gave his horse to the groom at the rectory gate, and walked along the gravel towards the door which opened on the garden. He knew that the rector always breakfasted in his study, and the study lay on the left hand of this door, opposite the dining-room. It was a small low room, belonging to the old part of the house—dark with the sombre covers of the books that lined the walls; yet it looked very cheery this morning as Arthur reached the open window. For the morning sun fell aslant on the great glass globe with gold fish in it, which stood on a scagliola pillar in front of the ready-spread bachelor breakfast-table, and by the side of this breakfast-table was a group which would have made any room enticing. In the crimson damask easy-chair sat Mr. Irwine, with that radiant freshness which he always had when he came from his morning toilet; his finely formed plump white hand was playing along Juno's brown curly back; and close to Juno's tail, which was wagging with calm matronly pleasure, the two brown pups were rolling over each other in an ecstatic duet of worrying noises. On a cushion a little removed sat Pug, with the air of a maiden lady, who looked on these familiarities as animal weaknesses, which she made as little show as possible of observing. On the table, at Mr. Irwine's elbow, lay the first volume of the Foulis Æschylus, which Arthur knew well by sight; and the silver coffee-pot, which Carroll was bringing in, sent forth a fragrant steam which completed the delights of a bachelor breakfast.

"Hallo, Arthur, that's a good fellow! You're just in time," said Mr. Irwine, as Arthur paused and stepped in over the low window-sill. "Carroll, we shall want more coffee and eggs, and haven't you got some cold fowl for us to eat with that ham? Why, this is like old days, Arthur; you haven't been to breakfast with me these five years."

"It was a tempting morning for a ride before breakfast," said Arthur; "and I used to like breakfasting with you so when I was reading with you. My grandfather is always a few degrees colder at breakfast than at any other hour in the day. I think his morning bath doesn't agree with him."

Arthur was anxious not to imply that he came with any special purpose. He had no sooner found himself in Mr. Irwine's presence than the confidence which he had thought quite easy before, suddenly appeared the most difficult thing in the world to him, and at the very moment of shaking hands he saw his purpose in quite a new light. How could he make Irwine understand his position unless he told him those little scenes in the wood; and how could he tell them without looking like a fool? And then his weakness in coming back from Gawaine's, and doing the very opposite of what he intended! Irwine would think him a shilly-shally fellow ever after. However, it must come out in an unpremeditated way; the conversation might lead up to it.

"I like breakfast-time better than any other moment in the day," said Mr. Irwine. "No dust has settled on one's mind then, and it presents a clear mirror to the rays of things. I always have a favourite book by me at breakfast, and I enjoy the bits I pick up then so much, that regularly every morning it seems to me as if I should certainly become studious again. But presently Dent brings up a poor fellow who has killed a hare, and when I've got through my 'justicing,' as Carroll calls it, I'm inclined for a ride round the glebe, and on my way back I meet with the master of the workhouse, who has got a long story of a mutinous pauper to tell me; and so the day goes on, and I'm always the same lazy fellow before evening sets in. Besides, one wants the stimulus of sympathy, and I have never had that since poor D'Oyley left Treddleston. If you had stuck to your books well, you rascal, I should have had a pleasanter prospect before me. But scholarship doesn't run in your family blood."

"No indeed. It's well if I can remember a little inapplicable Latin to adorn my maiden speech in Parliament six or seven years hence. 'Cras ingens iterabimus aequor,' and a few shreds of that sort, will perhaps stick to me, and I shall arrange my opinions so as to introduce them. But I don't think a knowledge of the classics is a pressing want to a country gentleman; as far as I can see, he'd much better have a knowledge of manures. I've been reading your friend Arthur Young's books lately, and there's nothing I should like better than to carry out some of his ideas in putting the farmers on a better management of their land; and, as he says, making what was a wild country, all of the same dark hue, bright and variegated with corn and cattle. My grandfather will never let me have any power while he lives, but there's nothing I should like better than to undertake the Stonyshire side of the estate—it's in a dismal condition—and set improvements on foot, and gallop about from one place to another and overlook them. I should like to know all the labourers, and see them touching their hats to me with a look of goodwill."

"Bravo, Arthur! A man who has no feeling for the classics couldn't make a better apology for coming into the world than by increasing the quantity of food to maintain scholars—and rectors who appreciate scholars. And whenever you enter on your career of model landlord may I be there to see. You'll want a portly rector to complete the picture, and take his tithe of all the respect and honour you get by your hard work. Only don't set your heart too strongly on the goodwill you are to get in consequence. I'm not sure that men are the fondest of those who try to be useful to them. You know Gawaine has got the curses of the whole neighbourhood upon him about that enclosure. You must make it quite clear to your mind which you are most bent upon, old boy—popularity or usefulness—else you may happen to miss both."

"Oh! Gawaine is harsh in his manners; he doesn't make himself personally agreeable to his tenants. I don't believe there's anything you can't prevail on people to do with kindness. For my part, I couldn't live in a neighbourhood where I was not respected and beloved. And it's very pleasant to go among the tenants here—they seem all so well inclined to me I suppose it seems only the other day to them since I was a little lad, riding on a pony about as big as a sheep. And if fair allowances were made to them, and their buildings attended to, one could persuade them to farm on a better plan, stupid as they are."

"Then mind you fall in love in the right place, and don't get a wife who will drain your purse and make you niggardly in spite of yourself. My mother and I have a little discussion about you sometimes: she says, 'I'll never risk a single prophecy on Arthur until I see the woman he falls in love with.' She thinks your lady-love will rule you as the moon rules the tides. But I feel bound to stand up for you, as my pupil you know, and I maintain that you're not of that watery quality. So mind you don't disgrace my judgment."

Arthur winced under this speech, for keen old Mrs. Irwine's opinion about him had the disagreeable effect of a sinister omen. This, to be sure, was only another reason for persevering in his intention, and getting an additional security against himself. Nevertheless, at this point in the conversation, he was conscious of increased disinclination to tell his story about Hetty. He was of an impressible nature, and lived a great deal in other people's opinions and feelings concerning himself; and the mere fact that he was in the presence of an intimate friend, who had not the slightest notion that he had had any such serious internal struggle as he came to confide, rather shook his own belief in the seriousness of the struggle. It was not, after all, a thing to make a fuss about; and what could Irwine do for him that he could not do for himself? He would go to Eagledale in spite of Meg's lameness—go on Rattler, and let Pym follow as well as he could on the old hack. That was his thought as he sugared his coffee; but the next minute, as he was lifting the cup to his lips, he remembered how thoroughly he had made up his mind last night to tell Irwine. No! He would not be vacillating again—he *would* do what he had meant to do, this time. So it would be well not to let the personal tone of the conversation altogether drop. If they went to quite indifferent topics, his difficulty would be heightened. It had required no noticeable pause for this rush and rebound of feeling, before he answered, "But I think it is hardly an argument against a man's general strength of character that he should be apt to be mastered by love. A fine constitution doesn't insure one against smallpox or any other of those inevitable diseases. A man may be very firm in other matters and yet be under a sort of witchery from a woman."

"Yes; but there's this difference between love and smallpox, or bewitchment either—that if you detect the disease at an early stage and try change of air, there is every chance of complete escape without any further development of symptoms. And there are certain alternative doses which a man may administer to himself by keeping unpleasant consequences before his mind: this gives you a sort of smoked glass through which you may look at the resplendent fair one and discern her true outline; though I'm afraid, by the by, the smoked glass is apt to be missing just at the moment it is most wanted. I daresay, now, even a man fortified with a knowledge of the classics might be lured into an imprudent marriage, in spite of the warning given him by the chorus in the Prometheus."

The smile that flitted across Arthur's face was a faint one, and instead of following Mr. Irwine's playful lead, he said, quite seriously—"Yes, that's the worst of it. It's a desperately vexatious thing, that after all one's reflections and quiet determinations, we should be ruled by moods that one can't calculate on beforehand. I don't think a man ought to be blamed so much if he is betrayed into doing things in that way, in spite of his resolutions."

"Ah, but the moods lie in his nature, my boy, just as much as his reflections did, and more. A man can never do anything at variance with his own nature. He carries within him the germ of his most exceptional action; and if we wise people make eminent fools of ourselves on any particular occasion, we must endure the legitimate conclusion that we carry a few grains of folly to our ounce of wisdom."

"Well, but one may be betrayed into doing things by a combination of circumstances, which one might never have done otherwise."

"Why, yes, a man can't very well steal a bank-note unless the bank-note lies within convenient reach; but he won't make us think him an honest man because he begins to howl at the bank-note for falling in his way."

"But surely you don't think a man who struggles against a temptation into which he falls at last as bad as the man who never struggles at all?"

"No, certainly; I pity him in proportion to his struggles, for they foreshadow the inward suffering which is the worst form of Nemesis. Consequences are unpitying. Our deeds carry their terrible consequences, quite apart from any fluctuations that went before—consequences that are hardly ever confined to ourselves. And it is best to fix our minds on that certainty, instead of considering what may be the elements of excuse for us. But I never knew you so inclined for moral discussion, Arthur? Is it some danger of your own that you are considering in this philosophical, general way?"

In asking this question, Mr. Irwine pushed his plate away, threw himself back in his chair, and looked straight at Arthur. He really suspected that Arthur wanted to tell him something, and thought of smoothing the way for him by this direct question. But he was mistaken. Brought suddenly and involuntarily to the brink of confession, Arthur shrank back and felt less disposed towards it than ever. The conversation had taken a more serious tone than he had intended—it would quite mislead Irwine—he would imagine there was a deep passion for Hetty, while there was no such thing. He was conscious of colouring, and was annoyed at his boyishness.

"Oh no, no danger," he said as indifferently as he could. "I don't know that I am more liable to irresolution than other people; only there are little incidents now and then that set one speculating on what might happen in the future."

Was there a motive at work under this strange reluctance of Arthur's which had a sort of backstairs influence, not admitted to himself? Our mental business is carried on much in the same way as the business of the State: a great deal of hard work is done by agents who are not acknowledged. In a piece of machinery, too, I believe there is often a small unnoticeable wheel which has a great deal to do with the motion of the large obvious ones. Possibly there was some such unrecognized agent secretly busy in Arthur's mind at this moment—possibly it was the fear lest he might hereafter find the fact of having made a confession to the rector a serious annoyance, in case he should *not* be able quite to carry out his good resolutions? I dare not assert that it was not so. The human soul is a very complex thing.

The idea of Hetty had just crossed Mr. Irwine's mind as he looked inquiringly at Arthur, but his disclaiming indifferent answer confirmed the thought which had quickly followed—that there could be nothing serious in that direction. There was no probability that Arthur ever saw her except at church, and at her own home under the eye of Mrs. Poyser; and the hint he had given Arthur about her the other day had no more serious meaning than to prevent him from noticing her so as to rouse the little chit's vanity, and in this way perturb the rustic drama of her life. Arthur would soon join his regiment, and be far away: no, there could be no danger in that quarter, even if Arthur's character had not been a strong security against it. His honest, patronizing pride in the good-will and respect of everybody about him was a safeguard even against foolish romance, still more against a lower kind of folly. If there had been anything special on Arthur's mind in the previous conversation, it was clear he was not inclined to enter into details, and Mr. Irwine was too delicate to imply even a friendly curiosity. He perceived a change of subject would be welcome, and said, "By the way, Arthur, at your colonel's birthday fête there were some transparencies that made a great effect in honour of Britannia, and Pitt, and the Loamshire Militia, and, above all, the 'generous youth,' the hero of the day. Don't you think you should get up something of the same sort to astonish our weak minds?"

The opportunity was gone. While Arthur was hesitating, the rope to which he might have clung had drifted away—he must trust now to his own swimming.

In ten minutes from that time, Mr. Irwine was called for on business, and Arthur, bidding him good-bye, mounted his horse again with a sense of dissatisfaction, which he tried to quell by determining to set off for Eagledale without an hour's delay.

BOOK SECOND

Chapter XVII
In Which the Story Pauses a Little

"This Rector of Broxton is little better than a pagan!" I hear one of my readers exclaim. "How much more edifying it would have been if you had made him give Arthur some truly spiritual advice! You might have put into his mouth the most beautiful things—quite as good as reading a sermon."

Certainly I could, if I held it the highest vocation of the novelist to represent things as they never have been and never will be. Then, of course, I might refashion life and character entirely after my own liking; I might select the most unexceptionable type of clergyman and put my own admirable opinions into his mouth on all occasions. But it happens, on the contrary, that my strongest effort is to avoid any such arbitrary picture, and to give a faithful account of men and things as they have mirrored themselves in my mind. The mirror is doubtless defective, the outlines will sometimes be disturbed, the reflection faint or confused; but I feel as much bound to tell you as precisely as I can what that reflection is, as if I were in the witness-box, narrating my experience on oath.

Sixty years ago—it is a long time, so no wonder things have changed—all clergymen were not zealous; indeed, there is reason to believe that the number of zealous clergymen was small, and it is probable that if one among the small minority had owned the livings of Broxton and Hayslope in the year 1799, you would have liked him no better than you like Mr. Irwine. Ten to one, you would have thought him a tasteless, indiscreet, methodistical man. It is so very rarely that facts hit that nice medium required by our own enlightened opinions and refined taste! Perhaps you will say, "Do improve the facts a little, then; make them more accordant with those correct views which it is our privilege to possess. The world is not just what we like; do touch it up with a tasteful pencil, and make believe it is not quite such a mixed entangled affair. Let all people who hold unexceptionable opinions act unexceptionably. Let your most faulty characters always be on the wrong side, and your virtuous ones on the right. Then we shall see at a glance whom we are to condemn and whom we are to approve. Then we shall be able to admire, without the slightest disturbance of our prepossessions: we shall hate and despise with that true ruminant relish which belongs to undoubting confidence."

But, my good friend, what will you do then with your fellow-parishioner who opposes your husband in the vestry? With your newly appointed vicar, whose style of preaching you find painfully below that of his regretted predecessor? With the honest servant who worries your soul with her one failing? With your neighbour, Mrs. Green, who was really kind to you in your last illness, but has said several ill-natured things about you since your convalescence? Nay, with your excellent husband himself, who has other irritating habits besides that of not wiping his shoes? These fellow-mortals, every one, must be accepted as they are: you can neither straighten their noses, nor brighten their wit, nor rectify their dispositions; and it is these people—amongst whom your life is passed—that it is needful you should tolerate, pity, and love: it is these more or less ugly, stupid, inconsistent people whose movements of goodness you should be able to admire—for whom you should cherish all possible hopes, all possible patience. And I would not, even if I had the choice, be the clever novelist who could create a world so much better than this, in which we get up in the morning to do our daily work, that you would be likely to turn a harder, colder eye on the dusty streets and the common green fields—on the real breathing men and women, who can be chilled by your indifference or injured by your prejudice; who can be cheered and helped onward by your fellow-feeling, your forbearance, your outspoken, brave justice.

So I am content to tell my simple story, without trying to make things seem better than they were; dreading nothing, indeed, but falsity, which, in spite of one's best efforts, there is reason to dread. Falsehood is so easy, truth so difficult. The pencil is conscious of a delightful facility in drawing a griffin—the longer the claws, and the larger the wings, the better; but that marvellous facility which we mistook for genius is apt to forsake us when we want to draw a real unexaggerated lion. Examine your words well, and you will find that even when you have no motive to be false, it is a very hard thing to say the exact truth, even about your own immediate feelings—much harder than to say something fine about them which is *not* the exact truth.

It is for this rare, precious quality of truthfulness that I delight in many Dutch paintings, which lofty-minded people despise. I find a source of delicious sympathy in these faithful pictures of a monotonous homely existence, which has been the fate of so many more among my fellow-mortals than a life of pomp or of absolute indigence, of tragic suffering or of world-stirring actions. I turn, without shrinking, from cloud-borne angels, from prophets, sibyls, and heroic warriors, to an old woman bending over her flower-pot, or eating her solitary dinner, while the noonday light, softened perhaps by a screen of leaves, falls on her mob-cap, and just touches the rim of her spinning-wheel, and her stone jug, and all those cheap common things which are the precious necessaries of life to her—or I turn to that village wedding, kept between four brown walls, where an awkward bridegroom opens the dance with a high-shouldered, broad-faced bride, while elderly and middle-aged friends look on, with very irregular noses and lips, and probably with quart-pots in their hands, but with an expression of unmistakable contentment and goodwill. “Foh!” says my idealistic friend, “what vulgar details! What good is there in taking all these pains to give an exact likeness of old women and clowns? What a low phase of life! What clumsy, ugly people!”

But bless us, things may be lovable that are not altogether handsome, I hope? I am not at all sure that the majority of the human race have not been ugly, and even among those “lords of their kind,” the British, squat figures, ill-shapen nostrils, and dingy complexions are not startling exceptions. Yet there is a great deal of family love amongst us. I have a friend or two whose class of features is such that the Apollo curl on the summit of their brows would be decidedly trying; yet to my certain knowledge tender hearts have beaten for them, and their miniatures—flattering, but still not lovely—are kissed in secret by motherly lips. I have seen many an excellent matron, who could have never in her best days have been handsome, and yet she had a packet of yellow love-letters in a private drawer, and sweet children showered kisses on her sallow cheeks. And I believe there have been plenty of young heroes, of middle stature and feeble beards, who have felt quite sure they could never love anything more insignificant than a Diana, and yet have found themselves in middle life happily settled with a wife who waddles. Yes! Thank God; human feeling is like the mighty rivers that bless the earth: it does not wait for beauty—it flows with resistless force and brings beauty with it.

All honour and reverence to the divine beauty of form! Let us cultivate it to the utmost in men, women, and children—in our gardens and in our houses. But let us love that other beauty too, which lies in no secret of proportion, but in the secret of deep human sympathy. Paint us an angel, if you can, with a floating violet robe, and a face paled by the celestial light; paint us yet oftener a Madonna, turning her mild face upward and opening her arms to welcome the divine glory; but do not impose on us any aesthetic rules which shall banish from the region of Art those old women scraping carrots with their work-worn hands, those heavy clowns taking holiday in a dingy pot-house, those rounded backs and stupid weather-beaten faces that have bent over the spade and done the rough work of the world—those homes with their tin pans, their brown pitchers, their rough curs, and their clusters of onions. In this world there are so many of these common coarse people, who have no picturesque sentimental wretchedness! It is so needful we should remember their existence, else we may happen to leave them quite out of our religion and philosophy and frame lofty theories which only fit a world of extremes. Therefore, let Art always remind us of them; therefore let us always have men ready to give the loving pains of a life to the faithful representing of commonplace things—men who see beauty in these commonplace things, and delight in showing how kindly the light of heaven falls on them. There are few prophets in the world; few sublimely beautiful women; few heroes. I can't afford to give all my love and reverence to such rarities: I want a great deal of those feelings for my every-day fellow-men, especially for the few in the foreground of the great multitude, whose faces I know, whose hands I touch, for whom I have to make way with kindly courtesy. Neither are picturesque lazzaroni or romantic criminals half so frequent as your common labourer, who gets his own bread and eats it vulgarly but creditably with his own pocket-knife. It is more needful that I should have a fibre of sympathy connecting me with that vulgar citizen who weighs out my sugar in a vilely assorted cravat and waistcoat, than with the handsomest rascal in red scarf and green feathers—more needful that my heart should swell with loving admiration at some trait of gentle goodness in the faulty people who sit at the same hearth with me, or in the clergyman of my own parish, who is perhaps rather too corpulent and in other respects is not an Oberlin or a Tillotson, than at the deeds of heroes whom I shall never know except by hearsay, or at the sublimest abstract of all clerical graces that was ever conceived by an able novelist.

And so I come back to Mr. Irwine, with whom I desire you to be in perfect charity, far as he may be from satisfying your demands on the clerical character. Perhaps you think he was not—as he ought to have been—a living demonstration of the benefits attached to a national church? But I am not sure of that; at least I know that the people in Broxton and Hayslope would have been very sorry to part with their clergyman, and that most faces brightened at his approach; and until it can be proved that hatred is a better thing for the soul than love, I must believe that Mr. Irwine's influence in his parish was a more wholesome one than that of the zealous Mr. Ryde, who came there twenty years afterwards, when Mr. Irwine had been gathered to his fathers. It is true, Mr. Ryde insisted strongly on the doctrines of the Reformation, visited his flock a great deal in their own homes, and was severe in rebuking the aberrations of the flesh—put a stop, indeed, to the Christmas rounds of the church singers, as promoting drunkenness and too light a handling of sacred things. But I gathered from Adam Bede, to whom I talked of these matters in his old age, that few clergymen could be less successful in winning the hearts of their parishioners than Mr. Ryde. They learned a great many notions about doctrine from him, so that almost every church-goer under fifty began to distinguish as well between the genuine gospel and what did not come precisely up to that standard, as if he had been born and bred a Dissenter; and for some time after his arrival there seemed to be quite a religious movement in that quiet rural district. "But," said Adam, "I've seen pretty clear, ever since I was a young un, as religion's something else besides notions. It isn't notions sets people doing the right thing—it's feelings. It's the same with the notions in religion as it is with math'matics—a man may be able to work problems straight off in's head as he sits by the fire and smokes his pipe, but if he has to make a machine or a building, he must have a will and a resolution and love something else better than his own ease. Somehow, the congregation began to fall off, and people began to speak light o' Mr. Ryde. I believe he meant right at bottom; but, you see, he was sourish-tempered, and was for beating down prices with the people as worked for him; and his preaching wouldn't go down well with that sauce. And he wanted to be like my lord judge i' the parish, punishing folks for doing wrong; and he scolded 'em from the pulpit as if he'd been a Ranter, and yet he couldn't abide the Dissenters, and was a deal more set against 'em than Mr. Irwine was. And then he didn't keep within his income, for he seemed to think at first go-off that six hundred a-year was to make him as big a man as Mr. Donnithorne. That's a sore mischief I've often seen with the poor curates jumping into a bit of a living all of a sudden. Mr. Ryde was a deal thought on at a distance, I believe, and he wrote books, but as for math'matics and the natur o' things, he was as ignorant as a woman. He was very knowing about doctrines, and used to call 'em the bulwarks of the Reformation; but I've always mistrusted that sort o' learning as leaves folks foolish and unreasonable about business. Now Mester Irwine was as different as could be: as quick!—he understood what you meant in a minute, and he knew all about building, and could see when you'd made a good job. And he behaved as much like a gentleman to the farmers, and th' old women, and the labourers, as he did to the gentry. You never saw *him* interfering and scolding, and trying to play th' emperor. Ah, he was a fine man as ever you set eyes on; and so kind to's mother and sisters. That poor sickly Miss Anne—he seemed to think more of her than of anybody else in the world. There wasn't a soul in the parish had a word to say against him; and his servants stayed with him till they were so old and pottering, he had to hire other folks to do their work."

"Well," I said, "that was an excellent way of preaching in the weekdays; but I daresay, if your old friend Mr. Irwine were to come to life again, and get into the pulpit next Sunday, you would be rather ashamed that he didn't preach better after all your praise of him."

"Nay, nay," said Adam, broadening his chest and throwing himself back in his chair, as if he were ready to meet all inferences, "nobody has ever heard me say Mr. Irwine was much of a preacher. He didn't go into deep speritial experience; and I know there s a deal in a man's inward life as you can't measure by the square, and say, 'Do this and that 'll follow,' and, 'Do that and this 'll follow.' There's things go on in the soul, and times when feelings come into you like a rushing mighty wind, as the Scripture says, and part your life in two a'most, so you look back on yourself as if you was somebody else. Those are things as you can't bottle up in a 'do this' and 'do that'; and I'll go so far with the strongest Methodist ever you'll find. That shows me there's deep speritial things in religion. You can't make much out wi' talking about it, but you feel it. Mr. Irwine didn't go into those things—he preached short moral sermons, and that was all.

But then he acted pretty much up to what he said; he didn't set up for being so different from other folks one day, and then be as like 'em as two peas the next. And he made folks love him and respect him, and that was better nor stirring up their gall wi' being overbusy. Mrs. Poyser used to say—you know she would have her word about everything—she said, Mr. Irwine was like a good meal o' victual, you were the better for him without thinking on it, and Mr. Ryde was like a dose o' physic, he gripped you and worreted you, and after all he left you much the same."

"But didn't Mr. Ryde preach a great deal more about that spiritual part of religion that you talk of, Adam? Couldn't you get more out of his sermons than out of Mr. Irwine's?"

"Eh, I knowna. He preached a deal about doctrines. But I've seen pretty clear, ever since I was a young un, as religion's something else besides doctrines and notions. I look at it as if the doctrines was like finding names for your feelings, so as you can talk of 'em when you've never known 'em, just as a man may talk o' tools when he knows their names, though he's never so much as seen 'em, still less handled 'em. I've heard a deal o' doctrine i' my time, for I used to go after the Dissenting preachers along wi' Seth, when I was a lad o' seventeen, and got puzzling myself a deal about th' Arminians and the Calvinists. The Wesleyans, you know, are strong Arminians; and Seth, who could never abide anything harsh and was always for hoping the best, held fast by the Wesleyans from the very first; but I thought I could pick a hole or two in their notions, and I got disputing wi' one o' the class leaders down at Treddles'on, and harassed him so, first o' this side and then o' that, till at last he said, 'Young man, it's the devil making use o' your pride and conceit as a weapon to war against the simplicity o' the truth.' I couldn't help laughing then, but as I was going home, I thought the man wasn't far wrong. I began to see as all this weighing and sifting what this text means and that text means, and whether folks are saved all by God's grace, or whether there goes an ounce o' their own will to't, was no part o' real religion at all. You may talk o' these things for hours on end, and you'll only be all the more coxy and conceited for't. So I took to going nowhere but to church, and hearing nobody but Mr. Irwine, for he said nothing but what was good and what you'd be the wiser for remembering. And I found it better for my soul to be humble before the mysteries o' God's dealings, and not be making a clatter about what I could never understand. And they're poor foolish questions after all; for what have we got either inside or outside of us but what comes from God? If we've got a resolution to do right, He gave it us, I reckon, first or last; but I see plain enough we shall never do it without a resolution, and that's enough for me."

Adam, you perceive, was a warm admirer, perhaps a partial judge, of Mr. Irwine, as, happily, some of us still are of the people we have known familiarly.

Doubtless it will be despised as a weakness by that lofty order of minds who pant after the ideal, and are oppressed by a general sense that their emotions are of too exquisite a character to find fit objects among their everyday fellowmen. I have often been favoured with the confidence of these select natures, and find them to concur in the experience that great men are overestimated and small men are insupportable; that if you would love a woman without ever looking back on your love as a folly, she must die while you are courting her; and if you would maintain the slightest belief in human heroism, you must never make a pilgrimage to see the hero. I confess I have often meanly shrunk from confessing to these accomplished and acute gentlemen what my own experience has been. I am afraid I have often smiled with hypocritical assent, and gratified them with an epigram on the fleeting nature of our illusions, which any one moderately acquainted with French literature can command at a moment's notice. Human converse, I think some wise man has remarked, is not rigidly sincere. But I herewith discharge my conscience, and declare that I have had quite enthusiastic movements of admiration towards old gentlemen who spoke the worst English, who were occasionally fretful in their temper, and who had never moved in a higher sphere of influence than that of parish overseer; and that the way in which I have come to the conclusion that human nature is lovable—the way I have learnt something of its deep pathos, its sublime mysteries—has been by living a great deal among people more or less commonplace and vulgar, of whom you would perhaps hear nothing very surprising if you were to inquire about them in the neighbourhoods where they dwelt. Ten to one most of the small shopkeepers in their vicinity saw nothing at all in them. For I have observed this remarkable coincidence, that the select natures who pant after the ideal, and find nothing in pantaloons or petticoats great enough to command their reverence and love, are curiously in unison with the narrowest and pettiest. For example, I have often heard Mr. Gedge, the landlord of the Royal Oak, who used to turn a bloodshot eye on his neighbours in the village of Shepperton, sum up his opinion of the people in his own parish—and they were all the people he knew—in these emphatic words: "Aye, sir, I've said it often, and I'll say it again, they're a poor lot i' this parish—a poor lot, sir, big and little." I think he had a dim idea that if he could migrate to a distant parish, he might find neighbours worthy of him; and indeed he did subsequently transfer himself to the Saracen's Head, which was doing a thriving business in the back street of a neighbouring market-town. But, oddly enough, he has found the people up that back street of precisely the same stamp as the inhabitants of Shepperton—"a poor lot, sir, big and little, and them as comes for a go o' gin are no better than them as comes for a pint o' twopenny—a poor lot."

Chapter XVIII
Church

"Hetty, Hetty, don't you know church begins at two, and it's gone half after one a'ready? Have you got nothing better to think on this good Sunday as poor old Thias Bede's to be put into the ground, and him drownded i' th' dead o' the night, as it's enough to make one's back run cold, but you must be 'dizening yourself as if there was a wedding i'stid of a funeral?"

"Well, Aunt," said Hetty, "I can't be ready so soon as everybody else, when I've got Totty's things to put on. And I'd ever such work to make her stand still."

Hetty was coming downstairs, and Mrs. Poyser, in her plain bonnet and shawl, was standing below. If ever a girl looked as if she had been made of roses, that girl was Hetty in her Sunday hat and frock. For her hat was trimmed with pink, and her frock had pink spots, sprinkled on a white ground. There was nothing but pink and white about her, except in her dark hair and eyes and her little buckled shoes. Mrs. Poyser was provoked at herself, for she could hardly keep from smiling, as any mortal is inclined to do at the sight of pretty round things. So she turned without speaking, and joined the group outside the house door, followed by Hetty, whose heart was fluttering so at the thought of some one she expected to see at church that she hardly felt the ground she trod on.

And now the little procession set off. Mr. Poyser was in his Sunday suit of drab, with a red-and-green waistcoat and a green watch-ribbon having a large cornelian seal attached, pendant like a plumb-line from that promontory where his watch-pocket was situated; a silk handkerchief of a yellow tone round his neck; and excellent grey ribbed stockings, knitted by Mrs. Poyser's own hand, setting off the proportions of his leg. Mr. Poyser had no reason to be ashamed of his leg, and suspected that the growing abuse of top-boots and other fashions tending to disguise the nether limbs had their origin in a pitiable degeneracy of the human calf. Still less had he reason to be ashamed of his round jolly face, which was good humour itself as he said, "Come, Hetty—come, little uns!" and giving his arm to his wife, led the way through the causeway gate into the yard.

The "little uns" addressed were Marty and Tommy, boys of nine and seven, in little fustian tailed coats and knee-breeches, relieved by rosy cheeks and black eyes, looking as much like their father as a very small elephant is like a very large one. Hetty walked between them, and behind came patient Molly, whose task it was to carry Totty through the yard and over all the wet places on the road; for Totty, having speedily recovered from her threatened fever, had insisted on going to church to-day, and especially on wearing her red-and-black necklace outside her tippet. And there were many wet places for her to be carried over this afternoon, for there had been heavy showers in the morning, though now the clouds had rolled off and lay in towering silvery masses on the horizon.

You might have known it was Sunday if you had only waked up in the farmyard. The cocks and hens seemed to know it, and made only crooning subdued noises; the very bull-dog looked less savage, as if he would have been satisfied with a smaller bite than usual. The sunshine seemed to call all things to rest and not to labour. It was asleep itself on the moss-grown cow-shed; on the group of white ducks nestling together with their bills tucked under their wings; on the old black sow stretched languidly on the straw, while her largest young one found an excellent spring-bed on his mother's fat ribs; on Alick, the shepherd, in his new smock-frock, taking an uneasy siesta, half-sitting, half-standing on the granary steps. Alick was of opinion that church, like other luxuries, was not to be indulged in often by a foreman who had the weather and the ewes on his mind. "Church! Nay—I'n gotten summat else to think on," was an answer which he often uttered in a tone of bitter significance that silenced further question. I feel sure Alick meant no irreverence; indeed, I know that his mind was not of a speculative, negative cast, and he would on no account have missed going to church on Christmas Day, Easter Sunday, and "Whissuntide." But he had a general impression that public worship and religious ceremonies, like other non-productive employments, were intended for people who had leisure.

"There's Father a-standing at the yard-gate," said Martin Poyser. "I reckon he wants to watch us down the field. It's wonderful what sight he has, and him turned seventy-five."

"Ah, I often think it's wi' th' old folks as it is wi' the babbies," said Mrs. Poyser; "they're satisfied wi' looking, no matter what they're looking at. It's God A'mighty's way o' quietening 'em, I reckon, afore they go to sleep."

Old Martin opened the gate as he saw the family procession approaching, and held it wide open, leaning on his stick—pleased to do this bit of work; for, like all old men whose life has been spent in labour, he liked to feel that he was still useful—that there was a better crop of onions in the garden because he was by at the sowing—and that the cows would be milked the better if he stayed at home on a Sunday afternoon to look on. He always went to church on Sacrament Sundays, but not very regularly at other times; on wet Sundays, or whenever he had a touch of rheumatism, he used to read the three first chapters of Genesis instead.

"They'll ha' putten Thias Bede i' the ground afore ye get to the churchyard," he said, as his son came up. "It 'ud ha' been better luck if they'd ha' buried him i' the forenoon when the rain was fallin'; there's no likelihoods of a drop now; an' the moon lies like a boat there, dost see? That's a sure sign o' fair weather—there's a many as is false but that's sure."

"Aye, aye," said the son, "I'm in hopes it'll hold up now."

"Mind what the parson says, mind what the parson says, my lads," said Grandfather to the black-eyed youngsters in knee-breeches, conscious of a marble or two in their pockets which they looked forward to handling, a little, secretly, during the sermon.

"Dood-bye, Dandad," said Totty. "Me doin' to church. Me dot my neklace on. Dive me a peppermint."

Grandad, shaking with laughter at this "deep little wench," slowly transferred his stick to his left hand, which held the gate open, and slowly thrust his finger into the waistcoat pocket on which Totty had fixed her eyes with a confident look of expectation.

And when they were all gone, the old man leaned on the gate again, watching them across the lane along the Home Close, and through the far gate, till they disappeared behind a bend in the hedge. For the hedgerows in those days shut out one's view, even on the better-managed farms; and this afternoon, the dog-roses were tossing out their pink wreaths, the nightshade was in its yellow and purple glory, the pale honeysuckle grew out of reach, peeping high up out of a holly bush, and over all an ash or a sycamore every now and then threw its shadow across the path.

There were acquaintances at other gates who had to move aside and let them pass: at the gate of the Home Close there was half the dairy of cows standing one behind the other, extremely slow to understand that their large bodies might be in the way; at the far gate there was the mare holding her head over the bars, and beside her the liver-coloured foal with its head towards its mother's flank, apparently still much embarrassed by its own straddling existence. The way lay entirely through Mr. Poyser's own fields till they reached the main road leading to the village, and he turned a keen eye on the stock and the crops as they went along, while Mrs. Poyser was ready to supply a running commentary on them all. The woman who manages a dairy has a large share in making the rent, so she may well be allowed to have her opinion on stock and their "keep"—an exercise which strengthens her understanding so much that she finds herself able to give her husband advice on most other subjects.

"There's that shorthorned Sally," she said, as they entered the Home Close, and she caught sight of the meek beast that lay chewing the cud and looking at her with a sleepy eye. "I begin to hate the sight o' the cow; and I say now what I said three weeks ago, the sooner we get rid of her the better, for there's that little yallow cow as doesn't give half the milk, and yet I've twice as much butter from her."

"Why, thee't not like the women in general," said Mr. Poyser; "they like the shorthorns, as give such a lot o' milk. There's Chowne's wife wants him to buy no other sort."

"What's it sinnify what Chowne's wife likes? A poor soft thing, wi' no more head-piece nor a sparrow. She'd take a big cullender to strain her lard wi', and then wonder as the scratchin's run through. I've seen enough of her to know as I'll niver take a servant from her house again—all hugger-mugger—and you'd niver know, when you went in, whether it was Monday or Friday, the wash draggin' on to th' end o' the week; and as for her cheese, I know well enough it rose like a loaf in a tin last year. And then she talks o' the weather bein' i' fault, as there's folks 'ud stand on their heads and then say the fault was i' their boots."

"Well, Chowne's been wanting to buy Sally, so we can get rid of her if thee lik'st," said Mr. Poyser, secretly proud of his wife's superior power of putting two and two together; indeed, on recent market-days he had more than once boasted of her discernment in this very matter of shorthorns. "Aye, them as choose a soft for a wife may's well buy up the shorthorns, for if you get your head stuck in a bog, your legs may's well go after it. Eh! Talk o' legs, there's legs for you," Mrs. Poyser continued, as Totty, who had been set down now the road was dry, toddled on in front of her father and mother. "There's shapes! An' she's got such a long foot, she'll be her father's own child."

"Aye, she'll be welly such a one as Hetty i' ten years' time, on'y she's got *thy* coloured eyes. I niver remember a blue eye i' my family; my mother had eyes as black as sloes, just like Hetty's."

"The child 'ull be none the worse for having summat as isn't like Hetty. An' I'm none for having her so overpretty. Though for the matter o' that, there's people wi' light hair an' blue eyes as pretty as them wi' black. If Dinah had got a bit o' colour in her cheeks, an' didn't stick that Methodist cap on her head, enough to frighten the cows, folks 'ud think her as pretty as Hetty."

"Nay, nay," said Mr. Poyser, with rather a contemptuous emphasis, "thee dostna know the pints of a woman. The men 'ud niver run after Dinah as they would after Hetty."

"What care I what the men 'ud run after? It's well seen what choice the most of 'em know how to make, by the poor draggle-tails o' wives you see, like bits o' gauze ribbin, good for nothing when the colour's gone."

"Well, well, thee canstna say but what I knowed how to make a choice when I married thee," said Mr. Poyser, who usually settled little conjugal disputes by a compliment of this sort; "and thee wast twice as buxom as Dinah ten year ago."

"I niver said as a woman had need to be ugly to make a good missis of a house. There's Chowne's wife ugly enough to turn the milk an' save the rennet, but she'll niver save nothing any other way. But as for Dinah, poor child, she's niver likely to be buxom as long as she'll make her dinner o' cake and water, for the sake o' giving to them as want. She provoked me past bearing sometimes; and, as I told her, she went clean again' the Scriptur', for that says, 'Love your neighbour as yourself'; 'but,' I said, 'if you loved your neighbour no better nor you do yourself, Dinah, it's little enough you'd do for him. You'd be thinking he might do well enough on a half-empty stomach.' Eh, I wonder where she is this blessed Sunday! Sitting by that sick woman, I daresay, as she'd set her heart on going to all of a sudden."

"Ah, it was a pity she should take such megrims into her head, when she might ha' stayed wi' us all summer, and eaten twice as much as she wanted, and it 'ud niver ha' been missed. She made no odds in th' house at all, for she sat as still at her sewing as a bird on the nest, and was uncommon nimble at running to fetch anything. If Hetty gets married, theed'st like to ha' Dinah wi' thee constant."

"It's no use thinking o' that," said Mrs. Poyser. "You might as well beckon to the flying swallow as ask Dinah to come an' live here comfortable, like other folks. If anything could turn her, *I* should ha' turned her, for I've talked to her for a hour on end, and scolded her too; for she's my own sister's child, and it behoves me to do what I can for her. But eh, poor thing, as soon as she'd said us 'good-bye' an' got into the cart, an' looked back at me with her pale face, as is welly like her Aunt Judith come back from heaven, I begun to be frightened to think o' the set-downs I'd given her; for it comes over you sometimes as if she'd a way o' knowing the rights o' things more nor other folks have. But I'll niver give in as that's 'cause she's a Methodist, no more nor a white calf's white 'cause it eats out o' the same bucket wi' a black un."

"Nay," said Mr. Poyser, with as near an approach to a snarl as his good-nature would allow; "I'm no opinion o' the Methodists. It's on'y tradesfolks as turn Methodists; you nuver knew a farmer bitten wi' them maggots. There's maybe a workman now an' then, as isn't overclever at's work, takes to preachin' an' that, like Seth Bede. But you see Adam, as has got one o' the best head-pieces hereabout, knows better; he's a good Churchman, else I'd never encourage him for a sweetheart for Hetty."

"Why, goodness me," said Mrs. Poyser, who had looked back while her husband was speaking, "look where Molly is with them lads! They're the field's length behind us. How *could* you let 'em do so, Hetty? Anybody might as well set a pictur' to watch the children as you. Run back and tell 'em to come on."

Mr. and Mrs. Poyser were now at the end of the second field, so they set Totty on the top of one of the large stones forming the true Loamshire stile, and awaited the loiterers; Totty observing with complacency, "Dey naughty, naughty boys—me dood."

The fact was that this Sunday walk through the fields was fraught with great excitement to Marty and Tommy, who saw a perpetual drama going on in the hedgerows, and could no more refrain from stopping and peeping than if they had been a couple of spaniels or terriers. Marty was quite sure he saw a yellow-hammer on the boughs of the great ash, and while he was peeping, he missed the sight of a white-throated stoat, which had run across the path and was described with much fervour by the junior Tommy. Then there was a little greenfinch, just fledged, fluttering along the ground, and it seemed quite possible to catch it, till it managed to flutter under the blackberry bush. Hetty could not be got to give any heed to these things, so Molly was called on for her ready sympathy, and peeped with open mouth wherever she was told, and said "Lawks!" whenever she was expected to wonder.

Molly hastened on with some alarm when Hetty had come back and called to them that her aunt was angry; but Marty ran on first, shouting, "We've found the speckled turkey's nest, Mother!" with the instinctive confidence that people who bring good news are never in fault.

"Ah," said Mrs. Poyser, really forgetting all discipline in this pleasant surprise, "that's a good lad; why, where is it?"

"Down in ever such a hole, under the hedge. I saw it first, looking after the greenfinch, and she sat on th' nest."

"You didn't frighten her, I hope," said the mother, "else she'll forsake it."

"No, I went away as still as still, and whispered to Molly—didn't I, Molly?"

"Well, well, now come on," said Mrs. Poyser, "and walk before Father and Mother, and take your little sister by the hand. We must go straight on now. Good boys don't look after the birds of a Sunday."

"But, Mother," said Marty, "you said you'd give half-a-crown to find the speckled turkey's nest. Mayn't I have the half-crown put into my money-box?"

"We'll see about that, my lad, if you walk along now, like a good boy."

The father and mother exchanged a significant glance of amusement at their eldest-born's acuteness; but on Tommy's round face there was a cloud.

"Mother," he said, half-crying, "Marty's got ever so much more money in his box nor I've got in mine."

"Munny, *me* want half-a-toun in *my* bots," said Totty.

"Hush, hush, hush," said Mrs. Poyser, "did ever anybody hear such naughty children? Nobody shall ever see their money-boxes any more, if they don't make haste and go on to church."

This dreadful threat had the desired effect, and through the two remaining fields the three pair of small legs trotted on without any serious interruption, notwithstanding a small pond full of tadpoles, alias "bullheads," which the lads looked at wistfully.

The damp hay that must be scattered and turned afresh to-morrow was not a cheering sight to Mr. Poyser, who during hay and corn harvest had often some mental struggles as to the benefits of a day of rest; but no temptation would have induced him to carry on any field-work, however early in the morning, on a Sunday; for had not Michael Holdsworth had a pair of oxen "sweltered" while he was ploughing on Good Friday? That was a demonstration that work on sacred days was a wicked thing; and with wickedness of any sort Martin Poyser was quite clear that he would have nothing to do, since money got by such means would never prosper.

"It a'most makes your fingers itch to be at the hay now the sun shines so," he observed, as they passed through the "Big Meadow." "But it's poor foolishness to think o' saving by going against your conscience. There's that Jim Wakefield, as they used to call 'Gentleman Wakefield,' used to do the same of a Sunday as o' weekdays, and took no heed to right or wrong, as if there was nayther God nor devil. An' what's he come to? Why, I saw him myself last market-day a-carrying a basket wi' oranges in't."

"Ah, to be sure," said Mrs. Poyser, emphatically, "you make but a poor trap to catch luck if you go and bait it wi' wickedness. The money as is got so's like to burn holes i' your pocket. I'd niver wish us to leave our lads a sixpence but what was got i' the rightful way. And as for the weather, there's One above makes it, and we must put up wi't: it's nothing of a plague to what the wenches are."

Notwithstanding the interruption in their walk, the excellent habit which Mrs. Poyser's clock had of taking time by the forelock had secured their arrival at the village while it was still a quarter to two, though almost every one who meant to go to church was already within the churchyard gates. Those who stayed at home were chiefly mothers, like Timothy's Bess, who stood at her own door nursing her baby and feeling as women feel in that position—that nothing else can be expected of them.

It was not entirely to see Thias Bede's funeral that the people were standing about the churchyard so long before service began; that was their common practice. The women, indeed, usually entered the church at once, and the farmers' wives talked in an undertone to each other, over the tall pews, about their illnesses and the total failure of doctor's stuff, recommending dandelion-tea, and other home-made specifics, as far preferable—about the servants, and their growing exorbitance as to wages, whereas the quality of their services declined from year to year, and there was no girl nowadays to be trusted any further than you could see her—about the bad price Mr. Dingall, the Treddleston grocer, was giving for butter, and the reasonable doubts that might be held as to his solvency, notwithstanding that Mrs. Dingall was a sensible woman, and they were all sorry for *her*, for she had very good kin. Meantime the men lingered outside, and hardly any of them except the singers, who had a humming and fragmentary rehearsal to go through, entered the church until Mr. Irwine was in the desk. They saw no reason for that premature entrance—what could they do in church if they were there before service began?—and they did not conceive that any power in the universe could take it ill of them if they stayed out and talked a little about "bus'ness."

Chad Cranage looks like quite a new acquaintance to-day, for he has got his clean Sunday face, which always makes his little granddaughter cry at him as a stranger. But an experienced eye would have fixed on him at once as the village blacksmith, after seeing the humble deference with which the big saucy fellow took off his hat and stroked his hair to the farmers; for Chad was accustomed to say that a working-man must hold a candle to a personage understood to be as black as he was himself on weekdays; by which evil-sounding rule of conduct he meant what was, after all, rather virtuous than otherwise, namely, that men who had horses to be shod must be treated with respect. Chad and the rougher sort of workmen kept aloof from the grave under the white thorn, where the burial was going forward; but Sandy Jim, and several of the farm-labourers, made a group round it, and stood with their hats off, as fellow-mourners with the mother and sons. Others held a midway position, sometimes watching the group at the grave, sometimes listening to the conversation of the farmers, who stood in a knot near the church door, and were now joined by Martin Poyser, while his family passed into the church. On the outside of this knot stood Mr. Casson, the landlord of the Donnithorne Arms, in his most striking attitude—that is to say, with the forefinger of his right hand thrust between the buttons of his waistcoat, his left hand in his breeches pocket, and his head very much on one side; looking, on the whole, like an actor who has only a mono-syllabic part entrusted to him, but feels sure that the audience discern his fitness for the leading business; curiously in contrast with old Jonathan Burge, who held his hands behind him and leaned forward, coughing asthmatically, with an inward scorn of all knowingness that could not be turned into cash. The talk was in rather a lower tone than usual to-day, hushed a little by the sound of Mr. Irwine's voice reading the final prayers of the burial-service. They had all had their word of pity for poor Thias, but now they had got upon the nearer subject of their own grievances against Satchell, the Squire's bailiff, who played the part of steward so far as it was not performed by old Mr. Donnithorne himself, for that gentleman had the meanness to receive his own rents and make bargains about his own timber. This subject of conversation was an additional reason for not being loud, since Satchell himself might presently be walking up the paved road to the church door. And soon they became suddenly silent; for Mr. Irwine's voice had ceased, and the group round the white thorn was dispersing itself towards the church.

They all moved aside, and stood with their hats off, while Mr. Irwine passed. Adam and Seth were coming next, with their mother between them; for Joshua Rann officiated as head sexton as well as clerk, and was not yet ready to follow the rector into the vestry. But there was a pause before the three mourners came on: Lisbeth had turned round to look again towards the grave! Ah! There was nothing now but the brown earth under the white thorn. Yet she cried less to-day than she had done any day since her husband's death. Along with all her grief there was mixed an unusual sense of her own importance in having a "burial," and in Mr. Irwine's reading a special service for her husband; and besides, she knew the funeral psalm was going to be sung for him. She felt this counter-excitement to her sorrow still more strongly as she walked with her sons towards the church door, and saw the friendly sympathetic nods of their fellow-parishioners.

The mother and sons passed into the church, and one by one the loiterers followed, though some still lingered without; the sight of Mr. Donnithorne's carriage, which was winding slowly up the hill, perhaps helping to make them feel that there was no need for haste.

But presently the sound of the bassoon and the key-bugles burst forth; the evening hymn, which always opened the service, had begun, and every one must now enter and take his place.

I cannot say that the interior of Hayslope Church was remarkable for anything except for the grey age of its oaken pews—great square pews mostly, ranged on each side of a narrow aisle. It was free, indeed, from the modern blemish of galleries. The choir had two narrow pews to themselves in the middle of the right-hand row, so that it was a short process for Joshua Rann to take his place among them as principal bass, and return to his desk after the singing was over. The pulpit and desk, grey and old as the pews, stood on one side of the arch leading into the chancel, which also had its grey square pews for Mr. Donnithorne's family and servants. Yet I assure you these grey pews, with the buff-washed walls, gave a very pleasing tone to this shabby interior, and agreed extremely well with the ruddy faces and bright waistcoats. And there were liberal touches of crimson toward the chancel, for the pulpit and Mr. Donnithorne's own pew had handsome crimson cloth cushions; and, to close the vista, there was a crimson altar-cloth, embroidered with golden rays by Miss Lydia's own hand.

But even without the crimson cloth, the effect must have been warm and cheering when Mr. Irwine was in the desk, looking benignly round on that simple congregation—on the hardy old men, with bent knees and shoulders, perhaps, but with vigour left for much hedge-clipping and thatching; on the tall stalwart frames and roughly cut bronzed faces of the stone-cutters and carpenters; on the half-dozen well-to-do farmers, with their apple-cheeked families; and on the clean old women, mostly farm-labourers' wives, with their bit of snow-white cap-border under their black bonnets, and with their withered arms, bare from the elbow, folded passively over their chests. For none of the old people held books—why should they? Not one of them could read. But they knew a few "good words" by heart, and their withered lips now and then moved silently, following the service without any very clear comprehension indeed, but with a simple faith in its efficacy to ward off harm and bring blessing. And now all faces were visible, for all were standing up—the little children on the seats peeping over the edge of the grey pews, while good Bishop Ken's evening hymn was being sung to one of those lively psalm-tunes which died out with the last generation of rectors and choral parish clerks. Melodies die out, like the pipe of Pan, with the ears that love them and listen for them. Adam was not in his usual place among the singers to-day, for he sat with his mother and Seth, and he noticed with surprise that Bartle Massey was absent too—all the more agreeable for Mr. Joshua Rann, who gave out his bass notes with unusual complacency and threw an extra ray of severity into the glances he sent over his spectacles at the recusant Will Maskery.

I beseech you to imagine Mr. Irwine looking round on this scene, in his ample white surplice that became him so well, with his powdered hair thrown back, his rich brown complexion, and his finely cut nostril and upper lip; for there was a certain virtue in that benignant yet keen countenance as there is in all human faces from which a generous soul beams out. And over all streamed the delicious June sunshine through the old windows, with their desultory patches of yellow, red, and blue, that threw pleasant touches of colour on the opposite wall.

I think, as Mr. Irwine looked round to-day, his eyes rested an instant longer than usual on the square pew occupied by Martin Poyser and his family. And there was another pair of dark eyes that found it impossible not to wander thither, and rest on that round pink-and-white figure. But Hetty was at that moment quite careless of any glances—she was absorbed in the thought that Arthur

Donnithorne would soon be coming into church, for the carriage must surely be at the church-gate by this time. She had never seen him since she parted with him in the wood on Thursday evening, and oh, how long the time had seemed! Things had gone on just the same as ever since that evening; the wonders that had happened then had brought no changes after them; they were already like a dream. When she heard the church door swinging, her heart beat so, she dared not look up. She felt that her aunt was curtsying; she curtsied herself. That must be old Mr. Donnithorne—he always came first, the wrinkled small old man, peering round with short-sighted glances at the bowing and curtsying congregation; then she knew Miss Lydia was passing, and though Hetty liked so much to look at her fashionable little coal-scuttle bonnet, with the wreath of small roses round it, she didn't mind it to-day. But there were no more curtsies—no, he was not come; she felt sure there was nothing else passing the pew door but the house-keeper's black bonnet and the lady's maid's beautiful straw hat that had once been Miss Lydia's, and then the powdered heads of the butler and footman. No, he was not there; yet she would look now—she might be mistaken—for, after all, she had not looked. So she lifted up her eyelids and glanced timidly at the cushioned pew in the chancel—there was no one but old Mr. Donnithorne rubbing his spectacles with his white handkerchief, and Miss Lydia opening the large gilt-edged prayer-book. The chill disappointment was too hard to bear. She felt herself turning pale, her lips trembling; she was ready to cry. Oh, what *should* she do? Everybody would know the reason; they would know she was crying because Arthur was not there. And Mr. Craig, with the wonderful hothouse plant in his button-hole, was staring at her, she knew. It was dreadfully long before the General Confession began, so that she could kneel down. Two great drops *would* fall then, but no one saw them except good-natured Molly, for her aunt and uncle knelt with their backs towards her. Molly, unable to imagine any cause for tears in church except faintness, of which she had a vague traditional knowledge, drew out of her pocket a queer little flat blue smelling-bottle, and after much labour in pulling the cork out, thrust the narrow neck against Hetty's nostrils. "It donna smell," she whispered, thinking this was a great advantage which old salts had over fresh ones: they did you good without biting your nose. Hetty pushed it away peevishly; but this little flash of temper did what the salts could not have done—it roused her to wipe away the traces of her tears, and try with all her might not to shed any more. Hetty had a certain strength in her vain little nature: she would have borne anything rather than be laughed at, or pointed at with any other feeling than admiration; she would have pressed her own nails into her tender flesh rather than people should know a secret she did not want them to know.

What fluctuations there were in her busy thoughts and feelings, while Mr. Irwine was pronouncing the solemn "Absolution" in her deaf ears, and through all the tones of petition that followed! Anger lay very close to disappointment, and soon won the victory over the conjectures her small ingenuity could devise to account for Arthur's absence on the supposition that he really wanted to come, really wanted to see her again. And by the time she rose from her knees mechanically, because all the rest were rising, the colour had returned to her cheeks even with a heightened glow, for she was framing little indignant speeches to herself, saying she hated Arthur for giving her this pain—she would like him to suffer too. Yet while this selfish tumult was going on in her soul, her eyes were bent down on her prayer-book, and the eyelids with their dark fringe looked as lovely as ever. Adam Bede thought so, as he glanced at her for a moment on rising from his knees.

But Adam's thoughts of Hetty did not deafen him to the service; they rather blended with all the other deep feelings for which the church service was a channel to him this afternoon, as a certain consciousness of our entire past and our imagined future blends itself with all our moments of keen sensibility. And to Adam the church service was the best channel he could have found for his mingled regret, yearning, and resignation; its interchange of beseeching cries for help with outbursts of faith and praise, its recurrent responses and the familiar rhythm of its collects, seemed to speak for him as no other form of worship could have done; as, to those early Christians who had worshipped from their childhood upwards in catacombs, the torch-light and shadows must have seemed nearer the Divine presence than the heathenish daylight of the streets. The secret of our emotions never lies in the bare object, but in its subtle relations to our own past: no wonder the secret escapes the unsympathizing observer, who might as well put on his spectacles to discern odours.

But there was one reason why even a chance comer would have found the service in Hayslope Church more impressive than in most other village nooks in the kingdom—a reason of which I am sure you have not the slightest suspicion. It was the reading of our friend Joshua Rann. Where that good shoemaker got his notion of reading from remained a mystery even to his most intimate acquaintances. I believe, after all, he got it chiefly from Nature, who had poured some of her music into this honest conceited soul, as she had been known to do into other narrow souls before his. She had given him, at least, a fine bass voice and a musical ear; but I cannot positively say whether these alone had sufficed to inspire him with the rich chant in which he delivered the responses. The way he rolled from a rich deep forte into a melancholy cadence, subsiding, at the end of the last word, into a sort of faint resonance, like the lingering vibrations of a fine violoncello, I can compare to nothing for its strong calm melancholy but the rush and cadence of the wind among the autumn boughs. This may seem a strange mode of speaking about the reading of a parish clerk—a man in rusty spectacles, with stubbly hair, a large occiput, and a prominent crown. But that is Nature's way: she will allow a gentleman of splendid physiognomy and poetic aspirations to sing woefully out of tune, and not give him the slightest hint of it; and takes care that some narrow-browed fellow, trolling a ballad in the corner of a pot-house, shall be as true to his intervals as a bird.

Joshua himself was less proud of his reading than of his singing, and it was always with a sense of heightened importance that he passed from the desk to the choir. Still more to-day: it was a special occasion, for an old man, familiar to all the parish, had died a sad death—not in his bed, a circumstance the most painful to the mind of the peasant—and now the funeral psalm was to be sung in memory of his sudden departure. Moreover, Bartle Massey was not at church, and Joshua's importance in the choir suffered no eclipse. It was a solemn minor strain they sang. The old psalm-tunes have many a wail among them, and the words—

"Thou sweep'st us off as with a flood;
We vanish hence like dreams"—

seemed to have a closer application than usual in the death of poor Thias. The mother and sons listened, each with peculiar feelings. Lisbeth had a vague belief that the psalm was doing her husband good; it was part of that decent burial which she would have thought it a greater wrong to withhold from him than to have caused him many unhappy days while he was living. The more there was said about her husband, the more there was done for him, surely the safer he would be. It was poor Lisbeth's blind way of feeling that human love and pity are a ground of faith in some other love. Seth, who was easily touched, shed tears, and tried to recall, as he had done continually since his father's death, all that he had heard of the possibility that a single moment of consciousness at the last might be a moment of pardon and reconcilement; for was it not written in the very psalm they were singing that the Divine dealings were not measured and circumscribed by time? Adam had never been unable to join in a psalm before. He had known plenty of trouble and vexation since he had been a lad, but this was the first sorrow that had hemmed in his voice, and strangely enough it was sorrow because the chief source of his past trouble and vexation was for ever gone out of his reach. He had not been able to press his father's hand before their parting, and say, "Father, you know it was all right between us; I never forgot what I owed you when I was a lad; you forgive me if I have been too hot and hasty now and then!" Adam thought but little to-day of the hard work and the earnings he had spent on his father: his thoughts ran constantly on what the old man's feelings had been in moments of humiliation, when he had held down his head before the rebukes of his son. When our indignation is borne in submissive silence, we are apt to feel twinges of doubt afterwards as to our own generosity, if not justice; how much more when the object of our anger has gone into everlasting silence, and we have seen his face for the last time in the meekness of death!

"Ah! I was always too hard," Adam said to himself. "It's a sore fault in me as I'm so hot and out o' patience with people when they do wrong, and my heart gets shut up against 'em, so as I can't bring myself to forgive 'em. I see clear enough there's more pride nor love in my soul, for I could sooner make a thousand strokes with th' hammer for my father than bring myself to say a kind word to him. And there went plenty o' pride and temper to the strokes, as the devil *will* be having his finger in what we call our duties as well as our sins. Mayhap the best thing I ever did in my life was only doing what was easiest for myself. It's allays been easier for me to work nor to sit still, but the real tough job for me 'ud be to master my own will and temper and go right against my own pride. It seems to me now, if I was to find Father at home to-night, I should behave different; but there's no knowing—perhaps nothing 'ud be a lesson to us if it didn't come too late. It's well we should feel as life's a reckoning we can't make twice over; there's no real making amends in this world, any more nor you can mend a wrong subtraction by doing your addition right."

This was the key-note to which Adam's thoughts had perpetually returned since his father's death, and the solemn wail of the funeral psalm was only an influence that brought back the old thoughts with stronger emphasis. So was the sermon, which Mr. Irwine had chosen with reference to Thias's funeral. It spoke briefly and simply of the words, "In the midst of life we are in death"—how the present moment is all we can call our own for works of mercy, of righteous dealing, and of family tenderness. All very old truths—but what we thought the oldest truth becomes the most startling to us in the week when we have looked on the dead face of one who has made a part of our own lives. For when men want to impress us with the effect of a new and wonderfully vivid light, do they not let it fall on the most familiar objects, that we may measure its intensity by remembering the former dimness?

Then came the moment of the final blessing, when the forever sublime words, "The peace of God, which passeth all understanding," seemed to blend with the calm afternoon sunshine that fell on the bowed heads of the congregation; and then the quiet rising, the mothers tying on the bonnets of the little maidens who had slept through the sermon, the fathers collecting the prayer-books, until all streamed out through the old archway into the green churchyard and began their neighbourly talk, their simple civilities, and their invitations to tea; for on a Sunday every one was ready to receive a guest—it was the day when all must be in their best clothes and their best humour.

Mr. and Mrs. Poyser paused a minute at the church gate: they were waiting for Adam to come up, not being contented to go away without saying a kind word to the widow and her sons.

"Well, Mrs. Bede," said Mrs. Poyser, as they walked on together, "you must keep up your heart; husbands and wives must be content when they've lived to rear their children and see one another's hair grey."

"Aye, aye," said Mr. Poyser; "they wonna have long to wait for one another then, anyhow. And ye've got two o' the strapping'st sons i' th' country; and well you may, for I remember poor Thias as fine a broad-shouldered fellow as need to be; and as for you, Mrs. Bede, why you're straighter i' the back nor half the young women now."

"Eh," said Lisbeth, "it's poor luck for the platter to wear well when it's broke i' two. The sooner I'm laid under the thorn the better. I'm no good to nobody now."

Adam never took notice of his mother's little unjust plaints; but Seth said, "Nay, Mother, thee mustna say so. Thy sons 'ull never get another mother."

"That's true, lad, that's true," said Mr. Poyser; "and it's wrong on us to give way to grief, Mrs. Bede; for it's like the children cryin' when the fathers and mothers take things from 'em. There's One above knows better nor us."

"Ah," said Mrs. Poyser, "an' it's poor work allays settin' the dead above the livin'. We shall all on us be dead some time, I reckon—it 'ud be better if folks 'ud make much on us beforehand, i'stid o' beginnin' when we're gone. It's but little good you'll do a-watering the last year's crop."

"Well, Adam," said Mr. Poyser, feeling that his wife's words were, as usual, rather incisive than soothing, and that it would be well to change the subject, "you'll come and see us again now, I hope. I hanna had a talk with you this long while, and the missis here wants you to see what can be done with her best spinning-wheel, for it's got broke, and it'll be a nice job to mend it—there'll want a bit o' turning. You'll come as soon as you can now, will you?"

Mr. Poyser paused and looked round while he was speaking, as if to see where Hetty was; for the children were running on before. Hetty was not without a companion, and she had, besides, more pink and white about her than ever, for she held in her hand the wonderful pink-and-white hot-house plant, with a very long name—a Scotch name, she supposed, since people said Mr. Craig the gardener was Scotch. Adam took the opportunity of looking round too; and I am sure you will not require of him that he should feel any vexation in observing a pouting expression on Hetty's face as she listened to the gardener's small talk. Yet in her secret heart she was glad to have him by her side, for she would perhaps learn from him how it was Arthur had not come to church. Not that she cared to ask him the question, but she hoped the information would be given spontaneously; for Mr. Craig, like a superior man, was very fond of giving information.

Mr. Craig was never aware that his conversation and advances were received coldly, for to shift one's point of view beyond certain limits is impossible to the most liberal and expansive mind; we are none of us aware of the impression we produce on Brazilian monkeys of feeble understanding—it is possible they see hardly anything in us. Moreover, Mr. Craig was a man of sober passions, and was already in his tenth year of hesitation as to the relative advantages of matrimony and bachelorhood. It is true that, now and then, when he had been a little heated by an extra glass of grog, he had been heard to say of Hetty that the "lass was well enough," and that "a man might do worse"; but on convivial occasions men are apt to express themselves strongly.

Martin Poyser held Mr. Craig in honour, as a man who "knew his business" and who had great lights concerning soils and compost; but he was less of a favourite with Mrs. Poyser, who had more than once said in confidence to her husband, "You're mighty fond o' Craig, but for my part, I think he's welly like a cock as thinks the sun's rose o' purpose to hear him crow." For the rest, Mr. Craig was an estimable gardener, and was not without reasons for having a high opinion of himself. He had also high shoulders and high cheek-bones and hung his head forward a little, as he walked along with his hands in his breeches pockets. I think it was his pedigree only that had the advantage of being Scotch, and not his "bringing up"; for except that he had a stronger burr in his accent, his speech differed little from that of the Loamshire people about him. But a gardener is Scotch, as a French teacher is Parisian.

"Well, Mr. Poyser," he said, before the good slow farmer had time to speak, "ye'll not be carrying your hay to-morrow, I'm thinking. The glass sticks at 'change,' and ye may rely upo' my word as we'll ha' more downfall afore twenty-four hours is past. Ye see that darkish-blue cloud there upo' the 'rizon—ye know what I mean by the 'rizon, where the land and sky seems to meet?"

"Aye, aye, I see the cloud," said Mr. Poyser, "'rizon or no 'rizon. It's right o'er Mike Holdsworth's fallow, and a foul fallow it is."

"Well, you mark my words, as that cloud 'ull spread o'er the sky pretty nigh as quick as you'd spread a tarpaulin over one o' your hay-ricks. It's a great thing to ha' studied the look o' the clouds. Lord bless you! Th' met'orological almanecks can learn me nothing, but there's a pretty sight o' things I could let *them* up to, if they'd just come to me. And how are *you*, Mrs. Poyser?—thinking o' getherin' the red currants soon, I reckon. You'd a deal better gether 'em afore they're o'erripe, wi' such weather as we've got to look forward to. How do ye do, Mistress Bede?" Mr. Craig continued, without a pause, nodding by the way to Adam and Seth. "I hope y' enjoyed them spinach and gooseberries as I sent Chester with th' other day. If ye want vegetables while ye're in trouble, ye know where to come to. It's well known I'm not giving other folks' things away, for when I've supplied the house, the garden's my own spekilation, and it isna every man th' old squire could get as 'ud be equil to the undertaking, let alone asking whether he'd be willing I've got to run my calkilation fine, I can tell you, to make sure o' getting back the money as I pay the squire. I should like to see some o' them fellows as make the almanecks looking as far before their noses as I've got to do every year as comes."

"They look pretty fur, though," said Mr. Poyser, turning his head on one side and speaking in rather a subdued reverential tone. "Why, what could come truer nor that pictur o' the cock wi' the big spurs, as has got its head knocked down wi' th' anchor, an' th' firin', an' the ships behind? Why, that pictur was made afore Christmas, and yit it's come as true as th' Bible. Why, th' cock's France, an' th' anchor's Nelson—an' they told us that beforehand."

"Pee—ee-eh!" said Mr. Craig. "A man doesna want to see fur to know as th' English 'ull beat the French. Why, I know upo' good authority as it's a big Frenchman as reaches five foot high, an' they live upo' spoon-meat mostly. I knew a man as his father had a particular knowledge o' the French. I should like to know what them grasshoppers are to do against such fine fellows as our young Captain Arthur. Why, it 'ud astonish a Frenchman only to look at him; his arm's thicker nor a Frenchman's body, I'll be bound, for they pinch theirsells in wi' stays; and it's easy enough, for they've got nothing i' their insides."

"Where is the captain, as he wasna at church to-day?" said Adam. "I was talking to him o' Friday, and he said nothing about his going away."

"Oh, he's only gone to Eagledale for a bit o' fishing; I reckon he'll be back again afore many days are o'er, for he's to be at all th' arranging and preparing o' things for the comin' o' age o' the 30th o' July. But he's fond o' getting away for a bit, now and then. Him and th' old squire fit one another like frost and flowers."

Mr. Craig smiled and winked slowly as he made this last observation, but the subject was not developed farther, for now they had reached the turning in the road where Adam and his companions must say "good-bye." The gardener, too, would have had to turn off in the same direction if he had not accepted Mr. Poyser's invitation to tea. Mrs. Poyser duly seconded the invitation, for she would have held it a deep disgrace not to make her neighbours welcome to her house: personal likes and dislikes must not interfere with that sacred custom. Moreover, Mr. Craig had always been full of civilities to the family at the Hall Farm, and Mrs. Poyser was scrupulous in declaring that she had "nothing to say again' him, on'y it was a pity he couldna be hatched o'er again, an' hatched different."

So Adam and Seth, with their mother between them, wound their way down to the valley and up again to the old house, where a saddened memory had taken the place of a long, long anxiety—where Adam would never have to ask again as he entered, "Where's Father?"

And the other family party, with Mr. Craig for company, went back to the pleasant bright house-place at the Hall Farm—all with quiet minds, except Hetty, who knew now where Arthur was gone, but was only the more puzzled and uneasy. For it appeared that his absence was quite voluntary; he need not have gone—he would not have gone if he had wanted to see her. She had a sickening sense that no lot could ever be pleasant to her again if her Thursday night's vision was not to be fulfilled; and in this moment of chill, bare, wintry disappointment and doubt, she looked towards the possibility of being with Arthur again, of meeting his loving glance, and hearing his soft words with that eager yearning which one may call the "growing pain" of passion.

Chapter XIX
Adam on a Working Day

Notwithstanding Mr. Craig's prophecy, the dark-blue cloud dispersed itself without having produced the threatened consequences. "The weather"—as he observed the next morning—"the weather, you see, 's a ticklish thing, an' a fool 'ull hit on't sometimes when a wise man misses; that's why the almanecks get so much credit. It's one o' them chancy things as fools thrive on."

This unreasonable behaviour of the weather, however, could displease no one else in Hayslope besides Mr. Craig. All hands were to be out in the meadows this morning as soon as the dew had risen; the wives and daughters did double work in every farmhouse, that the maids might give their help in tossing the hay; and when Adam was marching along the lanes, with his basket of tools over his shoulder, he caught the sound of jocose talk and ringing laughter from behind the hedges. The jocose talk of hay-makers is best at a distance; like those clumsy bells round the cows' necks, it has rather a coarse sound when it comes close, and may even grate on your ears painfully; but heard from far off, it mingles very prettily with the other joyous sounds of nature. Men's muscles move better when their souls are making merry music, though their merriment is of a poor blundering sort, not at all like the merriment of birds.

And perhaps there is no time in a summer's day more cheering than when the warmth of the sun is just beginning to triumph over the freshness of the morning—when there is just a lingering hint of early coolness to keep off languor under the delicious influence of warmth. The reason Adam was walking along the lanes at this time was because his work for the rest of the day lay at a country-house about three miles off, which was being put in repair for the son of a neighbouring squire; and he had been busy since early morning with the packing of panels, doors, and chimney-pieces, in a waggon which was now gone on before him, while Jonathan Burge himself had ridden to the spot on horseback, to await its arrival and direct the workmen.

This little walk was a rest to Adam, and he was unconsciously under the charm of the moment. It was summer morning in his heart, and he saw Hetty in the sunshine—a sunshine without glare, with slanting rays that tremble between the delicate shadows of the leaves. He thought, yesterday when he put out his hand to her as they came out of church, that there was a touch of melancholy kindness in her face, such as he had not seen before, and he took it as a sign that she had some sympathy with his family trouble. Poor fellow! That touch of melancholy came from quite another source, but how was he to know? We look at the one little woman's face we love as we look at the face of our mother earth, and see all sorts of answers to our own yearnings. It was impossible for Adam not to feel that what had happened in the last week had brought the prospect of marriage nearer to him. Hitherto he had felt keenly the danger that some other man might step in and get possession of Hetty's heart and hand, while he himself was still in a position that made him shrink from asking her to accept him. Even if he had had a strong hope that she was fond of him—and his hope was far from being strong—he had been too heavily burdened with other claims to provide a home for himself and Hetty—a home such as he could expect her to be content with after the comfort and plenty of the Farm. Like all strong natures, Adam had confidence in his ability to achieve something in the future; he felt sure he should some day, if he lived, be able to maintain a family and make a good broad path for himself; but he had too cool a head not to estimate to the full the obstacles that were to be overcome. And the time would be so long! And there was Hetty, like a bright-cheeked apple hanging over the orchard wall, within sight of everybody, and everybody must long for her! To be sure, if she loved him very much, she would be content to wait for him: but *did* she love him? His hopes had never risen so high that he had dared to ask her. He was clear-sighted enough to be aware that her uncle and aunt would have looked kindly on his suit, and indeed, without this encouragement he would never have persevered in going to the Farm; but it was impossible to come to any but fluctuating conclusions about Hetty's feelings. She was like a kitten, and had the same distractingly pretty looks, that meant nothing, for everybody that came near her.

But now he could not help saying to himself that the heaviest part of his burden was removed, and that even before the end of another year his circumstances might be brought into a shape that would allow him to think of marrying. It would always be a hard struggle with his mother, he knew: she would be jealous of any wife he might choose, and she had set her mind especially against Hetty—perhaps for no other reason than that she suspected Hetty to be the woman he *had* chosen. It would never do, he feared, for his mother to live in the same house with him when he was married; and yet how hard she would think it if he asked her to leave him! Yes, there was a great deal of pain to be gone through with his mother, but it was a case in which he must make her feel that his will was strong—it would be better for her in the end. For himself, he would have liked that they should all live together till Seth was married, and they might have built a bit themselves to the old house, and made more room. He did not like "to part wi' th' lad": they had hardly ever been separated for more than a day since they were born.

But Adam had no sooner caught his imagination leaping forward in this way—making arrangements for an uncertain future—than he checked himself. "A pretty building I'm making, without either bricks or timber. I'm up i' the garret a'ready, and haven't so much as dug the foundation." Whenever Adam was strongly convinced of any proposition, it took the form of a principle in his mind: it was knowledge to be acted on, as much as the knowledge that damp will cause rust. Perhaps here lay the secret of the hardness he had accused himself of: he had too little fellow-feeling with the weakness that errs in spite of foreseen consequences. Without this fellow-feeling, how are we to get enough patience and charity towards our stumbling, falling companions in the long and changeful journey? And there is but one way in which a strong determined soul can learn it—by getting his heart-strings bound round the weak and erring, so that he must share not only the outward consequence of their error, but their inward suffering. That is a long and hard lesson, and Adam had at present only learned the alphabet of it in his father's sudden death, which, by annihilating in an instant all that had stimulated his indignation, had sent a sudden rush of thought and memory over what had claimed his pity and tenderness.

But it was Adam's strength, not its correlative hardness, that influenced his meditations this morning. He had long made up his mind that it would be wrong as well as foolish for him to marry a blooming young girl, so long as he had no other prospect than that of growing poverty with a growing family. And his savings had been so constantly drawn upon (besides the terrible sweep of paying for Seth's substitute in the militia) that he had not enough money beforehand to furnish even a small cottage, and keep something in reserve against a rainy day. He had good hope that he should be "firmer on his legs" by and by; but he could not be satisfied with a vague confidence in his arm and brain; he must have definite plans, and set about them at once. The partnership with Jonathan Burge was not to be thought of at present—there were things implicitly tacked to it that he could not accept; but Adam thought that he and Seth might carry on a little business for themselves in addition to their journeyman's work, by buying a small stock of superior wood and making articles of household furniture, for which Adam had no end of contrivances. Seth might gain more by working at separate jobs under Adam's direction than by his journeyman's work, and Adam, in his overhours, could do all the "nice" work that required peculiar skill. The money gained in this way, with the good wages he received as foreman, would soon enable them to get beforehand with the world, so sparingly as they would all live now. No sooner had this little plan shaped itself in his mind than he began to be busy with exact calculations about the wood to be bought and the particular article of furniture that should be undertaken first—a kitchen cupboard of his own contrivance, with such an ingenious arrangement of sliding-doors and bolts, such convenient nooks for stowing household provender, and such a symmetrical result to the eye, that every good housewife would be in raptures with it, and fall through all the gradations of melancholy longing till her husband promised to buy it for her. Adam pictured to himself Mrs. Poyser examining it with her keen eye and trying in vain to find out a deficiency; and, of course, close to Mrs.

Poyser stood Hetty, and Adam was again beguiled from calculations and contrivances into dreams and hopes. Yes, he would go and see her this evening—it was so long since he had been at the Hall Farm. He would have liked to go to the night-school, to see why Bartle Massey had not been at church yesterday, for he feared his old friend was ill; but, unless he could manage both visits, this last must be put off till to-morrow—the desire to be near Hetty and to speak to her again was too strong.

As he made up his mind to this, he was coming very near to the end of his walk, within the sound of the hammers at work on the refitting of the old house. The sound of tools to a clever workman who loves his work is like the tentative sounds of the orchestra to the violinist who has to bear his part in the overture: the strong fibres begin their accustomed thrill, and what was a moment before joy, vexation, or ambition, begins its change into energy. All passion becomes strength when it has an outlet from the narrow limits of our personal lot in the labour of our right arm, the cunning of our right hand, or the still, creative activity of our thought. Look at Adam through the rest of the day, as he stands on the scaffolding with the two-feet ruler in his hand, whistling low while he considers how a difficulty about a floor-joist or a window-frame is to be overcome; or as he pushes one of the younger workmen aside and takes his place in upheaving a weight of timber, saying, "Let alone, lad! Thee'st got too much gristle i' thy bones yet"; or as he fixes his keen black eyes on the motions of a workman on the other side of the room and warns him that his distances are not right. Look at this broad-shouldered man with the bare muscular arms, and the thick, firm, black hair tossed about like trodden meadow-grass whenever he takes off his paper cap, and with the strong barytone voice bursting every now and then into loud and solemn psalm-tunes, as if seeking an outlet for superfluous strength, yet presently checking himself, apparently crossed by some thought which jars with the singing. Perhaps, if you had not been already in the secret, you might not have guessed what sad memories, what warm affection, what tender fluttering hopes, had their home in this athletic body with the broken finger-nails—in this rough man, who knew no better lyrics than he could find in the Old and New Version and an occasional hymn; who knew the smallest possible amount of profane history; and for whom the motion and shape of the earth, the course of the sun, and the changes of the seasons lay in the region of mystery just made visible by fragmentary knowledge. It had cost Adam a great deal of trouble and work in overhours to know what he knew over and above the secrets of his handicraft, and that acquaintance with mechanics and figures, and the nature of the materials he worked with, which was made easy to him by inborn inherited faculty—to get the mastery of his pen, and write a plain hand, to spell without any other mistakes than must in fairness be attributed to the unreasonable character of orthography rather than to any deficiency in the speller, and, moreover, to learn his musical notes and part-singing. Besides all this, he had read his Bible, including the apocryphal books; Poor Richard's Almanac, Taylor's Holy Living and Dying, The Pilgrim's Progress, with Bunyan's Life and Holy War, a great deal of Bailey's Dictionary, Valentine and Orson, and part of a History of Babylon, which Bartle Massey had lent him. He might have had many more books from Bartle Massey, but he had no time for reading "the commin print," as Lisbeth called it, so busy as he was with figures in all the leisure moments which he did not fill up with extra carpentry.

Adam, you perceive, was by no means a marvellous man, nor, properly speaking, a genius, yet I will not pretend that his was an ordinary character among workmen; and it would not be at all a safe conclusion that the next best man you may happen to see with a basket of tools over his shoulder and a paper cap on his head has the strong conscience and the strong sense, the blended susceptibility and self-command, of our friend Adam. He was not an average man. Yet such men as he are reared here and there in every generation of our peasant artisans—with an inheritance of affections nurtured by a simple family life of common need and common industry, and an inheritance of faculties trained in skilful courageous labour: they make their way upwards, rarely as geniuses, most commonly as painstaking honest men, with the skill and conscience to do well the tasks that lie before them. Their lives have no discernible echo beyond the neighbourhood where they dwelt, but you are almost sure to find there some good piece of road, some building, some application of mineral produce, some improvement in farming practice, some reform of parish abuses, with which their names are associated by one or two generations after them. Their employers were the richer for them, the work of their hands has worn well, and the work of their brains has guided well the hands of other men. They went about in their youth in flannel or paper caps, in coats black with coal-dust or streaked with lime and red paint; in old age their white hairs are seen in a place of honour at church and at market, and they tell their well-dressed sons and daughters, seated round the bright hearth on winter evenings, how pleased they were when they first earned their twopence a-day. Others there are who die poor and never put off the workman's coat on weekdays. They have not had the art of getting rich, but they are men of trust, and when they die before the work is all out of them, it is as if some main screw had got loose in a machine; the master who employed them says, "Where shall I find their like?"

Chapter XX
Adam Visits the Hall Farm

Adam came back from his work in the empty waggon—that was why he had changed his clothes—and was ready to set out to the Hall Farm when it still wanted a quarter to seven.

"What's thee got thy Sunday cloose on for?" said Lisbeth complainingly, as he came downstairs. "Thee artna goin' to th' school i' thy best coat?"

"No, Mother," said Adam, quietly. "I'm going to the Hall Farm, but mayhap I may go to the school after, so thee mustna wonder if I'm a bit late. Seth 'ull be at home in half an hour—he's only gone to the village; so thee wutna mind."

"Eh, an' what's thee got thy best cloose on for to go to th' Hall Farm? The Poyser folks see'd thee in 'em yesterday, I warrand. What dost mean by turnin' worki'day into Sunday a-that'n? It's poor keepin' company wi' folks as donna like to see thee i' thy workin' jacket."

"Good-bye, mother, I can't stay," said Adam, putting on his hat and going out.

But he had no sooner gone a few paces beyond the door than Lisbeth became uneasy at the thought that she had vexed him. Of course, the secret of her objection to the best clothes was her suspicion that they were put on for Hetty's sake; but deeper than all her peevishness lay the need that her son should love her. She hurried after him, and laid hold of his arm before he had got half-way down to the brook, and said, "Nay, my lad, thee wutna go away angered wi' thy mother, an' her got nought to do but to sit by hersen an' think on thee?"

"Nay, nay, Mother," said Adam, gravely, and standing still while he put his arm on her shoulder, "I'm not angered. But I wish, for thy own sake, thee'dst be more contented to let me do what I've made up my mind to do. I'll never be no other than a good son to thee as long as we live. But a man has other feelings besides what he owes to's father and mother, and thee oughtna to want to rule over me body and soul. And thee must make up thy mind as I'll not give way to thee where I've a right to do what I like. So let us have no more words about it."

"Eh," said Lisbeth, not willing to show that she felt the real bearing of Adam's words, "and' who likes to see thee i' thy best cloose better nor thy mother? An' when thee'st got thy face washed as clean as the smooth white pibble, an' thy hair combed so nice, and thy eyes a-sparklin'—what else is there as thy old mother should like to look at half so well? An' thee sha't put on thy Sunday cloose when thee lik'st for me—I'll ne'er plague thee no moor about'n."

"Well, well; good-bye, mother," said Adam, kissing her and hurrying away. He saw there was no other means of putting an end to the dialogue. Lisbeth stood still on the spot, shading her eyes and looking after him till he was quite out of sight. She felt to the full all the meaning that had lain in Adam's words, and, as she lost sight of him and turned back slowly into the house, she said aloud to herself—for it was her way to speak her thoughts aloud in the long days when her husband and sons were at their work—"Eh, he'll be tellin' me as he's goin' to bring her home one o' these days; an' she'll be missis o'er me, and I mun look on, belike, while she uses the blue-edged platters, and breaks 'em, mayhap, though there's ne'er been one broke sin' my old man an' me bought 'em at the fair twenty 'ear come next Whissuntide. Eh!" she went on, still louder, as she caught up her knitting from the table, "but she'll ne'er knit the lad's stockin's, nor foot 'em nayther, while I live; an' when I'm gone, he'll bethink him as nobody 'ull ne'er fit's leg an' foot as his old mother did. She'll know nothin' o' narrowin' an' heelin', I warrand, an' she'll make a long toe as he canna get's boot on. That's what comes o' marr'in' young wenches. I war gone thirty, an' th' feyther too, afore we war married; an' young enough too. She'll be a poor dratchell by then *she's* thirty, a-marr'in' a-that'n, afore her teeth's all come."

Adam walked so fast that he was at the yard-gate before seven. Martin Poyser and the grandfather were not yet come in from the meadow: every one was in the meadow, even to the black-and-tan terrier—no one kept watch in the yard but the bull-dog; and when Adam reached the house-door, which stood wide open, he saw there was no one in the bright clean house-place. But he guessed where Mrs. Poyser and some one else would be, quite within hearing; so he knocked on the door and said in his strong voice, "Mrs. Poyser within?"

"Come in, Mr. Bede, come in," Mrs. Poyser called out from the dairy. She always gave Adam this title when she received him in her own house. "You may come into the dairy if you will, for I canna justly leave the cheese."

Adam walked into the dairy, where Mrs. Poyser and Nancy were crushing the first evening cheese.

"Why, you might think you war come to a dead-house," said Mrs. Poyser, as he stood in the open doorway; "they're all i' the meadow; but Martin's sure to be in afore long, for they're leaving the hay cocked to-night, ready for carrying first thing to-morrow. I've been forced t' have Nancy in, upo' 'count as Hetty must gether the red currants to-night; the fruit allays ripens so contrairy, just when every hand's wanted. An' there's no trustin' the children to gether it, for they put more into their own mouths nor into the basket; you might as well set the wasps to gether the fruit."

Adam longed to say he would go into the garden till Mr. Poyser came in, but he was not quite courageous enough, so he said, “I could be looking at your spinning-wheel, then, and see what wants doing to it. Perhaps it stands in the house, where I can find it?”

“No, I’ve put it away in the right-hand parlour; but let it be till I can fetch it and show it you. I’d be glad now if you’d go into the garden and tell Hetty to send Totty in. The child ’ull run in if she’s told, an’ I know Hetty’s lettin’ her eat too many currants. I’ll be much obliged to you, Mr. Bede, if you’ll go and send her in; an’ there’s the York and Lankester roses beautiful in the garden now—you’ll like to see ’em. But you’d like a drink o’ whey first, p’r’aps; I know you’re fond o’ whey, as most folks is when they hanna got to crush it out.”

“Thank you, Mrs. Poyser,” said Adam; “a drink o’ whey’s allays a treat to me. I’d rather have it than beer any day.”

“Aye, aye,” said Mrs. Poyser, reaching a small white basin that stood on the shelf, and dipping it into the whey-tub, “the smell o’ bread’s sweet t’ everybody but the baker. The Miss Irwines allays say, ‘Oh, Mrs. Poyser, I envy you your dairy; and I envy you your chickens; and what a beautiful thing a farm-house is, to be sure!’ An’ I say, ‘Yes; a farm-house is a fine thing for them as look on, an’ don’t know the liftin’, an’ the stannin’, an’ the worritin’ o’ th’ inside as belongs to’t.’”

“Why, Mrs. Poyser, you wouldn’t like to live anywhere else but in a farm-house, so well as you manage it,” said Adam, taking the basin; “and there can be nothing to look at pleasanter nor a fine milch cow, standing up to’ts knees in pasture, and the new milk frothing in the pail, and the fresh butter ready for market, and the calves, and the poultry. Here’s to your health, and may you allays have strength to look after your own dairy, and set a pattern t’ all the farmers’ wives in the country.”

Mrs. Poyser was not to be caught in the weakness of smiling at a compliment, but a quiet complacency over-spread her face like a stealing sunbeam, and gave a milder glance than usual to her blue-grey eyes, as she looked at Adam drinking the whey. Ah! I think I taste that whey now—with a flavour so delicate that one can hardly distinguish it from an odour, and with that soft gliding warmth that fills one’s imagination with a still, happy dreaminess. And the light music of the dropping whey is in my ears, mingling with the twittering of a bird outside the wire network window—the window overlooking the garden, and shaded by tall Guelder roses.

“Have a little more, Mr. Bede?” said Mrs. Poyser, as Adam set down the basin.

“No, thank you; I’ll go into the garden now, and send in the little lass.”

“Aye, do; and tell her to come to her mother in the dairy.”

Adam walked round by the rick-yard, at present empty of ricks, to the little wooden gate leading into the garden—once the well-tended kitchen-garden of a manor-house; now, but for the handsome brick wall with stone coping that ran along one side of it, a true farmhouse garden, with hardy perennial flowers, unpruned fruit-trees, and kitchen vegetables growing together in careless, half-neglected abundance. In that leafy, flowery, bushy time, to look for any one in this garden was like playing at "hide-and-seek." There were the tall hollyhocks beginning to flower and dazzle the eye with their pink, white, and yellow; there were the syringas and Guelder roses, all large and disorderly for want of trimming; there were leafy walls of scarlet beans and late peas; there was a row of bushy filberts in one direction, and in another a huge apple-tree making a barren circle under its low-spreading boughs. But what signified a barren patch or two? The garden was so large. There was always a superfluity of broad beans—it took nine or ten of Adam's strides to get to the end of the uncut grass walk that ran by the side of them; and as for other vegetables, there was so much more room than was necessary for them that in the rotation of crops a large flourishing bed of groundsel was of yearly occurrence on one spot or other. The very rose-trees at which Adam stopped to pluck one looked as if they grew wild; they were all huddled together in bushy masses, now flaunting with wide-open petals, almost all of them of the streaked pink-and-white kind, which doubtless dated from the union of the houses of York and Lancaster. Adam was wise enough to choose a compact Provence rose that peeped out half-smothered by its flaunting scentless neighbours, and held it in his hand—he thought he should be more at ease holding something in his hand—as he walked on to the far end of the garden, where he remembered there was the largest row of currant-trees, not far off from the great yew-tree arbour.

But he had not gone many steps beyond the roses, when he heard the shaking of a bough, and a boy's voice saying, "Now, then, Totty, hold out your pinny—there's a duck."

The voice came from the boughs of a tall cherry-tree, where Adam had no difficulty in discerning a small blue-pinafored figure perched in a commodious position where the fruit was thickest. Doubtless Totty was below, behind the screen of peas. Yes—with her bonnet hanging down her back, and her fat face, dreadfully smeared with red juice, turned up towards the cherry-tree, while she held her little round hole of a mouth and her red-stained pinafore to receive the promised downfall. I am sorry to say, more than half the cherries that fell were hard and yellow instead of juicy and red; but Totty spent no time in useless regrets, and she was already sucking the third juiciest when Adam said, "There now, Totty, you've got your cherries. Run into the house with 'em to Mother—she wants you—she's in the dairy. Run in this minute—there's a good little girl."

He lifted her up in his strong arms and kissed her as he spoke, a ceremony which Totty regarded as a tiresome interruption to cherry-eating; and when he set her down she trotted off quite silently towards the house, sucking her cherries as she went along.

"Tommy, my lad, take care you're not shot for a little thieving bird," said Adam, as he walked on towards the currant-trees.

He could see there was a large basket at the end of the row: Hetty would not be far off, and Adam already felt as if she were looking at him. Yet when he turned the corner she was standing with her back towards him, and stooping to gather the low-hanging fruit. Strange that she had not heard him coming! Perhaps it was because she was making the leaves rustle. She started when she became conscious that some one was near—started so violently that she dropped the basin with the currants in it, and then, when she saw it was Adam, she turned from pale to deep red. That blush made his heart beat with a new happiness. Hetty had never blushed at seeing him before.

"I frightened you," he said, with a delicious sense that it didn't signify what he said, since Hetty seemed to feel as much as he did; "let *me* pick the currants up."

That was soon done, for they had only fallen in a tangled mass on the grass-plot, and Adam, as he rose and gave her the basin again, looked straight into her eyes with the subdued tenderness that belongs to the first moments of hopeful love.

Hetty did not turn away her eyes; her blush had subsided, and she met his glance with a quiet sadness, which contented Adam because it was so unlike anything he had seen in her before.

"There's not many more currants to get," she said; "I shall soon ha' done now."

"I'll help you," said Adam; and he fetched the large basket, which was nearly full of currants, and set it close to them.

Not a word more was spoken as they gathered the currants. Adam's heart was too full to speak, and he thought Hetty knew all that was in it. She was not indifferent to his presence after all; she had blushed when she saw him, and then there was that touch of sadness about her which must surely mean love, since it was the opposite of her usual manner, which had often impressed him as indifference. And he could glance at her continually as she bent over the fruit, while the level evening sunbeams stole through the thick apple-tree boughs, and rested on her round cheek and neck as if they too were in love with her. It was to Adam the time that a man can least forget in after-life, the time when he believes that the first woman he has ever loved betrays by a slight something—a word, a tone, a glance, the quivering of a lip or an eyelid—that she is at least beginning to love him in return. The sign is so slight, it is scarcely perceptible to the ear or eye—

he could describe it to no one—it is a mere feather-touch, yet it seems to have changed his whole being, to have merged an uneasy yearning into a delicious unconsciousness of everything but the present moment. So much of our early gladness vanishes utterly from our memory: we can never recall the joy with which we laid our heads on our mother's bosom or rode on our father's back in childhood. Doubtless that joy is wrought up into our nature, as the sunlight of long-past mornings is wrought up in the soft mellowness of the apricot, but it is gone for ever from our imagination, and we can only *believe* in the joy of childhood. But the first glad moment in our first love is a vision which returns to us to the last, and brings with it a thrill of feeling intense and special as the recurrent sensation of a sweet odour breathed in a far-off hour of happiness. It is a memory that gives a more exquisite touch to tenderness, that feeds the madness of jealousy and adds the last keenness to the agony of despair.

Hetty bending over the red bunches, the level rays piercing the screen of apple-tree boughs, the length of bushy garden beyond, his own emotion as he looked at her and believed that she was thinking of him, and that there was no need for them to talk—Adam remembered it all to the last moment of his life.

And Hetty? You know quite well that Adam was mistaken about her. Like many other men, he thought the signs of love for another were signs of love towards himself. When Adam was approaching unseen by her, she was absorbed as usual in thinking and wondering about Arthur's possible return. The sound of any man's footstep would have affected her just in the same way—she would have *felt* it might be Arthur before she had time to see, and the blood that forsook her cheek in the agitation of that momentary feeling would have rushed back again at the sight of any one else just as much as at the sight of Adam. He was not wrong in thinking that a change had come over Hetty: the anxieties and fears of a first passion, with which she was trembling, had become stronger than vanity, had given her for the first time that sense of helpless dependence on another's feeling which awakens the clinging deprecating womanhood even in the shallowest girl that can ever experience it, and creates in her a sensibility to kindness which found her quite hard before. For the first time Hetty felt that there was something soothing to her in Adam's timid yet manly tenderness. She wanted to be treated lovingly—oh, it was very hard to bear this blank of absence, silence, apparent indifference, after those moments of glowing love! She was not afraid that Adam would tease her with love-making and flattering speeches like her other admirers; he had always been so reserved to her; she could enjoy without any fear the sense that this strong brave man loved her and was near her. It never entered into her mind that Adam was pitiable too—that Adam too must suffer one day.

Hetty, we know, was not the first woman that had behaved more gently to the man who loved her in vain because she had herself begun to love another. It was a very old story, but Adam knew nothing about it, so he drank in the sweet delusion.

"That'll do," said Hetty, after a little while. "Aunt wants me to leave some on the trees. I'll take 'em in now."

"It's very well I came to carry the basket," said Adam "for it 'ud ha' been too heavy for your little arms."

"No; I could ha' carried it with both hands."

"Oh, I daresay," said Adam, smiling, "and been as long getting into the house as a little ant carrying a caterpillar. Have you ever seen those tiny fellows carrying things four times as big as themselves?"

"No," said Hetty, indifferently, not caring to know the difficulties of ant life.

"Oh, I used to watch 'em often when I was a lad. But now, you see, I can carry the basket with one arm, as if it was an empty nutshell, and give you th' other arm to lean on. Won't you? Such big arms as mine were made for little arms like yours to lean on."

Hetty smiled faintly and put her arm within his. Adam looked down at her, but her eyes were turned dreamily towards another corner of the garden.

"Have you ever been to Eagledale?" she said, as they walked slowly along.

"Yes," said Adam, pleased to have her ask a question about himself. "Ten years ago, when I was a lad, I went with father to see about some work there. It's a wonderful sight—rocks and caves such as you never saw in your life. I never had a right notion o' rocks till I went there."

"How long did it take to get there?"

"Why, it took us the best part o' two days' walking. But it's nothing of a day's journey for anybody as has got a first-rate nag. The captain 'ud get there in nine or ten hours, I'll be bound, he's such a rider. And I shouldn't wonder if he's back again to-morrow; he's too active to rest long in that lonely place, all by himself, for there's nothing but a bit of a inn i' that part where he's gone to fish. I wish he'd got th' estate in his hands; that 'ud be the right thing for him, for it 'ud give him plenty to do, and he'd do't well too, for all he's so young; he's got better notions o' things than many a man twice his age. He spoke very handsome to me th' other day about lending me money to set up i' business; and if things came round that way, I'd rather be beholding to him nor to any man i' the world."

Poor Adam was led on to speak about Arthur because he thought Hetty would be pleased to know that the young squire was so ready to befriend him; the fact entered into his future prospects, which he would like to seem promising in her eyes. And it was true that Hetty listened with an interest which brought a new light into her eyes and a half-smile upon her lips.

"How pretty the roses are now!" Adam continued, pausing to look at them. "See! I stole the prettiest, but I didna mean to keep it myself. I think these as are all pink, and have got a finer sort o' green leaves, are prettier than the striped uns, don't you?"

He set down the basket and took the rose from his button-hole.

"It smells very sweet," he said; "those striped uns have no smell. Stick it in your frock, and then you can put it in water after. It 'ud be a pity to let it fade."

Hetty took the rose, smiling as she did so at the pleasant thought that Arthur could so soon get back if he liked. There was a flash of hope and happiness in her mind, and with a sudden impulse of gaiety she did what she had very often done before—stuck the rose in her hair a little above the left ear. The tender admiration in Adam's face was slightly shadowed by reluctant disapproval. Hetty's love of finery was just the thing that would most provoke his mother, and he himself disliked it as much as it was possible for him to dislike anything that belonged to her.

"Ah," he said, "that's like the ladies in the pictures at the Chase; they've mostly got flowers or feathers or gold things i' their hair, but somehow I don't like to see 'em; they allays put me i' mind o' the painted women outside the shows at Treddles'on Fair. What can a woman have to set her off better than her own hair, when it curls so, like yours? If a woman's young and pretty, I think you can see her good looks all the better for her being plain dressed. Why, Dinah Morris looks very nice, for all she wears such a plain cap and gown. It seems to me as a woman's face doesna want flowers; it's almost like a flower itself. I'm sure yours is."

"Oh, very well," said Hetty, with a little playful pout, taking the rose out of her hair. "I'll put one o' Dinah's caps on when we go in, and you'll see if I look better in it. She left one behind, so I can take the pattern."

"Nay, nay, I don't want you to wear a Methodist cap like Dinah's. I daresay it's a very ugly cap, and I used to think when I saw her here as it was nonsense for her to dress different t' other people; but I never rightly noticed her till she came to see mother last week, and then I thought the cap seemed to fit her face somehow as th 'acorn-cup fits th' acorn, and I shouldn't like to see her so well without it. But you've got another sort o' face; I'd have you just as you are now, without anything t' interfere with your own looks. It's like when a man's singing a good tune—you don't want t' hear bells tinkling and interfering wi' the sound."

He took her arm and put it within his again, looking down on her fondly. He was afraid she should think he had lectured her, imagining, as we are apt to do, that she had perceived all the thoughts he had only half-expressed. And the thing he dreaded most was lest any cloud should come over this evening's happiness. For the world he would not have spoken of his love to Hetty yet, till this commencing kindness towards him should have grown into unmistakable love. In his imagination he saw long years of his future life stretching before him, blest with the right to call Hetty his own: he could be content with very little at present. So he took up the basket of currants once more, and they went on towards the house.

The scene had quite changed in the half-hour that Adam had been in the garden. The yard was full of life now: Marty was letting the screaming geese through the gate, and wickedly provoking the gander by hissing at him; the granary-door was groaning on its hinges as Alick shut it, after dealing out the corn; the horses were being led out to watering, amidst much barking of all the three dogs and many "whups" from Tim the ploughman, as if the heavy animals who held down their meek, intelligent heads, and lifted their shaggy feet so deliberately, were likely to rush wildly in every direction but the right. Everybody was come back from the meadow; and when Hetty and Adam entered the house-place, Mr. Poyser was seated in the three-cornered chair, and the grandfather in the large arm-chair opposite, looking on with pleasant expectation while the supper was being laid on the oak table. Mrs. Poyser had laid the cloth herself—a cloth made of homespun linen, with a shining checkered pattern on it, and of an agreeable whitey-brown hue, such as all sensible housewives like to see—none of your bleached "shop-rag" that would wear into holes in no time, but good homespun that would last for two generations. The cold veal, the fresh lettuces, and the stuffed chine might well look tempting to hungry men who had dined at half-past twelve o'clock. On the large deal table against the wall there were bright pewter plates and spoons and cans, ready for Alick and his companions; for the master and servants ate their supper not far off each other; which was all the pleasanter, because if a remark about to-morrow morning's work occurred to Mr. Poyser, Alick was at hand to hear it.

"Well, Adam, I'm glad to see ye," said Mr. Poyser. "What! ye've been helping Hetty to gether the curran's, eh? Come, sit ye down, sit ye down. Why, it's pretty near a three-week since y' had your supper with us; and the missis has got one of her rare stuffed chines. I'm glad ye're come."

"Hetty," said Mrs. Poyser, as she looked into the basket of currants to see if the fruit was fine, "run upstairs and send Molly down. She's putting Totty to bed, and I want her to draw th' ale, for Nancy's busy yet i' the dairy. You can see to the child. But whativer did you let her run away from you along wi' Tommy for, and stuff herself wi' fruit as she can't eat a bit o' good victual?"

This was said in a lower tone than usual, while her husband was talking to Adam; for Mrs. Poyser was strict in adherence to her own rules of propriety, and she considered that a young girl was not to be treated sharply in the presence of a respectable man who was courting her. That would not be fair-play: every woman was young in her turn, and had her chances of matrimony, which it was a point of honour for other women not to spoil—just as one market-woman who has sold her own eggs must not try to balk another of a customer.

Hetty made haste to run away upstairs, not easily finding an answer to her aunt's question, and Mrs. Poyser went out to see after Marty and Tommy and bring them in to supper.

Soon they were all seated—the two rosy lads, one on each side, by the pale mother, a place being left for Hetty between Adam and her uncle. Alick too was come in, and was seated in his far corner, eating cold broad beans out of a large dish with his pocket-knife, and finding a flavour in them which he would not have exchanged for the finest pineapple.

"What a time that gell is drawing th' ale, to be sure!" said Mrs. Poyser, when she was dispensing her slices of stuffed chine. "I think she sets the jug under and forgets to turn the tap, as there's nothing you can't believe o' them wenches: they'll set the empty kettle o' the fire, and then come an hour after to see if the water boils."

"She's drawin' for the men too," said Mr. Poyser. "Thee shouldst ha' told her to bring our jug up first."

"Told her?" said Mrs. Poyser. "Yes, I might spend all the wind i' my body, an' take the bellows too, if I was to tell them gells everything as their own sharpness wonna tell 'em. Mr. Bede, will you take some vinegar with your lettuce? Aye you're i' the right not. It spoils the flavour o' the chine, to my thinking. It's poor eating where the flavour o' the meat lies i' the cruets. There's folks as make bad butter and trusten to the salt t' hide it."

Mrs. Poyser's attention was here diverted by the appearance of Molly, carrying a large jug, two small mugs, and four drinking-cans, all full of ale or small beer—an interesting example of the prehensile power possessed by the human hand. Poor Molly's mouth was rather wider open than usual, as she walked along with her eyes fixed on the double cluster of vessels in her hands, quite innocent of the expression in her mistress's eye.

"Molly, I niver knew your equils—to think o' your poor mother as is a widow, an' I took you wi' as good as no character, an' the times an' times I've told you...."

Molly had not seen the lightning, and the thunder shook her nerves the more for the want of that preparation. With a vague alarmed sense that she must somehow comport herself differently, she hastened her step a little towards the far deal table, where she might set down her cans—caught her foot in her apron, which had become untied, and fell with a crash and a splash into a pool of beer; whereupon a tittering explosion from Marty and Tommy, and a serious "Ello!" from Mr. Poyser, who saw his draught of ale unpleasantly deferred.

"There you go!" resumed Mrs. Poyser, in a cutting tone, as she rose and went towards the cupboard while Molly began dolefully to pick up the fragments of pottery. "It's what I told you 'ud come, over and over again; and there's your month's wage gone, and more, to pay for that jug as I've had i' the house this ten year, and nothing ever happened to't before; but the crockery you've broke sin' here in th' house you've been 'ud make a parson swear—God forgi' me for saying so—an' if it had been boiling wort out o' the copper, it 'ud ha' been the same, and you'd ha' been scalded and very like lamed for life, as there's no knowing but what you will be some day if you go on; for anybody 'ud think you'd got the St. Vitus's Dance, to see the things you've throwed down. It's a pity but what the bits was stacked up for you to see, though it's neither seeing nor hearing as 'ull make much odds to you—anybody 'ud think you war case-hardened."

Poor Molly's tears were dropping fast by this time, and in her desperation at the lively movement of the beer-stream towards Alick's legs, she was converting her apron into a mop, while Mrs. Poyser, opening the cupboard, turned a blighting eye upon her.

"Ah," she went on, "you'll do no good wi' crying an' making more wet to wipe up. It's all your own wilfulness, as I tell you, for there's nobody no call to break anything if they'll only go the right way to work. But wooden folks had need ha' wooden things t' handle. And here must I take the brown-and-white jug, as it's niver been used three times this year, and go down i' the cellar myself, and belike catch my death, and be laid up wi' inflammation...."

Mrs. Poyser had turned round from the cupboard with the brown-and-white jug in her hand, when she caught sight of something at the other end of the kitchen; perhaps it was because she was already trembling and nervous that the apparition had so strong an effect on her; perhaps jug-breaking, like other crimes, has a contagious influence. However it was, she stared and started like a ghost-seer, and the precious brown-and-white jug fell to the ground, parting for ever with its spout and handle.

"Did ever anybody see the like?" she said, with a suddenly lowered tone, after a moment's bewildered glance round the room. "The jugs are bewitched, *I* think. It's them nasty glazed handles—they slip o'er the finger like a snail."

"Why, thee'st let thy own whip fly i' thy face," said her husband, who had now joined in the laugh of the young ones.

"It's all very fine to look on and grin," rejoined Mrs. Poyser; "but there's times when the crockery seems alive an' flies out o' your hand like a bird. It's like the glass, sometimes, 'ull crack as it stands. What is to be broke *will* be broke, for I never dropped a thing i' my life for want o' holding it, else I should never ha' kept the crockery all these 'ears as I bought at my own wedding. And Hetty, are you mad? Whativer do you mean by coming down i' that way, and making one think as there's a ghost a-walking i' th' house?"

A new outbreak of laughter, while Mrs. Poyser was speaking, was caused, less by her sudden conversion to a fatalistic view of jug-breaking than by that strange appearance of Hetty, which had startled her aunt. The little minx had found a black gown of her aunt's, and pinned it close round her neck to look like Dinah's, had made her hair as flat as she could, and had tied on one of Dinah's high-crowned borderless net caps. The thought of Dinah's pale grave face and mild grey eyes, which the sight of the gown and cap brought with it, made it a laughable surprise enough to see them replaced by Hetty's round rosy cheeks and coquettish dark eyes. The boys got off their chairs and jumped round her, clapping their hands, and even Alick gave a low ventral laugh as he looked up from his beans. Under cover of the noise, Mrs. Poyser went into the back kitchen to send Nancy into the cellar with the great pewter measure, which had some chance of being free from bewitchment.

"Why, Hetty, lass, are ye turned Methodist?" said Mr. Poyser, with that comfortable slow enjoyment of a laugh which one only sees in stout people. "You must pull your face a deal longer before you'll do for one; mustna she, Adam? How come you put them things on, eh?"

"Adam said he liked Dinah's cap and gown better nor my clothes," said Hetty, sitting down demurely. "He says folks looks better in ugly clothes."

"Nay, nay," said Adam, looking at her admiringly; "I only said they seemed to suit Dinah. But if I'd said you'd look pretty in 'em, I should ha' said nothing but what was true."

"Why, thee thought'st Hetty war a ghost, didstna?" said Mr. Poyser to his wife, who now came back and took her seat again. "Thee look'dst as scared as scared."

"It little sinnifies how I looked," said Mrs. Poyser; "looks 'ull mend no jugs, nor laughing neither, as I see. Mr. Bede, I'm sorry you've to wait so long for your ale, but it's coming in a minute. Make yourself at home wi' th' cold potatoes: I know you like 'em. Tommy, I'll send you to bed this minute, if you don't give over laughing. What is there to laugh at, I should like to know? I'd sooner cry nor laugh at the sight o' that poor thing's cap; and there's them as 'ud be better if they could make theirselves like her i' more ways nor putting on her cap. It little becomes anybody i' this house to make fun o' my sister's child, an' her just gone away from us, as it went to my heart to part wi' her. An' I know one thing, as if trouble was to come, an' I was to be laid up i' my bed, an' the children was to die—as there's no knowing but what they will—an' the murrain was to come among the cattle again, an' everything went to rack an' ruin, I say we might be glad to get sight o' Dinah's cap again, wi' her own face under it, border or no border. For she's one o' them things as looks the brightest on a rainy day, and loves you the best when you're most i' need on't."

Mrs. Poyser, you perceive, was aware that nothing would be so likely to expel the comic as the terrible. Tommy, who was of a susceptible disposition, and very fond of his mother, and who had, besides, eaten so many cherries as to have his feelings less under command than usual, was so affected by the dreadful picture she had made of the possible future that he began to cry; and the good-natured father, indulgent to all weaknesses but those of negligent farmers, said to Hetty, "You'd better take the things off again, my lass; it hurts your aunt to see 'em."

Hetty went upstairs again, and the arrival of the ale made an agreeable diversion; for Adam had to give his opinion of the new tap, which could not be otherwise than complimentary to Mrs. Poyser; and then followed a discussion on the secrets of good brewing, the folly of stinginess in "hopping," and the doubtful economy of a farmer's making his own malt. Mrs. Poyser had so many opportunities of expressing herself with weight on these subjects that by the time supper was ended, the ale-jug refilled, and Mr. Poyser's pipe alight she was once more in high good humour, and ready, at Adam's request, to fetch the broken spinning-wheel for his inspection.

"Ah," said Adam, looking at it carefully, "here's a nice bit o' turning wanted. It's a pretty wheel. I must have it up at the turning-shop in the village and do it there, for I've no convenence for turning at home. If you'll send it to Mr. Burge's shop i' the morning, I'll get it done for you by Wednesday. I've been turning it over in my mind," he continued, looking at Mr. Poyser, "to make a bit more convenence at home for nice jobs o' cabinet-making. I've always done a deal at such little things in odd hours, and they're profitable, for there's more workmanship nor material in 'em. I look for me and Seth to get a little business for ourselves i' that way, for I know a man at Rosseter as 'ull take as many things as we should make, besides what we could get orders for round about."

Mr. Poyser entered with interest into a project which seemed a step towards Adam's becoming a "master-man," and Mrs. Poyser gave her approbation to the scheme of the movable kitchen cupboard, which was to be capable of containing grocery, pickles, crockery, and house-linen in the utmost compactness without confusion. Hetty, once more in her own dress, with her neckerchief pushed a little backwards on this warm evening, was seated picking currants near the window, where Adam could see her quite well. And so the time passed pleasantly till Adam got up to go. He was pressed to come again soon, but not to stay longer, for at this busy time sensible people would not run the risk of being sleepy at five o'clock in the morning.

"I shall take a step farther," said Adam, "and go on to see Mester Massey, for he wasn't at church yesterday, and I've not seen him for a week past. I've never hardly known him to miss church before."

"Aye," said Mr. Poyser, "we've heared nothing about him, for it's the boys' hollodays now, so we can give you no account."

"But you'll niver think o' going there at this hour o' the night?" said Mrs. Poyser, folding up her knitting.

"Oh, Mester Massey sits up late," said Adam. "An' the night-school's not over yet. Some o' the men don't come till late—they've got so far to walk. And Bartle himself's never in bed till it's gone eleven."

"I wouldna have him to live wi' me, then," said Mrs. Poyser, "a-dropping candle-grease about, as you're like to tumble down o' the floor the first thing i' the morning."

"Aye, eleven o'clock's late—it's late," said old Martin. "I ne'er sot up so i' *my* life, not to say as it warna a marr'in', or a christenin', or a wake, or th' harvest supper. Eleven o'clock's late."

"Why, I sit up till after twelve often," said Adam, laughing, "but it isn't t' eat and drink extry, it's to work extry. Good-night, Mrs. Poyser; good-night, Hetty."

Hetty could only smile and not shake hands, for hers were dyed and damp with currant-juice; but all the rest gave a hearty shake to the large palm that was held out to them, and said, "Come again, come again!"

"Aye, think o' that now," said Mr. Poyser, when Adam was out of on the causeway. "Sitting up till past twelve to do extry work! Ye'll not find many men o' six-an' twenty as 'ull do to put i' the shafts wi' him. If you can catch Adam for a husband, Hetty, you'll ride i' your own spring-cart some day, I'll be your warrant."

Hetty was moving across the kitchen with the currants, so her uncle did not see the little toss of the head with which she answered him. To ride in a spring-cart seemed a very miserable lot indeed to her now.

Chapter XXI
The Night-School and the Schoolmaster

Bartle Massey's was one of a few scattered houses on the edge of a common, which was divided by the road to Treddleston. Adam reached it in a quarter of an hour after leaving the Hall Farm; and when he had his hand on the door-latch, he could see, through the curtainless window, that there were eight or nine heads bending over the desks, lighted by thin dips.

When he entered, a reading lesson was going forward and Bartle Massey merely nodded, leaving him to take his place where he pleased. He had not come for the sake of a lesson to-night, and his mind was too full of personal matters, too full of the last two hours he had passed in Hetty's presence, for him to amuse himself with a book till school was over; so he sat down in a corner and looked on with an absent mind. It was a sort of scene which Adam had beheld almost weekly for years; he knew by heart every arabesque flourish in the framed specimen of Bartle Massey's handwriting which hung over the schoolmaster's head, by way of keeping a lofty ideal before the minds of his pupils; he knew the backs of all the books on the shelf running along the whitewashed wall above the pegs for the slates; he knew exactly how many grains were gone out of the ear of Indian corn that hung from one of the rafters; he had long ago exhausted the resources of his imagination in trying to think how the bunch of leathery seaweed had looked and grown in its native element; and from the place where he sat, he could make nothing of the old map of England that hung against the opposite wall, for age had turned it of a fine yellow brown, something like that of a well-seasoned meerschaum. The drama that was going on was almost as familiar as the scene, nevertheless habit had not made him indifferent to it, and even in his present self-absorbed mood, Adam felt a momentary stirring of the old fellow-feeling, as he looked at the rough men painfully holding pen or pencil with their cramped hands, or humbly labouring through their reading lesson.

The reading class now seated on the form in front of the schoolmaster's desk consisted of the three most backward pupils. Adam would have known it only by seeing Bartle Massey's face as he looked over his spectacles, which he had shifted to the ridge of his nose, not requiring them for present purposes. The face wore its mildest expression: the grizzled bushy eyebrows had taken their more acute angle of compassionate kindness, and the mouth, habitually compressed with a pout of the lower lip, was relaxed so as to be ready to speak a helpful word or syllable in a moment. This gentle expression was the more interesting because the schoolmaster's nose, an irregular aquiline twisted a little on one side, had rather a formidable character; and his brow, moreover, had that peculiar tension which always impresses one as a sign of a keen impatient temperament: the blue veins stood out like cords under the transparent yellow skin, and this intimidating brow was softened by no tendency to baldness, for the grey bristly hair, cut down to about an inch in length, stood round it in as close ranks as ever.

"Nay, Bill, nay," Bartle was saying in a kind tone, as he nodded to Adam, "begin that again, and then perhaps, it'll come to you what d-r-y spells. It's the same lesson you read last week, you know."

"Bill" was a sturdy fellow, aged four-and-twenty, an excellent stone-sawyer, who could get as good wages as any man in the trade of his years; but he found a reading lesson in words of one syllable a harder matter to deal with than the hardest stone he had ever had to saw. The letters, he complained, were so "uncommon alike, there was no tellin' 'em one from another," the sawyer's business not being concerned with minute differences such as exist between a letter with its tail turned up and a letter with its tail turned down. But Bill had a firm determination that he would learn to read, founded chiefly on two reasons: first, that Tom Hazelow, his cousin, could read anything "right off," whether it was print or writing, and Tom had sent him a letter from twenty miles off, saying how he was prospering in the world and had got an overlooker's place; secondly, that Sam Phillips, who sawed with him, had learned to read when he was turned twenty, and what could be done by a little fellow like Sam Phillips, Bill considered, could be done by himself, seeing that he could pound Sam into wet clay if circumstances required it. So here he was, pointing his big finger towards three words at once, and turning his head on one side that he might keep better hold with his eye of the one word which was to be discriminated out of the group. The amount of knowledge Bartle Massey must possess was something so dim and vast that Bill's imagination recoiled before it: he would hardly have ventured to deny that the schoolmaster might have something to do in bringing about the regular return of daylight and the changes in the weather.

The man seated next to Bill was of a very different type: he was a Methodist brickmaker who, after spending thirty years of his life in perfect satisfaction with his ignorance, had lately "got religion," and along with it the desire to read the Bible. But with him, too, learning was a heavy business, and on his way out to-night he had offered as usual a special prayer for help, seeing that he had undertaken this hard task with a single eye to the nourishment of his soul—that he might have a greater abundance of texts and hymns wherewith to banish evil memories and the temptations of old habit—or, in brief language, the devil. For the brickmaker had been a notorious poacher, and was suspected, though there was no good evidence against him, of being the man who had shot a neighbouring gamekeeper in the leg. However that might be, it is certain that shortly after the accident referred to, which was coincident with the arrival of an awakening

Methodist preacher at Treddleston, a great change had been observed in the brickmaker; and though he was still known in the neighbourhood by his old sobriquet of "Brimstone," there was nothing he held in so much horror as any further transactions with that evil-smelling element. He was a broad-chested fellow with a fervid temperament, which helped him better in imbibing religious ideas than in the dry process of acquiring the mere human knowledge of the alphabet. Indeed, he had been already a little shaken in his resolution by a brother Methodist, who assured him that the letter was a mere obstruction to the Spirit, and expressed a fear that Brimstone was too eager for the knowledge that puffeth up.

The third beginner was a much more promising pupil. He was a tall but thin and wiry man, nearly as old as Brimstone, with a very pale face and hands stained a deep blue. He was a dyer, who in the course of dipping homespun wool and old women's petticoats had got fired with the ambition to learn a great deal more about the strange secrets of colour. He had already a high reputation in the district for his dyes, and he was bent on discovering some method by which he could reduce the expense of crimsons and scarlets. The druggist at Treddleston had given him a notion that he might save himself a great deal of labour and expense if he could learn to read, and so he had begun to give his spare hours to the night-school, resolving that his "little chap" should lose no time in coming to Mr. Massey's day-school as soon as he was old enough.

It was touching to see these three big men, with the marks of their hard labour about them, anxiously bending over the worn books and painfully making out, "The grass is green," "The sticks are dry," "The corn is ripe"—a very hard lesson to pass to after columns of single words all alike except in the first letter. It was almost as if three rough animals were making humble efforts to learn how they might become human. And it touched the tenderest fibre in Bartle Massey's nature, for such full-grown children as these were the only pupils for whom he had no severe epithets and no impatient tones. He was not gifted with an imperturbable temper, and on music-nights it was apparent that patience could never be an easy virtue to him; but this evening, as he glances over his spectacles at Bill Downes, the sawyer, who is turning his head on one side with a desperate sense of blankness before the letters d-r-y, his eyes shed their mildest and most encouraging light.

After the reading class, two youths between sixteen and nineteen came up with the imaginary bills of parcels, which they had been writing out on their slates and were now required to calculate "off-hand"—a test which they stood with such imperfect success that Bartle Massey, whose eyes had been glaring at them ominously through his spectacles for some minutes, at length burst out in a bitter, high-pitched tone, pausing between every sentence to rap the floor with a knobbed stick which rested between his legs.

"Now, you see, you don't do this thing a bit better than you did a fortnight ago, and I'll tell you what's the reason. You want to learn accounts—that's well and good. But you think all you need do to learn accounts is to come to me and do sums for an hour or so, two or three times a-week; and no sooner do you get your caps on and turn out of doors again than you sweep the whole thing clean out of your mind. You go whistling about, and take no more care what you're thinking of than if your heads were gutters for any rubbish to swill through that happened to be in the way; and if you get a good notion in 'em, it's pretty soon washed out again. You think knowledge is to be got cheap—you'll come and pay Bartle Massey sixpence a-week, and he'll make you clever at figures without your taking any trouble. But knowledge isn't to be got with paying sixpence, let me tell you. If you're to know figures, you must turn 'em over in your heads and keep your thoughts fixed on 'em. There's nothing you can't turn into a sum, for there's nothing but what's got number in it—even a fool. You may say to yourselves, 'I'm one fool, and Jack's another; if my fool's head weighed four pound, and Jack's three pound three ounces and three quarters, how many pennyweights heavier would my head be than Jack's?' A man that had got his heart in learning figures would make sums for himself and work 'em in his head. When he sat at his shoemaking, he'd count his stitches by fives, and then put a price on his stitches, say half a farthing, and then see how much money he could get in an hour; and then ask himself how much money he'd get in a day at that rate; and then how much ten workmen would get working three, or twenty, or a hundred years at that rate—and all the while his needle would be going just as fast as if he left his head empty for the devil to dance in. But the long and the short of it is—I'll have nobody in my night-school that doesn't strive to learn what he comes to learn, as hard as if he was striving to get out of a dark hole into broad daylight. I'll send no man away because he's stupid: if Billy Taft, the idiot, wanted to learn anything, I'd not refuse to teach him. But I'll not throw away good knowledge on people who think they can get it by the sixpenn'orth, and carry it away with 'em as they would an ounce of snuff. So never come to me again, if you can't show that you've been working with your own heads, instead of thinking that you can pay for mine to work for you. That's the last word I've got to say to you."

With this final sentence, Bartle Massey gave a sharper rap than ever with his knobbed stick, and the discomfited lads got up to go with a sulky look. The other pupils had happily only their writing-books to show, in various stages of progress from pot-hooks to round text; and mere pen-strokes, however perverse, were less exasperating to Bartle than false arithmetic. He was a little more severe than usual on Jacob Storey's Z's, of which poor Jacob had written a pageful, all with their tops turned the wrong way, with a puzzled sense that they were not right "somehow." But he observed in apology, that it was a letter you never wanted hardly, and he thought it had only been there "to finish off th' alphabet, like, though ampusand (&) would ha' done as well, for what he could see."

At last the pupils had all taken their hats and said their "Good-nights," and Adam, knowing his old master's habits, rose and said, "Shall I put the candles out, Mr. Massey?"

"Yes, my boy, yes, all but this, which I'll carry into the house; and just lock the outer door, now you're near it," said Bartle, getting his stick in the fitting angle to help him in descending from his stool. He was no sooner on the ground than it became obvious why the stick was necessary—the left leg was much shorter than the right. But the school-master was so active with his lameness that it was hardly thought of as a misfortune; and if you had seen him make his way along the schoolroom floor, and up the step into his kitchen, you would perhaps have understood why the naughty boys sometimes felt that his pace might be indefinitely quickened and that he and his stick might overtake them even in their swiftest run.

The moment he appeared at the kitchen door with the candle in his hand, a faint whimpering began in the chimney-corner, and a brown-and-tan-coloured bitch, of that wise-looking breed with short legs and long body, known to an unmechanical generation as turnspits, came creeping along the floor, wagging her tail, and hesitating at every other step, as if her affections were painfully divided between the hamper in the chimney-corner and the master, whom she could not leave without a greeting.

"Well, Vixen, well then, how are the babbies?" said the schoolmaster, making haste towards the chimney-corner and holding the candle over the low hamper, where two extremely blind puppies lifted up their heads towards the light from a nest of flannel and wool. Vixen could not even see her master look at them without painful excitement: she got into the hamper and got out again the next moment, and behaved with true feminine folly, though looking all the while as wise as a dwarf with a large old-fashioned head and body on the most abbreviated legs.

"Why, you've got a family, I see, Mr. Massey?" said Adam, smiling, as he came into the kitchen. "How's that? I thought it was against the law here."

"Law? What's the use o' law when a man's once such a fool as to let a woman into his house?" said Bartle, turning away from the hamper with some bitterness. He always called Vixen a woman, and seemed to have lost all consciousness that he was using a figure of speech. "If I'd known Vixen was a woman, I'd never have held the boys from drowning her; but when I'd got her into my hand, I was forced to take to her. And now you see what she's brought me to—the sly, hypocritical wench"—Bartle spoke these last words in a rasping tone of reproach, and looked at Vixen, who poked down her head and turned up her eyes towards him with a keen sense of opprobrium—"and contrived to be brought to bed on a Sunday at church-time. I've wished again and again I'd been a bloody minded man, that I could have strangled the mother and the brats with one cord."

"I'm glad it was no worse a cause kept you from church," said Adam. "I was afraid you must be ill for the first time i' your life. And I was particularly sorry not to have you at church yesterday."

"Ah, my boy, I know why, I know why," said Bartle kindly, going up to Adam and raising his hand up to the shoulder that was almost on a level with his own head. "You've had a rough bit o' road to get over since I saw you—a rough bit o' road. But I'm in hopes there are better times coming for you. I've got some news to tell you. But I must get my supper first, for I'm hungry, I'm hungry. Sit down, sit down."

Bartel went into his little pantry, and brought out an excellent home-baked loaf; for it was his one extravagance in these dear times to eat bread once a-day instead of oat-cake; and he justified it by observing, that what a schoolmaster wanted was brains, and oat-cake ran too much to bone instead of brains. Then came a piece of cheese and a quart jug with a crown of foam upon it. He placed them all on the round deal table which stood against his large arm-chair in the chimney-corner, with Vixen's hamper on one side of it and a window-shelf with a few books piled up in it on the other. The table was as clean as if Vixen had been an excellent housewife in a checkered apron; so was the quarry floor; and the old carved oaken press, table, and chairs, which in these days would be bought at a high price in aristocratic houses, though, in that period of spider-legs and inlaid cupids, Bartle had got them for an old song, were as free from dust as things could be at the end of a summer's day.

"Now, then, my boy, draw up, draw up. We'll not talk about business till we've had our supper. No man can be wise on an empty stomach. But," said Bartle, rising from his chair again, "I must give Vixen her supper too, confound her! Though she'll do nothing with it but nourish those unnecessary babbies. That's the way with these women—they've got no head-pieces to nourish, and so their food all runs either to fat or to brats."

He brought out of the pantry a dish of scraps, which Vixen at once fixed her eyes on, and jumped out of her hamper to lick up with the utmost dispatch.

"I've had my supper, Mr. Massey," said Adam, "so I'll look on while you eat yours. I've been at the Hall Farm, and they always have their supper betimes, you know: they don't keep your late hours."

"I know little about their hours," said Bartle dryly, cutting his bread and not shrinking from the crust. "It's a house I seldom go into, though I'm fond of the boys, and Martin Poyser's a good fellow. There's too many women in the house for me: I hate the sound of women's voices; they're always either a-buzz or a-squeak—always either a-buzz or a-squeak. Mrs. Poyser keeps at the top o' the talk like a fife; and as for the young lasses, I'd as soon look at water-grubs. I know what they'll turn to—stinging gnats, stinging gnats. Here, take some ale, my boy: it's been drawn for you—it's been drawn for you."

"Nay, Mr. Massey," said Adam, who took his old friend's whim more seriously than usual to-night, "don't be so hard on the creaturs God has made to be companions for us. A working-man 'ud be badly off without a wife to see to th' house and the victual, and make things clean and comfortable."

"Nonsense! It's the silliest lie a sensible man like you ever believed, to say a woman makes a house comfortable. It's a story got up because the women are there and something must be found for 'em to do. I tell you there isn't a thing under the sun that needs to be done at all, but what a man can do better than a woman, unless it's bearing children, and they do that in a poor make-shift way; it had better ha' been left to the men—it had better ha' been left to the men. I tell you, a woman 'ull bake you a pie every week of her life and never come to see that the hotter th' oven the shorter the time. I tell you, a woman 'ull make your porridge every day for twenty years and never think of measuring the proportion between the meal and the milk—a little more or less, she'll think, doesn't signify. The porridge *will* be awk'ard now and then: if it's wrong, it's summat in the meal, or it's summat in the milk, or it's summat in the water. Look at me! I make my own bread, and there's no difference between one batch and another from year's end to year's end; but if I'd got any other woman besides Vixen in the house, I must pray to the Lord every baking to give me patience if the bread turned out heavy. And as for cleanliness, my house is cleaner than any other house on the Common, though the half of 'em swarm with women. Will Baker's lad comes to help me in a morning, and we get as much cleaning done in one hour, without any fuss, as a woman 'ud get done in three, and all the while be sending buckets o' water after your ankles, and let the fender and the fire-irons stand in the middle o' the floor half the day for you to break your shins against 'em. Don't tell me about God having made such creatures to be companions for us! I don't say but He might make Eve to be a companion to Adam in Paradise—there was no cooking to be spoilt there, and no other woman to cackle with and make mischief, though you see what mischief she did as soon as she'd an opportunity. But it's an impious, unscriptural opinion to say a woman's a blessing to a man now; you might as well say adders and wasps, and foxes and wild beasts are a blessing, when they're only the evils that belong to this state o' probation, which it's lawful for a man to keep as clear of as he can in this life, hoping to get quit of 'em for ever in another—hoping to get quit of 'em for ever in another."

Bartle had become so excited and angry in the course of his invective that he had forgotten his supper, and only used the knife for the purpose of rapping the table with the haft. But towards the close, the raps became so sharp and frequent, and his voice so quarrelsome, that Vixen felt it incumbent on her to jump out of the hamper and bark vaguely.

"Quiet, Vixen!" snarled Bartle, turning round upon her. "You're like the rest o' the women—always putting in *your* word before you know why."

Vixen returned to her hamper again in humiliation, and her master continued his supper in a silence which Adam did not choose to interrupt; he knew the old man would be in a better humour when he had had his supper and lighted his pipe. Adam was used to hear him talk in this way, but had never learned so much of Bartle's past life as to know whether his view of married comfort was founded on experience. On that point Bartle was mute, and it was even a secret where he had lived previous to the twenty years in which happily for the peasants and artisans of this neighbourhood he had been settled among them as their only schoolmaster. If anything like a question was ventured on this subject, Bartle always replied, "Oh, I've seen many places—I've been a deal in the south," and the Loamshire men would as soon have thought of asking for a particular town or village in Africa as in "the south."

"Now then, my boy," said Bartle, at last, when he had poured out his second mug of ale and lighted his pipe, "now then, we'll have a little talk. But tell me first, have you heard any particular news to-day?"

"No," said Adam, "not as I remember."

"Ah, they'll keep it close, they'll keep it close, I daresay. But I found it out by chance; and it's news that may concern you, Adam, else I'm a man that don't know a superficial square foot from a solid."

Here Bartle gave a series of fierce and rapid puffs, looking earnestly the while at Adam. Your impatient loquacious man has never any notion of keeping his pipe alight by gentle measured puffs; he is always letting it go nearly out, and then punishing it for that negligence. At last he said, "Satchell's got a paralytic stroke. I found it out from the lad they sent to Treddleston for the doctor, before seven o'clock this morning. He's a good way beyond sixty, you know; it's much if he gets over it."

"Well," said Adam, "I daresay there'd be more rejoicing than sorrow in the parish at his being laid up. He's been a selfish, tale-bearing, mischievous fellow; but, after all, there's nobody he's done so much harm to as to th' old squire. Though it's the squire himself as is to blame—making a stupid fellow like that a sort o' man-of-all-work, just to save th' expense of having a proper steward to look after th' estate. And he's lost more by ill management o' the woods, I'll be bound, than 'ud pay for two stewards. If he's laid on the shelf, it's to be hoped he'll make way for a better man, but I don't see how it's like to make any difference to me."

"But I see it, but I see it," said Bartle, "and others besides me. The captain's coming of age now—you know that as well as I do—and it's to be expected he'll have a little more voice in things. And I know, and you know too, what 'ud be the captain's wish about the woods, if there was a fair opportunity for making a change. He's said in plenty of people's hearing that he'd make you manager of the woods to-morrow, if he'd the power. Why, Carroll, Mr. Irwine's butler, heard him say so to the parson not many days ago. Carroll looked in when we were smoking our pipes o' Saturday night at Casson's, and he told us about it; and whenever anybody says a good word for you, the parson's ready to back it, that I'll answer for. It was pretty well talked over, I can tell you, at Casson's, and one and another had their fling at you; for if donkeys set to work to sing, you're pretty sure what the tune'll be."

"Why, did they talk it over before Mr. Burge?" said Adam; "or wasn't he there o' Saturday?"

"Oh, he went away before Carroll came; and Casson—he's always for setting other folks right, you know—would have it Burge was the man to have the management of the woods. 'A substantial man,' says he, 'with pretty near sixty years' experience o' timber: it 'ud be all very well for Adam Bede to act under him, but it isn't to be supposed the squire 'ud appoint a young fellow like Adam, when there's his elders and betters at hand!' But I said, 'That's a pretty notion o' yours, Casson. Why, Burge is the man to *buy* timber; would you put the woods into his hands and let him make his own bargains? I think you don't leave your customers to score their own drink, do you? And as for age, what that's worth depends on the quality o' the liquor. It's pretty well known who's the backbone of Jonathan Burge's business.'"

"I thank you for your good word, Mr. Massey," said Adam. "But, for all that, Casson was partly i' the right for once. There's not much likelihood that th' old squire 'ud ever consent t' employ me. I offended him about two years ago, and he's never forgiven me."

"Why, how was that? You never told me about it," said Bartle.

"Oh, it was a bit o' nonsense. I'd made a frame for a screen for Miss Lyddy—she's allays making something with her worsted-work, you know—and she'd given me particular orders about this screen, and there was as much talking and measuring as if we'd been planning a house. However, it was a nice bit o' work, and I liked doing it for her. But, you know, those little friggling things take a deal o' time. I only worked at it in overhours—often late at night—and I had to go to Treddleston over an' over again about little bits o' brass nails and such gear; and I turned the little knobs and the legs, and carved th' open work, after a pattern, as nice as could be. And I was uncommon pleased with it when it was done. And when I took it home, Miss Lyddy sent for me to bring it into her drawing-room, so as she might give me directions about fastening on the work—very fine needlework, Jacob and Rachel a-kissing one another among the sheep, like a picture—and th' old squire was sitting there, for he mostly sits with her. Well, she was mighty pleased with the screen, and then she wanted to know what pay she was to give me. I didn't speak at random—you know it's not my way; I'd calculated pretty close, though I hadn't made out a bill, and I said, 'One pound thirteen.' That was paying for the mater'als and paying me, but none too much, for my work. Th' old squire looked up at this, and peered in his way at the screen, and said, 'One pound thirteen for a gimcrack like that! Lydia, my dear, if you must spend money on these things, why don't you get them at Rosseter, instead of paying double price for clumsy work here? Such things are not work for a carpenter like Adam. Give him a guinea, and no more.' Well, Miss Lyddy, I reckon, believed what he told her, and she's not overfond o' parting with the money herself—she's not a bad woman at bottom, but she's been brought up under his thumb; so she began fidgeting with her purse, and turned as red as her ribbon. But I made a bow, and said, 'No, thank you, madam; I'll make you a present o' the screen, if you please. I've charged the regular price for my work, and I know it's done well; and I know, begging His Honour's pardon, that you couldn't get such a screen at Rosseter under two guineas. I'm willing to give you my work—it's been done in my own time, and nobody's got anything to do with it but me; but if I'm paid, I can't take a smaller price than I asked, because that 'ud be like saying I'd asked more than was just. With your leave, madam, I'll bid you good-morning.' I made my bow and went out before she'd time to say any more, for she stood with the purse in her hand, looking almost foolish. I didn't mean to be disrespectful, and I spoke as polite as I could; but I can give in to no man, if he wants to make it out as I'm trying to overreach him. And in the evening the footman brought me the one pound thirteen wrapped in paper. But since then I've seen pretty clear as th' old squire can't abide me."

"That's likely enough, that's likely enough," said Bartle meditatively. "The only way to bring him round would be to show him what was for his own interest, and that the captain may do—that the captain may do."

"Nay, I don't know," said Adam; "the squire's 'cute enough but it takes something else besides 'cuteness to make folks see what'll be their interest in the long run. It takes some conscience and belief in right and wrong, I see that pretty clear. You'd hardly ever bring round th' old squire to believe he'd gain as much in a straightfor'ard way as by tricks and turns. And, besides, I've not much mind to work under him: I don't want to quarrel with any gentleman, more particular an old gentleman turned eighty, and I know we couldn't agree long. If the captain was master o' th' estate, it 'ud be different: he's got a conscience and a will to do right, and I'd sooner work for him nor for any man living."

"Well, well, my boy, if good luck knocks at your door, don't you put your head out at window and tell it to be gone about its business, that's all. You must learn to deal with odd and even in life, as well as in figures. I tell you now, as I told you ten years ago, when you pommelled young Mike Holdsworth for wanting to pass a bad shilling before you knew whether he was in jest or earnest—you're overhasty and proud, and apt to set your teeth against folks that don't square to your notions. It's no harm for me to be a bit fiery and stiff-backed—I'm an old schoolmaster, and shall never want to get on to a higher perch. But where's the use of all the time I've spent in teaching you writing and mapping and mensuration, if you're not to get for'ard in the world and show folks there's some advantage in having a head on your shoulders, instead of a turnip? Do you mean to go on turning up your nose at every opportunity because it's got a bit of a smell about it that nobody finds out but yourself? It's as foolish as that notion o' yours that a wife is to make a working-man comfortable. Stuff and nonsense! Stuff and nonsense! Leave that to fools that never got beyond a sum in simple addition. Simple addition enough! Add one fool to another fool, and in six years' time six fools more—they're all of the same denomination, big and little's nothing to do with the sum!"

During this rather heated exhortation to coolness and discretion the pipe had gone out, and Bartle gave the climax to his speech by striking a light furiously, after which he puffed with fierce resolution, fixing his eye still on Adam, who was trying not to laugh.

"There's a good deal o' sense in what you say, Mr. Massey," Adam began, as soon as he felt quite serious, "as there always is. But you'll give in that it's no business o' mine to be building on chances that may never happen. What I've got to do is to work as well as I can with the tools and mater'als I've got in my hands. If a good chance comes to me, I'll think o' what you've been saying; but till then, I've got nothing to do but to trust to my own hands and my own head-piece. I'm turning over a little plan for Seth and me to go into the cabinet-making a bit by ourselves, and win a extra pound or two in that way. But it's getting late now—it'll be pretty near eleven before I'm at home, and Mother may happen to lie awake; she's more fidgety nor usual now. So I'll bid you good-night."

"Well, well, we'll go to the gate with you—it's a fine night," said Bartle, taking up his stick. Vixen was at once on her legs, and without further words the three walked out into the starlight, by the side of Bartle's potato-beds, to the little gate.

"Come to the music o' Friday night, if you can, my boy," said the old man, as he closed the gate after Adam and leaned against it.

"Aye, aye," said Adam, striding along towards the streak of pale road. He was the only object moving on the wide common. The two grey donkeys, just visible in front of the gorse bushes, stood as still as limestone images—as still as the grey-thatched roof of the mud cottage a little farther on. Bartle kept his eye on the moving figure till it passed into the darkness, while Vixen, in a state of divided affection, had twice run back to the house to bestow a parenthetic lick on her puppies.

"Aye, aye," muttered the schoolmaster, as Adam disappeared, "there you go, stalking along—stalking along; but you wouldn't have been what you are if you hadn't had a bit of old lame Bartle inside you. The strongest calf must have something to suck at. There's plenty of these big, lumbering fellows 'ud never have known their A B C if it hadn't been for Bartle Massey. Well, well, Vixen, you foolish wench, what is it, what is it? I must go in, must I? Aye, aye, I'm never to have a will o' my own any more. And those pups—what do you think I'm to do with 'em, when they're twice as big as you? For I'm pretty sure the father was that hulking bull-terrier of Will Baker's—wasn't he now, eh, you sly hussy?"(Here Vixen tucked her tail between her legs and ran forward into the house. Subjects are sometimes broached which a well-bred female will ignore.)

"But where's the use of talking to a woman with babbies?" continued Bartle. "She's got no conscience—no conscience; it's all run to milk."

BOOK THIRD

Chapter XXII
Going to the Birthday Feast

The thirtieth of July was come, and it was one of those half-dozen warm days which sometimes occur in the middle of a rainy English summer. No rain had fallen for the last three or four days, and the weather was perfect for that time of the year: there was less dust than usual on the dark-green hedge-rows and on the wild camomile that starred the roadside, yet the grass was dry enough for the little children to roll on it, and there was no cloud but a long dash of light, downy ripple, high, high up in the far-off blue sky. Perfect weather for an outdoor July merry-making, yet surely not the best time of year to be born in. Nature seems to make a hot pause just then: all the loveliest flowers are gone; the sweet time of early growth and vague hopes is past; and yet the time of harvest and ingathering is not come, and we tremble at the possible storms that may ruin the precious fruit in the moment of its ripeness. The woods are all one dark monotonous green; the waggon-loads of hay no longer creep along the lanes, scattering their sweet-smelling fragments on the blackberry branches; the pastures are often a little tanned, yet the corn has not got its last splendour of red and gold; the lambs and calves have lost all traces of their innocent frisky prettiness, and have become stupid young sheep and cows. But it is a time of leisure on the farm—that pause between hay-and corn-harvest, and so the farmers and labourers in Hayslope and Broxton thought the captain did well to come of age just then, when they could give their undivided minds to the flavour of the great cask of ale which had been brewed the autumn after "the heir" was born, and was to be tapped on his twenty-first birthday. The air had been merry with the ringing of church-bells very early this morning, and every one had made haste to get through the needful work before twelve, when it would be time to think of getting ready to go to the Chase.

The midday sun was streaming into Hetty's bedchamber, and there was no blind to temper the heat with which it fell on her head as she looked at herself in the old specked glass. Still, that was the only glass she had in which she could see her neck and arms, for the small hanging glass she had fetched out of the next room—the room that had been Dinah's—would show her nothing below her little chin; and that beautiful bit of neck where the roundness of her cheek melted into another roundness shadowed by dark delicate curls. And to-day she thought more than usual about her neck and arms; for at the dance this evening she was not to wear any neckerchief, and she had been busy yesterday with her spotted pink-

and-white frock, that she might make the sleeves either long or short at will. She was dressed now just as she was to be in the evening, with a tucker made of "real" lace, which her aunt had lent her for this unparalleled occasion, but with no ornaments besides; she had even taken out her small round ear-rings which she wore every day. But there was something more to be done, apparently, before she put on her neckerchief and long sleeves, which she was to wear in the day-time, for now she unlocked the drawer that held her private treasures. It is more than a month since we saw her unlock that drawer before, and now it holds new treasures, so much more precious than the old ones that these are thrust into the corner. Hetty would not care to put the large coloured glass ear-rings into her ears now; for see! she has got a beautiful pair of gold and pearls and garnet, lying snugly in a pretty little box lined with white satin. Oh, the delight of taking out that little box and looking at the ear-rings! Do not reason about it, my philosphical reader, and say that Hetty, being very pretty, must have known that it did not signify whether she had on any ornaments or not; and that, moreover, to look at ear-rings which she could not possibly wear out of her bedroom could hardly be a satisfaction, the essence of vanity being a reference to the impressions produced on others; you will never understand women's natures if you are so excessively rational. Try rather to divest yourself of all your rational prejudices, as much as if you were studying the psychology of a canary bird, and only watch the movements of this pretty round creature as she turns her head on one side with an unconscious smile at the ear-rings nestled in the little box. Ah, you think, it is for the sake of the person who has given them to her, and her thoughts are gone back now to the moment when they were put into her hands. No; else why should she have cared to have ear-rings rather than anything else? And I know that she had longed for ear-rings from among all the ornaments she could imagine.

"Little, little ears!" Arthur had said, pretending to pinch them one evening, as Hetty sat beside him on the grass without her hat. "I wish I had some pretty ear-rings!" she said in a moment, almost before she knew what she was saying—the wish lay so close to her lips, it *would* flutter past them at the slightest breath. And the next day—it was only last week—Arthur had ridden over to Rosseter on purpose to buy them. That little wish so naively uttered seemed to him the prettiest bit of childishness; he had never heard anything like it before; and he had wrapped the box up in a great many covers, that he might see Hetty unwrapping it with growing curiosity, till at last her eyes flashed back their new delight into his.

No, she was not thinking most of the giver when she smiled at the ear-rings, for now she is taking them out of the box, not to press them to her lips, but to fasten them in her ears—only for one moment, to see how pretty they look, as she peeps at them in the glass against the wall, with first one position of the head and then another, like a listening bird. It is impossible to be wise on the subject of ear-rings as one looks at her; what should those delicate pearls and crystals be made for, if not for such ears? One cannot even find fault with the tiny round hole which they leave when they are taken out; perhaps water-nixies, and such lovely things without souls, have these little round holes in their ears by nature, ready to hang jewels in. And Hetty must be one of them: it is too painful to think that she is a woman, with a woman's destiny before her—a woman spinning in young ignorance a light web of folly and vain hopes which may one day close round her and press upon her, a rancorous poisoned garment, changing all at once her fluttering, trivial butterfly sensations into a life of deep human anguish.

But she cannot keep in the ear-rings long, else she may make her uncle and aunt wait. She puts them quickly into the box again and shuts them up. Some day she will be able to wear any ear-rings she likes, and already she lives in an invisible world of brilliant costumes, shimmering gauze, soft satin, and velvet, such as the lady's maid at the Chase has shown her in Miss Lydia's wardrobe. She feels the bracelets on her arms, and treads on a soft carpet in front of a tall mirror. But she has one thing in the drawer which she can venture to wear to-day, because she can hang it on the chain of dark-brown berries which she has been used to wear on grand days, with a tiny flat scent-bottle at the end of it tucked inside her frock; and she *must* put on her brown berries—her neck would look so unfinished without it. Hetty was not quite as fond of the locket as of the ear-rings, though it was a handsome large locket, with enamelled flowers at the back and a beautiful gold border round the glass, which showed a light-brown slightly waving lock, forming a background for two little dark rings. She must keep it under her clothes, and no one would see it. But Hetty had another passion, only a little less strong than her love of finery, and that other passion made her like to wear the locket even hidden in her bosom. She would always have worn it, if she had dared to encounter her aunt's questions about a ribbon round her neck. So now she slipped it on along her chain of dark-brown berries, and snapped the chain round her neck. It was not a very long chain, only allowing the locket to hang a little way below the edge of her frock. And now she had nothing to do but to put on her long sleeves, her new white gauze neckerchief, and her straw hat trimmed with white to-day instead of the pink, which had become rather faded under the July sun. That hat made the drop of bitterness in Hetty's cup to-day, for it was not quite new—everybody would see that it was a little tanned against the white ribbon—and Mary Burge, she felt sure, would have a new hat or bonnet on. She looked for consolation at her fine white cotton stockings: they really were very nice indeed, and she had given almost all her spare money for them. Hetty's dream of the future could not make her insensible to triumph in the present. To be sure, Captain Donnithorne loved her so that he would never care about looking at other people, but then those other people didn't know how he loved her, and she was not satisfied to appear shabby and insignificant in their eyes even for a short space.

The whole party was assembled in the house-place when Hetty went down, all of course in their Sunday clothes; and the bells had been ringing so this morning in honour of the captain's twenty-first birthday, and the work had all been got done so early, that Marty and Tommy were not quite easy in their minds until their mother had assured them that going to church was not part of the day's festivities. Mr. Poyser had once suggested that the house should be shut up and left to take care of itself; "for," said he, "there's no danger of anybody's breaking in—everybody'll be at the Chase, thieves an' all. If we lock th' house up, all the men can go: it's a day they wonna see twice i' their lives." But Mrs. Poyser answered with great decision: "I never left the house to take care of itself since I was a missis, and I never will. There's been ill-looking tramps enoo' about the place this last week, to carry off every ham an' every spoon we'n got; and they all collogue together, them tramps, as it's a mercy they hanna come and poisoned the dogs and murdered us all in our beds afore we knowed, some Friday night when we'n got the money in th' house to pay the men. And it's like enough the tramps know where we're going as well as we do oursens; for if Old Harry wants any work done, you may be sure he'll find the means."

"Nonsense about murdering us in our beds," said Mr. Poyser; "I've got a gun i' our room, hanna I? and thee'st got ears as 'ud find it out if a mouse was gnawing the bacon. Howiver, if thee wouldstna be easy, Alick can stay at home i' the forepart o' the day, and Tim can come back tow'rds five o'clock, and let Alick have his turn. They may let Growler loose if anybody offers to do mischief, and there's Alick's dog too, ready enough to set his tooth in a tramp if Alick gives him a wink."

Mrs. Poyser accepted this compromise, but thought it advisable to bar and bolt to the utmost; and now, at the last moment before starting, Nancy, the dairy-maid, was closing the shutters of the house-place, although the window, lying under the immediate observation of Alick and the dogs, might have been supposed the least likely to be selected for a burglarious attempt.

The covered cart, without springs, was standing ready to carry the whole family except the men-servants. Mr. Poyser and the grandfather sat on the seat in front, and within there was room for all the women and children; the fuller the cart the better, because then the jolting would not hurt so much, and Nancy's broad person and thick arms were an excellent cushion to be pitched on. But Mr. Poyser drove at no more than a walking pace, that there might be as little risk of jolting as possible on this warm day, and there was time to exchange greetings and remarks with the foot-passengers who were going the same way, specking the paths between the green meadows and the golden cornfields with bits of movable bright colour—a scarlet waistcoat to match the poppies that nodded a little too thickly among the corn, or a dark-blue neckerchief with ends flaunting across a brand-new white smock-frock. All Broxton and all Hayslope were to be at the Chase, and make merry there in honour of "th' heir"; and the old men and women, who had never been so far down this side of the hill for the last twenty years, were being brought from Broxton and Hayslope in one of the farmer's waggons, at Mr. Irwine's suggestion. The church-bells had struck up again now—a last tune, before the ringers came down the hill to have their share in the festival; and before the bells had finished, other music was heard approaching, so that even Old Brown, the sober horse that was drawing Mr. Poyser's cart, began to prick up his ears. It was the band of the Benefit Club, which had mustered in all its glory—that is to say, in bright-blue scarfs and blue favours, and carrying its banner with the motto, "Let brotherly love continue," encircling a picture of a stone-pit.

The carts, of course, were not to enter the Chase. Every one must get down at the lodges, and the vehicles must be sent back.

"Why, the Chase is like a fair a'ready," said Mrs. Poyser, as she got down from the cart, and saw the groups scattered under the great oaks, and the boys running about in the hot sunshine to survey the tall poles surmounted by the fluttering garments that were to be the prize of the successful climbers. "I should ha' thought there wasna so many people i' the two parishes. Mercy on us! How hot it is out o' the shade! Come here, Totty, else your little face 'ull be burnt to a scratchin'! They might ha' cooked the dinners i' that open space an' saved the fires. I shall go to Mrs. Best's room an' sit down."

"Stop a bit, stop a bit," said Mr. Poyser. "There's th' waggin coming wi' th' old folks in't; it'll be such a sight as wonna come o'er again, to see 'em get down an' walk along all together. You remember some on 'em i' their prime, eh, Father?"

"Aye, aye," said old Martin, walking slowly under the shade of the lodge porch, from which he could see the aged party descend. "I remember Jacob Taft walking fifty mile after the Scotch raybels, when they turned back from Stoniton."

He felt himself quite a youngster, with a long life before him, as he saw the Hayslope patriarch, old Feyther Taft, descend from the waggon and walk towards him, in his brown nightcap, and leaning on his two sticks.

"Well, Mester Taft," shouted old Martin, at the utmost stretch of his voice—for though he knew the old man was stone deaf, he could not omit the propriety of a greeting—"you're hearty yet. You can enjoy yoursen to-day, for-all you're ninety an' better."

"Your sarvant, mesters, your sarvant," said Feyther Taft in a treble tone, perceiving that he was in company.

The aged group, under care of sons or daughters, themselves worn and grey, passed on along the least-winding carriage-road towards the house, where a special table was prepared for them; while the Poyser party wisely struck across the grass under the shade of the great trees, but not out of view of the house-front, with its sloping lawn and flower-beds, or of the pretty striped marquee at the edge of the lawn, standing at right angles with two larger marquees on each side of the open green space where the games were to be played. The house would have been nothing but a plain square mansion of Queen Anne's time, but for the remnant of an old abbey to which it was united at one end, in much the same way as one may sometimes see a new farmhouse rising high and prim at the end of older and lower farm-offices. The fine old remnant stood a little backward and under the shadow of tall beeches, but the sun was now on the taller and more advanced front, the blinds were all down, and the house seemed asleep in the hot midday. It made Hetty quite sad to look at it: Arthur must be somewhere in the back rooms, with the grand company, where he could not possibly know that she was come, and she should not see him for a long, long while—not till after dinner, when they said he was to come up and make a speech.

But Hetty was wrong in part of her conjecture. No grand company was come except the Irwines, for whom the carriage had been sent early, and Arthur was at that moment not in a back room, but walking with the rector into the broad stone cloisters of the old abbey, where the long tables were laid for all the cottage tenants and the farm-servants. A very handsome young Briton he looked to-day, in high spirits and a bright-blue frock-coat, the highest mode—his arm no longer in a sling. So open-looking and candid, too; but candid people have their secrets, and secrets leave no lines in young faces.

"Upon my word," he said, as they entered the cool cloisters, "I think the cottagers have the best of it: these cloisters make a delightful dining-room on a hot day. That was capital advice of yours, Irwine, about the dinners—to let them be as orderly and comfortable as possible, and only for the tenants: especially as I had only a limited sum after all; for though my grandfather talked of a *carte blanche*, he couldn't make up his mind to trust me, when it came to the point."

"Never mind, you'll give more pleasure in this quiet way," said Mr. Irwine. "In this sort of thing people are constantly confounding liberality with riot and disorder. It sounds very grand to say that so many sheep and oxen were roasted whole, and everybody ate who liked to come; but in the end it generally happens that no one has had an enjoyable meal. If the people get a good dinner and a moderate quantity of ale in the middle of the day, they'll be able to enjoy the games as the day cools. You can't hinder some of them from getting too much towards evening, but drunkenness and darkness go better together than drunkenness and daylight."

"Well, I hope there won't be much of it. I've kept the Treddleston people away by having a feast for them in the town; and I've got Casson and Adam Bede and some other good fellows to look to the giving out of ale in the booths, and to take care things don't go too far. Come, let us go up above now and see the dinner-tables for the large tenants."

They went up the stone staircase leading simply to the long gallery above the cloisters, a gallery where all the dusty worthless old pictures had been banished for the last three generations—mouldy portraits of Queen Elizabeth and her ladies, General Monk with his eye knocked out, Daniel very much in the dark among the lions, and Julius Cæsar on horseback, with a high nose and laurel crown, holding his Commentaries in his hand.

"What a capital thing it is that they saved this piece of the old abbey!" said Arthur. "If I'm ever master here, I shall do up the gallery in first-rate style. We've got no room in the house a third as large as this. That second table is for the farmers' wives and children: Mrs. Best said it would be more comfortable for the mothers and children to be by themselves. I was determined to have the children, and make a regular family thing of it. I shall be 'the old squire' to those little lads and lasses some day, and they'll tell their children what a much finer young fellow I was than my own son. There's a table for the women and children below as well. But you will see them all—you will come up with me after dinner, I hope?"

"Yes, to be sure," said Mr. Irwine. "I wouldn't miss your maiden speech to the tenantry."

"And there will be something else you'll like to hear," said Arthur. "Let us go into the library and I'll tell you all about it while my grandfather is in the drawing-room with the ladies. Something that will surprise you," he continued, as they sat down. "My grandfather has come round after all."

"What, about Adam?"

"Yes; I should have ridden over to tell you about it, only I was so busy. You know I told you I had quite given up arguing the matter with him—I thought it was hopeless—but yesterday morning he asked me to come in here to him before I went out, and astonished me by saying that he had decided on all the new arrangements he should make in consequence of old Satchell being obliged to lay by work, and that he intended to employ Adam in superintending the woods at a salary of a guinea a-week, and the use of a pony to be kept here. I believe the secret of it is, he saw from the first it would be a profitable plan, but he had some particular dislike of Adam to get over—and besides, the fact that I propose a thing is generally a reason with him for rejecting it. There's the most curious contradiction in my grandfather: I know he means to leave me all the money he has saved, and he is likely enough to have cut off poor Aunt Lydia, who has been a slave to him all her life, with only five hundred a-year, for the sake of giving me all the more; and yet I sometimes think he positively hates me because I'm his heir. I believe if I were to break my neck, he would feel it the greatest misfortune that could befall him, and yet it seems a pleasure to him to make my life a series of petty annoyances."

"Ah, my boy, it is not only woman's love that is ἀπέρωτος ἔρως as old Æschylus calls it. There's plenty of 'unloving love' in the world of a masculine kind. But tell me about Adam. Has he accepted the post? I don't see that it can be much more profitable than his present work, though, to be sure, it will leave him a good deal of time on his own hands.

"Well, I felt some doubt about it when I spoke to him and he seemed to hesitate at first. His objection was that he thought he should not be able to satisfy my grandfather. But I begged him as a personal favour to me not to let any reason prevent him from accepting the place, if he really liked the employment and would not be giving up anything that was more profitable to him. And he assured me he should like it of all things—it would be a great step forward for him in business, and it would enable him to do what he had long wished to do, to give up working for Burge. He says he shall have plenty of time to superintend a little business of his own, which he and Seth will carry on, and will perhaps be able to enlarge by degrees. So he has agreed at last, and I have arranged that he shall dine with the large tenants to-day; and I mean to announce the appointment to them, and ask them to drink Adam's health. It's a little drama I've got up in honour of my friend Adam. He's a fine fellow, and I like the opportunity of letting people know that I think so."

"A drama in which friend Arthur piques himself on having a pretty part to play," said Mr. Irwine, smiling. But when he saw Arthur colour, he went on relentingly, "My part, you know, is always that of the old fogy who sees nothing to admire in the young folks. I don't like to admit that I'm proud of my pupil when he does graceful things. But I must play the amiable old gentleman for once, and second your toast in honour of Adam. Has your grandfather yielded on the other point too, and agreed to have a respectable man as steward?"

"Oh no," said Arthur, rising from his chair with an air of impatience and walking along the room with his hands in his pockets. "He's got some project or other about letting the Chase Farm and bargaining for a supply of milk and butter for the house. But I ask no questions about it—it makes me too angry. I believe he means to do all the business himself, and have nothing in the shape of a steward. It's amazing what energy he has, though."

"Well, we'll go to the ladies now," said Mr. Irwine, rising too. "I want to tell my mother what a splendid throne you've prepared for her under the marquee."

"Yes, and we must be going to luncheon too," said Arthur. "It must be two o'clock, for there is the gong beginning to sound for the tenants' dinners."

Chapter XXIII
Dinner-Time

When Adam heard that he was to dine upstairs with the large tenants, he felt rather uncomfortable at the idea of being exalted in this way above his mother and Seth, who were to dine in the cloisters below. But Mr. Mills, the butler, assured him that Captain Donnithorne had given particular orders about it, and would be very angry if Adam was not there.

Adam nodded and went up to Seth, who was standing a few yards off. "Seth, lad," he said, "the captain has sent to say I'm to dine upstairs—he wishes it particular, Mr. Mills says, so I suppose it 'ud be behaving ill for me not to go. But I don't like sitting up above thee and mother, as if I was better than my own flesh and blood. Thee't not take it unkind, I hope?"

"Nay, nay, lad," said Seth, "thy honour's our honour; and if thee get'st respect, thee'st won it by thy own deserts. The further I see thee above me, the better, so long as thee feel'st like a brother to me. It's because o' thy being appointed over the woods, and it's nothing but what's right. That's a place o' trust, and thee't above a common workman now."

"Aye," said Adam, "but nobody knows a word about it yet. I haven't given notice to Mr. Burge about leaving him, and I don't like to tell anybody else about it before he knows, for he'll be a good bit hurt, I doubt. People 'ull be wondering to see me there, and they'll like enough be guessing the reason and asking questions, for there's been so much talk up and down about my having the place, this last three weeks."

"Well, thee canst say thee wast ordered to come without being told the reason. That's the truth. And mother 'ull be fine and joyful about it. Let's go and tell her."

Adam was not the only guest invited to come upstairs on other grounds than the amount he contributed to the rent-roll. There were other people in the two parishes who derived dignity from their functions rather than from their pocket, and of these Bartle Massey was one. His lame walk was rather slower than usual on this warm day, so Adam lingered behind when the bell rang for dinner, that he might walk up with his old friend; for he was a little too shy to join the Poyser party on this public occasion. Opportunities of getting to Hetty's side would be sure to turn up in the course of the day, and Adam contented himself with that for he disliked any risk of being "joked" about Hetty—the big, outspoken, fearless man was very shy and diffident as to his love-making.

"Well, Mester Massey," said Adam, as Bartle came up "I'm going to dine upstairs with you to-day: the captain's sent me orders."

"Ah!" said Bartle, pausing, with one hand on his back. "Then there's something in the wind—there's something in the wind. Have you heard anything about what the old squire means to do?"

"Why, yes," said Adam; "I'll tell you what I know, because I believe you can keep a still tongue in your head if you like, and I hope you'll not let drop a word till it's common talk, for I've particular reasons against its being known."

"Trust to me, my boy, trust to me. I've got no wife to worm it out of me and then run out and cackle it in everybody's hearing. If you trust a man, let him be a bachelor—let him be a bachelor."

"Well, then, it was so far settled yesterday that I'm to take the management o' the woods. The captain sent for me t' offer it me, when I was seeing to the poles and things here and I've agreed to't. But if anybody asks any questions upstairs, just you take no notice, and turn the talk to something else, and I'll be obliged to you. Now, let us go on, for we're pretty nigh the last, I think."

"I know what to do, never fear," said Bartle, moving on. "The news will be good sauce to my dinner. Aye, aye, my boy, you'll get on. I'll back you for an eye at measuring and a head-piece for figures, against any man in this county and you've had good teaching—you've had good teaching."

When they got upstairs, the question which Arthur had left unsettled, as to who was to be president, and who vice, was still under discussion, so that Adam's entrance passed without remark.

"It stands to sense," Mr. Casson was saying, "as old Mr. Poyser, as is th' oldest man i' the room, should sit at top o' the table. I wasn't butler fifteen year without learning the rights and the wrongs about dinner."

"Nay, nay," said old Martin, "I'n gi'en up to my son; I'm no tenant now: let my son take my place. Th' ould foulks ha' had their turn: they mun make way for the young uns."

"I should ha' thought the biggest tenant had the best right, more nor th' oldest," said Luke Britton, who was not fond of the critical Mr. Poyser; "there's Mester Holdsworth has more land nor anybody else on th' estate."

"Well," said Mr. Poyser, "suppose we say the man wi' the foulest land shall sit at top; then whoever gets th' honour, there'll be no envying on him."

"Eh, here's Mester Massey," said Mr. Craig, who, being a neutral in the dispute, had no interest but in conciliation; "the schoolmaster ought to be able to tell you what's right. Who's to sit at top o' the table, Mr. Massey?"

"Why, the broadest man," said Bartle; "and then he won't take up other folks' room; and the next broadest must sit at bottom."

This happy mode of settling the dispute produced much laughter—a smaller joke would have sufficed for that. Mr. Casson, however, did not feel it compatible with his dignity and superior knowledge to join in the laugh, until it turned out that he was fixed on as the second broadest man. Martin Poyser the younger, as the broadest, was to be president, and Mr. Casson, as next broadest, was to be vice.

Owing to this arrangement, Adam, being, of course, at the bottom of the table, fell under the immediate observation of Mr. Casson, who, too much occupied with the question of precedence, had not hitherto noticed his entrance. Mr. Casson, we have seen, considered Adam "rather lifted up and peppery-like": he thought the gentry made more fuss about this young carpenter than was necessary; they made no fuss about Mr. Casson, although he had been an excellent butler for fifteen years.

"Well, Mr. Bede, you're one o' them as mounts hup'ards apace," he said, when Adam sat down. "You've niver dined here before, as I remember."

"No, Mr. Casson," said Adam, in his strong voice, that could be heard along the table; "I've never dined here before, but I come by Captain Donnithorne's wish, and I hope it's not disagreeable to anybody here."

"Nay, nay," said several voices at once, "we're glad ye're come. Who's got anything to say again' it?"

"And ye'll sing us 'Over the hills and far away,' after dinner, wonna ye?" said Mr. Chowne. "That's a song I'm uncommon fond on."

"Peeh!" said Mr. Craig; "it's not to be named by side o' the Scotch tunes. I've never cared about singing myself; I've had something better to do. A man that's got the names and the natur o' plants in's head isna likely to keep a hollow place t' hold tunes in. But a second cousin o' mine, a drovier, was a rare hand at remembering the Scotch tunes. He'd got nothing else to think on."

"The Scotch tunes!" said Bartle Massey, contemptuously; "I've heard enough o' the Scotch tunes to last me while I live. They're fit for nothing but to frighten the birds with—that's to say, the English birds, for the Scotch birds may sing Scotch for what I know. Give the lads a bagpipe instead of a rattle, and I'll answer for it the corn 'll be safe."

"Yes, there's folks as find a pleasure in undervallying what they know but little about," said Mr. Craig.

"Why, the Scotch tunes are just like a scolding, nagging woman," Bartle went on, without deigning to notice Mr. Craig's remark. "They go on with the same thing over and over again, and never come to a reasonable end. Anybody 'ud think the Scotch tunes had always been asking a question of somebody as deaf as old Taft, and had never got an answer yet."

Adam minded the less about sitting by Mr. Casson, because this position enabled him to see Hetty, who was not far off him at the next table. Hetty, however, had not even noticed his presence yet, for she was giving angry attention to Totty, who insisted on drawing up her feet on to the bench in antique fashion, and thereby threatened to make dusty marks on Hetty's pink-and-white frock. No sooner were the little fat legs pushed down than up they came again, for Totty's eyes were too busy in staring at the large dishes to see where the plum pudding was for her to retain any consciousness of her legs. Hetty got quite out of patience, and at last, with a frown and pout, and gathering tears, she said, "Oh dear, Aunt, I wish you'd speak to Totty; she keeps putting her legs up so, and messing my frock."

"What's the matter wi' the child? She can niver please you," said the mother. "Let her come by the side o' me, then. *I* can put up wi' her."

Adam was looking at Hetty, and saw the frown, and pout, and the dark eyes seeming to grow larger with pettish half-gathered tears. Quiet Mary Burge, who sat near enough to see that Hetty was cross and that Adam's eyes were fixed on her, thought that so sensible a man as Adam must be reflecting on the small value of beauty in a woman whose temper was bad. Mary was a good girl, not given to indulge in evil feelings, but she said to herself, that, since Hetty had a bad temper, it was better Adam should know it. And it was quite true that if Hetty had been plain, she would have looked very ugly and unamiable at that moment, and no one's moral judgment upon her would have been in the least beguiled. But really there was something quite charming in her pettishness: it looked so much more like innocent distress than ill humour; and the severe Adam felt no movement of disapprobation; he only felt a sort of amused pity, as if he had seen a kitten setting up its back, or a little bird with its feathers ruffled. He could not gather what was vexing her, but it was impossible to him to feel otherwise than that she was the prettiest thing in the world, and that if he could have his way, nothing should ever vex her any more. And presently, when Totty was gone, she caught his eye, and her face broke into one of its brightest smiles, as she nodded to him. It was a bit of flirtation—she knew Mary Burge was looking at them. But the smile was like wine to Adam.

Chapter XXIV
The Health-Drinking

When the dinner was over, and the first draughts from the great cask of birthday ale were brought up, room was made for the broad Mr. Poyser at the side of the table, and two chairs were placed at the head. It had been settled very definitely what Mr. Poyser was to do when the young squire should appear, and for the last five minutes he had been in a state of abstraction, with his eyes fixed on the dark picture opposite, and his hands busy with the loose cash and other articles in his breeches pockets.

When the young squire entered, with Mr. Irwine by his side, every one stood up, and this moment of homage was very agreeable to Arthur. He liked to feel his own importance, and besides that, he cared a great deal for the good-will of these people: he was fond of thinking that they had a hearty, special regard for him. The pleasure he felt was in his face as he said, "My grandfather and I hope all our friends here have enjoyed their dinner, and find my birthday ale good. Mr. Irwine and I are come to taste it with you, and I am sure we shall all like anything the better that the rector shares with us."

All eyes were now turned on Mr. Poyser, who, with his hands still busy in his pockets, began with the deliberateness of a slow-striking clock. "Captain, my neighbours have put it upo' me to speak for 'em to-day, for where folks think pretty much alike, one spokesman's as good as a score. And though we've mayhappen got contrairy ways o' thinking about a many things—one man lays down his land one way an' another another—an' I'll not take it upon me to speak to no man's farming, but my own—this I'll say, as we're all o' one mind about our young squire. We've pretty nigh all on us known you when you war a little un, an' we've niver known anything on you but what was good an' honorable. You speak fair an' y' act fair, an' we're joyful when we look forrard to your being our landlord, for we 'lieve you mean to do right by everybody, an' 'ull make no man's bread bitter to him if you can help it. That's what I mean, an' that's what we all mean; and when a man's said what he means, he'd better stop, for th' ale 'ull be none the better for stannin'. An' I'll not say how we like th' ale yet, for we couldna well taste it till we'd drunk your health in it; but the dinner was good, an' if there's anybody hasna enjoyed it, it must be the fault of his own inside. An' as for the rector's company, it's well known as that's welcome t' all the parish wherever he may be; an' I hope, an' we all hope, as he'll live to see us old folks, an' our children grown to men an' women an' Your Honour a family man. I've no more to say as concerns the present time, an' so we'll drink our young squire's health—three times three."

Hereupon a glorious shouting, a rapping, a jingling, a clattering, and a shouting, with plentiful *da capo*, pleasanter than a strain of sublimest music in the ears that receive such a tribute for the first time. Arthur had felt a twinge of conscience during Mr. Poyser's speech, but it was too feeble to nullify the pleasure he felt in being praised. Did he not deserve what was said of him on the whole? If there was something in his conduct that Poyser wouldn't have liked if he had known it, why, no man's conduct will bear too close an inspection; and Poyser was not likely to know it; and, after all, what had he done? Gone a little too far, perhaps, in flirtation, but another man in his place would have acted much worse; and no harm would come—no harm *should* come, for the next time he was alone with Hetty, he would explain to her that she must not think seriously of him or of what had passed. It was necessary to Arthur, you perceive, to be satisfied with himself. Uncomfortable thoughts must be got rid of by good intentions for the future, which can be formed so rapidly that he had time to be uncomfortable and to become easy again before Mr. Poyser's slow speech was finished, and when it was time for him to speak he was quite light-hearted.

"I thank you all, my good friends and neighbours," Arthur said, "for the good opinion of me, and the kind feelings towards me which Mr. Poyser has been expressing on your behalf and on his own, and it will always be my heartiest wish to deserve them. In the course of things we may expect that, if I live, I shall one day or other be your landlord; indeed, it is on the ground of that expectation that my grandfather has wished me to celebrate this day and to come among you now; and I look forward to this position, not merely as one of power and pleasure for myself, but as a means of benefiting my neighbours. It hardly becomes so young a man as I am to talk much about farming to you, who are most of you so much older, and are men of experience; still, I have interested myself a good deal in such matters, and learned as much about them as my opportunities have allowed; and when the course of events shall place the estate in my hands, it will be my first desire to afford my tenants all the encouragement a landlord can give them, in improving their land and trying to bring about a better practice of husbandry. It will be my wish to be looked on by all my deserving tenants as their best friend, and nothing would make me so happy as to be able to respect every man on the estate, and to be respected by him in return. It is not my place at present to enter into particulars; I only meet your good hopes concerning me by telling you that my own hopes correspond to them—that what you expect from me I desire to fulfil; and I am quite of Mr. Poyser's opinion, that when a man has said what he means, he had better stop. But the pleasure I feel in having my own health drunk by you would not be perfect if we did not drink the health of my grandfather, who has filled the place of both parents to me. I will say no more, until you have joined me in drinking his health on a day when he has wished me to appear among you as the future representative of his name and family."

Perhaps there was no one present except Mr. Irwine who thoroughly understood and approved Arthur's graceful mode of proposing his grandfather's health. The farmers thought the young squire knew well enough that they hated the old squire, and Mrs. Poyser said, "he'd better not ha' stirred a kettle o' sour broth." The bucolic mind does not readily apprehend the refinements of good taste. But the toast could not be rejected and when it had been drunk, Arthur said, "I thank you, both for my grandfather and myself; and now there is one more thing I wish to tell you, that you may share my pleasure about it, as I hope and believe you will. I think there can be no man here who has not a respect, and some of you, I am sure, have a very high regard, for my friend Adam Bede. It is well known to every one in this neighbourhood that there is no man whose word can be more depended on than his; that whatever he undertakes to do, he does well, and is as careful for the interests of those who employ him as for his own. I'm proud to say that I was very fond of Adam when I was a little boy, and I have never lost my old feeling for him—I think that shows that I know a good fellow when I find him. It has long been my wish that he should have the management of the woods on the estate, which happen to be very valuable, not only because I think so highly of his character, but because he has the knowledge and the skill which fit him for the place. And I am happy to tell you that it is my grandfather's wish too, and it is now settled that Adam shall manage the woods—a change which I am sure will be very much for the advantage of the estate; and I hope you will by and by join me in drinking his health, and in wishing him all the prosperity in life that he deserves. But there is a still older friend of mine than Adam Bede present, and I need not tell you that it is Mr. Irwine. I'm sure you will agree with me that we must drink no other person's health until we have drunk his. I know you have all reason to love him, but no one of his parishioners has so much reason as I. Come, charge your glasses, and let us drink to our excellent rector—three times three!"

This toast was drunk with all the enthusiasm that was wanting to the last, and it certainly was the most picturesque moment in the scene when Mr. Irwine got up to speak, and all the faces in the room were turned towards him. The superior refinement of his face was much more striking than that of Arthur's when seen in comparison with the people round them. Arthur's was a much commoner British face, and the splendour of his new-fashioned clothes was more akin to the young farmer's taste in costume than Mr. Irwine's powder and the well-brushed but well-worn black, which seemed to be his chosen suit for great occasions; for he had the mysterious secret of never wearing a new-looking coat.

"This is not the first time, by a great many," he said, "that I have had to thank my parishioners for giving me tokens of their goodwill, but neighbourly kindness is among those things that are the more precious the older they get. Indeed, our pleasant meeting to-day is a proof that when what is good comes of age and is likely to live, there is reason for rejoicing, and the relation between us as clergyman and parishioners came of age two years ago, for it is three-and-twenty years since I first came among you, and I see some tall fine-looking young men here, as well as some blooming young women, that were far from looking as pleasantly at me when I christened them as I am happy to see them looking now. But I'm sure you will not wonder when I say that among all those young men, the one in whom I have the strongest interest is my friend Mr. Arthur Donnithorne, for whom you have just expressed your regard. I had the pleasure of being his tutor for several years, and have naturally had opportunities of knowing him intimately which cannot have occurred to any one else who is present; and I have some pride as well as pleasure in assuring you that I share your high hopes concerning him, and your confidence in his possession of those qualities which will make him an excellent landlord when the time shall come for him to take that important position among you. We feel alike on most matters on which a man who is getting towards fifty can feel in common with a young man of one-and-twenty, and he has just been expressing a feeling which I share very heartily, and I would not willingly omit the opportunity of saying so. That feeling is his value and respect for Adam Bede. People in a high station are of course more thought of and talked about and have their virtues more praised, than those whose lives are passed in humble everyday work; but every sensible man knows how necessary that humble everyday work is, and how important it is to us that it should be done well. And I agree with my friend Mr. Arthur Donnithorne in feeling that when a man whose duty lies in that sort of work shows a character which would make him an example in any station, his merit should be acknowledged. He is one of those to whom honour is due, and his friends should delight to honour him. I know Adam Bede well—I know what he is as a workman, and what he has been as a son and brother—and I am saying the simplest truth when I say that I respect him as much as I respect any man living. But I am not speaking to you about a stranger; some of you are his intimate friends, and I believe there is not one here who does not know enough of him to join heartily in drinking his health."

As Mr. Irwine paused, Arthur jumped up and, filling his glass, said, "A bumper to Adam Bede, and may he live to have sons as faithful and clever as himself!"

No hearer, not even Bartle Massey, was so delighted with this toast as Mr. Poyser. "Tough work" as his first speech had been, he would have started up to make another if he had not known the extreme irregularity of such a course. As it was, he found an outlet for his feeling in drinking his ale unusually fast, and setting down his glass with a swing of his arm and a determined rap. If Jonathan Burge and a few others felt less comfortable on the occasion, they tried their best to look contented, and so the toast was drunk with a goodwill apparently unanimous.

Adam was rather paler than usual when he got up to thank his friends. He was a good deal moved by this public tribute—very naturally, for he was in the presence of all his little world, and it was uniting to do him honour. But he felt no shyness about speaking, not being troubled with small vanity or lack of words; he looked neither awkward nor embarrassed, but stood in his usual firm upright attitude, with his head thrown a little backward and his hands perfectly still, in that rough dignity which is peculiar to intelligent, honest, well-built workmen, who are never wondering what is their business in the world.

"I'm quite taken by surprise," he said. "I didn't expect anything o' this sort, for it's a good deal more than my wages. But I've the more reason to be grateful to you, Captain, and to you, Mr. Irwine, and to all my friends here, who've drunk my health and wished me well. It 'ud be nonsense for me to be saying, I don't at all deserve th' opinion you have of me; that 'ud be poor thanks to you, to say that you've known me all these years and yet haven't sense enough to find out a great deal o' the truth about me. You think, if I undertake to do a bit o' work, I'll do it well, be my pay big or little—and that's true. I'd be ashamed to stand before you here if it wasna true. But it seems to me that's a man's plain duty, and nothing to be conceited about, and it's pretty clear to me as I've never done more than my duty; for let us do what we will, it's only making use o' the sperrit and the powers that ha' been given to us. And so this kindness o' yours, I'm sure, is no debt you owe me, but a free gift, and as such I accept it and am thankful. And as to this new employment I've taken in hand, I'll only say that I took it at Captain Donnithorne's desire, and that I'll try to fulfil his expectations. I'd wish for no better lot than to work under him, and to know that while I was getting my own bread I was taking care of his int'rests. For I believe he's one o' those gentlemen as wishes to do the right thing, and to leave the world a bit better than he found it, which it's my belief every man may do, whether he's gentle or simple, whether he sets a good bit o' work going and finds the money, or whether he does the work with his own hands. There's no occasion for me to say any more about what I feel towards him: I hope to show it through the rest o' my life in my actions."

There were various opinions about Adam's speech: some of the women whispered that he didn't show himself thankful enough, and seemed to speak as proud as could be; but most of the men were of opinion that nobody could speak more straightfor'ard, and that Adam was as fine a chap as need to be. While such observations were being buzzed about, mingled with wonderings as to what the old squire meant to do for a bailiff, and whether he was going to have a steward, the two gentlemen had risen, and were walking round to the table where the wives and children sat. There was none of the strong ale here, of course, but wine and dessert—sparkling gooseberry for the young ones, and some good sherry for the mothers. Mrs. Poyser was at the head of this table, and Totty was now seated in her lap, bending her small nose deep down into a wine-glass in search of the nuts floating there.

"How do you do, Mrs. Poyser?" said Arthur. "Weren't you pleased to hear your husband make such a good speech to-day?"

"Oh, sir, the men are mostly so tongue-tied—you're forced partly to guess what they mean, as you do wi' the dumb creaturs."

"What! you think you could have made it better for him?" said Mr. Irwine, laughing.

"Well, sir, when I want to say anything, I can mostly find words to say it in, thank God. Not as I'm a-finding faut wi' my husband, for if he's a man o' few words, what he says he'll stand to."

"I'm sure I never saw a prettier party than this," Arthur said, looking round at the apple-cheeked children. "My aunt and the Miss Irwines will come up and see you presently. They were afraid of the noise of the toasts, but it would be a shame for them not to see you at table."

He walked on, speaking to the mothers and patting the children, while Mr. Irwine satisfied himself with standing still and nodding at a distance, that no one's attention might be disturbed from the young squire, the hero of the day. Arthur did not venture to stop near Hetty, but merely bowed to her as he passed along the opposite side. The foolish child felt her heart swelling with discontent; for what woman was ever satisfied with apparent neglect, even when she knows it to be the mask of love? Hetty thought this was going to be the most miserable day she had had for a long while, a moment of chill daylight and reality came across her dream: Arthur, who had seemed so near to her only a few hours before, was separated from her, as the hero of a great procession is separated from a small outsider in the crowd.

Chapter XXV
The Games

The great dance was not to begin until eight o'clock, but for any lads and lasses who liked to dance on the shady grass before then, there was music always at hand—for was not the band of the Benefit Club capable of playing excellent jigs, reels, and hornpipes? And, besides this, there was a grand band hired from Rosseter, who, with their wonderful wind-instruments and puffed-out cheeks, were themselves a delightful show to the small boys and girls. To say nothing of Joshua Rann's fiddle, which, by an act of generous forethought, he had provided himself with, in case any one should be of sufficiently pure taste to prefer dancing to a solo on that instrument.

Meantime, when the sun had moved off the great open space in front of the house, the games began. There were, of course, well-soaped poles to be climbed by the boys and youths, races to be run by the old women, races to be run in sacks, heavy weights to be lifted by the strong men, and a long list of challenges to such ambitious attempts as that of walking as many yards possible on one leg—feats in which it was generally remarked that Wiry Ben, being "the lissom'st, springest fellow i' the country," was sure to be pre-eminent. To crown all, there was to be a donkey-race—that sublimest of all races, conducted on the grand socialistic idea of everybody encouraging everybody else's donkey, and the sorriest donkey winning.

And soon after four o'clock, splendid old Mrs. Irwine, in her damask satin and jewels and black lace, was led out by Arthur, followed by the whole family party, to her raised seat under the striped marquee, where she was to give out the prizes to the victors. Staid, formal Miss Lydia had requested to resign that queenly office to the royal old lady, and Arthur was pleased with this opportunity of gratifying his godmother's taste for stateliness. Old Mr. Donnithorne, the delicately clean, finely scented, withered old man, led out Miss Irwine, with his air of punctilious, acid politeness; Mr. Gawaine brought Miss Lydia, looking neutral and stiff in an elegant peach-blossom silk; and Mr. Irwine came last with his pale sister Anne. No other friend of the family, besides Mr. Gawaine, was invited to-day; there was to be a grand dinner for the neighbouring gentry on the morrow, but to-day all the forces were required for the entertainment of the tenants.

There was a sunk fence in front of the marquee, dividing the lawn from the park, but a temporary bridge had been made for the passage of the victors, and the groups of people standing, or seated here and there on benches, stretched on each side of the open space from the white marquees up to the sunk fence.

"Upon my word it's a pretty sight," said the old lady, in her deep voice, when she was seated, and looked round on the bright scene with its dark-green background; "and it's the last fête-day I'm likely to see, unless you make haste and get married, Arthur. But take care you get a charming bride, else I would rather die without seeing her."

"You're so terribly fastidious, Godmother," said Arthur, "I'm afraid I should never satisfy you with my choice."

"Well, I won't forgive you if she's not handsome. I can't be put off with amiability, which is always the excuse people are making for the existence of plain people. And she must not be silly; that will never do, because you'll want managing, and a silly woman can't manage you. Who is that tall young man, Dauphin, with the mild face? There, standing without his hat, and taking such care of that tall old woman by the side of him—his mother, of course. I like to see that."

"What, don't you know him, Mother?" said Mr. Irwine. "That is Seth Bede, Adam's brother—a Methodist, but a very good fellow. Poor Seth has looked rather down-hearted of late; I thought it was because of his father's dying in that sad way, but Joshua Rann tells me he wanted to marry that sweet little Methodist preacher who was here about a month ago, and I suppose she refused him."

"Ah, I remember hearing about her. But there are no end of people here that I don't know, for they're grown up and altered so since I used to go about."

"What excellent sight you have!" said old Mr. Donnithorne, who was holding a double glass up to his eyes, "to see the expression of that young man's face so far off. His face is nothing but a pale blurred spot to me. But I fancy I have the advantage of you when we come to look close. I can read small print without spectacles."

"Ah, my dear sir, you began with being very near-sighted, and those near-sighted eyes always wear the best. I want very strong spectacles to read with, but then I think my eyes get better and better for things at a distance. I suppose if I could live another fifty years, I should be blind to everything that wasn't out of other people's sight, like a man who stands in a well and sees nothing but the stars."

"See," said Arthur, "the old women are ready to set out on their race now. Which do you bet on, Gawaine?"

"The long-legged one, unless they're going to have several heats, and then the little wiry one may win."

"There are the Poysers, Mother, not far off on the right hand," said Miss Irwine. "Mrs. Poyser is looking at you. Do take notice of her."

"To be sure I will," said the old lady, giving a gracious bow to Mrs. Poyser. "A woman who sends me such excellent cream-cheese is not to be neglected. Bless me! What a fat child that is she is holding on her knee! But who is that pretty girl with dark eyes?"

"That is Hetty Sorrel," said Miss Lydia Donnithorne, "Martin Poyser's niece—a very likely young person, and well-looking too. My maid has taught her fine needlework, and she has mended some lace of mine very respectably indeed—very respectably."

"Why, she has lived with the Poysers six or seven years, Mother; you must have seen her," said Miss Irwine.

"No, I've never seen her, child—at least not as she is now," said Mrs. Irwine, continuing to look at Hetty. "Well-looking, indeed! She's a perfect beauty! I've never seen anything so pretty since my young days. What a pity such beauty as that should be thrown away among the farmers, when it's wanted so terribly among the good families without fortune! I daresay, now, she'll marry a man who would have thought her just as pretty if she had had round eyes and red hair."

Arthur dared not turn his eyes towards Hetty while Mrs. Irwine was speaking of her. He feigned not to hear, and to be occupied with something on the opposite side. But he saw her plainly enough without looking; saw her in heightened beauty, because he heard her beauty praised—for other men's opinion, you know, was like a native climate to Arthur's feelings: it was the air on which they thrived the best, and grew strong. Yes! She *was* enough to turn any man's head: any man in his place would have done and felt the same. And to give her up after all, as he was determined to do, would be an act that he should always look back upon with pride.

"No, Mother," and Mr. Irwine, replying to her last words; "I can't agree with you there. The common people are not quite so stupid as you imagine. The commonest man, who has his ounce of sense and feeling, is conscious of the difference between a lovely, delicate woman and a coarse one. Even a dog feels a difference in their presence. The man may be no better able than the dog to explain the influence the more refined beauty has on him, but he feels it."

"Bless me, Dauphin, what does an old bachelor like you know about it?"

"Oh, that is one of the matters in which old bachelors are wiser than married men, because they have time for more general contemplation. Your fine critic of woman must never shackle his judgment by calling one woman his own. But, as an example of what I was saying, that pretty Methodist preacher I mentioned just now told me that she had preached to the roughest miners and had never been treated with anything but the utmost respect and kindness by them. The reason is—though she doesn't know it—that there's so much tenderness, refinement, and purity about her. Such a woman as that brings with her 'airs from heaven' that the coarsest fellow is not insensible to."

"Here's a delicate bit of womanhood, or girlhood, coming to receive a prize, I suppose," said Mr. Gawaine. "She must be one of the racers in the sacks, who had set off before we came."

The "bit of womanhood" was our old acquaintance Bessy Cranage, otherwise Chad's Bess, whose large red cheeks and blowsy person had undergone an exaggeration of colour, which, if she had happened to be a heavenly body, would have made her sublime. Bessy, I am sorry to say, had taken to her ear-rings again since Dinah's departure, and was otherwise decked out in such small finery as she could muster. Any one who could have looked into poor Bessy's heart would have seen a striking resemblance between her little hopes and anxieties and Hetty's. The advantage, perhaps, would have been on Bessy's side in the matter of feeling. But then, you see, they were so very different outside! You would have been inclined to box Bessy's ears, and you would have longed to kiss Hetty.

Bessy had been tempted to run the arduous race, partly from mere hedonish gaiety, partly because of the prize. Some one had said there were to be cloaks and other nice clothes for prizes, and she approached the marquee, fanning herself with her handkerchief, but with exultation sparkling in her round eyes.

"Here is the prize for the first sack-race," said Miss Lydia, taking a large parcel from the table where the prizes were laid and giving it to Mrs. Irwine before Bessy came up, "an excellent grogram gown and a piece of flannel."

"You didn't think the winner was to be so young, I suppose, Aunt?" said Arthur. "Couldn't you find something else for this girl, and save that grim-looking gown for one of the older women?"

"I have bought nothing but what is useful and substantial," said Miss Lydia, adjusting her own lace; "I should not think of encouraging a love of finery in young women of that class. I have a scarlet cloak, but that is for the old woman who wins."

This speech of Miss Lydia's produced rather a mocking expression in Mrs. Irwine's face as she looked at Arthur, while Bessy came up and dropped a series of curtsies.

"This is Bessy Cranage, mother," said Mr. Irwine, kindly, "Chad Cranage's daughter. You remember Chad Cranage, the blacksmith?"

"Yes, to be sure," said Mrs. Irwine. "Well, Bessy, here is your prize—excellent warm things for winter. I'm sure you have had hard work to win them this warm day."

Bessy's lip fell as she saw the ugly, heavy gown—which felt so hot and disagreeable too, on this July day, and was such a great ugly thing to carry. She dropped her curtsies again, without looking up, and with a growing tremulousness about the corners of her mouth, and then turned away.

"Poor girl," said Arthur; "I think she's disappointed. I wish it had been something more to her taste."

"She's a bold-looking young person," observed Miss Lydia. "Not at all one I should like to encourage."

Arthur silently resolved that he would make Bessy a present of money before the day was over, that she might buy something more to her mind; but she, not aware of the consolation in store for her, turned out of the open space, where she was visible from the marquee, and throwing down the odious bundle under a tree, began to cry—very much tittered at the while by the small boys. In this situation she was descried by her discreet matronly cousin, who lost no time in coming up, having just given the baby into her husband's charge.

"What's the matter wi' ye?" said Bess the matron, taking up the bundle and examining it. "Ye'n sweltered yoursen, I reckon, running that fool's race. An' here, they'n gi'en you lots o' good grogram and flannel, as should ha' been gi'en by good rights to them as had the sense to keep away from such foolery. Ye might spare me a bit o' this grogram to make clothes for the lad—ye war ne'er ill-natured, Bess; I ne'er said that on ye."

"Ye may take it all, for what I care," said Bess the maiden, with a pettish movement, beginning to wipe away her tears and recover herself.

"Well, I could do wi't, if so be ye want to get rid on't," said the disinterested cousin, walking quickly away with the bundle, lest Chad's Bess should change her mind.

But that bonny-cheeked lass was blessed with an elasticity of spirits that secured her from any rankling grief; and by the time the grand climax of the donkey-race came on, her disappointment was entirely lost in the delightful excitement of attempting to stimulate the last donkey by hisses, while the boys applied the argument of sticks. But the strength of the donkey mind lies in adopting a course inversely as the arguments urged, which, well considered, requires as great a mental force as the direct sequence; and the present donkey proved the first-rate order of his intelligence by coming to a dead standstill just when the blows were thickest. Great was the shouting of the crowd, radiant the grinning of Bill Downes the stone-sawyer and the fortunate rider of this superior beast, which stood calm and stiff-legged in the midst of its triumph.

Arthur himself had provided the prizes for the men, and Bill was made happy with a splendid pocket-knife, supplied with blades and gimlets enough to make a man at home on a desert island. He had hardly returned from the marquee with the prize in his hand, when it began to be understood that Wiry Ben proposed to amuse the company, before the gentry went to dinner, with an impromptu and gratuitous performance—namely, a hornpipe, the main idea of which was doubtless borrowed; but this was to be developed by the dancer in so peculiar and complex a manner that no one could deny him the praise of originality. Wiry Ben's pride in his dancing—an accomplishment productive of great effect at the yearly Wake—had needed only slightly elevating by an extra quantity of good ale to convince him that the gentry would be very much struck with his performance of his hornpipe; and he had been decidedly encouraged in this idea by Joshua Rann, who observed that it was nothing but right to do something to please the young squire, in return for what he had done for them. You will be the less surprised at this opinion in so grave a personage when you learn that Ben had requested Mr. Rann to accompany him on the fiddle, and Joshua felt quite sure that though there might not be much in the dancing, the music would make up for it. Adam Bede, who was present in one of the large marquees, where the plan was being discussed, told Ben he had better not make a fool of himself—a remark which at once fixed Ben's determination: he was not going to let anything alone because Adam Bede turned up his nose at it.

"What's this, what's this?" said old Mr. Donnithorne. "Is it something you've arranged, Arthur? Here's the clerk coming with his fiddle, and a smart fellow with a nosegay in his button-hole."

"No," said Arthur; "I know nothing about it. By Jove, he's going to dance! It's one of the carpenters—I forget his name at this moment."

"It's Ben Cranage—Wiry Ben, they call him," said Mr. Irwine; "rather a loose fish, I think. Anne, my dear, I see that fiddle-scraping is too much for you: you're getting tired. Let me take you in now, that you may rest till dinner."

Miss Anne rose assentingly, and the good brother took her away, while Joshua's preliminary scrapings burst into the "White Cockade," from which he intended to pass to a variety of tunes, by a series of transitions which his good ear really taught him to execute with some skill. It would have been an exasperating fact to him, if he had known it, that the general attention was too thoroughly absorbed by Ben's dancing for any one to give much heed to the music.

Have you ever seen a real English rustic perform a solo dance? Perhaps you have only seen a ballet rustic, smiling like a merry countryman in crockery, with graceful turns of the haunch and insinuating movements of the head. That is as much like the real thing as the "Bird Waltz" is like the song of birds. Wiry Ben never smiled: he looked as serious as a dancing monkey—as serious as if he had been an experimental philosopher ascertaining in his own person the amount of shaking and the varieties of angularity that could be given to the human limbs.

To make amends for the abundant laughter in the striped marquee, Arthur clapped his hands continually and cried "Bravo!" But Ben had one admirer whose eyes followed his movements with a fervid gravity that equalled his own. It was Martin Poyser, who was seated on a bench, with Tommy between his legs.

"What dost think o' that?" he said to his wife. "He goes as pat to the music as if he was made o' clockwork. I used to be a pretty good un at dancing myself when I was lighter, but I could niver ha' hit it just to th' hair like that."

"It's little matter what his limbs are, to my thinking," re-turned Mrs. Poyser. "He's empty enough i' the upper story, or he'd niver come jigging an' stamping i' that way, like a mad grasshopper, for the gentry to look at him. They're fit to die wi' laughing, I can see."

"Well, well, so much the better, it amuses 'em," said Mr. Poyser, who did not easily take an irritable view of things. "But they're going away now, t' have their dinner, I reckon. We'll move about a bit, shall we, and see what Adam Bede's doing. He's got to look after the drinking and things: I doubt he hasna had much fun."

Chapter XXVI
The Dance

Arthur had chosen the entrance-hall for the ballroom: very wisely, for no other room could have been so airy, or would have had the advantage of the wide doors opening into the garden, as well as a ready entrance into the other rooms. To be sure, a stone floor was not the pleasantest to dance on, but then, most of the dancers had known what it was to enjoy a Christmas dance on kitchen quarries. It was one of those entrance-halls which make the surrounding rooms look like closets—with stucco angels, trumpets, and flower-wreaths on the lofty ceiling, and great medallions of miscellaneous heroes on the walls, alternating with statues in niches. Just the sort of place to be ornamented well with green boughs, and Mr. Craig had been proud to show his taste and his hothouse plants on the occasion. The broad steps of the stone staircase were covered with cushions to serve as seats for the children, who were to stay till half-past nine with the servant-maids to see the dancing, and as this dance was confined to the chief tenants, there was abundant room for every one. The lights were charmingly disposed in coloured-paper lamps, high up among green boughs, and the farmers' wives and daughters, as they peeped in, believed no scene could be more splendid; they knew now quite well in what sort of rooms the king and queen lived, and their thoughts glanced with some pity towards cousins and acquaintances who had not this fine opportunity of knowing how things went on in the great world. The lamps were already lit, though the sun had not long set, and there was that calm light out of doors in which we seem to see all objects more distinctly than in the broad day.

It was a pretty scene outside the house: the farmers and their families were moving about the lawn, among the flowers and shrubs, or along the broad straight road leading from the east front, where a carpet of mossy grass spread on each side, studded here and there with a dark flat-boughed cedar, or a grand pyramidal fir sweeping the ground with its branches, all tipped with a fringe of paler green. The groups of cottagers in the park were gradually diminishing, the young ones being attracted towards the lights that were beginning to gleam from the windows of the gallery in the abbey, which was to be their dancing-room, and some of the sober elder ones thinking it time to go home quietly. One of these was Lisbeth Bede, and Seth went with her—not from filial attention only, for his conscience would not let him join in dancing. It had been rather a melancholy day to Seth: Dinah had never been more constantly present with him than in this scene, where everything was so unlike her. He saw her all the more vividly after looking at the thoughtless faces and gay-coloured dresses of the young women—just as one feels the beauty and the greatness of a pictured Madonna the more when it has been for a moment screened from us by a vulgar head in a bonnet. But this presence of Dinah in his mind only helped him to bear the better with his mother's mood, which had been becoming more and more querulous for the last hour. Poor Lisbeth was suffering from a strange conflict of feelings. Her joy and pride in the honour paid to her darling son Adam was beginning to be worsted in the conflict with the jealousy and fretfulness which had revived when Adam came to tell her that Captain Donnithorne desired him to join the dancers in the hall. Adam was getting more and more out of her reach; she wished all the old troubles back again, for then it mattered more to Adam what his mother said and did.

"Eh, it's fine talkin' o' dancin'," she said, "an' thy father not a five week in's grave. An' I wish I war there too, i'stid o' bein' left to take up merrier folks's room above ground."

"Nay, don't look at it i' that way, Mother," said Adam, who was determined to be gentle to her to-day. "I don't mean to dance—I shall only look on. And since the captain wishes me to be there, it 'ud look as if I thought I knew better than him to say as I'd rather not stay. And thee know'st how he's behaved to me to-day."

"Eh, thee't do as thee lik'st, for thy old mother's got no right t' hinder thee. She's nought but th' old husk, and thee'st slipped away from her, like the ripe nut."

"Well, Mother," said Adam, "I'll go and tell the captain as it hurts thy feelings for me to stay, and I'd rather go home upo' that account: he won't take it ill then, I daresay, and I'm willing." He said this with some effort, for he really longed to be near Hetty this evening.

"Nay, nay, I wonna ha' thee do that—the young squire 'ull be angered. Go an' do what thee't ordered to do, an' me and Seth 'ull go whome. I know it's a grit honour for thee to be so looked on—an' who's to be prouder on it nor thy mother? Hadna she the cumber o' rearin' thee an' doin' for thee all these 'ears?"

"Well, good-bye, then, Mother—good-bye, lad—remember Gyp when you get home," said Adam, turning away towards the gate of the pleasure-grounds, where he hoped he might be able to join the Poysers, for he had been so occupied throughout the afternoon that he had had no time to speak to Hetty. His eye soon detected a distant group, which he knew to be the right one, returning to the house along the broad gravel road, and he hastened on to meet them.

"Why, Adam, I'm glad to get sight on y' again," said Mr. Poyser, who was carrying Totty on his arm. "You're going t' have a bit o' fun, I hope, now your work's all done. And here's Hetty has promised no end o' partners, an' I've just been askin' her if she'd agreed to dance wi' you, an' she says no."

"Well, I didn't think o' dancing to-night," said Adam, already tempted to change his mind, as he looked at Hetty.

"Nonsense!" said Mr. Poyser. "Why, everybody's goin' to dance to-night, all but th' old squire and Mrs. Irwine. Mrs. Best's been tellin' us as Miss Lyddy and Miss Irwine 'ull dance, an' the young squire 'ull pick my wife for his first partner, t' open the ball: so she'll be forced to dance, though she's laid by ever sin' the Christmas afore the little un was born. You canna for shame stand still, Adam, an' you a fine young fellow and can dance as well as anybody."

"Nay, nay," said Mrs. Poyser, "it 'ud be unbecomin'. I know the dancin's nonsense, but if you stick at everything because it's nonsense, you wonna go far i' this life. When your broth's ready-made for you, you mun swallow the thickenin', or else let the broth alone."

"Then if Hetty 'ull dance with me," said Adam, yielding either to Mrs. Poyser's argument or to something else, "I'll dance whichever dance she's free."

"I've got no partner for the fourth dance," said Hetty; "I'll dance that with you, if you like."

"Ah," said Mr. Poyser, "but you mun dance the first dance, Adam, else it'll look partic'ler. There's plenty o' nice partners to pick an' choose from, an' it's hard for the gells when the men stan' by and don't ask 'em."

Adam felt the justice of Mr. Poyser's observation: it would not do for him to dance with no one besides Hetty; and remembering that Jonathan Burge had some reason to feel hurt to-day, he resolved to ask Miss Mary to dance with him the first dance, if she had no other partner.

"There's the big clock strikin' eight," said Mr. Poyser; "we must make haste in now, else the squire and the ladies 'ull be in afore us, an' that wouldna look well."

When they had entered the hall, and the three children under Molly's charge had been seated on the stairs, the folding-doors of the drawing-room were thrown open, and Arthur entered in his regimentals, leading Mrs. Irwine to a carpet-covered dais ornamented with hot-house plants, where she and Miss Anne were to be seated with old Mr. Donnithorne, that they might look on at the dancing, like the kings and queens in the plays. Arthur had put on his uniform to please the tenants, he said, who thought as much of his militia dignity as if it had been an elevation to the premiership. He had not the least objection to gratify them in that way: his uniform was very advantageous to his figure.

The old squire, before sitting down, walked round the hall to greet the tenants and make polite speeches to the wives: he was always polite; but the farmers had found out, after long puzzling, that this polish was one of the signs of hardness.

It was observed that he gave his most elaborate civility to Mrs. Poyser to-night, inquiring particularly about her health, recommending her to strengthen herself with cold water as he did, and avoid all drugs. Mrs. Poyser curtsied and thanked him with great self-command, but when he had passed on, she whispered to her husband, "I'll lay my life he's brewin' some nasty turn against us. Old Harry doesna wag his tail so for nothin'." Mr. Poyser had no time to answer, for now Arthur came up and said, "Mrs. Poyser, I'm come to request the favour of your hand for the first dance; and, Mr. Poyser, you must let me take you to my aunt, for she claims you as her partner."

The wife's pale cheek flushed with a nervous sense of unwonted honour as Arthur led her to the top of the room; but Mr. Poyser, to whom an extra glass had restored his youthful confidence in his good looks and good dancing, walked along with them quite proudly, secretly flattering himself that Miss Lydia had never had a partner in *her* life who could lift her off the ground as he would. In order to balance the honours given to the two parishes, Miss Irwine danced with Luke Britton, the largest Broxton farmer, and Mr. Gawaine led out Mrs. Britton. Mr. Irwine, after seating his sister Anne, had gone to the abbey gallery, as he had agreed with Arthur beforehand, to see how the merriment of the cottagers was prospering. Meanwhile, all the less distinguished couples had taken their places: Hetty was led out by the inevitable Mr. Craig, and Mary Burge by Adam; and now the music struck up, and the glorious country-dance, best of all dances, began.

Pity it was not a boarded floor! Then the rhythmic stamping of the thick shoes would have been better than any drums. That merry stamping, that gracious nodding of the head, that waving bestowal of the hand—where can we see them now? That simple dancing of well-covered matrons, laying aside for an hour the cares of house and dairy, remembering but not affecting youth, not jealous but proud of the young maidens by their side—that holiday sprightliness of portly husbands paying little compliments to their wives, as if their courting days were come again—those lads and lasses a little confused and awkward with their partners, having nothing to say—it would be a pleasant variety to see all that sometimes, instead of low dresses and large skirts, and scanning glances exploring costumes, and languid men in lacquered boots smiling with double meaning.

There was but one thing to mar Martin Poyser's pleasure in this dance: it was that he was always in close contact with Luke Britton, that slovenly farmer. He thought of throwing a little glazed coldness into his eye in the crossing of hands; but then, as Miss Irwine was opposite to him instead of the offensive Luke, he might freeze the wrong person. So he gave his face up to hilarity, unchilled by moral judgments.

How Hetty's heart beat as Arthur approached her! He had hardly looked at her to-day: now he *must* take her hand. Would he press it? Would he look at her? She thought she would cry if he gave her no sign of feeling. Now he was there—he had taken her hand—yes, he was pressing it. Hetty turned pale as she looked up at him for an instant and met his eyes, before the dance carried him away. That pale look came upon Arthur like the beginning of a dull pain, which clung to him, though he must dance and smile and joke all the same. Hetty would look so, when he told her what he had to tell her; and he should never be able to bear it—he should be a fool and give way again. Hetty's look did not really mean so much as he thought: it was only the sign of a struggle between the desire for him to notice her and the dread lest she should betray the desire to others. But Hetty's face had a language that transcended her feelings. There are faces which nature charges with a meaning and pathos not belonging to the single human soul that flutters beneath them, but speaking the joys and sorrows of foregone generations—eyes that tell of deep love which doubtless has been and is somewhere, but not paired with these eyes—perhaps paired with pale eyes that can say nothing; just as a national language may be instinct with poetry unfelt by the lips that use it. That look of Hetty's oppressed Arthur with a dread which yet had something of a terrible unconfessed delight in it, that she loved him too well. There was a hard task before him, for at that moment he felt he would have given up three years of his youth for the happiness of abandoning himself without remorse to his passion for Hetty.

These were the incongruous thoughts in his mind as he led Mrs. Poyser, who was panting with fatigue, and secretly resolving that neither judge nor jury should force her to dance another dance, to take a quiet rest in the dining-room, where supper was laid out for the guests to come and take it as they chose.

"I've desired Hetty to remember as she's got to dance wi' you, sir," said the good innocent woman; "for she's so thoughtless, she'd be like enough to go an' engage herself for ivery dance. So I told her not to promise too many."

"Thank you, Mrs. Poyser," said Arthur, not without a twinge. "Now, sit down in this comfortable chair, and here is Mills ready to give you what you would like best."

He hurried away to seek another matronly partner, for due honour must be paid to the married women before he asked any of the young ones; and the country-dances, and the stamping, and the gracious nodding, and the waving of the hands, went on joyously.

At last the time had come for the fourth dance—longed for by the strong, grave Adam, as if he had been a delicate-handed youth of eighteen; for we are all very much alike when we are in our first love; and Adam had hardly ever touched

Hetty's hand for more than a transient greeting—had never danced with her but once before. His eyes had followed her eagerly to-night in spite of himself, and had taken in deeper draughts of love. He thought she behaved so prettily, so quietly; she did not seem to be flirting at all, she smiled less than usual; there was almost a sweet sadness about her. "God bless her!" he said inwardly; "I'd make her life a happy 'un, if a strong arm to work for her, and a heart to love her, could do it."

And then there stole over him delicious thoughts of coming home from work, and drawing Hetty to his side, and feeling her cheek softly pressed against his, till he forgot where he was, and the music and the tread of feet might have been the falling of rain and the roaring of the wind, for what he knew.

But now the third dance was ended, and he might go up to her and claim her hand. She was at the far end of the hall near the staircase, whispering with Molly, who had just given the sleeping Totty into her arms before running to fetch shawls and bonnets from the landing. Mrs. Poyser had taken the two boys away into the dining-room to give them some cake before they went home in the cart with Grandfather and Molly was to follow as fast as possible.

"Let me hold her," said Adam, as Molly turned upstairs; "the children are so heavy when they're asleep."

Hetty was glad of the relief, for to hold Totty in her arms, standing, was not at all a pleasant variety to her. But this second transfer had the unfortunate effect of rousing Totty, who was not behind any child of her age in peevishness at an unseasonable awaking. While Hetty was in the act of placing her in Adam's arms, and had not yet withdrawn her own, Totty opened her eyes, and forthwith fought out with her left fist at Adam's arm, and with her right caught at the string of brown beads round Hetty's neck. The locket leaped out from her frock, and the next moment the string was broken, and Hetty, helpless, saw beads and locket scattered wide on the floor.

"My locket, my locket!" she said, in a loud frightened whisper to Adam; "never mind the beads."

Adam had already seen where the locket fell, for it had attracted his glance as it leaped out of her frock. It had fallen on the raised wooden dais where the band sat, not on the stone floor; and as Adam picked it up, he saw the glass with the dark and light locks of hair under it. It had fallen that side upwards, so the glass was not broken. He turned it over on his hand, and saw the enamelled gold back.

"It isn't hurt," he said, as he held it towards Hetty, who was unable to take it because both her hands were occupied with Totty.

“Oh, it doesn’t matter, I don’t mind about it,” said Hetty, who had been pale and was now red.

“Not matter?” said Adam, gravely. “You seemed very frightened about it. I’ll hold it till you’re ready to take it,” he added, quietly closing his hand over it, that she might not think he wanted to look at it again.

By this time Molly had come with bonnet and shawl, and as soon as she had taken Totty, Adam placed the locket in Hetty’s hand. She took it with an air of indifference and put it in her pocket, in her heart vexed and angry with Adam because he had seen it, but determined now that she would show no more signs of agitation.

“See,” she said, “they’re taking their places to dance; let us go.”

Adam assented silently. A puzzled alarm had taken possession of him. Had Hetty a lover he didn’t know of? For none of her relations, he was sure, would give her a locket like that; and none of her admirers, with whom he was acquainted, was in the position of an accepted lover, as the giver of that locket must be. Adam was lost in the utter impossibility of finding any person for his fears to alight on. He could only feel with a terrible pang that there was something in Hetty’s life unknown to him; that while he had been rocking himself in the hope that she would come to love him, she was already loving another. The pleasure of the dance with Hetty was gone; his eyes, when they rested on her, had an uneasy questioning expression in them; he could think of nothing to say to her; and she too was out of temper and disinclined to speak. They were both glad when the dance was ended.

Adam was determined to stay no longer; no one wanted him, and no one would notice if he slipped away. As soon as he got out of doors, he began to walk at his habitual rapid pace, hurrying along without knowing why, busy with the painful thought that the memory of this day, so full of honour and promise to him, was poisoned for ever. Suddenly, when he was far on through the Chase, he stopped, startled by a flash of reviving hope. After all, he might be a fool, making a great misery out of a trifle. Hetty, fond of finery as she was, might have bought the thing herself. It looked too expensive for that—it looked like the things on white satin in the great jeweller’s shop at Rosseter. But Adam had very imperfect notions of the value of such things, and he thought it could certainly not cost more than a guinea. Perhaps Hetty had had as much as that in Christmas boxes, and there was no knowing but she might have been childish enough to spend it in that way; she was such a young thing, and she couldn’t help loving finery! But then, why had she been so frightened about it at first, and changed colour so, and afterwards pretended not to care? Oh, that was because she was ashamed of his seeing that she had such a smart thing—she was conscious that it was wrong for her to spend her money on it, and she knew that Adam disapproved of finery. It was a proof she cared about what he liked and disliked. She must have thought from his silence and gravity afterwards that he was very much displeased with her, that he was inclined to be harsh and severe towards her foibles. And as he walked on more quietly, chewing the cud of this new hope, his only uneasiness was that he had behaved in a way which might chill Hetty's feeling towards him. For this last view of the matter *must* be the true one. How could Hetty have an accepted lover, quite unknown to him? She was never away from her uncle's house for more than a day; she could have no acquaintances that did not come there, and no intimacies unknown to her uncle and aunt. It would be folly to believe that the locket was given to her by a lover. The little ring of dark hair he felt sure was her own; he could form no guess about the light hair under it, for he had not seen it very distinctly. It might be a bit of her father's or mother's, who had died when she was a child, and she would naturally put a bit of her own along with it.

And so Adam went to bed comforted, having woven for himself an ingenious web of probabilities—the surest screen a wise man can place between himself and the truth. His last waking thoughts melted into a dream that he was with Hetty again at the Hall Farm, and that he was asking her to forgive him for being so cold and silent.

And while he was dreaming this, Arthur was leading Hetty to the dance and saying to her in low hurried tones, "I shall be in the wood the day after to-morrow at seven; come as early as you can." And Hetty's foolish joys and hopes, which had flown away for a little space, scared by a mere nothing, now all came fluttering back, unconscious of the real peril. She was happy for the first time this long day, and wished that dance would last for hours. Arthur wished it too; it was the last weakness he meant to indulge in; and a man never lies with more delicious languor under the influence of a passion than when he has persuaded himself that he shall subdue it to-morrow.

But Mrs. Poyser's wishes were quite the reverse of this, for her mind was filled with dreary forebodings as to the retardation of to-morrow morning's cheese in consequence of these late hours. Now that Hetty had done her duty and danced one dance with the young squire, Mr. Poyser must go out and see if the cart was come back to fetch them, for it was half-past ten o'clock, and notwithstanding a mild suggestion on his part that it would be bad manners for them to be the first to go, Mrs. Poyser was resolute on the point, "manners or no manners."

"What! Going already, Mrs. Poyser?" said old Mr. Donnithorne, as she came to curtsy and take leave; "I thought we should not part with any of our guests till eleven. Mrs. Irwine and I, who are elderly people, think of sitting out the dance till then."

"Oh, Your Honour, it's all right and proper for gentlefolks to stay up by candlelight—they've got no cheese on their minds. We're late enough as it is, an' there's no lettin' the cows know as they mustn't want to be milked so early to-morrow mornin'. So, if you'll please t' excuse us, we'll take our leave."

"Eh!" she said to her husband, as they set off in the cart, "I'd sooner ha' brewin' day and washin' day together than one o' these pleasurin' days. There's no work so tirin' as danglin' about an' starin' an' not rightly knowin' what you're goin' to do next; and keepin' your face i' smilin' order like a grocer o' market-day for fear people shouldna think you civil enough. An' you've nothing to show for't when it's done, if it isn't a yallow face wi' eatin' things as disagree."

"Nay, nay," said Mr. Poyser, who was in his merriest mood, and felt that he had had a great day, "a bit o' pleasuring's good for thee sometimes. An' thee danc'st as well as any of 'em, for I'll back thee against all the wives i' the parish for a light foot an' ankle. An' it was a great honour for the young squire to ask thee first—I reckon it was because I sat at th' head o' the table an' made the speech. An' Hetty too—*she* never had such a partner before—a fine young gentleman in reg'mentals. It'll serve you to talk on, Hetty, when you're an old woman—how you danced wi' th' young squire the day he come o' age."

BOOK FOURTH

Chapter XXVII
A crisis

It was beyond the middle of August—nearly three weeks after the birthday feast. The reaping of the wheat had begun in our north midland county of Loamshire, but the harvest was likely still to be retarded by the heavy rains, which were causing inundations and much damage throughout the country. From this last trouble the Broxton and Hayslope farmers, on their pleasant uplands and in their brook-watered valleys, had not suffered, and as I cannot pretend that they were such exceptional farmers as to love the general good better than their own, you will infer that they were not in very low spirits about the rapid rise in the price of bread, so long as there was hope of gathering in their own corn undamaged; and occasional days of sunshine and drying winds flattered this hope.

The eighteenth of August was one of these days when the sunshine looked brighter in all eyes for the gloom that went before. Grand masses of cloud were hurried across the blue, and the great round hills behind the Chase seemed alive with their flying shadows; the sun was hidden for a moment, and then shone out warm again like a recovered joy; the leaves, still green, were tossed off the hedgerow trees by the wind; around the farmhouses there was a sound of clapping doors; the apples fell in the orchards; and the stray horses on the green sides of the lanes and on the common had their manes blown about their faces. And yet the wind seemed only part of the general gladness because the sun was shining. A merry day for the children, who ran and shouted to see if they could top the wind with their voices; and the grown-up people too were in good spirits, inclined to believe in yet finer days, when the wind had fallen. If only the corn were not ripe enough to be blown out of the husk and scattered as untimely seed!

And yet a day on which a blighting sorrow may fall upon a man. For if it be true that Nature at certain moments seems charged with a presentiment of one individual lot must it not also be true that she seems unmindful, unconscious of another? For there is no hour that has not its births of gladness and despair, no morning brightness that does not bring new sickness to desolation as well as new forces to genius and love. There are so many of us, and our lots are so different, what wonder that Nature's mood is often in harsh contrast with the great crisis of our lives? We are children of a large family, and must learn, as such children do, not to expect that our hurts will be made much of—to be content with little nurture and caressing, and help each other the more.

It was a busy day with Adam, who of late had done almost double work, for he was continuing to act as foreman for Jonathan Burge, until some satisfactory person could be found to supply his place, and Jonathan was slow to find that person. But he had done the extra work cheerfully, for his hopes were buoyant again about Hetty. Every time she had seen him since the birthday, she had seemed to make an effort to behave all the more kindly to him, that she might make him understand she had forgiven his silence and coldness during the dance. He had never mentioned the locket to her again; too happy that she smiled at him—still happier because he observed in her a more subdued air, something that he interpreted as the growth of womanly tenderness and seriousness. "Ah!" he thought, again and again, "she's only seventeen; she'll be thoughtful enough after a while. And her aunt allays says how clever she is at the work. She'll make a wife as Mother'll have no occasion to grumble at, after all." To be sure, he had only seen her at home twice since the birthday; for one Sunday, when he was intending to go from church to the Hall Farm, Hetty had joined the party of upper servants from the Chase and had gone home with them—almost as if she were inclined to encourage Mr. Craig. "She's takin' too much likin' to them folks i' the housekeeper's room," Mrs. Poyser remarked. "For my part, I was never overfond o' gentlefolks's servants—they're mostly like the fine ladies' fat dogs, nayther good for barking nor butcher's meat, but on'y for show." And another evening she was gone to Treddleston to buy some things; though, to his great surprise, as he was returning home, he saw her at a distance getting over a stile quite out of the Treddleston road. But, when he hastened to her, she was very kind, and asked him to go in again when he had taken her to the yard gate. She had gone a little farther into the fields after coming from Treddleston because she didn't want to go in, she said: it was so nice to be out of doors, and her aunt always made such a fuss about it if she wanted to go out. "Oh, do come in with me!" she said, as he was going to shake hands with her at the gate, and he could not resist that. So he went in, and Mrs. Poyser was contented with only a slight remark on Hetty's being later than was expected; while Hetty, who had looked out of spirits when he met her, smiled and talked and waited on them all with unusual promptitude.

That was the last time he had seen her; but he meant to make leisure for going to the Farm to-morrow. To-day, he knew, was her day for going to the Chase to sew with the lady's maid, so he would get as much work done as possible this evening, that the next might be clear.

One piece of work that Adam was superintending was some slight repairs at the Chase Farm, which had been hitherto occupied by Satchell, as bailiff, but which it was now rumoured that the old squire was going to let to a smart man in top-boots, who had been seen to ride over it one day. Nothing but the desire to get a tenant could account for the squire's undertaking repairs, though the Saturday-evening party at Mr. Casson's agreed over their pipes that no man in his senses would take the Chase Farm unless there was a bit more ploughland laid to it. However that might be, the repairs were ordered to be executed with all dispatch, and Adam, acting for Mr. Burge, was carrying out the order with his usual energy. But to-day, having been occupied elsewhere, he had not been able to arrive at the Chase Farm till late in the afternoon, and he then discovered that some old roofing, which he had calculated on preserving, had given way. There was clearly no good to be done with this part of the building without pulling it all down, and Adam immediately saw in his mind a plan for building it up again, so as to make the most convenient of cow-sheds and calf-pens, with a hovel for implements; and all without any great expense for materials. So, when the workmen were gone, he sat down, took out his pocket-book, and busied himself with sketching a plan, and making a specification of the expenses that he might show it to Burge the next morning, and set him on persuading the squire to consent. To "make a good job" of anything, however small, was always a pleasure to Adam, and he sat on a block, with his book resting on a planing-table, whistling low every now and then and turning his head on one side with a just perceptible smile of gratification—of pride, too, for if Adam loved a bit of good work, he loved also to think, "I did it!" And I believe the only people who are free from that weakness are those who have no work to call their own. It was nearly seven before he had finished and put on his jacket again; and on giving a last look round, he observed that Seth, who had been working here to-day, had left his basket of tools behind him. "Why, th' lad's forgot his tools," thought Adam, "and he's got to work up at the shop to-morrow. There never was such a chap for wool-gathering; he'd leave his head behind him, if it was loose. However, it's lucky I've seen 'em; I'll carry 'em home."

The buildings of the Chase Farm lay at one extremity of the Chase, at about ten minutes' walking distance from the Abbey. Adam had come thither on his pony, intending to ride to the stables and put up his nag on his way home. At the stables he encountered Mr. Craig, who had come to look at the captain's new horse, on which he was to ride away the day after to-morrow; and Mr. Craig detained him to tell how all the servants were to collect at the gate of the courtyard to wish the young squire luck as he rode out; so that by the time Adam had got into the Chase, and was striding along with the basket of tools over his shoulder, the sun was on the point of setting, and was sending level crimson rays among the great trunks of the old oaks, and touching every bare patch of ground with a transient glory that made it look like a jewel dropt upon the grass. The wind had fallen now, and there was only enough breeze to stir the delicate-stemmed leaves. Any one who had been sitting in the house all day would have been glad to walk now; but Adam had been quite enough in the open air to wish to shorten his way home, and he bethought himself that he might do so by striking across the Chase and going through the Grove, where he had never been for years. He hurried on across the Chase, stalking along the narrow paths between the fern, with Gyp at his heels, not lingering to watch the magnificent changes of the light—hardly once thinking of it—yet feeling its presence in a certain calm happy awe which mingled itself with his busy working-day thoughts. How could he help feeling it? The very deer felt it, and were more timid.

Presently Adam's thoughts recurred to what Mr. Craig had said about Arthur Donnithorne, and pictured his going away, and the changes that might take place before he came back; then they travelled back affectionately over the old scenes of boyish companionship, and dwelt on Arthur's good qualities, which Adam had a pride in, as we all have in the virtues of the superior who honours us. A nature like Adam's, with a great need of love and reverence in it, depends for so much of its happiness on what it can believe and feel about others! And he had no ideal world of dead heroes; he knew little of the life of men in the past; he must find the beings to whom he could cling with loving admiration among those who came within speech of him. These pleasant thoughts about Arthur brought a milder expression than usual into his keen rough face: perhaps they were the reason why, when he opened the old green gate leading into the Grove, he paused to pat Gyp and say a kind word to him.

After that pause, he strode on again along the broad winding path through the Grove. What grand beeches! Adam delighted in a fine tree of all things; as the fisherman's sight is keenest on the sea, so Adam's perceptions were more at home with trees than with other objects. He kept them in his memory, as a painter does, with all the flecks and knots in their bark, all the curves and angles of their boughs, and had often calculated the height and contents of a trunk to a nicety, as he stood looking at it. No wonder that, not-withstanding his desire to get on, he could not help pausing to look at a curious large beech which he had seen standing before him at a turning in the road, and convince himself that it was not two trees wedded together, but only one. For the rest of his life he remembered that moment when he was calmly examining the beech, as a man remembers his last glimpse of the home where his youth was passed, before the road turned, and he saw it no more. The beech stood at the last turning before the Grove ended in an archway of boughs that let in the eastern light; and as Adam stepped away from the tree to continue his walk, his eyes fell on two figures about twenty yards before him.

He remained as motionless as a statue, and turned almost as pale. The two figures were standing opposite to each other, with clasped hands about to part; and while they were bending to kiss, Gyp, who had been running among the brushwood, came out, caught sight of them, and gave a sharp bark. They separated with a start—one hurried through the gate out of the Grove, and the other, turning round, walked slowly, with a sort of saunter, towards Adam who still stood transfixed and pale, clutching tighter the stick with which he held the basket of tools over his shoulder, and looking at the approaching figure with eyes in which amazement was fast turning to fierceness.

Arthur Donnithorne looked flushed and excited; he had tried to make unpleasant feelings more bearable by drinking a little more wine than usual at dinner to-day, and was still enough under its flattering influence to think more lightly of this unwished-for rencontre with Adam than he would otherwise have done. After all, Adam was the best person who could have happened to see him and Hetty together—he was a sensible fellow, and would not babble about it to other people. Arthur felt confident that he could laugh the thing off and explain it away. And so he sauntered forward with elaborate carelessness—his flushed face, his evening dress of fine cloth and fine linen, his hands half-thrust into his waistcoat pockets, all shone upon by the strange evening light which the light clouds had caught up even to the zenith, and were now shedding down between the topmost branches above him.

Adam was still motionless, looking at him as he came up. He understood it all now—the locket and everything else that had been doubtful to him: a terrible scorching light showed him the hidden letters that changed the meaning of the past. If he had moved a muscle, he must inevitably have sprung upon Arthur like a tiger; and in the conflicting emotions that filled those long moments, he had told himself that he would not give loose to passion, he would only speak the right thing. He stood as if petrified by an unseen force, but the force was his own strong will.

"Well, Adam," said Arthur, "you've been looking at the fine old beeches, eh? They're not to be come near by the hatchet, though; this is a sacred grove. I overtook pretty little Hetty Sorrel as I was coming to my den—the Hermitage, there. She ought not to come home this way so late. So I took care of her to the gate, and asked for a kiss for my pains. But I must get back now, for this road is confoundedly damp. Good-night, Adam. I shall see you to-morrow—to say good-bye, you know."

Arthur was too much preoccupied with the part he was playing himself to be thoroughly aware of the expression in Adam's face. He did not look directly at Adam, but glanced carelessly round at the trees and then lifted up one foot to look at the sole of his boot. He cared to say no more—he had thrown quite dust enough into honest Adam's eyes—and as he spoke the last words, he walked on.

"Stop a bit, sir," said Adam, in a hard peremptory voice, without turning round. "I've got a word to say to you."

Arthur paused in surprise. Susceptible persons are more affected by a change of tone than by unexpected words, and Arthur had the susceptibility of a nature at once affectionate and vain. He was still more surprised when he saw that Adam had not moved, but stood with his back to him, as if summoning him to return. What did he mean? He was going to make a serious business of this affair. Arthur felt his temper rising. A patronising disposition always has its meaner side, and in the confusion of his irritation and alarm there entered the feeling that a man to whom he had shown so much favour as to Adam was not in a position to criticize his conduct. And yet he was dominated, as one who feels himself in the wrong always is, by the man whose good opinion he cares for. In spite of pride and temper, there was as much deprecation as anger in his voice when he said, "What do you mean, Adam?"

"I mean, sir"—answered Adam, in the same harsh voice, still without turning round—"I mean, sir, that you don't deceive me by your light words. This is not the first time you've met Hetty Sorrel in this grove, and this is not the first time you've kissed her."

Arthur felt a startled uncertainty how far Adam was speaking from knowledge, and how far from mere inference. And this uncertainty, which prevented him from contriving a prudent answer, heightened his irritation. He said, in a high sharp tone, "Well, sir, what then?"

"Why, then, instead of acting like th' upright, honourable man we've all believed you to be, you've been acting the part of a selfish light-minded scoundrel. You know as well as I do what it's to lead to when a gentleman like you kisses and makes love to a young woman like Hetty, and gives her presents as she's frightened for other folks to see. And I say it again, you're acting the part of a selfish light-minded scoundrel though it cuts me to th' heart to say so, and I'd rather ha' lost my right hand."

"Let me tell you, Adam," said Arthur, bridling his growing anger and trying to recur to his careless tone, "you're not only devilishly impertinent, but you're talking nonsense. Every pretty girl is not such a fool as you, to suppose that when a gentleman admires her beauty and pays her a little attention, he must mean something particular. Every man likes to flirt with a pretty girl, and every pretty girl likes to be flirted with. The wider the distance between them, the less harm there is, for then she's not likely to deceive herself."

"I don't know what you mean by flirting," said Adam, "but if you mean behaving to a woman as if you loved her, and yet not loving her all the while, I say that's not th' action of an honest man, and what isn't honest does come t' harm. I'm not a fool, and you're not a fool, and you know better than what you're saying. You know it couldn't be made public as you've behaved to Hetty as y' have done without her losing her character and bringing shame and trouble on her and her relations. What if you meant nothing by your kissing and your presents? Other folks won't believe as you've meant nothing; and don't tell me about her not deceiving herself. I tell you as you've filled her mind so with the thought of you as it'll mayhap poison her life, and she'll never love another man as 'ud make her a good husband."

Arthur had felt a sudden relief while Adam was speaking; he perceived that Adam had no positive knowledge of the past, and that there was no irrevocable damage done by this evening's unfortunate rencontre. Adam could still be deceived. The candid Arthur had brought himself into a position in which successful lying was his only hope. The hope allayed his anger a little.

"Well, Adam," he said, in a tone of friendly concession, "you're perhaps right. Perhaps I've gone a little too far in taking notice of the pretty little thing and stealing a kiss now and then. You're such a grave, steady fellow, you don't understand the temptation to such trifling. I'm sure I wouldn't bring any trouble or annoyance on her and the good Poysers on any account if I could help it. But I think you look a little too seriously at it. You know I'm going away immediately, so I shan't make any more mistakes of the kind. But let us say good-night"—Arthur here turned round to walk on—"and talk no more about the matter. The whole thing will soon be forgotten."

"No, by God!" Adam burst out with rage that could be controlled no longer, throwing down the basket of tools and striding forward till he was right in front of Arthur. All his jealousy and sense of personal injury, which he had been hitherto trying to keep under, had leaped up and mastered him. What man of us, in the first moments of a sharp agony, could ever feel that the fellow-man who has been the medium of inflicting it did not mean to hurt us? In our instinctive rebellion against pain, we are children again, and demand an active will to wreak our vengeance on. Adam at this moment could only feel that he had been robbed of Hetty—robbed treacherously by the man in whom he had trusted—and he stood close in front of Arthur, with fierce eyes glaring at him, with pale lips and clenched hands, the hard tones in which he had hitherto been constraining himself to express no more than a just indignation giving way to a deep agitated voice that seemed to shake him as he spoke.

"No, it'll not be soon forgot, as you've come in between her and me, when she might ha' loved me—it'll not soon be forgot as you've robbed me o' my happiness, while I thought you was my best friend, and a noble-minded man, as I was proud to work for. And you've been kissing her, and meaning nothing, have you? And I never kissed her i' my life—but I'd ha' worked hard for years for the right to kiss her. And you make light of it. You think little o' doing what may damage other folks, so as you get your bit o' trifling, as means nothing. I throw back your favours, for you're not the man I took you for. I'll never count you my friend any more. I'd rather you'd act as my enemy, and fight me where I stand—it's all th' amends you can make me."

Poor Adam, possessed by rage that could find no other vent, began to throw off his coat and his cap, too blind with passion to notice the change that had taken place in Arthur while he was speaking. Arthur's lips were now as pale as Adam's; his heart was beating violently. The discovery that Adam loved Hetty was a shock which made him for the moment see himself in the light of Adam's indignation, and regard Adam's suffering as not merely a consequence, but an element of his error. The words of hatred and contempt—the first he had ever heard in his life—seemed like scorching missiles that were making ineffaceable scars on him. All screening self-excuse, which rarely falls quite away while others respect us, forsook him for an instant, and he stood face to face with the first great irrevocable evil he had ever committed. He was only twenty-one, and three months ago—nay, much later—he had thought proudly that no man should ever be able to reproach him justly. His first impulse, if there had been time for it, would perhaps have been to utter words of propitiation; but Adam had no sooner thrown off his coat and cap than he became aware that Arthur was standing pale and motionless, with his hands still thrust in his waistcoat pockets.

"What!" he said, "won't you fight me like a man? You know I won't strike you while you stand so."

"Go away, Adam," said Arthur, "I don't want to fight you."

"No," said Adam, bitterly; "you don't want to fight me—you think I'm a common man, as you can injure without answering for it."

"I never meant to injure you," said Arthur, with returning anger. "I didn't know you loved her."

"But you've made her love *you*," said Adam. "You're a double-faced man—I'll never believe a word you say again."

"Go away, I tell you," said Arthur, angrily, "or we shall both repent."

"No," said Adam, with a convulsed voice, "I swear I won't go away without fighting you. Do you want provoking any more? I tell you you're a coward and a scoundrel, and I despise you."

The colour had all rushed back to Arthur's face; in a moment his right hand was clenched, and dealt a blow like lightning, which sent Adam staggering backward. His blood was as thoroughly up as Adam's now, and the two men, forgetting the emotions that had gone before, fought with the instinctive fierceness of panthers in the deepening twilight darkened by the trees. The delicate-handed gentleman was a match for the workman in everything but strength, and Arthur's skill enabled him to protract the struggle for some long moments. But between unarmed men the battle is to the strong, where the strong is no blunderer, and Arthur must sink under a well-planted blow of Adam's as a steel rod is broken by an iron bar. The blow soon came, and Arthur fell, his head lying concealed in a tuft of fern, so that Adam could only discern his darkly clad body.

He stood still in the dim light waiting for Arthur to rise.

The blow had been given now, towards which he had been straining all the force of nerve and muscle—and what was the good of it? What had he done by fighting? Only satisfied his own passion, only wreaked his own vengeance. He had not rescued Hetty, nor changed the past—there it was, just as it had been, and he sickened at the vanity of his own rage.

But why did not Arthur rise? He was perfectly motionless, and the time seemed long to Adam. Good God! had the blow been too much for him? Adam shuddered at the thought of his own strength, as with the oncoming of this dread he knelt down by Arthur's side and lifted his head from among the fern. There was no sign of life: the eyes and teeth were set. The horror that rushed over Adam completely mastered him, and forced upon him its own belief. He could feel nothing but that death was in Arthur's face, and that he was helpless before it. He made not a single movement, but knelt like an image of despair gazing at an image of death.

Chapter XXVIII
A Dilemma

It was only a few minutes measured by the clock—though Adam always thought it had been a long while—before he perceived a gleam of consciousness in Arthur's face and a slight shiver through his frame. The intense joy that flooded his soul brought back some of the old affection with it.

"Do you feel any pain, sir?" he said, tenderly, loosening Arthur's cravat.

Arthur turned his eyes on Adam with a vague stare which gave way to a slightly startled motion as if from the shock of returning memory. But he only shivered again and said nothing.

"Do you feel any hurt, sir?" Adam said again, with a trembling in his voice.

Arthur put his hand up to his waistcoat buttons, and when Adam had unbuttoned it, he took a longer breath. "Lay my head down," he said, faintly, "and get me some water if you can."

Adam laid the head down gently on the fern again, and emptying the tools out of the flag-basket, hurried through the trees to the edge of the Grove bordering on the Chase, where a brook ran below the bank.

When he returned with his basket leaking, but still half-full, Arthur looked at him with a more thoroughly reawakened consciousness.

"Can you drink a drop out o' your hand, sir?" said Adam, kneeling down again to lift up Arthur's head.

"No," said Arthur, "dip my cravat in and souse it on my head."

The water seemed to do him some good, for he presently raised himself a little higher, resting on Adam's arm.

"Do you feel any hurt inside sir?" Adam asked again

"No—no hurt," said Arthur, still faintly, "but rather done up."

After a while he said, "I suppose I fainted away when you knocked me down."

"Yes, sir, thank God," said Adam. "I thought it was worse."

"What! You thought you'd done for me, eh? Come help me on my legs."

"I feel terribly shaky and dizzy," Arthur said, as he stood leaning on Adam's arm; "that blow of yours must have come against me like a battering-ram. I don't believe I can walk alone."

"Lean on me, sir; I'll get you along," said Adam. "Or, will you sit down a bit longer, on my coat here, and I'll prop y' up. You'll perhaps be better in a minute or two."

"No," said Arthur. "I'll go to the Hermitage—I think I've got some brandy there. There's a short road to it a little farther on, near the gate. If you'll just help me on."

They walked slowly, with frequent pauses, but without speaking again. In both of them, the concentration in the present which had attended the first moments of Arthur's revival had now given way to a vivid recollection of the previous scene. It was nearly dark in the narrow path among the trees, but within the circle of fir-trees round the Hermitage there was room for the growing moonlight to enter in at the windows. Their steps were noiseless on the thick carpet of fir-needles, and the outward stillness seemed to heighten their inward consciousness, as Arthur took the key out of his pocket and placed it in Adam's hand, for him to open the door. Adam had not known before that Arthur had furnished the old Hermitage and made it a retreat for himself, and it was a surprise to him when he opened the door to see a snug room with all the signs of frequent habitation.

Arthur loosed Adam's arm and threw himself on the ottoman. "You'll see my hunting-bottle somewhere," he said. "A leather case with a bottle and glass in."

Adam was not long in finding the case. "There's very little brandy in it, sir," he said, turning it downwards over the glass, as he held it before the window; "hardly this little glassful."

"Well, give me that," said Arthur, with the peevishness of physical depression. When he had taken some sips, Adam said, "Hadn't I better run to th' house, sir, and get some more brandy? I can be there and back pretty soon. It'll be a stiff walk home for you, if you don't have something to revive you."

"Yes—go. But don't say I'm ill. Ask for my man Pym, and tell him to get it from Mills, and not to say I'm at the Hermitage. Get some water too."

Adam was relieved to have an active task—both of them were relieved to be apart from each other for a short time. But Adam's swift pace could not still the eager pain of thinking—of living again with concentrated suffering through the last wretched hour, and looking out from it over all the new sad future.

Arthur lay still for some minutes after Adam was gone, but presently he rose feebly from the ottoman and peered about slowly in the broken moonlight, seeking something. It was a short bit of wax candle that stood amongst a confusion of writing and drawing materials. There was more searching for the means of lighting the candle, and when that was done, he went cautiously round the room, as if wishing to assure himself of the presence or absence of something.

At last he had found a slight thing, which he put first in his pocket, and then, on a second thought, took out again and thrust deep down into a waste-paper basket. It was a woman's little, pink, silk neckerchief. He set the candle on the table, and threw himself down on the ottoman again, exhausted with the effort.

When Adam came back with his supplies, his entrance awoke Arthur from a doze.

"That's right," Arthur said; "I'm tremendously in want of some brandy-vigour."

"I'm glad to see you've got a light, sir," said Adam. "I've been thinking I'd better have asked for a lanthorn."

"No, no; the candle will last long enough—I shall soon be up to walking home now."

"I can't go before I've seen you safe home, sir," said Adam, hesitatingly.

"No: it will be better for you to stay—sit down."

Adam sat down, and they remained opposite to each other in uneasy silence, while Arthur slowly drank brandy-and-water, with visibly renovating effect. He began to lie in a more voluntary position, and looked as if he were less overpowered by bodily sensations. Adam was keenly alive to these indications, and as his anxiety about Arthur's condition began to be allayed, he felt more of that impatience which every one knows who has had his just indignation suspended by the physical state of the culprit. Yet there was one thing on his mind to be done before he could recur to remonstrance: it was to confess what had been unjust in his own words. Perhaps he longed all the more to make this confession, that his indignation might be free again; and as he saw the signs of returning ease in Arthur, the words again and again came to his lips and went back, checked by the thought that it would be better to leave everything till to-morrow. As long as they were silent they did not look at each other, and a foreboding came across Adam that if they began to speak as though they remembered the past—if they looked at each other with full recognition—they must take fire again. So they sat in silence till the bit of wax candle flickered low in the socket, the silence all the while becoming more irksome to Adam. Arthur had just poured out some more brandy-and-water, and he threw one arm behind his head and drew up one leg in an attitude of recovered ease, which was an irresistible temptation to Adam to speak what was on his mind.

"You begin to feel more yourself again, sir," he said, as the candle went out and they were half-hidden from each other in the faint moonlight.

"Yes: I don't feel good for much—very lazy, and not inclined to move; but I'll go home when I've taken this dose."

There was a slight pause before Adam said, "My temper got the better of me, and I said things as wasn't true. I'd no right to speak as if you'd known you was doing me an injury: you'd no grounds for knowing it; I've always kept what I felt for her as secret as I could."

He paused again before he went on.

"And perhaps I judged you too harsh—I'm apt to be harsh—and you may have acted out o' thoughtlessness more than I should ha' believed was possible for a man with a heart and a conscience. We're not all put together alike, and we may misjudge one another. God knows, it's all the joy I could have now, to think the best of you."

Arthur wanted to go home without saying any more—he was too painfully embarrassed in mind, as well as too weak in body, to wish for any further explanation to-night. And yet it was a relief to him that Adam reopened the subject in a way the least difficult for him to answer. Arthur was in the wretched position of an open, generous man who has committed an error which makes deception seem a necessity. The native impulse to give truth in return for truth, to meet trust with frank confession, must be suppressed, and duty was becoming a question of tactics. His deed was reacting upon him—was already governing him tyrannously and forcing him into a course that jarred with his habitual feelings. The only aim that seemed admissible to him now was to deceive Adam to the utmost: to make Adam think better of him than he deserved. And when he heard the words of honest retractation—when he heard the sad appeal with which Adam ended—he was obliged to rejoice in the remains of ignorant confidence it implied. He did not answer immediately, for he had to be judicious and not truthful.

"Say no more about our anger, Adam," he said, at last, very languidly, for the labour of speech was unwelcome to him; "I forgive your momentary injustice—it was quite natural, with the exaggerated notions you had in your mind. We shall be none the worse friends in future, I hope, because we've fought. You had the best of it, and that was as it should be, for I believe I've been most in the wrong of the two. Come, let us shake hands."

Arthur held out his hand, but Adam sat still.

"I don't like to say 'No' to that, sir," he said, "but I can't shake hands till it's clear what we mean by't. I was wrong when I spoke as if you'd done me an injury knowingly, but I wasn't wrong in what I said before, about your behaviour t' Hetty, and I can't shake hands with you as if I held you my friend the same as ever till you've cleared that up better."

Arthur swallowed his pride and resentment as he drew back his hand. He was silent for some moments, and then said, as indifferently as he could, "I don't know what you mean by clearing up, Adam. I've told you already that you think too seriously of a little flirtation. But if you are right in supposing there is any danger in it—I'm going away on Saturday, and there will be an end of it. As for the pain it has given you, I'm heartily sorry for it. I can say no more."

Adam said nothing, but rose from his chair and stood with his face towards one of the windows, as if looking at the blackness of the moonlit fir-trees; but he was in reality conscious of nothing but the conflict within him. It was of no use now—his resolution not to speak till to-morrow. He must speak there and then. But it was several minutes before he turned round and stepped nearer to Arthur, standing and looking down on him as he lay.

"It'll be better for me to speak plain," he said, with evident effort, "though it's hard work. You see, sir, this isn't a trifle to me, whatever it may be to you. I'm none o' them men as can go making love first to one woman and then t' another, and don't think it much odds which of 'em I take. What I feel for Hetty's a different sort o' love, such as I believe nobody can know much about but them as feel it and God as has given it to 'em. She's more nor everything else to me, all but my conscience and my good name. And if it's true what you've been saying all along—and if it's only been trifling and flirting as you call it, as 'll be put an end to by your going away—why, then, I'd wait, and hope her heart 'ud turn to me after all. I'm loath to think you'd speak false to me, and I'll believe your word, however things may look."

"You would be wronging Hetty more than me not to believe it," said Arthur, almost violently, starting up from the ottoman and moving away. But he threw himself into a chair again directly, saying, more feebly, "You seem to forget that, in suspecting me, you are casting imputations upon her."

"Nay, sir," Adam said, in a calmer voice, as if he were half-relieved—for he was too straightforward to make a distinction between a direct falsehood and an indirect one—"Nay, sir, things don't lie level between Hetty and you. You're acting with your eyes open, whatever you may do; but how do you know what's been in her mind? She's all but a child—as any man with a conscience in him ought to feel bound to take care on. And whatever you may think, I know you've disturbed her mind. I know she's been fixing her heart on you, for there's a many things clear to me now as I didn't understand before. But you seem to make light o' what *she* may feel—you don't think o' that."

"Good God, Adam, let me alone!" Arthur burst out impetuously; "I feel it enough without your worrying me."

He was aware of his indiscretion as soon as the words had escaped him.

"Well, then, if you feel it," Adam rejoined, eagerly; "if you feel as you may ha' put false notions into her mind, and made her believe as you loved her, when all the while you meant nothing, I've this demand to make of you—I'm not speaking for myself, but for her. I ask you t' undeceive her before you go away. Y'aren't going away for ever, and if you leave her behind with a notion in her head o' your feeling about her the same as she feels about you, she'll be hankering after you, and the mischief may get worse. It may be a smart to her now, but it'll save her pain i' th' end. I ask you to write a letter—you may trust to my seeing as she gets it. Tell her the truth, and take blame to yourself for behaving as you'd no right to do to a young woman as isn't your equal. I speak plain, sir, but I can't speak any other way. There's nobody can take care o' Hetty in this thing but me."

"I can do what I think needful in the matter," said Arthur, more and more irritated by mingled distress and perplexity, "without giving promises to you. I shall take what measures I think proper."

"No," said Adam, in an abrupt decided tone, "that won't do. I must know what ground I'm treading on. I must be safe as you've put an end to what ought never to ha' been begun. I don't forget what's owing to you as a gentleman, but in this thing we're man and man, and I can't give up."

There was no answer for some moments. Then Arthur said, "I'll see you to-morrow. I can bear no more now; I'm ill." He rose as he spoke, and reached his cap, as if intending to go.

"You won't see her again!" Adam exclaimed, with a flash of recurring anger and suspicion, moving towards the door and placing his back against it. "Either tell me she can never be my wife—tell me you've been lying—or else promise me what I've said."

Adam, uttering this alternative, stood like a terrible fate before Arthur, who had moved forward a step or two, and now stopped, faint, shaken, sick in mind and body. It seemed long to both of them—that inward struggle of Arthur's—before he said, feebly, "I promise; let me go."

Adam moved away from the door and opened it, but when Arthur reached the step, he stopped again and leaned against the door-post.

"You're not well enough to walk alone, sir," said Adam. "Take my arm again."

Arthur made no answer, and presently walked on, Adam following. But, after a few steps, he stood still again, and said, coldly, "I believe I must trouble you. It's getting late now, and there may be an alarm set up about me at home."

Adam gave his arm, and they walked on without uttering a word, till they came where the basket and the tools lay.

"I must pick up the tools, sir," Adam said. "They're my brother's. I doubt they'll be rusted. If you'll please to wait a minute."

Arthur stood still without speaking, and no other word passed between them till they were at the side entrance, where he hoped to get in without being seen by any one. He said then, "Thank you; I needn't trouble you any further."

"What time will it be conven'ent for me to see you to-morrow, sir?" said Adam.

"You may send me word that you're here at five o'clock," said Arthur; "not before."

"Good-night, sir," said Adam. But he heard no reply; Arthur had turned into the house.

Chapter XXIX
The Next Morning

Arthur did not pass a sleepless night; he slept long and well. For sleep comes to the perplexed—if the perplexed are only weary enough. But at seven he rang his bell and astonished Pym by declaring he was going to get up, and must have breakfast brought to him at eight.

"And see that my mare is saddled at half-past eight, and tell my grandfather when he's down that I'm better this morning and am gone for a ride."

He had been awake an hour, and could rest in bed no longer. In bed our yesterdays are too oppressive: if a man can only get up, though it be but to whistle or to smoke, he has a present which offers some resistance to the past—sensations which assert themselves against tyrannous memories. And if there were such a thing as taking averages of feeling, it would certainly be found that in the hunting and shooting seasons regret, self-reproach, and mortified pride weigh lighter on country gentlemen than in late spring and summer. Arthur felt that he should be more of a man on horseback. Even the presence of Pym, waiting on him with the usual deference, was a reassurance to him after the scenes of yesterday. For, with Arthur's sensitiveness to opinion, the loss of Adam's respect was a shock to his self-contentment which suffused his imagination with the sense that he had sunk in all eyes—as a sudden shock of fear from some real peril makes a nervous woman afraid even to step, because all her perceptions are suffused with a sense of danger.

Arthur's, as you know, was a loving nature. Deeds of kindness were as easy to him as a bad habit: they were the common issue of his weaknesses and good qualities, of his egoism and his sympathy. He didn't like to witness pain, and he liked to have grateful eyes beaming on him as the giver of pleasure. When he was a lad of seven, he one day kicked down an old gardener's pitcher of broth, from no motive but a kicking impulse, not reflecting that it was the old man's dinner; but on learning that sad fact, he took his favourite pencil-case and a silver-hafted knife out of his pocket and offered them as compensation. He had been the same Arthur ever since, trying to make all offences forgotten in benefits. If there were any bitterness in his nature, it could only show itself against the man who refused to be conciliated by him. And perhaps the time was come for some of that bitterness to rise. At the first moment, Arthur had felt pure distress and self-reproach at discovering that Adam's happiness was involved in his relation to Hetty. If there had been a possibility of making Adam tenfold amends—if deeds of gift, or any other deeds, could have restored Adam's contentment and regard for him as a benefactor, Arthur would not only have executed them without hesitation, but would have felt bound all the more closely to Adam, and would never have been weary of making retribution. But Adam could receive no amends; his suffering could not be cancelled; his respect and affection could not be recovered by any prompt deeds of atonement. He stood like an immovable obstacle against which no pressure could avail; an embodiment of what Arthur most shrank from believing in—the irrevocableness of his own wrongdoing. The words of scorn, the refusal to shake hands, the mastery asserted over him in their last conversation in the Hermitage—above all, the sense of having been knocked down, to which a man does not very well reconcile himself, even under the most heroic circumstances—pressed on him with a galling pain which was stronger than compunction. Arthur would so gladly have persuaded himself that he had done no harm! And if no one had told him the contrary, he could have persuaded himself so much better. Nemesis can seldom forge a sword for herself out of our consciences—out of the suffering we feel in the suffering we may have caused: there is rarely metal enough there to make an effective weapon. Our moral sense learns the manners of good society and smiles when others smile, but when some rude person gives rough names to our actions, she is apt to take part against us. And so it was with Arthur: Adam's judgment of him, Adam's grating words, disturbed his self-soothing arguments.

Not that Arthur had been at ease before Adam's discovery. Struggles and resolves had transformed themselves into compunction and anxiety. He was distressed for Hetty's sake, and distressed for his own, that he must leave her behind. He had always, both in making and breaking resolutions, looked beyond his passion and seen that it must speedily end in separation; but his nature was too ardent and tender for him not to suffer at this parting; and on Hetty's account he was filled with uneasiness. He had found out the dream in which she was living—that she was to be a lady in silks and satins—and when he had first talked to her about his going away, she had asked him tremblingly to let her go with him and be married. It was his painful knowledge of this which had given the most exasperating sting to Adam's reproaches. He had said no word with the purpose of deceiving her—her vision was all spun by her own childish fancy—but he was obliged to confess to himself that it was spun half out of his own actions. And to increase the mischief, on this last evening he had not dared to hint the truth to Hetty; he had been obliged to soothe her with tender, hopeful words, lest he should throw her into violent distress. He felt the situation acutely, felt the sorrow of the dear thing in the present, and thought with a darker anxiety of the tenacity which her feelings might have in the future. That was the one sharp point which pressed against him; every other he could evade by hopeful self-persuasion. The whole thing had been secret; the Poysers had not the shadow of a suspicion. No one, except Adam, knew anything of what had passed—no one else was likely to know; for Arthur had impressed on Hetty that it would be fatal to betray, by word or look, that there had been the least intimacy between them; and Adam, who knew half their secret, would rather help them to keep it than betray it. It was an unfortunate business altogether, but there was no use in making it worse than it was by imaginary exaggerations and forebodings of evil that might never come. The temporary sadness for Hetty was the worst consequence; he resolutely turned away his eyes from any bad consequence that was not demonstrably inevitable. But—but Hetty might have had the trouble in some other way if not in this. And perhaps hereafter he might be able to do a great deal for her and make up to her for all the tears she would shed about him. She would owe the advantage of his care for her in future years to the sorrow she had incurred now. *So* good comes out of evil. Such is the beautiful arrangement of things!

Are you inclined to ask whether this can be the same Arthur who, two months ago, had that freshness of feeling, that delicate honour which shrinks from wounding even a sentiment, and does not contemplate any more positive offence as possible for it?—who thought that his own self-respect was a higher tribunal than any external opinion? The same, I assure you, only under different conditions. Our deeds determine us, as much as we determine our deeds, and until we know what has been or will be the peculiar combination of outward with inward facts, which constitutes a man's critical actions, it will be better not to think ourselves wise about his character. There is a terrible coercion in our deeds, which may first turn the honest man into a deceiver and then reconcile him to the change, for this reason—that the second wrong presents itself to him in the guise of the only practicable right. The action which before commission has been seen with that blended common sense and fresh untarnished feeling which is the healthy eye of the soul, is looked at afterwards with the lens of apologetic ingenuity, through which all things that men call beautiful and ugly are seen to be made up of textures very much alike. Europe adjusts itself to a *fait accompli*, and so does an individual character—until the placid adjustment is disturbed by a convulsive retribution.

No man can escape this vitiating effect of an offence against his own sentiment of right, and the effect was the stronger in Arthur because of that very need of self-respect which, while his conscience was still at ease, was one of his best safeguards. Self-accusation was too painful to him—he could not face it. He must persuade himself that he had not been very much to blame; he began even to pity himself for the necessity he was under of deceiving Adam—it was a course so opposed to the honesty of his own nature. But then, it was the only right thing to do.

Well, whatever had been amiss in him, he was miserable enough in consequence: miserable about Hetty; miserable about this letter that he had promised to write, and that seemed at one moment to be a gross barbarity, at another perhaps the greatest kindness he could do to her. And across all this reflection would dart every now and then a sudden impulse of passionate defiance towards all consequences. He would carry Hetty away, and all other considerations might go to....

In this state of mind the four walls of his room made an intolerable prison to him; they seemed to hem in and press down upon him all the crowd of contradictory thoughts and conflicting feelings, some of which would fly away in the open air. He had only an hour or two to make up his mind in, and he must get clear and calm. Once on Meg's back, in the fresh air of that fine morning, he should be more master of the situation.

The pretty creature arched her bay neck in the sunshine, and pawed the gravel, and trembled with pleasure when her master stroked her nose, and patted her, and talked to her even in a more caressing tone than usual. He loved her the better because she knew nothing of his secrets. But Meg was quite as well acquainted with her master's mental state as many others of her sex with the mental condition of the nice young gentlemen towards whom their hearts are in a state of fluttering expectation.

Arthur cantered for five miles beyond the Chase, till he was at the foot of a hill where there were no hedges or trees to hem in the road. Then he threw the bridle on Meg's neck and prepared to make up his mind.

Hetty knew that their meeting yesterday must be the last before Arthur went away—there was no possibility of their contriving another without exciting suspicion—and she was like a frightened child, unable to think of anything, only able to cry at the mention of parting, and then put her face up to have the tears kissed away. He *could* do nothing but comfort her, and lull her into dreaming on. A letter would be a dreadfully abrupt way of awakening her! Yet there was truth in what Adam said—that it would save her from a lengthened delusion, which might be worse than a sharp immediate pain. And it was the only way of satisfying Adam, who *must* be satisfied, for more reasons than one. If he could have seen her again! But that was impossible; there was such a thorny hedge of hindrances between them, and an imprudence would be fatal. And yet, if he *could* see her again, what good would it do? Only cause him to suffer more from the sight of her distress and the remembrance of it. Away from him she was surrounded by all the motives to self-control.

A sudden dread here fell like a shadow across his imagination—the dread lest she should do something violent in her grief; and close upon that dread came another, which deepened the shadow. But he shook them off with the force of youth and hope. What was the ground for painting the future in that dark way? It was just as likely to be the reverse. Arthur told himself he did not deserve that things should turn out badly. He had never meant beforehand to do anything his conscience disapproved; he had been led on by circumstances. There was a sort of implicit confidence in him that he was really such a good fellow at bottom, Providence would not treat him harshly.

At all events, he couldn't help what would come now: all he could do was to take what seemed the best course at the present moment. And he persuaded himself that that course was to make the way open between Adam and Hetty. Her heart might really turn to Adam, as he said, after a while; and in that case there would have been no great harm done, since it was still Adam's ardent wish to make her his wife. To be sure, Adam was deceived—deceived in a way that Arthur would have resented as a deep wrong if it had been practised on himself. That was a reflection that marred the consoling prospect. Arthur's cheeks even burned in mingled shame and irritation at the thought. But what could a man do in such a dilemma? He was bound in honour to say no word that could injure Hetty: his first duty was to guard *her*. He would never have told or acted a lie on his own account. Good God! What a miserable fool he was to have brought himself into such a dilemma; and yet, if ever a man had excuses, he had. (Pity that consequences are determined not by excuses but by actions!)

Well, the letter must be written; it was the only means that promised a solution of the difficulty. The tears came into Arthur's eyes as he thought of Hetty reading it; but it would be almost as hard for him to write it; he was not doing anything easy to himself; and this last thought helped him to arrive at a conclusion. He could never deliberately have taken a step which inflicted pain on another and left himself at ease. Even a movement of jealousy at the thought of giving up Hetty to Adam went to convince him that he was making a sacrifice.

When once he had come to this conclusion, he turned Meg round and set off home again in a canter. The letter should be written the first thing, and the rest of the day would be filled up with other business: he should have no time to look behind him. Happily, Irwine and Gawaine were coming to dinner, and by twelve o'clock the next day he should have left the Chase miles behind him. There was some security in this constant occupation against an uncontrollable impulse seizing him to rush to Hetty and thrust into her hand some mad proposition that would undo everything. Faster and faster went the sensitive Meg, at every slight sign from her rider, till the canter had passed into a swift gallop.

"I thought they said th' young mester war took ill last night," said sour old John, the groom, at dinner-time in the servants' hall. "He's been ridin' fit to split the mare i' two this forenoon."

"That's happen one o' the symptims, John," said the facetious coachman.

"Then I wish he war let blood for 't, that's all," said John, grimly.

Adam had been early at the Chase to know how Arthur was, and had been relieved from all anxiety about the effects of his blow by learning that he was gone out for a ride. At five o'clock he was punctually there again, and sent up word of his arrival. In a few minutes Pym came down with a letter in his hand and gave it to Adam, saying that the captain was too busy to see him, and had written everything he had to say. The letter was directed to Adam, but he went out of doors again before opening it. It contained a sealed enclosure directed to Hetty. On the inside of the cover Adam read:

"In the enclosed letter I have written everything you wish. I leave it to you to decide whether you will be doing best to deliver it to Hetty or to return it to me. Ask yourself once more whether you are not taking a measure which may pain her more than mere silence.

"There is no need for our seeing each other again now. We shall meet with better feelings some months hence.

"A.D."

"Perhaps he's i' th' right on 't not to see me," thought Adam. "It's no use meeting to say more hard words, and it's no use meeting to shake hands and say we're friends again. We're not friends, an' it's better not to pretend it. I know forgiveness is a man's duty, but, to my thinking, that can only mean as you're to give up all thoughts o' taking revenge: it can never mean as you're t' have your old feelings back again, for that's not possible. He's not the same man to me, and I can't *feel* the same towards him. God help me! I don't know whether I feel the same towards anybody: I seem as if I'd been measuring my work from a false line, and had got it all to measure over again."

But the question about delivering the letter to Hetty soon absorbed Adam's thoughts. Arthur had procured some relief to himself by throwing the decision on Adam with a warning; and Adam, who was not given to hesitation, hesitated here. He determined to feel his way—to ascertain as well as he could what was Hetty's state of mind before he decided on delivering the letter.

Chapter XXX
The Delivery of the Letter

The next Sunday Adam joined the Poysers on their way out of church, hoping for an invitation to go home with them. He had the letter in his pocket, and was anxious to have an opportunity of talking to Hetty alone. He could not see her face at church, for she had changed her seat, and when he came up to her to shake hands, her manner was doubtful and constrained. He expected this, for it was the first time she had met him since she had been aware that he had seen her with Arthur in the Grove.

"Come, you'll go on with us, Adam," Mr. Poyser said when they reached the turning; and as soon as they were in the fields Adam ventured to offer his arm to Hetty. The children soon gave them an opportunity of lingering behind a little, and then Adam said:

"Will you contrive for me to walk out in the garden a bit with you this evening, if it keeps fine, Hetty? I've something partic'lar to talk to you about."

Hetty said, "Very well." She was really as anxious as Adam was that she should have some private talk with him. She wondered what he thought of her and Arthur. He must have seen them kissing, she knew, but she had no conception of the scene that had taken place between Arthur and Adam. Her first feeling had been that Adam would be very angry with her, and perhaps would tell her aunt and uncle, but it never entered her mind that he would dare to say anything to Captain Donnithorne. It was a relief to her that he behaved so kindly to her to-day, and wanted to speak to *her* alone; for she had trembled when she found he was going home with them lest he should mean "to tell." But, now he wanted to talk to her by herself, she should learn what he thought and what he meant to do. She felt a certain confidence that she could persuade him not to do anything she did not want him to do; she could perhaps even make him believe that she didn't care for Arthur; and as long as Adam thought there was any hope of her having him, he would do just what she liked, she knew. Besides, she *must* go on seeming to encourage Adam, lest her uncle and aunt should be angry and suspect her of having some secret lover.

Hetty's little brain was busy with this combination as she hung on Adam's arm and said "yes" or "no" to some slight observations of his about the many hawthorn-berries there would be for the birds this next winter, and the low-hanging clouds that would hardly hold up till morning. And when they rejoined her aunt and uncle, she could pursue her thoughts without interruption, for Mr. Poyser held that though a young man might like to have the woman he was courting on his arm, he would nevertheless be glad of a little reasonable talk about business the while; and, for his own part, he was curious to hear the most recent news about the Chase Farm. So, through the rest of the walk, he claimed Adam's conversation for himself, and Hetty laid her small plots and imagined her little scenes of cunning blandishment, as she walked along by the hedgerows on honest Adam's arm, quite as well as if she had been an elegantly clad coquette alone in her boudoir. For if a country beauty in clumsy shoes be only shallow-hearted enough, it is astonishing how closely her mental processes may resemble those of a lady in society and crinoline, who applies her refined intellect to the problem of committing indiscretions without compromising herself. Perhaps the resemblance was not much the less because Hetty felt very unhappy all the while. The parting with Arthur was a double pain to her—mingling with the tumult of passion and vanity there was a dim undefined fear that the future might shape itself in some way quite unlike her dream. She clung to the comforting hopeful words Arthur had uttered in their last meeting—"I shall come again at Christmas, and then we will see what can be done." She clung to the belief that he was so fond of her, he would never be happy without her; and she still hugged her secret—that a great gentleman loved her—with gratified pride, as a superiority over all the girls she knew. But the uncertainty of the future, the possibilities to which she could give no shape, began to press upon her like the invisible weight of air; she was alone on her little island of dreams, and all around her was the dark unknown water where Arthur was gone. She could gather no elation of spirits now by looking forward, but only by looking backward to build confidence on past words and caresses. But occasionally, since Thursday evening, her dim anxieties had been almost lost behind the more definite fear that Adam might betray what he knew to her uncle and aunt, and his sudden proposition to talk with her alone had set her thoughts to work in a new way. She was eager not to lose this evening's opportunity; and after tea, when the boys were going into the garden and Totty begged to go with them, Hetty said, with an alacrity that surprised Mrs. Poyser, "I'll go with her, Aunt."

It did not seem at all surprising that Adam said he would go too, and soon he and Hetty were left alone together on the walk by the filbert-trees, while the boys were busy elsewhere gathering the large unripe nuts to play at "cob-nut" with, and Totty was watching them with a puppylike air of contemplation. It was but a short time—hardly two months—since Adam had had his mind filled with delicious hopes as he stood by Hetty's side in this garden. The remembrance of that scene had often been with him since Thursday evening: the sunlight through the apple-tree boughs, the red bunches, Hetty's sweet blush. It came importunately now, on this sad evening, with the low-hanging clouds, but he tried to suppress it, lest some emotion should impel him to say more than was needful for Hetty's sake.

"After what I saw on Thursday night, Hetty," he began, "you won't think me making too free in what I'm going to say. If you was being courted by any man as 'ud make you his wife, and I'd known you was fond of him and meant to have him, I should have no right to speak a word to you about it; but when I see you're being made love to by a gentleman as can never marry you, and doesna think o' marrying you, I feel bound t' interfere for you. I can't speak about it to them as are i' the place o' your parents, for that might bring worse trouble than's needful."

Adam's words relieved one of Hetty's fears, but they also carried a meaning which sickened her with a strengthened foreboding. She was pale and trembling, and yet she would have angrily contradicted Adam, if she had dared to betray her feelings. But she was silent.

"You're so young, you know, Hetty," he went on, almost tenderly, "and y' haven't seen much o' what goes on in the world. It's right for me to do what I can to save you from getting into trouble for want o' your knowing where you're being led to. If anybody besides me knew what I know about your meeting a gentleman and having fine presents from him, they'd speak light on you, and you'd lose your character. And besides that, you'll have to suffer in your feelings, wi' giving your love to a man as can never marry you, so as he might take care of you all your life."

Adam paused and looked at Hetty, who was plucking the leaves from the filbert-trees and tearing them up in her hand. Her little plans and preconcerted speeches had all forsaken her, like an ill-learnt lesson, under the terrible agitation produced by Adam's words. There was a cruel force in their calm certainty which threatened to grapple and crush her flimsy hopes and fancies. She wanted to resist them—she wanted to throw them off with angry contradiction—but the determination to conceal what she felt still governed her. It was nothing more than a blind prompting now, for she was unable to calculate the effect of her words.

"You've no right to say as I love him," she said, faintly, but impetuously, plucking another rough leaf and tearing it up. She was very beautiful in her paleness and agitation, with her dark childish eyes dilated and her breath shorter than usual. Adam's heart yearned over her as he looked at her. Ah, if he could but comfort her, and soothe her, and save her from this pain; if he had but some sort of strength that would enable him to rescue her poor troubled mind, as he would have rescued her body in the face of all danger!

"I doubt it must be so, Hetty," he said, tenderly; "for I canna believe you'd let any man kiss you by yourselves, and give you a gold box with his hair, and go a-walking i' the Grove to meet him, if you didna love him. I'm not blaming you, for I know it 'ud begin by little and little, till at last you'd not be able to throw it off. It's him I blame for stealing your love i' that way, when he knew he could never make you the right amends. He's been trifling with you, and making a plaything of you, and caring nothing about you as a man ought to care."

"Yes, he does care for me; I know better nor you," Hetty burst out. Everything was forgotten but the pain and anger she felt at Adam's words.

"Nay, Hetty," said Adam, "if he'd cared for you rightly, he'd never ha' behaved so. He told me himself he meant nothing by his kissing and presents, and he wanted to make me believe as you thought light of 'em too. But I know better nor that. I can't help thinking as you've been trusting to his loving you well enough to marry you, for all he's a gentleman. And that's why I must speak to you about it, Hetty, for fear you should be deceiving yourself. It's never entered his head the thought o' marrying you."

"How do you know? How durst you say so?" said Hetty, pausing in her walk and trembling. The terrible decision of Adam's tone shook her with fear. She had no presence of mind left for the reflection that Arthur would have his reasons for not telling the truth to Adam. Her words and look were enough to determine Adam: he must give her the letter.

"Perhaps you can't believe me, Hetty, because you think too well of him—because you think he loves you better than he does. But I've got a letter i' my pocket, as he wrote himself for me to give you. I've not read the letter, but he says he's told you the truth in it. But before I give you the letter, consider, Hetty, and don't let it take too much hold on you. It wouldna ha' been good for you if he'd wanted to do such a mad thing as marry you: it 'ud ha' led to no happiness i' th' end."

Hetty said nothing; she felt a revival of hope at the mention of a letter which Adam had not read. There would be something quite different in it from what he thought.

Adam took out the letter, but he held it in his hand still, while he said, in a tone of tender entreaty, "Don't you bear me ill will, Hetty, because I'm the means o' bringing you this pain. God knows I'd ha' borne a good deal worse for the sake o' sparing it you. And think—there's nobody but me knows about this, and I'll take care of you as if I was your brother. You're the same as ever to me, for I don't believe you've done any wrong knowingly."

Hetty had laid her hand on the letter, but Adam did not loose it till he had done speaking. She took no notice of what he said—she had not listened; but when he loosed the letter, she put it into her pocket, without opening it, and then began to walk more quickly, as if she wanted to go in.

"You're in the right not to read it just yet," said Adam. "Read it when you're by yourself. But stay out a little bit longer, and let us call the children: you look so white and ill, your aunt may take notice of it."

Hetty heard the warning. It recalled to her the necessity of rallying her native powers of concealment, which had half given way under the shock of Adam's words. And she had the letter in her pocket: she was sure there was comfort in that letter in spite of Adam. She ran to find Totty, and soon reappeared with recovered colour, leading Totty, who was making a sour face because she had been obliged to throw away an unripe apple that she had set her small teeth in.

"Hegh, Totty," said Adam, "come and ride on my shoulder—ever so high—you'll touch the tops o' the trees."

What little child ever refused to be comforted by that glorious sense of being seized strongly and swung upward? I don't believe Ganymede cried when the eagle carried him away, and perhaps deposited him on Jove's shoulder at the end. Totty smiled down complacently from her secure height, and pleasant was the sight to the mother's eyes, as she stood at the house door and saw Adam coming with his small burden.

"Bless your sweet face, my pet," she said, the mother's strong love filling her keen eyes with mildness, as Totty leaned forward and put out her arms. She had no eyes for Hetty at that moment, and only said, without looking at her, "You go and draw some ale, Hetty; the gells are both at the cheese."

After the ale had been drawn and her uncle's pipe lighted, there was Totty to be taken to bed, and brought down again in her night-gown because she would cry instead of going to sleep. Then there was supper to be got ready, and Hetty must be continually in the way to give help. Adam stayed till he knew Mrs. Poyser expected him to go, engaging her and her husband in talk as constantly as he could, for the sake of leaving Hetty more at ease. He lingered, because he wanted to see her safely through that evening, and he was delighted to find how much self-command she showed. He knew she had not had time to read the letter, but he did not know she was buoyed up by a secret hope that the letter would contradict everything he had said. It was hard work for him to leave her—hard to think that he should not know for days how she was bearing her trouble. But he must go at last, and all he could do was to press her hand gently as he said "Good-bye," and hope she would take that as a sign that if his love could ever be a refuge for her, it was there the same as ever. How busy his thoughts were, as he walked home, in devising pitying excuses for her folly, in referring all her weakness to the sweet lovingness of her nature, in blaming Arthur, with less and less inclination to admit that *his* conduct might be extenuated too! His exasperation at Hetty's suffering—and also at the sense that she was possibly thrust for ever out of his own reach—deafened him to any plea for the miscalled friend who had wrought this misery. Adam was a clear-sighted, fair-minded man—a fine fellow, indeed, morally as well as physically. But if Aristides the Just was ever in love and jealous, he was at that moment not perfectly magnanimous. And I cannot pretend that Adam, in these painful days, felt nothing but righteous indignation and loving pity. He was bitterly jealous, and in proportion as his love made him indulgent in his judgment of Hetty, the bitterness found a vent in his feeling towards Arthur.

"Her head was allays likely to be turned," he thought, "when a gentleman, with his fine manners, and fine clothes, and his white hands, and that way o' talking gentlefolks have, came about her, making up to her in a bold way, as a man couldn't do that was only her equal; and it's much if she'll ever like a common man now." He could not help drawing his own hands out of his pocket and looking at them—at the hard palms and the broken finger-nails. "I'm a roughish fellow, altogether; I don't know, now I come to think on't, what there is much for a woman to like about me; and yet I might ha' got another wife easy enough, if I hadn't set my heart on her. But it's little matter what other women think about me, if she can't love me. She might ha' loved me, perhaps, as likely as any other man—there's nobody hereabouts as I'm afraid of, if *he* hadn't come between us; but now I shall belike be hateful to her because I'm so different to him. And yet there's no telling—she may turn round the other way, when she finds he's made light of her all the while. She may come to feel the vally of a man as 'ud be thankful to be bound to her all his life. But I must put up with it whichever way it is—I've only to be thankful it's been no worse. I am not th' only man that's got to do without much happiness i' this life. There's many a good bit o' work done with a bad heart. It's God's will, and that's enough for us: we shouldn't know better how things ought to be than He does, I reckon, if we was to spend our lives i' puzzling. But it 'ud ha' gone near to spoil my work for me, if I'd seen her brought to sorrow and shame, and through the man as I've always been proud to think on. Since I've been spared that, I've no right to grumble. When a man's got his limbs whole, he can bear a smart cut or two."

As Adam was getting over a stile at this point in his reflections, he perceived a man walking along the field before him. He knew it was Seth, returning from an evening preaching, and made haste to overtake him.

"I thought thee'dst be at home before me," he said, as Seth turned round to wait for him, "for I'm later than usual to-night."

"Well, I'm later too, for I got into talk, after meeting, with John Barnes, who has lately professed himself in a state of perfection, and I'd a question to ask him about his experience. It's one o' them subjects that lead you further than y' expect—they don't lie along the straight road."

They walked along together in silence two or three minutes. Adam was not inclined to enter into the subtleties of religious experience, but he was inclined to interchange a word or two of brotherly affection and confidence with Seth. That was a rare impulse in him, much as the brothers loved each other. They hardly ever spoke of personal matters, or uttered more than an allusion to their family troubles. Adam was by nature reserved in all matters of feeling, and Seth felt a certain timidity towards his more practical brother.

"Seth, lad," Adam said, putting his arm on his brother's shoulder, "hast heard anything from Dinah Morris since she went away?"

"Yes," said Seth. "She told me I might write her word after a while, how we went on, and how mother bore up under her trouble. So I wrote to her a fortnight ago, and told her about thee having a new employment, and how Mother was more contented; and last Wednesday, when I called at the post at Treddles'on, I found a letter from her. I think thee'dst perhaps like to read it, but I didna say anything about it because thee'st seemed so full of other things. It's quite easy t' read—she writes wonderful for a woman."

Seth had drawn the letter from his pocket and held it out to Adam, who said, as he took it, "Aye, lad, I've got a tough load to carry just now—thee mustna take it ill if I'm a bit silenter and crustier nor usual. Trouble doesna make me care the less for thee. I know we shall stick together to the last."

"I take nought ill o' thee, Adam. I know well enough what it means if thee't a bit short wi' me now and then."

"There's Mother opening the door to look out for us," said Adam, as they mounted the slope. "She's been sitting i' the dark as usual. Well, Gyp, well, art glad to see me?"

Lisbeth went in again quickly and lighted a candle, for she had heard the welcome rustling of footsteps on the grass, before Gyp's joyful bark.

"Eh, my lads! Th' hours war ne'er so long sin' I war born as they'n been this blessed Sunday night. What can ye both ha' been doin' till this time?"

"Thee shouldstna sit i' the dark, Mother," said Adam; "that makes the time seem longer."

"Eh, what am I to do wi' burnin' candle of a Sunday, when there's on'y me an' it's sin to do a bit o' knittin'? The daylight's long enough for me to stare i' the booke as I canna read. It 'ud be a fine way o' shortenin' the time, to make it waste the good candle. But which on you's for ha'in' supper? Ye mun ayther be clemmed or full, I should think, seein' what time o' night it is."

“I’m hungry, Mother,” said Seth, seating himself at the little table, which had been spread ever since it was light.

“I’ve had my supper,” said Adam. “Here, Gyp,” he added, taking some cold potato from the table and rubbing the rough grey head that looked up towards him.

“Thee needstna be gi’in’ th’ dog,” said Lisbeth; “I’n fed him well a’ready. I’m not like to forget him, I reckon, when he’s all o’ thee I can get sight on.”

“Come, then, Gyp,” said Adam, “we’ll go to bed. Good-night, Mother; I’m very tired.”

“What ails him, dost know?” Lisbeth said to Seth, when Adam was gone upstairs. “He’s like as if he was struck for death this day or two—he’s so cast down. I found him i’ the shop this forenoon, arter thee wast gone, a-sittin’ an’ doin’ nothin’—not so much as a booke afore him.”

“He’s a deal o’ work upon him just now, Mother,” said Seth, “and I think he’s a bit troubled in his mind. Don’t you take notice of it, because it hurts him when you do. Be as kind to him as you can, Mother, and don’t say anything to vex him.”

“Eh, what dost talk o’ my vexin’ him? An’ what am I like to be but kind? I’ll ma’ him a kettle-cake for breakfast i’ the mornin’.”

Adam, meanwhile, was reading Dinah’s letter by the light of his dip candle.

DEAR BROTHER SETH—Your letter lay three days beyond my knowing of it at the post, for I had not money enough by me to pay the carriage, this being a time of great need and sickness here, with the rains that have fallen, as if the windows of heaven were opened again; and to lay by money, from day to day, in such a time, when there are so many in present need of all things, would be a want of trust like the laying up of the manna. I speak of this, because I would not have you think me slow to answer, or that I had small joy in your rejoicing at the worldly good that has befallen your brother Adam. The honour and love you bear him is nothing but meet, for God has given him great gifts, and he uses them as the patriarch Joseph did, who, when he was exalted to a place of power and trust, yet yearned with tenderness towards his parent and his younger brother.

“My heart is knit to your aged mother since it was granted me to be near her in the day of trouble. Speak to her of me, and tell her I often bear her in my thoughts at evening time, when I am sitting in the dim light as I did with her, and we held one another’s hands, and I spoke the words of comfort that were given to me. Ah, that is a blessed time, isn’t it, Seth, when the outward light is fading, and the body is a little wearied with its work and its labour. Then the inward light shines the brighter, and we have a deeper sense of resting on the Divine strength. I sit on my chair in the dark room and close my eyes, and it is as if I was out of the body and could feel no want for evermore. For then, the very hardship, and the sorrow, and the blindness, and the sin I have beheld and been ready to weep over—yea, all the anguish of the children of men, which sometimes wraps me round like sudden darkness—I can bear with a willing pain, as if I was sharing the Redeemer's cross. For I feel it, I feel it—infinite love is suffering too—yea, in the fulness of knowledge it suffers, it yearns, it mourns; and that is a blind self-seeking which wants to be freed from the sorrow wherewith the whole creation groaneth and travaileth. Surely it is not true blessedness to be free from sorrow, while there is sorrow and sin in the world: sorrow is then a part of love, and love does not seek to throw it off. It is not the spirit only that tells me this—I see it in the whole work and word of the Gospel. Is there not pleading in heaven? Is not the Man of Sorrows there in that crucified body wherewith he ascended? And is He not one with the Infinite Love itself—as our love is one with our sorrow?

"These thoughts have been much borne in on me of late, and I have seen with new clearness the meaning of those words, 'If any man love me, let him take up my cross.' I have heard this enlarged on as if it meant the troubles and persecutions we bring on ourselves by confessing Jesus. But surely that is a narrow thought. The true cross of the Redeemer was the sin and sorrow of this world—*that* was what lay heavy on his heart—and that is the cross we shall share with him, that is the cup we must drink of with him, if we would have any part in that Divine Love which is one with his sorrow.

"In my outward lot, which you ask about, I have all things and abound. I have had constant work in the mill, though some of the other hands have been turned off for a time, and my body is greatly strengthened, so that I feel little weariness after long walking and speaking. What you say about staying in your own country with your mother and brother shows me that you have a true guidance; your lot is appointed there by a clear showing, and to seek a greater blessing elsewhere would be like laying a false offering on the altar and expecting the fire from heaven to kindle it. My work and my joy are here among the hills, and I sometimes think I cling too much to my life among the people here, and should be rebellious if I was called away.

"I was thankful for your tidings about the dear friends at the Hall Farm, for though I sent them a letter, by my aunt's desire, after I came back from my sojourn among them, I have had no word from them. My aunt has not the pen of a ready writer, and the work of the house is sufficient for the day, for she is weak in body. My heart cleaves to her and her children as the nearest of all to me in the flesh—yea, and to all in that house. I am carried away to them continually in my sleep, and often in the midst of work, and even of speech, the thought of them is borne in on me as if they were in need and trouble, which yet is dark to me. There may be some leading here; but I wait to be taught. You say they are all well.

"We shall see each other again in the body, I trust, though, it may be, not for a long while; for the brethren and sisters at Leeds are desirous to have me for a short space among them, when I have a door opened me again to leave Snowfield.

"Farewell, dear brother—and yet not farewell. For those children of God whom it has been granted to see each other face to face, and to hold communion together, and to feel the same spirit working in both can never more be sundered though the hills may lie between. For their souls are enlarged for evermore by that union, and they bear one another about in their thoughts continually as it were a new strength.—Your faithful Sister and fellow-worker in Christ,

"DINAH MORRIS."

"I have not skill to write the words so small as you do and my pen moves slow. And so I am straitened, and say but little of what is in my mind. Greet your mother for me with a kiss. She asked me to kiss her twice when we parted."

Adam had refolded the letter, and was sitting meditatively with his head resting on his arm at the head of the bed, when Seth came upstairs.

"Hast read the letter?" said Seth.

"Yes," said Adam. "I don't know what I should ha' thought of her and her letter if I'd never seen her: I daresay I should ha' thought a preaching woman hateful. But she's one as makes everything seem right she says and does, and I seemed to see her and hear her speaking when I read the letter. It's wonderful how I remember her looks and her voice. She'd make thee rare and happy, Seth; she's just the woman for thee."

"It's no use thinking o' that," said Seth, despondingly. "She spoke so firm, and she's not the woman to say one thing and mean another."

"Nay, but her feelings may grow different. A woman may get to love by degrees—the best fire dosna flare up the soonest. I'd have thee go and see her by and by: I'd make it convenient for thee to be away three or four days, and it 'ud be no walk for thee—only between twenty and thirty mile."

"I should like to see her again, whether or no, if she wouldna be displeased with me for going," said Seth.

"She'll be none displeased," said Adam emphatically, getting up and throwing off his coat. "It might be a great happiness to us all if she'd have thee, for mother took to her so wonderful and seemed so contented to be with her."

"Aye," said Seth, rather timidly, "and Dinah's fond o' Hetty too; she thinks a deal about her."

Adam made no reply to that, and no other word but "good-night" passed between them.

Chapter XXXI
In Hetty's Bed-Chamber

It was no longer light enough to go to bed without a candle, even in Mrs. Poyser's early household, and Hetty carried one with her as she went up at last to her bedroom soon after Adam was gone, and bolted the door behind her.

Now she would read her letter. It must—it must have comfort in it. How was Adam to know the truth? It was always likely he should say what he did say.

She set down the candle and took out the letter. It had a faint scent of roses, which made her feel as if Arthur were close to her. She put it to her lips, and a rush of remembered sensations for a moment or two swept away all fear. But her heart began to flutter strangely, and her hands to tremble as she broke the seal. She read slowly; it was not easy for her to read a gentleman's handwriting, though Arthur had taken pains to write plainly.

"DEAREST HETTY—I have spoken truly when I have said that I loved you, and I shall never forget our love. I shall be your true friend as long as life lasts, and I hope to prove this to you in many ways. If I say anything to pain you in this letter, do not believe it is for want of love and tenderness towards you, for there is nothing I would not do for you, if I knew it to be really for your happiness. I cannot bear to think of my little Hetty shedding tears when I am not there to kiss them away; and if I followed only my own inclinations, I should be with her at this moment instead of writing. It is very hard for me to part from her—harder still for me to write words which may seem unkind, though they spring from the truest kindness.

"Dear, dear Hetty, sweet as our love has been to me, sweet as it would be to me for you to love me always, I feel that it would have been better for us both if we had never had that happiness, and that it is my duty to ask you to love me and care for me as little as you can. The fault has all been mine, for though I have been unable to resist the longing to be near you, I have felt all the while that your affection for me might cause you grief. I ought to have resisted my feelings. I should have done so, if I had been a better fellow than I am; but now, since the past cannot be altered, I am bound to save you from any evil that I have power to prevent. And I feel it would be a great evil for you if your affections continued so fixed on me that you could think of no other man who might be able to make you happier by his love than I ever can, and if you continued to look towards something in the future which cannot possibly happen. For, dear Hetty, if I were to do what you one day spoke of, and make you my wife, I should do what you yourself would come to feel was for your misery instead of your welfare. I know you can never be happy except by marrying a man in your own station; and if I were to marry you now, I should only be adding to any wrong I have done, besides offending against my duty in the other relations of life. You know nothing, dear Hetty, of the world in which I must always live, and you would soon begin to dislike me, because there would be so little in which we should be alike.

"And since I cannot marry you, we must part—we must try not to feel like lovers any more. I am miserable while I say this, but nothing else can be. Be angry with me, my sweet one, I deserve it; but do not believe that I shall not always care for you—always be grateful to you—always remember my Hetty; and if any trouble should come that we do not now foresee, trust in me to do everything that lies in my power.

"I have told you where you are to direct a letter to, if you want to write, but I put it down below lest you should have forgotten. Do not write unless there is something I can really do for you; for, dear Hetty, we must try to think of each other as little as we can. Forgive me, and try to forget everything about me, except that I shall be, as long as I live, your affectionate friend,

"ARTHUR DONNITHORNE."

Slowly Hetty had read this letter; and when she looked up from it there was the reflection of a blanched face in the old dim glass—a white marble face with rounded childish forms, but with something sadder than a child's pain in it. Hetty did not see the face—she saw nothing—she only felt that she was cold and sick and trembling. The letter shook and rustled in her hand. She laid it down. It was a horrible sensation—this cold and trembling. It swept away the very ideas that produced it, and Hetty got up to reach a warm cloak from her clothes-press, wrapped it round her, and sat as if she were thinking of nothing but getting warm. Presently she took up the letter with a firmer hand, and began to read it through again. The tears came this time—great rushing tears that blinded her and blotched the paper. She felt nothing but that Arthur was cruel—cruel to write so, cruel not to marry her. Reasons why he could not marry her had no existence for her mind; how could she believe in any misery that could come to her from the fulfilment of all she had been longing for and dreaming of? She had not the ideas that could make up the notion of that misery.

As she threw down the letter again, she caught sight of her face in the glass; it was reddened now, and wet with tears; it was almost like a companion that she might complain to—that would pity her. She leaned forward on her elbows, and looked into those dark overflooding eyes and at the quivering mouth, and saw how the tears came thicker and thicker, and how the mouth became convulsed with sobs.

The shattering of all her little dream-world, the crushing blow on her new-born passion, afflicted her pleasure-craving nature with an overpowering pain that annihilated all impulse to resistance, and suspended her anger. She sat sobbing till the candle went out, and then, wearied, aching, stupefied with crying, threw herself on the bed without undressing and went to sleep.

There was a feeble dawn in the room when Hetty awoke, a little after four o'clock, with a sense of dull misery, the cause of which broke upon her gradually as she began to discern the objects round her in the dim light. And then came the frightening thought that she had to conceal her misery as well as to bear it, in this dreary daylight that was coming. She could lie no longer. She got up and went towards the table: there lay the letter. She opened her treasure-drawer: there lay the ear-rings and the locket—the signs of all her short happiness—the signs of the lifelong dreariness that was to follow it. Looking at the little trinkets which she had once eyed and fingered so fondly as the earnest of her future paradise of finery, she lived back in the moments when they had been given to her with such tender caresses, such strangely pretty words, such glowing looks, which filled her with a bewildering delicious surprise—they were so much sweeter than she had thought anything could be. And the Arthur who had spoken to her and looked at her in this way, who was present with her now—whose arm she felt round her, his cheek against hers, his very breath upon her—was the cruel, cruel Arthur who had written that letter, that letter which she snatched and crushed and then opened again, that she might read it once more. The half-benumbed mental condition which was the effect of the last night's violent crying made it necessary to her to look again and see if her wretched thoughts were actually true—if the letter was really so cruel. She had to hold it close to the window, else she could not have read it by the faint light. Yes! It was worse—it was more cruel. She crushed it up again in anger. She hated the writer of that letter—hated him for the very reason that she hung upon him with all her love—all the girlish passion and vanity that made up her love.

She had no tears this morning. She had wept them all away last night, and now she felt that dry-eyed morning misery, which is worse than the first shock because it has the future in it as well as the present. Every morning to come, as far as her imagination could stretch, she would have to get up and feel that the day would have no joy for her. For there is no despair so absolute as that which comes with the first moments of our first great sorrow, when we have not yet known what it is to have suffered and be healed, to have despaired and to have recovered hope. As Hetty began languidly to take off the clothes she had worn all the night, that she might wash herself and brush her hair, she had a sickening sense that her life would go on in this way. She should always be doing things she had no pleasure in, getting up to the old tasks of work, seeing people she cared nothing about, going to church, and to Treddleston, and to tea with Mrs. Best, and carrying no happy thought with her. For her short poisonous delights had spoiled for ever all the little joys that had once made the sweetness of her life—the new frock ready for Treddleston Fair, the party at Mr. Britton's at Broxton wake, the beaux that she would say "No" to for a long while, and the prospect of the wedding that was to come at last when she would have a silk gown and a great many clothes all at once. These things were all flat and dreary to her now; everything would be a weariness, and she would carry about for ever a hopeless thirst and longing.

She paused in the midst of her languid undressing and leaned against the dark old clothes-press. Her neck and arms were bare, her hair hung down in delicate rings—and they were just as beautiful as they were that night two months ago, when she walked up and down this bed-chamber glowing with vanity and hope. She was not thinking of her neck and arms now; even her own beauty was indifferent to her. Her eyes wandered sadly over the dull old chamber, and then looked out vacantly towards the growing dawn. Did a remembrance of Dinah come across her mind? Of her foreboding words, which had made her angry? Of Dinah's affectionate entreaty to think of her as a friend in trouble? No, the impression had been too slight to recur. Any affection or comfort Dinah could have given her would have been as indifferent to Hetty this morning as everything else was except her bruised passion. She was only thinking she could never stay here and go on with the old life—she could better bear something quite new than sinking back into the old everyday round. She would like to run away that very morning, and never see any of the old faces again. But Hetty's was not a nature to face difficulties—to dare to loose her hold on the familiar and rush blindly on some unknown condition. Hers was a luxurious and vain nature—not a passionate one—and if she were ever to take any violent measure, she must be urged to it by the desperation of terror. There was not much room for her thoughts to travel in the narrow circle of her imagination, and she soon fixed on the one thing she would do to get away from her old life: she would ask her uncle to let her go to be a lady's maid. Miss Lydia's maid would help her to get a situation, if she knew Hetty had her uncle's leave.

When she had thought of this, she fastened up her hair and began to wash: it seemed more possible to her to go downstairs and try to behave as usual. She would ask her uncle this very day. On Hetty's blooming health it would take a great deal of such mental suffering as hers to leave any deep impress; and when she was dressed as neatly as usual in her working-dress, with her hair tucked up under her little cap, an indifferent observer would have been more struck with the young roundness of her cheek and neck and the darkness of her eyes and eyelashes than with any signs of sadness about her. But when she took up the crushed letter and put it in her drawer, that she might lock it out of sight, hard smarting tears, having no relief in them as the great drops had that fell last night, forced their way into her eyes. She wiped them away quickly: she must not cry in the day-time. Nobody should find out how miserable she was, nobody should know she was disappointed about anything; and the thought that the eyes of her aunt and uncle would be upon her gave her the self-command which often accompanies a great dread. For Hetty looked out from her secret misery towards the possibility of their ever knowing what had happened, as the sick and weary prisoner might think of the possible pillory. They would think her conduct shameful, and shame was torture. That was poor little Hetty's conscience.

So she locked up her drawer and went away to her early work.

In the evening, when Mr. Poyser was smoking his pipe, and his good-nature was therefore at its superlative moment, Hetty seized the opportunity of her aunt's absence to say, "Uncle, I wish you'd let me go for a lady's maid."

Mr. Poyser took the pipe from his mouth and looked at Hetty in mild surprise for some moments. She was sewing, and went on with her work industriously.

"Why, what's put that into your head, my wench?" he said at last, after he had given one conservative puff.

"I should like it—I should like it better than farm-work."

"Nay, nay; you fancy so because you donna know it, my wench. It wouldn't be half so good for your health, nor for your luck i' life. I'd like you to stay wi' us till you've got a good husband: you're my own niece, and I wouldn't have you go to service, though it was a gentleman's house, as long as I've got a home for you."

Mr. Poyser paused, and puffed away at his pipe.

"I like the needlework," said Hetty, "and I should get good wages."

"Has your aunt been a bit sharp wi' you?" said Mr. Poyser, not noticing Hetty's further argument. "You mustna mind that, my wench—she does it for your good. She wishes you well; an' there isn't many aunts as are no kin to you 'ud ha' done by you as she has."

"No, it isn't my aunt," said Hetty, "but I should like the work better."

"It was all very well for you to learn the work a bit—an' I gev my consent to that fast enough, sin' Mrs. Pomfret was willing to teach you. For if anything was t' happen, it's well to know how to turn your hand to different sorts o' things. But I niver meant you to go to service, my wench; my family's ate their own bread and cheese as fur back as anybody knows, hanna they, Father? You wouldna like your grand-child to take wage?"

"Na-a-y," said old Martin, with an elongation of the word, meant to make it bitter as well as negative, while he leaned forward and looked down on the floor. "But the wench takes arter her mother. I'd hard work t' hould *her* in, an' she married i' spite o' me—a feller wi' on'y two head o' stock when there should ha' been ten on's farm—she might well die o' th' inflammation afore she war thirty."

It was seldom the old man made so long a speech, but his son's question had fallen like a bit of dry fuel on the embers of a long unextinguished resentment, which had always made the grandfather more indifferent to Hetty than to his son's children. Her mother's fortune had been spent by that good-for-nought Sorrel, and Hetty had Sorrel's blood in her veins.

"Poor thing, poor thing!" said Martin the younger, who was sorry to have provoked this retrospective harshness. "She'd but bad luck. But Hetty's got as good a chance o' getting a solid, sober husband as any gell i' this country."

After throwing out this pregnant hint, Mr. Poyser recurred to his pipe and his silence, looking at Hetty to see if she did not give some sign of having renounced her ill-advised wish. But instead of that, Hetty, in spite of herself, began to cry, half out of ill temper at the denial, half out of the day's repressed sadness.

"Hegh, hegh!" said Mr. Poyser, meaning to check her playfully, "don't let's have any crying. Crying's for them as ha' got no home, not for them as want to get rid o' one. What dost think?" he continued to his wife, who now came back into the house-place, knitting with fierce rapidity, as if that movement were a necessary function, like the twittering of a crab's antennæ.

"Think? Why, I think we shall have the fowl stole before we are much older, wi' that gell forgetting to lock the pens up o' nights. What's the matter now, Hetty? What are you crying at?"

"Why, she's been wanting to go for a lady's maid," said Mr. Poyser. "I tell her we can do better for her nor that."

"I thought she'd got some maggot in her head, she's gone about wi' her mouth buttoned up so all day. It's all wi' going so among them servants at the Chase, as we war fools for letting her. She thinks it 'ud be a finer life than being wi' them as are akin to her and ha' brought her up sin' she war no bigger nor Marty. She thinks there's nothing belongs to being a lady's maid but wearing finer clothes nor she was born to, I'll be bound. It's what rag she can get to stick on her as she's thinking on from morning till night, as I often ask her if she wouldn't like to be the mawkin i' the field, for then she'd be made o' rags inside and out. I'll never gi' my consent to her going for a lady's maid, while she's got good friends to take care on her till she's married to somebody better nor one o' them valets, as is neither a common man nor a gentleman, an' must live on the fat o' the land, an's like enough to stick his hands under his coat-tails and expect his wife to work for him."

"Aye, aye," said Mr. Poyser, "we must have a better husband for her nor that, and there's better at hand. Come, my wench, give over crying and get to bed. I'll do better for you nor letting you go for a lady's maid. Let's hear no more on't."

When Hetty was gone upstairs he said, "I canna make it out as she should want to go away, for I thought she'd got a mind t' Adam Bede. She's looked like it o' late."

"Eh, there's no knowing what she's got a liking to, for things take no more hold on her than if she was a dried pea. I believe that gell, Molly—as is aggravatin' enough, for the matter o' that—but I believe she'd care more about leaving us and the children, for all she's been here but a year come Michaelmas, nor Hetty would. But she's got this notion o' being a lady's maid wi' going among them servants—we might ha' known what it 'ud lead to when we let her go to learn the fine work. But I'll put a stop to it pretty quick."

"Thee'dst be sorry to part wi' her, if it wasn't for her good," said Mr. Poyser. "She's useful to thee i' the work."

"Sorry? Yes, I'm fonder on her nor she deserves—a little hard-hearted hussy, wanting to leave us i' that way. I can't ha' had her about me these seven year, I reckon, and done for her, and taught her everything wi'out caring about her. An' here I'm having linen spun, an' thinking all the while it'll make sheeting and table-clothing for her when she's married, an' she'll live i' the parish wi' us, and never go out of our sights—like a fool as I am for thinking aught about her, as is no better nor a cherry wi' a hard stone inside it."

"Nay, nay, thee mustna make much of a trifle," said Mr. Poyser, soothingly. "She's fond on us, I'll be bound; but she's young, an' gets things in her head as she can't rightly give account on. Them young fillies 'ull run away often wi'out knowing why."

Her uncle's answers, however, had had another effect on Hetty besides that of disappointing her and making her cry. She knew quite well whom he had in his mind in his allusions to marriage, and to a sober, solid husband; and when she was in her bedroom again, the possibility of her marrying Adam presented itself to her in a new light. In a mind where no strong sympathies are at work, where there is no supreme sense of right to which the agitated nature can cling and steady itself to quiet endurance, one of the first results of sorrow is a desperate vague clutching after any deed that will change the actual condition. Poor Hetty's vision of consequences, at no time more than a narrow fantastic calculation of her own probable pleasures and pains, was now quite shut out by reckless irritation under present suffering, and she was ready for one of those convulsive, motiveless actions by which wretched men and women leap from a temporary sorrow into a lifelong misery.

Why should she not marry Adam? She did not care what she did, so that it made some change in her life. She felt confident that he would still want to marry her, and any further thought about Adam's happiness in the matter had never yet visited her.

"Strange!" perhaps you will say, "this rush of impulse towards a course that might have seemed the most repugnant to her present state of mind, and in only the second night of her sadness!"

Yes, the actions of a little trivial soul like Hetty's, struggling amidst the serious sad destinies of a human being, *are* strange. So are the motions of a little vessel without ballast tossed about on a stormy sea. How pretty it looked with its parti-coloured sail in the sunlight, moored in the quiet bay!

"Let that man bear the loss who loosed it from its moorings."

But that will not save the vessel—the pretty thing that might have been a lasting joy.

Chapter XXXII
Mrs. Poyser "Has Her Say Out"

The next Saturday evening there was much excited discussion at the Donnithorne Arms concerning an incident which had occurred that very day—no less than a second appearance of the smart man in top-boots said by some to be a mere farmer in treaty for the Chase Farm, by others to be the future steward, but by Mr. Casson himself, the personal witness to the stranger's visit, pronounced contemptuously to be nothing better than a bailiff, such as Satchell had been before him. No one had thought of denying Mr. Casson's testimony to the fact that he had seen the stranger; nevertheless, he proffered various corroborating circumstances.

"I see him myself," he said; "I see him coming along by the Crab-tree Meadow on a bald-faced hoss. I'd just been t' hev a pint—it was half after ten i' the fore-noon, when I hev my pint as reg'lar as the clock—and I says to Knowles, as druv up with his waggon, 'You'll get a bit o' barley to-day, Knowles,' I says, 'if you look about you'; and then I went round by the rick-yard, and towart the Treddles'on road, and just as I come up by the big ash-tree, I see the man i' top-boots coming along on a bald-faced hoss—I wish I may never stir if I didn't. And I stood still till he come up, and I says, 'Good morning, sir,' I says, for I wanted to hear the turn of his tongue, as I might know whether he was a this-country man; so I says, 'Good morning, sir: it 'll 'old hup for the barley this morning, I think. There'll be a bit got hin, if we've good luck.' And he says, 'Eh, ye may be raight, there's noo tallin',' he says, and I knowed by that"—here Mr. Casson gave a wink—"as he didn't come from a hundred mile off. I daresay he'd think me a hodd talker, as you Loamshire folks allays does hany one as talks the right language."

"The right language!" said Bartle Massey, contemptuously. "You're about as near the right language as a pig's squeaking is like a tune played on a key-bugle."

"Well, I don't know," answered Mr. Casson, with an angry smile. "I should think a man as has lived among the gentry from a by, is likely to know what's the right language pretty nigh as well as a schoolmaster."

"Ay, ay, man," said Bartle, with a tone of sarcastic consolation, "you talk the right language for *you*. When Mike Holdsworth's goat says ba-a-a, it's all right—it 'ud be unnatural for it to make any other noise."

The rest of the party being Loamshire men, Mr. Casson had the laugh strongly against him, and wisely fell back on the previous question, which, far from being exhausted in a single evening, was renewed in the churchyard, before service, the next day, with the fresh interest conferred on all news when there is a fresh person to hear it; and that fresh hearer was Martin Poyser, who, as his wife said, "never went boozin' with that set at Casson's, a-sittin' soakin' in drink, and looking as wise as a lot o' cod-fish wi' red faces."

It was probably owing to the conversation she had had with her husband on their way from church concerning this problematic stranger that Mrs. Poyser's thoughts immediately reverted to him when, a day or two afterwards, as she was standing at the house-door with her knitting, in that eager leisure which came to her when the afternoon cleaning was done, she saw the old squire enter the yard on his black pony, followed by John the groom. She always cited it afterwards as a case of prevision, which really had something more in it than her own remarkable penetration, that the moment she set eyes on the squire she said to herself, "I shouldna wonder if he's come about that man as is a-going to take the Chase Farm, wanting Poyser to do something for him without pay. But Poyser's a fool if he does."

Something unwonted must clearly be in the wind, for the old squire's visits to his tenantry were rare; and though Mrs. Poyser had during the last twelvemonth recited many imaginary speeches, meaning even more than met the ear, which she was quite determined to make to him the next time he appeared within the gates of the Hall Farm, the speeches had always remained imaginary.

"Good-day, Mrs. Poyser," said the old squire, peering at her with his short-sighted eyes—a mode of looking at her which, as Mrs. Poyser observed, "allays aggravated me: it was as if you was a insect, and he was going to dab his finger-nail on you."

However, she said, "Your servant, sir," and curtsied with an air of perfect deference as she advanced towards him: she was not the woman to misbehave towards her betters, and fly in the face of the catechism, without severe provocation.

"Is your husband at home, Mrs. Poyser?"

"Yes, sir; he's only i' the rick-yard. I'll send for him in a minute, if you'll please to get down and step in."

"Thank you; I will do so. I want to consult him about a little matter; but you are quite as much concerned in it, if not more. I must have your opinion too."

"Hetty, run and tell your uncle to come in," said Mrs. Poyser, as they entered the house, and the old gentleman bowed low in answer to Hetty's curtsy; while Totty, conscious of a pinafore stained with gooseberry jam, stood hiding her face against the clock and peeping round furtively.

"What a fine old kitchen this is!" said Mr. Donnithorne, looking round admiringly. He always spoke in the same deliberate, well-chiselled, polite way, whether his words were sugary or venomous. "And you keep it so exquisitely clean, Mrs. Poyser. I like these premises, do you know, beyond any on the estate."

"Well, sir, since you're fond of 'em, I should be glad if you'd let a bit o' repairs be done to 'em, for the boarding's i' that state as we're like to be eaten up wi' rats and mice; and the cellar, you may stan' up to your knees i' water in't, if you like to go down; but perhaps you'd rather believe my words. Won't you please to sit down, sir?"

"Not yet; I must see your dairy. I have not seen it for years, and I hear on all hands about your fine cheese and butter," said the squire, looking politely unconscious that there could be any question on which he and Mrs. Poyser might happen to disagree. "I think I see the door open, there. You must not be surprised if I cast a covetous eye on your cream and butter. I don't expect that Mrs. Satchell's cream and butter will bear comparison with yours."

"I can't say, sir, I'm sure. It's seldom I see other folks's butter, though there's some on it as one's no need to see—the smell's enough."

"Ah, now this I like," said Mr. Donnithorne, looking round at the damp temple of cleanliness, but keeping near the door. "I'm sure I should like my breakfast better if I knew the butter and cream came from this dairy. Thank you, that really is a pleasant sight. Unfortunately, my slight tendency to rheumatism makes me afraid of damp: I'll sit down in your comfortable kitchen. Ah, Poyser, how do you do? In the midst of business, I see, as usual. I've been looking at your wife's beautiful dairy—the best manager in the parish, is she not?"

Mr. Poyser had just entered in shirt-sleeves and open waistcoat, with a face a shade redder than usual, from the exertion of "pitching." As he stood, red, rotund, and radiant, before the small, wiry, cool old gentleman, he looked like a prize apple by the side of a withered crab.

"Will you please to take this chair, sir?" he said, lifting his father's arm-chair forward a little: "you'll find it easy."

"No, thank you, I never sit in easy-chairs," said the old gentleman, seating himself on a small chair near the door. "Do you know, Mrs. Poyser—sit down, pray, both of you—I've been far from contented, for some time, with Mrs. Satchell's dairy management. I think she has not a good method, as you have."

"Indeed, sir, I can't speak to that," said Mrs. Poyser in a hard voice, rolling and unrolling her knitting and looking icily out of the window, as she continued to stand opposite the squire. Poyser might sit down if he liked, she thought; *she* wasn't going to sit down, as if she'd give in to any such smooth-tongued palaver. Mr. Poyser, who looked and felt the reverse of icy, did sit down in his three-cornered chair.

"And now, Poyser, as Satchell is laid up, I am intending to let the Chase Farm to a respectable tenant. I'm tired of having a farm on my own hands—nothing is made the best of in such cases, as you know. A satisfactory bailiff is hard to find; and I think you and I, Poyser, and your excellent wife here, can enter into a little arrangement in consequence, which will be to our mutual advantage."

"Oh," said Mr. Poyser, with a good-natured blankness of imagination as to the nature of the arrangement.

"If I'm called upon to speak, sir," said Mrs. Poyser, after glancing at her husband with pity at his softness, "you know better than me; but I don't see what the Chase Farm is t' us—we've cumber enough wi' our own farm. Not but what I'm glad to hear o' anybody respectable coming into the parish; there's some as ha' been brought in as hasn't been looked on i' that character."

"You're likely to find Mr. Thurle an excellent neighbour, I assure you—such a one as you will feel glad to have accommodated by the little plan I'm going to mention, especially as I hope you will find it as much to your own advantage as his."

"Indeed, sir, if it's anything t' our advantage, it'll be the first offer o' the sort I've heared on. It's them as take advantage that get advantage i' this world, *I* think: folks have to wait long enough afore it's brought to 'em."

"The fact is, Poyser," said the squire, ignoring Mrs. Poyser's theory of worldly prosperity, "there is too much dairy land, and too little plough land, on the Chase Farm to suit Thurle's purpose—indeed, he will only take the farm on condition of some change in it: his wife, it appears, is not a clever dairy-woman, like yours. Now, the plan I'm thinking of is to effect a little exchange. If you were to have the Hollow Pastures, you might increase your dairy, which must be so profitable under your wife's management; and I should request you, Mrs. Poyser, to supply my house with milk, cream, and butter at the market prices. On the other hand, Poyser, you might let Thurle have the Lower and Upper Ridges, which really, with our wet seasons, would be a good riddance for you. There is much less risk in dairy land than corn land."

Mr. Poyser was leaning forward, with his elbows on his knees, his head on one side, and his mouth screwed up—apparently absorbed in making the tips of his fingers meet so as to represent with perfect accuracy the ribs of a ship. He was much too acute a man not to see through the whole business, and to foresee perfectly what would be his wife's view of the subject; but he disliked giving unpleasant answers. Unless it was on a point of farming practice, he would rather give up than have a quarrel, any day; and, after all, it mattered more to his wife than to him. So, after a few moments' silence, he looked up at her and said mildly, "What dost say?"

Mrs. Poyser had had her eyes fixed on her husband with cold severity during his silence, but now she turned away her head with a toss, looked icily at the opposite roof of the cow-shed, and spearing her knitting together with the loose pin, held it firmly between her clasped hands.

"Say? Why, I say you may do as you like about giving up any o' your corn-land afore your lease is up, which it won't be for a year come next Michaelmas, but I'll not consent to take more dairy work into my hands, either for love or money; and there's nayther love nor money here, as I can see, on'y other folks's love o' theirselves, and the money as is to go into other folks's pockets. I know there's them as is born t' own the land, and them as is born to sweat on't"—here Mrs. Poyser paused to gasp a little—"and I know it's christened folks's duty to submit to their betters as fur as flesh and blood 'ull bear it; but I'll not make a martyr o' myself, and wear myself to skin and bone, and worret myself as if I was a churn wi' butter a-coming in't, for no landlord in England, not if he was King George himself."

"No, no, my dear Mrs. Poyser, certainly not," said the squire, still confident in his own powers of persuasion, "you must not overwork yourself; but don't you think your work will rather be lessened than increased in this way? There is so much milk required at the Abbey that you will have little increase of cheese and butter making from the addition to your dairy; and I believe selling the milk is the most profitable way of disposing of dairy produce, is it not?"

"Aye, that's true," said Mr. Poyser, unable to repress an opinion on a question of farming profits, and forgetting that it was not in this case a purely abstract question.

"I daresay," said Mrs. Poyser bitterly, turning her head half-way towards her husband and looking at the vacant arm-chair—"I daresay it's true for men as sit i' th' chimney-corner and make believe as everything's cut wi' ins an' outs to fit int' everything else. If you could make a pudding wi' thinking o' the batter, it 'ud be easy getting dinner. How do I know whether the milk 'ull be wanted constant? What's to make me sure as the house won't be put o' board wage afore we're many months older, and then I may have to lie awake o' nights wi' twenty gallons o' milk on my mind—and Dingall 'ull take no more butter, let alone paying for it; and we must fat pigs till we're obliged to beg the butcher on our knees to buy 'em, and lose half of 'em wi' the measles. And there's the fetching and carrying, as 'ud be welly half a day's work for a man an' hoss—*that's* to be took out o' the profits, I reckon? But there's folks 'ud hold a sieve under the pump and expect to carry away the water."

"That difficulty—about the fetching and carrying—you will not have, Mrs. Poyser," said the squire, who thought that this entrance into particulars indicated a distant inclination to compromise on Mrs. Poyser's part. "Bethell will do that regularly with the cart and pony."

"Oh, sir, begging your pardon, I've never been used t' having gentlefolks's servants coming about my back places, a-making love to both the gells at once and keeping 'em with their hands on their hips listening to all manner o' gossip when they should be down on their knees a-scouring. If we're to go to ruin, it shanna be wi' having our back kitchen turned into a public."

"Well, Poyser," said the squire, shifting his tactics and looking as if he thought Mrs. Poyser had suddenly withdrawn from the proceedings and left the room, "you can turn the Hollows into feeding-land. I can easily make another arrangement about supplying my house. And I shall not forget your readiness to accommodate your landlord as well as a neighbour. I know you will be glad to have your lease renewed for three years, when the present one expires; otherwise, I daresay Thurle, who is a man of some capital, would be glad to take both the farms, as they could be worked so well together. But I don't want to part with an old tenant like you."

To be thrust out of the discussion in this way would have been enough to complete Mrs. Poyser's exasperation, even without the final threat. Her husband, really alarmed at the possibility of their leaving the old place where he had been bred and born—for he believed the old squire had small spite enough for anything—was beginning a mild remonstrance explanatory of the inconvenience he should find in having to buy and sell more stock, with, "Well, sir, I think as it's rether hard..." when Mrs. Poyser burst in with the desperate determination to have her say out this once, though it were to rain notices to quit and the only shelter were the work-house.

"Then, sir, if I may speak—as, for all I'm a woman, and there's folks as thinks a woman's fool enough to stan' by an' look on while the men sign her soul away, I've a right to speak, for I make one quarter o' the rent, and save another quarter—I say, if Mr. Thurle's so ready to take farms under you, it's a pity but what he should take this, and see if he likes to live in a house wi' all the plagues o' Egypt in't—wi' the cellar full o' water, and frogs and toads hoppin' up the steps by dozens—and the floors rotten, and the rats and mice gnawing every bit o' cheese, and runnin' over our heads as we lie i' bed till we expect 'em to eat us up alive—as it's a mercy they hanna eat the children long ago. I should like to see if there's another tenant besides Poyser as 'ud put up wi' never having a bit o' repairs done till a place tumbles down—and not then, on'y wi' begging and praying and having to pay half—and being strung up wi' the rent as it's much if he gets enough out o' the land to pay, for all he's put his own money into the ground beforehand. See if you'll get a stranger to lead such a life here as that: a maggot must be born i' the rotten cheese to like it, I reckon. You may run away from my words, sir," continued Mrs. Poyser, following the old squire beyond the door—for after the first moments of stunned surprise he had got up, and, waving his hand towards her with a smile, had walked out towards his pony. But it was impossible for him to get away immediately, for John was walking the pony up and down the yard, and was some distance from the causeway when his master beckoned.

"You may run away from my words, sir, and you may go spinnin' underhand ways o' doing us a mischief, for you've got Old Harry to your friend, though nobody else is, but I tell you for once as we're not dumb creatures to be abused and made money on by them as ha' got the lash i' their hands, for want o' knowing how t' undo the tackle. An' if I'm th' only one as speaks my mind, there's plenty o' the same way o' thinking i' this parish and the next to 't, for your name's no better than a brimstone match in everybody's nose—if it isna two-three old folks as you think o' saving your soul by giving 'em a bit o' flannel and a drop o' porridge. An' you may be right i' thinking it'll take but little to save your soul, for it'll be the smallest savin' y' iver made, wi' all your scrapin'."

There are occasions on which two servant-girls and a waggoner may be a formidable audience, and as the squire rode away on his black pony, even the gift of short-sightedness did not prevent him from being aware that Molly and Nancy and Tim were grinning not far from him. Perhaps he suspected that sour old John was grinning behind him—which was also the fact. Meanwhile the bull-dog, the black-and-tan terrier, Alick's sheep-dog, and the gander hissing at a safe distance from the pony's heels carried out the idea of Mrs. Poyser's solo in an impressive quartet.

Mrs. Poyser, however, had no sooner seen the pony move off than she turned round, gave the two hilarious damsels a look which drove them into the back kitchen, and unspearing her knitting, began to knit again with her usual rapidity as she re-entered the house.

"Thee'st done it now," said Mr. Poyser, a little alarmed and uneasy, but not without some triumphant amusement at his wife's outbreak.

"Yes, I know I've done it," said Mrs. Poyser; "but I've had my say out, and I shall be th' easier for't all my life. There's no pleasure i' living if you're to be corked up for ever, and only dribble your mind out by the sly, like a leaky barrel. I shan't repent saying what I think, if I live to be as old as th' old squire; and there's little likelihood—for it seems as if them as aren't wanted here are th' only folks as aren't wanted i' th' other world."

"But thee wutna like moving from th' old place, this Michaelmas twelvemonth," said Mr. Poyser, "and going into a strange parish, where thee know'st nobody. It'll be hard upon us both, and upo' Father too."

"Eh, it's no use worreting; there's plenty o' things may happen between this and Michaelmas twelvemonth. The captain may be master afore them, for what we know," said Mrs. Poyser, inclined to take an unusually hopeful view of an embarrassment which had been brought about by her own merit and not by other people's fault.

"*I'm* none for worreting," said Mr. Poyser, rising from his three-cornered chair and walking slowly towards the door; "but I should be loath to leave th' old place, and the parish where I was bred and born, and Father afore me. We should leave our roots behind us, I doubt, and niver thrive again."

Chapter XXXIII
More Links

The barley was all carried at last, and the harvest suppers went by without waiting for the dismal black crop of beans. The apples and nuts were gathered and stored; the scent of whey departed from the farm-houses, and the scent of brewing came in its stead. The woods behind the Chase, and all the hedgerow trees, took on a solemn splendour under the dark low-hanging skies. Michaelmas was come, with its fragrant basketfuls of purple damsons, and its paler purple daisies, and its lads and lasses leaving or seeking service and winding along between the yellow hedges, with their bundles under their arms. But though Michaelmas was come, Mr. Thurle, that desirable tenant, did not come to the Chase Farm, and the old squire, after all, had been obliged to put in a new bailiff. It was known throughout the two parishes that the squire's plan had been frustrated because the Poysers had refused to be "put upon," and Mrs. Poyser's outbreak was discussed in all the farm-houses with a zest which was only heightened by frequent repetition. The news that "Bony" was come back from Egypt was comparatively insipid, and the repulse of the French in Italy was nothing to Mrs. Poyser's repulse of the old squire. Mr. Irwine had heard a version of it in every parishioner's house, with the one exception of the Chase. But since he had always, with marvellous skill, avoided any quarrel with Mr. Donnithorne, he could not allow himself the pleasure of laughing at the old gentleman's discomfiture with any one besides his mother, who declared that if she were rich she should like to allow Mrs. Poyser a pension for life, and wanted to invite her to the parsonage that she might hear an account of the scene from Mrs. Poyser's own lips.

"No, no, Mother," said Mr. Irwine; "it was a little bit of irregular justice on Mrs. Poyser's part, but a magistrate like me must not countenance irregular justice. There must be no report spread that I have taken notice of the quarrel, else I shall lose the little good influence I have over the old man."

"Well, I like that woman even better than her cream-cheeses," said Mrs. Irwine. "She has the spirit of three men, with that pale face of hers. And she says such sharp things too."

"Sharp! Yes, her tongue is like a new-set razor. She's quite original in her talk too; one of those untaught wits that help to stock a country with proverbs. I told you that capital thing I heard her say about Craig—that he was like a cock, who thought the sun had risen to hear him crow. Now that's an Æsop's fable in a sentence."

"But it will be a bad business if the old gentleman turns them out of the farm next Michaelmas, eh?" said Mrs. Irwine.

"Oh, that must not be; and Poyser is such a good tenant that Donnithorne is likely to think twice, and digest his spleen rather than turn them out. But if he should give them notice at Lady Day, Arthur and I must move heaven and earth to mollify him. Such old parishioners as they are must not go."

"Ah, there's no knowing what may happen before Lady day," said Mrs. Irwine. "It struck me on Arthur's birthday that the old man was a little shaken: he's eighty-three, you know. It's really an unconscionable age. It's only women who have a right to live as long as that."

"When they've got old-bachelor sons who would be forlorn without them," said Mr. Irwine, laughing, and kissing his mother's hand.

Mrs. Poyser, too, met her husband's occasional forebodings of a notice to quit with "There's no knowing what may happen before Lady day"—one of those undeniable general propositions which are usually intended to convey a particular meaning very far from undeniable. But it is really too hard upon human nature that it should be held a criminal offence to imagine the death even of the king when he is turned eighty-three. It is not to be believed that any but the dullest Britons can be good subjects under that hard condition.

Apart from this foreboding, things went on much as usual in the Poyser household. Mrs. Poyser thought she noticed a surprising improvement in Hetty. To be sure, the girl got "closer tempered, and sometimes she seemed as if there'd be no drawing a word from her with cart-ropes," but she thought much less about her dress, and went after the work quite eagerly, without any telling. And it was wonderful how she never wanted to go out now—indeed, could hardly be persuaded to go; and she bore her aunt's putting a stop to her weekly lesson in fine-work at the Chase without the least grumbling or pouting. It must be, after all, that she had set her heart on Adam at last, and her sudden freak of wanting to be a lady's maid must have been caused by some little pique or misunderstanding between them, which had passed by. For whenever Adam came to the Hall Farm, Hetty seemed to be in better spirits and to talk more than at other times, though she was almost sullen when Mr. Craig or any other admirer happened to pay a visit there.

Adam himself watched her at first with trembling anxiety, which gave way to surprise and delicious hope. Five days after delivering Arthur's letter, he had ventured to go to the Hall Farm again—not without dread lest the sight of him might be painful to her. She was not in the house-place when he entered, and he sat talking to Mr. and Mrs. Poyser for a few minutes with a heavy fear on his heart that they might presently tell him Hetty was ill. But by and by there came a light step that he knew, and when Mrs. Poyser said, "Come, Hetty, where have you been?" Adam was obliged to turn round, though he was afraid to see the changed look there must be in her face. He almost started when he saw her smiling as if she were pleased to see him—looking the same as ever at a first glance, only that she had her cap on, which he had never seen her in before when he came of an evening. Still, when he looked at her again and again as she moved about or sat at her work, there was a change: the cheeks were as pink as ever, and she smiled as much as she had ever done of late, but there was something different in her eyes, in the expression of her face, in all her movements, Adam thought—something harder, older, less child-like. "Poor thing!" he said to himself, "that's allays likely. It's because she's had her first heartache. But she's got a spirit to bear up under it. Thank God for that."

As the weeks went by, and he saw her always looking pleased to see him—turning up her lovely face towards him as if she meant him to understand that she was glad for him to come—and going about her work in the same equable way, making no sign of sorrow, he began to believe that her feeling towards Arthur must have been much slighter than he had imagined in his first indignation and alarm, and that she had been able to think of her girlish fancy that Arthur was in love with her and would marry her as a folly of which she was timely cured. And it perhaps was, as he had sometimes in his more cheerful moments hoped it would be—her heart was really turning with all the more warmth towards the man she knew to have a serious love for her.

Possibly you think that Adam was not at all sagacious in his interpretations, and that it was altogether extremely unbecoming in a sensible man to behave as he did—falling in love with a girl who really had nothing more than her beauty to recommend her, attributing imaginary virtues to her, and even condescending to cleave to her after she had fallen in love with another man, waiting for her kind looks as a patient trembling dog waits for his master's eye to be turned upon him. But in so complex a thing as human nature, we must consider, it is hard to find rules without exceptions. Of course, I know that, as a rule, sensible men fall in love with the most sensible women of their acquaintance, see through all the pretty deceits of coquettish beauty, never imagine themselves loved when they are not loved, cease loving on all proper occasions, and marry the woman most fitted for them in every respect—indeed, so as to compel the approbation of all the maiden ladies in their neighbourhood. But even to this rule an exception will occur now and then in the lapse of centuries, and my friend Adam was one. For my own part, however, I respect him none the less—nay, I think the deep love he had for that sweet, rounded, blossom-like, dark-eyed Hetty, of whose inward self he was really very ignorant, came out of the very strength of his nature and not out of any inconsistent weakness. Is it any weakness, pray, to be wrought on by exquisite music? To feel its wondrous harmonies searching the subtlest windings of your soul, the delicate fibres of life where no memory can penetrate, and binding together your whole being past and present in one unspeakable vibration, melting you in one moment with all the tenderness, all the love that has been scattered through the toilsome years, concentrating in one emotion of heroic courage or resignation all the hard-learnt lessons of self-renouncing sympathy, blending your present joy with past sorrow and your present sorrow with all your past joy? If not, then neither is it a weakness to be so wrought upon by the exquisite curves of a woman's cheek and neck and arms, by the liquid depths of her beseeching eyes, or the sweet childish pout of her lips. For the beauty of a lovely woman is like music: what can one say more? Beauty has an expression beyond and far above the one woman's soul that it clothes, as the words of genius have a wider meaning than the thought that prompted them. It is more than a woman's love that moves us in a woman's eyes—it seems to be a far-off mighty love that has come near to us, and made speech for itself there; the rounded neck, the dimpled arm, move us by something more than their prettiness—by their close kinship with all we have known of tenderness and peace. The noblest nature sees the most of this *impersonal* expression in beauty (it is needless to say that there are gentlemen with whiskers dyed and undyed who see none of it whatever), and for this reason, the noblest nature is often the most blinded to the character of the one woman's soul that the beauty clothes. Whence, I fear, the tragedy of human life is likely to continue for a long time to come, in spite of mental philosophers who are ready with the best receipts for avoiding all mistakes of the kind.

Our good Adam had no fine words into which he could put his feeling for Hetty: he could not disguise mystery in this way with the appearance of knowledge; he called his love frankly a mystery, as you have heard him. He only knew that the sight and memory of her moved him deeply, touching the spring of all love and tenderness, all faith and courage within him. How could he imagine narrowness, selfishness, hardness in her? He created the mind he believed in out of his own, which was large, unselfish, tender.

The hopes he felt about Hetty softened a little his feeling towards Arthur. Surely his attentions to Hetty must have been of a slight kind; they were altogether wrong, and such as no man in Arthur's position ought to have allowed himself, but they must have had an air of playfulness about them, which had probably blinded him to their danger and had prevented them from laying any strong hold on Hetty's heart. As the new promise of happiness rose for Adam, his indignation and jealousy began to die out. Hetty was not made unhappy; he almost believed that she liked him best; and the thought sometimes crossed his mind that the friendship which had once seemed dead for ever might revive in the days to come, and he would not have to say "good-bye" to the grand old woods, but would like them better because they were Arthur's. For this new promise of happiness following so quickly on the shock of pain had an intoxicating effect on the sober Adam, who had all his life been used to much hardship and moderate hope. Was he really going to have an easy lot after all? It seemed so, for at the beginning of November, Jonathan Burge, finding it impossible to replace Adam, had at last made up his mind to offer him a share in the business, without further condition than that he should continue to give his energies to it and renounce all thought of having a separate business of his own. Son-in-law or no son-in-law, Adam had made himself too necessary to be parted with, and his headwork was so much more important to Burge than his skill in handicraft that his having the management of the woods made little difference in the value of his services; and as to the bargains about the squire's timber, it would be easy to call in a third person. Adam saw here an opening into a broadening path of prosperous work such as he had thought of with ambitious longing ever since he was a lad: he might come to build a bridge, or a town hall, or a factory, for he had always said to himself that Jonathan Burge's building business was like an acorn, which might be the mother of a great tree. So he gave his hand to Burge on that bargain, and went home with his mind full of happy visions, in which (my refined reader will perhaps be shocked when I say it) the image of Hetty hovered, and smiled over plans for seasoning timber at a trifling expense, calculations as to the cheapening of bricks per thousand by water-carriage, and a favourite scheme for the strengthening of roofs and walls with a peculiar form of iron girder. What then? Adam's enthusiasm lay in these things; and our love is inwrought in our enthusiasm as electricity is inwrought in the air, exalting its power by a subtle presence.

Adam would be able to take a separate house now, and provide for his mother in the old one; his prospects would justify his marrying very soon, and if Dinah consented to have Seth, their mother would perhaps be more contented to live apart from Adam. But he told himself that he would not be hasty—he would not try Hetty's feeling for him until it had had time to grow strong and firm. However, tomorrow, after church, he would go to the Hall Farm and tell them the news. Mr. Poyser, he knew, would like it better than a five-pound note, and he should see if Hetty's eyes brightened at it. The months would be short with all he had to fill his mind, and this foolish eagerness which had come over him of late must not hurry him into any premature words. Yet when he got home and told his mother the good news, and ate his supper, while she sat by almost crying for joy and wanting him to eat twice as much as usual because of this good-luck, he could not help preparing her gently for the coming change by talking of the old house being too small for them all to go on living in it always.

Chapter XXXIV
The Betrothal

It was a dry Sunday, and really a pleasant day for the 2d of November. There was no sunshine, but the clouds were high, and the wind was so still that the yellow leaves which fluttered down from the hedgerow elms must have fallen from pure decay. Nevertheless, Mrs. Poyser did not go to church, for she had taken a cold too serious to be neglected; only two winters ago she had been laid up for weeks with a cold; and since his wife did not go to church, Mr. Poyser considered that on the whole it would be as well for him to stay away too and "keep her company." He could perhaps have given no precise form to the reasons that determined this conclusion, but it is well known to all experienced minds that our firmest convictions are often dependent on subtle impressions for which words are quite too coarse a medium. However it was, no one from the Poyser family went to church that afternoon except Hetty and the boys; yet Adam was bold enough to join them after church, and say that he would walk home with them, though all the way through the village he appeared to be chiefly occupied with Marty and Tommy, telling them about the squirrels in Binton Coppice, and promising to take them there some day. But when they came to the fields he said to the boys, "Now, then, which is the stoutest walker? Him as gets to th' home-gate first shall be the first to go with me to Binton Coppice on the donkey. But Tommy must have the start up to the next stile, because he's the smallest."

Adam had never behaved so much like a determined lover before. As soon as the boys had both set off, he looked down at Hetty and said, "Won't you hang on my arm, Hetty?" in a pleading tone, as if he had already asked her and she had refused. Hetty looked up at him smilingly and put her round arm through his in a moment. It was nothing to her, putting her arm through Adam's, but she knew he cared a great deal about having her arm through his, and she wished him to care. Her heart beat no faster, and she looked at the half-bare hedgerows and the ploughed field with the same sense of oppressive dulness as before. But Adam scarcely felt that he was walking. He thought Hetty must know that he was pressing her arm a little—a very little. Words rushed to his lips that he dared not utter—that he had made up his mind not to utter yet—and so he was silent for the length of that field. The calm patience with which he had once waited for Hetty's love, content only with her presence and the thought of the future, had forsaken him since that terrible shock nearly three months ago. The agitations of jealousy had given a new restlessness to his passion—had made fear and uncertainty too hard almost to bear. But though he might not speak to Hetty of his love, he would tell her about his new prospects and see if she would be pleased. So when he was enough master of himself to talk, he said, "I'm going to tell your uncle some news that'll surprise him, Hetty; and I think he'll be glad to hear it too."

"What's that?" Hetty said indifferently.

"Why, Mr. Burge has offered me a share in his business, and I'm going to take it."

There was a change in Hetty's face, certainly not produced by any agreeable impression from this news. In fact she felt a momentary annoyance and alarm, for she had so often heard it hinted by her uncle that Adam might have Mary Burge and a share in the business any day, if he liked, that she associated the two objects now, and the thought immediately occurred that perhaps Adam had given her up because of what had happened lately, and had turned towards Mary Burge. With that thought, and before she had time to remember any reasons why it could not be true, came a new sense of forsakenness and disappointment. The one thing—the one person—her mind had rested on in its dull weariness, had slipped away from her, and peevish misery filled her eyes with tears. She was looking on the ground, but Adam saw her face, saw the tears, and before he had finished saying, "Hetty, dear Hetty, what are you crying for?" his eager rapid thought had flown through all the causes conceivable to him, and had at last alighted on half the true one. Hetty thought he was going to marry Mary Burge—she didn't like him to marry—perhaps she didn't like him to marry any one but herself? All caution was swept away—all reason for it was gone, and Adam could feel nothing but trembling joy. He leaned towards her and took her hand, as he said:

"I could afford to be married now, Hetty—I could make a wife comfortable; but I shall never want to be married if you won't have me."

Hetty looked up at him and smiled through her tears, as she had done to Arthur that first evening in the wood, when she had thought he was not coming, and yet he came. It was a feebler relief, a feebler triumph she felt now, but the great dark eyes and the sweet lips were as beautiful as ever, perhaps more beautiful, for there was a more luxuriant womanliness about Hetty of late. Adam could hardly believe in the happiness of that moment. His right hand held her left, and he pressed her arm close against his heart as he leaned down towards her.

"Do you really love me, Hetty? Will you be my own wife, to love and take care of as long as I live?"

Hetty did not speak, but Adam's face was very close to hers, and she put up her round cheek against his, like a kitten. She wanted to be caressed—she wanted to feel as if Arthur were with her again.

Adam cared for no words after that, and they hardly spoke through the rest of the walk. He only said, "I may tell your uncle and aunt, mayn't I, Hetty?" and she said, "Yes."

The red fire-light on the hearth at the Hall Farm shone on joyful faces that evening, when Hetty was gone upstairs and Adam took the opportunity of telling Mr. and Mrs. Poyser and the grandfather that he saw his way to maintaining a wife now, and that Hetty had consented to have him.

"I hope you have no objections against me for her husband," said Adam; "I'm a poor man as yet, but she shall want nothing as I can work for."

"Objections?" said Mr. Poyser, while the grandfather leaned forward and brought out his long "Nay, nay." "What objections can we ha' to you, lad? Never mind your being poorish as yet; there's money in your head-piece as there's money i' the sown field, but it must ha' time. You'n got enough to begin on, and we can do a deal tow'rt the bit o' furniture you'll want. Thee'st got feathers and linen to spare—plenty, eh?"

This question was of course addressed to Mrs. Poyser, who was wrapped up in a warm shawl and was too hoarse to speak with her usual facility. At first she only nodded emphatically, but she was presently unable to resist the temptation to be more explicit.

"It ud be a poor tale if I hadna feathers and linen," she said, hoarsely, "when I never sell a fowl but what's plucked, and the wheel's a-going every day o' the week."

"Come, my wench," said Mr. Poyser, when Hetty came down, "come and kiss us, and let us wish you luck."

Hetty went very quietly and kissed the big good-natured man.

"There!" he said, patting her on the back, "go and kiss your aunt and your grandfather. I'm as wishful t' have you settled well as if you was my own daughter; and so's your aunt, I'll be bound, for she's done by you this seven 'ear, Hetty, as if you'd been her own. Come, come, now," he went on, becoming jocose, as soon as Hetty had kissed her aunt and the old man, "Adam wants a kiss too, I'll warrant, and he's a right to one now."

Hetty turned away, smiling, towards her empty chair.

"Come, Adam, then, take one," persisted Mr. Poyser, "else y' arena half a man."

Adam got up, blushing like a small maiden—great strong fellow as he was—and, putting his arm round Hetty stooped down and gently kissed her lips.

It was a pretty scene in the red fire-light; for there were no candles—why should there be, when the fire was so bright and was reflected from all the pewter and the polished oak? No one wanted to work on a Sunday evening. Even Hetty felt something like contentment in the midst of all this love. Adam's attachment to her, Adam's caress, stirred no passion in her, were no longer enough to satisfy her vanity, but they were the best her life offered her now—they promised her some change.

There was a great deal of discussion before Adam went away, about the possibility of his finding a house that would do for him to settle in. No house was empty except the one next to Will Maskery's in the village, and that was too small for Adam now. Mr. Poyser insisted that the best plan would be for Seth and his mother to move and leave Adam in the old home, which might be enlarged after a while, for there was plenty of space in the woodyard and garden; but Adam objected to turning his mother out.

"Well, well," said Mr. Poyser at last, "we needna fix everything to-night. We must take time to consider. You canna think o' getting married afore Easter. I'm not for long courtships, but there must be a bit o' time to make things comfortable."

"Aye, to be sure," said Mrs. Poyser, in a hoarse whisper; "Christian folks can't be married like cuckoos, I reckon."

"I'm a bit daunted, though," said Mr. Poyser, "when I think as we may have notice to quit, and belike be forced to take a farm twenty mile off."

"Eh," said the old man, staring at the floor and lifting his hands up and down, while his arms rested on the elbows of his chair, "it's a poor tale if I mun leave th' ould spot an be buried in a strange parish. An' you'll happen ha' double rates to pay," he added, looking up at his son.

"Well, thee mustna fret beforehand, father," said Martin the younger. "Happen the captain 'ull come home and make our peace wi' th' old squire. I build upo' that, for I know the captain 'll see folks righted if he can."

Chapter XXXV
The Hidden Dread

It was a busy time for Adam—the time between the beginning of November and the beginning of February, and he could see little of Hetty, except on Sundays. But a happy time, nevertheless, for it was taking him nearer and nearer to March, when they were to be married, and all the little preparations for their new housekeeping marked the progress towards the longed-for day. Two new rooms had been "run up" to the old house, for his mother and Seth were to live with them after all. Lisbeth had cried so piteously at the thought of leaving Adam that he had gone to Hetty and asked her if, for the love of him, she would put up with his mother's ways and consent to live with her. To his great delight, Hetty said, "Yes; I'd as soon she lived with us as not." Hetty's mind was oppressed at that moment with a worse difficulty than poor Lisbeth's ways; she could not care about them. So Adam was consoled for the disappointment he had felt when Seth had come back from his visit to Snowfield and said "it was no use—Dinah's heart wasna turned towards marrying." For when he told his mother that Hetty was willing they should all live together and there was no more need of them to think of parting, she said, in a more contented tone than he had heard her speak in since it had been settled that he was to be married, "Eh, my lad, I'll be as still as th' ould tabby, an' ne'er want to do aught but th' offal work, as *she* wonna like t' do. An' then we needna part the platters an' things, as ha' stood on the shelf together sin' afore thee wast born."

There was only one cloud that now and then came across Adam's sunshine: Hetty seemed unhappy sometimes. But to all his anxious, tender questions, she replied with an assurance that she was quite contented and wished nothing different; and the next time he saw her she was more lively than usual. It might be that she was a little overdone with work and anxiety now, for soon after Christmas Mrs. Poyser had taken another cold, which had brought on inflammation, and this illness had confined her to her room all through January. Hetty had to manage everything downstairs, and half-supply Molly's place too, while that good damsel waited on her mistress, and she seemed to throw herself so entirely into her new functions, working with a grave steadiness which was new in her, that Mr. Poyser often told Adam she was wanting to show him what a good housekeeper he would have; but he "doubted the lass was o'erdoing it—she must have a bit o' rest when her aunt could come downstairs."

This desirable event of Mrs. Poyser's coming downstairs happened in the early part of February, when some mild weather thawed the last patch of snow on the Binton Hills. On one of these days, soon after her aunt came down, Hetty went to Treddleston to buy some of the wedding things which were wanting, and which Mrs. Poyser had scolded her for neglecting, observing that she supposed "it was because they were not for th' outside, else she'd ha' bought 'em fast enough."

It was about ten o'clock when Hetty set off, and the slight hoar-frost that had whitened the hedges in the early morning had disappeared as the sun mounted the cloudless sky. Bright February days have a stronger charm of hope about them than any other days in the year. One likes to pause in the mild rays of the sun, and look over the gates at the patient plough-horses turning at the end of the furrow, and think that the beautiful year is all before one. The birds seem to feel just the same: their notes are as clear as the clear air. There are no leaves on the trees and hedgerows, but how green all the grassy fields are! And the dark purplish brown of the ploughed earth and of the bare branches is beautiful too. What a glad world this looks like, as one drives or rides along the valleys and over the hills! I have often thought so when, in foreign countries, where the fields and woods have looked to me like our English Loamshire—the rich land tilled with just as much care, the woods rolling down the gentle slopes to the green meadows—I have come on something by the roadside which has reminded me that I am not in Loamshire: an image of a great agony—the agony of the Cross. It has stood perhaps by the clustering apple-blossoms, or in the broad sunshine by the cornfield, or at a turning by the wood where a clear brook was gurgling below; and surely, if there came a traveller to this world who knew nothing of the story of man's life upon it, this image of agony would seem to him strangely out of place in the midst of this joyous nature. He would not know that hidden behind the apple-blossoms, or among the golden corn, or under the shrouding boughs of the wood, there might be a human heart beating heavily with anguish—perhaps a young blooming girl, not knowing where to turn for refuge from swift-advancing shame, understanding no more of this life of ours than a foolish lost lamb wandering farther and farther in the nightfall on the lonely heath, yet tasting the bitterest of life's bitterness.

Such things are sometimes hidden among the sunny fields and behind the blossoming orchards; and the sound of the gurgling brook, if you came close to one spot behind a small bush, would be mingled for your ear with a despairing human sob. No wonder man's religion has much sorrow in it: no wonder he needs a suffering God.

Hetty, in her red cloak and warm bonnet, with her basket in her hand, is turning towards a gate by the side of the Treddleston road, but not that she may have a more lingering enjoyment of the sunshine and think with hope of the long unfolding year. She hardly knows that the sun is shining; and for weeks, now, when she has hoped at all, it has been for something at which she herself trembles and shudders. She only wants to be out of the high-road, that she may walk slowly and not care how her face looks, as she dwells on wretched thoughts; and through this gate she can get into a field-path behind the wide thick hedgerows. Her great dark eyes wander blankly over the fields like the eyes of one who is desolate, homeless, unloved, not the promised bride of a brave tender man. But there are no tears in them: her tears were all wept away in the weary night, before she went to sleep. At the next stile the pathway branches off: there are two roads before her—one along by the hedgerow, which will by and by lead her into the road again, the other across the fields, which will take her much farther out of the way into the Scantlands, low shrouded pastures where she will see nobody. She chooses this and begins to walk a little faster, as if she had suddenly thought of an object towards which it was worth while to hasten. Soon she is in the Scantlands, where the grassy land slopes gradually downwards, and she leaves the level ground to follow the slope. Farther on there is a clump of trees on the low ground, and she is making her way towards it. No, it is not a clump of trees, but a dark shrouded pool, so full with the wintry rains that the under boughs of the elder-bushes lie low beneath the water. She sits down on the grassy bank, against the stooping stem of the great oak that hangs over the dark pool. She has thought of this pool often in the nights of the month that has just gone by, and now at last she is come to see it. She clasps her hands round her knees, and leans forward, and looks earnestly at it, as if trying to guess what sort of bed it would make for her young round limbs.

No, she has not courage to jump into that cold watery bed, and if she had, they might find her—they might find out why she had drowned herself. There is but one thing left to her: she must go away, go where they can't find her.

After the first on-coming of her great dread, some weeks after her betrothal to Adam, she had waited and waited, in the blind vague hope that something would happen to set her free from her terror; but she could wait no longer. All the force of her nature had been concentrated on the one effort of concealment, and she had shrunk with irresistible dread from every course that could tend towards a betrayal of her miserable secret. Whenever the thought of writing to Arthur had occurred to her, she had rejected it. He could do nothing for her that would shelter her from discovery and scorn among the relatives and neighbours who once more made all her world, now her airy dream had vanished. Her imagination no longer saw happiness with Arthur, for he could do nothing that would satisfy or soothe her pride. No, something else would happen—something *must* happen—to set her free from this dread. In young, childish, ignorant souls there is constantly this blind trust in some unshapen chance: it is as hard to a boy or girl to believe that a great wretchedness will actually befall them as to believe that they will die.

But now necessity was pressing hard upon her—now the time of her marriage was close at hand—she could no longer rest in this blind trust. She must run away; she must hide herself where no familiar eyes could detect her; and then the terror of wandering out into the world, of which she knew nothing, made the possibility of going to Arthur a thought which brought some comfort with it. She felt so helpless now, so unable to fashion the future for herself, that the prospect of throwing herself on him had a relief in it which was stronger than her pride. As she sat by the pool and shuddered at the dark cold water, the hope that he would receive her tenderly—that he would care for her and think for her—was like a sense of lulling warmth, that made her for the moment indifferent to everything else; and she began now to think of nothing but the scheme by which she should get away.

She had had a letter from Dinah lately, full of kind words about the coming marriage, which she had heard of from Seth; and when Hetty had read this letter aloud to her uncle, he had said, "I wish Dinah 'ud come again now, for she'd be a comfort to your aunt when you're gone. What do you think, my wench, o' going to see her as soon as you can be spared and persuading her to come back wi' you? You might happen persuade her wi' telling her as her aunt wants her, for all she writes o' not being able to come." Hetty had not liked the thought of going to Snowfield, and felt no longing to see Dinah, so she only said, "It's so far off, Uncle." But now she thought this proposed visit would serve as a pretext for going away. She would tell her aunt when she got home again that she should like the change of going to Snowfield for a week or ten days. And then, when she got to Stoniton, where nobody knew her, she would ask for the coach that would take her on the way to Windsor. Arthur was at Windsor, and she would go to him.

As soon as Hetty had determined on this scheme, she rose from the grassy bank of the pool, took up her basket, and went on her way to Treddleston, for she must buy the wedding things she had come out for, though she would never want them. She must be careful not to raise any suspicion that she was going to run away.

Mrs. Poyser was quite agreeably surprised that Hetty wished to go and see Dinah and try to bring her back to stay over the wedding. The sooner she went the better, since the weather was pleasant now; and Adam, when he came in the evening, said, if Hetty could set off to-morrow, he would make time to go with her to Treddleston and see her safe into the Stoniton coach.

"I wish I could go with you and take care of you, Hetty," he said, the next morning, leaning in at the coach door; "but you won't stay much beyond a week—the time 'ull seem long."

He was looking at her fondly, and his strong hand held hers in its grasp. Hetty felt a sense of protection in his presence—she was used to it now: if she could have had the past undone and known no other love than her quiet liking for Adam! The tears rose as she gave him the last look.

"God bless her for loving me," said Adam, as he went on his way to work again, with Gyp at his heels.

But Hetty's tears were not for Adam—not for the anguish that would come upon him when he found she was gone from him for ever. They were for the misery of her own lot, which took her away from this brave tender man who offered up his whole life to her, and threw her, a poor helpless suppliant, on the man who would think it a misfortune that she was obliged to cling to him.

At three o'clock that day, when Hetty was on the coach that was to take her, they said, to Leicester—part of the long, long way to Windsor—she felt dimly that she might be travelling all this weary journey towards the beginning of new misery.

Yet Arthur was at Windsor; he would surely not be angry with her. If he did not mind about her as he used to do, he had promised to be good to her.

BOOK FIFTH

Chapter XXXVI
The Journey of Hope

A long, lonely journey, with sadness in the heart; away from the familiar to the strange: that is a hard and dreary thing even to the rich, the strong, the instructed; a hard thing, even when we are called by duty, not urged by dread.

What was it then to Hetty? With her poor narrow thoughts, no longer melting into vague hopes, but pressed upon by the chill of definite fear, repeating again and again the same small round of memories—shaping again and again the same childish, doubtful images of what was to come—seeing nothing in this wide world but the little history of her own pleasures and pains; with so little money in her pocket, and the way so long and difficult. Unless she could afford always to go in the coaches—and she felt sure she could not, for the journey to Stoniton was more expensive than she had expected—it was plain that she must trust to carriers' carts or slow waggons; and what a time it would be before she could get to the end of her journey! The burly old coachman from Oakbourne, seeing such a pretty young woman among the outside passengers, had invited her to come and sit beside him; and feeling that it became him as a man and a coachman to open the dialogue with a joke, he applied himself as soon as they were off the stones to the elaboration of one suitable in all respects. After many cuts with his whip and glances at Hetty out of the corner of his eye, he lifted his lips above the edge of his wrapper and said, "He's pretty nigh six foot, I'll be bound, isna he, now?"

"Who?" said Hetty, rather startled.

"Why, the sweetheart as you've left behind, or else him as you're goin' arter—which is it?"

Hetty felt her face flushing and then turning pale. She thought this coachman must know something about her. He must know Adam, and might tell him where she was gone, for it is difficult to country people to believe that those who make a figure in their own parish are not known everywhere else, and it was equally difficult to Hetty to understand that chance words could happen to apply closely to her circumstances. She was too frightened to speak.

"Hegh, hegh!" said the coachman, seeing that his joke was not so gratifying as he had expected, "you munna take it too ser'ous; if he's behaved ill, get another. Such a pretty lass as you can get a sweetheart any day."

Hetty's fear was allayed by and by, when she found that the coachman made no further allusion to her personal concerns; but it still had the effect of preventing her from asking him what were the places on the road to Windsor. She told him she was only going a little way out of Stoniton, and when she got down at the inn where the coach stopped, she hastened away with her basket to another part of the town. When she had formed her plan of going to Windsor, she had not foreseen any difficulties except that of getting away, and after she had overcome this by proposing the visit to Dinah, her thoughts flew to the meeting with Arthur and the question how he would behave to her—not resting on any probable incidents of the journey. She was too entirely ignorant of traveling to imagine any of its details, and with all her store of money—her three guineas—in her pocket, she thought herself amply provided. It was not until she found how much it cost her to get to Stoniton that she began to be alarmed about the journey, and then, for the first time, she felt her ignorance as to the places that must be passed on her way. Oppressed with this new alarm, she walked along the grim Stoniton streets, and at last turned into a shabby little inn, where she hoped to get a cheap lodging for the night. Here she asked the landlord if he could tell her what places she must go to, to get to Windsor.

"Well, I can't rightly say. Windsor must be pretty nigh London, for it's where the king lives," was the answer. "Anyhow, you'd best go t' Ashby next—that's south'ard. But there's as many places from here to London as there's houses in Stoniton, by what I can make out. I've never been no traveller myself. But how comes a lone young woman like you to be thinking o' taking such a journey as that?"

"I'm going to my brother—he's a soldier at Windsor," said Hetty, frightened at the landlord's questioning look. "I can't afford to go by the coach; do you think there's a cart goes toward Ashby in the morning?"

"Yes, there may be carts if anybody knowed where they started from; but you might run over the town before you found out. You'd best set off and walk, and trust to summat overtaking you."

Every word sank like lead on Hetty's spirits; she saw the journey stretch bit by bit before her now. Even to get to Ashby seemed a hard thing: it might take the day, for what she knew, and that was nothing to the rest of the journey. But it must be done—she must get to Arthur. Oh, how she yearned to be again with somebody who would care for her! She who had never got up in the morning without the certainty of seeing familiar faces, people on whom she had an acknowledged claim; whose farthest journey had been to Rosseter on the pillion with her uncle; whose thoughts had always been taking holiday in dreams of pleasure, because all the business of her life was managed for her—this kittenlike Hetty, who till a few months ago had never felt any other grief than that of envying Mary Burge a new ribbon, or being girded at by her aunt for neglecting Totty, must now make her toilsome way in loneliness, her peaceful home left behind for ever, and nothing but a tremulous hope of distant refuge before her. Now for the first time, as she lay down to-night in the strange hard bed, she felt that her home had been a happy one, that her uncle had been very good to her, that her quiet lot at Hayslope among the things and people she knew, with her little pride in her one best gown and bonnet, and nothing to hide from any one, was what she would like to wake up to as a reality, and find that all the feverish life she had known besides was a short nightmare. She thought of all she had left behind with yearning regret for her own sake. Her own misery filled her heart—there was no room in it for other people's sorrow. And yet, before the cruel letter, Arthur had been so tender and loving. The memory of that had still a charm for her, though it was no more than a soothing draught that just made pain bearable. For Hetty could conceive no other existence for herself in future than a hidden one, and a hidden life, even with love, would have had no delights for her; still less a life mingled with shame. She knew no romances, and had only a feeble share in the feelings which are the source of romance, so that well-read ladies may find it difficult to understand her state of mind. She was too ignorant of everything beyond the simple notions and habits in which she had been brought up to have any more definite idea of her probable future than that Arthur would take care of her somehow, and shelter her from anger and scorn. He would not marry her and make her a lady; and apart from that she could think of nothing he could give towards which she looked with longing and ambition.

The next morning she rose early, and taking only some milk and bread for her breakfast, set out to walk on the road towards Ashby, under a leaden-coloured sky, with a narrowing streak of yellow, like a departing hope, on the edge of the horizon. Now in her faintness of heart at the length and difficulty of her journey, she was most of all afraid of spending her money, and becoming so destitute that she would have to ask people's charity; for Hetty had the pride not only of a proud nature but of a proud class—the class that pays the most poor-rates, and most shudders at the idea of profiting by a poor-rate. It had not yet occurred to her that she might get money for her locket and earrings which she carried with her, and she applied all her small arithmetic and knowledge of prices to calculating how many meals and how many rides were contained in her two guineas, and the odd shillings, which had a melancholy look, as if they were the pale ashes of the other bright-flaming coin.

For the first few miles out of Stoniton, she walked on bravely, always fixing on some tree or gate or projecting bush at the most distant visible point in the road as a goal, and feeling a faint joy when she had reached it. But when she came to the fourth milestone, the first she had happened to notice among the long grass by the roadside, and read that she was still only four miles beyond Stoniton, her courage sank. She had come only this little way, and yet felt tired, and almost hungry again in the keen morning air; for though Hetty was accustomed to much movement and exertion indoors, she was not used to long walks which produced quite a different sort of fatigue from that of household activity. As she was looking at the milestone she felt some drops falling on her face—it was beginning to rain. Here was a new trouble which had not entered into her sad thoughts before, and quite weighed down by this sudden addition to her burden, she sat down on the step of a stile and began to sob hysterically. The beginning of hardship is like the first taste of bitter food—it seems for a moment unbearable; yet, if there is nothing else to satisfy our hunger, we take another bite and find it possible to go on. When Hetty recovered from her burst of weeping, she rallied her fainting courage: it was raining, and she must try to get on to a village where she might find rest and shelter. Presently, as she walked on wearily, she heard the rumbling of heavy wheels behind her; a covered waggon was coming, creeping slowly along with a slouching driver cracking his whip beside the horses. She waited for it, thinking that if the waggoner were not a very sour-looking man, she would ask him to take her up. As the waggon approached her, the driver had fallen behind, but there was something in the front of the big vehicle which encouraged her. At any previous moment in her life she would not have noticed it, but now, the new susceptibility that suffering had awakened in her caused this object to impress her strongly. It was only a small white-and-liver-coloured spaniel which sat on the front ledge of the waggon, with large timid eyes, and an incessant trembling in the body, such as you may have seen in some of these small creatures. Hetty cared little for animals, as you know, but at this moment she felt as if the helpless timid creature had some fellowship with her, and without being quite aware of the reason, she was less doubtful about speaking to the driver, who now came forward—a large ruddy man, with a sack over his shoulders, by way of scarf or mantle.

"Could you take me up in your waggon, if you're going towards Ashby?" said Hetty. "I'll pay you for it."

"Aw," said the big fellow, with that slowly dawning smile which belongs to heavy faces, "I can take y' up fawst enough wi'out bein' paid for't if you dooant mind lyin' a bit closish a-top o' the wool-packs. Where do you coom from? And what do you want at Ashby?"

"I come from Stoniton. I'm going a long way—to Windsor."

"What! Arter some service, or what?"

"Going to my brother—he's a soldier there."

"Well, I'm going no furder nor Leicester—and fur enough too—but I'll take you, if you dooant mind being a bit long on the road. Th' hosses wooant feel *your* weight no more nor they feel the little doog there, as I puck up on the road a fortni't agoo. He war lost, I b'lieve, an's been all of a tremble iver sin'. Come, gi' us your basket an' come behind and let me put y' in."

To lie on the wool-packs, with a cranny left between the curtains of the awning to let in the air, was luxury to Hetty now, and she half-slept away the hours till the driver came to ask her if she wanted to get down and have "some victual"; he himself was going to eat his dinner at this "public." Late at night they reached Leicester, and so this second day of Hetty's journey was past. She had spent no money except what she had paid for her food, but she felt that this slow journeying would be intolerable for her another day, and in the morning she found her way to a coach-office to ask about the road to Windsor, and see if it would cost her too much to go part of the distance by coach again. Yes! The distance was too great—the coaches were too dear—she must give them up; but the elderly clerk at the office, touched by her pretty anxious face, wrote down for her the names of the chief places she must pass through. This was the only comfort she got in Leicester, for the men stared at her as she went along the street, and for the first time in her life Hetty wished no one would look at her. She set out walking again; but this day she was fortunate, for she was soon overtaken by a carrier's cart which carried her to Hinckley, and by the help of a return chaise, with a drunken postilion—who frightened her by driving like Jehu the son of Nimshi, and shouting hilarious remarks at her, twisting himself backwards on his saddle—she was before night in the heart of woody Warwickshire: but still almost a hundred miles from Windsor, they told her. Oh what a large world it was, and what hard work for her to find her way in it! She went by mistake to Stratford-on-Avon, finding Stratford set down in her list of places, and then she was told she had come a long way out of the right road. It was not till the fifth day that she got to Stony Stratford. That seems but a slight journey as you look at the map, or remember your own pleasant travels to and from the meadowy banks of the Avon. But how wearily long it was to Hetty! It seemed to her as if this country of flat fields, and hedgerows, and dotted houses, and villages, and market-towns—all so much alike to her indifferent eyes—must have no end, and she must go on wandering among them for ever, waiting tired at toll-gates for some cart to come, and then finding the cart went only a little way—a very little way—to the miller's a mile off perhaps; and she hated going into the public houses, where she must go to get food and ask questions, because there were always men lounging there, who stared at her and joked her rudely. Her body was very weary too with these days of new fatigue and anxiety; they had made her look more pale and worn than all the time of hidden dread she had gone through at home. When at last she reached Stony Stratford, her impatience and weariness had become too strong for her economical caution; she determined to take the coach for the rest of the way, though it should cost her all her remaining money.

She would need nothing at Windsor but to find Arthur. When she had paid the fare for the last coach, she had only a shilling; and as she got down at the sign of the Green Man in Windsor at twelve o'clock in the middle of the seventh day, hungry and faint, the coachman came up, and begged her to "remember him." She put her hand in her pocket and took out the shilling, but the tears came with the sense of exhaustion and the thought that she was giving away her last means of getting food, which she really required before she could go in search of Arthur. As she held out the shilling, she lifted up her dark tear-filled eyes to the coachman's face and said, "Can you give me back sixpence?"

"No, no," he said, gruffly, "never mind—put the shilling up again."

The landlord of the Green Man had stood near enough to witness this scene, and he was a man whose abundant feeding served to keep his good nature, as well as his person, in high condition. And that lovely tearful face of Hetty's would have found out the sensitive fibre in most men.

"Come, young woman, come in," he said, "and have a drop o' something; you're pretty well knocked up, I can see that."

He took her into the bar and said to his wife, "Here, missis, take this young woman into the parlour; she's a little overcome"—for Hetty's tears were falling fast. They were merely hysterical tears: she thought she had no reason for weeping now, and was vexed that she was too weak and tired to help it. She was at Windsor at last, not far from Arthur.

She looked with eager, hungry eyes at the bread and meat and beer that the landlady brought her, and for some minutes she forgot everything else in the delicious sensations of satisfying hunger and recovering from exhaustion. The landlady sat opposite to her as she ate, and looked at her earnestly. No wonder: Hetty had thrown off her bonnet, and her curls had fallen down. Her face was all the more touching in its youth and beauty because of its weary look, and the good woman's eyes presently wandered to her figure, which in her hurried dressing on her journey she had taken no pains to conceal; moreover, the stranger's eye detects what the familiar unsuspecting eye leaves unnoticed.

"Why, you're not very fit for travelling," she said, glancing while she spoke at Hetty's ringless hand. "Have you come far?"

"Yes," said Hetty, roused by this question to exert more self-command, and feeling the better for the food she had taken. "I've come a good long way, and it's very tiring. But I'm better now. Could you tell me which way to go to this place?" Here Hetty took from her pocket a bit of paper: it was the end of Arthur's letter on which he had written his address.

While she was speaking, the landlord had come in and had begun to look at her as earnestly as his wife had done. He took up the piece of paper which Hetty handed across the table, and read the address.

"Why, what do you want at this house?" he said. It is in the nature of innkeepers and all men who have no pressing business of their own to ask as many questions as possible before giving any information.

"I want to see a gentleman as is there," said Hetty.

"But there's no gentleman there," returned the landlord. "It's shut up—been shut up this fortnight. What gentleman is it you want? Perhaps I can let you know where to find him."

"It's Captain Donnithorne," said Hetty tremulously, her heart beginning to beat painfully at this disappointment of her hope that she should find Arthur at once.

"Captain Donnithorne? Stop a bit," said the landlord, slowly. "Was he in the Loamshire Militia? A tall young officer with a fairish skin and reddish whiskers—and had a servant by the name o' Pym?"

"Oh yes," said Hetty; "you know him—where is he?"

"A fine sight o' miles away from here. The Loamshire Militia's gone to Ireland; it's been gone this fortnight."

"Look there! She's fainting," said the landlady, hastening to support Hetty, who had lost her miserable consciousness and looked like a beautiful corpse. They carried her to the sofa and loosened her dress.

"Here's a bad business, I suspect," said the landlord, as he brought in some water.

"Ah, it's plain enough what sort of business it is," said the wife. "She's not a common flaunting dratchell, I can see that. She looks like a respectable country girl, and she comes from a good way off, to judge by her tongue. She talks something like that ostler we had that come from the north. He was as honest a fellow as we ever had about the house—they're all honest folks in the north."

"I never saw a prettier young woman in my life," said the husband. "She's like a pictur in a shop-winder. It goes to one's 'eart to look at her."

"It 'ud have been a good deal better for her if she'd been uglier and had more conduct," said the landlady, who on any charitable construction must have been supposed to have more "conduct" than beauty. "But she's coming to again. Fetch a drop more water."

Chapter XXXVII
The Journey in Despair

Hetty was too ill through the rest of that day for any questions to be addressed to her—too ill even to think with any distinctness of the evils that were to come. She only felt that all her hope was crushed, and that instead of having found a refuge she had only reached the borders of a new wilderness where no goal lay before her. The sensations of bodily sickness, in a comfortable bed, and with the tendance of the good-natured landlady, made a sort of respite for her; such a respite as there is in the faint weariness which obliges a man to throw himself on the sand instead of toiling onward under the scorching sun.

But when sleep and rest had brought back the strength necessary for the keenness of mental suffering—when she lay the next morning looking at the growing light which was like a cruel task-master returning to urge from her a fresh round of hated hopeless labour—she began to think what course she must take, to remember that all her money was gone, to look at the prospect of further wandering among strangers with the new clearness shed on it by the experience of her journey to Windsor. But which way could she turn? It was impossible for her to enter into any service, even if she could obtain it. There was nothing but immediate beggary before her. She thought of a young woman who had been found against the church wall at Hayslope one Sunday, nearly dead with cold and hunger—a tiny infant in her arms. The woman was rescued and taken to the parish. "The parish!" You can perhaps hardly understand the effect of that word on a mind like Hetty's, brought up among people who were somewhat hard in their feelings even towards poverty, who lived among the fields, and had little pity for want and rags as a cruel inevitable fate such as they sometimes seem in cities, but held them a mark of idleness and vice—and it was idleness and vice that brought burdens on the parish. To Hetty the "parish" was next to the prison in obloquy, and to ask anything of strangers—to beg—lay in the same far-off hideous region of intolerable shame that Hetty had all her life thought it impossible she could ever come near. But now the remembrance of that wretched woman whom she had seen herself, on her way from church, being carried into Joshua Rann's, came back upon her with the new terrible sense that there was very little now to divide *her* from the same lot. And the dread of bodily hardship mingled with the dread of shame; for Hetty had the luxurious nature of a round soft-coated pet animal.

How she yearned to be back in her safe home again, cherished and cared for as she had always been! Her aunt's scolding about trifles would have been music to her ears now; she longed for it; she used to hear it in a time when she had only trifles to hide. Could she be the same Hetty that used to make up the butter in the dairy with the Guelder roses peeping in at the window—she, a runaway whom her friends would not open their doors to again, lying in this strange bed, with the knowledge that she had no money to pay for what she received, and must offer those strangers some of the clothes in her basket? It was then she thought of her locket and ear-rings, and seeing her pocket lie near, she reached it and spread the contents on the bed before her. There were the locket and ear-rings in the little velvet-lined boxes, and with them there was a beautiful silver thimble which Adam had bought her, the words "Remember me" making the ornament of the border; a steel purse, with her one shilling in it; and a small red-leather case, fastening with a strap. Those beautiful little ear-rings, with their delicate pearls and garnet, that she had tried in her ears with such longing in the bright sunshine on the 30th of July! She had no longing to put them in her ears now: her head with its dark rings of hair lay back languidly on the pillow, and the sadness that rested about her brow and eyes was something too hard for regretful memory. Yet she put her hands up to her ears: it was because there were some thin gold rings in them, which were also worth a little money. Yes, she could surely get some money for her ornaments: those Arthur had given her must have cost a great deal of money. The landlord and landlady had been good to her; perhaps they would help her to get the money for these things.

But this money would not keep her long. What should she do when it was gone? Where should she go? The horrible thought of want and beggary drove her once to think she would go back to her uncle and aunt and ask them to forgive her and have pity on her. But she shrank from that idea again, as she might have shrunk from scorching metal. She could never endure that shame before her uncle and aunt, before Mary Burge, and the servants at the Chase, and the people at Broxton, and everybody who knew her. They should never know what had happened to her. What *could* she do? She would go away from Windsor—travel again as she had done the last week, and get among the flat green fields with the high hedges round them, where nobody could see her or know her; and there, perhaps, when there was nothing else she could do, she should get courage to drown herself in some pond like that in the Scantlands. Yes, she would get away from Windsor as soon as possible: she didn't like these people at the inn to know about her, to know that she had come to look for Captain Donnithorne. She must think of some reason to tell them why she had asked for him.

With this thought she began to put the things back into her pocket, meaning to get up and dress before the landlady came to her. She had her hand on the red-leather case, when it occurred to her that there might be something in this case which she had forgotten—something worth selling; for without knowing what she should do with her life, she craved the means of living as long as possible; and when we desire eagerly to find something, we are apt to search for it in hopeless places. No, there was nothing but common needles and pins, and dried tulip-petals between the paper leaves where she had written down her little money-accounts. But on one of these leaves there was a name, which, often as she had seen it before, now flashed on Hetty's mind like a newly discovered message. The name was—*Dinah Morris, Snowfield*. There was a text above it, written, as well as the name, by Dinah's own hand with a little pencil, one evening that they were sitting together and Hetty happened to have the red case lying open before her. Hetty did not read the text now: she was only arrested by the name. Now, for the first time, she remembered without indifference the affectionate kindness Dinah had shown her, and those words of Dinah in the bed-chamber—that Hetty must think of her as a friend in trouble. Suppose she were to go to Dinah, and ask her to help her? Dinah did not think about things as other people did. She was a mystery to Hetty, but Hetty knew she was always kind. She couldn't imagine Dinah's face turning away from her in dark reproof or scorn, Dinah's voice willingly speaking ill of her, or rejoicing in her misery as a punishment. Dinah did not seem to belong to that world of Hetty's, whose glance she dreaded like scorching fire. But even to her Hetty shrank from beseeching and confession. She could not prevail on herself to say, "I will go to Dinah": she only thought of that as a possible alternative, if she had not courage for death.

The good landlady was amazed when she saw Hetty come downstairs soon after herself, neatly dressed, and looking resolutely self-possessed. Hetty told her she was quite well this morning. She had only been very tired and overcome with her journey, for she had come a long way to ask about her brother, who had run away, and they thought he was gone for a soldier, and Captain Donnithorne might know, for he had been very kind to her brother once. It was a lame story, and the landlady looked doubtfully at Hetty as she told it; but there was a resolute air of self-reliance about her this morning, so different from the helpless prostration of yesterday, that the landlady hardly knew how to make a remark that might seem like prying into other people's affairs. She only invited her to sit down to breakfast with them, and in the course of it Hetty brought out her ear-rings and locket, and asked the landlord if he could help her to get money for them. Her journey, she said, had cost her much more than she expected, and now she had no money to get back to her friends, which she wanted to do at once.

It was not the first time the landlady had seen the ornaments, for she had examined the contents of Hetty's pocket yesterday, and she and her husband had discussed the fact of a country girl having these beautiful things, with a stronger conviction than ever that Hetty had been miserably deluded by the fine young officer.

"Well," said the landlord, when Hetty had spread the precious trifles before him, "we might take 'em to the jeweller's shop, for there's one not far off; but Lord bless you, they wouldn't give you a quarter o' what the things are worth. And you wouldn't like to part with 'em?" he added, looking at her inquiringly.

"Oh, I don't mind," said Hetty, hastily, "so as I can get money to go back."

"And they might think the things were stolen, as you wanted to sell 'em," he went on, "for it isn't usual for a young woman like you to have fine jew'llery like that."

The blood rushed to Hetty's face with anger. "I belong to respectable folks," she said; "I'm not a thief."

"No, that you aren't, I'll be bound," said the landlady; "and you'd no call to say that," looking indignantly at her husband. "The things were gev to her: that's plain enough to be seen."

"I didn't mean as I thought so," said the husband, apologetically, "but I said it was what the jeweller might think, and so he wouldn't be offering much money for 'em."

"Well," said the wife, "suppose you were to advance some money on the things yourself, and then if she liked to redeem 'em when she got home, she could. But if we heard nothing from her after two months, we might do as we liked with 'em."

I will not say that in this accommodating proposition the landlady had no regard whatever to the possible reward of her good nature in the ultimate possession of the locket and ear-rings: indeed, the effect they would have in that case on the mind of the grocer's wife had presented itself with remarkable vividness to her rapid imagination. The landlord took up the ornaments and pushed out his lips in a meditative manner. He wished Hetty well, doubtless; but pray, how many of your well-wishers would decline to make a little gain out of you? Your landlady is sincerely affected at parting with you, respects you highly, and will really rejoice if any one else is generous to you; but at the same time she hands you a bill by which she gains as high a percentage as possible.

"How much money do you want to get home with, young woman?" said the well-wisher, at length.

"Three guineas," answered Hetty, fixing on the sum she set out with, for want of any other standard, and afraid of asking too much.

"Well, I've no objections to advance you three guineas," said the landlord; "and if you like to send it me back and get the jewellery again, you can, you know. The Green Man isn't going to run away."

"Oh yes, I'll be very glad if you'll give me that," said Hetty, relieved at the thought that she would not have to go to the jeweller's and be stared at and questioned.

"But if you want the things again, you'll write before long," said the landlady, "because when two months are up, we shall make up our minds as you don't want 'em."

"Yes," said Hetty indifferently.

The husband and wife were equally content with this arrangement. The husband thought, if the ornaments were not redeemed, he could make a good thing of it by taking them to London and selling them. The wife thought she would coax the good man into letting her keep them. And they were accommodating Hetty, poor thing—a pretty, respectable-looking young woman, apparently in a sad case. They declined to take anything for her food and bed: she was quite welcome. And at eleven o'clock Hetty said "Good-bye" to them with the same quiet, resolute air she had worn all the morning, mounting the coach that was to take her twenty miles back along the way she had come.

There is a strength of self-possession which is the sign that the last hope has departed. Despair no more leans on others than perfect contentment, and in despair pride ceases to be counteracted by the sense of dependence.

Hetty felt that no one could deliver her from the evils that would make life hateful to her; and no one, she said to herself, should ever know her misery and humiliation. No; she would not confess even to Dinah. She would wander out of sight, and drown herself where her body would never be found, and no one should know what had become of her.

When she got off this coach, she began to walk again, and take cheap rides in carts, and get cheap meals, going on and on without distinct purpose, yet strangely, by some fascination, taking the way she had come, though she was determined not to go back to her own country. Perhaps it was because she had fixed her mind on the grassy Warwickshire fields, with the bushy tree-studded hedgerows that made a hiding-place even in this leafless season. She went more slowly than she came, often getting over the stiles and sitting for hours under the hedgerows, looking before her with blank, beautiful eyes; fancying herself at the edge of a hidden pool, low down, like that in the Scantlands; wondering if it were very painful to be drowned, and if there would be anything worse after death than what she dreaded in life. Religious doctrines had taken no hold on Hetty's mind. She was one of those numerous people who have had godfathers and godmothers, learned their catechism, been confirmed, and gone to church every Sunday, and yet, for any practical result of strength in life, or trust in death, have never appropriated a single Christian idea or Christian feeling. You would misunderstand her thoughts during these wretched days, if you imagined that they were influenced either by religious fears or religious hopes.

She chose to go to Stratford-on-Avon again, where she had gone before by mistake, for she remembered some grassy fields on her former way towards it—fields among which she thought she might find just the sort of pool she had in her mind. Yet she took care of her money still; she carried her basket; death seemed still a long way off, and life was so strong in her. She craved food and rest—she hastened towards them at the very moment she was picturing to herself the bank from which she would leap towards death. It was already five days since she had left Windsor, for she had wandered about, always avoiding speech or questioning looks, and recovering her air of proud self-dependence whenever she was under observation, choosing her decent lodging at night, and dressing herself neatly in the morning, and setting off on her way steadily, or remaining under shelter if it rained, as if she had a happy life to cherish.

And yet, even in her most self-conscious moments, the face was sadly different from that which had smiled at itself in the old specked glass, or smiled at others when they glanced at it admiringly. A hard and even fierce look had come in the eyes, though their lashes were as long as ever, and they had all their dark brightness. And the cheek was never dimpled with smiles now. It was the same rounded, pouting, childish prettiness, but with all love and belief in love departed from it—the sadder for its beauty, like that wondrous Medusa-face, with the passionate, passionless lips.

At last she was among the fields she had been dreaming of, on a long narrow pathway leading towards a wood. If there should be a pool in that wood! It would be better hidden than one in the fields. No, it was not a wood, only a wild brake, where there had once been gravel-pits, leaving mounds and hollows studded with brushwood and small trees. She roamed up and down, thinking there was perhaps a pool in every hollow before she came to it, till her limbs were weary, and she sat down to rest. The afternoon was far advanced, and the leaden sky was darkening, as if the sun were setting behind it. After a little while Hetty started up again, feeling that darkness would soon come on; and she must put off finding the pool till to-morrow, and make her way to some shelter for the night. She had quite lost her way in the fields, and might as well go in one direction as another, for aught she knew. She walked through field after field, and no village, no house was in sight; but *there*, at the corner of this pasture, there was a break in the hedges; the land seemed to dip down a little, and two trees leaned towards each other across the opening. Hetty's heart gave a great beat as she thought there must be a pool there. She walked towards it heavily over the tufted grass, with pale lips and a sense of trembling. It was as if the thing were come in spite of herself, instead of being the object of her search.

There it was, black under the darkening sky: no motion, no sound near. She set down her basket, and then sank down herself on the grass, trembling. The pool had its wintry depth now: by the time it got shallow, as she remembered the pools did at Hayslope, in the summer, no one could find out that it was her body. But then there was her basket—she must hide that too. She must throw it into the water—make it heavy with stones first, and then throw it in. She got up to look about for stones, and soon brought five or six, which she laid down beside her basket, and then sat down again. There was no need to hurry—there was all the night to drown herself in. She sat leaning her elbow on the basket. She was weary, hungry. There were some buns in her basket—three, which she had supplied herself with at the place where she ate her dinner. She took them out now and ate them eagerly, and then sat still again, looking at the pool. The soothed sensation that came over her from the satisfaction of her hunger, and this fixed dreamy attitude, brought on drowsiness, and presently her head sank down on her knees. She was fast asleep.

When she awoke it was deep night, and she felt chill. She was frightened at this darkness—frightened at the long night before her. If she *could* but throw herself into the water! No, not yet. She began to walk about that she might get warm again, as if she would have more resolution then. Oh how long the time was in that darkness! The bright hearth and the warmth and the voices of home, the secure uprising and lying down, the familiar fields, the familiar people, the Sundays and holidays with their simple joys of dress and feasting—all the sweets of her young life rushed before her now, and she seemed to be stretching her arms towards them across a great gulf. She set her teeth when she thought of Arthur. She cursed him, without knowing what her cursing would do. She wished he too might know desolation, and cold, and a life of shame that he dared not end by death.

The horror of this cold, and darkness, and solitude—out of all human reach—became greater every long minute. It was almost as if she were dead already, and knew that she was dead, and longed to get back to life again. But no: she was alive still; she had not taken the dreadful leap. She felt a strange contradictory wretchedness and exultation: wretchedness, that she did not dare to face death; exultation, that she was still in life—that she might yet know light and warmth again. She walked backwards and forwards to warm herself, beginning to discern something of the objects around her, as her eyes became accustomed to the night—the darker line of the hedge, the rapid motion of some living creature—perhaps a field-mouse—rushing across the grass. She no longer felt as if the darkness hedged her in. She thought she could walk back across the field, and get over the stile; and then, in the very next field, she thought she remembered there was a hovel of furze near a sheepfold. If she could get into that hovel, she would be warmer. She could pass the night there, for that was what Alick did at

Hayslope in lambing-time. The thought of this hovel brought the energy of a new hope. She took up her basket and walked across the field, but it was some time before she got in the right direction for the stile. The exercise and the occupation of finding the stile were a stimulus to her, however, and lightened the horror of the darkness and solitude. There were sheep in the next field, and she startled a group as she set down her basket and got over the stile; and the sound of their movement comforted her, for it assured her that her impression was right—this *was* the field where she had seen the hovel, for it was the field where the sheep were. Right on along the path, and she would get to it. She reached the opposite gate, and felt her way along its rails and the rails of the sheep-fold, till her hand encountered the pricking of the gorsy wall. Delicious sensation! She had found the shelter. She groped her way, touching the prickly gorse, to the door, and pushed it open. It was an ill-smelling close place, but warm, and there was straw on the ground. Hetty sank down on the straw with a sense of escape. Tears came—she had never shed tears before since she left Windsor—tears and sobs of hysterical joy that she had still hold of life, that she was still on the familiar earth, with the sheep near her. The very consciousness of her own limbs was a delight to her: she turned up her sleeves, and kissed her arms with the passionate love of life. Soon warmth and weariness lulled her in the midst of her sobs, and she fell continually into dozing, fancying herself at the brink of the pool again—fancying that she had jumped into the water, and then awaking with a start, and wondering where she was. But at last deep dreamless sleep came; her head, guarded by her bonnet, found a pillow against the gorsy wall, and the poor soul, driven to and fro between two equal terrors, found the one relief that was possible to it—the relief of unconsciousness.

Alas! That relief seems to end the moment it has begun. It seemed to Hetty as if those dozen dreams had only passed into another dream—that she was in the hovel, and her aunt was standing over her with a candle in her hand. She trembled under her aunt's glance, and opened her eyes. There was no candle, but there was light in the hovel—the light of early morning through the open door. And there was a face looking down on her; but it was an unknown face, belonging to an elderly man in a smock-frock.

"Why, what do you do here, young woman?" the man said roughly.

Hetty trembled still worse under this real fear and shame than she had done in her momentary dream under her aunt's glance. She felt that she was like a beggar already—found sleeping in that place. But in spite of her trembling, she was so eager to account to the man for her presence here, that she found words at once.

"I lost my way," she said. "I'm travelling—north'ard, and I got away from the road into the fields, and was overtaken by the dark. Will you tell me the way to the nearest village?"

She got up as she was speaking, and put her hands to her bonnet to adjust it, and then laid hold of her basket.

The man looked at her with a slow bovine gaze, without giving her any answer, for some seconds. Then he turned away and walked towards the door of the hovel, but it was not till he got there that he stood still, and, turning his shoulder half-round towards her, said, "Aw, I can show you the way to Norton, if you like. But what do you do gettin' out o' the highroad?" he added, with a tone of gruff reproof. "Y'ull be gettin' into mischief, if you dooant mind."

"Yes," said Hetty, "I won't do it again. I'll keep in the road, if you'll be so good as show me how to get to it."

"Why dooant you keep where there's a finger-poasses an' folks to ax the way on?" the man said, still more gruffly. "Anybody 'ud think you was a wild woman, an' look at yer."

Hetty was frightened at this gruff old man, and still more at this last suggestion that she looked like a wild woman. As she followed him out of the hovel she thought she would give him a sixpence for telling her the way, and then he would not suppose she was wild. As he stopped to point out the road to her, she put her hand in her pocket to get the six-pence ready, and when he was turning away, without saying good-morning, she held it out to him and said, "Thank you; will you please to take something for your trouble?"

He looked slowly at the sixpence, and then said, "I want none o' your money. You'd better take care on't, else you'll get it stool from yer, if you go trapesin' about the fields like a mad woman a-thatway."

The man left her without further speech, and Hetty held on her way. Another day had risen, and she must wander on. It was no use to think of drowning herself—she could not do it, at least while she had money left to buy food and strength to journey on. But the incident on her waking this morning heightened her dread of that time when her money would be all gone; she would have to sell her basket and clothes then, and she would really look like a beggar or a wild woman, as the man had said. The passionate joy in life she had felt in the night, after escaping from the brink of the black cold death in the pool, was gone now. Life now, by the morning light, with the impression of that man's hard wondering look at her, was as full of dread as death—it was worse; it was a dread to which she felt chained, from which she shrank and shrank as she did from the black pool, and yet could find no refuge from it.

She took out her money from her purse, and looked at it. She had still two-and-twenty shillings; it would serve her for many days more, or it would help her to get on faster to Stonyshire, within reach of Dinah. The thought of Dinah urged itself more strongly now, since the experience of the night had driven her shuddering imagination away from the pool. If it had been only going to Dinah—if nobody besides Dinah would ever know—Hetty could have made up her mind to go to her. The soft voice, the pitying eyes, would have drawn her. But afterwards the other people must know, and she could no more rush on that shame than she could rush on death.

She must wander on and on, and wait for a lower depth of despair to give her courage. Perhaps death would come to her, for she was getting less and less able to bear the day's weariness. And yet—such is the strange action of our souls, drawing us by a lurking desire towards the very ends we dread—Hetty, when she set out again from Norton, asked the straightest road northwards towards Stonyshire, and kept it all that day.

Poor wandering Hetty, with the rounded childish face and the hard, unloving, despairing soul looking out of it—with the narrow heart and narrow thoughts, no room in them for any sorrows but her own, and tasting that sorrow with the more intense bitterness! My heart bleeds for her as I see her toiling along on her weary feet, or seated in a cart, with her eyes fixed vacantly on the road before her, never thinking or caring whither it tends, till hunger comes and makes her desire that a village may be near.

What will be the end, the end of her objectless wandering, apart from all love, caring for human beings only through her pride, clinging to life only as the hunted wounded brute clings to it?

God preserve you and me from being the beginners of such misery!

Chapter XXXVIII
The Quest

The first ten days after Hetty's departure passed as quietly as any other days with the family at the Hall Farm, and with Adam at his daily work. They had expected Hetty to stay away a week or ten days at least, perhaps a little longer if Dinah came back with her, because there might then be something to detain them at Snowfield. But when a fortnight had passed they began to feel a little surprise that Hetty did not return; she must surely have found it pleasanter to be with Dinah than any one could have supposed. Adam, for his part, was getting very impatient to see her, and he resolved that, if she did not appear the next day (Saturday), he would set out on Sunday morning to fetch her. There was no coach on a Sunday, but by setting out before it was light, and perhaps getting a lift in a cart by the way, he would arrive pretty early at Snowfield, and bring back Hetty the next day—Dinah too, if she were coming. It was quite time Hetty came home, and he would afford to lose his Monday for the sake of bringing her.

His project was quite approved at the Farm when he went there on Saturday evening. Mrs. Poyser desired him emphatically not to come back without Hetty, for she had been quite too long away, considering the things she had to get ready by the middle of March, and a week was surely enough for any one to go out for their health. As for Dinah, Mrs. Poyser had small hope of their bringing her, unless they could make her believe the folks at Hayslope were twice as miserable as the folks at Snowfield. "Though," said Mrs. Poyser, by way of conclusion, "you might tell her she's got but one aunt left, and *she's* wasted pretty nigh to a shadder; and we shall p'rhaps all be gone twenty mile farther off her next Michaelmas, and shall die o' broken hearts among strange folks, and leave the children fatherless and motherless."

"Nay, nay," said Mr. Poyser, who certainly had the air of a man perfectly heart-whole, "it isna so bad as that. Thee't looking rarely now, and getting flesh every day. But I'd be glad for Dinah t' come, for she'd help thee wi' the little uns: they took t' her wonderful."

So at daybreak, on Sunday, Adam set off. Seth went with him the first mile or two, for the thought of Snowfield and the possibility that Dinah might come again made him restless, and the walk with Adam in the cold morning air, both in their best clothes, helped to give him a sense of Sunday calm. It was the last morning in February, with a low grey sky, and a slight hoar-frost on the green border of the road and on the black hedges. They heard the gurgling of the full brooklet hurrying down the hill, and the faint twittering of the early birds. For they walked in silence, though with a pleased sense of companionship.

"Good-bye, lad," said Adam, laying his hand on Seth's shoulder and looking at him affectionately as they were about to part. "I wish thee wast going all the way wi' me, and as happy as I am."

"I'm content, Addy, I'm content," said Seth cheerfully. "I'll be an old bachelor, belike, and make a fuss wi' thy children."

They turned away from each other, and Seth walked leisurely homeward, mentally repeating one of his favourite hymns—he was very fond of hymns:

"Dark and cheerless is the morn
Unaccompanied by thee:
Joyless is the day's return
Till thy mercy's beams I see:
Till thou inward light impart,
Glad my eyes and warm my heart.

Visit, then, this soul of mine,
Pierce the gloom of sin and grief—
Fill me, Radiancy Divine,
Scatter all my unbelief.
More and more thyself display,
Shining to the perfect day."

Adam walked much faster, and any one coming along the Oakbourne road at sunrise that morning must have had a pleasant sight in this tall broad-chested man, striding along with a carriage as upright and firm as any soldier's, glancing with keen glad eyes at the dark-blue hills as they began to show themselves on his way. Seldom in Adam's life had his face been so free from any cloud of anxiety as it was this morning; and this freedom from care, as is usual with constructive practical minds like his, made him all the more observant of the objects round him and all the more ready to gather suggestions from them towards his own favourite plans and ingenious contrivances. His happy love—the knowledge that his steps were carrying him nearer and nearer to Hetty, who was so soon to be his—was to his thoughts what the sweet morning air was to his sensations: it gave him a consciousness of well-being that made activity delightful. Every now and then there was a rush of more intense feeling towards her, which chased away other images than Hetty; and along with that would come a wondering thankfulness that all this happiness was given to him—that this life of ours had such sweetness in it. For Adam had a devout mind, though he was perhaps rather impatient of devout words, and his tenderness lay very close to his reverence, so that the one could hardly be stirred without the other. But after feeling had welled up and poured itself out in this way, busy thought would come back with the greater vigour; and this morning it was intent on schemes by which the roads might be improved that were so imperfect all through the country, and on picturing all the benefits that might come from the exertions of a single country gentleman, if he would set himself to getting the roads made good in his own district.

It seemed a very short walk, the ten miles to Oakbourne, that pretty town within sight of the blue hills, where he break-fasted. After this, the country grew barer and barer: no more rolling woods, no more wide-branching trees near frequent homesteads, no more bushy hedgerows, but greystone walls intersecting the meagre pastures, and dismal wide-scattered greystone houses on broken lands where mines had been and were no longer. "A hungry land," said Adam to himself. "I'd rather go south'ard, where they say it's as flat as a table, than come to live here; though if Dinah likes to live in a country where she can be the most comfort to folks, she's i' the right to live o' this side; for she must look as if she'd come straight from heaven, like th' angels in the desert, to strengthen them as ha' got nothing t' eat." And when at last he came in sight of Snowfield, he thought it looked like a town that was "fellow to the country," though the stream through the valley where the great mill stood gave a pleasant greenness to the lower fields. The town lay, grim, stony, and unsheltered, up the side of a steep hill, and Adam did not go forward to it at present, for Seth had told him where to find Dinah. It was at a thatched cottage outside the town, a little way from the mill—an old cottage, standing sideways towards the road, with a little bit of potato-ground before it. Here Dinah lodged with an elderly couple; and if she and Hetty happened to be out, Adam could learn where they were gone, or when they would be at home again. Dinah might be out on some preaching errand, and perhaps she would have left Hetty at home. Adam could not help hoping this, and as he recognized the cottage by the roadside before him, there shone out in his face that involuntary smile which belongs to the expectation of a near joy.

He hurried his step along the narrow causeway, and rapped at the door. It was opened by a very clean old woman, with a slow palsied shake of the head.

"Is Dinah Morris at home?" said Adam.

"Eh?... no," said the old woman, looking up at this tall stranger with a wonder that made her slower of speech than usual. "Will you please to come in?" she added, retiring from the door, as if recollecting herself. "Why, ye're brother to the young man as come afore, arena ye?"

"Yes," said Adam, entering. "That was Seth Bede. I'm his brother Adam. He told me to give his respects to you and your good master."

"Aye, the same t' him. He was a gracious young man. An' ye feature him, on'y ye're darker. Sit ye down i' th' arm-chair. My man isna come home from meeting."

Adam sat down patiently, not liking to hurry the shaking old woman with questions, but looking eagerly towards the narrow twisting stairs in one corner, for he thought it was possible Hetty might have heard his voice and would come down them.

"So you're come to see Dinah Morris?" said the old woman, standing opposite to him. "An' you didn' know she was away from home, then?"

"No," said Adam, "but I thought it likely she might be away, seeing as it's Sunday. But the other young woman—is she at home, or gone along with Dinah?"

The old woman looked at Adam with a bewildered air.

"Gone along wi' her?" she said. "Eh, Dinah's gone to Leeds, a big town ye may ha' heared on, where there's a many o' the Lord's people. She's been gone sin' Friday was a fortnight: they sent her the money for her journey. You may see her room here," she went on, opening a door and not noticing the effect of her words on Adam. He rose and followed her, and darted an eager glance into the little room with its narrow bed, the portrait of Wesley on the wall, and the few books lying on the large Bible. He had had an irrational hope that Hetty might be there. He could not speak in the first moment after seeing that the room was empty; an undefined fear had seized him—something had happened to Hetty on the journey. Still the old woman was so slow of speech and apprehension, that Hetty might be at Snowfield after all.

"It's a pity ye didna know," she said. "Have ye come from your own country o' purpose to see her?"

"But Hetty—Hetty Sorrel," said Adam, abruptly; "Where is *she?*"

"I know nobody by that name," said the old woman, wonderingly. "Is it anybody ye've heared on at Snowfield?"

"Did there come no young woman here—very young and pretty—Friday was a fortnight, to see Dinah Morris?"

"Nay; I'n seen no young woman."

"Think; are you quite sure? A girl, eighteen years old, with dark eyes and dark curly hair, and a red cloak on, and a basket on her arm? You couldn't forget her if you saw her."

"Nay; Friday was a fortnight—it was the day as Dinah went away—there come nobody. There's ne'er been nobody asking for her till you come, for the folks about know as she's gone. Eh dear, eh dear, is there summat the matter?"

The old woman had seen the ghastly look of fear in Adam's face. But he was not stunned or confounded: he was thinking eagerly where he could inquire about Hetty.

"Yes; a young woman started from our country to see Dinah, Friday was a fortnight. I came to fetch her back. I'm afraid something has happened to her. I can't stop. Good-bye."

He hastened out of the cottage, and the old woman followed him to the gate, watching him sadly with her shaking head as he almost ran towards the town. He was going to inquire at the place where the Oakbourne coach stopped.

No! No young woman like Hetty had been seen there. Had any accident happened to the coach a fortnight ago? No. And there was no coach to take him back to Oakbourne that day. Well, he would walk: he couldn't stay here, in wretched inaction. But the innkeeper, seeing that Adam was in great anxiety, and entering into this new incident with the eagerness of a man who passes a great deal of time with his hands in his pockets looking into an obstinately monotonous street, offered to take him back to Oakbourne in his own "taxed cart" this very evening. It was not five o'clock; there was plenty of time for Adam to take a meal and yet to get to Oakbourne before ten o'clock. The innkeeper declared that he really wanted to go to Oakbourne, and might as well go to-night; he should have all Monday before him then. Adam, after making an ineffectual attempt to eat, put the food in his pocket, and, drinking a draught of ale, declared himself ready to set off. As they approached the cottage, it occurred to him that he would do well to learn from the old woman where Dinah was to be found in Leeds: if there was trouble at the Hall Farm—he only half-admitted the foreboding that there would be—the Poysers might like to send for Dinah. But Dinah had not left any address, and the old woman, whose memory for names was infirm, could not recall the name of the "blessed woman" who was Dinah's chief friend in the Society at Leeds.

During that long, long journey in the taxed cart, there was time for all the conjectures of importunate fear and struggling hope. In the very first shock of discovering that Hetty had not been to Snowfield, the thought of Arthur had darted through Adam like a sharp pang, but he tried for some time to ward off its return by busying himself with modes of accounting for the alarming fact, quite apart from that intolerable thought. Some accident had happened. Hetty had, by some strange chance, got into a wrong vehicle from Oakbourne: she had been taken ill, and did not want to frighten them by letting them know. But this frail fence of vague improbabilities was soon hurled down by a rush of distinct agonizing fears. Hetty had been deceiving herself in thinking that she could love and marry him: she had been loving Arthur all the while; and now, in her desperation at the nearness of their marriage, she had run away. And she was gone to *him*. The old indignation and jealousy rose again, and prompted the suspicion that Arthur had been dealing falsely—had written to Hetty—had tempted her to come to him—being unwilling, after all, that she should belong to another man besides himself. Perhaps the whole thing had been contrived by him, and he had given her directions how to follow him to Ireland—for Adam knew that Arthur had been gone thither three weeks ago, having recently learnt it at the Chase. Every sad look of Hetty's, since she had been engaged to Adam, returned upon him now with all the exaggeration of painful retrospect. He had been foolishly sanguine and confident. The poor thing hadn't perhaps known her own mind for a long while; had thought that she could forget Arthur; had been momentarily drawn towards the man who offered her a protecting, faithful love. He couldn't bear to blame her: she never meant to cause him this dreadful pain. The blame lay with that man who had selfishly played with her heart—had perhaps even deliberately lured her away.

At Oakbourne, the ostler at the Royal Oak remembered such a young woman as Adam described getting out of the Treddleston coach more than a fortnight ago—wasn't likely to forget such a pretty lass as that in a hurry—was sure she had not gone on by the Buxton coach that went through Snowfield, but had lost sight of her while he went away with the horses and had never set eyes on her again. Adam then went straight to the house from which the Stoniton coach started: Stoniton was the most obvious place for Hetty to go to first, whatever might be her destination, for she would hardly venture on any but the chief coach-roads. She had been noticed here too, and was remembered to have sat on the box by the coachman; but the coachman could not be seen, for another man had been driving on that road in his stead the last three or four days. He could probably be seen at Stoniton, through inquiry at the inn where the coach put up. So the anxious heart-stricken Adam must of necessity wait and try to rest till morning—nay, till eleven o'clock, when the coach started.

At Stoniton another delay occurred, for the old coachman who had driven Hetty would not be in the town again till night. When he did come he remembered Hetty well, and remembered his own joke addressed to her, quoting it many times to Adam, and observing with equal frequency that he thought there was something more than common, because Hetty had not laughed when he joked her. But he declared, as the people had done at the inn, that he had lost sight of Hetty directly she got down. Part of the next morning was consumed in inquiries at every house in the town from which a coach started—(all in vain, for you know Hetty did not start from Stoniton by coach, but on foot in the grey morning)—and then in walking out to the first toll-gates on the different lines of road, in the forlorn hope of finding some recollection of her there. No, she was not to be traced any farther; and the next hard task for Adam was to go home and carry the wretched tidings to the Hall Farm. As to what he should do beyond that, he had come to two distinct resolutions amidst the tumult of thought and feeling which was going on within him while he went to and fro. He would not mention what he knew of Arthur Donnithorne's behaviour to Hetty till there was a clear necessity for it: it was still possible Hetty might come back, and the disclosure might be an injury or an offence to her. And as soon as he had been home and done what was necessary there to prepare for his further absence, he would start off to Ireland: if he found no trace of Hetty on the road, he would go straight to Arthur Donnithorne and make himself certain how far he was acquainted with her movements. Several times the thought occurred to him that he would consult Mr. Irwine, but that would be useless unless he told him all, and so betrayed the secret about Arthur. It seems strange that Adam, in the incessant occupation of his mind about Hetty, should never have alighted on the probability that she had gone to Windsor, ignorant that Arthur was no longer there. Perhaps the reason was that he could not conceive Hetty's throwing herself on Arthur uncalled; he imagined no cause that could have driven her to such a step, after that letter written in August. There were but two alternatives in his mind: either Arthur had written to her again and enticed her away, or she had simply fled from her approaching marriage with himself because she found, after all, she could not love him well enough, and yet was afraid of her friends' anger if she retracted.

With this last determination on his mind, of going straight to Arthur, the thought that he had spent two days in inquiries which had proved to be almost useless, was torturing to Adam; and yet, since he would not tell the Poysers his conviction as to where Hetty was gone, or his intention to follow her thither, he must be able to say to them that he had traced her as far as possible.

It was after twelve o'clock on Tuesday night when Adam reached Treddleston; and, unwilling to disturb his mother and Seth, and also to encounter their questions at that hour, he threw himself without undressing on a bed at the "Waggon Overthrown," and slept hard from pure weariness. Not more than four hours, however, for before five o'clock he set out on his way home in the faint morning twilight. He always kept a key of the workshop door in his pocket, so that he could let himself in; and he wished to enter without awaking his mother, for he was anxious to avoid telling her the new trouble himself by seeing Seth first, and asking him to tell her when it should be necessary. He walked gently along the yard, and turned the key gently in the door; but, as he expected, Gyp, who lay in the workshop, gave a sharp bark. It subsided when he saw Adam, holding up his finger at him to impose silence, and in his dumb, tailless joy he must content himself with rubbing his body against his master's legs.

Adam was too heart-sick to take notice of Gyp's fondling. He threw himself on the bench and stared dully at the wood and the signs of work around him, wondering if he should ever come to feel pleasure in them again, while Gyp, dimly aware that there was something wrong with his master, laid his rough grey head on Adam's knee and wrinkled his brows to look up at him. Hitherto, since Sunday afternoon, Adam had been constantly among strange people and in strange places, having no associations with the details of his daily life, and now that by the light of this new morning he was come back to his home and surrounded by the familiar objects that seemed for ever robbed of their charm, the reality—the hard, inevitable reality of his troubles pressed upon him with a new weight. Right before him was an unfinished chest of drawers, which he had been making in spare moments for Hetty's use, when his home should be hers.

Seth had not heard Adam's entrance, but he had been roused by Gyp's bark, and Adam heard him moving about in the room above, dressing himself. Seth's first thoughts were about his brother: he would come home to-day, surely, for the business would be wanting him sadly by to-morrow, but it was pleasant to think he had had a longer holiday than he had expected. And would Dinah come too? Seth felt that that was the greatest happiness he could look forward to for himself, though he had no hope left that she would ever love him well enough to marry him; but he had often said to himself, it was better to be Dinah's friend and brother than any other woman's husband. If he could but be always near her, instead of living so far off!

He came downstairs and opened the inner door leading from the kitchen into the workshop, intending to let out Gyp; but he stood still in the doorway, smitten with a sudden shock at the sight of Adam seated listlessly on the bench, pale, unwashed, with sunken blank eyes, almost like a drunkard in the morning. But Seth felt in an instant what the marks meant—not drunkenness, but some great calamity. Adam looked up at him without speaking, and Seth moved forward towards the bench, himself trembling so that speech did not come readily.

"God have mercy on us, Addy," he said, in a low voice, sitting down on the bench beside Adam, "what is it?"

Adam was unable to speak. The strong man, accustomed to suppress the signs of sorrow, had felt his heart swell like a child's at this first approach of sympathy. He fell on Seth's neck and sobbed.

Seth was prepared for the worst now, for, even in his recollections of their boyhood, Adam had never sobbed before.

"Is it death, Adam? Is she dead?" he asked, in a low tone, when Adam raised his head and was recovering himself.

"No, lad; but she's gone—gone away from us. She's never been to Snowfield. Dinah's been gone to Leeds ever since last Friday was a fortnight, the very day Hetty set out. I can't find out where she went after she got to Stoniton."

Seth was silent from utter astonishment: he knew nothing that could suggest to him a reason for Hetty's going away.

"Hast any notion what she's done it for?" he said, at last.

"She can't ha' loved me. She didn't like our marriage when it came nigh—that must be it," said Adam. He had determined to mention no further reason.

"I hear Mother stirring," said Seth. "Must we tell her?"

"No, not yet," said Adam, rising from the bench and pushing the hair from his face, as if he wanted to rouse himself. "I can't have her told yet; and I must set out on another journey directly, after I've been to the village and th' Hall Farm. I can't tell thee where I'm going, and thee must say to her I'm gone on business as nobody is to know anything about. I'll go and wash myself now." Adam moved towards the door of the workshop, but after a step or two he turned round, and, meeting Seth's eyes with a calm sad glance, he said, "I must take all the money out o' the tin box, lad; but if anything happens to me, all the rest 'll be thine, to take care o' Mother with."

Seth was pale and trembling: he felt there was some terrible secret under all this. "Brother," he said, faintly—he never called Adam "Brother" except in solemn moments—"I don't believe you'll do anything as you can't ask God's blessing on."

"Nay, lad," said Adam, "don't be afraid. I'm for doing nought but what's a man's duty."

The thought that if he betrayed his trouble to his mother, she would only distress him by words, half of blundering affection, half of irrepressible triumph that Hetty proved as unfit to be his wife as she had always foreseen, brought back some of his habitual firmness and self-command. He had felt ill on his journey home—he told her when she came down—had stayed all night at Tredddleston for that reason; and a bad headache, that still hung about him this morning, accounted for his paleness and heavy eyes.

He determined to go to the village, in the first place, attend to his business for an hour, and give notice to Burge of his being obliged to go on a journey, which he must beg him not to mention to any one; for he wished to avoid going to the Hall Farm near breakfast-time, when the children and servants would be in the house-place, and there must be exclamations in their hearing about his having returned without Hetty. He waited until the clock struck nine before he left the work-yard at the village, and set off, through the fields, towards the Farm. It was an immense relief to him, as he came near the Home Close, to see Mr. Poyser advancing towards him, for this would spare him the pain of going to the house. Mr. Poyser was walking briskly this March morning, with a sense of spring business on his mind: he was going to cast the master's eye on the shoeing of a new cart-horse, carrying his spud as a useful companion by the way. His surprise was great when he caught sight of Adam, but he was not a man given to presentiments of evil.

"Why, Adam, lad, is't you? Have ye been all this time away and not brought the lasses back, after all? Where are they?"

"No, I've not brought 'em," said Adam, turning round, to indicate that he wished to walk back with Mr. Poyser.

"Why," said Martin, looking with sharper attention at Adam, "ye look bad. Is there anything happened?"

"Yes," said Adam, heavily. "A sad thing's happened. I didna find Hetty at Snowfield."

Mr. Poyser's good-natured face showed signs of troubled astonishment. "Not find her? What's happened to her?" he said, his thoughts flying at once to bodily accident.

"That I can't tell, whether anything's happened to her. She never went to Snowfield—she took the coach to Stoniton, but I can't learn nothing of her after she got down from the Stoniton coach."

"Why, you donna mean she's run away?" said Martin, standing still, so puzzled and bewildered that the fact did not yet make itself felt as a trouble by him.

"She must ha' done," said Adam. "She didn't like our marriage when it came to the point—that must be it. She'd mistook her feelings."

Martin was silent for a minute or two, looking on the ground and rooting up the grass with his spud, without knowing what he was doing. His usual slowness was always trebled when the subject of speech was painful. At last he looked up, right in Adam's face, saying, "Then she didna deserve t' ha' ye, my lad. An' I feel i' fault myself, for she was my niece, and I was allays hot for her marr'ing ye. There's no amends I can make ye, lad—the more's the pity: it's a sad cut-up for ye, I doubt."

Adam could say nothing; and Mr. Poyser, after pursuing his walk for a little while, went on, "I'll be bound she's gone after trying to get a lady's maid's place, for she'd got that in her head half a year ago, and wanted me to gi' my consent. But I'd thought better on her"—he added, shaking his head slowly and sadly—"I'd thought better on her, nor to look for this, after she'd gi'en y' her word, an' everything been got ready."

Adam had the strongest motives for encouraging this supposition in Mr. Poyser, and he even tried to believe that it might possibly be true. He had no warrant for the *certainty* that she was gone to Arthur.

"It was better it should be so," he said, as quietly as he could, "if she felt she couldn't like me for a husband. Better run away before than repent after. I hope you won't look harshly on her if she comes back, as she may do if she finds it hard to get on away from home."

"I canna look on her as I've done before," said Martin decisively. "She's acted bad by you, and by all of us. But I'll not turn my back on her: she's but a young un, and it's the first harm I've knowed on her. It'll be a hard job for me to tell her aunt. Why didna Dinah come back wi' ye? She'd ha' helped to pacify her aunt a bit."

"Dinah wasn't at Snowfield. She's been gone to Leeds this fortnight, and I couldn't learn from th' old woman any direction where she is at Leeds, else I should ha' brought it you."

"She'd a deal better be staying wi' her own kin," said Mr. Poyser, indignantly, "than going preaching among strange folks a-that'n."

"I must leave you now, Mr. Poyser," said Adam, "for I've a deal to see to."

"Aye, you'd best be after your business, and I must tell the missis when I go home. It's a hard job."

"But," said Adam, "I beg particular, you'll keep what's happened quiet for a week or two. I've not told my mother yet, and there's no knowing how things may turn out."

"Aye, aye; least said, soonest mended. We'n no need to say why the match is broke off, an' we may hear of her after a bit. Shake hands wi' me, lad: I wish I could make thee amends."

There was something in Martin Poyser's throat at that moment which caused him to bring out those scanty words in rather a broken fashion. Yet Adam knew what they meant all the better, and the two honest men grasped each other's hard hands in mutual understanding.

There was nothing now to hinder Adam from setting off. He had told Seth to go to the Chase and leave a message for the squire, saying that Adam Bede had been obliged to start off suddenly on a journey—and to say as much, and no more, to any one else who made inquiries about him. If the Poysers learned that he was gone away again, Adam knew they would infer that he was gone in search of Hetty.

He had intended to go right on his way from the Hall Farm, but now the impulse which had frequently visited him before—to go to Mr. Irwine, and make a confidant of him—recurred with the new force which belongs to a last opportunity. He was about to start on a long journey—a difficult one—by sea—and no soul would know where he was gone. If anything happened to him? Or, if he absolutely needed help in any matter concerning Hetty? Mr. Irwine was to be trusted; and the feeling which made Adam shrink from telling anything which was *her* secret must give way before the need there was that she should have some one else besides himself who would be prepared to defend her in the worst extremity. Towards Arthur, even though he might have incurred no new guilt, Adam felt that he was not bound to keep silence when Hetty's interest called on him to speak.

"I must do it," said Adam, when these thoughts, which had spread themselves through hours of his sad journeying, now rushed upon him in an instant, like a wave that had been slowly gathering; "it's the right thing. I can't stand alone in this way any longer."

Chapter XXXIX
The Tidings

Adam turned his face towards Broxton and walked with his swiftest stride, looking at his watch with the fear that Mr. Irwine might be gone out—hunting, perhaps. The fear and haste together produced a state of strong excitement before he reached the rectory gate, and outside it he saw the deep marks of a recent hoof on the gravel.

But the hoofs were turned towards the gate, not away from it, and though there was a horse against the stable door, it was not Mr. Irwine's: it had evidently had a journey this morning, and must belong to some one who had come on business. Mr. Irwine was at home, then; but Adam could hardly find breath and calmness to tell Carroll that he wanted to speak to the rector. The double suffering of certain and uncertain sorrow had begun to shake the strong man. The butler looked at him wonderingly, as he threw himself on a bench in the passage and stared absently at the clock on the opposite wall. The master had somebody with him, he said, but he heard the study door open—the stranger seemed to be coming out, and as Adam was in a hurry, he would let the master know at once.

Adam sat looking at the clock: the minute-hand was hurrying along the last five minutes to ten with a loud, hard, indifferent tick, and Adam watched the movement and listened to the sound as if he had had some reason for doing so. In our times of bitter suffering there are almost always these pauses, when our consciousness is benumbed to everything but some trivial perception or sensation. It is as if semi-idiocy came to give us rest from the memory and the dread which refuse to leave us in our sleep.

Carroll, coming back, recalled Adam to the sense of his burden. He was to go into the study immediately. "I can't think what that strange person's come about," the butler added, from mere incontinence of remark, as he preceded Adam to the door, "he's gone i' the dining-room. And master looks unaccountable—as if he was frightened." Adam took no notice of the words: he could not care about other people's business. But when he entered the study and looked in Mr. Irwine's face, he felt in an instant that there was a new expression in it, strangely different from the warm friendliness it had always worn for him before. A letter lay open on the table, and Mr. Irwine's hand was on it, but the changed glance he cast on Adam could not be owing entirely to preoccupation with some disagreeable business, for he was looking eagerly towards the door, as if Adam's entrance were a matter of poignant anxiety to him.

"You want to speak to me, Adam," he said, in that low constrainedly quiet tone which a man uses when he is determined to suppress agitation. "Sit down here." He pointed to a chair just opposite to him, at no more than a yard's distance from his own, and Adam sat down with a sense that this cold manner of Mr. Irwine's gave an additional unexpected difficulty to his disclosure. But when Adam had made up his mind to a measure, he was not the man to renounce it for any but imperative reasons.

"I come to you, sir," he said, "as the gentleman I look up to most of anybody. I've something very painful to tell you—something as it'll pain you to hear as well as me to tell. But if I speak o' the wrong other people have done, you'll see I didn't speak till I'd good reason."

Mr. Irwine nodded slowly, and Adam went on rather tremulously, "You was t' ha' married me and Hetty Sorrel, you know, sir, o' the fifteenth o' this month. I thought she loved me, and I was th' happiest man i' the parish. But a dreadful blow's come upon me."

Mr. Irwine started up from his chair, as if involuntarily, but then, determined to control himself, walked to the window and looked out.

"She's gone away, sir, and we don't know where. She said she was going to Snowfield o' Friday was a fortnight, and I went last Sunday to fetch her back; but she'd never been there, and she took the coach to Stoniton, and beyond that I can't trace her. But now I'm going a long journey to look for her, and I can't trust t' anybody but you where I'm going."

Mr. Irwine came back from the window and sat down.

"Have you no idea of the reason why she went away?" he said.

"It's plain enough she didn't want to marry me, sir," said Adam. "She didn't like it when it came so near. But that isn't all, I doubt. There's something else I must tell you, sir. There's somebody else concerned besides me."

A gleam of something—it was almost like relief or joy—came across the eager anxiety of Mr. Irwine's face at that moment. Adam was looking on the ground, and paused a little: the next words were hard to speak. But when he went on, he lifted up his head and looked straight at Mr. Irwine. He would do the thing he had resolved to do, without flinching.

"You know who's the man I've reckoned my greatest friend," he said, "and used to be proud to think as I should pass my life i' working for him, and had felt so ever since we were lads...."

Mr. Irwine, as if all self-control had forsaken him, grasped Adam's arm, which lay on the table, and, clutching it tightly like a man in pain, said, with pale lips and a low hurried voice, "No, Adam, no—don't say it, for God's sake!"

Adam, surprised at the violence of Mr. Irwine's feeling, repented of the words that had passed his lips and sat in distressed silence. The grasp on his arm gradually relaxed, and Mr. Irwine threw himself back in his chair, saying, "Go on—I must know it."

"That man played with Hetty's feelings, and behaved to her as he'd no right to do to a girl in her station o' life—made her presents and used to go and meet her out a-walking. I found it out only two days before he went away—found him a-kissing her as they were parting in the Grove. There'd been nothing said between me and Hetty then, though I'd loved her for a long while, and she knew it. But I reproached him with his wrong actions, and words and blows passed between us; and he said solemnly to me, after that, as it had been all nonsense and no more than a bit o' flirting. But I made him write a letter to tell Hetty he'd meant nothing, for I saw clear enough, sir, by several things as I hadn't understood at the time, as he'd got hold of her heart, and I thought she'd belike go on thinking of him and never come to love another man as wanted to marry her. And I gave her the letter, and she seemed to bear it all after a while better than I'd expected... and she behaved kinder and kinder to me... I daresay she didn't know her own feelings then, poor thing, and they came back upon her when it was too late... I don't want to blame her... I can't think as she meant to deceive me. But I was encouraged to think she loved me, and—you know the rest, sir. But it's on my mind as he's been false to me, and 'ticed her away, and she's gone to him—and I'm going now to see, for I can never go to work again till I know what's become of her."

During Adam's narrative, Mr. Irwine had had time to recover his self-mastery in spite of the painful thoughts that crowded upon him. It was a bitter remembrance to him now—that morning when Arthur breakfasted with him and seemed as if he were on the verge of a confession. It was plain enough *now* what he had wanted to confess. And if their words had taken another turn... if he himself had been less fastidious about intruding on another man's secrets... it was cruel to think how thin a film had shut out rescue from all this guilt and misery. He saw the whole history now by that terrible illumination which the present sheds back upon the past. But every other feeling as it rushed upon him was thrown into abeyance by pity, deep respectful pity, for the man who sat before him—already so bruised, going forth with sad blind resignedness to an unreal sorrow, while a real one was close upon him, too far beyond the range of common trial for him ever to have feared it. His own agitation was quelled by a certain awe that comes over us in the presence of a great anguish, for the anguish he must inflict on Adam was already present to him. Again he put his hand on the arm that lay on the table, but very gently this time, as he said solemnly:

"Adam, my dear friend, you have had some hard trials in your life. You can bear sorrow manfully, as well as act manfully. God requires both tasks at our hands. And there is a heavier sorrow coming upon you than any you have yet known. But you are not guilty—you have not the worst of all sorrows. God help him who has!"

The two pale faces looked at each other; in Adam's there was trembling suspense, in Mr. Irwine's hesitating, shrinking pity. But he went on.

"I have had news of Hetty this morning. She is not gone to *him*. She is in Stonyshire—at Stoniton."

Adam started up from his chair, as if he thought he could have leaped to her that moment. But Mr. Irwine laid hold of his arm again and said, persuasively, "Wait, Adam, wait." So he sat down.

"She is in a very unhappy position—one which will make it worse for you to find her, my poor friend, than to have lost her for ever."

Adam's lips moved tremulously, but no sound came. They moved again, and he whispered, "Tell me."

"She has been arrested... she is in prison."

It was as if an insulting blow had brought back the spirit of resistance into Adam. The blood rushed to his face, and he said, loudly and sharply, "For what?"

"For a great crime—the murder of her child."

"It *can't be!*" Adam almost shouted, starting up from his chair and making a stride towards the door; but he turned round again, setting his back against the bookcase, and looking fiercely at Mr. Irwine. "It isn't possible. She never had a child. She can't be guilty. *Who* says it?"

"God grant she may be innocent, Adam. We can still hope she is."

"But who says she is guilty?" said Adam violently. "Tell me everything."

"Here is a letter from the magistrate before whom she was taken, and the constable who arrested her is in the dining-room. She will not confess her name or where she comes from; but I fear, I fear, there can be no doubt it is Hetty. The description of her person corresponds, only that she is said to look very pale and ill. She had a small red-leather pocket-book in her pocket with two names written in it—one at the beginning, 'Hetty Sorrel, Hayslope,' and the other near the end, 'Dinah Morris, Snowfield.' She will not say which is her own name—she denies everything, and will answer no questions, and application has been made to me, as a magistrate, that I may take measures for identifying her, for it was thought probable that the name which stands first is her own name."

"But what proof have they got against her, if it *is* Hetty?" said Adam, still violently, with an effort that seemed to shake his whole frame. "I'll not believe it. It couldn't ha' been, and none of us know it."

"Terrible proof that she was under the temptation to commit the crime; but we have room to hope that she did not really commit it. Try and read that letter, Adam."

Adam took the letter between his shaking hands and tried to fix his eyes steadily on it. Mr. Irwine meanwhile went out to give some orders. When he came back, Adam's eyes were still on the first page—he couldn't read—he could not put the words together and make out what they meant. He threw it down at last and clenched his fist.

"It's *his* doing," he said; "if there's been any crime, it's at his door, not at hers. *He* taught her to deceive—*he* deceived me first. Let 'em put *him* on his trial—let him stand in court beside her, and I'll tell 'em how he got hold of her heart, and 'ticed her t' evil, and then lied to me. Is *he* to go free, while they lay all the punishment on her... so weak and young?"

The image called up by these last words gave a new direction to poor Adam's maddened feelings. He was silent, looking at the corner of the room as if he saw something there. Then he burst out again, in a tone of appealing anguish,

"I *can't* bear it... O God, it's too hard to lay upon me—it's too hard to think she's wicked."

Mr. Irwine had sat down again in silence. He was too wise to utter soothing words at present, and indeed, the sight of Adam before him, with that look of sudden age which sometimes comes over a young face in moments of terrible emotion—the hard bloodless look of the skin, the deep lines about the quivering mouth, the furrows in the brow—the sight of this strong firm man shattered by the invisible stroke of sorrow, moved him so deeply that speech was not easy. Adam stood motionless, with his eyes vacantly fixed in this way for a minute or two; in that short space he was living through all his love again.

"She can't ha' done it," he said, still without moving his eyes, as if he were only talking to himself: "it was fear made her hide it... I forgive her for deceiving me... I forgive thee, Hetty... thee wast deceived too... it's gone hard wi' thee, my poor Hetty... but they'll never make me believe it."

He was silent again for a few moments, and then he said, with fierce abruptness, "I'll go to him—I'll bring him back—I'll make him go and look at her in her misery—he shall look at her till he can't forget it—it shall follow him night and day—as long as he lives it shall follow him—he shan't escape wi' lies this time—I'll fetch him, I'll drag him myself."

In the act of going towards the door, Adam paused automatically and looked about for his hat, quite unconscious where he was or who was present with him. Mr. Irwine had followed him, and now took him by the arm, saying, in a quiet but decided tone,

"No, Adam, no; I'm sure you will wish to stay and see what good can be done for *her*, instead of going on a useless errand of vengeance. The punishment will surely fall without your aid. Besides, he is no longer in Ireland. He must be on his way home—or would be, long before you arrived, for his grandfather, I know, wrote for him to come at least ten days ago. I want you now to go with me to Stoniton. I have ordered a horse for you to ride with us, as soon as you can compose yourself."

While Mr. Irwine was speaking, Adam recovered his consciousness of the actual scene. He rubbed his hair off his forehead and listened.

"Remember," Mr. Irwine went on, "there are others to think of, and act for, besides yourself, Adam: there are Hetty's friends, the good Poysers, on whom this stroke will fall more heavily than I can bear to think. I expect it from your strength of mind, Adam—from your sense of duty to God and man—that you will try to act as long as action can be of any use."

In reality, Mr. Irwine proposed this journey to Stoniton for Adam's own sake. Movement, with some object before him, was the best means of counteracting the violence of suffering in these first hours.

"You *will* go with me to Stoniton, Adam?" he said again, after a moment's pause. "We have to see if it is really Hetty who is there, you know."

"Yes, sir," said Adam, "I'll do what you think right. But the folks at th' Hall Farm?"

"I wish them not to know till I return to tell them myself. I shall have ascertained things then which I am uncertain about now, and I shall return as soon as possible. Come now, the horses are ready."

Chapter XL
The Bitter Waters Spread

Mr. Irwine returned from Stoniton in a post-chaise that night, and the first words Carroll said to him, as he entered the house, were, that Squire Donnithorne was dead—found dead in his bed at ten o'clock that morning—and that Mrs. Irwine desired him to say she should be awake when Mr. Irwine came home, and she begged him not to go to bed without seeing her.

"Well, Dauphin," Mrs. Irwine said, as her son entered her room, "you're come at last. So the old gentleman's fidgetiness and low spirits, which made him send for Arthur in that sudden way, really meant something. I suppose Carroll has told you that Donnithorne was found dead in his bed this morning. You will believe my prognostications another time, though I daresay I shan't live to prognosticate anything but my own death."

"What have they done about Arthur?" said Mr. Irwine. "Sent a messenger to await him at Liverpool?"

"Yes, Ralph was gone before the news was brought to us. Dear Arthur, I shall live now to see him master at the Chase, and making good times on the estate, like a generous-hearted fellow as he is. He'll be as happy as a king now."

Mr. Irwine could not help giving a slight groan: he was worn with anxiety and exertion, and his mother's light words were almost intolerable.

"What are you so dismal about, Dauphin? Is there any bad news? Or are you thinking of the danger for Arthur in crossing that frightful Irish Channel at this time of year?"

"No, Mother, I'm not thinking of that; but I'm not prepared to rejoice just now."

"You've been worried by this law business that you've been to Stoniton about. What in the world is it, that you can't tell me?"

"You will know by and by, mother. It would not be right for me to tell you at present. Good-night: you'll sleep now you have no longer anything to listen for."

Mr. Irwine gave up his intention of sending a letter to meet Arthur, since it would not now hasten his return: the news of his grandfather's death would bring him as soon as he could possibly come. He could go to bed now and get some needful rest, before the time came for the morning's heavy duty of carrying his sickening news to the Hall Farm and to Adam's home.

Adam himself was not come back from Stoniton, for though he shrank from seeing Hetty, he could not bear to go to a distance from her again.

"It's no use, sir," he said to the rector, "it's no use for me to go back. I can't go to work again while she's here, and I couldn't bear the sight o' the things and folks round home. I'll take a bit of a room here, where I can see the prison walls, and perhaps I shall get, in time, to bear seeing *her*."

Adam had not been shaken in his belief that Hetty was innocent of the crime she was charged with, for Mr. Irwine, feeling that the belief in her guilt would be a crushing addition to Adam's load, had kept from him the facts which left no hope in his own mind. There was not any reason for thrusting the whole burden on Adam at once, and Mr. Irwine, at parting, only said, "If the evidence should tell too strongly against her, Adam, we may still hope for a pardon. Her youth and other circumstances will be a plea for her."

"Ah, and it's right people should know how she was tempted into the wrong way," said Adam, with bitter earnestness. "It's right they should know it was a fine gentleman made love to her, and turned her head wi' notions. You'll remember, sir, you've promised to tell my mother, and Seth, and the people at the farm, who it was as led her wrong, else they'll think harder of her than she deserves. You'll be doing her a hurt by sparing him, and I hold him the guiltiest before God, let her ha' done what she may. If you spare him, I'll expose him!"

"I think your demand is just, Adam," said Mr. Irwine, "but when you are calmer, you will judge Arthur more mercifully. I say nothing now, only that his punishment is in other hands than ours."

Mr. Irwine felt it hard upon him that he should have to tell of Arthur's sad part in the story of sin and sorrow—he who cared for Arthur with fatherly affection, who had cared for him with fatherly pride. But he saw clearly that the secret must be known before long, even apart from Adam's determination, since it was scarcely to be supposed that Hetty would persist to the end in her obstinate silence. He made up his mind to withhold nothing from the Poysers, but to tell them the worst at once, for there was no time to rob the tidings of their suddenness. Hetty's trial must come on at the Lent assizes, and they were to be held at Stoniton the next week. It was scarcely to be hoped that Martin Poyser could escape the pain of being called as a witness, and it was better he should know everything as long beforehand as possible.

Before ten o'clock on Thursday morning the home at the Hall Farm was a house of mourning for a misfortune felt to be worse than death. The sense of family dishonour was too keen even in the kind-hearted Martin Poyser the younger to leave room for any compassion towards Hetty. He and his father were simple-minded farmers, proud of their untarnished character, proud that they came of a family which had held up its head and paid its way as far back as its name was in the parish register; and Hetty had brought disgrace on them all—disgrace that could never be wiped out. That was the all-conquering feeling in the mind both of father and son—the scorching sense of disgrace, which neutralised all other sensibility—and Mr. Irwine was struck with surprise to observe that Mrs. Poyser was less severe than her husband. We are often startled by the severity of mild people on exceptional occasions; the reason is, that mild people are most liable to be under the yoke of traditional impressions.

"I'm willing to pay any money as is wanted towards trying to bring her off," said Martin the younger when Mr. Irwine was gone, while the old grandfather was crying in the opposite chair, "but I'll not go nigh her, nor ever see her again, by my own will. She's made our bread bitter to us for all our lives to come, an' we shall ne'er hold up our heads i' this parish nor i' any other. The parson talks o' folks pitying us: it's poor amends pity 'ull make us."

"Pity?" said the grandfather, sharply. "I ne'er wanted folks's pity i' *my* life afore... an' I mun begin to be looked down on now, an' me turned seventy-two last St. Thomas's, an' all th' underbearers and pall-bearers as I'n picked for my funeral are i' this parish and the next to 't.... It's o' no use now... I mun be ta'en to the grave by strangers."

"Don't fret so, father," said Mrs. Poyser, who had spoken very little, being almost overawed by her husband's unusual hardness and decision. "You'll have your children wi' you; an' there's the lads and the little un 'ull grow up in a new parish as well as i' th' old un."

"Ah, there's no staying i' this country for us now," said Mr. Poyser, and the hard tears trickled slowly down his round cheeks. "We thought it 'ud be bad luck if the old squire gave us notice this Lady day, but I must gi' notice myself now, an' see if there can anybody be got to come an' take to the crops as I'n put i' the ground; for I wonna stay upo' that man's land a day longer nor I'm forced to't. An' me, as thought him such a good upright young man, as I should be glad when he come to be our landlord. I'll ne'er lift my hat to him again, nor sit i' the same church wi' him... a man as has brought shame on respectable folks... an' pretended to be such a friend t' everybody.... Poor Adam there... a fine friend he's been t' Adam, making speeches an' talking so fine, an' all the while poisoning the lad's life, as it's much if he can stay i' this country any more nor we can."

"An' you t' ha' to go into court, and own you're akin t' her," said the old man. "Why, they'll cast it up to the little un, as isn't four 'ear old, some day—they'll cast it up t' her as she'd a cousin tried at the 'sizes for murder."

"It'll be their own wickedness, then," said Mrs. Poyser, with a sob in her voice. "But there's One above 'ull take care o' the innicent child, else it's but little truth they tell us at church. It'll be harder nor ever to die an' leave the little uns, an' nobody to be a mother to 'em."

“We’d better ha’ sent for Dinah, if we’d known where she is,” said Mr. Poyser; “but Adam said she’d left no direction where she’d be at Leeds.”

“Why, she’d be wi’ that woman as was a friend t’ her Aunt Judith,” said Mrs. Poyser, comforted a little by this suggestion of her husband. “I’ve often heard Dinah talk of her, but I can’t remember what name she called her by. But there’s Seth Bede; he’s like enough to know, for she’s a preaching woman as the Methodists think a deal on.”

“I’ll send to Seth,” said Mr. Poyser. “I’ll send Alick to tell him to come, or else to send up word o’ the woman’s name, an’ thee canst write a letter ready to send off to Treddles’on as soon as we can make out a direction.”

“It’s poor work writing letters when you want folks to come to you i’ trouble,” said Mrs. Poyser. “Happen it’ll be ever so long on the road, an’ never reach her at last.”

Before Alick arrived with the message, Lisbeth’s thoughts too had already flown to Dinah, and she had said to Seth, “Eh, there’s no comfort for us i’ this world any more, wi’out thee couldst get Dinah Morris to come to us, as she did when my old man died. I’d like her to come in an’ take me by th’ hand again, an’ talk to me. She’d tell me the rights on’t, belike—she’d happen know some good i’ all this trouble an’ heart-break comin’ upo’ that poor lad, as ne’er done a bit o’ wrong in’s life, but war better nor anybody else’s son, pick the country round. Eh, my lad... Adam, my poor lad!”

“Thee wouldstna like me to leave thee, to go and fetch Dinah?” said Seth, as his mother sobbed and rocked herself to and fro.

“Fetch her?” said Lisbeth, looking up and pausing from her grief, like a crying child who hears some promise of consolation. “Why, what place is’t she’s at, do they say?”

“It’s a good way off, mother—Leeds, a big town. But I could be back in three days, if thee couldst spare me.”

“Nay, nay, I canna spare thee. Thee must go an’ see thy brother, an’ bring me word what he’s a-doin’. Mester Irwine said he’d come an’ tell me, but I canna make out so well what it means when he tells me. Thee must go thysen, sin’ Adam wonna let me go to him. Write a letter to Dinah canstna? Thee’t fond enough o’ writin’ when nobody wants thee.”

“I’m not sure where she’d be i’ that big town,” said Seth. “If I’d gone myself, I could ha’ found out by asking the members o’ the Society. But perhaps if I put Sarah Williamson, Methodist preacher, Leeds, o’ th’ outside, it might get to her; for most like she’d be wi’ Sarah Williamson.”

Alick came now with the message, and Seth, finding that Mrs. Poyser was writing to Dinah, gave up the intention of writing himself; but he went to the Hall Farm to tell them all he could suggest about the address of the letter, and warn them that there might be some delay in the delivery, from his not knowing an exact direction.

On leaving Lisbeth, Mr. Irwine had gone to Jonathan Burge, who had also a claim to be acquainted with what was likely to keep Adam away from business for some time; and before six o'clock that evening there were few people in Broxton and Hayslope who had not heard the sad news. Mr. Irwine had not mentioned Arthur's name to Burge, and yet the story of his conduct towards Hetty, with all the dark shadows cast upon it by its terrible consequences, was presently as well known as that his grandfather was dead, and that he was come into the estate. For Martin Poyser felt no motive to keep silence towards the one or two neighbours who ventured to come and shake him sorrowfully by the hand on the first day of his trouble; and Carroll, who kept his ears open to all that passed at the rectory, had framed an inferential version of the story, and found early opportunities of communicating it.

One of those neighbours who came to Martin Poyser and shook him by the hand without speaking for some minutes was Bartle Massey. He had shut up his school, and was on his way to the rectory, where he arrived about half-past seven in the evening, and, sending his duty to Mr. Irwine, begged pardon for troubling him at that hour, but had something particular on his mind. He was shown into the study, where Mr. Irwine soon joined him.

"Well, Bartle?" said Mr. Irwine, putting out his hand. That was not his usual way of saluting the schoolmaster, but trouble makes us treat all who feel with us very much alike. "Sit down."

"You know what I'm come about as well as I do, sir, I daresay," said Bartle.

"You wish to know the truth about the sad news that has reached you... about Hetty Sorrel?"

"Nay, sir, what I wish to know is about Adam Bede. I understand you left him at Stoniton, and I beg the favour of you to tell me what's the state of the poor lad's mind, and what he means to do. For as for that bit o' pink-and-white they've taken the trouble to put in jail, I don't value her a rotten nut—not a rotten nut—only for the harm or good that may come out of her to an honest man—a lad I've set such store by—trusted to, that he'd make my bit o' knowledge go a good way in the world.... Why, sir, he's the only scholar I've had in this stupid country that ever had the will or the head-piece for mathematics. If he hadn't had so much hard work to do, poor fellow, he might have gone into the higher branches, and then this might never have happened—might never have happened."

Bartle was heated by the exertion of walking fast in an agitated frame of mind, and was not able to check himself on this first occasion of venting his feelings. But he paused now to rub his moist forehead, and probably his moist eyes also.

"You'll excuse me, sir," he said, when this pause had given him time to reflect, "for running on in this way about my own feelings, like that foolish dog of mine howling in a storm, when there's nobody wants to listen to me. I came to hear you speak, not to talk myself—if you'll take the trouble to tell me what the poor lad's doing."

"Don't put yourself under any restraint, Bartle," said Mr. Irwine. "The fact is, I'm very much in the same condition as you just now; I've a great deal that's painful on my mind, and I find it hard work to be quite silent about my own feelings and only attend to others. I share your concern for Adam, though he is not the only one whose sufferings I care for in this affair. He intends to remain at Stoniton till after the trial: it will come on probably a week to-morrow. He has taken a room there, and I encouraged him to do so, because I think it better he should be away from his own home at present; and, poor fellow, he still believes Hetty is innocent—he wants to summon up courage to see her if he can; he is unwilling to leave the spot where she is."

"Do you think the creatur's guilty, then?" said Bartle. "Do you think they'll hang her?""I'm afraid it will go hard with her. The evidence is very strong. And one bad symptom is that she denies everything—denies that she has had a child in the face of the most positive evidence. I saw her myself, and she was obstinately silent to me; she shrank up like a frightened animal when she saw me. I was never so shocked in my life as at the change in her. But I trust that, in the worst case, we may obtain a pardon for the sake of the innocent who are involved."

"Stuff and nonsense!" said Bartle, forgetting in his irritation to whom he was speaking. "I beg your pardon, sir, I mean it's stuff and nonsense for the innocent to care about her being hanged. For my own part, I think the sooner such women are put out o' the world the better; and the men that help 'em to do mischief had better go along with 'em for that matter. What good will you do by keeping such vermin alive, eating the victual that 'ud feed rational beings? But if Adam's fool enough to care about it, I don't want him to suffer more than's needful.... Is he very much cut up, poor fellow?" Bartle added, taking out his spectacles and putting them on, as if they would assist his imagination.

"Yes, I'm afraid the grief cuts very deep," said Mr. Irwine. "He looks terribly shattered, and a certain violence came over him now and then yesterday, which made me wish I could have remained near him. But I shall go to Stoniton again to-morrow, and I have confidence enough in the strength of Adam's principle to trust that he will be able to endure the worst without being driven to anything rash." Mr. Irwine, who was involuntarily uttering his own thoughts rather than addressing Bartle Massey in the last sentence, had in his mind the possibility that the spirit of vengeance towards Arthur, which was the form Adam's anguish was continually taking, might make him seek an encounter that was likely to end more fatally than the one in the Grove. This possibility heightened the anxiety with which he looked forward to Arthur's arrival. But Bartle thought Mr. Irwine was referring to suicide, and his face wore a new alarm.

"I'll tell you what I have in my head, sir," he said, "and I hope you'll approve of it. I'm going to shut up my school—if the scholars come, they must go back again, that's all—and I shall go to Stoniton and look after Adam till this business is over. I'll pretend I'm come to look on at the assizes; he can't object to that. What do you think about it, sir?"

"Well," said Mr. Irwine, rather hesitatingly, "there would be some real advantages in that... and I honour you for your friendship towards him, Bartle. But... you must be careful what you say to him, you know. I'm afraid you have too little fellow-feeling in what you consider his weakness about Hetty."

"Trust to me, sir—trust to me. I know what you mean. I've been a fool myself in my time, but that's between you and me. I shan't thrust myself on him only keep my eye on him, and see that he gets some good food, and put in a word here and there."

"Then," said Mr. Irwine, reassured a little as to Bartle's discretion, "I think you'll be doing a good deed; and it will be well for you to let Adam's mother and brother know that you're going."

"Yes, sir, yes," said Bartle, rising, and taking off his spectacles, "I'll do that, I'll do that; though the mother's a whimpering thing—I don't like to come within earshot of her; however, she's a straight-backed, clean woman, none of your slatterns. I wish you good-bye, sir, and thank you for the time you've spared me. You're everybody's friend in this business—everybody's friend. It's a heavy weight you've got on your shoulders."

"Good-bye, Bartle, till we meet at Stoniton, as I daresay we shall."

Bartle hurried away from the rectory, evading Carroll's conversational advances, and saying in an exasperated tone to Vixen, whose short legs pattered beside him on the gravel, "Now, I shall be obliged to take you with me, you good-for-nothing woman. You'd go fretting yourself to death if I left you—you know you would, and perhaps get snapped up by some tramp. And you'll be running into bad company, I expect, putting your nose in every hole and corner where you've no business! But if you do anything disgraceful, I'll disown you—mind that, madam, mind that!"

Chapter XLI
The Eve of the Trial

An upper room in a dull Stoniton street, with two beds in it—one laid on the floor. It is ten o'clock on Thursday night, and the dark wall opposite the window shuts out the moonlight that might have struggled with the light of the one dip candle by which Bartle Massey is pretending to read, while he is really looking over his spectacles at Adam Bede, seated near the dark window.

You would hardly have known it was Adam without being told. His face has got thinner this last week: he has the sunken eyes, the neglected beard of a man just risen from a sick-bed. His heavy black hair hangs over his forehead, and there is no active impulse in him which inclines him to push it off, that he may be more awake to what is around him. He has one arm over the back of the chair, and he seems to be looking down at his clasped hands. He is roused by a knock at the door.

"There he is," said Bartle Massey, rising hastily and unfastening the door. It was Mr. Irwine. Adam rose from his chair with instinctive respect, as Mr. Irwine approached him and took his hand.

"I'm late, Adam," he said, sitting down on the chair which Bartle placed for him, "but I was later in setting off from Broxton than I intended to be, and I have been incessantly occupied since I arrived. I have done everything now, however—everything that can be done to-night, at least. Let us all sit down."

Adam took his chair again mechanically, and Bartle, for whom there was no chair remaining, sat on the bed in the background.

"Have you seen her, sir?" said Adam tremulously.

"Yes, Adam; I and the chaplain have both been with her this evening."

"Did you ask her, sir... did you say anything about me?"

"Yes," said Mr. Irwine, with some hesitation, "I spoke of you. I said you wished to see her before the trial, if she consented."

As Mr. Irwine paused, Adam looked at him with eager, questioning eyes.

"You know she shrinks from seeing any one, Adam. It is not only you—some fatal influence seems to have shut up her heart against her fellow-creatures. She has scarcely said anything more than 'No' either to me or the chaplain. Three or four days ago, before you were mentioned to her, when I asked her if there was any one of her family whom she would like to see—to whom she could open her mind—she said, with a violent shudder, 'Tell them not to come near me—I won't see any of them.'"

Adam's head was hanging down again, and he did not speak. There was silence for a few minutes, and then Mr. Irwine said, "I don't like to advise you against your own feelings, Adam, if they now urge you strongly to go and see her to-morrow morning, even without her consent. It is just possible, notwithstanding appearances to the contrary, that the interview might affect her favourably. But I grieve to say I have scarcely any hope of that. She didn't seem agitated when I mentioned your name; she only said 'No,' in the same cold, obstinate way as usual. And if the meeting had no good effect on her, it would be pure, useless suffering to you—severe suffering, I fear. She is very much changed..." Adam started up from his chair and seized his hat, which lay on the table. But he stood still then, and looked at Mr. Irwine, as if he had a question to ask which it was yet difficult to utter. Bartle Massey rose quietly, turned the key in the door, and put it in his pocket.

"Is he come back?" said Adam at last.

"No, he is not," said Mr. Irwine, quietly. "Lay down your hat, Adam, unless you like to walk out with me for a little fresh air. I fear you have not been out again to-day."

"You needn't deceive me, sir," said Adam, looking hard at Mr. Irwine and speaking in a tone of angry suspicion. "You needn't be afraid of me. I only want justice. I want him to feel what she feels. It's his work... she was a child as it 'ud ha' gone t' anybody's heart to look at... I don't care what she's done... it was him brought her to it. And he shall know it... he shall feel it... if there's a just God, he shall feel what it is t' ha' brought a child like her to sin and misery."

"I'm not deceiving you, Adam," said Mr. Irwine. "Arthur Donnithorne is not come back—was not come back when I left. I have left a letter for him: he will know all as soon as he arrives."

"But you don't mind about it," said Adam indignantly. "You think it doesn't matter as she lies there in shame and misery, and he knows nothing about it—he suffers nothing."

"Adam, he *will* know—he *will* suffer, long and bitterly. He has a heart and a conscience: I can't be entirely deceived in his character. I am convinced—I am sure he didn't fall under temptation without a struggle. He may be weak, but he is not callous, not coldly selfish. I am persuaded that this will be a shock of which he will feel the effects all his life. Why do you crave vengeance in this way? No amount of torture that you could inflict on *him* could benefit *her*."

"No—O God, no," Adam groaned out, sinking on his chair again; "but then, that's the deepest curse of all... that's what makes the blackness of it... *it can never be undone*. My poor Hetty... she can never be my sweet Hetty again... the prettiest thing God had made—smiling up at me... I thought she loved me... and was good..." Adam's voice had been gradually sinking into a hoarse undertone, as if he were only talking to himself; but now he said abruptly, looking at Mr. Irwine, "But she isn't as guilty as they say? You don't think she is, sir? She can't ha' done it."

"That perhaps can never be known with certainty, Adam," Mr. Irwine answered gently. "In these cases we sometimes form our judgment on what seems to us strong evidence, and yet, for want of knowing some small fact, our judgment is wrong. But suppose the worst: you have no right to say that the guilt of her crime lies with him, and that he ought to bear the punishment. It is not for us men to apportion the shares of moral guilt and retribution. We find it impossible to avoid mistakes even in determining who has committed a single criminal act, and the problem how far a man is to be held responsible for the unforeseen consequences of his own deed is one that might well make us tremble to look into it. The evil consequences that may lie folded in a single act of selfish indulgence is a thought so awful that it ought surely to awaken some feeling less presumptuous than a rash desire to punish. You have a mind that can understand this fully, Adam, when you are calm. Don't suppose I can't enter into the anguish that drives you into this state of revengeful hatred. But think of this: if you were to obey your passion—for it *is* passion, and you deceive yourself in calling it justice—it might be with you precisely as it has been with Arthur; nay, worse; your passion might lead you yourself into a horrible crime."

"No—not worse," said Adam, bitterly; "I don't believe it's worse—I'd sooner do it—I'd sooner do a wickedness as I could suffer for by myself than ha' brought *her* to do wickedness and then stand by and see 'em punish her while they let me alone; and all for a bit o' pleasure, as, if he'd had a man's heart in him, he'd ha' cut his hand off sooner than he'd ha' taken it. What if he didn't foresee what's happened? He foresaw enough; he'd no right to expect anything but harm and shame to her. And then he wanted to smooth it off wi' lies. No—there's plenty o' things folks are hanged for not half so hateful as that. Let a man do what he will, if he knows he's to bear the punishment himself, he isn't half so bad as a mean selfish coward as makes things easy t' himself and knows all the while the punishment 'll fall on somebody else."

"There again you partly deceive yourself, Adam. There is no sort of wrong deed of which a man can bear the punishment alone; you can't isolate yourself and say that the evil which is in you shall not spread. Men's lives are as thoroughly blended with each other as the air they breathe: evil spreads as necessarily as disease. I know, I feel the terrible extent of suffering this sin of Arthur's has caused to others; but so does every sin cause suffering to others besides those who commit it. An act of vengeance on your part against Arthur would simply be another evil added to those we are suffering under: you could not bear the punishment alone; you would entail the worst sorrows on every one who loves you. You would have committed an act of blind fury that would leave all the present evils just as they were and add worse evils to them. You may tell me that you meditate no fatal act of vengeance, but the feeling in your mind is what gives birth to such actions, and as long as you indulge it, as long as you do not see that to fix your mind on Arthur's punishment is revenge, and not justice, you are in danger of being led on to the commission of some great wrong. Remember what you told me about your feelings after you had given that blow to Arthur in the Grove."

Adam was silent: the last words had called up a vivid image of the past, and Mr. Irwine left him to his thoughts, while he spoke to Bartle Massey about old Mr. Donnithorne's funeral and other matters of an indifferent kind. But at length Adam turned round and said, in a more subdued tone, "I've not asked about 'em at th' Hall Farm, sir. Is Mr. Poyser coming?" "He is come; he is in Stoniton to-night. But I could not advise him to see you, Adam. His own mind is in a very perturbed state, and it is best he should not see you till you are calmer."

"Is Dinah Morris come to 'em, sir? Seth said they'd sent for her."

"No. Mr. Poyser tells me she was not come when he left. They're afraid the letter has not reached her. It seems they had no exact address." Adam sat ruminating a little while, and then said, "I wonder if Dinah 'ud ha' gone to see her. But perhaps the Poysers would ha' been sorely against it, since they won't come nigh her themselves. But I think she would, for the Methodists are great folks for going into the prisons; and Seth said he thought she would. She'd a very tender way with her, Dinah had; I wonder if she could ha' done any good. You never saw her, sir, did you?"

"Yes, I did. I had a conversation with her—she pleased me a good deal. And now you mention it, I wish she would come, for it is possible that a gentle mild woman like her might move Hetty to open her heart. The jail chaplain is rather harsh in his manner."

"But it's o' no use if she doesn't come," said Adam sadly.

"If I'd thought of it earlier, I would have taken some measures for finding her out," said Mr. Irwine, "but it's too late now, I fear... Well, Adam, I must go now. Try to get some rest to-night. God bless you. I'll see you early to-morrow morning."

Chapter XLII
The Morning of the Trial

At one o'clock the next day, Adam was alone in his dull upper room; his watch lay before him on the table, as if he were counting the long minutes. He had no knowledge of what was likely to be said by the witnesses on the trial, for he had shrunk from all the particulars connected with Hetty's arrest and accusation. This brave active man, who would have hastened towards any danger or toil to rescue Hetty from an apprehended wrong or misfortune, felt himself powerless to contemplate irremediable evil and suffering. The susceptibility which would have been an impelling force where there was any possibility of action became helpless anguish when he was obliged to be passive, or else sought an active outlet in the thought of inflicting justice on Arthur. Energetic natures, strong for all strenuous deeds, will often rush away from a hopeless sufferer, as if they were hard-hearted. It is the overmastering sense of pain that drives them. They shrink by an ungovernable instinct, as they would shrink from laceration. Adam had brought himself to think of seeing Hetty, if she would consent to see him, because he thought the meeting might possibly be a good to her—might help to melt away this terrible hardness they told him of. If she saw he bore her no ill will for what she had done to him, she might open her heart to him. But this resolution had been an immense effort—he trembled at the thought of seeing her changed face, as a timid woman trembles at the thought of the surgeon's knife, and he chose now to bear the long hours of suspense rather than encounter what seemed to him the more intolerable agony of witnessing her trial.

Deep unspeakable suffering may well be called a baptism, a regeneration, the initiation into a new state. The yearning memories, the bitter regret, the agonized sympathy, the struggling appeals to the Invisible Right—all the intense emotions which had filled the days and nights of the past week, and were compressing themselves again like an eager crowd into the hours of this single morning, made Adam look back on all the previous years as if they had been a dim sleepy existence, and he had only now awaked to full consciousness. It seemed to him as if he had always before thought it a light thing that men should suffer, as if all that he had himself endured and called sorrow before was only a moment's stroke that had never left a bruise. Doubtless a great anguish may do the work of years, and we may come out from that baptism of fire with a soul full of new awe and new pity.

"O God," Adam groaned, as he leaned on the table and looked blankly at the face of the watch, "and men have suffered like this before... and poor helpless young things have suffered like her.... Such a little while ago looking so happy and so pretty... kissing 'em all, her grandfather and all of 'em, and they wishing her luck.... O my poor, poor Hetty... dost think on it now?"

Adam started and looked round towards the door. Vixen had begun to whimper, and there was a sound of a stick and a lame walk on the stairs. It was Bartle Massey come back. Could it be all over?

Bartle entered quietly, and, going up to Adam, grasped his hand and said, "I'm just come to look at you, my boy, for the folks are gone out of court for a bit."

Adam's heart beat so violently he was unable to speak—he could only return the pressure of his friend's hand—and Bartle, drawing up the other chair, came and sat in front of him, taking off his hat and his spectacles.

"That's a thing never happened to me before," he observed, "to go out o' the door with my spectacles on. I clean forgot to take 'em off."

The old man made this trivial remark, thinking it better not to respond at all to Adam's agitation: he would gather, in an indirect way, that there was nothing decisive to communicate at present.

"And now," he said, rising again, "I must see to your having a bit of the loaf, and some of that wine Mr. Irwine sent this morning. He'll be angry with me if you don't have it. Come, now," he went on, bringing forward the bottle and the loaf and pouring some wine into a cup, "I must have a bit and a sup myself. Drink a drop with me, my lad—drink with me."

Adam pushed the cup gently away and said, entreatingly, "Tell me about it, Mr. Massey—tell me all about it. Was she there? Have they begun?"

"Yes, my boy, yes—it's taken all the time since I first went; but they're slow, they're slow; and there's the counsel they've got for her puts a spoke in the wheel whenever he can, and makes a deal to do with cross-examining the witnesses and quarrelling with the other lawyers. That's all he can do for the money they give him; and it's a big sum—it's a big sum. But he's a 'cute fellow, with an eye that 'ud pick the needles out of the hay in no time. If a man had got no feelings, it 'ud be as good as a demonstration to listen to what goes on in court; but a tender heart makes one stupid. I'd have given up figures for ever only to have had some good news to bring to you, my poor lad."

"But does it seem to be going against her?" said Adam. "Tell me what they've said. I must know it now—I must know what they have to bring against her."

"Why, the chief evidence yet has been the doctors; all but Martin Poyser—poor Martin. Everybody in court felt for him—it was like one sob, the sound they made when he came down again. The worst was when they told him to look at the prisoner at the bar. It was hard work, poor fellow—it was hard work. Adam, my boy, the blow falls heavily on him as well as you; you must help poor Martin; you must show courage. Drink some wine now, and show me you mean to bear it like a man."

Bartle had made the right sort of appeal. Adam, with an air of quiet obedience, took up the cup and drank a little.

"Tell me how *she* looked," he said presently.

"Frightened, very frightened, when they first brought her in; it was the first sight of the crowd and the judge, poor creatur. And there's a lot o' foolish women in fine clothes, with gewgaws all up their arms and feathers on their heads, sitting near the judge: they've dressed themselves out in that way, one 'ud think, to be scarecrows and warnings against any man ever meddling with a woman again. They put up their glasses, and stared and whispered. But after that she stood like a white image, staring down at her hands and seeming neither to hear nor see anything. And she's as white as a sheet. She didn't speak when they asked her if she'd plead 'guilty' or 'not guilty,' and they pleaded 'not guilty' for her. But when she heard her uncle's name, there seemed to go a shiver right through her; and when they told him to look at her, she hung her head down, and cowered, and hid her face in her hands. He'd much ado to speak poor man, his voice trembled so. And the counsellors—who look as hard as nails mostly—I saw, spared him as much as they could. Mr. Irwine put himself near him and went with him out o' court. Ah, it's a great thing in a man's life to be able to stand by a neighbour and uphold him in such trouble as that."

"God bless him, and you too, Mr. Massey," said Adam, in a low voice, laying his hand on Bartle's arm.

"Aye, aye, he's good metal; he gives the right ring when you try him, our parson does. A man o' sense—says no more than's needful. He's not one of those that think they can comfort you with chattering, as if folks who stand by and look on knew a deal better what the trouble was than those who have to bear it. I've had to do with such folks in my time—in the south, when I was in trouble myself. Mr. Irwine is to be a witness himself, by and by, on her side, you know, to speak to her character and bringing up."

"But the other evidence... does it go hard against her!" said Adam. "What do you think, Mr. Massey? Tell me the truth."

"Yes, my lad, yes. The truth is the best thing to tell. It must come at last. The doctors' evidence is heavy on her—is heavy. But she's gone on denying she's had a child from first to last. These poor silly women-things—they've not the sense to know it's no use denying what's proved. It'll make against her with the jury, I doubt, her being so obstinate: they may be less for recommending her to mercy, if the verdict's against her. But Mr. Irwine 'ull leave no stone unturned with the judge—you may rely upon that, Adam."

"Is there nobody to stand by her and seem to care for her in the court?" said Adam.

"There's the chaplain o' the jail sits near her, but he's a sharp ferrety-faced man—another sort o' flesh and blood to Mr. Irwine. They say the jail chaplains are mostly the fag-end o' the clergy."

"There's one man as ought to be there," said Adam bitterly. Presently he drew himself up and looked fixedly out of the window, apparently turning over some new idea in his mind.

"Mr. Massey," he said at last, pushing the hair off his forehead, "I'll go back with you. I'll go into court. It's cowardly of me to keep away. I'll stand by her—I'll own her—for all she's been deceitful. They oughtn't to cast her off—her own flesh and blood. We hand folks over to God's mercy, and show none ourselves. I used to be hard sometimes: I'll never be hard again. I'll go, Mr. Massey—I'll go with you."

There was a decision in Adam's manner which would have prevented Bartle from opposing him, even if he had wished to do so. He only said, "Take a bit, then, and another sup, Adam, for the love of me. See, I must stop and eat a morsel. Now, you take some."

Nerved by an active resolution, Adam took a morsel of bread and drank some wine. He was haggard and unshaven, as he had been yesterday, but he stood upright again, and looked more like the Adam Bede of former days.

Chapter XLIII
The Verdict

The place fitted up that day as a court of justice was a grand old hall, now destroyed by fire. The midday light that fell on the close pavement of human heads was shed through a line of high pointed windows, variegated with the mellow tints of old painted glass. Grim dusty armour hung in high relief in front of the dark oaken gallery at the farther end, and under the broad arch of the great mullioned window opposite was spread a curtain of old tapestry, covered with dim melancholy figures, like a dozing indistinct dream of the past. It was a place that through the rest of the year was haunted with the shadowy memories of old kings and queens, unhappy, discrowned, imprisoned; but to-day all those shadows had fled, and not a soul in the vast hall felt the presence of any but a living sorrow, which was quivering in warm hearts.

But that sorrow seemed to have made it itself feebly felt hitherto, now when Adam Bede's tall figure was suddenly seen being ushered to the side of the prisoner's dock. In the broad sunlight of the great hall, among the sleek shaven faces of other men, the marks of suffering in his face were startling even to Mr. Irwine, who had last seen him in the dim light of his small room; and the neighbours from Hayslope who were present, and who told Hetty Sorrel's story by their firesides in their old age, never forgot to say how it moved them when Adam Bede, poor fellow, taller by the head than most of the people round him, came into court and took his place by her side.

But Hetty did not see him. She was standing in the same position Bartle Massey had described, her hands crossed over each other and her eyes fixed on them. Adam had not dared to look at her in the first moments, but at last, when the attention of the court was withdrawn by the proceedings he turned his face towards her with a resolution not to shrink.

Why did they say she was so changed? In the corpse we love, it is the *likeness* we see—it is the likeness, which makes itself felt the more keenly because something else *was* and *is not*. There they were—the sweet face and neck, with the dark tendrils of hair, the long dark lashes, the rounded cheek and the pouting lips—pale and thin, yes, but like Hetty, and only Hetty. Others thought she looked as if some demon had cast a blighting glance upon her, withered up the woman's soul in her, and left only a hard despairing obstinacy. But the mother's yearning, that completest type of the life in another life which is the essence of real human love, feels the presence of the cherished child even in the debased, degraded man; and to Adam, this pale, hard-looking culprit was the Hetty who had smiled at him in the garden under the apple-tree boughs—she was that Hetty's corpse, which he had trembled to look at the first time, and then was unwilling to turn away his eyes from.

But presently he heard something that compelled him to listen, and made the sense of sight less absorbing. A woman was in the witness-box, a middle-aged woman, who spoke in a firm distinct voice. She said, "My name is Sarah Stone. I am a widow, and keep a small shop licensed to sell tobacco, snuff, and tea in Church Lane, Stoniton. The prisoner at the bar is the same young woman who came, looking ill and tired, with a basket on her arm, and asked for a lodging at my house on Saturday evening, the 27th of February. She had taken the house for a public, because there was a figure against the door. And when I said I didn't take in lodgers, the prisoner began to cry, and said she was too tired to go anywhere else, and she only wanted a bed for one night. And her prettiness, and her condition, and something respectable about her clothes and looks, and the trouble she seemed to be in made me as I couldn't find in my heart to send her away at once. I asked her to sit down, and gave her some tea, and asked her where she was going, and where her friends were. She said she was going home to her friends: they were farming folks a good way off, and she'd had a long journey that had cost her more money than she expected, so as she'd hardly any money left in her pocket, and was afraid of going where it would cost her much. She had been obliged to sell most of the things out of her basket, but she'd thankfully give a shilling for a bed. I saw no reason why I shouldn't take the young woman in for the night. I had only one room, but there were two beds in it, and I told her she might stay with me. I thought she'd been led wrong, and got into trouble, but if she was going to her friends, it would be a good work to keep her out of further harm."

The witness then stated that in the night a child was born, and she identified the baby-clothes then shown to her as those in which she had herself dressed the child.

"Those are the clothes. I made them myself, and had kept them by me ever since my last child was born. I took a deal of trouble both for the child and the mother. I couldn't help taking to the little thing and being anxious about it. I didn't send for a doctor, for there seemed no need. I told the mother in the day-time she must tell me the name of her friends, and where they lived, and let me write to them. She said, by and by she would write herself, but not to-day. She would have no nay, but she would get up and be dressed, in spite of everything I could say. She said she felt quite strong enough; and it was wonderful what spirit she showed. But I wasn't quite easy what I should do about her, and towards evening I made up my mind I'd go, after Meeting was over, and speak to our minister about it. I left the house about half-past eight o'clock. I didn't go out at the shop door, but at the back door, which opens into a narrow alley. I've only got the ground-floor of the house, and the kitchen and bedroom both look into the alley. I left the prisoner sitting up by the fire in the kitchen with the baby on her lap. She hadn't cried or seemed low at all, as she did the night before. I thought she had a strange look with her eyes, and she got a bit flushed towards evening. I was afraid of the fever, and I thought I'd call and ask an acquaintance of mine, an experienced woman, to come back with me when I went out. It was a very dark night. I didn't fasten the door behind me; there was no lock; it was a latch with a bolt inside, and when there was nobody in the house I always went out at the shop door. But I thought there was no danger in leaving it unfastened that little while. I was longer than I meant to be, for I had to wait for the woman that came back with me. It was an hour and a half before we got back, and when we went in, the candle was standing burning just as I left it, but the prisoner and the baby were both gone. She'd taken her cloak and bonnet, but she'd left the basket and the things in it.... I was dreadful frightened, and angry with her for going. I didn't go to give information, because I'd no thought she meant to do any harm, and I knew she had money in her pocket to buy her food and lodging. I didn't like to set the constable after her, for she'd a right to go from me if she liked."

The effect of this evidence on Adam was electrical; it gave him new force. Hetty could not be guilty of the crime—her heart must have clung to her baby—else why should she have taken it with her? She might have left it behind. The little creature had died naturally, and then she had hidden it. Babies were so liable to death—and there might be the strongest suspicions without any proof of guilt. His mind was so occupied with imaginary arguments against such suspicions, that he could not listen to the cross-examination by Hetty's counsel, who tried, without result, to elicit evidence that the prisoner had shown some movements of maternal affection towards the child. The whole time this witness was being examined, Hetty had stood as motionless as before: no word seemed to arrest her ear. But the sound of the next witness's voice touched a chord that was still sensitive, she gave a start and a frightened look towards him, but immediately turned away her head and looked down at her hands as before. This witness was a man, a rough peasant. He said:

"My name is John Olding. I am a labourer, and live at Tedd's Hole, two miles out of Stoniton. A week last Monday, towards one o'clock in the afternoon, I was going towards Hetton Coppice, and about a quarter of a mile from the coppice I saw the prisoner, in a red cloak, sitting under a bit of a haystack not far off the stile. She got up when she saw me, and seemed as if she'd be walking on the other way. It was a regular road through the fields, and nothing very uncommon to see a young woman there, but I took notice of her because she looked white and scared. I should have thought she was a beggar-woman, only for her good clothes. I thought she looked a bit crazy, but it was no business of mine. I stood and looked back after her, but she went right on while she was in sight. I had to go to the other side of the coppice to look after some stakes. There's a road right through it, and bits of openings here and there, where the trees have been cut down, and some of 'em not carried away. I didn't go straight along the road, but turned off towards the middle, and took a shorter way towards the spot I wanted to get to. I hadn't got far out of the road into one of the open places before I heard a strange cry. I thought it didn't come from any animal I knew, but I wasn't for stopping to look about just then. But it went on, and seemed so strange to me in that place, I couldn't help stopping to look. I began to think I might make some money of it, if it was a new thing. But I had hard work to tell which way it came from, and for a good while I kept looking up at the boughs. And then I thought it came from the ground; and there was a lot of timber-choppings lying about, and loose pieces of turf, and a trunk or two. And I looked about among them, but could find nothing, and at last the cry stopped. So I was for giving it up, and I went on about my business. But when I came back the same way pretty nigh an hour after, I couldn't help laying down my stakes to have another look. And just as I was stooping and laying down the stakes, I saw something odd and round and whitish lying on the ground under a nut-bush by the side of me. And I stooped down on hands and knees to pick it up. And I saw it was a little baby's hand."

At these words a thrill ran through the court. Hetty was visibly trembling; now, for the first time, she seemed to be listening to what a witness said.

"There was a lot of timber-choppings put together just where the ground went hollow, like, under the bush, and the hand came out from among them. But there was a hole left in one place and I could see down it and see the child's head; and I made haste and did away the turf and the choppings, and took out the child. It had got comfortable clothes on, but its body was cold, and I thought it must be dead. I made haste back with it out of the wood, and took it home to my wife. She said it was dead, and I'd better take it to the parish and tell the constable. And I said, 'I'll lay my life it's that young woman's child as I met going to the coppice.' But she seemed to be gone clean out of sight. And I took the child on to Hetton parish and told the constable, and we went on to Justice Hardy. And then we went looking after the young woman till dark at night, and we went and gave information at Stoniton, as they might stop her. And the next morning, another constable came to me, to go with him to the spot where I found the child. And when we got there, there was the prisoner a-sitting against the bush where I found the child; and she cried out when she saw us, but she never offered to move. She'd got a big piece of bread on her lap."

Adam had given a faint groan of despair while this witness was speaking. He had hidden his face on his arm, which rested on the boarding in front of him. It was the supreme moment of his suffering: Hetty was guilty; and he was silently calling to God for help. He heard no more of the evidence, and was unconscious when the case for the prosecution had closed—unconscious that Mr. Irwine was in the witness-box, telling of Hetty's unblemished character in her own parish and of the virtuous habits in which she had been brought up. This testimony could have no influence on the verdict, but it was given as part of that plea for mercy which her own counsel would have made if he had been allowed to speak for her—a favour not granted to criminals in those stern times.

At last Adam lifted up his head, for there was a general movement round him. The judge had addressed the jury, and they were retiring. The decisive moment was not far off. Adam felt a shuddering horror that would not let him look at Hetty, but she had long relapsed into her blank hard indifference. All eyes were strained to look at her, but she stood like a statue of dull despair.

There was a mingled rustling, whispering, and low buzzing throughout the court during this interval. The desire to listen was suspended, and every one had some feeling or opinion to express in undertones. Adam sat looking blankly before him, but he did not see the objects that were right in front of his eyes—the counsel and attorneys talking with an air of cool business, and Mr. Irwine in low earnest conversation with the judge—did not see Mr. Irwine sit down again in agitation and shake his head mournfully when somebody whispered to him. The inward action was too intense for Adam to take in outward objects until some strong sensation roused him.

It was not very long, hardly more than a quarter of an hour, before the knock which told that the jury had come to their decision fell as a signal for silence on every ear. It is sublime—that sudden pause of a great multitude which tells that one soul moves in them all. Deeper and deeper the silence seemed to become, like the deepening night, while the jurymen's names were called over, and the prisoner was made to hold up her hand, and the jury were asked for their verdict.

"Guilty."

It was the verdict every one expected, but there was a sigh of disappointment from some hearts that it was followed by no recommendation to mercy. Still the sympathy of the court was not with the prisoner. The unnaturalness of her crime stood out the more harshly by the side of her hard immovability and obstinate silence. Even the verdict, to distant eyes, had not appeared to move her, but those who were near saw her trembling.

The stillness was less intense until the judge put on his black cap, and the chaplain in his canonicals was observed behind him. Then it deepened again, before the crier had had time to command silence. If any sound were heard, it must have been the sound of beating hearts. The judge spoke, "Hester Sorrel...."

The blood rushed to Hetty's face, and then fled back again as she looked up at the judge and kept her wide-open eyes fixed on him, as if fascinated by fear. Adam had not yet turned towards her, there was a deep horror, like a great gulf, between them. But at the words "and then to be hanged by the neck till you be dead," a piercing shriek rang through the hall. It was Hetty's shriek. Adam started to his feet and stretched out his arms towards her. But the arms could not reach her: she had fallen down in a fainting-fit, and was carried out of court.

Chapter XLIV
Arthur's Return

When Arthur Donnithorne landed at Liverpool and read the letter from his Aunt Lydia, briefly announcing his grand-father's death, his first feeling was, "Poor Grandfather! I wish I could have got to him to be with him when he died. He might have felt or wished something at the last that I shall never know now. It was a lonely death."

It is impossible to say that his grief was deeper than that. Pity and softened memory took place of the old antagonism, and in his busy thoughts about the future, as the chaise carried him rapidly along towards the home where he was now to be master, there was a continually recurring effort to remember anything by which he could show a regard for his grandfather's wishes, without counteracting his own cherished aims for the good of the tenants and the estate. But it is not in human nature—only in human pretence—for a young man like Arthur, with a fine constitution and fine spirits, thinking well of himself, believing that others think well of him, and having a very ardent intention to give them more and more reason for that good opinion—it is not possible for such a young man, just coming into a splendid estate through the death of a very old man whom he was not fond of, to feel anything very different from exultant joy. *Now* his real life was beginning; now he would have room and opportunity for action, and he would use them. He would show the Loamshire people what a fine country gentleman was; he would not exchange that career for any other under the sun. He felt himself riding over the hills in the breezy autumn days, looking after favourite plans of drainage and enclosure; then admired on sombre mornings as the best rider on the best horse in the hunt; spoken well of on market-days as a first-rate landlord; by and by making speeches at election dinners, and showing a wonderful knowledge of agriculture; the patron of new ploughs and drills, the severe upbraider of negligent landowners, and withal a jolly fellow that everybody must like—happy faces greeting him everywhere on his own estate, and the neighbouring families on the best terms with him. The Irwines should dine with him every week, and have their own carriage to come in, for in some very delicate way that Arthur would devise, the lay-impropriator of the Hayslope tithes would insist on paying a couple of hundreds more to the vicar; and his aunt should be as comfortable as possible, and go on living at the Chase, if she liked, in spite of her old-maidish ways—at least until he was married, and that event lay in the indistinct background, for Arthur had not yet seen the woman who would play the lady-wife to the first-rate country gentleman.

These were Arthur's chief thoughts, so far as a man's thoughts through hours of travelling can be compressed into a few sentences, which are only like the list of names telling you what are the scenes in a long long panorama full of colour, of detail, and of life. The happy faces Arthur saw greeting him were not pale abstractions, but real ruddy faces, long familiar to him: Martin Poyser was there—the whole Poyser family.

What—Hetty?

Yes; for Arthur was at ease about Hetty—not quite at ease about the past, for a certain burning of the ears would come whenever he thought of the scenes with Adam last August, but at ease about her present lot. Mr. Irwine, who had been a regular correspondent, telling him all the news about the old places and people, had sent him word nearly three months ago that Adam Bede was not to marry Mary Burge, as he had thought, but pretty Hetty Sorrel. Martin Poyser and Adam himself had both told Mr. Irwine all about it—that Adam had been deeply in love with Hetty these two years, and that now it was agreed they were to be married in March. That stalwart rogue Adam was more susceptible than the rector had thought; it was really quite an idyllic love affair; and if it had not been too long to tell in a letter, he would have liked to describe to Arthur the blushing looks and the simple strong words with which the fine honest fellow told his secret. He knew Arthur would like to hear that Adam had this sort of happiness in prospect.

Yes, indeed! Arthur felt there was not air enough in the room to satisfy his renovated life, when he had read that passage in the letter. He threw up the windows, he rushed out of doors into the December air, and greeted every one who spoke to him with an eager gaiety, as if there had been news of a fresh Nelson victory. For the first time that day since he had come to Windsor, he was in true boyish spirits. The load that had been pressing upon him was gone, the haunting fear had vanished. He thought he could conquer his bitterness towards Adam now—could offer him his hand, and ask to be his friend again, in spite of that painful memory which would still make his ears burn. He had been knocked down, and he had been forced to tell a lie: such things make a scar, do what we will. But if Adam were the same again as in the old days, Arthur wished to be the same too, and to have Adam mixed up with his business and his future, as he had always desired before the accursed meeting in August. Nay, he would do a great deal more for Adam than he should otherwise have done, when he came into the estate; Hetty's husband had a special claim on him—Hetty herself should feel that any pain she had suffered through Arthur in the past was compensated to her a hundredfold. For really she could not have felt much, since she had so soon made up her mind to marry Adam.

You perceive clearly what sort of picture Adam and Hetty made in the panorama of Arthur's thoughts on his journey homeward. It was March now; they were soon to be married: perhaps they were already married. And *now* it was actually in his power to do a great deal for them. Sweet—sweet little Hetty! The little puss hadn't cared for him half as much as he cared for her; for he was a great fool about her still—was almost afraid of seeing her—indeed, had not cared much to look at any other woman since he parted from her. That little figure coming towards him in the Grove, those dark-fringed childish eyes, the lovely lips put up to kiss him—that picture had got no fainter with the lapse of months. And she would look just the same. It was impossible to think how he could meet her: he should certainly tremble. Strange, how long this sort of influence lasts, for he was certainly not in love with Hetty now. He had been earnestly desiring, for months, that she should marry Adam, and there was nothing that contributed more to his happiness in these moments than the thought of their marriage. It was the exaggerating effect of imagination that made his heart still beat a little more quickly at the thought of her. When he saw the little thing again as she really was, as Adam's wife, at work quite prosaically in her new home, he should perhaps wonder at the possibility of his past feelings. Thank heaven it had turned out so well! He should have plenty of affairs and interests to fill his life now, and not be in danger of playing the fool again.

Pleasant the crack of the post-boy's whip! Pleasant the sense of being hurried along in swift ease through English scenes, so like those round his own home, only not quite so charming. Here was a market-town—very much like Treddleston—where the arms of the neighbouring lord of the manor were borne on the sign of the principal inn; then mere fields and hedges, their vicinity to a market-town carrying an agreeable suggestion of high rent, till the land began to assume a trimmer look, the woods were more frequent, and at length a white or red mansion looked down from a moderate eminence, or allowed him to be aware of its parapet and chimneys among the dense-looking masses of oaks and elms—masses reddened now with early buds. And close at hand came the village: the small church, with its red-tiled roof, looking humble even among the faded half-timbered houses; the old green gravestones with nettles round them; nothing fresh and bright but the children, opening round eyes at the swift post-chaise; nothing noisy and busy but the gaping curs of mysterious pedigree. What a much prettier village Hayslope was! And it should not be neglected like this place: vigorous repairs should go on everywhere among farm-buildings and cottages, and travellers in post-chaises, coming along the Rosseter road, should do nothing but admire as they went. And Adam Bede should superintend all the repairs, for he had a share in Burge's business now, and, if he liked, Arthur would put some money into the concern and buy the old man out in another year or two. That was an ugly fault in Arthur's life, that affair last summer, but the future should make amends. Many men would have retained a feeling of vindictiveness towards Adam, but *he* would not—he would resolutely overcome all littleness of that kind, for he had certainly been very much in the wrong; and though Adam had been harsh and violent, and had thrust on him a painful dilemma, the poor fellow was in love, and had real provocation. No, Arthur had not an evil feeling in his mind towards any human being: he was happy, and would make every one else happy that came within his reach.

And here was dear old Hayslope at last, sleeping, on the hill, like a quiet old place as it was, in the late afternoon sunlight, and opposite to it the great shoulders of the Binton Hills, below them the purplish blackness of the hanging woods, and at last the pale front of the Abbey, looking out from among the oaks of the Chase, as if anxious for the heir's return. "Poor Grandfather! And he lies dead there. *He* was a young fellow once, coming into the estate and making his plans. So the world goes round! Aunt Lydia must feel very desolate, poor thing; but she shall be indulged as much as she indulges her fat Fido."

The wheels of Arthur's chaise had been anxiously listened for at the Chase, for to-day was Friday, and the funeral had already been deferred two days. Before it drew up on the gravel of the courtyard, all the servants in the house were assembled to receive him with a grave, decent welcome, befitting a house of death. A month ago, perhaps, it would have been difficult for them to have maintained a suitable sadness in their faces, when Mr. Arthur was come to take possession; but the hearts of the head-servants were heavy that day for another cause than the death of the old squire, and more than one of them was longing to be twenty miles away, as Mr. Craig was, knowing what was to become of Hetty Sorrel—pretty Hetty Sorrel—whom they used to see every week. They had the partisanship of household servants who like their places, and were not inclined to go the full length of the severe indignation felt against him by the farming tenants, but rather to make excuses for him; nevertheless, the upper servants, who had been on terms of neighbourly intercourse with the Poysers for many years, could not help feeling that the longed-for event of the young squire's coming into the estate had been robbed of all its pleasantness.

To Arthur it was nothing surprising that the servants looked grave and sad: he himself was very much touched on seeing them all again, and feeling that he was in a new relation to them. It was that sort of pathetic emotion which has more pleasure than pain in it—which is perhaps one of the most delicious of all states to a good-natured man, conscious of the power to satisfy his good nature. His heart swelled agreeably as he said, "Well, Mills, how is my aunt?"

But now Mr. Bygate, the lawyer, who had been in the house ever since the death, came forward to give deferential greetings and answer all questions, and Arthur walked with him towards the library, where his Aunt Lydia was expecting him. Aunt Lydia was the only person in the house who knew nothing about Hetty. Her sorrow as a maiden daughter was unmixed with any other thoughts than those of anxiety about funeral arrangements and her own future lot; and, after the manner of women, she mourned for the father who had made her life important, all the more because she had a secret sense that there was little mourning for him in other hearts.

But Arthur kissed her tearful face more tenderly than he had ever done in his life before.

"Dear Aunt," he said affectionately, as he held her hand, "*your* loss is the greatest of all, but you must tell me how to try and make it up to you all the rest of your life."

"It was so sudden and so dreadful, Arthur," poor Miss Lydia began, pouring out her little plaints, and Arthur sat down to listen with impatient patience. When a pause came, he said:

"Now, Aunt, I'll leave you for a quarter of an hour just to go to my own room, and then I shall come and give full attention to everything."

"My room is all ready for me, I suppose, Mills?" he said to the butler, who seemed to be lingering uneasily about the entrance-hall.

"Yes, sir, and there are letters for you; they are all laid on the writing-table in your dressing-room."

On entering the small anteroom which was called a dressing-room, but which Arthur really used only to lounge and write in, he just cast his eyes on the writing-table, and saw that there were several letters and packets lying there; but he was in the uncomfortable dusty condition of a man who has had a long hurried journey, and he must really refresh himself by attending to his toilette a little, before he read his letters. Pym was there, making everything ready for him, and soon, with a delightful freshness about him, as if he were prepared to begin a new day, he went back into his dressing-room to open his letters. The level rays of the low afternoon sun entered directly at the window, and as Arthur seated himself in his velvet chair with their pleasant warmth upon him, he was conscious of that quiet well-being which perhaps you and I have felt on a sunny afternoon when, in our brightest youth and health, life has opened a new vista for us, and long to-morrows of activity have stretched before us like a lovely plain which there was no need for hurrying to look at, because it was all our own.

The top letter was placed with its address upwards: it was in Mr. Irwine's handwriting, Arthur saw at once; and below the address was written, "To be delivered as soon as he arrives." Nothing could have been less surprising to him than a letter from Mr. Irwine at that moment: of course, there was something he wished Arthur to know earlier than it was possible for them to see each other. At such a time as that it was quite natural that Irwine should have something pressing to say. Arthur broke the seal with an agreeable anticipation of soon seeing the writer.

"I send this letter to meet you on your arrival, Arthur, because I may then be at Stoniton, whither I am called by the most painful duty it has ever been given me to perform, and it is right that you should know what I have to tell you without delay.

I will not attempt to add by one word of reproach to the retribution that is now falling on you: any other words that I could write at this moment must be weak and unmeaning by the side of those in which I must tell you the simple fact. Hetty Sorrel is in prison, and will be tried on Friday for the crime of child-murder."...

Arthur read no more. He started up from his chair and stood for a single minute with a sense of violent convulsion in his whole frame, as if the life were going out of him with horrible throbs; but the next minute he had rushed out of the room, still clutching the letter—he was hurrying along the corridor, and down the stairs into the hall. Mills was still there, but Arthur did not see him, as he passed like a hunted man across the hall and out along the gravel. The butler hurried out after him as fast as his elderly limbs could run: he guessed, he knew, where the young squire was going.

When Mills got to the stables, a horse was being saddled, and Arthur was forcing himself to read the remaining words of the letter. He thrust it into his pocket as the horse was led up to him, and at that moment caught sight of Mills' anxious face in front of him.

"Tell them I'm gone—gone to Stoniton," he said in a muffled tone of agitation—sprang into the saddle, and set off at a gallop.

Chapter XLV
In the Prison

Near sunset that evening an elderly gentleman was standing with his back against the smaller entrance-door of Stoniton jail, saying a few last words to the departing chaplain. The chaplain walked away, but the elderly gentleman stood still, looking down on the pavement and stroking his chin with a ruminating air, when he was roused by a sweet clear woman's voice, saying, "Can I get into the prison, if you please?"

He turned his head and looked fixedly at the speaker for a few moments without answering.

"I have seen you before," he said at last. "Do you remember preaching on the village green at Hayslope in Loamshire?"

"Yes, sir, surely. Are you the gentleman that stayed to listen on horseback?"

"Yes. Why do you want to go into the prison?"

"I want to go to Hetty Sorrel, the young woman who has been condemned to death—and to stay with her, if I may be permitted. Have you power in the prison, sir?"

"Yes; I am a magistrate, and can get admittance for you. But did you know this criminal, Hetty Sorrel?"

"Yes, we are kin. My own aunt married her uncle, Martin Poyser. But I was away at Leeds, and didn't know of this great trouble in time to get here before to-day. I entreat you, sir, for the love of our heavenly Father, to let me go to her and stay with her."

"How did you know she was condemned to death, if you are only just come from Leeds?"

"I have seen my uncle since the trial, sir. He is gone back to his home now, and the poor sinner is forsaken of all. I beseech you to get leave for me to be with her."

"What! Have you courage to stay all night in the prison? She is very sullen, and will scarcely make answer when she is spoken to."

"Oh, sir, it may please God to open her heart still. Don't let us delay."

"Come, then," said the elderly gentleman, ringing and gaining admission, "I know you have a key to unlock hearts."

Dinah mechanically took off her bonnet and shawl as soon as they were within the prison court, from the habit she had of throwing them off when she preached or prayed, or visited the sick; and when they entered the jailer's room, she laid them down on a chair unthinkingly. There was no agitation visible in her, but a deep concentrated calmness, as if, even when she was speaking, her soul was in prayer reposing on an unseen support.

After speaking to the jailer, the magistrate turned to her and said, "The turnkey will take you to the prisoner's cell and leave you there for the night, if you desire it, but you can't have a light during the night—it is contrary to rules. My name is Colonel Townley: if I can help you in anything, ask the jailer for my address and come to me. I take some interest in this Hetty Sorrel, for the sake of that fine fellow, Adam Bede. I happened to see him at Hayslope the same evening I heard you preach, and recognized him in court to-day, ill as he looked."

"Ah, sir, can you tell me anything about him? Can you tell me where he lodges? For my poor uncle was too much weighed down with trouble to remember."

"Close by here. I inquired all about him of Mr. Irwine. He lodges over a tinman's shop, in the street on the right hand as you entered the prison. There is an old school-master with him. Now, good-bye: I wish you success."

"Farewell, sir. I am grateful to you."

As Dinah crossed the prison court with the turnkey, the solemn evening light seemed to make the walls higher than they were by day, and the sweet pale face in the cap was more than ever like a white flower on this background of gloom. The turnkey looked askance at her all the while, but never spoke. He somehow felt that the sound of his own rude voice would be grating just then. He struck a light as they entered the dark corridor leading to the condemned cell, and then said in his most civil tone, "It'll be pretty nigh dark in the cell a'ready, but I can stop with my light a bit, if you like."

"Nay, friend, thank you," said Dinah. "I wish to go in alone."

"As you like," said the jailer, turning the harsh key in the lock and opening the door wide enough to admit Dinah. A jet of light from his lantern fell on the opposite corner of the cell, where Hetty was sitting on her straw pallet with her face buried in her knees. It seemed as if she were asleep, and yet the grating of the lock would have been likely to waken her.

The door closed again, and the only light in the cell was that of the evening sky, through the small high grating—enough to discern human faces by. Dinah stood still for a minute, hesitating to speak because Hetty might be asleep, and looking at the motionless heap with a yearning heart. Then she said, softly, "Hetty!"

There was a slight movement perceptible in Hetty's frame—a start such as might have been produced by a feeble electrical shock—but she did not look up. Dinah spoke again, in a tone made stronger by irrepressible emotion, "Hetty... it's Dinah."

Again there was a slight startled movement through Hetty's frame, and without uncovering her face, she raised her head a little, as if listening.

"Hetty... Dinah is come to you."

After a moment's pause, Hetty lifted her head slowly and timidly from her knees and raised her eyes. The two pale faces were looking at each other: one with a wild hard despair in it, the other full of sad yearning love. Dinah unconsciously opened her arms and stretched them out.

"Don't you know me, Hetty? Don't you remember Dinah? Did you think I wouldn't come to you in trouble?"

Hetty kept her eyes fixed on Dinah's face—at first like an animal that gazes, and gazes, and keeps aloof.

"I'm come to be with you, Hetty—not to leave you—to stay with you—to be your sister to the last."

Slowly, while Dinah was speaking, Hetty rose, took a step forward, and was clasped in Dinah's arms.

They stood so a long while, for neither of them felt the impulse to move apart again. Hetty, without any distinct thought of it, hung on this something that was come to clasp her now, while she was sinking helpless in a dark gulf; and Dinah felt a deep joy in the first sign that her love was welcomed by the wretched lost one. The light got fainter as they stood, and when at last they sat down on the straw pallet together, their faces had become indistinct.

Not a word was spoken. Dinah waited, hoping for a spontaneous word from Hetty, but she sat in the same dull despair, only clutching the hand that held hers and leaning her cheek against Dinah's. It was the human contact she clung to, but she was not the less sinking into the dark gulf.

Dinah began to doubt whether Hetty was conscious who it was that sat beside her. She thought suffering and fear might have driven the poor sinner out of her mind. But it was borne in upon her, as she afterwards said, that she must not hurry God's work: we are overhasty to speak—as if God did not manifest himself by our silent feeling, and make his love felt through ours. She did not know how long they sat in that way, but it got darker and darker, till there was only a pale patch of light on the opposite wall: all the rest was darkness. But she felt the Divine presence more and more—nay, as if she herself were a part of it, and it was the Divine pity that was beating in her heart and was willing the rescue of this helpless one. At last she was prompted to speak and find out how far Hetty was conscious of the present.

"Hetty," she said gently, "do you know who it is that sits by your side?"

"Yes," Hetty answered slowly, "it's Dinah."

"And do you remember the time when we were at the Hall Farm together, and that night when I told you to be sure and think of me as a friend in trouble?"

"Yes," said Hetty. Then, after a pause, she added, "But you can do nothing for me. You can't make 'em do anything. They'll hang me o' Monday—it's Friday now."

As Hetty said the last words, she clung closer to Dinah, shuddering.

"No, Hetty, I can't save you from that death. But isn't the suffering less hard when you have somebody with you, that feels for you—that you can speak to, and say what's in your heart?... Yes, Hetty: you lean on me: you are glad to have me with you."

"You won't leave me, Dinah? You'll keep close to me?"

"No, Hetty, I won't leave you. I'll stay with you to the last.... But, Hetty, there is some one else in this cell besides me, some one close to you."

Hetty said, in a frightened whisper, "Who?"

"Some one who has been with you through all your hours of sin and trouble—who has known every thought you have had—has seen where you went, where you lay down and rose up again, and all the deeds you have tried to hide in darkness. And on Monday, when I can't follow you—when my arms can't reach you—when death has parted us—He who is with us now, and knows all, will be with you then. It makes no difference—whether we live or die, we are in the presence of God."

"Oh, Dinah, won't nobody do anything for me? *Will* they hang me for certain?... I wouldn't mind if they'd let me live."

"My poor Hetty, death is very dreadful to you. I know it's dreadful. But if you had a friend to take care of you after death—in that other world—some one whose love is greater than mine—who can do everything?... If God our Father was your friend, and was willing to save you from sin and suffering, so as you should neither know wicked feelings nor pain again? If you could believe he loved you and would help you, as you believe I love you and will help you, it wouldn't be so hard to die on Monday, would it?"

"But I can't know anything about it," Hetty said, with sullen sadness.

"Because, Hetty, you are shutting up your soul against him, by trying to hide the truth. God's love and mercy can overcome all things—our ignorance, and weakness, and all the burden of our past wickedness—all things but our wilful sin, sin that we cling to, and will not give up. You believe in my love and pity for you, Hetty, but if you had not let me come near you, if you wouldn't have looked at me or spoken to me, you'd have shut me out from helping you. I couldn't have made you feel my love; I couldn't have told you what I felt for you. Don't shut God's love out in that way, by clinging to sin.... He can't bless you while you have one falsehood in your soul; his pardoning mercy can't reach you until you open your heart to him, and say, 'I have done this great wickedness; O God, save me, make me pure from sin.' While you cling to one sin and will not part with it, it must drag you down to misery after death, as it has dragged you to misery here in this world, my poor, poor Hetty. It is sin that brings dread, and darkness, and despair: there is light and blessedness for us as soon as we cast it off. God enters our souls then, and teaches us, and brings us strength and peace. Cast it off now, Hetty—now: confess the wickedness you have done—the sin you have been guilty of against your Heavenly Father. Let us kneel down together, for we are in the presence of God."

Hetty obeyed Dinah's movement, and sank on her knees. They still held each other's hands, and there was long silence. Then Dinah said, "Hetty, we are before God. He is waiting for you to tell the truth."

Still there was silence. At last Hetty spoke, in a tone of beseeching—

"Dinah... help me... I can't feel anything like you...my heart is hard."

Dinah held the clinging hand, and all her soul went forth in her voice:

"Jesus, thou present Saviour! Thou hast known the depths of all sorrow: thou hast entered that black darkness where God is not, and hast uttered the cry of the forsaken. Come Lord, and gather of the fruits of thy travail and thy pleading. Stretch forth thy hand, thou who art mighty to save to the uttermost, and rescue this lost one. She is clothed round with thick darkness. The fetters of her sin are upon her, and she cannot stir to come to thee. She can only feel her heart is hard, and she is helpless. She cries to me, thy weak creature.... Saviour! It is a blind cry to thee. Hear it! Pierce the darkness! Look upon her with thy face of love and sorrow that thou didst turn on him who denied thee, and melt her hard heart.

"See, Lord, I bring her, as they of old brought the sick and helpless, and thou didst heal them. I bear her on my arms and carry her before thee. Fear and trembling have taken hold on her, but she trembles only at the pain and death of the body. Breathe upon her thy life-giving Spirit, and put a new fear within her—

the fear of her sin. Make her dread to keep the accursed thing within her soul. Make her feel the presence of the living God, who beholds all the past, to whom the darkness is as noonday; who is waiting now, at the eleventh hour, for her to turn to him, and confess her sin, and cry for mercy—now, before the night of death comes, and the moment of pardon is for ever fled, like yesterday that returneth not.

"Saviour! It is yet time—time to snatch this poor soul from everlasting darkness. I believe—I believe in thy infinite love. What is *my* love or *my* pleading? It is quenched in thine. I can only clasp her in my weak arms and urge her with my weak pity. Thou—thou wilt breathe on the dead soul, and it shall arise from the unanswering sleep of death.

"Yea, Lord, I see thee, coming through the darkness, coming, like the morning, with healing on thy wings. The marks of thy agony are upon thee—I see, I see thou art able and willing to save—thou wilt not let her perish for ever. Come, mighty Saviour! Let the dead hear thy voice. Let the eyes of the blind be opened. Let her see that God encompasses her. Let her tremble at nothing but at the sin that cuts her off from him. Melt the hard heart. Unseal the closed lips: make her cry with her whole soul, 'Father, I have sinned.'..."

"Dinah," Hetty sobbed out, throwing her arms round Dinah's neck, "I will speak... I will tell... I won't hide it any more."

But the tears and sobs were too violent. Dinah raised her gently from her knees and seated her on the pallet again, sitting down by her side. It was a long time before the convulsed throat was quiet, and even then they sat some time in stillness and darkness, holding each other's hands. At last Hetty whispered, "I did do it, Dinah... I buried it in the wood... the little baby... and it cried... I heard it cry... ever such a way off... all night... and I went back because it cried."

She paused, and then spoke hurriedly in a louder, pleading tone.

"But I thought perhaps it wouldn't die—there might somebody find it. I didn't kill it—I didn't kill it myself. I put it down there and covered it up, and when I came back it was gone.... It was because I was so very miserable, Dinah... I didn't know where to go... and I tried to kill myself before, and I couldn't. Oh, I tried so to drown myself in the pool, and I couldn't. I went to Windsor—I ran away—did you know? I went to find him, as he might take care of me; and he was gone; and then I didn't know what to do. I daredn't go back home again—I couldn't bear it. I couldn't have bore to look at anybody, for they'd have scorned me. I thought o' you sometimes, and thought I'd come to you, for I didn't think you'd be cross with me, and cry shame on me. I thought I could tell you. But then the other folks 'ud come to know it at last, and I couldn't bear that. It was partly thinking o' you made me come toward Stoniton; and, besides, I was so frightened at going wandering about till I was a beggar-woman, and had nothing; and sometimes it seemed as if I must go back to the farm sooner than that. Oh, it was so dreadful, Dinah... I was so miserable... I wished I'd never been born into this world. I should never like to go into the green fields again—I hated 'em so in my misery."

Hetty paused again, as if the sense of the past were too strong upon her for words.

"And then I got to Stoniton, and I began to feel frightened that night, because I was so near home. And then the little baby was born, when I didn't expect it; and the thought came into my mind that I might get rid of it and go home again. The thought came all of a sudden, as I was lying in the bed, and it got stronger and stronger... I longed so to go back again... I couldn't bear being so lonely and coming to beg for want. And it gave me strength and resolution to get up and dress myself. I felt I must do it... I didn't know how... I thought I'd find a pool, if I could, like that other, in the corner of the field, in the dark. And when the woman went out, I felt as if I was strong enough to do anything... I thought I should get rid of all my misery, and go back home, and never let 'em know why I ran away. I put on my bonnet and shawl, and went out into the dark street, with the baby under my cloak; and I walked fast till I got into a street a good way off, and there was a public, and I got some warm stuff to drink and some bread. And I walked on and on, and I hardly felt the ground I trod on; and it got lighter, for there came the moon—oh, Dinah, it frightened me when it first looked at me out o' the clouds—it never looked so before; and I turned out of the road into the fields, for I was afraid o' meeting anybody with the moon shining on me. And I came to a haystack, where I thought I could lie down and keep myself warm all night. There was a place cut into it, where I could make me a bed, and I lay comfortable, and the baby was warm against me; and I must have gone to sleep for a good while, for when I woke it was morning, but not very light, and the baby was crying. And I saw a wood a little way off... I thought there'd perhaps be a ditch or a pond there... and it was so early I thought I could hide the child there, and get a long way off before folks was up. And then I thought I'd go home—I'd get rides in carts and go home and tell 'em I'd been to try and see for a place, and couldn't get one. I longed so for it, Dinah, I longed so to be safe at home. I don't know how I felt about the baby. I seemed to hate it—it was like a heavy weight hanging round my neck; and yet its crying went through me, and I daredn't look at its little hands and face. But I went on to the wood, and I walked about, but there was no water...."

Hetty shuddered. She was silent for some moments, and when she began again, it was in a whisper.

"I came to a place where there was lots of chips and turf, and I sat down on the trunk of a tree to think what I should do. And all of a sudden I saw a hole under the nut-tree, like a little grave. And it darted into me like lightning—I'd lay the baby there and cover it with the grass and the chips. I couldn't kill it any other way. And I'd done it in a minute; and, oh, it cried so, Dinah—I *couldn't* cover it quite up—I thought perhaps somebody 'ud come and take care of it, and then it wouldn't die. And I made haste out of the wood, but I could hear it crying all the while; and when I got out into the fields, it was as if I was held fast—I couldn't go away, for all I wanted so to go. And I sat against the haystack to watch if anybody 'ud come. I was very hungry, and I'd only a bit of bread left, but I couldn't go away. And after ever such a while—hours and hours—the man came—him in a smock-frock, and he looked at me so, I was frightened, and I made haste and went on. I thought he was going to the wood and would perhaps find the baby. And I went right on, till I came to a village, a long way off from the wood, and I was very sick, and faint, and hungry. I got something to eat there, and bought a loaf. But I was frightened to stay. I heard the baby crying, and thought the other folks heard it too—and I went on. But I was so tired, and it was getting towards dark. And at last, by the roadside there was a barn—ever such a way off any house—like the barn in Abbot's Close, and I thought I could go in there and hide myself among the hay and straw, and nobody 'ud be likely to come. I went in, and it was half full o' trusses of straw, and there was some hay too. And I made myself a bed, ever so far behind, where nobody could find me; and I was so tired and weak, I went to sleep.... But oh, the baby's crying kept waking me, and I thought that man as looked at me so was come and laying hold of me. But I must have slept a long while at last, though I didn't know, for when I got up and went out of the barn, I didn't know whether it was night or morning. But it was morning, for it kept getting lighter, and I turned back the way I'd come. I couldn't help it, Dinah; it was the baby's crying made me go—and yet I was frightened to death. I thought that man in the smock-frock 'ud see me and know I put the baby there. But I went on, for all that. I'd left off thinking about going home—it had gone out o' my mind. I saw nothing but that place in the wood where I'd buried the baby... I see it now. Oh Dinah! shall I allays see it?"

Hetty clung round Dinah and shuddered again. The silence seemed long before she went on.

"I met nobody, for it was very early, and I got into the wood.... I knew the way to the place... the place against the nut-tree; and I could hear it crying at every step.... I thought it was alive.... I don't know whether I was frightened or glad... I don't know what I felt. I only know I was in the wood and heard the cry. I don't know what I felt till I saw the baby was gone. And when I'd put it there, I thought I should like somebody to find it and save it from dying; but when I saw it was gone, I was struck like a stone, with fear. I never thought o' stirring, I felt so weak. I knew I couldn't run away, and everybody as saw me 'ud know about the baby. My heart went like a stone. I couldn't wish or try for anything; it seemed like as if I should stay there for ever, and nothing 'ud ever change. But they came and took me away."

Hetty was silent, but she shuddered again, as if there was still something behind; and Dinah waited, for her heart was so full that tears must come before words. At last Hetty burst out, with a sob, "Dinah, do you think God will take away that crying and the place in the wood, now I've told everything?""Let us pray, poor sinner. Let us fall on our knees again, and pray to the God of all mercy."

Chapter XLVI
The Hours of Suspense

On Sunday morning, when the church bells in Stoniton were ringing for morning service, Bartle Massey re-entered Adam's room, after a short absence, and said, "Adam, here's a visitor wants to see you."

Adam was seated with his back towards the door, but he started up and turned round instantly, with a flushed face and an eager look. His face was even thinner and more worn than we have seen it before, but he was washed and shaven this Sunday morning.

"Is it any news?" he said.

"Keep yourself quiet, my lad," said Bartle; "keep quiet. It's not what you're thinking of. It's the young Methodist woman come from the prison. She's at the bottom o' the stairs, and wants to know if you think well to see her, for she has something to say to you about that poor castaway; but she wouldn't come in without your leave, she said. She thought you'd perhaps like to go out and speak to her. These preaching women are not so back'ard commonly," Bartle muttered to himself.

"Ask her to come in," said Adam.

He was standing with his face towards the door, and as Dinah entered, lifting up her mild grey eyes towards him, she saw at once the great change that had come since the day when she had looked up at the tall man in the cottage. There was a trembling in her clear voice as she put her hand into his and said, "Be comforted, Adam Bede, the Lord has not forsaken her."

"Bless you for coming to her," Adam said. "Mr. Massey brought me word yesterday as you was come."

They could neither of them say any more just yet, but stood before each other in silence; and Bartle Massey, too, who had put on his spectacles, seemed transfixed, examining Dinah's face. But he recovered himself first, and said, "Sit down, young woman, sit down," placing the chair for her and retiring to his old seat on the bed.

"Thank you, friend; I won't sit down," said Dinah, "for I must hasten back. She entreated me not to stay long away. What I came for, Adam Bede, was to pray you to go and see the poor sinner and bid her farewell. She desires to ask your forgiveness, and it is meet you should see her to-day, rather than in the early morning, when the time will be short."

Adam stood trembling, and at last sank down on his chair again.

"It won't be," he said, "it'll be put off—there'll perhaps come a pardon. Mr. Irwine said there was hope. He said, I needn't quite give it up."

"That's a blessed thought to me," said Dinah, her eyes filling with tears. "It's a fearful thing hurrying her soul away so fast."

"But let what will be," she added presently. "You will surely come, and let her speak the words that are in her heart. Although her poor soul is very dark and discerns little beyond the things of the flesh, she is no longer hard. She is contrite, she has confessed all to me. The pride of her heart has given way, and she leans on me for help and desires to be taught. This fills me with trust, for I cannot but think that the brethren sometimes err in measuring the Divine love by the sinner's knowledge. She is going to write a letter to the friends at the Hall Farm for me to give them when she is gone, and when I told her you were here, she said, 'I should like to say good-bye to Adam and ask him to forgive me.' You will come, Adam? Perhaps you will even now come back with me."

"I can't," Adam said. "I can't say good-bye while there's any hope. I'm listening, and listening—I can't think o' nothing but that. It can't be as she'll die that shameful death—I can't bring my mind to it."

He got up from his chair again and looked away out of the window, while Dinah stood with compassionate patience. In a minute or two he turned round and said,

"I *will* come, Dinah... to-morrow morning... if it must be. I may have more strength to bear it, if I know it *must* be. Tell her, I forgive her; tell her I will come—at the very last."

"I will not urge you against the voice of your own heart," said Dinah. "I must hasten back to her, for it is wonderful how she clings now, and was not willing to let me out of her sight. She used never to make any return to my affection before, but now tribulation has opened her heart. Farewell, Adam. Our heavenly Father comfort you and strengthen you to bear all things." Dinah put out her hand, and Adam pressed it in silence.

Bartle Massey was getting up to lift the stiff latch of the door for her, but before he could reach it, she had said gently, "Farewell, friend," and was gone, with her light step down the stairs.

"Well," said Bartle, taking off his spectacles and putting them into his pocket, "if there must be women to make trouble in the world, it's but fair there should be women to be comforters under it; and she's one—she's one. It's a pity she's a Methodist; but there's no getting a woman without some foolishness or other."

Adam never went to bed that night. The excitement of suspense, heightening with every hour that brought him nearer the fatal moment, was too great, and in spite of his entreaties, in spite of his promises that he would be perfectly quiet, the schoolmaster watched too.

"What does it matter to me, lad?" Bartle said: "a night's sleep more or less? I shall sleep long enough, by and by, underground. Let me keep thee company in trouble while I can."

It was a long and dreary night in that small chamber. Adam would sometimes get up and tread backwards and forwards along the short space from wall to wall; then he would sit down and hide his face, and no sound would be heard but the ticking of the watch on the table, or the falling of a cinder from the fire which the schoolmaster carefully tended. Sometimes he would burst out into vehement speech,

"If I could ha' done anything to save her—if my bearing anything would ha' done any good... but t' have to sit still, and know it, and do nothing... it's hard for a man to bear... and to think o' what might ha' been now, if it hadn't been for *him*.... O God, it's the very day we should ha' been married."

"Aye, my lad," said Bartle tenderly, "it's heavy—it's heavy. But you must remember this: when you thought of marrying her, you'd a notion she'd got another sort of a nature inside her. You didn't think she could have got hardened in that little while to do what she's done."

"I know—I know that," said Adam. "I thought she was loving and tender-hearted, and wouldn't tell a lie, or act deceitful. How could I think any other way? And if he'd never come near her, and I'd married her, and been loving to her, and took care of her, she might never ha' done anything bad. What would it ha' signified—my having a bit o' trouble with her? It 'ud ha' been nothing to this."

"There's no knowing, my lad—there's no knowing what might have come. The smart's bad for you to bear now: you must have time—you must have time. But I've that opinion of you, that you'll rise above it all and be a man again, and there may good come out of this that we don't see."

"Good come out of it!" said Adam passionately. "That doesn't alter th' evil: *her* ruin can't be undone. I hate that talk o' people, as if there was a way o' making amends for everything. They'd more need be brought to see as the wrong they do can never be altered. When a man's spoiled his fellow-creatur's life, he's no right to comfort himself with thinking good may come out of it. Somebody else's good doesn't alter her shame and misery."

"Well, lad, well," said Bartle, in a gentle tone, strangely in contrast with his usual peremptoriness and impatience of contradiction, "it's likely enough I talk foolishness. I'm an old fellow, and it's a good many years since I was in trouble myself. It's easy finding reasons why other folks should be patient."

"Mr. Massey," said Adam penitently, "I'm very hot and hasty. I owe you something different; but you mustn't take it ill of me."

"Not I, lad—not I."

So the night wore on in agitation till the chill dawn and the growing light brought the tremulous quiet that comes on the brink of despair. There would soon be no more suspense.

"Let us go to the prison now, Mr. Massey," said Adam, when he saw the hand of his watch at six. "If there's any news come, we shall hear about it."

The people were astir already, moving rapidly, in one direction, through the streets. Adam tried not to think where they were going, as they hurried past him in that short space between his lodging and the prison gates. He was thankful when the gates shut him in from seeing those eager people.

No; there was no news come—no pardon—no reprieve.

Adam lingered in the court half an hour before he could bring himself to send word to Dinah that he was come. But a voice caught his ear: he could not shut out the words.

"The cart is to set off at half-past seven."

It must be said—the last good-bye: there was no help.

In ten minutes from that time, Adam was at the door of the cell. Dinah had sent him word that she could not come to him; she could not leave Hetty one moment; but Hetty was prepared for the meeting.

He could not see her when he entered, for agitation deadened his senses, and the dim cell was almost dark to him. He stood a moment after the door closed behind him, trembling and stupefied.

But he began to see through the dimness—to see the dark eyes lifted up to him once more, but with no smile in them. O God, how sad they looked! The last time they had met his was when he parted from her with his heart full of joyous hopeful love, and they looked out with a tearful smile from a pink, dimpled, childish face. The face was marble now; the sweet lips were pallid and half-open and quivering; the dimples were all gone—all but one, that never went; and the eyes—O, the worst of all was the likeness they had to Hetty's. They were Hetty's eyes looking at him with that mournful gaze, as if she had come back to him from the dead to tell him of her misery.

She was clinging close to Dinah; her cheek was against Dinah's. It seemed as if her last faint strength and hope lay in that contact, and the pitying love that shone out from Dinah's face looked like a visible pledge of the Invisible Mercy.

When the sad eyes met—when Hetty and Adam looked at each other—she felt the change in him too, and it seemed to strike her with fresh fear. It was the first time she had seen any being whose face seemed to reflect the change in herself: Adam was a new image of the dreadful past and the dreadful present. She trembled more as she looked at him.

"Speak to him, Hetty," Dinah said; "tell him what is in your heart."

Hetty obeyed her, like a little child.

"Adam... I'm very sorry... I behaved very wrong to you... will you forgive me... before I die?"

Adam answered with a half-sob, "Yes, I forgive thee Hetty. I forgave thee long ago."

It had seemed to Adam as if his brain would burst with the anguish of meeting Hetty's eyes in the first moments, but the sound of her voice uttering these penitent words touched a chord which had been less strained. There was a sense of relief from what was becoming unbearable, and the rare tears came—they had never come before, since he had hung on Seth's neck in the beginning of his sorrow.

Hetty made an involuntary movement towards him, some of the love that she had once lived in the midst of was come near her again. She kept hold of Dinah's hand, but she went up to Adam and said timidly, "Will you kiss me again, Adam, for all I've been so wicked?"

Adam took the blanched wasted hand she put out to him, and they gave each other the solemn unspeakable kiss of a lifelong parting.

"And tell him," Hetty said, in rather a stronger voice, "tell him... for there's nobody else to tell him... as I went after him and couldn't find him... and I hated him and cursed him once... but Dinah says I should forgive him... and I try... for else God won't forgive me."

There was a noise at the door of the cell now—the key was being turned in the lock, and when the door opened, Adam saw indistinctly that there were several faces there. He was too agitated to see more—even to see that Mr. Irwine's face was one of them. He felt that the last preparations were beginning, and he could stay no longer. Room was silently made for him to depart, and he went to his chamber in loneliness, leaving Bartle Massey to watch and see the end.

Chapter XLVII
The Last Moment

It was a sight that some people remembered better even than their own sorrows—the sight in that grey clear morning, when the fatal cart with the two young women in it was descried by the waiting watching multitude, cleaving its way towards the hideous symbol of a deliberately inflicted sudden death.

All Stoniton had heard of Dinah Morris, the young Methodist woman who had brought the obstinate criminal to confess, and there was as much eagerness to see her as to see the wretched Hetty.

But Dinah was hardly conscious of the multitude. When Hetty had caught sight of the vast crowd in the distance, she had clutched Dinah convulsively.

"Close your eyes, Hetty," Dinah said, "and let us pray without ceasing to God."

And in a low voice, as the cart went slowly along through the midst of the gazing crowd, she poured forth her soul with the wrestling intensity of a last pleading, for the trembling creature that clung to her and clutched her as the only visible sign of love and pity.

Dinah did not know that the crowd was silent, gazing at her with a sort of awe—she did not even know how near they were to the fatal spot, when the cart stopped, and she shrank appalled at a loud shout hideous to her ear, like a vast yell of demons. Hetty's shriek mingled with the sound, and they clasped each other in mutual horror.

But it was not a shout of execration—not a yell of exultant cruelty.

It was a shout of sudden excitement at the appearance of a horseman cleaving the crowd at full gallop. The horse is hot and distressed, but answers to the desperate spurring; the rider looks as if his eyes were glazed by madness, and he saw nothing but what was unseen by others. See, he has something in his hand—he is holding it up as if it were a signal.

The Sheriff knows him: it is Arthur Donnithorne, carrying in his hand a hard-won release from death.

Chapter XLVIII
Another Meeting in the Wood

The next day, at evening, two men were walking from opposite points towards the same scene, drawn thither by a common memory. The scene was the Grove by Donnithorne Chase: you know who the men were.

The old squire's funeral had taken place that morning, the will had been read, and now in the first breathing-space, Arthur Donnithorne had come out for a lonely walk, that he might look fixedly at the new future before him and confirm himself in a sad resolution. He thought he could do that best in the Grove.

Adam too had come from Stoniton on Monday evening, and to-day he had not left home, except to go to the family at the Hall Farm and tell them everything that Mr. Irwine had left untold. He had agreed with the Poysers that he would follow them to their new neighbourhood, wherever that might be, for he meant to give up the management of the woods, and, as soon as it was practicable, he would wind up his business with Jonathan Burge and settle with his mother and Seth in a home within reach of the friends to whom he felt bound by a mutual sorrow.

"Seth and me are sure to find work," he said. "A man that's got our trade at his finger-ends is at home everywhere; and we must make a new start. My mother won't stand in the way, for she's told me, since I came home, she'd made up her mind to being buried in another parish, if I wished it, and if I'd be more comfortable elsewhere. It's wonderful how quiet she's been ever since I came back. It seems as if the very greatness o' the trouble had quieted and calmed her. We shall all be better in a new country, though there's some I shall be loath to leave behind. But I won't part from you and yours, if I can help it, Mr. Poyser. Trouble's made us kin."

"Aye, lad," said Martin. "We'll go out o' hearing o' that man's name. But I doubt we shall ne'er go far enough for folks not to find out as we've got them belonging to us as are transported o'er the seas, and were like to be hanged. We shall have that flyin' up in our faces, and our children's after us."

That was a long visit to the Hall Farm, and drew too strongly on Adam's energies for him to think of seeing others, or re-entering on his old occupations till the morrow. "But to-morrow," he said to himself, "I'll go to work again. I shall learn to like it again some time, maybe; and it's right whether I like it or not."

This evening was the last he would allow to be absorbed by sorrow: suspense was gone now, and he must bear the unalterable. He was resolved not to see

Arthur Donnithorne again, if it were possible to avoid him. He had no message to deliver from Hetty now, for Hetty had seen Arthur. And Adam distrusted himself—he had learned to dread the violence of his own feeling. That word of Mr. Irwine's—that he must remember what he had felt after giving the last blow to Arthur in the Grove—had remained with him.

These thoughts about Arthur, like all thoughts that are charged with strong feeling, were continually recurring, and they always called up the image of the Grove—of that spot under the overarching boughs where he had caught sight of the two bending figures, and had been possessed by sudden rage.

"I'll go and see it again to-night for the last time," he said; "it'll do me good; it'll make me feel over again what I felt when I'd knocked him down. I felt what poor empty work it was, as soon as I'd done it, *before* I began to think he might be dead."

In this way it happened that Arthur and Adam were walking towards the same spot at the same time.

Adam had on his working-dress again, now, for he had thrown off the other with a sense of relief as soon as he came home; and if he had had the basket of tools over his shoulder, he might have been taken, with his pale wasted face, for the spectre of the Adam Bede who entered the Grove on that August evening eight months ago. But he had no basket of tools, and he was not walking with the old erectness, looking keenly round him; his hands were thrust in his side pockets, and his eyes rested chiefly on the ground. He had not long entered the Grove, and now he paused before a beech. He knew that tree well; it was the boundary mark of his youth—the sign, to him, of the time when some of his earliest, strongest feelings had left him. He felt sure they would never return. And yet, at this moment, there was a stirring of affection at the remembrance of that Arthur Donnithorne whom he had believed in before he had come up to this beech eight months ago. It was affection for the dead: *that* Arthur existed no longer.

He was disturbed by the sound of approaching footsteps, but the beech stood at a turning in the road, and he could not see who was coming until the tall slim figure in deep mourning suddenly stood before him at only two yards' distance. They both started, and looked at each other in silence. Often, in the last fortnight, Adam had imagined himself as close to Arthur as this, assailing him with words that should be as harrowing as the voice of remorse, forcing upon him a just share in the misery he had caused; and often, too, he had told himself that such a meeting had better not be. But in imagining the meeting he had always seen Arthur, as he had met him on that evening in the Grove, florid, careless, light of speech; and the figure before him touched him with the signs of suffering. Adam knew what suffering was—he could not lay a cruel finger on a bruised man. He felt no impulse that he needed to resist. Silence was more just than reproach. Arthur was the first to speak.

"Adam," he said, quietly, "it may be a good thing that we have met here, for I wished to see you. I should have asked to see you to-morrow."

He paused, but Adam said nothing.

"I know it is painful to you to meet me," Arthur went on, "but it is not likely to happen again for years to come."

"No, sir," said Adam, coldly, "that was what I meant to write to you to-morrow, as it would be better all dealings should be at an end between us, and somebody else put in my place."

Arthur felt the answer keenly, and it was not without an effort that he spoke again.

"It was partly on that subject I wished to speak to you. I don't want to lessen your indignation against me, or ask you to do anything for my sake. I only wish to ask you if you will help me to lessen the evil consequences of the past, which is unchangeable. I don't mean consequences to myself, but to others. It is but little I can do, I know. I know the worst consequences will remain; but something may be done, and you can help me. Will you listen to me patiently?"

"Yes, sir," said Adam, after some hesitation; "I'll hear what it is. If I can help to mend anything, I will. Anger 'ull mend nothing, I know. We've had enough o' that."

"I was going to the Hermitage," said Arthur. "Will you go there with me and sit down? We can talk better there."

The Hermitage had never been entered since they left it together, for Arthur had locked up the key in his desk. And now, when he opened the door, there was the candle burnt out in the socket; there was the chair in the same place where Adam remembered sitting; there was the waste-paper basket full of scraps, and deep down in it, Arthur felt in an instant, there was the little pink silk handkerchief. It would have been painful to enter this place if their previous thoughts had been less painful.

They sat down opposite each other in the old places, and Arthur said, "I'm going away, Adam; I'm going into the army."

Poor Arthur felt that Adam ought to be affected by this announcement—ought to have a movement of sympathy towards him. But Adam's lips remained firmly closed, and the expression of his face unchanged.

"What I want to say to you," Arthur continued, "is this: one of my reasons for going away is that no one else may leave Hayslope—may leave their home on my account. I would do anything, there is no sacrifice I would not make, to prevent any further injury to others through my—through what has happened."

Arthur's words had precisely the opposite effect to that he had anticipated. Adam thought he perceived in them that notion of compensation for irretrievable wrong, that self-soothing attempt to make evil bear the same fruits as good, which most of all roused his indignation. He was as strongly impelled to look painful facts right in the face as Arthur was to turn away his eyes from them. Moreover, he had the wakeful suspicious pride of a poor man in the presence of a rich man. He felt his old severity returning as he said, "The time's past for that, sir. A man should make sacrifices to keep clear of doing a wrong; sacrifices won't undo it when it's done. When people's feelings have got a deadly wound, they can't be cured with favours."

"Favours!" said Arthur, passionately; "no; how can you suppose I meant that? But the Poysers—Mr. Irwine tells me the Poysers mean to leave the place where they have lived so many years—for generations. Don't you see, as Mr. Irwine does, that if they could be persuaded to overcome the feeling that drives them away, it would be much better for them in the end to remain on the old spot, among the friends and neighbours who know them?"

"That's true," said Adam coldly. "But then, sir, folks's feelings are not so easily overcome. It'll be hard for Martin Poyser to go to a strange place, among strange faces, when he's been bred up on the Hall Farm, and his father before him; but then it 'ud be harder for a man with his feelings to stay. I don't see how the thing's to be made any other than hard. There's a sort o' damage, sir, that can't be made up for."

Arthur was silent some moments. In spite of other feelings dominant in him this evening, his pride winced under Adam's mode of treating him. Wasn't he himself suffering? Was not he too obliged to renounce his most cherished hopes? It was now as it had been eight months ago—Adam was forcing Arthur to feel more intensely the irrevocableness of his own wrong-doing. He was presenting the sort of resistance that was the most irritating to Arthur's eager ardent nature. But his anger was subdued by the same influence that had subdued Adam's when they first confronted each other—by the marks of suffering in a long familiar face. The momentary struggle ended in the feeling that he could bear a great deal from Adam, to whom he had been the occasion of bearing so much; but there was a touch of pleading, boyish vexation in his tone as he said, "But people may make injuries worse by unreasonable conduct—by giving way to anger and satisfying that for the moment, instead of thinking what will be the effect in the future.

"If I were going to stay here and act as landlord," he added presently, with still more eagerness—"if I were careless about what I've done—what I've been the cause of, you would have some excuse, Adam, for going away and encouraging others to go. You would have some excuse then for trying to make the evil worse. But when I tell you I'm going away for years—when you know what that means for me, how it cuts off every plan of happiness I've ever formed—it is impossible for a sensible man like you to believe that there is any real ground for the Poysers refusing to remain. I know their feeling about disgrace—Mr. Irwine has told me all; but he is of opinion that they might be persuaded out of this idea that they are disgraced in the eyes of their neighbours, and that they can't remain on my estate, if you would join him in his efforts—if you would stay yourself and go on managing the old woods."

Arthur paused a moment and then added, pleadingly, "You know that's a good work to do for the sake of other people, besides the owner. And you don't know but that they may have a better owner soon, whom you will like to work for. If I die, my cousin Tradgett will have the estate and take my name. He is a good fellow."

Adam could not help being moved: it was impossible for him not to feel that this was the voice of the honest warm-hearted Arthur whom he had loved and been proud of in old days; but nearer memories would not be thrust away. He was silent; yet Arthur saw an answer in his face that induced him to go on, with growing earnestness.

"And then, if you would talk to the Poysers—if you would talk the matter over with Mr. Irwine—he means to see you to-morrow—and then if you would join your arguments to his to prevail on them not to go.... I know, of course, that they would not accept any favour from me—I mean nothing of that kind—but I'm sure they would suffer less in the end. Irwine thinks so too. And Mr. Irwine is to have the chief authority on the estate—he has consented to undertake that. They will really be under no man but one whom they respect and like. It would be the same with you, Adam, and it could be nothing but a desire to give me worse pain that could incline you to go."

Arthur was silent again for a little while, and then said, with some agitation in his voice, "I wouldn't act so towards you, I know. If you were in my place and I in yours, I should try to help you to do the best."

Adam made a hasty movement on his chair and looked on the ground. Arthur went on, "Perhaps you've never done anything you've had bitterly to repent of in your life, Adam; if you had, you would be more generous. You would know then that it's worse for me than for you."

Arthur rose from his seat with the last words, and went to one of the windows, looking out and turning his back on Adam, as he continued, passionately,

"Haven't *I* loved her too? Didn't I see her yesterday? Shan't I carry the thought of her about with me as much as you will? And don't you think you would suffer more if you'd been in fault?"

There was silence for several minutes, for the struggle in Adam's mind was not easily decided. Facile natures, whose emotions have little permanence, can hardly understand how much inward resistance he overcame before he rose from his seat and turned towards Arthur. Arthur heard the movement, and turning round, met the sad but softened look with which Adam said,

"It's true what you say, sir. I'm hard—it's in my nature. I was too hard with my father, for doing wrong. I've been a bit hard t' everybody but *her*. I felt as if nobody pitied her enough—her suffering cut into me so; and when I thought the folks at the farm were too hard with her, I said I'd never be hard to anybody myself again. But feeling overmuch about her has perhaps made me unfair to you. I've known what it is in my life to repent and feel it's too late. I felt I'd been too harsh to my father when he was gone from me—I feel it now, when I think of him. I've no right to be hard towards them as have done wrong and repent."

Adam spoke these words with the firm distinctness of a man who is resolved to leave nothing unsaid that he is bound to say; but he went on with more hesitation.

"I wouldn't shake hands with you once, sir, when you asked me—but if you're willing to do it now, for all I refused then..."

Arthur's white hand was in Adam's large grasp in an instant, and with that action there was a strong rush, on both sides, of the old, boyish affection.

"Adam," Arthur said, impelled to full confession now, "it would never have happened if I'd known you loved her. That would have helped to save me from it. And I *did* struggle: I never meant to injure her. I deceived you afterwards—and that led on to worse; but I thought it was forced upon me, I thought it was the best thing I could do. And in that letter I told her to let me know if she were in any trouble: don't think I would not have done everything I could. But I was all wrong from the very first, and horrible wrong has come of it. God knows, I'd give my life if I could undo it."

They sat down again opposite each other, and Adam said, tremulously, "How did she seem when you left her, sir?"

"Don't ask me, Adam," Arthur said; "I feel sometimes as if I should go mad with thinking of her looks and what she said to me, and then, that I couldn't get a full pardon—that I couldn't save her from that wretched fate of being transported—that I can do nothing for her all those years; and she may die under it, and never know comfort any more."

"Ah, sir," said Adam, for the first time feeling his own pain merged in sympathy for Arthur, "you and me'll often be thinking o' the same thing, when we're a long way off one another. I'll pray God to help you, as I pray him to help me."

"But there's that sweet woman—that Dinah Morris," Arthur said, pursuing his own thoughts and not knowing what had been the sense of Adam's words, "she says she shall stay with her to the very last moment—till she goes; and the poor thing clings to her as if she found some comfort in her. I could worship that woman; I don't know what I should do if she were not there. Adam, you will see her when she comes back. I could say nothing to her yesterday—nothing of what I felt towards her. Tell her," Arthur went on hurriedly, as if he wanted to hide the emotion with which he spoke, while he took off his chain and watch, "tell her I asked you to give her this in remembrance of me—of the man to whom she is the one source of comfort, when he thinks of... I know she doesn't care about such things—or anything else I can give her for its own sake. But she will use the watch—I shall like to think of her using it."

"I'll give it to her, sir," Adam said, "and tell her your words. She told me she should come back to the people at the Hall Farm."

"And you *will* persuade the Poysers to stay, Adam?" said Arthur, reminded of the subject which both of them had forgotten in the first interchange of revived friendship. "You *will* stay yourself, and help Mr. Irwine to carry out the repairs and improvements on the estate?"

"There's one thing, sir, that perhaps you don't take account of," said Adam, with hesitating gentleness, "and that was what made me hang back longer. You see, it's the same with both me and the Poysers: if we stay, it's for our own worldly interest, and it looks as if we'd put up with anything for the sake o' that. I know that's what they'll feel, and I can't help feeling a little of it myself. When folks have got an honourable independent spirit, they don't like to do anything that might make 'em seem base-minded."

"But no one who knows you will think that, Adam. That is not a reason strong enough against a course that is really more generous, more unselfish than the other. And it will be known—it shall be made known, that both you and the Poysers stayed at my entreaty. Adam, don't try to make things worse for me; I'm punished enough without that."

"No, sir, no," Adam said, looking at Arthur with mournful affection. "God forbid I should make things worse for you. I used to wish I could do it, in my passion—but that was when I thought you didn't feel enough. I'll stay, sir, I'll do the best I can. It's all I've got to think of now—to do my work well and make the world a bit better place for them as can enjoy it."

"Then we'll part now, Adam. You will see Mr. Irwine to-morrow, and consult with him about everything."

"Are you going soon, sir?" said Adam.

"As soon as possible—after I've made the necessary arrangements. Good-bye, Adam. I shall think of you going about the old place."

"Good-bye, sir. God bless you."

The hands were clasped once more, and Adam left the Hermitage, feeling that sorrow was more bearable now hatred was gone.

As soon as the door was closed behind him, Arthur went to the waste-paper basket and took out the little pink silk handkerchief.

BOOK SIXTH

Chapter XLIX
At the Hall Farm

The first autumnal afternoon sunshine of 1801—more than eighteen months after that parting of Adam and Arthur in the Hermitage—was on the yard at the Hall Farm; and the bull-dog was in one of his most excited moments, for it was that hour of the day when the cows were being driven into the yard for their afternoon milking. No wonder the patient beasts ran confusedly into the wrong places, for the alarming din of the bull-dog was mingled with more distant sounds which the timid feminine creatures, with pardonable superstition, imagined also to have some relation to their own movements—with the tremendous crack of the waggoner's whip, the roar of his voice, and the booming thunder of the waggon, as it left the rick-yard empty of its golden load.

The milking of the cows was a sight Mrs. Poyser loved, and at this hour on mild days she was usually standing at the house door, with her knitting in her hands, in quiet contemplation, only heightened to a keener interest when the vicious yellow cow, who had once kicked over a pailful of precious milk, was about to undergo the preventive punishment of having her hinder-legs strapped.

To-day, however, Mrs. Poyser gave but a divided attention to the arrival of the cows, for she was in eager discussion with Dinah, who was stitching Mr. Poyser's shirt-collars, and had borne patiently to have her thread broken three times by Totty pulling at her arm with a sudden insistence that she should look at "Baby," that is, at a large wooden doll with no legs and a long skirt, whose bald head Totty, seated in her small chair at Dinah's side, was caressing and pressing to her fat cheek with much fervour. Totty is larger by more than two years' growth than when you first saw her, and she has on a black frock under her pinafore. Mrs. Poyser too has on a black gown, which seems to heighten the family likeness between her and Dinah. In other respects there is little outward change now discernible in our old friends, or in the pleasant house-place, bright with polished oak and pewter.

"I never saw the like to you, Dinah," Mrs. Poyser was saying, "when you've once took anything into your head: there's no more moving you than the rooted tree. You may say what you like, but I don't believe *that's* religion; for what's the Sermon on the Mount about, as you're so fond o' reading to the boys, but doing what other folks 'ud have you do? But if it was anything unreasonable they wanted you to do, like taking your cloak off and giving it to 'em, or letting 'em slap you i' the face, I daresay you'd be ready enough. It's only when one 'ud have you do what's plain common sense and good for yourself, as you're obstinate th' other way."

"Nay, dear Aunt," said Dinah, smiling slightly as she went on with her work, "I'm sure your wish 'ud be a reason for me to do anything that I didn't feel it was wrong to do."

"Wrong! You drive me past bearing. What is there wrong, I should like to know, i' staying along wi' your own friends, as are th' happier for having you with 'em an' are willing to provide for you, even if your work didn't more nor pay 'em for the bit o' sparrow's victual y' eat and the bit o' rag you put on? An' who is it, I should like to know, as you're bound t' help and comfort i' the world more nor your own flesh and blood—an' me th' only aunt you've got above-ground, an' am brought to the brink o' the grave welly every winter as comes, an' there's the child as sits beside you 'ull break her little heart when you go, an' the grandfather not been dead a twelvemonth, an' your uncle 'ull miss you so as never was—a-lighting his pipe an' waiting on him, an' now I can trust you wi' the butter, an' have had all the trouble o' teaching you, and there's all the sewing to be done, an' I must have a strange gell out o' Treddles'on to do it—an' all because you must go back to that bare heap o' stones as the very crows fly over an' won't stop at."

"Dear Aunt Rachel," said Dinah, looking up in Mrs. Poyser's face, "it's your kindness makes you say I'm useful to you. You don't really want me now, for Nancy and Molly are clever at their work, and you're in good health now, by the blessing of God, and my uncle is of a cheerful countenance again, and you have neighbours and friends not a few—some of them come to sit with my uncle almost daily. Indeed, you will not miss me; and at Snowfield there are brethren and sisters in great need, who have none of those comforts you have around you. I feel that I am called back to those amongst whom my lot was first cast. I feel drawn again towards the hills where I used to be blessed in carrying the word of life to the sinful and desolate."

"You feel! Yes," said Mrs. Poyser, returning from a parenthetic glance at the cows, "that's allays the reason I'm to sit down wi', when you've a mind to do anything contrairy. What do you want to be preaching for more than you're preaching now? Don't you go off, the Lord knows where, every Sunday a-preaching and praying? An' haven't you got Methodists enow at Treddles'on to go and look at, if church-folks's faces are too handsome to please you? An' isn't there them i' this parish as you've got under hand, and they're like enough to make friends wi' Old Harry again as soon as your back's turned? There's that Bessy Cranage—she'll be flaunting i' new finery three weeks after you're gone, I'll be bound. She'll no more go on in her new ways without you than a dog 'ull stand on its hind-legs when there's nobody looking. But I suppose it doesna matter so much about folks's souls i' this country, else you'd be for staying with your own aunt, for she's none so good but what you might help her to be better."

There was a certain something in Mrs. Poyser's voice just then, which she did not wish to be noticed, so she turned round hastily to look at the clock, and said: "See there! It's tea-time; an' if Martin's i' the rick-yard, he'll like a cup. Here, Totty, my chicken, let mother put your bonnet on, and then you go out into the rick-yard and see if Father's there, and tell him he mustn't go away again without coming t' have a cup o' tea; and tell your brothers to come in too."

Totty trotted off in her flapping bonnet, while Mrs. Poyser set out the bright oak table and reached down the tea-cups.

"You talk o' them gells Nancy and Molly being clever i' their work," she began again; "it's fine talking. They're all the same, clever or stupid—one can't trust 'em out o' one's sight a minute. They want somebody's eye on 'em constant if they're to be kept to their work. An' suppose I'm ill again this winter, as I was the winter before last? Who's to look after 'em then, if you're gone? An' there's that blessed child—something's sure t' happen to her—they'll let her tumble into the fire, or get at the kettle wi' the boiling lard in't, or some mischief as 'ull lame her for life; an' it'll be all your fault, Dinah."

"Aunt," said Dinah, "I promise to come back to you in the winter if you're ill. Don't think I will ever stay away from you if you're in real want of me. But, indeed, it is needful for my own soul that I should go away from this life of ease and luxury in which I have all things too richly to enjoy—at least that I should go away for a short space. No one can know but myself what are my inward needs, and the besetments I am most in danger from. Your wish for me to stay is not a call of duty which I refuse to hearken to because it is against my own desires; it is a temptation that I must resist, lest the love of the creature should become like a mist in my soul shutting out the heavenly light."

"It passes my cunning to know what you mean by ease and luxury," said Mrs. Poyser, as she cut the bread and butter. "It's true there's good victual enough about you, as nobody shall ever say I don't provide enough and to spare, but if there's ever a bit o' odds an' ends as nobody else 'ud eat, you're sure to pick it out... but look there! There's Adam Bede a-carrying the little un in. I wonder how it is he's come so early."

Mrs. Poyser hastened to the door for the pleasure of looking at her darling in a new position, with love in her eyes but reproof on her tongue.

"Oh for shame, Totty! Little gells o' five year old should be ashamed to be carried. Why, Adam, she'll break your arm, such a big gell as that; set her down—for shame!"

"Nay, nay," said Adam, "I can lift her with my hand—I've no need to take my arm to it."

Totty, looking as serenely unconscious of remark as a fat white puppy, was set down at the door-place, and the mother enforced her reproof with a shower of kisses.

"You're surprised to see me at this hour o' the day," said Adam.

"Yes, but come in," said Mrs. Poyser, making way for him; "there's no bad news, I hope?"

"No, nothing bad," Adam answered, as he went up to Dinah and put out his hand to her. She had laid down her work and stood up, instinctively, as he approached her. A faint blush died away from her pale cheek as she put her hand in his and looked up at him timidly.

"It's an errand to you brought me, Dinah," said Adam, apparently unconscious that he was holding her hand all the while; "mother's a bit ailing, and she's set her heart on your coming to stay the night with her, if you'll be so kind. I told her I'd call and ask you as I came from the village. She overworks herself, and I can't persuade her to have a little girl t' help her. I don't know what's to be done."

Adam released Dinah's hand as he ceased speaking, and was expecting an answer, but before she had opened her lips Mrs. Poyser said, "Look there now! I told you there was folks enow t' help i' this parish, wi'out going further off. There's Mrs. Bede getting as old and cas'alty as can be, and she won't let anybody but you go a-nigh her hardly. The folks at Snowfield have learnt by this time to do better wi'out you nor she can."

"I'll put my bonnet on and set off directly, if you don't want anything done first, Aunt," said Dinah, folding up her work.

"Yes, I do want something done. I want you t' have your tea, child; it's all ready—and you'll have a cup, Adam, if y' arena in too big a hurry."

"Yes, I'll have a cup, please; and then I'll walk with Dinah. I'm going straight home, for I've got a lot o' timber valuations to write out."

"Why, Adam, lad, are you here?" said Mr. Poyser, entering warm and coatless, with the two black-eyed boys behind him, still looking as much like him as two small elephants are like a large one. "How is it we've got sight o' you so long before foddering-time?"

"I came on an errand for Mother," said Adam. "She's got a touch of her old complaint, and she wants Dinah to go and stay with her a bit."

"Well, we'll spare her for your mother a little while," said Mr. Poyser. "But we wonna spare her for anybody else, on'y her husband."

"Husband!" said Marty, who was at the most prosaic and literal period of the boyish mind. "Why, Dinah hasn't got a husband."

"Spare her?" said Mrs. Poyser, placing a seed-cake on the table and then seating herself to pour out the tea. "But we must spare her, it seems, and not for a husband neither, but for her own megrims. Tommy, what are you doing to your little sister's doll? Making the child naughty, when she'd be good if you'd let her. You shanna have a morsel o' cake if you behave so."

Tommy, with true brotherly sympathy, was amusing himself by turning Dolly's skirt over her bald head and exhibiting her truncated body to the general scorn—an indignity which cut Totty to the heart.

"What do you think Dinah's been a-telling me since dinner-time?" Mrs. Poyser continued, looking at her husband.

"Eh! I'm a poor un at guessing," said Mr. Poyser.

"Why, she means to go back to Snowfield again, and work i' the mill, and starve herself, as she used to do, like a creatur as has got no friends."

Mr. Poyser did not readily find words to express his unpleasant astonishment; he only looked from his wife to Dinah, who had now seated herself beside Totty, as a bulwark against brotherly playfulness, and was busying herself with the children's tea. If he had been given to making general reflections, it would have occurred to him that there was certainly a change come over Dinah, for she never used to change colour; but, as it was, he merely observed that her face was flushed at that moment. Mr. Poyser thought she looked the prettier for it: it was a flush no deeper than the petal of a monthly rose. Perhaps it came because her uncle was looking at her so fixedly; but there is no knowing, for just then Adam was saying, with quiet surprise, "Why, I hoped Dinah was settled among us for life. I thought she'd given up the notion o' going back to her old country."

"Thought! Yes," said Mrs. Poyser, "and so would anybody else ha' thought, as had got their right end up'ards. But I suppose you must *be* a Methodist to know what a Methodist 'ull do. It's ill guessing what the bats are flying after."

"Why, what have we done to you. Dinah, as you must go away from us?" said Mr. Poyser, still pausing over his tea-cup. "It's like breaking your word, welly, for your aunt never had no thought but you'd make this your home."

"Nay, Uncle," said Dinah, trying to be quite calm. "When I first came, I said it was only for a time, as long as I could be of any comfort to my aunt."

"Well, an' who said you'd ever left off being a comfort to me?" said Mrs. Poyser. "If you didna mean to stay wi' me, you'd better never ha' come. Them as ha' never had a cushion don't miss it."

"Nay, nay," said Mr. Poyser, who objected to exaggerated views. "Thee mustna say so; we should ha' been ill off wi'out her, Lady day was a twelvemont'. We mun be thankful for that, whether she stays or no. But I canna think what she mun leave a good home for, to go back int' a country where the land, most on't, isna worth ten shillings an acre, rent and profits."

"Why, that's just the reason she wants to go, as fur as she can give a reason," said Mrs. Poyser. "She says this country's too comfortable, an' there's too much t' eat, an' folks arena miserable enough. And she's going next week. I canna turn her, say what I will. It's allays the way wi' them meek-faced people; you may's well pelt a bag o' feathers as talk to 'em. But I say it isna religion, to be so obstinate—is it now, Adam?"

Adam saw that Dinah was more disturbed than he had ever seen her by any matter relating to herself, and, anxious to relieve her, if possible, he said, looking at her affectionately, "Nay, I can't find fault with anything Dinah does. I believe her thoughts are better than our guesses, let 'em be what they may. I should ha' been thankful for her to stay among us, but if she thinks well to go, I wouldn't cross her, or make it hard to her by objecting. We owe her something different to that."

As it often happens, the words intended to relieve her were just too much for Dinah's susceptible feelings at this moment. The tears came into the grey eyes too fast to be hidden and she got up hurriedly, meaning it to be understood that she was going to put on her bonnet.

"Mother, what's Dinah crying for?" said Totty. "She isn't a naughty dell."

"Thee'st gone a bit too fur," said Mr. Poyser. "We've no right t' interfere with her doing as she likes. An' thee'dst be as angry as could be wi' me, if I said a word against anything she did."

"Because you'd very like be finding fault wi'out reason," said Mrs. Poyser. "But there's reason i' what I say, else I shouldna say it. It's easy talking for them as can't love her so well as her own aunt does. An' me got so used to her! I shall feel as uneasy as a new sheared sheep when she's gone from me. An' to think of her leaving a parish where she's so looked on. There's Mr. Irwine makes as much of her as if she was a lady, for all her being a Methodist, an' wi' that maggot o' preaching in her head—God forgi'e me if I'm i' the wrong to call it so."

"Aye," said Mr. Poyser, looking jocose; "but thee dostna tell Adam what he said to thee about it one day. The missis was saying, Adam, as the preaching was the only fault to be found wi' Dinah, and Mr. Irwine says, 'But you mustn't find fault with her for that, Mrs. Poyser; you forget she's got no husband to preach to. I'll answer for it, you give Poyser many a good sermon.' The parson had thee there," Mr. Poyser added, laughing unctuously. "I told Bartle Massey on it, an' he laughed too."

"Yes, it's a small joke sets men laughing when they sit a-staring at one another with a pipe i' their mouths," said Mrs. Poyser. "Give Bartle Massey his way and he'd have all the sharpness to himself. If the chaff-cutter had the making of us, we should all be straw, I reckon. Totty, my chicken, go upstairs to cousin Dinah, and see what she's doing, and give her a pretty kiss."

This errand was devised for Totty as a means of checking certain threatening symptoms about the corners of the mouth; for Tommy, no longer expectant of cake, was lifting up his eyelids with his forefingers and turning his eyeballs towards Totty in a way that she felt to be disagreeably personal.

"You're rare and busy now—eh, Adam?" said Mr. Poyser. "Burge's getting so bad wi' his asthmy, it's well if he'll ever do much riding about again."

"Yes, we've got a pretty bit o' building on hand now," said Adam, "what with the repairs on th' estate, and the new houses at Treddles'on."

"I'll bet a penny that new house Burge is building on his own bit o' land is for him and Mary to go to," said Mr. Poyser. "He'll be for laying by business soon, I'll warrant, and be wanting you to take to it all and pay him so much by th' 'ear. We shall see you living on th' hill before another twelvemont's over."

"Well," said Adam, "I should like t' have the business in my own hands. It isn't as I mind much about getting any more money. We've enough and to spare now, with only our two selves and mother; but I should like t' have my own way about things—I could try plans then, as I can't do now."

"You get on pretty well wi' the new steward, I reckon?" said Mr. Poyser.

"Yes, yes; he's a sensible man enough; understands farming—he's carrying on the draining, and all that, capital. You must go some day towards the Stonyshire side and see what alterations they're making. But he's got no notion about buildings. You can so seldom get hold of a man as can turn his brains to more nor one thing; it's just as if they wore blinkers like th' horses and could see nothing o' one side of 'em. Now, there's Mr. Irwine has got notions o' building more nor most architects; for as for th' architects, they set up to be fine fellows, but the most of 'em don't know where to set a chimney so as it shan't be quarrelling with a door. My notion is, a practical builder that's got a bit o' taste makes the best architect for common things; and I've ten times the pleasure i' seeing after the work when I've made the plan myself."

Mr. Poyser listened with an admiring interest to Adam's discourse on building, but perhaps it suggested to him that the building of his corn-rick had been proceeding a little too long without the control of the master's eye, for when Adam had done speaking, he got up and said, "Well, lad, I'll bid you good-bye now, for I'm off to the rick-yard again."

Adam rose too, for he saw Dinah entering, with her bonnet on and a little basket in her hand, preceded by Totty.

"You're ready, I see, Dinah," Adam said; "so we'll set off, for the sooner I'm at home the better."

"Mother," said Totty, with her treble pipe, "Dinah was saying her prayers and crying ever so."

"Hush, hush," said the mother, "little gells mustn't chatter."

Whereupon the father, shaking with silent laughter, set Totty on the white deal table and desired her to kiss him. Mr. and Mrs. Poyser, you perceive, had no correct principles of education.

"Come back to-morrow if Mrs. Bede doesn't want you, Dinah," said Mrs. Poyser: "but you can stay, you know, if she's ill."

So, when the good-byes had been said, Dinah and Adam left the Hall Farm together.

Chapter L
In the Cottage

Adam did not ask Dinah to take his arm when they got out into the lane. He had never yet done so, often as they had walked together, for he had observed that she never walked arm-in-arm with Seth, and he thought, perhaps, that kind of support was not agreeable to her. So they walked apart, though side by side, and the close poke of her little black bonnet hid her face from him.

"You can't be happy, then, to make the Hall Farm your home, Dinah?" Adam said, with the quiet interest of a brother, who has no anxiety for himself in the matter. "It's a pity, seeing they're so fond of you."

"You know, Adam, my heart is as their heart, so far as love for them and care for their welfare goes, but they are in no present need. Their sorrows are healed, and I feel that I am called back to my old work, in which I found a blessing that I have missed of late in the midst of too abundant worldly good. I know it is a vain thought to flee from the work that God appoints us, for the sake of finding a greater blessing to our own souls, as if we could choose for ourselves where we shall find the fulness of the Divine Presence, instead of seeking it where alone it is to be found, in loving obedience. But now, I believe, I have a clear showing that my work lies elsewhere—at least for a time. In the years to come, if my aunt's health should fail, or she should otherwise need me, I shall return."

"You know best, Dinah," said Adam. "I don't believe you'd go against the wishes of them that love you, and are akin to you, without a good and sufficient reason in your own conscience. I've no right to say anything about my being sorry: you know well enough what cause I have to put you above every other friend I've got; and if it had been ordered so that you could ha' been my sister, and lived with us all our lives, I should ha' counted it the greatest blessing as could happen to us now. But Seth tells me there's no hope o' that: your feelings are different, and perhaps I'm taking too much upon me to speak about it."

Dinah made no answer, and they walked on in silence for some yards, till they came to the stone stile, where, as Adam had passed through first and turned round to give her his hand while she mounted the unusually high step, she could not prevent him from seeing her face. It struck him with surprise, for the grey eyes, usually so mild and grave, had the bright uneasy glance which accompanies suppressed agitation, and the slight flush in her cheeks, with which she had come downstairs, was heightened to a deep rose-colour. She looked as if she were only sister to Dinah. Adam was silent with surprise and conjecture for some moments, and then he said, "I hope I've not hurt or displeased you by what I've said, Dinah.

Perhaps I was making too free. I've no wish different from what you see to be best, and I'm satisfied for you to live thirty mile off, if you think it right. I shall think of you just as much as I do now, for you're bound up with what I can no more help remembering than I can help my heart beating."

Poor Adam! Thus do men blunder. Dinah made no answer, but she presently said, "Have you heard any news from that poor young man, since we last spoke of him?"

Dinah always called Arthur so; she had never lost the image of him as she had seen him in the prison.

"Yes," said Adam. "Mr. Irwine read me part of a letter from him yesterday. It's pretty certain, they say, that there'll be a peace soon, though nobody believes it'll last long; but he says he doesn't mean to come home. He's no heart for it yet, and it's better for others that he should keep away. Mr. Irwine thinks he's in the right not to come. It's a sorrowful letter. He asks about you and the Poysers, as he always does. There's one thing in the letter cut me a good deal: 'You can't think what an old fellow I feel,' he says; 'I make no schemes now. I'm the best when I've a good day's march or fighting before me.'"

"He's of a rash, warm-hearted nature, like Esau, for whom I have always felt great pity," said Dinah. "That meeting between the brothers, where Esau is so loving and generous, and Jacob so timid and distrustful, notwithstanding his sense of the Divine favour, has always touched me greatly. Truly, I have been tempted sometimes to say that Jacob was of a mean spirit. But that is our trial: we must learn to see the good in the midst of much that is unlovely."

"Ah," said Adam, "I like to read about Moses best, in th' Old Testament. He carried a hard business well through, and died when other folks were going to reap the fruits. A man must have courage to look at his life so, and think what'll come of it after he's dead and gone. A good solid bit o' work lasts: if it's only laying a floor down, somebody's the better for it being done well, besides the man as does it."

They were both glad to talk of subjects that were not personal, and in this way they went on till they passed the bridge across the Willow Brook, when Adam turned round and said, "Ah, here's Seth. I thought he'd be home soon. Does he know of you're going, Dinah?"

"Yes, I told him last Sabbath."

Adam remembered now that Seth had come home much depressed on Sunday evening, a circumstance which had been very unusual with him of late, for the happiness he had in seeing Dinah every week seemed long to have outweighed the pain of knowing she would never marry him. This evening he had his habitual air of dreamy benignant contentment, until he came quite close to Dinah and saw the traces of tears on her delicate eyelids and eyelashes. He gave one rapid glance at his brother, but Adam was evidently quite outside the current of emotion that had shaken Dinah: he wore his everyday look of unexpectant calm. Seth tried not to let Dinah see that he had noticed her face, and only said, "I'm thankful you're come, Dinah, for Mother's been hungering after the sight of you all day. She began to talk of you the first thing in the morning."

When they entered the cottage, Lisbeth was seated in her arm-chair, too tired with setting out the evening meal, a task she always performed a long time beforehand, to go and meet them at the door as usual, when she heard the approaching footsteps.

"Coom, child, thee't coom at last," she said, when Dinah went towards her. "What dost mane by lavin' me a week an' ne'er coomin' a-nigh me?"

"Dear friend," said Dinah, taking her hand, "you're not well. If I'd known it sooner, I'd have come."

"An' how's thee t' know if thee dostna coom? Th' lads on'y know what I tell 'em. As long as ye can stir hand and foot the men think ye're hearty. But I'm none so bad, on'y a bit of a cold sets me achin'. An' th' lads tease me so t' ha' somebody wi' me t' do the work—they make me ache worse wi' talkin'. If thee'dst come and stay wi' me, they'd let me alone. The Poysers canna want thee so bad as I do. But take thy bonnet off, an' let me look at thee."

Dinah was moving away, but Lisbeth held her fast, while she was taking off her bonnet, and looked at her face as one looks into a newly gathered snowdrop, to renew the old impressions of purity and gentleness.

"What's the matter wi' thee?" said Lisbeth, in astonishment; "thee'st been a-cryin'."

"It's only a grief that'll pass away," said Dinah, who did not wish just now to call forth Lisbeth's remonstrances by disclosing her intention to leave Hayslope. "You shall know about it shortly—we'll talk of it to-night. I shall stay with you to-night."

Lisbeth was pacified by this prospect. And she had the whole evening to talk with Dinah alone; for there was a new room in the cottage, you remember, built nearly two years ago, in the expectation of a new inmate; and here Adam always sat when he had writing to do or plans to make. Seth sat there too this evening, for he knew his mother would like to have Dinah all to herself.

There were two pretty pictures on the two sides of the wall in the cottage. On one side there was the broad-shouldered, large-featured, hardy old woman, in her blue jacket and buff kerchief, with her dim-eyed anxious looks turned continually on the lily face and the slight form in the black dress that were either moving lightly about in helpful activity, or seated close by the old woman's arm-chair, holding her withered hand, with eyes lifted up towards her to speak a language which Lisbeth understood far better than the Bible or the hymn-book. She would scarcely listen to reading at all to-night. "Nay, nay, shut the book," she said. "We mun talk. I want t' know what thee was cryin' about. Hast got troubles o' thy own, like other folks?"

On the other side of the wall there were the two brothers so like each other in the midst of their unlikeness: Adam with knit brows, shaggy hair, and dark vigorous colour, absorbed in his "figuring"; Seth, with large rugged features, the close copy of his brother's, but with thin, wavy, brown hair and blue dreamy eyes, as often as not looking vaguely out of the window instead of at his book, although it was a newly bought book—Wesley's abridgment of Madame Guyon's life, which was full of wonder and interest for him. Seth had said to Adam, "Can I help thee with anything in here to-night? I don't want to make a noise in the shop."

"No, lad," Adam answered, "there's nothing but what I must do myself. Thee'st got thy new book to read."

And often, when Seth was quite unconscious, Adam, as he paused after drawing a line with his ruler, looked at his brother with a kind smile dawning in his eyes. He knew "th' lad liked to sit full o' thoughts he could give no account of; they'd never come t' anything, but they made him happy," and in the last year or so, Adam had been getting more and more indulgent to Seth. It was part of that growing tenderness which came from the sorrow at work within him.

For Adam, though you see him quite master of himself, working hard and delighting in his work after his inborn inalienable nature, had not outlived his sorrow—had not felt it slip from him as a temporary burden, and leave him the same man again. Do any of us? God forbid. It would be a poor result of all our anguish and our wrestling if we won nothing but our old selves at the end of it—if we could return to the same blind loves, the same self-confident blame, the same light thoughts of human suffering, the same frivolous gossip over blighted human lives, the same feeble sense of that Unknown towards which we have sent forth irrepressible cries in our loneliness. Let us rather be thankful that our sorrow lives in us as an indestructible force, only changing its form, as forces do, and passing from pain into sympathy—the one poor word which includes all our best insight and our best love. Not that this transformation of pain into sympathy had completely taken place in Adam yet. There was still a great remnant of pain, and this he felt would subsist as long as *her* pain was not a memory, but an existing thing, which he must think of as renewed with the light of every new morning.

But we get accustomed to mental as well as bodily pain, without, for all that, losing our sensibility to it. It becomes a habit of our lives, and we cease to imagine a condition of perfect ease as possible for us. Desire is chastened into submission, and we are contented with our day when we have been able to bear our grief in silence and act as if we were not suffering. For it is at such periods that the sense of our lives having visible and invisible relations, beyond any of which either our present or prospective self is the centre, grows like a muscle that we are obliged to lean on and exert.

That was Adam's state of mind in this second autumn of his sorrow. His work, as you know, had always been part of his religion, and from very early days he saw clearly that good carpentry was God's will—was that form of God's will that most immediately concerned him. But now there was no margin of dreams for him beyond this daylight reality, no holiday-time in the working-day world, no moment in the distance when duty would take off her iron glove and breast-plate and clasp him gently into rest. He conceived no picture of the future but one made up of hard-working days such as he lived through, with growing contentment and intensity of interest, every fresh week. Love, he thought, could never be anything to him but a living memory—a limb lopped off, but not gone from consciousness. He did not know that the power of loving was all the while gaining new force within him; that the new sensibilities bought by a deep experience were so many new fibres by which it was possible, nay, necessary to him, that his nature should intertwine with another. Yet he was aware that common affection and friendship were more precious to him than they used to be—that he clung more to his mother and Seth, and had an unspeakable satisfaction in the sight or imagination of any small addition to their happiness. The Poysers, too—hardly three or four days passed but he felt the need of seeing them and interchanging words and looks of friendliness with them. He would have felt this, probably, even if Dinah had not been with them, but he had only said the simplest truth in telling Dinah that he put her above all other friends in the world. Could anything be more natural? For in the darkest moments of memory the thought of her always came as the first ray of returning comfort. The early days of gloom at the Hall Farm had been gradually turned into soft moonlight by her presence; and in the cottage, too, for she had come at every spare moment to soothe and cheer poor Lisbeth, who had been stricken with a fear that subdued even her querulousness at the sight of her darling Adam's grief-worn face. He had become used to watching her light quiet movements, her pretty loving ways to the children, when he went to the Hall Farm; to listen for her voice as for a recurrent music; to think everything she said and did was just right, and could not have been better. In spite of his wisdom, he could not find fault with her for her overindulgence of the children, who had managed to convert Dinah the preacher, before whom a circle of rough men had often trembled a little, into a convenient household slave—though Dinah herself was rather ashamed of this weakness, and had some inward conflict as to her departure from the precepts of Solomon. Yes, there was one thing that might have been better; she might have loved Seth and consented to marry him. He felt a little vexed, for his brother's sake, and he could not help thinking regretfully how Dinah, as Seth's wife, would have made their home as happy as it could be for them all—how she was the one being that would have soothed their mother's last days into peacefulness and rest.

"It's wonderful she doesn't love th' lad," Adam had said sometimes to himself, "for anybody 'ud think he was just cut out for her. But her heart's so taken up with other things. She's one o' those women that feel no drawing towards having a husband and children o' their own. She thinks she should be filled up with her own life then, and she's been used so to living in other folks's cares, she can't bear the thought of her heart being shut up from 'em. I see how it is, well enough. She's cut out o' different stuff from most women: I saw that long ago. She's never easy but when she's helping somebody, and marriage 'ud interfere with her ways—that's true. I've no right to be contriving and thinking it 'ud be better if she'd have Seth, as if I was wiser than she is—or than God either, for He made her what she is, and that's one o' the greatest blessings I've ever had from His hands, and others besides me."

This self-reproof had recurred strongly to Adam's mind when he gathered from Dinah's face that he had wounded her by referring to his wish that she had accepted Seth, and so he had endeavoured to put into the strongest words his confidence in her decision as right—his resignation even to her going away from them and ceasing to make part of their life otherwise than by living in their thoughts, if that separation were chosen by herself. He felt sure she knew quite well enough how much he cared to see her continually—to talk to her with the silent consciousness of a mutual great remembrance. It was not possible she should hear anything but self-renouncing affection and respect in his assurance that he was contented for her to go away; and yet there remained an uneasy feeling in his mind that he had not said quite the right thing—that, somehow, Dinah had not understood him.

Dinah must have risen a little before the sun the next morning, for she was downstairs about five o'clock. So was Seth, for, through Lisbeth's obstinate refusal to have any woman-helper in the house, he had learned to make himself, as Adam said, "very handy in the housework," that he might save his mother from too great weariness; on which ground I hope you will not think him unmanly, any more than you can have thought the gallant Colonel Bath unmanly when he made the gruel for his invalid sister. Adam, who had sat up late at his writing, was still asleep, and was not likely, Seth said, to be down till breakfast-time. Often as Dinah had visited Lisbeth during the last eighteen months, she had never slept in the cottage since that night after Thias's death, when, you remember, Lisbeth praised her deft movements and even gave a modified approval to her porridge. But in that long interval Dinah had made great advances in household cleverness, and this morning, since Seth was there to help, she was bent on bringing everything to a pitch of cleanliness and order that would have satisfied her Aunt Poyser. The cottage was far from that standard at present, for Lisbeth's rheumatism had forced her to give up her old habits of dilettante scouring and polishing. When the kitchen was to her mind, Dinah went into the new room, where Adam had been writing the night before, to see what sweeping and dusting were needed there. She opened the window and let in the fresh morning air, and the smell of the sweet-brier, and the bright low-slanting rays of the early sun, which made a glory about her pale face and pale auburn hair as she held the long brush, and swept, singing to herself in a very low tone—like a sweet summer murmur that you have to listen for very closely—one of Charles Wesley's hymns:

Eternal Beam of Light Divine,
Fountain of unexhausted love,
In whom the Father's glories shine,
Through earth beneath and heaven above;

Jesus! the weary wanderer's rest,
Give me thy easy yoke to bear;
With steadfast patience arm my breast,
With spotless love and holy fear.

Speak to my warring passions, "Peace!"
Say to my trembling heart, "Be still!"
Thy power my strength and fortress is,
For all things serve thy sovereign will.

She laid by the brush and took up the duster; and if you had ever lived in Mrs. Poyser's household, you would know how the duster behaved in Dinah's hand—how it went into every small corner, and on every ledge in and out of sight—how it went again and again round every bar of the chairs, and every leg, and under and over everything that lay on the table, till it came to Adam's papers and rulers and the open desk near them. Dinah dusted up to the very edge of these and then hesitated, looking at them with a longing but timid eye. It was painful to see how much dust there was among them. As she was looking in this way, she heard Seth's step just outside the open door, towards which her back was turned, and said, raising her clear treble, "Seth, is your brother wrathful when his papers are stirred?"

"Yes, very, when they are not put back in the right places," said a deep strong voice, not Seth's.

It was as if Dinah had put her hands unawares on a vibrating chord. She was shaken with an intense thrill, and for the instant felt nothing else; then she knew her cheeks were glowing, and dared not look round, but stood still, distressed because she could not say good-morning in a friendly way. Adam, finding that she did not look round so as to see the smile on his face, was afraid she had thought him serious about his wrathfulness, and went up to her, so that she was obliged to look at him.

"What! You think I'm a cross fellow at home, Dinah?" he said, smilingly.

"Nay," said Dinah, looking up with timid eyes, "not so. But you might be put about by finding things meddled with; and even the man Moses, the meekest of men, was wrathful sometimes."

"Come, then," said Adam, looking at her affectionately, "I'll help you move the things, and put 'em back again, and then they can't get wrong. You're getting to be your aunt's own niece, I see, for particularness."

They began their little task together, but Dinah had not recovered herself sufficiently to think of any remark, and Adam looked at her uneasily. Dinah, he thought, had seemed to disapprove him somehow lately; she had not been so kind and open to him as she used to be. He wanted her to look at him, and be as pleased as he was himself with doing this bit of playful work. But Dinah did not look at him—it was easy for her to avoid looking at the tall man—and when at last there was no more dusting to be done and no further excuse for him to linger near her, he could bear it no longer, and said, in rather a pleading tone, "Dinah, you're not displeased with me for anything, are you? I've not said or done anything to make you think ill of me?"

The question surprised her, and relieved her by giving a new course to her feeling. She looked up at him now, quite earnestly, almost with the tears coming, and said, "Oh, no, Adam! how could you think so?"

"I couldn't bear you not to feel as much a friend to me as I do to you," said Adam. "And you don't know the value I set on the very thought of you, Dinah. That was what I meant yesterday, when I said I'd be content for you to go, if you thought right. I meant, the thought of you was worth so much to me, I should feel I ought to be thankful, and not grumble, if you see right to go away. You know I do mind parting with you, Dinah?"

"Yes, dear friend," said Dinah, trembling, but trying to speak calmly, "I know you have a brother's heart towards me, and we shall often be with one another in spirit; but at this season I am in heaviness through manifold temptations. You must not mark me. I feel called to leave my kindred for a while; but it is a trial—the flesh is weak."

Adam saw that it pained her to be obliged to answer.

"I hurt you by talking about it, Dinah," he said. "I'll say no more. Let's see if Seth's ready with breakfast now."

That is a simple scene, reader. But it is almost certain that you, too, have been in love—perhaps, even, more than once, though you may not choose to say so to all your feminine friends. If so, you will no more think the slight words, the timid looks, the tremulous touches, by which two human souls approach each other gradually, like two little quivering rain-streams, before they mingle into one—you will no more think these things trivial than you will think the first-detected signs of coming spring trivial, though they be but a faint indescribable something in the air and in the song of the birds, and the tiniest perceptible budding on the hedge-row branches. Those slight words and looks and touches are part of the soul's language; and the finest language, I believe, is chiefly made up of unimposing words, such as "light," "sound," "stars," "music"—words really not worth looking at, or hearing, in themselves, any more than "chips" or "sawdust." It is only that they happen to be the signs of something unspeakably great and beautiful. I am of opinion that love is a great and beautiful thing too, and if you agree with me, the smallest signs of it will not be chips and sawdust to you: they will rather be like those little words, "light" and "music," stirring the long-winding fibres of your memory and enriching your present with your most precious past.

Chapter LI
Sunday Morning

Lisbeth's touch of rheumatism could not be made to appear serious enough to detain Dinah another night from the Hall Farm, now she had made up her mind to leave her aunt so soon, and at evening the friends must part. "For a long while," Dinah had said, for she had told Lisbeth of her resolve.

"Then it'll be for all my life, an' I shall ne'er see thee again," said Lisbeth. "Long while! I'n got no long while t' live. An' I shall be took bad an' die, an' thee canst ne'er come a-nigh me, an' I shall die a-longing for thee."

That had been the key-note of her wailing talk all day; for Adam was not in the house, and so she put no restraint on her complaining. She had tried poor Dinah by returning again and again to the question, why she must go away; and refusing to accept reasons, which seemed to her nothing but whim and "contrairiness"; and still more, by regretting that she "couldna' ha' one o' the lads" and be her daughter.

"Thee couldstna put up wi' Seth," she said. "He isna cliver enough for thee, happen, but he'd ha' been very good t' thee—he's as handy as can be at doin' things for me when I'm bad, an' he's as fond o' the Bible an' chappellin' as thee art thysen. But happen, thee'dst like a husband better as isna just the cut o' thysen: the runnin' brook isna athirst for th' rain. Adam 'ud ha' done for thee—I know he would—an' he might come t' like thee well enough, if thee'dst stop. But he's as stubborn as th' iron bar—there's no bending him no way but's own. But he'd be a fine husband for anybody, be they who they will, so looked-on an' so cliver as he is. And he'd be rare an' lovin': it does me good on'y a look o' the lad's eye when he means kind tow'rt me."

Dinah tried to escape from Lisbeth's closest looks and questions by finding little tasks of housework that kept her moving about, and as soon as Seth came home in the evening she put on her bonnet to go. It touched Dinah keenly to say the last good-bye, and still more to look round on her way across the fields and see the old woman still standing at the door, gazing after her till she must have been the faintest speck in the dim aged eyes. "The God of love and peace be with them," Dinah prayed, as she looked back from the last stile. "Make them glad according to the days wherein thou hast afflicted them, and the years wherein they have seen evil. It is thy will that I should part from them; let me have no will but thine."

Lisbeth turned into the house at last and sat down in the workshop near Seth, who was busying himself there with fitting some bits of turned wood he had brought from the village into a small work-box, which he meant to give to Dinah before she went away.

"Thee't see her again o' Sunday afore she goes," were her first words. "If thee wast good for anything, thee'dst make her come in again o' Sunday night wi' thee, and see me once more."

"Nay, Mother," said Seth. "Dinah 'ud be sure to come again if she saw right to come. I should have no need to persuade her. She only thinks it 'ud be troubling thee for nought, just to come in to say good-bye over again."

"She'd ne'er go away, I know, if Adam 'ud be fond on her an' marry her, but everything's so contrairy," said Lisbeth, with a burst of vexation.

Seth paused a moment and looked up, with a slight blush, at his mother's face. "What! Has she said anything o' that sort to thee, Mother?" he said, in a lower tone.

"Said? Nay, she'll say nothin'. It's on'y the men as have to wait till folks say things afore they find 'em out."

"Well, but what makes thee think so, Mother? What's put it into thy head?"

"It's no matter what's put it into my head. My head's none so hollow as it must get in, an' nought to put it there. I know she's fond on him, as I know th' wind's comin' in at the door, an' that's anoof. An' he might be willin' to marry her if he know'd she's fond on him, but he'll ne'er think on't if somebody doesna put it into's head."

His mother's suggestion about Dinah's feeling towards Adam was not quite a new thought to Seth, but her last words alarmed him, lest she should herself undertake to open Adam's eyes. He was not sure about Dinah's feeling, and he thought he *was* sure about Adam's.

"Nay, Mother, nay," he said, earnestly, "thee mustna think o' speaking o' such things to Adam. Thee'st no right to say what Dinah's feelings are if she hasna told thee, and it 'ud do nothing but mischief to say such things to Adam. He feels very grateful and affectionate toward Dinah, but he's no thoughts towards her that 'ud incline him to make her his wife, and I don't believe Dinah 'ud marry him either. I don't think she'll marry at all."

"Eh," said Lisbeth, impatiently. "Thee think'st so 'cause she wouldna ha' thee. She'll ne'er marry thee; thee mightst as well like her t' ha' thy brother."

Seth was hurt. "Mother," he said, in a remonstrating tone, "don't think that of me. I should be as thankful t' have her for a sister as thee wouldst t' have her for a daughter. I've no more thoughts about myself in that thing, and I shall take it hard if ever thee say'st it again."

"Well, well, then thee shouldstna cross me wi' sayin' things arena as I say they are."

"But, Mother," said Seth, "thee'dst be doing Dinah a wrong by telling Adam what thee think'st about her. It 'ud do nothing but mischief, for it 'ud make Adam uneasy if he doesna feel the same to her. And I'm pretty sure he feels nothing o' the sort."

"Eh, donna tell me what thee't sure on; thee know'st nought about it. What's he allays goin' to the Poysers' for, if he didna want t' see her? He goes twice where he used t' go once. Happen he knowsna as he wants t' see her; he knowsna as I put salt in's broth, but he'd miss it pretty quick if it warna there. He'll ne'er think o' marrying if it isna put into's head, an' if thee'dst any love for thy mother, thee'dst put him up to't an' not let her go away out o' my sight, when I might ha' her to make a bit o' comfort for me afore I go to bed to my old man under the white thorn."

"Nay, Mother," said Seth, "thee mustna think me unkind, but I should be going against my conscience if I took upon me to say what Dinah's feelings are. And besides that, I think I should give offence to Adam by speaking to him at all about marrying; and I counsel thee not to do't. Thee may'st be quite deceived about Dinah. Nay, I'm pretty sure, by words she said to me last Sabbath, as she's no mind to marry."

"Eh, thee't as contrairy as the rest on 'em. If it war summat I didna want, it 'ud be done fast enough."

Lisbeth rose from the bench at this, and went out of the workshop, leaving Seth in much anxiety lest she should disturb Adam's mind about Dinah. He consoled himself after a time with reflecting that, since Adam's trouble, Lisbeth had been very timid about speaking to him on matters of feeling, and that she would hardly dare to approach this tenderest of all subjects. Even if she did, he hoped Adam would not take much notice of what she said.

Seth was right in believing that Lisbeth would be held in restraint by timidity, and during the next three days, the intervals in which she had an opportunity of speaking to Adam were too rare and short to cause her any strong temptation. But in her long solitary hours she brooded over her regretful thoughts about Dinah, till they had grown very near that point of unmanageable strength when thoughts are apt to take wing out of their secret nest in a startling manner. And on Sunday morning, when Seth went away to chapel at Treddleston, the dangerous opportunity came.

Sunday morning was the happiest time in all the week to Lisbeth, for as there was no service at Hayslope church till the afternoon, Adam was always at home, doing nothing but reading, an occupation in which she could venture to interrupt him. Moreover, she had always a better dinner than usual to prepare for her sons—very frequently for Adam and herself alone, Seth being often away the entire day—and the smell of the roast meat before the clear fire in the clean kitchen, the clock ticking in a peaceful Sunday manner, her darling Adam seated near her in his best clothes, doing nothing very important, so that she could go and stroke her hand across his hair if she liked, and see him look up at her and smile, while Gyp, rather jealous, poked his muzzle up between them—all these things made poor Lisbeth's earthly paradise.

The book Adam most often read on a Sunday morning was his large pictured Bible, and this morning it lay open before him on the round white deal table in the kitchen; for he sat there in spite of the fire, because he knew his mother liked to have him with her, and it was the only day in the week when he could indulge her in that way. You would have liked to see Adam reading his Bible. He never opened it on a weekday, and so he came to it as a holiday book, serving him for history, biography, and poetry. He held one hand thrust between his waistcoat buttons, and the other ready to turn the pages, and in the course of the morning you would have seen many changes in his face. Sometimes his lips moved in semi-articulation—it was when he came to a speech that he could fancy himself uttering, such as Samuel's dying speech to the people; then his eyebrows would be raised, and the corners of his mouth would quiver a little with sad sympathy—something, perhaps old Isaac's meeting with his son, touched him closely; at other times, over the New Testament, a very solemn look would come upon his face, and he would every now and then shake his head in serious assent, or just lift up his hand and let it fall again. And on some mornings, when he read in the Apocrypha, of which he was very fond, the son of Sirach's keen-edged words would bring a delighted smile, though he also enjoyed the freedom of occasionally differing from an Apocryphal writer. For Adam knew the Articles quite well, as became a good churchman.

Lisbeth, in the pauses of attending to her dinner, always sat opposite to him and watched him, till she could rest no longer without going up to him and giving him a caress, to call his attention to her. This morning he was reading the Gospel according to St. Matthew, and Lisbeth had been standing close by him for some minutes, stroking his hair, which was smoother than usual this morning, and looking down at the large page with silent wonderment at the mystery of letters. She was encouraged to continue this caress, because when she first went up to him, he had thrown himself back in his chair to look at her affectionately and say, "Why, Mother, thee look'st rare and hearty this morning. Eh, Gyp wants me t' look at him. He can't abide to think I love thee the best." Lisbeth said nothing, because she wanted to say so many things. And now there was a new leaf to be turned over, and it was a picture—that of the angel seated on the great stone that has been rolled away from the sepulchre. This picture had one strong association in Lisbeth's memory, for she had been reminded of it when she first saw Dinah, and Adam had no sooner turned the page, and lifted the book sideways that they might look at the angel, than she said, "That's her—that's Dinah."

Adam smiled, and, looking more intently at the angel's face, said,

"It *is* a bit like her; but Dinah's prettier, I think."

"Well, then, if thee think'st her so pretty, why arn't fond on her?"

Adam looked up in surprise. "Why, Mother, dost think I don't set store by Dinah?"

"Nay," said Lisbeth, frightened at her own courage, yet feeling that she had broken the ice, and the waters must flow, whatever mischief they might do. "What's th' use o' settin' store by things as are thirty mile off? If thee wast fond enough on her, thee wouldstna let her go away."

"But I've no right t' hinder her, if she thinks well," said Adam, looking at his book as if he wanted to go on reading. He foresaw a series of complaints tending to nothing. Lisbeth sat down again in the chair opposite to him, as she said:

"But she wouldna think well if thee wastna so contrairy." Lisbeth dared not venture beyond a vague phrase yet.

"Contrairy, mother?" Adam said, looking up again in some anxiety. "What have I done? What dost mean?"

"Why, thee't never look at nothin', nor think o' nothin', but thy figurin, an' thy work," said Lisbeth, half-crying. "An' dost think thee canst go on so all thy life, as if thee wast a man cut out o' timber? An' what wut do when thy mother's gone, an' nobody to take care on thee as thee gett'st a bit o' victual comfortable i' the mornin'?"

"What hast got i' thy mind, Mother?" said Adam, vexed at this whimpering. "I canna see what thee't driving at. Is there anything I could do for thee as I don't do?"

"Aye, an' that there is. Thee might'st do as I should ha' somebody wi' me to comfort me a bit, an' wait on me when I'm bad, an' be good to me."

"Well, Mother, whose fault is it there isna some tidy body i' th' house t' help thee? It isna by my wish as thee hast a stroke o' work to do. We can afford it—I've told thee often enough. It 'ud be a deal better for us."

“Eh, what’s the use o’ talking o’ tidy bodies, when thee mean’st one o’ th’ wenches out o’ th’ village, or somebody from Treddles’on as I ne’er set eyes on i’ my life? I’d sooner make a shift an’ get into my own coffin afore I die, nor ha’ them folks to put me in.”

Adam was silent, and tried to go on reading. That was the utmost severity he could show towards his mother on a Sunday morning. But Lisbeth had gone too far now to check herself, and after scarcely a minute’s quietness she began again.

“Thee mightst know well enough who ’tis I’d like t’ ha’ wi’ me. It isna many folks I send for t’ come an’ see me. I reckon. An’ thee’st had the fetchin’ on her times enow.”

“Thee mean’st Dinah, Mother, I know,” said Adam. “But it’s no use setting thy mind on what can’t be. If Dinah ’ud be willing to stay at Hayslope, it isn’t likely she can come away from her aunt’s house, where they hold her like a daughter, and where she’s more bound than she is to us. If it had been so that she could ha’ married Seth, that ’ud ha’ been a great blessing to us, but we can’t have things just as we like in this life. Thee must try and make up thy mind to do without her.”

“Nay, but I canna ma’ up my mind, when she’s just cut out for thee; an’ nought shall ma’ me believe as God didna make her an’ send her there o’ purpose for thee. What’s it sinnify about her bein’ a Methody! It ’ud happen wear out on her wi’ marryin’.”

Adam threw himself back in his chair and looked at his mother. He understood now what she had been aiming at from the beginning of the conversation. It was as unreasonable, impracticable a wish as she had ever urged, but he could not help being moved by so entirely new an idea. The chief point, however, was to chase away the notion from his mother’s mind as quickly as possible.

“Mother,” he said, gravely, “thee’t talking wild. Don’t let me hear thee say such things again. It’s no good talking o’ what can never be. Dinah’s not for marrying; she’s fixed her heart on a different sort o’ life.”

“Very like,” said Lisbeth, impatiently, “very like she’s none for marr’ing, when them as she’d be willin’ t’ marry wonna ax her. I shouldna ha’ been for marr’ing thy feyther if he’d ne’er axed me; an’ she’s as fond o’ thee as e’er I war o’ Thias, poor fellow.”

The blood rushed to Adam’s face, and for a few moments he was not quite conscious where he was. His mother and the kitchen had vanished for him, and he saw nothing but Dinah’s face turned up towards his. It seemed as if there were a resurrection of his dead joy. But he woke up very speedily from that dream (the waking was chill and sad), for it would have been very foolish in him to believe his mother's words—she could have no ground for them. He was prompted to express his disbelief very strongly—perhaps that he might call forth the proofs, if there were any to be offered.

"What dost say such things for, Mother, when thee'st got no foundation for 'em? Thee know'st nothing as gives thee a right to say that."

"Then I knowna nought as gi'es me a right to say as the year's turned, for all I feel it fust thing when I get up i' th' morning. She isna fond o' Seth, I reckon, is she? She doesna want to marry *him?* But I can see as she doesna behave tow'rt thee as she daes tow'rt Seth. She makes no more o' Seth's coming a-nigh her nor if he war Gyp, but she's all of a tremble when thee't a-sittin' down by her at breakfast an' a-looking at her. Thee think'st thy mother knows nought, but she war alive afore thee wast born."

"But thee canstna be sure as the trembling means love?" said Adam anxiously.

"Eh, what else should it mane? It isna hate, I reckon. An' what should she do but love thee? Thee't made to be loved—for where's there a straighter cliverer man? An' what's it sinnify her bein' a Methody? It's on'y the marigold i' th' parridge."

Adam had thrust his hands in his pockets, and was looking down at the book on the table, without seeing any of the letters. He was trembling like a gold-seeker who sees the strong promise of gold but sees in the same moment a sickening vision of disappointment. He could not trust his mother's insight; she had seen what she wished to see. And yet—and yet, now the suggestion had been made to him, he remembered so many things, very slight things, like the stirring of the water by an imperceptible breeze, which seemed to him some confirmation of his mother's words.

Lisbeth noticed that he was moved. She went on, "An' thee't find out as thee't poorly aff when she's gone. Thee't fonder on her nor thee know'st. Thy eyes follow her about, welly as Gyp's follow thee."

Adam could sit still no longer. He rose, took down his hat, and went out into the fields.

The sunshine was on them: that early autumn sunshine which we should know was not summer's, even if there were not the touches of yellow on the lime and chestnut; the Sunday sunshine too, which has more than autumnal calmness for the working man; the morning sunshine, which still leaves the dew-crystals on the fine gossamer webs in the shadow of the bushy hedgerows.

Adam needed the calm influence; he was amazed at the way in which this new thought of Dinah's love had taken possession of him, with an overmastering power that made all other feelings give way before the impetuous desire to know that the thought was true. Strange, that till that moment the possibility of their ever being lovers had never crossed his mind, and yet now, all his longing suddenly went out towards that possibility. He had no more doubt or hesitation as to his own wishes than the bird that flies towards the opening through which the daylight gleams and the breath of heaven enters.

The autumnal Sunday sunshine soothed him, but not by preparing him with resignation to the disappointment if his mother—if he himself—proved to be mistaken about Dinah. It soothed him by gentle encouragement of his hopes. Her love was so like that calm sunshine that they seemed to make one presence to him, and he believed in them both alike. And Dinah was so bound up with the sad memories of his first passion that he was not forsaking them, but rather giving them a new sacredness by loving her. Nay, his love for her had grown out of that past: it was the noon of that morning.

But Seth? Would the lad be hurt? Hardly; for he had seemed quite contented of late, and there was no selfish jealousy in him; he had never been jealous of his mother's fondness for Adam. But had *he* seen anything of what their mother talked about? Adam longed to know this, for he thought he could trust Seth's observation better than his mother's. He must talk to Seth before he went to see Dinah, and, with this intention in his mind, he walked back to the cottage and said to his mother, "Did Seth say anything to thee about when he was coming home? Will he be back to dinner?"

"Aye, lad, he'll be back for a wonder. He isna gone to Treddles'on. He's gone somewhere else a-preachin' and a-prayin'."

"Hast any notion which way he's gone?" said Adam.

"Nay, but he aften goes to th' Common. Thee know'st more o's goings nor I do."

Adam wanted to go and meet Seth, but he must content himself with walking about the near fields and getting sight of him as soon as possible. That would not be for more than an hour to come, for Seth would scarcely be at home much before their dinner-time, which was twelve o'clock. But Adam could not sit down to his reading again, and he sauntered along by the brook and stood leaning against the stiles, with eager intense eyes, which looked as if they saw something very vividly; but it was not the brook or the willows, not the fields or the sky. Again and again his vision was interrupted by wonder at the strength of his own feeling, at the strength and sweetness of this new love—almost like the wonder a man feels at the added power he finds in himself for an art which he had laid aside for a space. How is it that the poets have said so many fine things about our first love, so few about our later love? Are their first poems their best? Or are not those the best which come from their fuller thought, their larger experience, their deeper-rooted affections? The boy's flutelike voice has its own spring charm; but the man should yield a richer deeper music.

At last, there was Seth, visible at the farthest stile, and Adam hastened to meet him. Seth was surprised, and thought something unusual must have happened, but when Adam came up, his face said plainly enough that it was nothing alarming.

"Where hast been?" said Adam, when they were side by side.

"I've been to the Common," said Seth. "Dinah's been speaking the Word to a little company of hearers at Brimstone's, as they call him. They're folks as never go to church hardly—them on the Common—but they'll go and hear Dinah a bit. She's been speaking with power this forenoon from the words, 'I came not to call the righteous, but sinners to repentance.' And there was a little thing happened as was pretty to see. The women mostly bring their children with 'em, but to-day there was one stout curly headed fellow about three or four year old, that I never saw there before. He was as naughty as could be at the beginning while I was praying, and while we was singing, but when we all sat down and Dinah began to speak, th' young un stood stock still all at once, and began to look at her with's mouth open, and presently he ran away from's mother and went to Dinah, and pulled at her, like a little dog, for her to take notice of him. So Dinah lifted him up and held th' lad on her lap, while she went on speaking; and he was as good as could be till he went to sleep—and the mother cried to see him."

"It's a pity she shouldna be a mother herself," said Adam, "so fond as the children are of her. Dost think she's quite fixed against marrying, Seth? Dost think nothing 'ud turn her?"

There was something peculiar in his brother's tone, which made Seth steal a glance at his face before he answered.

"It 'ud be wrong of me to say nothing 'ud turn her," he answered. "But if thee mean'st it about myself, I've given up all thoughts as she can ever be *my* wife. She calls me her brother, and that's enough."

"But dost think she might ever get fond enough of anybody else to be willing to marry 'em?" said Adam rather shyly.

"Well," said Seth, after some hesitation, "it's crossed my mind sometimes o' late as she might; but Dinah 'ud let no fondness for the creature draw her out o' the path as she believed God had marked out for her. If she thought the leading was not from Him, she's not one to be brought under the power of it. And she's allays seemed clear about that—as her work was to minister t' others, and make no home for herself i' this world."

"But suppose," said Adam, earnestly, "suppose there was a man as 'ud let her do just the same and not interfere with her—she might do a good deal o' what she does now, just as well when she was married as when she was single. Other women of her sort have married—that's to say, not just like her, but women as preached and attended on the sick and needy. There's Mrs. Fletcher as she talks of."

A new light had broken in on Seth. He turned round, and laying his hand on Adam's shoulder, said, "Why, wouldst like her to marry *thee*, brother?"

Adam looked doubtfully at Seth's inquiring eyes and said, "Wouldst be hurt if she was to be fonder o' me than o' thee?"

"Nay," said Seth warmly, "how canst think it? Have I felt thy trouble so little that I shouldna feel thy joy?"

There was silence a few moments as they walked on, and then Seth said, "I'd no notion as thee'dst ever think of her for a wife."

"But is it o' any use to think of her?" said Adam. "What dost say? Mother's made me as I hardly know where I am, with what she's been saying to me this forenoon. She says she's sure Dinah feels for me more than common, and 'ud be willing t' have me. But I'm afraid she speaks without book. I want to know if thee'st seen anything."

"It's a nice point to speak about," said Seth, "and I'm afraid o' being wrong; besides, we've no right t' intermeddle with people's feelings when they wouldn't tell 'em themselves."

Seth paused.

"But thee mightst ask her," he said presently. "She took no offence at *me* for asking, and thee'st more right than I had, only thee't not in the Society. But Dinah doesn't hold wi' them as are for keeping the Society so strict to themselves. She doesn't mind about making folks enter the Society, so as they're fit t' enter the kingdom o' God. Some o' the brethren at Treddles'on are displeased with her for that."

"Where will she be the rest o' the day?" said Adam.

"She said she shouldn't leave the farm again to-day," said Seth, "because it's her last Sabbath there, and she's going t' read out o' the big Bible wi' the children."

Adam thought—but did not say—"Then I'll go this afternoon; for if I go to church, my thoughts 'ull be with her all the while. They must sing th' anthem without me to-day."

Chapter LII
Adam and Dinah

It was about three o'clock when Adam entered the farmyard and roused Alick and the dogs from their Sunday dozing. Alick said everybody was gone to church "but th' young missis"—so he called Dinah—but this did not disappoint Adam, although the "everybody" was so liberal as to include Nancy the dairymaid, whose works of necessity were not unfrequently incompatible with church-going.

There was perfect stillness about the house. The doors were all closed, and the very stones and tubs seemed quieter than usual. Adam heard the water gently dripping from the pump—that was the only sound—and he knocked at the house door rather softly, as was suitable in that stillness.

The door opened, and Dinah stood before him, colouring deeply with the great surprise of seeing Adam at this hour, when she knew it was his regular practice to be at church. Yesterday he would have said to her without any difficulty, "I came to see you, Dinah: I knew the rest were not at home." But to-day something prevented him from saying that, and he put out his hand to her in silence. Neither of them spoke, and yet both wished they could speak, as Adam entered, and they sat down. Dinah took the chair she had just left; it was at the corner of the table near the window, and there was a book lying on the table, but it was not open. She had been sitting perfectly still, looking at the small bit of clear fire in the bright grate. Adam sat down opposite her, in Mr. Poyser's three-cornered chair.

"Your mother is not ill again, I hope, Adam?" Dinah said, recovering herself. "Seth said she was well this morning."

"No, she's very hearty to-day," said Adam, happy in the signs of Dinah's feeling at the sight of him, but shy.

"There's nobody at home, you see," Dinah said; "but you'll wait. You've been hindered from going to church to-day, doubtless."

"Yes," Adam said, and then paused, before he added, "I was thinking about you: that was the reason."

This confession was very awkward and sudden, Adam felt, for he thought Dinah must understand all he meant. But the frankness of the words caused her immediately to interpret them into a renewal of his brotherly regrets that she was going away, and she answered calmly, "Do not be careful and troubled for me, Adam. I have all things and abound at Snowfield. And my mind is at rest, for I am not seeking my own will in going."

“But if things were different, Dinah,” said Adam, hesitatingly. “If you knew things that perhaps you don’t know now....”

Dinah looked at him inquiringly, but instead of going on, he reached a chair and brought it near the corner of the table where she was sitting. She wondered, and was afraid—and the next moment her thoughts flew to the past: was it something about those distant unhappy ones that she didn’t know?

Adam looked at her. It was so sweet to look at her eyes, which had now a self-forgetful questioning in them—for a moment he forgot that he wanted to say anything, or that it was necessary to tell her what he meant.

“Dinah,” he said suddenly, taking both her hands between his, “I love you with my whole heart and soul. I love you next to God who made me.”

Dinah’s lips became pale, like her cheeks, and she trembled violently under the shock of painful joy. Her hands were cold as death between Adam’s. She could not draw them away, because he held them fast.

“Don’t tell me you can’t love me, Dinah. Don’t tell me we must part and pass our lives away from one another.”

The tears were trembling in Dinah’s eyes, and they fell before she could answer. But she spoke in a quiet low voice.

“Yes, dear Adam, we must submit to another Will. We must part.”

“Not if you love me, Dinah—not if you love me,” Adam said passionately. “Tell me—tell me if you can love me better than a brother?”

Dinah was too entirely reliant on the Supreme guidance to attempt to achieve any end by a deceptive concealment. She was recovering now from the first shock of emotion, and she looked at Adam with simple sincere eyes as she said, “Yes, Adam, my heart is drawn strongly towards you; and of my own will, if I had no clear showing to the contrary, I could find my happiness in being near you and ministering to you continually. I fear I should forget to rejoice and weep with others; nay, I fear I should forget the Divine presence, and seek no love but yours.”

Adam did not speak immediately. They sat looking at each other in delicious silence—for the first sense of mutual love excludes other feelings; it will have the soul all to itself.

“Then, Dinah,” Adam said at last, “how can there be anything contrary to what’s right in our belonging to one another and spending our lives together? Who put this great love into our hearts? Can anything be holier than that? For we can help one another in everything as is good. I’d never think o’ putting myself between you and God, and saying you oughtn't to do this and you oughtn't to do that. You'd follow your conscience as much as you do now."

"Yes, Adam," Dinah said, "I know marriage is a holy state for those who are truly called to it, and have no other drawing; but from my childhood upwards I have been led towards another path; all my peace and my joy have come from having no life of my own, no wants, no wishes for myself, and living only in God and those of his creatures whose sorrows and joys he has given me to know. Those have been very blessed years to me, and I feel that if I was to listen to any voice that would draw me aside from that path, I should be turning my back on the light that has shone upon me, and darkness and doubt would take hold of me. We could not bless each other, Adam, if there were doubts in my soul, and if I yearned, when it was too late, after that better part which had once been given me and I had put away from me."

"But if a new feeling has come into your mind, Dinah, and if you love me so as to be willing to be nearer to me than to other people, isn't that a sign that it's right for you to change your life? Doesn't the love make it right when nothing else would?"

"Adam, my mind is full of questionings about that; for now, since you tell me of your strong love towards me, what was clear to me has become dark again. I felt before that my heart was too strongly drawn towards you, and that your heart was not as mine; and the thought of you had taken hold of me, so that my soul had lost its freedom, and was becoming enslaved to an earthly affection, which made me anxious and careful about what should befall myself. For in all other affection I had been content with any small return, or with none; but my heart was beginning to hunger after an equal love from you. And I had no doubt that I must wrestle against that as a great temptation, and the command was clear that I must go away."

"But now, dear, dear Dinah, now you know I love you better than you love me... it's all different now. You won't think o' going. You'll stay, and be my dear wife, and I shall thank God for giving me my life as I never thanked him before."

"Adam, it's hard to me to turn a deaf ear... you know it's hard; but a great fear is upon me. It seems to me as if you were stretching out your arms to me, and beckoning me to come and take my ease and live for my own delight, and Jesus, the Man of Sorrows, was standing looking towards me, and pointing to the sinful, and suffering, and afflicted. I have seen that again and again when I have been sitting in stillness and darkness, and a great terror has come upon me lest I should become hard, and a lover of self, and no more bear willingly the Redeemer's cross."

Dinah had closed her eyes, and a faint shudder went through her. "Adam," she went on, "you wouldn't desire that we should seek a good through any unfaithfulness to the light that is in us; you wouldn't believe that could be a good. We are of one mind in that."

"Yes, Dinah," said Adam sadly, "I'll never be the man t' urge you against your conscience. But I can't give up the hope that you may come to see different. I don't believe your loving me could shut up your heart—it's only adding to what you've been before, not taking away from it. For it seems to me it's the same with love and happiness as with sorrow—the more we know of it the better we can feel what other people's lives are or might be, and so we shall only be more tender to 'em, and wishful to help 'em. The more knowledge a man has, the better he'll do's work; and feeling's a sort o' knowledge."

Dinah was silent; her eyes were fixed in contemplation of something visible only to herself. Adam went on presently with his pleading, "And you can do almost as much as you do now. I won't ask you to go to church with me of a Sunday. You shall go where you like among the people, and teach 'em; for though I like church best, I don't put my soul above yours, as if my words was better for you to follow than your own conscience. And you can help the sick just as much, and you'll have more means o' making 'em a bit comfortable; and you'll be among all your own friends as love you, and can help 'em and be a blessing to 'em till their dying day. Surely, Dinah, you'd be as near to God as if you was living lonely and away from me."

Dinah made no answer for some time. Adam was still holding her hands and looking at her with almost trembling anxiety, when she turned her grave loving eyes on his and said, in rather a sad voice, "Adam there is truth in what you say, and there's many of the brethren and sisters who have greater strength than I have, and find their hearts enlarged by the cares of husband and kindred. But I have not faith that it would be so with me, for since my affections have been set above measure on you, I have had less peace and joy in God. I have felt as it were a division in my heart. And think how it is with me, Adam. That life I have led is like a land I have trodden in blessedness since my childhood; and if I long for a moment to follow the voice which calls me to another land that I know not, I cannot but fear that my soul might hereafter yearn for that early blessedness which I had forsaken; and where doubt enters there is not perfect love. I must wait for clearer guidance. I must go from you, and we must submit ourselves entirely to the Divine Will. We are sometimes required to lay our natural lawful affections on the altar."

Adam dared not plead again, for Dinah's was not the voice of caprice or insincerity. But it was very hard for him; his eyes got dim as he looked at her.

"But you may come to feel satisfied... to feel that you may come to me again, and we may never part, Dinah?"

"We must submit ourselves, Adam. With time, our duty will be made clear. It may be when I have entered on my former life, I shall find all these new thoughts and wishes vanish, and become as things that were not. Then I shall know that my calling is not towards marriage. But we must wait."

"Dinah," said Adam mournfully, "you can't love me so well as I love you, else you'd have no doubts. But it's natural you shouldn't, for I'm not so good as you. I can't doubt it's right for me to love the best thing God's ever given me to know."

"Nay, Adam. It seems to me that my love for you is not weak, for my heart waits on your words and looks, almost as a little child waits on the help and tenderness of the strong on whom it depends. If the thought of you took slight hold of me, I should not fear that it would be an idol in the temple. But you will strengthen me—you will not hinder me in seeking to obey to the uttermost."

"Let us go out into the sunshine, Dinah, and walk together. I'll speak no word to disturb you."

They went out and walked towards the fields, where they would meet the family coming from church. Adam said, "Take my arm, Dinah," and she took it. That was the only change in their manner to each other since they were last walking together. But no sadness in the prospect of her going away—in the uncertainty of the issue—could rob the sweetness from Adam's sense that Dinah loved him. He thought he would stay at the Hall Farm all that evening. He would be near her as long as he could.

"Hey-day! There's Adam along wi' Dinah," said Mr. Poyser, as he opened the far gate into the Home Close. "I couldna think how he happened away from church. Why," added good Martin, after a moment's pause, "what dost think has just jumped into my head?"

"Summat as hadna far to jump, for it's just under our nose. You mean as Adam's fond o' Dinah."

"Aye! hast ever had any notion of it before?"

"To be sure I have," said Mrs. Poyser, who always declined, if possible, to be taken by surprise. "I'm not one o' those as can see the cat i' the dairy an' wonder what she's come after."

"Thee never saidst a word to me about it."

"Well, I aren't like a bird-clapper, forced to make a rattle when the wind blows on me. I can keep my own counsel when there's no good i' speaking."

"But Dinah 'll ha' none o' him. Dost think she will?"

"Nay," said Mrs. Poyser, not sufficiently on her guard against a possible surprise, "she'll never marry anybody, if he isn't a Methodist and a cripple."

"It 'ud ha' been a pretty thing though for 'em t' marry," said Martin, turning his head on one side, as if in pleased contemplation of his new idea. "Thee'dst ha' liked it too, wouldstna?"

"Ah! I should. I should ha' been sure of her then, as she wouldn't go away from me to Snowfield, welly thirty mile off, and me not got a creatur to look to, only neighbours, as are no kin to me, an' most of 'em women as I'd be ashamed to show my face, if *my* dairy things war like their'n. There may well be streaky butter i' the market. An' I should be glad to see the poor thing settled like a Christian woman, with a house of her own over her head; and we'd stock her well wi' linen and feathers, for I love her next to my own children. An' she makes one feel safer when she's i' the house, for she's like the driven snow: anybody might sin for two as had her at their elbow."

"Dinah," said Tommy, running forward to meet her, "mother says you'll never marry anybody but a Methodist cripple. What a silly you must be!" a comment which Tommy followed up by seizing Dinah with both arms, and dancing along by her side with incommodious fondness.

"Why, Adam, we missed you i' the singing to-day," said Mr. Poyser. "How was it?"

"I wanted to see Dinah—she's going away so soon," said Adam.

"Ah, lad! Can you persuade her to stop somehow? Find her a good husband somewhere i' the parish. If you'll do that, we'll forgive you for missing church. But, anyway, she isna going before the harvest supper o' Wednesday, and you must come then. There's Bartle Massey comin', an' happen Craig. You'll be sure an' come, now, at seven? The missis wunna have it a bit later."

"Aye," said Adam, "I'll come if I can. But I can't often say what I'll do beforehand, for the work often holds me longer than I expect. You'll stay till the end o' the week, Dinah?"

"Yes, yes!" said Mr. Poyser. "We'll have no nay."

"She's no call to be in a hurry," observed Mrs. Poyser. "Scarceness o' victual 'ull keep: there's no need to be hasty wi' the cooking. An' scarceness is what there's the biggest stock of i' that country."

Dinah smiled, but gave no promise to stay, and they talked of other things through the rest of the walk, lingering in the sunshine to look at the great flock of geese grazing, at the new corn-ricks, and at the surprising abundance of fruit on the old pear-tree; Nancy and Molly having already hastened home, side by side, each holding, carefully wrapped in her pocket-handkerchief, a prayer-book, in which she could read little beyond the large letters and the Amens.

Surely all other leisure is hurry compared with a sunny walk through the fields from "afternoon church"—as such walks used to be in those old leisurely times, when the boat, gliding sleepily along the canal, was the newest locomotive wonder; when Sunday books had most of them old brown-leather covers, and opened with remarkable precision always in one place. Leisure is gone—gone where the spinning-wheels are gone, and the pack-horses, and the slow waggons, and the pedlars, who brought bargains to the door on sunny afternoons. Ingenious philosophers tell you, perhaps, that the great work of the steam-engine is to create leisure for mankind. Do not believe them: it only creates a vacuum for eager thought to rush in. Even idleness is eager now—eager for amusement; prone to excursion-trains, art museums, periodical literature, and exciting novels; prone even to scientific theorizing and cursory peeps through microscopes. Old Leisure was quite a different personage. He only read one newspaper, innocent of leaders, and was free from that periodicity of sensations which we call post-time. He was a contemplative, rather stout gentleman, of excellent digestion; of quiet perceptions, undiseased by hypothesis; happy in his inability to know the causes of things, preferring the things themselves. He lived chiefly in the country, among pleasant seats and homesteads, and was fond of sauntering by the fruit-tree wall and scenting the apricots when they were warmed by the morning sunshine, or of sheltering himself under the orchard boughs at noon, when the summer pears were falling. He knew nothing of weekday services, and thought none the worse of the Sunday sermon if it allowed him to sleep from the text to the blessing; liking the afternoon service best, because the prayers were the shortest, and not ashamed to say so; for he had an easy, jolly conscience, broad-backed like himself, and able to carry a great deal of beer or port-wine, not being made squeamish by doubts and qualms and lofty aspirations. Life was not a task to him, but a sinecure. He fingered the guineas in his pocket, and ate his dinners, and slept the sleep of the irresponsible, for had he not kept up his character by going to church on the Sunday afternoons?

Fine old Leisure! Do not be severe upon him, and judge him by our modern standard. He never went to Exeter Hall, or heard a popular preacher, or read *Tracts for the Times* or *Sartor Resartus*.

Chapter LIII
The Harvest Supper

As Adam was going homeward, on Wednesday evening, in the six o'clock sunlight, he saw in the distance the last load of barley winding its way towards the yard-gate of the Hall Farm, and heard the chant of "Harvest Home!" rising and sinking like a wave. Fainter and fainter, and more musical through the growing distance, the falling dying sound still reached him, as he neared the Willow Brook. The low westering sun shone right on the shoulders of the old Binton Hills, turning the unconscious sheep into bright spots of light; shone on the windows of the cottage too, and made them a-flame with a glory beyond that of amber or amethyst. It was enough to make Adam feel that he was in a great temple, and that the distant chant was a sacred song.

"It's wonderful," he thought, "how that sound goes to one's heart almost like a funeral bell, for all it tells one o' the joyfullest time o' the year, and the time when men are mostly the thankfullest. I suppose it's a bit hard to us to think anything's over and gone in our lives; and there's a parting at the root of all our joys. It's like what I feel about Dinah. I should never ha' come to know that her love 'ud be the greatest o' blessings to me, if what I counted a blessing hadn't been wrenched and torn away from me, and left me with a greater need, so as I could crave and hunger for a greater and a better comfort."

He expected to see Dinah again this evening, and get leave to accompany her as far as Oakbourne; and then he would ask her to fix some time when he might go to Snowfield, and learn whether the last best hope that had been born to him must be resigned like the rest. The work he had to do at home, besides putting on his best clothes, made it seven before he was on his way again to the Hall Farm, and it was questionable whether, with his longest and quickest strides, he should be there in time even for the roast beef, which came after the plum pudding, for Mrs. Poyser's supper would be punctual.

Great was the clatter of knives and pewter plates and tin cans when Adam entered the house, but there was no hum of voices to this accompaniment: the eating of excellent roast beef, provided free of expense, was too serious a business to those good farm-labourers to be performed with a divided attention, even if they had had anything to say to each other—which they had not. And Mr. Poyser, at the head of the table, was too busy with his carving to listen to Bartle Massey's or Mr. Craig's ready talk.

"Here, Adam," said Mrs. Poyser, who was standing and looking on to see that Molly and Nancy did their duty as waiters, "here's a place kept for you between

Mr. Massey and the boys. It's a poor tale you couldn't come to see the pudding when it was whole."

Adam looked anxiously round for a fourth woman's figure, but Dinah was not there. He was almost afraid of asking about her; besides, his attention was claimed by greetings, and there remained the hope that Dinah was in the house, though perhaps disinclined to festivities on the eve of her departure.

It was a goodly sight—that table, with Martin Poyser's round good-humoured face and large person at the head of it helping his servants to the fragrant roast beef and pleased when the empty plates came again. Martin, though usually blest with a good appetite, really forgot to finish his own beef to-night—it was so pleasant to him to look on in the intervals of carving and see how the others enjoyed their supper; for were they not men who, on all the days of the year except Christmas Day and Sundays, ate their cold dinner, in a makeshift manner, under the hedgerows, and drank their beer out of wooden bottles—with relish certainly, but with their mouths towards the zenith, after a fashion more endurable to ducks than to human bipeds. Martin Poyser had some faint conception of the flavour such men must find in hot roast beef and fresh-drawn ale. He held his head on one side and screwed up his mouth, as he nudged Bartle Massey, and watched half-witted Tom Tholer, otherwise known as "Tom Saft," receiving his second plateful of beef. A grin of delight broke over Tom's face as the plate was set down before him, between his knife and fork, which he held erect, as if they had been sacred tapers. But the delight was too strong to continue smouldering in a grin—it burst out the next instant in a long-drawn "haw, haw!" followed by a sudden collapse into utter gravity, as the knife and fork darted down on the prey. Martin Poyser's large person shook with his silent unctuous laugh. He turned towards Mrs. Poyser to see if she too had been observant of Tom, and the eyes of husband and wife met in a glance of good-natured amusement.

"Tom Saft" was a great favourite on the farm, where he played the part of the old jester, and made up for his practical deficiencies by his success in repartee. His hits, I imagine, were those of the flail, which falls quite at random, but nevertheless smashes an insect now and then. They were much quoted at sheep-shearing and haymaking times, but I refrain from recording them here, lest Tom's wit should prove to be like that of many other bygone jesters eminent in their day—rather of a temporary nature, not dealing with the deeper and more lasting relations of things.

Tom excepted, Martin Poyser had some pride in his servants and labourers, thinking with satisfaction that they were the best worth their pay of any set on the estate. There was Kester Bale, for example (Beale, probably, if the truth were known, but he was called Bale, and was not conscious of any claim to a fifth letter), the old man with the close leather cap and the network of wrinkles on his sun-browned face. Was there any man in Loamshire who knew better the "natur" of all farming work? He was one of those invaluable labourers who can not only turn their hand to everything, but excel in everything they turn their hand to. It is true Kester's knees were much bent outward by this time, and he walked with a perpetual curtsy, as if he were among the most reverent of men. And so he was; but I am obliged to admit that the object of his reverence was his own skill, towards which he performed some rather affecting acts of worship. He always thatched the ricks—for if anything were his forte more than another, it was thatching—and when the last touch had been put to the last beehive rick, Kester, whose home lay at some distance from the farm, would take a walk to the rick-yard in his best clothes on a Sunday morning and stand in the lane, at a due distance, to contemplate his own thatching, walking about to get each rick from the proper point of view. As he curtsied along, with his eyes upturned to the straw knobs imitative of golden globes at the summits of the beehive ricks, which indeed were gold of the best sort, you might have imagined him to be engaged in some pagan act of adoration. Kester was an old bachelor and reputed to have stockings full of coin, concerning which his master cracked a joke with him every pay-night: not a new unseasoned joke, but a good old one, that had been tried many times before and had worn well. "Th' young measter's a merry mon," Kester frequently remarked; for having begun his career by frightening away the crows under the last Martin Poyser but one, he could never cease to account the reigning Martin a young master. I am not ashamed of commemorating old Kester. You and I are indebted to the hard hands of such men—hands that have long ago mingled with the soil they tilled so faithfully, thriftily making the best they could of the earth's fruits, and receiving the smallest share as their own wages.

Then, at the end of the table, opposite his master, there was Alick, the shepherd and head-man, with the ruddy face and broad shoulders, not on the best terms with old Kester; indeed, their intercourse was confined to an occasional snarl, for though they probably differed little concerning hedging and ditching and the treatment of ewes, there was a profound difference of opinion between them as to their own respective merits. When Tityrus and Meliboeus happen to be on the same farm, they are not sentimentally polite to each other. Alick, indeed, was not by any means a honeyed man. His speech had usually something of a snarl in it, and his broad-shouldered aspect something of the bull-dog expression—"Don't you meddle with me, and I won't meddle with you." But he was honest even to the splitting of an oat-grain rather than he would take beyond his acknowledged share, and as "close-fisted" with his master's property as if it had been his own—throwing very small handfuls of damaged barley to the chickens, because a large handful affected his imagination painfully with a sense of profusion. Good-tempered Tim, the waggoner, who loved his horses, had his grudge against Alick in the matter of corn. They rarely spoke to each other, and never looked at each other, even over their dish of cold potatoes; but then, as this was their usual mode of behaviour towards all mankind, it would be an unsafe conclusion that they had more than transient fits of unfriendliness. The bucolic character at Hayslope, you perceive, was not of that entirely genial, merry, broad-grinning sort, apparently observed in most districts visited by artists. The mild radiance of a smile was a rare sight on a field-labourer's face, and there was seldom any gradation between bovine gravity and a laugh. Nor was every labourer so honest as our friend Alick. At this very table, among Mr. Poyser's men, there is that big Ben Tholoway, a very powerful thresher, but detected more than once in carrying away his master's corn in his pockets—an action which, as Ben was not a philosopher, could hardly be ascribed to absence of mind. However, his master had forgiven him, and continued to employ him, for the Tholoways had lived on the Common time out of mind, and had always worked for the Poysers. And on the whole, I daresay, society was not much the worse because Ben had not six months of it at the treadmill, for his views of depredation were narrow, and the House of Correction might have enlarged them. As it was, Ben ate his roast beef to-night with a serene sense of having stolen nothing more than a few peas and beans as seed for his garden since the last harvest supper, and felt warranted in thinking that Alick's suspicious eye, for ever upon him, was an injury to his innocence.

But *now* the roast beef was finished and the cloth was drawn, leaving a fair large deal table for the bright drinking-cans, and the foaming brown jugs, and the bright brass candlesticks, pleasant to behold. *Now*, the great ceremony of the evening was to begin—the harvest-song, in which every man must join. He might be in tune, if he liked to be singular, but he must not sit with closed lips. The movement was obliged to be in triple time; the rest was *ad libitum*.

As to the origin of this song—whether it came in its actual state from the brain of a single rhapsodist, or was gradually perfected by a school or succession of rhapsodists, I am ignorant. There is a stamp of unity, of individual genius upon it, which inclines me to the former hypothesis, though I am not blind to the consideration that this unity may rather have arisen from that consensus of many minds which was a condition of primitive thought, foreign to our modern consciousness. Some will perhaps think that they detect in the first quatrain an indication of a lost line, which later rhapsodists, failing in imaginative vigour, have supplied by the feeble device of iteration. Others, however, may rather maintain that this very iteration is an original felicity, to which none but the most prosaic minds can be insensible.

The ceremony connected with the song was a drinking ceremony. (That is perhaps a painful fact, but then, you know, we cannot reform our forefathers.) During the first and second quatrain, sung decidedly *forte*, no can was filled.

"Here's a health unto our master,
The founder of the feast;
Here's a health unto our master
And to our mistress!

And may his doings prosper,
Whate'er he takes in hand,
For we are all his servants,
And are at his command."

But now, immediately before the third quatrain or chorus, sung *fortissimo*, with emphatic raps of the table, which gave the effect of cymbals and drum together, Alick's can was filled, and he was bound to empty it before the chorus ceased.

"Then drink, boys, drink!
And see ye do not spill,
For if ye do, ye shall drink two,
For 'tis our master's will."

When Alick had gone successfully through this test of steady-handed manliness, it was the turn of old Kester, at his right hand—and so on, till every man had drunk his initiatory pint under the stimulus of the chorus. Tom Saft—the rogue—took care to spill a little by accident; but Mrs. Poyser (too officiously, Tom thought) interfered to prevent the exaction of the penalty.

To any listener outside the door it would have been the reverse of obvious why the "Drink, boys, drink!" should have such an immediate and often-repeated encore; but once entered, he would have seen that all faces were at present sober, and most of them serious—it was the regular and respectable thing for those excellent farm-labourers to do, as much as for elegant ladies and gentlemen to smirk and bow over their wine-glasses. Bartle Massey, whose ears were rather sensitive, had gone out to see what sort of evening it was at an early stage in the ceremony, and had not finished his contemplation until a silence of five minutes declared that "Drink, boys, drink!" was not likely to begin again for the next twelvemonth. Much to the regret of the boys and Totty: on them the stillness fell rather flat, after that glorious thumping of the table, towards which Totty, seated on her father's knee, contributed with her small might and small fist.

When Bartle re-entered, however, there appeared to be a general desire for solo music after the choral. Nancy declared that Tim the waggoner knew a song and was "allays singing like a lark i' the stable," whereupon Mr. Poyser said encouragingly, "Come, Tim, lad, let's hear it." Tim looked sheepish, tucked down his head, and said he couldn't sing, but this encouraging invitation of the master's was echoed all round the table. It was a conversational opportunity: everybody could say, “Come, Tim,” except Alick, who never relaxed into the frivolity of unnecessary speech. At last, Tim’s next neighbour, Ben Tholoway, began to give emphasis to his speech by nudges, at which Tim, growing rather savage, said, “Let me alooan, will ye? Else I’ll ma’ ye sing a toon ye wonna like.” A good-tempered waggoner’s patience has limits, and Tim was not to be urged further.

“Well, then, David, ye’re the lad to sing,” said Ben, willing to show that he was not discomfited by this check. “Sing ‘My loove’s a roos wi’out a thorn.’”

The amatory David was a young man of an unconscious abstracted expression, which was due probably to a squint of superior intensity rather than to any mental characteristic; for he was not indifferent to Ben’s invitation, but blushed and laughed and rubbed his sleeve over his mouth in a way that was regarded as a symptom of yielding. And for some time the company appeared to be much in earnest about the desire to hear David’s song. But in vain. The lyricism of the evening was in the cellar at present, and was not to be drawn from that retreat just yet.

Meanwhile the conversation at the head of the table had taken a political turn. Mr. Craig was not above talking politics occasionally, though he piqued himself rather on a wise insight than on specific information. He saw so far beyond the mere facts of a case that really it was superfluous to know them.

“I’m no reader o’ the paper myself,” he observed to-night, as he filled his pipe, “though I might read it fast enough if I liked, for there’s Miss Lyddy has ’em and ’s done with ’em i’ no time. But there’s Mills, now, sits i’ the chimney-corner and reads the paper pretty nigh from morning to night, and when he’s got to th’ end on’t he’s more addle-headed than he was at the beginning. He’s full o’ this peace now, as they talk on; he’s been reading and reading, and thinks he’s got to the bottom on’t. ‘Why, Lor’ bless you, Mills,’ says I, ‘you see no more into this thing nor you can see into the middle of a potato. I’ll tell you what it is: you think it’ll be a fine thing for the country. And I’m not again’ it—mark my words—I’m not again’ it. But it’s my opinion as there’s them at the head o’ this country as are worse enemies to us nor Bony and all the mounseers he’s got at ’s back; for as for the mounseers, you may skewer half-a-dozen of ’em at once as if they war frogs.’”

“Aye, aye,” said Martin Poyser, listening with an air of much intelligence and edification, “they ne’er ate a bit o’ beef i’ their lives. Mostly sallet, I reckon.”

“And says I to Mills,” continued Mr. Craig, “‘Will *you* try to make me believe as furriners like them can do us half th’ harm them ministers do with their bad government? If King George ’ud turn ’em all away and govern by himself, he’d see everything righted. He might take on Billy Pitt again if he liked; but I don’t see myself what we want wi' anybody besides King and Parliament. It's that nest o' ministers does the mischief, I tell you.'"

"Ah, it's fine talking," observed Mrs. Poyser, who was now seated near her husband, with Totty on her lap—"it's fine talking. It's hard work to tell which is Old Harry when everybody's got boots on."

"As for this peace," said Mr. Poyser, turning his head on one side in a dubitative manner and giving a precautionary puff to his pipe between each sentence, "I don't know. Th' war's a fine thing for the country, an' how'll you keep up prices wi'out it? An' them French are a wicked sort o' folks, by what I can make out. What can you do better nor fight 'em?"

"Ye're partly right there, Poyser," said Mr. Craig, "but I'm not again' the peace—to make a holiday for a bit. We can break it when we like, an' *I'm* in no fear o' Bony, for all they talk so much o' his cliverness. That's what I says to Mills this morning. Lor' bless you, he sees no more through Bony!... why, I put him up to more in three minutes than he gets from's paper all the year round. Says I, 'Am I a gardener as knows his business, or arn't I, Mills? Answer me that.' 'To be sure y' are, Craig,' says he—he's not a bad fellow, Mills isn't, for a butler, but weak i' the head. 'Well,' says I, 'you talk o' Bony's cliverness; would it be any use my being a first-rate gardener if I'd got nought but a quagmire to work on?' 'No,' says he. 'Well,' I says, 'that's just what it is wi' Bony. I'll not deny but he may be a bit cliver—he's no Frenchman born, as I understand—but what's he got at's back but mounseers?'"

Mr. Craig paused a moment with an emphatic stare after this triumphant specimen of Socratic argument, and then added, thumping the table rather fiercely, "Why, it's a sure thing—and there's them 'ull bear witness to't—as i' one regiment where there was one man a-missing, they put the regimentals on a big monkey, and they fit him as the shell fits the walnut, and you couldn't tell the monkey from the mounseers!"

"Ah! Think o' that, now!" said Mr. Poyser, impressed at once with the political bearings of the fact and with its striking interest as an anecdote in natural history.

"Come, Craig," said Adam, "that's a little too strong. You don't believe that. It's all nonsense about the French being such poor sticks. Mr. Irwine's seen 'em in their own country, and he says they've plenty o' fine fellows among 'em. And as for knowledge, and contrivances, and manufactures, there's a many things as we're a fine sight behind 'em in. It's poor foolishness to run down your enemies. Why, Nelson and the rest of 'em 'ud have no merit i' beating 'em, if they were such offal as folks pretend."

Mr. Poyser looked doubtfully at Mr. Craig, puzzled by this opposition of authorities. Mr. Irwine's testimony was not to be disputed; but, on the other hand, Craig was a knowing fellow, and his view was less startling. Martin had never "heard tell" of the French being good for much. Mr. Craig had found no answer but such as was implied in taking a long draught of ale and then looking down fixedly at the proportions of his own leg, which he turned a little outward for that purpose, when Bartle Massey returned from the fireplace, where he had been smoking his first pipe in quiet, and broke the silence by saying, as he thrust his forefinger into the canister, "Why, Adam, how happened you not to be at church on Sunday? Answer me that, you rascal. The anthem went limping without you. Are you going to disgrace your schoolmaster in his old age?"

"No, Mr. Massey," said Adam. "Mr. and Mrs. Poyser can tell you where I was. I was in no bad company."

"She's gone, Adam—gone to Snowfield," said Mr. Poyser, reminded of Dinah for the first time this evening. "I thought you'd ha' persuaded her better. Nought 'ud hold her, but she must go yesterday forenoon. The missis has hardly got over it. I thought she'd ha' no sperrit for th' harvest supper."

Mrs. Poyser had thought of Dinah several times since Adam had come in, but she had had "no heart" to mention the bad news.

"What!" said Bartle, with an air of disgust. "Was there a woman concerned? Then I give you up, Adam."

"But it's a woman you'n spoke well on, Bartle," said Mr. Poyser. "Come now, you canna draw back; you said once as women wouldna ha' been a bad invention if they'd all been like Dinah."

"I meant her voice, man—I meant her voice, that was all," said Bartle. "I can bear to hear her speak without wanting to put wool in my ears. As for other things, I daresay she's like the rest o' the women—thinks two and two 'll come to make five, if she cries and bothers enough about it."

"Aye, aye!" said Mrs. Poyser; "one 'ud think, an' hear some folks talk, as the men war 'cute enough to count the corns in a bag o' wheat wi' only smelling at it. They can see through a barn-door, *they* can. Perhaps that's the reason they can see so little o' this side on't."

Martin Poyser shook with delighted laughter and winked at Adam, as much as to say the schoolmaster was in for it now.

"Ah!" said Bartle sneeringly, "the women are quick enough—they're quick enough. They know the rights of a story before they hear it, and can tell a man what his thoughts are before he knows 'em himself."

“Like enough,” said Mrs. Poyser, “for the men are mostly so slow, their thoughts overrun ’em, an’ they can only catch ’em by the tail. I can count a stocking-top while a man’s getting’s tongue ready an’ when he outs wi’ his speech at last, there’s little broth to be made on’t. It’s your dead chicks take the longest hatchin’. Howiver, I’m not denyin’ the women are foolish: God Almighty made ’em to match the men.”

“Match!” said Bartle. “Aye, as vinegar matches one’s teeth. If a man says a word, his wife ’ll match it with a contradiction; if he’s a mind for hot meat, his wife ’ll match it with cold bacon; if he laughs, she’ll match him with whimpering. She’s such a match as the horse-fly is to th’ horse: she’s got the right venom to sting him with—the right venom to sting him with.”

“Yes,” said Mrs. Poyser, “I know what the men like—a poor soft, as ’ud simper at ’em like the picture o’ the sun, whether they did right or wrong, an’ say thank you for a kick, an’ pretend she didna know which end she stood uppermost, till her husband told her. That’s what a man wants in a wife, mostly; he wants to make sure o’ one fool as ’ull tell him he’s wise. But there’s some men can do wi’out that—they think so much o’ themselves a’ready. An’ that’s how it is there’s old bachelors.”

“Come, Craig,” said Mr. Poyser jocosely, “you mun get married pretty quick, else you’ll be set down for an old bachelor; an’ you see what the women ’ull think on you.”

“Well,” said Mr. Craig, willing to conciliate Mrs. Poyser and setting a high value on his own compliments, “*I* like a cleverish woman—a woman o’ sperrit—a managing woman.”

“You’re out there, Craig,” said Bartle, dryly; “you’re out there. You judge o’ your garden-stuff on a better plan than that. You pick the things for what they can excel in—for what they can excel in. You don’t value your peas for their roots, or your carrots for their flowers. Now, that’s the way you should choose women. Their cleverness ’ll never come to much—never come to much—but they make excellent simpletons, ripe and strong-flavoured.”

“What dost say to that?” said Mr. Poyser, throwing himself back and looking merrily at his wife.

“Say!” answered Mrs. Poyser, with dangerous fire kindling in her eye. “Why, I say as some folks’ tongues are like the clocks as run on strikin’, not to tell you the time o’ the day, but because there’s summat wrong i’ their own inside...”

Mrs. Poyser would probably have brought her rejoinder to a further climax, if every one’s attention had not at this moment been called to the other end of the table, where the lyricism, which had at first only manifested itself by

David's *sotto voce* performance of "My love's a rose without a thorn," had gradually assumed a rather deafening and complex character. Tim, thinking slightly of David's vocalization, was impelled to supersede that feeble buzz by a spirited commencement of "Three Merry Mowers," but David was not to be put down so easily, and showed himself capable of a copious crescendo, which was rendering it doubtful whether the rose would not predominate over the mowers, when old Kester, with an entirely unmoved and immovable aspect, suddenly set up a quavering treble—as if he had been an alarum, and the time was come for him to go off.

The company at Alick's end of the table took this form of vocal entertainment very much as a matter of course, being free from musical prejudices; but Bartle Massey laid down his pipe and put his fingers in his ears; and Adam, who had been longing to go ever since he had heard Dinah was not in the house, rose and said he must bid good-night.

"I'll go with you, lad," said Bartle; "I'll go with you before my ears are split."

"I'll go round by the Common and see you home, if you like, Mr. Massey," said Adam.

"Aye, aye!" said Bartle; "then we can have a bit o' talk together. I never get hold of you now."

"Eh! It's a pity but you'd sit it out," said Martin Poyser. "They'll all go soon, for th' missis niver lets 'em stay past ten." But Adam was resolute, so the good-nights were said, and the two friends turned out on their starlight walk together.

"There's that poor fool, Vixen, whimpering for me at home," said Bartle. "I can never bring her here with me for fear she should be struck with Mrs. Poyser's eye, and the poor bitch might go limping for ever after."

"I've never any need to drive Gyp back," said Adam, laughing. "He always turns back of his own head when he finds out I'm coming here."

"Aye, aye," said Bartle. "A terrible woman!—made of needles, made of needles. But I stick to Martin—I shall always stick to Martin. And he likes the needles, God help him! He's a cushion made on purpose for 'em."

"But she's a downright good-natur'd woman, for all that," said Adam, "and as true as the daylight. She's a bit cross wi' the dogs when they offer to come in th' house, but if they depended on her, she'd take care and have 'em well fed. If her tongue's keen, her heart's tender: I've seen that in times o' trouble. She's one o' those women as are better than their word."

"Well, well," said Bartle, "I don't say th' apple isn't sound at the core; but it sets my teeth on edge—it sets my teeth on edge."

Chapter LIV
The Meeting on the Hill

Adam understood Dinah's haste to go away, and drew hope rather than discouragement from it. She was fearful lest the strength of her feeling towards him should hinder her from waiting and listening faithfully for the ultimate guiding voice from within.

"I wish I'd asked her to write to me, though," he thought. "And yet even that might disturb her a bit, perhaps. She wants to be quite quiet in her old way for a while. And I've no right to be impatient and interrupting her with my wishes. She's told me what her mind is, and she's not a woman to say one thing and mean another. I'll wait patiently."

That was Adam's wise resolution, and it throve excellently for the first two or three weeks on the nourishment it got from the remembrance of Dinah's confession that Sunday afternoon. There is a wonderful amount of sustenance in the first few words of love. But towards the middle of October the resolution began to dwindle perceptibly, and showed dangerous symptoms of exhaustion. The weeks were unusually long: Dinah must surely have had more than enough time to make up her mind. Let a woman say what she will after she has once told a man that she loves him, he is a little too flushed and exalted with that first draught she offers him to care much about the taste of the second. He treads the earth with a very elastic step as he walks away from her, and makes light of all difficulties. But that sort of glow dies out: memory gets sadly diluted with time, and is not strong enough to revive us. Adam was no longer so confident as he had been. He began to fear that perhaps Dinah's old life would have too strong a grasp upon her for any new feeling to triumph. If she had not felt this, she would surely have written to him to give him some comfort; but it appeared that she held it right to discourage him. As Adam's confidence waned, his patience waned with it, and he thought he must write himself. He must ask Dinah not to leave him in painful doubt longer than was needful. He sat up late one night to write her a letter, but the next morning he burnt it, afraid of its effect. It would be worse to have a discouraging answer by letter than from her own lips, for her presence reconciled him to her will.

You perceive how it was: Adam was hungering for the sight of Dinah, and when that sort of hunger reaches a certain stage, a lover is likely to still it though he may have to put his future in pawn.

But what harm could he do by going to Snowfield? Dinah could not be displeased with him for it. She had not forbidden him to go. She must surely expect that he would go before long. By the second Sunday in October this view of the case had become so clear to Adam that he was already on his way to Snowfield, on horseback this time, for his hours were precious now, and he had borrowed Jonathan Burge's good nag for the journey.

What keen memories went along the road with him! He had often been to Oakbourne and back since that first journey to Snowfield, but beyond Oakbourne the greystone walls, the broken country, the meagre trees, seemed to be telling him afresh the story of that painful past which he knew so well by heart. But no story is the same to us after a lapse of time—or rather, we who read it are no longer the same interpreters—and Adam this morning brought with him new thoughts through that grey country, thoughts which gave an altered significance to its story of the past.

That is a base and selfish, even a blasphemous, spirit which rejoices and is thankful over the past evil that has blighted or crushed another, because it has been made a source of unforeseen good to ourselves. Adam could never cease to mourn over that mystery of human sorrow which had been brought so close to him; he could never thank God for another's misery. And if I were capable of that narrow-sighted joy in Adam's behalf, I should still know he was not the man to feel it for himself. He would have shaken his head at such a sentiment and said, "Evil's evil, and sorrow's sorrow, and you can't alter it's natur by wrapping it up in other words. Other folks were not created for my sake, that I should think all square when things turn out well for me."

But it is not ignoble to feel that the fuller life which a sad experience has brought us is worth our own personal share of pain. Surely it is not possible to feel otherwise, any more than it would be possible for a man with cataract to regret the painful process by which his dim blurred sight of men as trees walking had been exchanged for clear outline and effulgent day. The growth of higher feeling within us is like the growth of faculty, bringing with it a sense of added strength. We can no more wish to return to a narrower sympathy than a painter or a musician can wish to return to his cruder manner, or a philosopher to his less complete formula.

Something like this sense of enlarged being was in Adam's mind this Sunday morning, as he rode along in vivid recollection of the past. His feeling towards Dinah, the hope of passing his life with her, had been the distant unseen point towards which that hard journey from Snowfield eighteen months ago had been leading him. Tender and deep as his love for Hetty had been—so deep that the roots of it would never be torn away—his love for Dinah was better and more precious to him, for it was the outgrowth of that fuller life which had come to him from his acquaintance with deep sorrow. "It's like as if it was a new strength to me," he said to himself, "to love her and know as she loves me. I shall look t' her to help me to see things right. For she's better than I am—there's less o' self in her, and pride. And it's a feeling as gives you a sort o' liberty, as if you could walk more fearless, when you've more trust in another than y' have in yourself. I've always been thinking I knew better than them as belonged to me, and that's a poor sort o' life, when you can't look to them nearest to you t' help you with a bit better thought than what you've got inside you a'ready."

It was more than two o'clock in the afternoon when Adam came in sight of the grey town on the hill-side and looked searchingly towards the green valley below, for the first glimpse of the old thatched roof near the ugly red mill. The scene looked less harsh in the soft October sunshine than it had in the eager time of early spring, and the one grand charm it possessed in common with all wide-stretching woodless regions—that it filled you with a new consciousness of the overarching sky—had a milder, more soothing influence than usual, on this almost cloudless day. Adam's doubts and fears melted under this influence as the delicate weblike clouds had gradually melted away into the clear blue above him. He seemed to see Dinah's gentle face assuring him, with its looks alone, of all he longed to know.

He did not expect Dinah to be at home at this hour, but he got down from his horse and tied it at the little gate, that he might ask where she was gone to-day. He had set his mind on following her and bringing her home. She was gone to Sloman's End, a hamlet about three miles off, over the hill, the old woman told him—had set off directly after morning chapel, to preach in a cottage there, as her habit was. Anybody at the town would tell him the way to Sloman's End. So Adam got on his horse again and rode to the town, putting up at the old inn and taking a hasty dinner there in the company of the too chatty landlord, from whose friendly questions and reminiscences he was glad to escape as soon as possible and set out towards Sloman's End. With all his haste it was nearly four o'clock before he could set off, and he thought that as Dinah had gone so early, she would perhaps already be near returning. The little, grey, desolate-looking hamlet, unscreened by sheltering trees, lay in sight long before he reached it, and as he came near he could hear the sound of voices singing a hymn. "Perhaps that's the last hymn before they come away," Adam thought. "I'll walk back a bit and turn again to meet her, farther off the village." He walked back till he got nearly to the top of the hill again, and seated himself on a loose stone, against the low wall, to watch till he should see the little black figure leaving the hamlet and winding up the hill. He chose this spot, almost at the top of the hill, because it was away from all eyes—no house, no cattle, not even a nibbling sheep near—no presence but the still lights and shadows and the great embracing sky.

She was much longer coming than he expected. He waited an hour at least watching for her and thinking of her, while the afternoon shadows lengthened and the light grew softer. At last he saw the little black figure coming from between the grey houses and gradually approaching the foot of the hill. Slowly, Adam thought, but Dinah was really walking at her usual pace, with a light quiet step. Now she was beginning to wind along the path up the hill, but Adam would not move yet; he would not meet her too soon; he had set his heart on meeting her in this assured loneliness. And now he began to fear lest he should startle her too much. "Yet," he thought, "she's not one to be overstartled; she's always so calm and quiet, as if she was prepared for anything."

What was she thinking of as she wound up the hill? Perhaps she had found complete repose without him, and had ceased to feel any need of his love. On the verge of a decision we all tremble: hope pauses with fluttering wings.

But now at last she was very near, and Adam rose from the stone wall. It happened that just as he walked forward, Dinah had paused and turned round to look back at the village—who does not pause and look back in mounting a hill? Adam was glad, for, with the fine instinct of a lover, he felt that it would be best for her to hear his voice before she saw him. He came within three paces of her and then said, "Dinah!" She started without looking round, as if she connected the sound with no place. "Dinah!" Adam said again. He knew quite well what was in her mind. She was so accustomed to think of impressions as purely spiritual monitions that she looked for no material visible accompaniment of the voice.

But this second time she looked round. What a look of yearning love it was that the mild grey eyes turned on the strong dark-eyed man! She did not start again at the sight of him; she said nothing, but moved towards him so that his arm could clasp her round.And they walked on so in silence, while the warm tears fell. Adam was content, and said nothing. It was Dinah who spoke first.

"Adam," she said, "it is the Divine Will. My soul is so knit to yours that it is but a divided life I live without you. And this moment, now you are with me, and I feel that our hearts are filled with the same love. I have a fulness of strength to bear and do our heavenly Father's Will that I had lost before."

Adam paused and looked into her sincere eyes.

"Then we'll never part any more, Dinah, till death parts us."

And they kissed each other with a deep joy.

What greater thing is there for two human souls than to feel that they are joined for life—to strengthen each other in all labour, to rest on each other in all sorrow, to minister to each other in all pain, to be one with each other in silent unspeakable memories at the moment of the last parting?

Chapter LV
Marriage Bells

In little more than a month after that meeting on the hill—on a rimy morning in departing November—Adam and Dinah were married.

It was an event much thought of in the village. All Mr. Burge's men had a holiday, and all Mr. Poyser's, and most of those who had a holiday appeared in their best clothes at the wedding. I think there was hardly an inhabitant of Hayslope specially mentioned in this history and still resident in the parish on this November morning who was not either in church to see Adam and Dinah married, or near the church door to greet them as they came forth. Mrs. Irwine and her daughters were waiting at the churchyard gates in their carriage (for they had a carriage now) to shake hands with the bride and bridegroom and wish them well; and in the absence of Miss Lydia Donnithorne at Bath, Mrs. Best, Mr. Mills, and Mr. Craig had felt it incumbent on them to represent "the family" at the Chase on the occasion. The churchyard walk was quite lined with familiar faces, many of them faces that had first looked at Dinah when she preached on the Green. And no wonder they showed this eager interest on her marriage morning, for nothing like Dinah and the history which had brought her and Adam Bede together had been known at Hayslope within the memory of man.

Bessy Cranage, in her neatest cap and frock, was crying, though she did not exactly know why; for, as her cousin Wiry Ben, who stood near her, judiciously suggested, Dinah was not going away, and if Bessy was in low spirits, the best thing for her to do was to follow Dinah's example and marry an honest fellow who was ready to have her. Next to Bessy, just within the church door, there were the Poyser children, peeping round the corner of the pews to get a sight of the mysterious ceremony; Totty's face wearing an unusual air of anxiety at the idea of seeing cousin Dinah come back looking rather old, for in Totty's experience no married people were young.

I envy them all the sight they had when the marriage was fairly ended and Adam led Dinah out of church. She was not in black this morning, for her Aunt Poyser would by no means allow such a risk of incurring bad luck, and had herself made a present of the wedding dress, made all of grey, though in the usual Quaker form, for on this point Dinah could not give way. So the lily face looked out with sweet gravity from under a grey Quaker bonnet, neither smiling nor blushing, but with lips trembling a little under the weight of solemn feelings. Adam, as he pressed her arm to his side, walked with his old erectness and his head thrown rather backward as if to face all the world better. But it was not because he was particularly proud this morning, as is the wont of bridegrooms, for his happiness was of a kind that had little reference to men's opinion of it. There was a tinge of sadness in his deep joy; Dinah knew it, and did not feel aggrieved.

There were three other couples, following the bride and bridegroom: first, Martin Poyser, looking as cheery as a bright fire on this rimy morning, led quiet Mary Burge, the bridesmaid; then came Seth serenely happy, with Mrs. Poyser on his arm; and last of all Bartle Massey, with Lisbeth—Lisbeth in a new gown and bonnet, too busy with her pride in her son and her delight in possessing the one daughter she had desired to devise a single pretext for complaint.

Bartle Massey had consented to attend the wedding at Adam's earnest request, under protest against marriage in general and the marriage of a sensible man in particular. Nevertheless, Mr. Poyser had a joke against him after the wedding dinner, to the effect that in the vestry he had given the bride one more kiss than was necessary.

Behind this last couple came Mr. Irwine, glad at heart over this good morning's work of joining Adam and Dinah. For he had seen Adam in the worst moments of his sorrow; and what better harvest from that painful seed-time could there be than this? The love that had brought hope and comfort in the hour of despair, the love that had found its way to the dark prison cell and to poor Hetty's darker soul—this strong gentle love was to be Adam's companion and helper till death.

There was much shaking of hands mingled with "God bless you's" and other good wishes to the four couples, at the churchyard gate, Mr. Poyser answering for the rest with unwonted vivacity of tongue, for he had all the appropriate wedding-day jokes at his command. And the women, he observed, could never do anything but put finger in eye at a wedding. Even Mrs. Poyser could not trust herself to speak as the neighbours shook hands with her, and Lisbeth began to cry in the face of the very first person who told her she was getting young again.

Mr. Joshua Rann, having a slight touch of rheumatism, did not join in the ringing of the bells this morning, and, looking on with some contempt at these informal greetings which required no official co-operation from the clerk, began to hum in his musical bass, "Oh what a joyful thing it is," by way of preluding a little to the effect he intended to produce in the wedding psalm next Sunday.

"That's a bit of good news to cheer Arthur," said Mr. Irwine to his mother, as they drove off. "I shall write to him the first thing when we get home."

Epilogue

It is near the end of June, in 1807. The workshops have been shut up half an hour or more in Adam Bede's timber-yard, which used to be Jonathan Burge's, and the mellow evening light is falling on the pleasant house with the buff walls and the soft grey thatch, very much as it did when we saw Adam bringing in the keys on that June evening nine years ago.

There is a figure we know well, just come out of the house, and shading her eyes with her hands as she looks for something in the distance, for the rays that fall on her white borderless cap and her pale auburn hair are very dazzling. But now she turns away from the sunlight and looks towards the door.

We can see the sweet pale face quite well now: it is scarcely at all altered—only a little fuller, to correspond to her more matronly figure, which still seems light and active enough in the plain black dress.

"I see him, Seth," Dinah said, as she looked into the house. "Let us go and meet him. Come, Lisbeth, come with Mother."

The last call was answered immediately by a small fair creature with pale auburn hair and grey eyes, little more than four years old, who ran out silently and put her hand into her mother's.

"Come, Uncle Seth," said Dinah.

"Aye, aye, we're coming," Seth answered from within, and presently appeared stooping under the doorway, being taller than usual by the black head of a sturdy two-year-old nephew, who had caused some delay by demanding to be carried on uncle's shoulder.

"Better take him on thy arm, Seth," said Dinah, looking fondly at the stout black-eyed fellow. "He's troublesome to thee so."

"Nay, nay: Addy likes a ride on my shoulder. I can carry him so for a bit." A kindness which young Addy acknowledged by drumming his heels with promising force against Uncle Seth's chest. But to walk by Dinah's side, and be tyrannized over by Dinah's and Adam's children, was Uncle Seth's earthly happiness.

"Where didst see him?" asked Seth, as they walked on into the adjoining field. "I can't catch sight of him anywhere."

"Between the hedges by the roadside," said Dinah. "I saw his hat and his shoulder. There he is again."

"Trust thee for catching sight of him if he's anywhere to be seen," said Seth, smiling. "Thee't like poor mother used to be. She was always on the look out for Adam, and could see him sooner than other folks, for all her eyes got dim."

"He's been longer than he expected," said Dinah, taking Arthur's watch from a small side pocket and looking at it; "it's nigh upon seven now."

"Aye, they'd have a deal to say to one another," said Seth, "and the meeting 'ud touch 'em both pretty closish. Why, it's getting on towards eight years since they parted."

"Yes," said Dinah, "Adam was greatly moved this morning at the thought of the change he should see in the poor young man, from the sickness he has undergone, as well as the years which have changed us all. And the death of the poor wanderer, when she was coming back to us, has been sorrow upon sorrow."

"See, Addy," said Seth, lowering the young one to his arm now and pointing, "there's Father coming—at the far stile."

Dinah hastened her steps, and little Lisbeth ran on at her utmost speed till she clasped her father's leg. Adam patted her head and lifted her up to kiss her, but Dinah could see the marks of agitation on his face as she approached him, and he put her arm within his in silence.

"Well, youngster, must I take you?" he said, trying to smile, when Addy stretched out his arms—ready, with the usual baseness of infancy, to give up his Uncle Seth at once, now there was some rarer patronage at hand.

"It's cut me a good deal, Dinah," Adam said at last, when they were walking on.

"Didst find him greatly altered?" said Dinah.

"Why, he's altered and yet not altered. I should ha' known him anywhere. But his colour's changed, and he looks sadly. However, the doctors say he'll soon be set right in his own country air. He's all sound in th' inside; it's only the fever shattered him so. But he speaks just the same, and smiles at me just as he did when he was a lad. It's wonderful how he's always had just the same sort o' look when he smiles."

"I've never seen him smile, poor young man," said Dinah.

"But thee *wilt* see him smile, to-morrow," said Adam. "He asked after thee the first thing when he began to come round, and we could talk to one another. 'I hope she isn't altered,' he said, 'I remember her face so well.' I told him 'no,'" Adam continued, looking fondly at the eyes that were turned towards his, "only a bit plumper, as thee'dst a right to be after seven year. 'I may come and see her to-morrow, mayn't I?' he said; 'I long to tell her how I've thought of her all these years.'"

"Didst tell him I'd always used the watch?" said Dinah.

"Aye; and we talked a deal about thee, for he says he never saw a woman a bit like thee. 'I shall turn Methodist some day,' he said, 'when she preaches out of doors, and go to hear her.' And I said, 'Nay, sir, you can't do that, for Conference has forbid the women preaching, and she's given it up, all but talking to the people a bit in their houses.'"

"Ah," said Seth, who could not repress a comment on this point, "and a sore pity it was o' Conference; and if Dinah had seen as I did, we'd ha' left the Wesleyans and joined a body that 'ud put no bonds on Christian liberty."

"Nay, lad, nay," said Adam, "she was right and thee wast wrong. There's no rules so wise but what it's a pity for somebody or other. Most o' the women do more harm nor good with their preaching—they've not got Dinah's gift nor her sperrit—and she's seen that, and she thought it right to set th' example o' submitting, for she's not held from other sorts o' teaching. And I agree with her, and approve o' what she did."Seth was silent. This was a standing subject of difference rarely alluded to, and Dinah, wishing to quit it at once, said, "Didst remember, Adam, to speak to Colonel Donnithorne the words my uncle and aunt entrusted to thee?"

"Yes, and he's going to the Hall Farm with Mr. Irwine the day after to-morrow. Mr. Irwine came in while we were talking about it, and he would have it as the Colonel must see nobody but thee to-morrow. He said—and he's in the right of it—as it'll be bad for him t' have his feelings stirred with seeing many people one after another. 'We must get you strong and hearty,' he said, 'that's the first thing to be done Arthur, and then you shall have your own way. But I shall keep you under your old tutor's thumb till then.' Mr. Irwine's fine and joyful at having him home again."

Adam was silent a little while, and then said, "It was very cutting when we first saw one another. He'd never heard about poor Hetty till Mr. Irwine met him in London, for the letters missed him on his journey. The first thing he said to me, when we'd got hold o' one another's hands was, 'I could never do anything for her, Adam—she lived long enough for all the suffering—and I'd thought so of the time when I might do something for her. But you told me the truth when you said to me once, "There's a sort of wrong that can never be made up for."'"

"Why, there's Mr. and Mrs. Poyser coming in at the yard gate," said Seth.

"So there is," said Dinah. "Run, Lisbeth, run to meet Aunt Poyser. Come in, Adam, and rest; it has been a hard day for thee."

Printed at Repro India Ltd.